The **Rough Guide** to

Boston

written and researched by

David Fagundes and Anthony Grant

this edition researched and updated by

James Ellis

ROUGH GUIDES

NEW YORK • LONDON • DELHI

www.roughguides.com

▲ John Hancock Tower and Trinity Church

Contents

3

Introduction to

Boston

Boston is as close to the Old World as the New World gets, an American city that proudly trades on its colonial past, having served a crucial role in the country's development from a few wayward pilgrims right through to the Revolutionary War. While it occasionally takes its past a bit too seriously – what might pass for a faded relic anywhere else becomes a plaque-covered tourist sight here – none of that detracts from the city's overriding historic charm, nor its present-day energy.

 The first four years of the new millennium saw a major renaissance in Boston. The completion of the seemingly never-ending Big Dig project, the Red Sox triumph in the 2004 World Series, the Patriots' repeated Super Bowl victories, local boy John Kerry's bid for the US presidency, and frequent openings of new restaurants, bars, clubs, and boutiques have all contributed to the feeling that Boston's future is even stronger than its past.

Despite the occasional wearisome touch, no other city in America gives a better feel for the events and persons behind the nation's birth, all played out in Boston's wealth of emblematic and evocative colonial-era sights, conveniently linked by the self-guided walking tour (one of a handful in the city) known as the Freedom Trail. As well, the city's cafés and shops, its attractive public spaces, and the diversity of its neighborhoods – student hives, ethnic enclaves, and stately districts of preserved townhouses – are similarly alluring and go some way to answering the twin accusations of elitism and provincialism that Boston often faces.

Boston is also at the center of the American university system: more than sixty colleges call the area home, including illustrious Harvard and MIT, in the neighboring town of Cambridge, just across the Charles River. This academic connection has played a key part in the city's long left-leaning political tradition, which has spawned, most famously, the Kennedy family. Steeped in Puritan roots, local residents often display a slightly anachronistic Yankee pride, but it's one which has served to protect the city's identity. Indeed, the districts around Boston Common exude an almost small-town atmosphere, and, until the past decade or so, were relatively unmarred by chain stores and fast-food joints. Meanwhile, groups of Irish and Italian descent have carved out authentic and often equally unchanged communities in areas like the North End, Charlestown, and South Boston.

No other city in America gives a better feel for the events and persons behind the nation's birth

Today, Boston's relatively small size – both physically and in terms of population (at under 600,000, it ranks well below most other similarly important US cities) – and its provincial feel actually serve to the city's advantage. Though it has expanded significantly through landfills and annexation since it was settled in 1630, it has never lost its core, which remains a

▲ Marlborough Street townhouses

Yankee cooking

Despite all sorts of strides made by flash chefs and trendy eateries, traditional cuisine remains strong in Boston, built on the unfussiness of the Puritan ethic and the city's proximity to the Atlantic Ocean. This distinctive brand of Yankee cooking – few other places think baked beans is an appropriate sidedish for lobster, for example – can be as comforting as comfort food gets. Fishcakes, seafood chowder, shortcakes, and cream pies are the foundations of Boston's cuisine, the best of which can be had at *Durgin-Park* (p.196) and the *Union Oyster House* (p.198). Food names can be confusing, however. Scrod, for one, a bastardization of "cod," is a small, mysterious fish that could be either cod or haddock – it all depends on what costs less at the market that day. New England clam chowder is more self-explanatory; however, if you're offered a bulkie along with your bowl, know that it's Boston slang for a kaiser-like roll, and that it's the perfect thing to sop up the soup.

▼ Freedom Trail signage

tangle of streets over old cowpaths clustered around Boston Common (which was itself originally used as cattle pasture). Delightfully, this center can really only be explored properly on foot; for even as Boston has evolved from busy port to blighted city to the rejuvenated and prosperous place it is today, it has remained, fundamentally, a city on a human scale.

What to see

The city's epicenter is **Boston Common**, a large public green (and the country's first public park) that orients **Downtown** and is near many of Boston's most historic sights, including the Old State House, the Old Granary Burying Ground, and

Boston nicknames, past and present

Boston has inspired many nicknames over the centuries, from the dignified to the inane. Originally called Tremontaine, after the three hills that
punctuated the skyline when the Puritans arrived in the early 1600s
(but which have since been razed and used for landfill), the newcomers
renamed the spot Boston – itself a shortening of St Botolph – after their
hometown, one hundred miles north of London. The name stuck, but
other, less deferential, monikers took Boston's place. These range from
the earnest ("Athens of America," after the sixty-plus universities that
call the city home), to the hokey ("Beantown," reflecting its inhabitants'
storied love affair with baked beans), to the overblown ("The Hub," after
Oliver Wendell Holmes's famous 1857 reference to the Massachusetts
State House as the "hub of the solar system").

the Old South Meeting House. Little, however, captures the spirit of the
city better than nearby **Faneuil Hall**, the so-called "Cradle of Liberty,"
and the always-animated Quincy Market, adjacent to the hall. Due north,
an incomparable sense of Boston's original layout can be found in the
cramped **Blackstone Block**. Boston's **waterfront**, on the edge of Downtown, offers its fair share of diversions, mostly ideal for traveling families;
the action is centered on Long Wharf.

The **North End**, modern Boston's Little Italy, occupies the northeast
corner of the peninsula, and was cut off from the rest of the city by the
old elevated I-93 before the
completion of the main section of the Big Dig in 2004.
The North End is home to a
few notable relics, such as **Old
North Church** and the **Paul
Revere House**, but is equally
worth visiting for its animated
streetlife, fueled, in large part,
by the strong cups of espresso
proffered by numerous Italian
caffes. Just across Boston Inner
Harbor from the North End lies
Charlestown, the quiet berth
of the world's oldest commissioned warship, the USS *Constitution*, as well as the site of
the **Bunker Hill Monument**,
an obelisk commemorating

▲ Downtown skyline

7

▲ Duck tour boats

the famous battle that bolstered American morale in the fight for independence.

North of the common, vintage gaslights and red-brick Federalist townhouses line the streets of **Beacon Hill**, the city's most exclusive residential neighborhood; it's anchored by the gold-domed **State House**, designed, as were numerous area houses, by Charles Bulfinch. Charles Street runs south from the hill and separates Boston Common from the **Public Garden**, which marks the eastern edge of **Back Bay**, a similarly well-heeled neighborhood which features opulent rowhouses alongside modern landmarks like the **John Hancock Tower**, New England's tallest skyscraper. The neighborhood also hosts some of the city's best shopping along **Newbury Street**. Additionally, the stylish enclave of the **South End**, known for its restaurants and streetlife, as well as the ornate ironwork gracing its well-maintained homes, is also worth a visit.

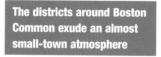

The districts around Boston Common exude an almost small-town atmosphere

The student domains of **Kenmore Square** and **the Fenway** are found west of Back Bay and the South End: the former is largely overrun with college kids from nearby Boston University; the latter spreads west of Massachusetts Avenue and southwest along Huntington Avenue, and is home to heavyweight local institutions like the **Museum of Fine Arts**, the **Isabella Stewart Gardner Museum**, and **Fenway Park**. Below all these neighborhoods are Boston's vast **southern districts**, which hold little of interest besides the **John F. Kennedy Library and Museum** and the southerly links in Frederick Law Olmsted's series of parks, known as the **Emerald Necklace**; it includes the spectacular **Arnold Arboretum** as well as **Franklin Park**, setting for the Franklin Zoo. Across the Charles River from Boston is **Cambridge**, synonymous with venerable Harvard University and tech-oriented MIT, but also boasting some of the area's best nightlife and a lively café scene, especially around Harvard Square, which spills over into neighboring **Somerville** to the north.

The waterfront's Long Wharf doubles as a jumping-off point for escaping the city altogether, on cruises to the idyllic Harbor Islands, or to happening **Provincetown**, Cape Cod's foremost destination. Inland, nearby battle sites in **Lexington** and **Concord** make for easy day-trips, as does a jaunt up the coast to **Salem** and its witch-trials sights, or further on to seafaring towns like **Gloucester** and **Rockport**.

▷ Eating at Quincy Market

Sports fanaticism

You'd be hard-pressed to come up with a city as fanatical about its sports as Boston. The Red Sox winning the 2004 World Series, so ending the 86-year-old "Curse of the Bambino," and the New England Patriots' Super Bowl victories in 2002, 2004, and 2005 have gone a long way to making locals forget that the Celtics haven't won a championship since 1986, and the Bruins haven't brought home the Stanley Cup since 1972. Professional sports are such an integral part of citizens' day-to-day existence here that many upscale restaurants have a television or two just so their patrons can catch the game. For first-hand experience of Bostonians' enthusiasm, head to a Red Sox game at Fenway Park (see p.115). The ruckus will be especially vicious if they're playing the New York Yankees – if you're a Yankees fan, be prepared to be taken to task for cheering on the Bronx Bombers; it might be a good idea to just keep it quiet and enjoy the sunshine.

The Big Dig

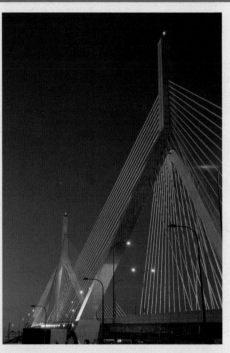

In a city whose roads follow the logic of colonial cowpaths, the added confusion wreaked by Boston's "Big Dig" highway reconstruction project – the largest and most expensive in US history – soured the idea of driving here for more than a decade. Thankfully, that's a thing of the past, and the final phase of the project, landscaping the space formerly occupied by the unsightly elevated Central Artery (I-93), is due to be completed in late 2005. The Big Dig's initial budget of $2.6 billion may have more than quadrupled, but the project – as most Bostonians will tell you – was worth both the cost and the wait. The project pumped millions of construction dollars into the city, birthed new structures like the Leonard P. Zakim Bunker Hill Bridge, and has freed up 150 acres of land for park and recreational use, while supplying dirt to cap landfills where toxins once seeped into Boston Harbor. Visit ⓦwww.bigdig.com, which has all the history, trivia, artwork, plans, politics, and gossip connected with the project; it's an interesting site, and has a lot more personality than you might expect.

When to go

While there's no official high season in Boston, the city is at its most enjoyable in the **fall** (September through early November), when the weather is cooler and the long lines have somewhat abated; and in the **spring** (April through mid-May), when the magnolia trees blossom along Commonwealth Avenue and the parks spring back to life. **Summer**, meanwhile, is certainly the most popular time to visit Boston, both for the warmer weather and frequent festivals. However, July and August can be uncomfortably humid, and you'll have to contend with large student-related influxes around graduation (early June) and the beginning of school (around Labor Day).

At the other end of the spectrum, Boston **winters** can be harsh affairs: they tend to run from late November through March, but, thanks to the moderating influence of the Atlantic, mild spells often break the monotony of long cold stretches, and snowfall is lighter than in the interior regions of New England. No matter when you go, though, be prepared for sudden changes in the weather in the space of a single day: a December morning snow squall could easily be followed by afternoon sunshine and temperatures in the 50s (Fahrenheit).

Boston climate

	Jan	Feb	Mar	Apr	May	Jun	July	Aug	Sept	Oct	Nov	Dec
Average daily max temp												
(°F)	36	39	46	56	67	77	82	80	73	62	52	42
(°C)	2.2	3.9	7.8	13.3	19.4	25	27.8	26.7	22.8	16.7	11.1	5.6
Average daily min temp												
(°F)	22	24	31	41	50	59	65	64	57	46	38	28
(°C)	-5.6	-4.5	-0.6	5	10	15	18.3	17.8	13.9	7.8	3.3	-2.2
Average rainfall												
(in)	3.9	3.3	3.9	3.6	3.2	3.2	3.1	3.4	3.5	3.8	4.0	3.7
(mm)	99.6	83.8	97.8	91.4	82.3	81.8	77.7	85.6	88.1	96.3	101.1	94.7

things not to miss

It's not possible to see everything that Boston has to offer in one trip – and we don't suggest you try. What follows is a selective and subjective taste of the city's highlights, from impressive museums and bucolic parks to wonderful food and engaging cultural events. They're arranged in five color-coded categories to help you find the very best things to see, do, and experience. All entries have a page reference to take you straight into the text, where you can find out more.

01 Isabella Stewart Gardner Museum Page **125** • The eccentric Gardner's stunning collection is housed around a beautiful courtyard in her former mansion.

02 Shopping on Newbury Street
Page **98** • Back Bay's poshest commercial stretch, with everything from colorful boutiques to hip cafés, housed in elegant rowhouses.

04 The Omni Parker House
Page **177** • This opulent old Boston hotel – birthplace of the divine Boston cream pie – merits a look whether you stay there or not.

06 Sevens Ale House Page **211**
• While *Cheers* might be more popular, this neighborhood bar in Beacon Hill is the real thing.

03 Museum of Fine Arts
Page **118** • New England's premier art space features the works of Sargent and Copley, Impressionist painters, and one of the world's best collections of art from the ancient world and Asia.

05 A game at Fenway Park
Page **115** • The country's oldest ballpark is home to the beloved Red Sox and the 37-foot-tall "Green Monster."

07 The USS Constitution
Page **79** • Navy sailors give tours of "Old Ironsides," the oldest commissioned warship in the world.

08 Bonsais at Arnold Arboretum
Page **136** • The highlight of Jamaica Plain's Arnold Arboretum is the Larz Anderson Bonsai Collection, boasting one of the largest assortments of the species outside Asia.

09 Eating in the North End
Pages **184**, **189**, & **198** • Experience the vibrant cafés, bakeries, and restaurants in Boston's most authentically Italian neighborhood.

10 Union Oyster House
Page **198** • One of the best spots in Boston to get fresh seafood is also the oldest continuously operating restaurant in the country.

11 The Ware collection
Page **148** • The Harvard Botanical Museum's awesome collection of glass flowers, plants, and herbs is truly one of a kind.

12 The Head of the Charles
Page **253** • The annual rowing regatta draws countless spectators to the banks of the Charles River in Cambridge.

13 Historic burying grounds Pages 52, 54, & 150 •
Holding everyone from revolutionary heroes to literary titans, Boston's colonial burying grounds are peaceful spots to contemplate their contributions.

15 A visit to Provincetown
Page 167 • Though out at the tip of Cape Cod, P-town is an easy day-trip from the city, its beaches and streetlife popular with families and gay visitors alike.

14 The houses of Beacon Hill Page 86 • Be on the lookout
for purple-tinted windowpanes, a former status symbol, as you stroll this elegant upper-class neighborhood.

16 A day in the Public Garden Page 96
• Take the kids down to Back Bay's idyllic Public Garden for a picnic and a ride on the Swan Boats; you might enjoy it as much as they do.

17 Faneuil Hall Page 60
• Get a good sense of Boston's celebrated history at this vaunted meetingplace, abutting the restaurants and shops of Quincy Market.

18 Gibson House Museum

Page **97** • Packed with Victorian-era curios, this 1860 Italian Renaissance townhouse preserves the Back Bay home of socialite Catherine Hammond Gibson.

19 Old North Church

Page **74** • The oldest church in Boston, this North End landmark is where the famous lanterns were hung on the night of April 18, 1775, to warn of the advancing British troops.

20 Charles Bulfinch architecture

Page **89** • Among the country's most influential architects, Bulfinch merged Federal and Classical styles to create a distinctly Bostonian "look," most notable in the glorious gold-domed Massachusetts State House.

21 Walking the Black Heritage Trail

Page **91** • The 1.6-mile Black Heritage Trail, beginning at the striking Robert Gould Shaw Memorial, is the country's foremost site devoted to pre-Civil War African-American history.

22 A concert at Symphony Hall

Page **221** • Home to the Boston Symphony Orchestra, which has been going strong for more than 120 years, this gilded hall is the perfect place in which to hear classical music.

Basics

Basics

Getting there

Flying is not only the fastest but, most often, the least expensive option in getting to Boston, especially if you land a last-minute deal, which can save you more than half the regular airfare. Upon arrival, you'll be pleased to find that the Boston airport, Logan International (BOS), is conveniently situated near subways and water taxis that provide fast and efficient city access.

If you're not into flying, or have already arrived from abroad somewhere in the US or Canada, the **railroad** is a decent second option for getting to the city, particularly for visitors traveling along the east coast. **Amtrak** has reliable high-speed service between Washington DC and Boston (which includes New York City); from elsewhere in the country, though, the approaches to Beantown are leisurely at best.

For budget travelers, the **Greyhound** and **Peter Pan bus companies** are good options, and they tend to have more flexible departure times than either train or plane. Keep in mind, though, that long-haul buses can be uncomfortable, and that, unlike on rail or by plane, you're at the mercy of the traffic.

Lastly, there's **driving**, probably the least palatable option, as car rental in the US is not cheap. If you insist on getting to Boston via car, plan on parking your vehicle once you get into the city and leaving it for the duration of your stay; you'll neither want (as Boston is a great walking city) nor need the thing again until you leave town.

On a final note, overseas visitors can buy **air**, **train**, and **bus passes** for **discounted travel** throughout the United States; these normally have to be purchased before your trip, and from within your home country. Below, all prices in this section are given in **US dollars**, unless otherwise stated.

Shopping for air tickets and passes

Competition on major routes keeps plane fares at a reasonable level, though prices do vary according to various factors. Within the US, prices for **domestic flights** to Boston are generally determined by the time of departure and seat availability, especially on the busy

Northeastern commuter routes between Washington, New York, and Boston.

Special seasonal deals or discount fares for students and anyone under 26 can bring the price down, but by far the best deals around are **last-minute fares** for long weekend travel, usually announced mid-week by airlines that haven't filled their full-fare seats. Of course, there's no guarantee that Boston will make the cut on any given week, but if it does, you can count on substantial savings – though ticketing restrictions will affect your departure and return times. You can get first crack at the cheap seats by signing up for email notification at most major airline websites.

From **overseas**, seasonal variations in price are common, with flights at their most expensive from June to August (actually the hottest and most humid time to visit Boston). Spring and autumn are slightly less pricey, while winter (excluding the Christmas and New Year holiday period) is the cheapest time to fly.

Whatever your departure point, if you want to travel during the **major American holiday periods** (around the Fourth of July, Thanksgiving, Christmas, and New Year's Day), you should book well in advance, and expect to pay more. The same is true if you're planning to visit in May or early June, when Boston area universities hold their graduation ceremonies.

Remember also to allow for the extra cost of government **duty fees and airport taxes** whenever, and from wherever, you travel – you'll be quoted an all-inclusive price when you pay for your ticket, but not necessarily when you first make inquiries. On the plus side, Logan doesn't charge a **departure tax** – yet.

Rather than contacting all the separate airlines, you'll save yourself a lot of time, and possibly money, too, by checking out the various **discount travel and flight agents**, which often advertise in the travel sections of the daily and weekend press. Some, such as STA, Travel Cuts, and Usit Campus, specialize in **youth/student fares**, but even if you don't fit into that category, they'll do their best to find you the cheapest available flight.

Overseas travelers should also keep in mind that many American carriers offer **air passes** for flights within the US; these passes are good for people who plan to make a lot of stops but only have a limited amount of time. Passes must be bought in advance and require that you arrive in the US via the airline issuing the passes. All the deals are broadly similar, involving the purchase of at least three coupons (costing up to $1000 for the first three coupons, and $100 for each additional one), each valid for a one-way flight of any duration within the US.

If you **book your tickets online**, keep in mind that you'll need to be flexible about your departure and return dates to get the best prices from these sites. Make sure you read the small print before buying, too, as it can be difficult, if not impossible, to claim refunds or change your ticket, especially on last-minute deals.

Online booking agents and general travel sites

ⓦ **www.cheapflights.com** and ⓦ **www .cheapflights.co.uk** Flight deals, travel agents, and links to other travel sites.

ⓦ **www.cheaptickets.com** American discount flight specialists.

ⓦ **www.ebookers.com** and ⓦ **www.ebookers .ie** Low fares on an extensive selection of scheduled flights from the UK and Ireland.

ⓦ **www.etn.nl/discount.** A hub of consolidator and discount-agent Web links.

ⓦ **www.expedia.com** Discount airfares, all-airline search engine, and daily deals.

ⓦ **www.flyaow.com** UK online air travel info and reservations site.

ⓦ **www.hotwire.com** Bookings from the US only. Last-minute savings of up to forty percent on regular published fares.

ⓦ **www.lastminute.com (in UK),** ⓦ **www .lastminute.com.au (in Australia),** and ⓦ **www.lastminute.co.nz (in New Zealand).** Good last-minute holiday package and flight-only deals.

ⓦ **www.orbitz.com** US bookings for cut-rate international and domestic flights.

ⓦ **www.priceline.com** and ⓦ **www.priceline .co.uk** Name-your-own-price website that has deals at around forty percent off standard fares. You can't specify flight times (although you do specify dates). If your bid is accepted, it"s considered binding and your credit card will be charged.

ⓦ **www.skyauction.com** Bookings from the US only. Auctions tickets and travel packages using a "second bid" scheme. The best strategy is to bid the maximum you're willing to pay, since if you win you'll pay just enough to beat the runner-up.

ⓦ **www.smilinjack.com/airlines** Lists an up-to-date compilation of airline website addresses.

ⓦ **www.travel.com.au** and ⓦ **www.travel .co.nz** Discount fares and destination advice for Australian/New Zealand travelers.

ⓦ **www.travelocity.com** and ⓦ **www .travelocity.co.uk** Destination guides along with deals for car rental, lodging, and airfares.

ⓦ **www.travelshop.com.au** Australian website offering discounted flights, packages, insurance, and online bookings.

ⓦ **travel.yahoo.com** Information about places to eat, sleep, and so on.

From the US and Canada

While getting to Boston from most places in North America is fastest and easiest by **plane**, the city is very easily accessible by **bus**, **train**, or **car**.

By plane

Boston's only airport, **Logan International**, is New England's busiest and has been undergoing an expansion project for the last few years: the international Terminal E opened in 2004, while Delta is opening a newly refurbished Terminal A in April 2005. Most service comes from **East Coast shuttles** originating at New York's La Guardia, JFK, and Newark airports (Delta Airlines; Mon–Fri every 30–60min 6am–9.30pm, Sat & Sun every 2hr 8.30am–8.30pm) and Washington DC's Dulles and Reagan National airports (US Airways; Mon–Sat every 30–60min 7.30am–9.25pm, Sun every 30–60mins 8.30am–9.25pm).

The following airlines also offer regular, **daily service** to Boston: Air Canada (from Montréal, Ottawa, Toronto, and Vancouver),

American Airlines (from Chicago, Dallas, Miami, Philadelphia, and St Louis), Continental (from Houston, Chicago, Miami, Newark, and Seattle), Delta (from Atlanta, Dallas, and Tampa), United (from Chicago, Los Angeles, and San Francisco), Northwest (from Detroit, Memphis, Minneapolis, San Diego, and Vancouver), and US Airways (from Fort Lauderdale, Orlando, and Philadelphia).

Fares are lowest in the heavily trafficked Northeast corridor; a round-trip fare **from New York** can cost as little as $90–100, although $120–170 is the more usual price fare; **from Washington DC** and **Miami**, the range is usually $200–250; from **Chicago**, $260–300. The price of flights **from the West Coast** is more likely to fluctuate – round-trip fares from LA, San Francisco, or Seattle typically cost $450–550, but can go as low as $300. **From Canada**, be prepared to pay around Can$400–500 from Toronto and Montréal, and closer to Can$700, and as high as Can$1200, from Vancouver.

Plenty of travel operators offer **tours** and **camping trips** that typically feature a day or two in Boston as part of a seven-day itinerary that includes several New England destinations. Though these are considerably more expensive than a mere weekend in the city (and prices vary wildly according to what's being offered), the Boston element of the trip makes a great backgrounder to a provincial New England vacation.

Airlines

Air Canada ☎1-888/247-2262, 🌐www.aircanada.ca

Air Tran ☎1-800/247-8726, 🌐www.airtran.com

America West ☎1-800/235-9292, 🌐www.americawest.com

American Airlines and American Eagle ☎1-800/433-7300, 🌐www.aa.com

American Trans Air ☎1-800/225-2995, 🌐www.ata.com

Cape Air ☎1-800/352-0714, 🌐www.flycapeair.com

Continental ☎1-800/523-3273, 🌐www.continental.com

Delta and Delta Shuttle ☎1-800/221-1212, 🌐www.delta.com

Delta Express ☎1-800/221-1212, 🌐www.flydlx.com

Frontier ☎1-800/432-1359, 🌐www.frontierairlines.com

Midwest Express ☎1-800/452-2022, 🌐www.midwestexpress.com

Northwest/KLM ☎1-800/225-2525, 🌐www.nwa.com

United ☎1-800/241-6522, 🌐www.ual.com

US Airways, US Airways Express, and US Airways Shuttle ☎1-800/428-4322, 🌐www.usairways.com

Discount travel agents

Airtech ☎212/219-7000, 🌐www.airtech.com. Standby seat broker.

Now Voyager ☎1-800/255-6951, 🌐www.nowvoyager.com. San Francisco-based gay- and lesbian-friendly consolidator with Boston-based tours and packages.

Skylink US ☎1-800/247-6659 or 212/573-8980, Canada ☎1-800/759-5465, 🌐www.skylinkus.com. Consolidator with multiple offices throughout the US and Canada.

STA Travel ☎1-800/781-4040, 🌐www.sta-travel.com. Worldwide specialists in independent travel; also furnish student IDs, travel insurance, and car rental.

TFI Tours International ☎1-800/745-8000 or 212/736-1140, 🌐www.lowestairprice.com. Consolidator with flights to Boston from Canadian and US cities.

Travelers Advantage ☎1-877/259-2691, 🌐www.travelersadvantage.com. Discount travel club; annual membership fee required (currently $1 for 3 months' trial).

Travel Cuts Canada ☎1-800/667-2887, US ☎1-866/246-9762, 🌐www.travelcuts.com. Canadian student-travel organization.

Worldtek Travel ☎1/800/243-1723, 🌐www.worldtek.com. Discount travel agency for worldwide travel.

Tour operators

American Express Vacations ☎1-800/346-3607, 🌐www.americanexpress.com/travel. Flights, hotels, last-minute specials, city-break packages, and specialty tours.

Amtrak Vacations ☎1-800/321-8684, 🌐www.amtrakvacations.com. Train or Amtrak Air-Rail trips through the Northeast, along with hotel reservations, car rental, and sightseeing tours.

Collette Vacations ☎1-800/340-5158, 🌐www.collettevacations.com. Boston figures in various escorted or independent tour permutations; from the seven-night "Islands of New England" option, which includes Boston, Nantucket, and Martha's Vineyard (from $1269), to the "New England Foliage" tour, which also covers provincial towns like Lexington,

Concord, and Killington (from $1269); prices include meals but exclude airfare/travel to Boston.

Contiki Holidays ☎1-888/CONTIKI, ⌨www .contiki.com. Trips for the 18–35-year-old crowd; the twelve-day "North by Northeast" tour (from $1178, airfare not included) takes in Boston and Cape Cod.

Globus and Cosmos ⌨www.globusandcosmos .com. Deluxe escorted tours. The "Eastern US & Canada Discovery" tour (twelve days, from $1999) includes significant time in Boston; the land-only prices include meals. Request brochures online or via a listed travel agent.

Suntrek Tours ☎1-800/SUN-TREK, ⌨www .suntrek.com. A six-day "Eastern Trails" tour includes a couple of days in the Boston region ($459).

Trek America ☎1-800/221-0596 ⌨www .trekamerica.com. Trekking company geared to 18–38-year-olds with seven- to fourteen-day camping tours through the eastern US, many with a Canadian leg thrown in (from $478).

By train

For those heading to Boston from within the Washington DC and New York shuttle flight radius, **train** travel is a decent – but probably no less expensive – alternative. On the plus side, the Amtrak trains (☎1-800/USA-RAIL, ⌨www.amtrak.com) that service the Washington-to-Boston corridor are the fleet's most reliable, and usually stick to their official schedules. Fares **from New York** to Boston are $128 round-trip, with travel taking between four and five hours; $198 gets you a seat on the cushier Acela Express, which, its name notwithstanding, only shaves about thirty minutes off the trip time. **From Washington DC,** the regular train runs just shy of eight hours ($178 return) while the express gets you there in 6.5 hours ($282 round-trip).

Although it's possible to haul yourself long-distance **from the West Coast**, the Midwest, or the South, the trip is anything but fast – count on three days and up from California – nor is it cost-effective, at around $350 for a round-trip ticket. The same applies to visitors trying to approach Boston **from Canada** using Via Rail (☎1-888/842-7245, ⌨www.viarail.ca); you can do so only by connecting in New York City, and on an indirect itinerary at best. The rail journey can take anywhere from twelve to twenty hours from Toronto and Montréal, and over three days from Vancouver. Fares start around Can$400 return from the closer points – and at those prices, you may as well fly.

By bus

Given how expensive rail travel is in the US, getting to Boston by **bus** can be an appealing – if less comfortable – option, especially as the buses quite often get there faster than the train does, given the notorious unreliability of rail travel outside of the Northeast corridor. Boston is an especially common stop coming **from New York** or **Washington DC**; barring rush-hour traffic and highway accidents, one-way trips typically take four-and-a-half hours from New York and ten-and-a-half hours from Washington, with round-trip fares costing $55 and $132, respectively – though nonrefundable and seven-day advance fares from New York can drop the round-trip price as low as $30. The rates can go down even further in the summer, when the two main carriers, **Greyhound** (☎1-800/231-2222, ⌨www.greyhound .com) and **Peter Pan** (☎1-800/237-8747, ⌨www.peterpanbus.com) lose their best income source – Boston university students – and tempt full-time residents with cut-rate deals. The only hitch is that these cheap tickets must be purchased in Boston; even so, you can still save by buying a one-way ticket to Boston and getting your return on arrival.

Visitors leaving **from New York** have two additional choices when it comes to bus travel. There's **Bonanza** (☎1-888/751-8800, ⌨www.bonanzabus.com), which has cheaper tickets year-round (though there's a stop in Providence, Rhode Island, for a total of five hours' travel time), and the **Chinatown** buses (☎1-888-881-0887, ⌨www .luckystarbus.com), which offer rates as low as $15 one-way for fully air-conditioned coaches.

Coming from Canada, several daily buses **from Toronto** reach Boston with at least one changeover – usually in Syracuse, New York – contributing to a minimum twelve-hour ride (Can$147 return). Buses **from Montréal** take around seven hours and have the added benefit of direct service (Can$122 return). In both cases, contact Greyhound (☎1-800/661-87447, ◉www.greyhound.com).

By car

Coming into Boston by car used to be a nightmare, but road access has improved, somewhat, with the completion of the Big Dig (see p.10), which has put the dreaded I-93 underground. Despite the old flyover being torn down, contruction continues on landscaping work above ground, meaning the occasional snarl-up is still possible. If you insist on driving, stay informed of road closures and reroutings by tuning in to 1030 AM (reports every ten minutes 5am–7pm; every half-hour 7pm–5am) and prepare for interminable jams and detours.

Two other highways lead into town: **I-95**, which circumscribes the Boston area (and is also known as Route-128 between Gloucester and Boston), and **I-90** (the Massachusetts Turnpike, or "Masspike"), which approaches Boston from the west and is popular with those arriving from New York state.

Once you get into Boston, if you're lucky enough to get rerouted to a street with a 24-hour **parking lot**, use it: you'll probably never want to drive your car again. For more on driving in town, see p.36.

From the UK and Ireland

Five airlines make the nonstop seven-hour flight from **the UK and Ireland** to Boston; most leave early to mid-afternoon and arrive in the late afternoon or evening, though the odd red-eye flight leaves the UK at 8pm and arrives later the same night in Boston. Returning to the UK and Ireland, you're looking at an early morning or early evening departure; the prevailing winds tend to make the trip back modestly shorter than the one over.

British Airways, Continental, Virgin Atlantic, and American Airlines fly from London's Heathrow Airport; travelers from elsewhere in the UK will have to connect in London. Aer Lingus and American Airlines operate nonstop services from Ireland.

As there's not a lot of price differentiation between the major airlines, you'll have to shop around to get the best deals. The standard option, the **Apex** ticket, is a nonrefundable return ticket that must be purchased 21 days in advance and requires a minimum seven-night stay, up to a maximum of one month; changing departure dates usually incurs a penalty. With or without an Apex ticket, fares **from London** hover around £200 in low season (Oct–Feb), £250 in the spring, and £300 in high season (May–Sept). All fares are subject to a £63 tax, and weekend flights incur additional surcharges. Flights **from Ireland** (Dublin, Shannon, or Cork) are somewhat cheaper, and can range from €200 in low season to €400 in high season.

If you're really penny-pinching and must go to Boston in high season, consider flying as a **courier**. In return for cheaper rates, you'd be responsible for checking a package through with your (carry-on only) luggage. Given heightened security following the events of September 11, 2001 though, the extra hassle over your relation to the package's contents may not be worth the trouble. To offer your services, call Flight Masters (☎020/7462 0022) or Bridges Worldwide (☎01895/465 065). You can also join the International Association of Air Travel Couriers (☎0800/746 481 or 01305/216 920, ◉www.aircourier.co.uk). Flights leave from either Gatwick or Heathrow, with high-season costs reduced to fares nearing spring rates.

Distances and driving times to Boston

From Chicago: 982 miles (16 hrs 30mins)

From Miami: 1488 miles (25 hrs)

From Montréal: 310 miles (6 hrs)

From New York: 216 miles (4 hrs)

From San Francisco: 3100 miles (52 hrs)

From Toronto: 552 miles (9 hrs 30 mins)

Airlines

Aer Lingus UK ☎0845/084 4444, Republic of Ireland ☎0818/365000, ◉www.aerlingus.ie
American Airlines UK ☎0845/778 9789, ◉www.americanairlines.co.uk

British Airways UK ☎ 0845/773 3377, Republic of Ireland ☎ 1800/626 747, ⓦ www .british-airways.com
Continental UK ☎ 0800/776 464, Republic of Ireland ☎ 1890/925 252, ⓦ www.continental.com
Delta UK ☎ 0800/414 767, Republic of Ireland ☎ 01/407 3165, ⓦ www.delta.com
KLM/Northwest UK ☎ 08705/074 074, ⓦ www .klm.com/uk_en/
United Airlines UK ☎ 0845/844 4777, Republic of Ireland ☎ 1800/535 300, ⓦ www.ual.com
US Airways UK ☎ 0845/600 3300, Republic of Ireland ☎ 1890/925 065, ⓦ www.usairways.com
Virgin Atlantic UK ☎ 08705 747 747, Republic of Ireland ☎ 01/873 3388, ⓦ www .virgin-atlantic.com

Travel agents

Apex Travel Dublin ☎ 012418000, ⓦ www .apextravel.ie. Specialists in flights to Australia, East Asia, and the US. Consolidators for British Airways, American, and SAS Scandinavian.
Bridge the World ☎ 0870/814 4400, ⓦ www .bridgetheworld.com. Specializing in round-the-world tickets, with good deals aimed at the backpacker market.
CIE Tours International Dublin ☎ 01/703 1888, ⓦ www.cietours.ie. General flight and tour agent.
Destination Group ☎ 0871 222 3423, ⓦ www .destination-group.com. Discount airfares, as well as inclusive packages for US travel.
Dial A Flight ☎ 0870/333 4488, ⓦ www .dialaflight.com. Discounts on airfares, as well as car rental, hotels, and insurance.
Flightbookers ☎ 0870 814 0000, ⓦ www .ebookers.com. Low fares on an extensive selection of scheduled flights.
Flight Centre ☎ 0870/499 0040, ⓦ www .flightcentre.co.uk. Guarantees lowest airfares.
Flightfinders ☎ 0870 1201 7476, ⓦ www .flightfinders.co.uk. Discount flight specialists.
Flynow ☎ 0870/660 003, ⓦ www.flynow.com. Wide range of discounted tickets.
Joe Walsh Tours Dublin ☎ 01/241 0800, Cork ☎ 021/427 7959, ⓦ www.joewalshtours.ie. Long-established travel agency and tour operator.
McCarthy's Travel Cork ☎ 021/427 0127, ⓦ www.mccarthystravel.ie. General flight agent.
North South Travel ☎ 01245/608 291, ⓦ www. northsouthtravel.co.uk. Discounted fares worldwide; profits are used to support projects in the developing world, especially the promotion of sustainable tourism.
Premier Travel Derry ☎ 028/7126 3333, ⓦ www .premiertravel.uk.com. Group travel, business travel, car rentals, travel insurance, and daily specials.

Quest Worldwide ☎ 0870 442 35422, ⓦ www .questtravel.com. Specialists in round-the-world discount fares.
Rosetta Travel Belfast ☎ 028/9064 4996, ⓦ www.rosettatravel.com. Travel bargains with flights leaving from Belfast.
STA Travel ☎ 08701/600 599, ⓦ www.statravel .co.uk. Worldwide specialists in low-cost flights and tours for students and under-26s (other customers welcome); Amtrak passes also available.
Top Deck Travel ☎ 020 8879 6789, ⓦ www .topdecktravel.co.uk. Adventure travel specialists.
Trailfinders UK ☎ 020 7292 1888, ⓦ www .trailfinders.com. Dublin ☎ 01/677 7888, ⓦ www .trailfinders.ie. One of the best-informed and most efficient agents for independent travelers; Amtrak passes also available.
Travel Bag ☎ 0870/814 4441, ⓦ www.travelbag .co.uk. Independent travel agency whose consultants specialize in specific destinations.
Twohigs Travel Dublin ☎ 01/648 0800, ⓦ www .twohigs.com. General flight and travel agent.
Usit Now Belfast ☎ 028/9032 7111, Dublin t01/602 1600, Cork ☎ 021/427 0900, ⓦ www .usitnow.ie. Student and youth travel specialists offering flights and Amtrak train passes.
World Travel Centre Dublin ☎ 01/416 7007, ⓦ www.worldtravel.ie. Experts in long-haul flights from Ireland.

Package tours

There are plenty of companies running package deals **from the UK** to Boston, mostly short city breaks that span three to five days. For a three-day trip, typical rates will run to around £600 per person in summer, though prices drop to around £450 out of high season, and sometimes less than that. It's usually around £100 more for the five-star or superior-grade hotel package. If you plan to see more of the country than just Boston, **fly-drive** deals – which include car rental when buying a transatlantic ticket from an airline or tour operator – are always cheaper than renting a car on the spot. Most of the specialist companies offer fly-drive packages, though watch out for hidden extras, such as local taxes, "drop-off" charges, and extra insurance.

Specialist tour operators

American Holidays Belfast ☎ 02890/238 762, Dublin ☎ 01/ 6733840, ⓦ www.american-holidays

.com. Package deals from Ireland to all parts of the US and Canada; three nights in Boston, including airfare, starts around €400.

British Airways Holidays UK ☎0870/242 4245, ⓦ www.baholidays.co.uk. Offers quality package and tailor-made Boston-area holidays by phone.

Contiki Tours UK ☎0208/290 6777, ⓦ www .contiki.com. Trips for the 18–35-year-old crowd; the twelve-day "North by Northeast" tour (from £654, airfare not included) takes in Boston and Cape Cod.

First Choice/Unijet UK ☎0870/600 8009, ⓦ www.firstchoice.co.uk/unijet. City breaks, hotel reservations, and car rental.

Funway USA UK ☎0870/444 0770, ⓦ www .funwayholidays.co.uk. Boston city breaks, flight-only deals, and car rental.

Kuoni Travel UK ☎01306/740 888, ⓦ www .kuoni.co.uk. Flexible package holidays to Boston in a number of price ranges; good family offers.

Media Travel UK ☎0870 027 3008, ⓦ www .mediatravel.co.uk. Tour operator with Boston city breaks and longer-stay New England packages.

Thomas Cook UK ☎0870/566 6222 or 0870/750 5701, ⓦ www.thomascook.com. One-stop 24-hour travel agency for package holidays, city breaks, and scheduled flights, with bureau de change issuing Thomas Cook travelers' checks, travel insurance, and car rental.

TrekAmerica UK ☎01295/256 777, ⓦ www .trekamerica.co.uk. Camping tours catering to 18–38-year-olds, with Boston included in seven- to fourteen-day tours through the eastern US (sometimes including Canada). From £309.

United Vacations UK ☎0870/606 2222, ⓦ www.unitedvacations.co.uk. One-stop agent for tailor-made holidays, city breaks, fly-drive deals, pre-booked sightseeing tours, and more. One week fly-drives to Boston start from £309.

Virgin Holidays UK ☎0870/220 2788, ⓦ www .virginholidays.co.uk. City breaks with hotels in Downtown, Back Bay, and Cambridge; flights are with Virgin Atlantic.

World Travel Centre Dublin ☎01/416 7007, ⓦ www.worldtravel.ie. Specialists in flights and packages to the US.

From Australia and New Zealand

Flights from **Australia** and **New Zealand** fly to the West Coast before continuing on to Boston, making for a pretty long trip (about ten hours, plus another six).

Return fares from eastern Australian cities are usually around $A2000/$NZ2900 in low season (mid-January to February and October–November), while tickets from Perth and Darwin can cost up to Aus$400 more. You might do better purchasing a direct ticket to either San Francisco or LA and using an air pass to get to Boston. If you choose this route, you must buy a minimum of three flight coupons (at a cost of $800 total) before leaving your home country. The best connections through the West Coast tend to be with United, Air New Zealand, and Qantas.

Airlines

Air New Zealand Australia ☎13 24 76, New Zealand ☎0800/737 000, ⓦ www.airnz.com

American Airlines Australia ☎1300/650 747, New Zealand ☎0800/887 997, ⓦ www.aa.com

British Airways Australia ☎02/8904 8800, New Zealand ☎09/356 8690, ⓦ www.british -airways.com

Continental Airlines Australia ☎02/9244 2242, New Zealand ☎09/308 3350, ⓦ www.continental .com

Delta Air Lines Australia ☎800/500 992, ⓦ www.delta.com

Japan Airlines (JAL) Australia ☎02/9272 1111, New Zealand ☎09/379 9906, ⓦ www.jall.com

Round-the-world tickets

If Boston is only one stop on a longer journey, you might want to consider buying a **round-the-world (RTW) ticket**. Some travel agents can sell you an "off-the-shelf" RTW ticket that will have you touching down in about half a dozen cities (Boston does figure on some standard itineraries, though New York is a more usual US East Coast stopover). You can also have an agent assemble a tailor-made ticket, though it's apt to be more expensive. Figure on a minimum of Aus$2200/$NZ2800 for a RTW ticket – the most it'll cost you is Aus$2800/NZ$3500. Travelers from the US can expect to pay in the neighborhood of $1250 for a similar ticket, while Europeans can expect to pay about €1300.

KLM/Northwest Australia ☎1300/303 747,
New Zealand ☎09/309 1782, ⓦwww.klm.com,
ⓦwww.nwa.com

Qantas Australia ☎13 13 13, New Zealand
☎0800/808 767, ⓦwww.qantas.com.au

United Airlines Australia ☎13 17 77, New
Zealand ☎09/379 3800, ⓦwww.ual.com

Virgin Atlantic Australia ☎02/9244 2747,
New Zealand ☎09/308 3377, ⓦwww.virgin
-atlantic.com

Travel agents

Anywhere Travel Australia ☎02/9663 0411 or
018/401 014, ⓦwww.anywheretravel.com.au.
General fares agent.

Budget Travel New Zealand ☎0800/80 84 80,
ⓦwww.budgettravel.co.nz. Flights, RTW fares,
and tours.

Destinations Unlimited New Zealand
☎09/4141685, ⓦwww.holiday.co.nz. RTW fares.

Flight Centre Australia ☎133 133, ⓦwww
.flightcentre.com.au; New Zealand ☎0800 24 35
44, ⓦwww.flightcentre.co.nz. Specialist agent for
budget flights, especially RTW. Guarantees lowest
airfares.

STA Travel Australia ☎1300/733 035, ⓦwww
.statravel.com.au; New Zealand ☎0508/782
872, ⓦwww.statravel.co.nz. Discount flights,
travel passes, and more for youth/student and other
independent travelers.

Student Uni Travel Australia ☎02/9232 8444
ⓦwww.sut.com.au; New Zealand ☎0508/
STUDENT, ⓦwww.sut.co.nz. Caters to student, youth,
and backpacker markets. RTW tickets, adventure tours,
traveler's insurance, and travel passes.

Trailfinders Australia ☎1300/780 212, ⓦwww
.trailfinders.com.au. One of the best-informed and
most efficient agents for independent travelers;
Amtrak passes also available.

Usit Beyond New Zealand ☎0800/874 823,
ⓦwww.usitbeyond.co.nz. Youth/student travel

specialist; also RTW tickets, train passes, and other
services.

Walshes World New Zealand ☎09/379 3708.
Agent for Amtrak rail passes.

Tour operators

Adventure World Australia ☎02/8913 0755 or
08/9226 4524 or 1300/363 055, ⓦwww
.adventureworld.com.au; New Zealand ☎09/524
5118, ⓦwww.adventureworld.co.nz. Boston hotel
bookings, car rental, and organized tours.

Australian Pacific Tours Australia ☎03/9277
8444 or 1800/675 222, New Zealand ☎09/279
6077. Package tours and independent travel to the
US.

Canada and America Travel Specialists
Australia ☎02/9922 4600, ⓦwww.canam.com.au.
Flights and accommodation in North America, plus
Greyhound Ameripasses and Amtrak passes.

Contiki Holidays Australia ☎02/9511 2200,
New Zealand ☎09/309 8824, ⓦwww.contiki
.com. Trips for the 18–35-year-old crowd; the
twelve-day "North by Northeast" tour (from £654,
Aus$1600, NZ$1760, airfare not included) takes in
Boston and Cape Cod.

Creative Holidays Australia ☎02/9386 2111,
ⓦwww.creativeholidays.com.au. City breaks and
other packages.

Journeys Worldwide Australia ☎1300 734 788.
All aspects of travel to the US.

Spectrum Holidays Australia ☎03/9877 3322,
ⓦwww.spectrumholidays.com.au. Tailor-made
trips and city breaks with accommodation and car
rental.

Sydney International Travel Centre ☎02/9250
9320, ⓦwww.sydneytravel.com.au. US flights,
accommodation, city breaks, and car rental.

United Vacations ☎02/9324 1000, ⓦwww
.unitedvacations.com. Tailor-made city stays or
wider American holidays, with departures from
several Australian airports.

Red tape and visas

Heightened security concerns after the events of September 11, 2001, have prompted a review of the US's entrance formalities. As of 2004, under the Visa Waiver Program (VWP), if you're a citizen of the UK, Ireland, Australia, New Zealand, most Western European states, or other selected countries like Singapore, Japan, and Brunei (27 in all), and visiting the United States for less than ninety days, you need an onward or return ticket, a Machine Readable Passport, and a visa waiver form (or I-94W), which will be provided either by your travel agency or by the airline during check-in or on the plane.

The new requirements apply to both adults and children – who must have their own passports. Passports must be valid for the duration of your stay, and entrants are also required to be photographed and finger-scanned. Some travelers who have been arrested or have criminal records will not be allowed to enter under the VWP; check with your local US embassy before making your trip, and visit the US State Department website (⊛travel.state.gov) for the latest information.

Canadian citizens can continue to visit the US for up to six months, as long as they present proof of citizenship (a passport or birth certificate and photo ID). Questions may be put to the US embassy at 490 Sussex Drive, Ottawa, ON, K1N 1G8 (☎613/238-5335, ⊛www.usembassycanada.gov). If you're planning a work- or study-related visit, you will need to get a visa.

Foreign consulates in Boston are listed in the Directory on p.255.

US embassies abroad

Australia 21 Moonah Place, Yarralumla, Canberra, ACT 2600 ☎02/6214 5600, ⊛usembassy-australia.state.gov
Canada 490 Sussex Drive, Ottawa, ON K1P 5T1 ☎613/238 5335, ⊛www.usembassycanada.gov
Ireland 42 Elgin Rd, Ballsbridge, Dublin 4 ☎01/688 8777, ⊛dublin.usembassy.gov

New Zealand 29 Fitzherbert Terrace, Thorndon, Wellington ☎04/462 6000, ⊛www.usembassy.org.nz
UK 24–31 Grosvenor Square, London, W1A 1AE ☎020/7499 9000, 24hr visa hotline ☎09068/200 290 (60p/min), ⊛www.usembassy.org.uk

Insurance

Getting travel insurance is definitely recommended, especially if you're coming from abroad and are at all concerned about your health – prices for medical attention in the US can be exorbitant. A secondary benefit is that most policies also cover against theft and loss, which can be useful if you're toting around a laptop or other expensive gear.

Before paying for a new policy, **check to see if you're already covered**: credit card companies, home-insurance policies, and private medical plans sometimes cover you and your belongings when you're abroad. In Canada, provincial health plans usually provide partial cover for medical mishaps outside of the country, while holders of official student/teacher/youth cards are entitled to meager accident coverage and hospital in-patient benefits. After exhausting the possibilities above, you might want to contact a specialist travel insurance company, or consider the travel insurance deal offered by Rough Guides (see box). A typical **travel insurance policy** usually provides cover for the loss of baggage, tickets, and – up to a certain limit – cash or checks, as well as cancellation or curtailment of your journey. Many policies can be adapted to reflect the coverage you want – for example, sickness and accident benefits can often be excluded or included at will. If you do take medical coverage, ascertain whether benefits will be paid as treatment proceeds or only after return home, and whether there is a 24-hour medical emergency number. When securing baggage cover, make sure that the per-article limit – typically under $500 – will cover your most valuable possession. If you need to make a claim, you should keep receipts for medicines and medical treatment, and in the event you have anything stolen, you must file an official police report.

Rough Guides travel insurance

Rough Guides has teamed up with Columbus Direct to offer you travel insurance that can be tailored to suit your needs. Readers can choose from many different travel insurance products, including a low-cost backpacker option for long stays; a short break option for city getaways; a typical holiday package option; and may others. There are also annual multi-trip policies for those who travel regularly, with variable levels of cover available. Different sports and activities (trekking, skiing, etc) can be covered if required on most policies.

Rough Guides travel insurance is available to the residents of 36 different countries with different language options to choose from via our website - ⓦwww .roughguidesinsurance.com where you can also purchase the insurance.

Alternatively, UK residents should call ☎0800 083 9507; US citizens should call ☎1-800 749-4922; Australians should call ☎1-300 669 999. All other nationalities should call ☎+44 870 890 2543.

Health

Visitors from Europe, Australia, New Zealand, and Canada don't require any vaccinations to enter the US, and there aren't any out-of-the-ordinary health concerns to consider when coming to the city, other than your own safety; turn to p.42 for a rundown of precautions.

Doctors, pharmacies, and hospitals

For emergencies or ambulances, dial ☎**911**. If you have medical or dental problems that don't require an ambulance, most hospitals will have a walk-in **emergency room**; for the nearest hospital, check with your hotel or dial ☎**411**. Should you need to see a **doctor**, the Massachusetts General Physician Referral Service (Mon–Fri 8.30am–5pm; ☎617/726-5800) puts you in touch with physicians at Massachusetts General Hospital. For immediate care, Inn-House Doctor (839 Beacon Street, Suite B, ☎617/267-9407 or 859-1776, ⓦwww.inn-housedoctor .net) makes 24-hour house calls; rates are $150–250 and prescriptions cost more. Gay and lesbian visitors can drop into the Fenway Community Health Center, 7 Haviland St (☎617/267-0900 or 1-888/242-0900, ⓦwww.fenwayhealth.org), which offers HIV testing during weekdays.

Prescriptions can be filled at the CVS **drugstore** chain (see p.256 in Directory, for branches). You can also pick up over-the-counter analgesics here, though international travelers should bear in mind that if you're partial to a particular brand back home, you should bring some with you – you might not find it in the US (this is especially true of codeine-based painkillers, which require a prescription in the US).

Should you be in an accident, an ambulance will take you to a **hospital** and charge you later. For walk-in emergencies, the Massachusetts General Hospital, 55 Fruit St (☎617/726-2000, ⓦwww.mgh .harvard.edu; Charles/MGH **T**); Beth Israel Deaconess Medical Center, 330 Brookline Ave (☎617/667-7000, ⓦwww.bidmc .harvard.edu; Longwood **T**); and New England Medical Center, 800 Washington St (☎617/636-5000, ⓦwww.nemc.org; NE Medical **T**); all have 24-hour emergency rooms. **Women travelers** with urgent needs can visit the Women's Hospital, 75 Francis St (☎617/732-5500 or 1-800/BWH-9999, ⓦwww.bwh.partners.org; Longwood or Brigham Circle **T**). Parents can take their kids to the Children's Hospital, 300 Longwood Ave (☎617/355-6000, ⓦwww.tch .harvard.edu; Longwood **T**).

Information, websites, and maps

The best source of information for Boston is the Greater Boston Convention and Visitors Bureau's (GBCVB) website, Ⓦwww.bostonusa.com, which maintains up-to-date information on events about town, a terrific list of special deals, and an online reservation service; agents can also make recommendations and bookings for you (call Ⓦ1-888/SEE BOSTON).

Information

The **GBCVB** produces the free *Guidebook to Boston*, a 100-page overview of restaurants, hotels, and sights, and a slimmer *Travel Planner* booklet; both can be mailed to you by request. For information once there, you can stop by the two GBCVB-run tourism centers: one is in Boston Common, west of the Park **T** stop, facing Tremont Street, and the other is in the Prudential Center, at 800 Boylston St. Both are open daily from 9am to 5pm.

Visitors to **Cambridge** can get all the information they need from the Cambridge Office of Tourism (Ⓣ1-800/862-5678, Ⓦwww.cambridge-usa.org), which maintains a well-stocked kiosk in Harvard Square (Mon–Sat 9am–5pm).

The state-wide **Massachusetts Office of Travel and Tourism** (Ⓣ617/727-3201 or 1-800/447-6277, Ⓦwww.massvacation.com) produces *Getaway Guide*, a free magazine featuring reviews of hotels, restaurants, and sights, and offers a telephone reservation service. Though by no means as comprehensive as the GBCVB, the state tourist office does have a UK phone number (Ⓣ020/7978 7429).

Useful websites

Many **websites** contain travel information about Boston. What follows is a short list of both informative and irreverent sites that'll give you the low-down on what's going on around town, local trivia, neighborhood profiles, and other Boston ephemera.

Boston Online Ⓦwww.boston-online.com
General info on the city, including a dictionary of Bostonian English and a guide to public bathrooms.
Boston Phoenix Ⓦwww.bostonphoenix.com
Easily searched site from the city's alternative weekly, with up-to-date arts, music, and nightlife listings, restaurant reviews, and lots of cool links.
The Bostonian Society Ⓦwww.bostonhistory.org
The official historical society of the city has info on its museum (see p.56) as well as a complete transcript of the Boston Massacre trial.
The Greater Boston CVB Ⓦwww.bostonusa.com
Everything you'd expect from the city's official site, plus lots of handy links to other sites.
Link Pink Ⓦwww.linkpink.com
Comprehensive listings of businesses, hotels, shops, and services catering to New England's gay and lesbian community.
Massachusetts Office of Travel and Tourism Ⓦwww.massvacation.com The state-wide tourism bureau is especially useful if you're planning side trips to Cape Cod, Nantucket, or Martha's Vineyard.

Maps

The **maps** in this book, and those given out at Boston tourism kiosks, should satisfy most of your needs; if you want something more comprehensive, best is the rip-proof, waterproof **Rough Guide Map to Boston** ($8.95), a street atlas that pinpoints recommended restaurants, bars, sights, and shops along the way.

Cyclists might want to pick up the Massachusetts Bicycle Coalition Boston **bike map** ($4.95), available at the Globe Corner Bookstore (28 Church St, Ⓣ617/497-6277; Harvard **T**) and online at Ⓦwww.massbikeboston.org.

Arrival

Those traveling to Boston by airplane will arrive at the city's Logan International Airport, located on Boston's easternmost peninsula, a landfill sticking far out into Boston Harbor. From there, you can catch the subway or a water shuttle to Downtown; taking a taxi is another option. For visitors coming into Boston by bus or train, you'll arrive at South Station, near the waterfront at Summer Street and Atlantic Avenue; from there, it's just a short walk or subway ride to Downtown.

By air

Busy **Logan International** – the closest airport to a downtown area in the US – services both domestic and international flights; it has five terminals, lettered A through E, that are connected by a series of courtesy buses. You'll find currency exchange in terminals C and E (daily 10am–5pm), plus information booths, car rental, and Automatic Teller Machines (ATMs) in all five.

After arriving into Logan, the most convenient way downtown is by **subway**. The Airport stop is a short ride away on courtesy bus #11, which you can catch outside on the arrival level of all five terminals. From there, you can take the Blue Line to State or Government Center **T** stations in the heart of Downtown, and transfer to the Red, Orange, and Green lines to reach other points; the ride to Downtown lasts about fifteen minutes ($1.25).

Just as quick, but a lot more fun, is the Harbor Express **water shuttle** that whisks you to either Rowes or Long Wharf near the Blue Line Aquarium **T** station (Mon–Fri 5.45am–11.25pm; Sat 8am–11.40pm; Sun 8am–10.15pm, departure times vary; $12 one-way). From the airport, courtesy bus #66 will take you to the pier.

By comparison, taking a **taxi** is expensive – the airport to a Downtown destination costs $20, plus an extra $4.50 or so in tolls – and time-consuming, given Boston's notorious traffic jams. Save yourself the trouble and avoid them.

By bus or train

The main terminus for both **buses** and **trains** to Boston is **South Station**, in the southeast corner of Downtown at Summer Street and Atlantic Avenue. **Amtrak trains** arrive at one end, in a station with an information booth, newsstands, a food court, and several ATMs (but no currency exchange); **bus carriers** arrive at the clean and modern terminal next door, from where it's a bit of a trek to reach the subway (the Red Line), which is through the Amtrak station and down a level. Those with sizable baggage will find the walk particularly awkward, as there are no porters or handcarts. Note that despite its modernity, the bus terminal's departure and arrival screens are anything but up-to-date – confirm your gate with an agent to be sure. Trains also make a second stop at Boston's **Back Bay Station**, 145 Dartmouth St, on the **T**'s Orange Line. If you've taken a **Chinatown bus** from New York (see p.22), you'll arrive at 33 Harrison St, a block from the Chinatown **T** and the Orange Line. Finally, Amtrak's Downeaster train – which connects Portland, Maine with Boston and points in-between – arrives at **North Station**, which is located in the West End near the FleetCenter.

By car

Driving into Boston is the absolute worst way to get there and is sure to put a damper on your trip if you're a first-time visitor. Nevertheless, two highways provide direct access to the city, **I-90** (on which you can drive from Seattle to Boston without hitting a traffic light) and **I-93**. The latter, which cuts north-south through the heart of the city, has been put underground by the "Big Dig" construction project. The completion of this ten-lane 7.5-mile tunnel has made the city, less congested and driving in Boston much easier than in the past.

A third highway, **I-95**, circumnavigates Boston, and is more useful to drivers trying to avoid the city altogether.

Costs, money, and banks

Boston ranks among the top five most expensive cities in the US to visit. While the high cost of accommodation, food, and drink is compensated for, somewhat, by a wealth of inexpensive (and occasionally free) activities, there's no getting around the fact that the former are going to eat up a lot of your budget. Most of your major purchases, whether hotel or car rental, will require a credit card deposit, even if you wind up paying the total in cash.

Average costs

Hotels are, by far, the biggest money-grubbers: expect to fork out somewhere in the $200 range per night just for the privilege of staying in a Boston hotel. This is due somewhat to the limited accommodation the city provides, met by a fairly constant demand. The city's B&Bs do cost less (around $150 a night) and often have more atmosphere than the chain hotels that make up most of Boston's market; long-term accommodation and hostels can take the price down even further.

Food costs are more reasonable – you could get by on $20 a day, if you stay in a hotel with complimentary breakfast, grab an order of scrod at Faneuil Hall for lunch, and eat only at budget restaurants for dinner. That said, scrimping on food costs when Boston has such terrific restaurants – especially the seafood ones – seems almost a waste of a trip.

The best way to stretch your dollar is to book your hotel through a discount agency like Quickbook (www.quickbook.com), and check the Greater Boston Convention and Visitor Bureau website (www.bostonusa.com) for deals. You'll also save on admission prices if you have a **student ID card**: most attractions in town give discounts when shown an American college ID card or the International Student Identification Card (ISIC; www.isiccard.com). The ISIC is available through most student travel agencies for $22 for Americans; Can$16 for Canadians; Aus$18 for Australians; NZ$20 for New Zealanders; and £7 for UK citizens. For the same price, an International Youth Travel Card (IYTC) is available and offers similar discounts to travelers under 26.

Otherwise, save money by traveling Oct–March, outside of peak season.

Currency

US currency comes in **bills** of $1, $5, $10, $20, $50, and $100, plus various larger (and rarer) denominations. All are the same size and same green color (except for twenties, which now have almost aesthetically pleasing splashes of pink, blue, and yellow in the middle), making it necessary to check each bill carefully. The dollar is made up of 100 cents (¢) in coins of 1 cent (usually called a penny), 5 cents (a nickel), 10 cents (a dime), 25 cents (a quarter), 50 cents (a half dollar), and one dollar. The $2 bill and the half-dollar and dollar coins are seldom seen. Change – especially quarters – is needed for buses, vending machines, and telephones, so always carry plenty. For current exchange rates check www.x-rates.com.

Debit cards and travelers' checks

Once in Boston, you can withdraw funds from your home account using your **debit card** at any ATM machine equipped with the Cirrus or Plus sign (as most are); conveniently, the machines typically give out $20 bills.

Otherwise, you can purchase **travelers' checks**, which have the added security of being replaceable should they be lost or stolen. Checks from Thomas Cook, American Express, and Visa are widely accepted in stores, restaurants, and gas stations, though you should always ask before using them, and pay using the low denominations. Make sure to keep the purchase agreement and a record of the check serial numbers

Visa TravelMoney

A compromise between travelers' checks and plastic is **Visa TravelMoney**, a disposable pre-paid debit card with a PIN, which works in all ATMs that take Visa cards. You load up your account with funds before leaving home, and when they run out, you simply throw the card away. You can buy up to nine cards to access the same funds – useful for couples or families traveling together – and it's a good idea to buy at least one extra as a back-up in case of loss or theft. The card is available in most countries from branches of Thomas Cook and Citicorp, and there's a helpful 24-hour toll-free customer assistance number (☎1-800/847-2911). For more information, check the Visa TravelMoney website at ⓦusa.visa.com /personal/cards/visa_travel_money.

safe and separate from the checks themselves. In the event that your checks are lost or stolen, the issuing company will expect you to report the loss forthwith to their office in Boston; most companies claim to replace lost or stolen checks within 24 hours. Foreign travelers should bring checks issued in US dollars.

Wiring money

Having money wired from home should be a last resort, since you (or, at least, the sender of the money) will pay for the privilege. The fee depends on the amount sent, where it's being sent from and to, and the speed of the service. The quickest way is to have someone take cash to the office of a money-wiring service and have it wired to the office nearest you; within ten to fifteen minutes, the cash should reach you in the US (be sure to bring ID with you).

This service is offered by **Travelers' Express Moneygram** (also available at participating **Thomas Cook** branches) and **Western Union**. See Directory (p.256) for the contact details of local Western Union offices in Boston.

Financial services

American Express UK ☎0870/600 1060, ⓦwww.americanexpress.co.uk; US and Canada ☎1-888/269-6669, ⓦwww.americanexpress.com **Thomas Cook** Canada ☎1-877/894-4333, ⓦwww.thomascook.ca; UK ☎0870/566 6222, 0870/750 5701, ⓦwww.thomascook.com; US ☎1-800/CURRENCY, ⓦwww.fx4travel.com

Travelers' Express Moneygram Canada ☎1-800/933-3278; UK ☎0800/6663 9472; US ☎1-800/926-9400; ⓦwww.moneygram.com **Western Union** Australia ☎1800/649 565 or 1800/501 500; New Zealand ☎09/270 0050; Republic of Ireland ☎1800/395 395; UK ☎0800/833 833; US ☎1-800/325-6000; ⓦwww .westernunion.com

Banks and exchange

Banking hours typically run Mon–Fri 9am–3pm; some banks stay open later on Thursdays and Fridays, and even fewer have Saturday hours. Major banks like Fleet and Bank of Boston will exchange travelers' checks and currencies at the standard exchange rate (one or two percent). Outside of banks, you're limited to exchange bureaus in Cambridge, Boston, and the airport, which set their own, often higher, commission and rates.

Lost credit cards or travelers' checks

American Express checks ☎1-800/221-7282 American Express cards ☎1-800/528-4800 Citicorp/Citibank ☎1-800/645-6556 Diners Club ☎1-800/234-6377 MasterCard cards ☎1-800/826-2181 Thomas Cook/MasterCard checks ☎1-800/223-9920 Visa cards ☎1-800/336-8472 Visa checks ☎1-800/227-6811

City transportation

Much of the pleasure of visiting Boston comes from being in a city built long before cars were invented. Walking around the narrow, winding streets can be a joy; conversely, driving around them can be a nightmare. Be particularly cautious in traffic circles known as "rotaries": when entering, always yield the right of way. If you have a car, better park it for the duration of your trip (see p.36) and get around either by foot or public transit – a system of subway lines, buses, and ferries run by the Massachusetts Bay Transportation Authority (MBTA, known as the "T"; ☎1-800/392-6100, ⊛www.mbta.com).

The subway (T)

While not the most modern system, Boston's subway is cheap, efficient, and charmingly antiquated – its Green Line was America's first underground train, built in the late nineteenth century, and riding it today is akin to riding a tram – albeit, underground.

Four **subway** lines transect Boston and continue out into some of its more proximate neighbors. Each line is color coded and passes through Downtown before continuing on to other districts. The **Red Line**, which serves Harvard, is the most frequent, intersecting South Boston and Dorchester to the south and Cambridge to the north. The **Green Line** hits Back Bay, Kenmore Square, the Fenway, and Brookline. The **Blue Line** heads into East Boston and is most useful for its stop at Logan Airport. The less frequent **Orange Line** traverses the South End and continues down to Roxbury and Jamaica Plain.

All trains travel either **inbound** (towards the quadrant made up of State, Downtown Crossing, Park Street, and Government Center stops) or **outbound** (away from the quadrant). If you're confused about whether you're going in or out, the train's terminus is also designated on the train itself; for instance, trains to Harvard from South Station will be on the "Inbound" platform and heading towards "Alewife."

The four lines are supplemented by a bus rapid transit (BRT) route, the Silver Line, which runs above ground along Washington Street from Downtown Crossing **T**. More of a fast bus than a subway, the line cuts through the heart of South End. In 2005 it

will be extended, with a tunnelled loop connection from the South End to the airport.

The fare to board the **T** is $1.25, payable by tokens purchased at the station or by exact change; when boarding a subway at a station with no token-seller, you can squeeze your dollar bill into the slot at the bottom left of the **T** conductor's till. If you're planning to use public transit a lot, it's a good idea to buy a **visitor's pass** for one ($7.50), three ($18), or seven days ($35) of unlimited subway, bus, commuter rail (zones 1A and 1B), and harbor ferry use. A cheaper alternative is to buy a seven-day Combo pass (valid Sun–Sat), which includes all the above, bar harbor ferry, for $16 – though for bus rides above $2.20 a supplement must be paid.

The biggest drawback to the **T** is the relatively limited hours of operation (Mon–Sat 5.15am–12.30am, Sun 6am–12.30am); the 12.30am closing time means you'll be stuck taking a taxi home after last-call. Free transit maps are available at any station; there's also a subway map at the back of this book.

Buses

The MBTA manages an impressive 170 **bus** routes both in and around Boston. Though the buses run less frequently than the subway and are harder to navigate, they bear two main advantages: they're cheaper (90¢, exact change only) and they provide service to many more points. It's a service used, however, primarily by natives who've grown familiar with the byzantine system of routes. If you're transferring from the **T**, you'll have to pay the full fare, as the two

Color scheming

Each of the **T**'s subway lines is colored after a characteristic of the area it covers. The **Red Line** evokes Harvard's crimson sports jerseys; the **Green Line** refers to the Emerald Necklace (see box, p.124); the **Blue Line** reflects its waterfront proximity; and the **Orange Line** is so named because the street under which it runs, Washington Street, used to be called Orange Street, after King William of Orange. The newer **Silver Line** is the only exception to the color scheme: it's colored for speed – like a silver bullet.

don't combine fares; transferring between buses is free, however, as long as you have a transfer from your original bus. The **T**'s visitor pass (see opposite), includes unlimited bus access over one, three, or seven days in its package, as does the seven-day Combo pass. Be sure to arm yourself with the *Official Public Transport Map*, available at all subway stations, before heading out. Most buses run from 5.30am to 1am, but a few "night owl" buses run until 2.30am, all leaving from the Government Center **T**.

Taxis

Given Boston's small scale and the efficiency (at least during the day) of its public transit, **taxis** aren't as necessary or prevalent as in cities like New York or London. If you do find yourself in need, you can generally hail one along the streets of Downtown or Back Bay, though competition gets pretty stiff after 12.30am when the subway has stopped running and bars and clubs begin to close. If desperate, go to a hotel where cabs cluster, or where, at the very least, a bellhop can arrange one. In Cambridge, taxis mostly congregate around Harvard Square.

Boston Cab (☎617/262-2227) and Bay State Taxi Service (☎617/566-5000) have 24-hour service and accept major credit cards. Other cab companies include Checker Taxi (☎617/536-7000) and Town Taxi (☎617/536-5000). In Cambridge, call the dispatcher (☎617/495-8294) for Yellow Cabs or Ambassador Cabs. As a general rule, the rate starts at $1.75 and goes up by 30¢ per 1/8th mile.

Ferries

Of all the MBTA transportation options, the Inner Harbor **ferry** is by far the most scenic:

$1.50 gets you a ten-minute boat ride with excellent views of Downtown Boston. The boats, covered 100-seaters with exposed upper decks, navigate several waterfront routes by day, though the one most useful to visitors is that connecting Long Wharf with Charlestown (every 30min Mon–Fri 6.30am–8pm, Sat & Sun 10am–6pm).

Another popular harbor route is the **water shuttle** between Logan Airport and Downtown's Long Wharf, a seven-minute trip that makes for a stunning arrival ($10; ☎617/951-0255, ⊛www.massport.com); bus #66 (free) from Logan Airport will get you to the quay.

Several larger **passenger boats** cruise across the harbor and beyond to reach beach destinations such as Provincetown, at the tip of Cape Cod. Two companies make the ninety-minute trip across Massachusetts Bay:

Boston Harbor Cruises depart from Long Wharf daily late May to mid-June departing 9am, returning 4pm; late June to early Sept Mon–Wed departing 9am and 2pm, returning 11am and 4pm; Thurs–Sun departing 9am, 2pm, and 6.30pm, returning 11am, 4pm; and 8.30pm; early Sept to early Oct Mon departing 9am and 2pm, returning 11am and 4pm; Tues and Wed departing 9am returning 4pm; Thurs departing 9am and 6.30pm returning 4pm and 8.30pm; Fri–Sun departing 9am, 2pm, and 6.30pm and returning 11am, 4pm, and 8.30pm; $58 return; ☎617/227-4321, ⊛www.bostonharborcruises.com; Aquarium **T**).

From the west side of the World Trade Center pier, **Bay State Cruises** leave daily late May to early Oct departing 8am, 1pm, & 5.30pm, returning 2hr later; $58 return; ☎617/748-1428, ⊛boston-ptown.com.

Bay State Cruises has an excellent **excursion fare** for weekend day-tripping, as well: $29 will get you to Provincetown and back with a three-hour window to tool around in – keep in mind, though, that the boats take three hours each way (late May to early Sept Fri–Sun departing 9.30am, returning 3.30pm).

Commuter rail

The only time you're likely to travel by **rail** in Boston is if you're making a day-trip to historical Salem, Revolutionary battlefields in Concord, or South Shore spots like Plymouth. All have stations on the MBTA's **commuter rail** (☏617/222-3200 or 1-800/392-6100), a faster, glossier subway than the **T**, with similarly frequent service. Most lines of interest depart from **North Station T**: Rockport, Goucester, and Salem lie on the **Rockport Line** (15min–1hr; $1.25–$6 one-way), while Concord is about midway on the **Fitchburg Line** (20min; $4.50 one-way). The exception, Plymouth, is the last stop on the **Plymouth Line** that leaves from **South Station** (55min; $5.50 one-way). Tickets can be bought in advance or aboard the train itself, though doing the latter incurs a service fee of $1.50 to $2, depending on the time of day.

Driving

A few years ago we would have said don't even try it. The charm of a city that bases its layout on the meandering routes of one-time cowpaths quickly loses its appeal when **driving** enters the picture, but, thanks to the completion of the Big Dig construction project, the situation is somewhat better today. Still, should you want to pull off the road for a while, the price of parking garages is virtually a highway robbery ($25–30 per evening and more overnight). There are metered spots on main streets like Newbury, Boylston, and Charles, but the chances of finding an empty one on any given evening are slim at best.

If you must drive, bear these rules in mind: driving is on the right, seatbelt wearing is mandatory, and the ubiquitous "Permit Parking Only" signs along residential streets must be obeyed – without the requisite parking sticker, you will be ticketed $40 or towed (expect to pay well over $50 to get

your car back). Should you get a ticket, you can try sweet-talking the Office of the Parking Clerk (☏617/635-4410), but it probably won't help.

The cheapest **parking lots** Downtown are Center Plaza Garage, at the corner of Cambridge and New Sudbury streets ($9/hr up to $25 max; ☏617/742-7807), and Garage at Post Office Square ($3.50/30min up to $29 max; ☏617/423-1430). The parking limit at nonmetered spots is two hours, whether posted or not.

As with parking, the cost of **renting a car** in Boston can add up, especially as extra charges, like the $10 Convention Center Finance Fee levied on all rentals, get tacked on to your bill. If you still insist on getting your own wheels, the agencies we list below will happily supply them. A compact car with unlimited mileage will ring in around $42/ day ($30 plus $12 in taxes) before insurance ($10).

Car rental agencies

Alamo ☏ 1-800/522-9696, ⓦ www.alamo.com
Avis ☏1-800/331-1084, ⓦwww.avis.com
Budget ☏1-800/527-0700, ⓦwww .budgetrentacar.com
Dollar ☏1-800/800-4000, ⓦwww.dollar.com
Enterprise Rent-a-Car ☏1-800/325-8007, ⓦwww.enterprise.com
Hertz ☏1-800/654-3001, ⓦwww.hertz.com
National ☏1-800/227-7368, ⓦwww.nationalcar .com
Thrifty ☏1-800/367-2277, ⓦwww.thrifty.com

Cycling

Cycling runs a close second to walking as the preferred mode of city transportation. It's especially popular along the riverside promenades in Cambridge, though hustling along Downtown streets is quite agreeable by bike as well. The usual precautions – wearing a helmet and carrying a whistle – are advised.

You can **rent a bike** starting at around $25/day from Community Bicycle Supply, at 496 Tremont St (☏617/542-8623, ⓦwww .communitybicycle.com; Copley **T**); Back Bay Bicycles, at 333 Newbury St (☏617/247-2336, ⓦwww.backbaybicycles.com; Hynes **T**); or Wheelworks Bicycle Workshop, at 259 Massachusetts Ave, Cambridge (☏617/876-6555; Central **T**). Wheelworks also does **repairs**.

Tours

It's hard to avoid Boston's role in Revolutionary American history – it's proclaimed by landmarks and placards virtually everywhere you go. You could very well spend your entire visit reading every last totem yourself, but a far more enjoyable way to experience the city's lore is by guided tour. Mind you, the walking and bus tours listed below aren't just limited to covering colonial-era Americana; you can also examine the architecture of Charles Bullfinch (Boston by Foot) or the city's literary legacy (Literary Trail). There are also two **multi-tour passes** in the city (see below), which offer discounted packages to several attractions.

Tour companies

Beantown Trolley ☎1-800/343-1328, ☎781/986 6100, ⓦwww.brushhilltours.com. One of the oldest and most popular history tours, covering everything from waterfront wharfs to Beacon Hill Brahmins, with multiple pick-up and drop-off points around town. A 45-minute harbor boat tour is included. $26.

Boston Bike Tours ☎ 617/308-5902, ⓦwww.BostonBikeTours.com. Tours of Boston, Cambridge, and surrounds, departing from Boston Common. May–Oct Sat & Sun 11am; $20–25 including equipment rental and map.

Boston by Foot ☎617/367-2345, ⓦwww.bostonbyfoot.com. Informative ninety-minute walking tours focusing on the architecture and history of Beacon Hill, Copley Square, the South End, North End, and the **T**, including disused stations. May–Oct; $10.

Boston Duck Tours ☎617/267-DUCK, ⓦwww.bostonducktours.com. Excellent tours that take to the streets and the Charles River in restored World War II amphibious landing vehicles; kids get to skipper the bus/boat in the water. Tours depart every half-hour from the Prudential Center, at 101 Huntington Ave; reservations advised in summer. $24.

Boston National Historical Park Visitors Center Freedom Trail Tours ☎617/242-5642, ⓦwww.nps.gov/bost/freedom_trail. Educational walking tours of National Landmark sites; the Black Heritage Trail tour is highly recommended. Sept–May call for hours and reservations; June–July 10am, noon & 2pm. Free.

Brush Hill Grayline Tours ☎1-800/343-1328 or 781/986 6100, ⓦwww.brushhilltours.com. Day-long coach tours to surrounding towns such as Lexington, Concord, Plymouth, and Salem. Late March to Nov; $26–45.

Charles River Wheelmen ☎617/332-8546 or 617/325-BIKE, ⓦwww.crw.org. Organizes free weekly cycling events, ranging from delightful Wednesday Night Ice Cream rides to hardcore weekend morning fitness rides.

Discover Boston Multilingual Trolley Tours ☎617/742-2194, ⓦwww.discoverbostontours.com/trolleytours. Tours of Boston and Cambridge in English; audio devices available with Spanish, French, German, Italian, Japanese, and Russian. Multiple pick-up and drop-off points. $24.

Literary Trail ☎617/350-0358, ⓦwww.lit-trail.org. A three-hour bus tour that takes in all the local hotshots from Henry Wadsworth Longfellow to Henry David Thoreau. $30.

Mass Bay Lines Whale Watch ☎617/542-8000, ⓦwww.massbaylines.com/whalewatch/default. Guaranteed whale sightings or you get another trip. May–June weekends only; late June–early Sept Mon–Fri 10.30am, Sat & Sun 9.30am & 1.30pm; $29.

MYTOWN ☎617/536-2891 ⓦwww.mytowninc.com. Multicultural Youth Tour of What's Now is an organization offering 90-minute youth-led historical walking tours of the South End. May–June Tues & Wed 3.30pm; July–Aug Tues & Wed 10am & 1pm, Fri 10am; Sept–Nov by appointment; $15.

North End Market Tour ☎617/523-6032, ⓦwww.northendmarkettours.com. Award-winning walking and tasting tours of the North End's Italian salumerias, pasticcerias, and enotecas. Reserve well in advance. Wed & Sat 10am & 2pm, Fri 10am & 3pm; $47.25.

Old Town Trolley Tours ☎617/269-7010, ⓦwww.trolleytours.com. Another hop-on, hop-off trolley tour of Boston, this one on ubiquitous orange-and-green trolleys with thematic routes like Sons and Daughters of Liberty and Ghosts and Gravestones. $26.

Photowalks ☎617/851-2273, ⓦwww.photowalks.com. Walking tours that point out the perfect places to point and shoot. Tour themes include Beacon Hill Masterpieces, Postcards of

Boston, Footseteps to Freedom, and the Waterfront. Times vary. $25 each.

Multi-tour passes

Boston CityPass ☎1- 888-330-500, ⓦcitypass .com. Tickets to the Museum of Science, New England Aquarium, Skywalk Observatory, Museum of Fine Arts, Harvard Museum of Natural History, and John F Kennedy Library and Museum for $36.75 – a 50 percent saving.

Go Boston Card ☎617/742-5950, ⓦwww .gobostoncard.com. Unlimited admission to fifty attractions and tours, plus discounts on shopping and dining. One day $45, two day $75, three day $95, five day $115. Discounted prices are available online.

Phones, email, and mail

Staying in touch with friends and family back home won't be a problem in Boston. Every hotel room comes equipped with a phone (though these can be expensive to use), public pay phones are widespread, and many Internet outlets allow you to check your email for free (if you have a laptop with a wireless card, there are also a number of coffee shops and malls where you can sit down and connect). You can buy stamps at post offices all over town and in Cambridge, and mailboxes are easy to find.

Telephones

Boston's area code is ☎617; you can reach the city from elsewhere in the US or Canada by dialing ☎1-617 before the seven-digit number; from abroad, dial your country's international access code, then ☎1-617 and the seven-digit number.

Local calls cost 35¢ in coin-operated public phones; when making a local call, compose all ten digits, including the area code. Operator assistance (☎0) and directory information (☎411) are toll-free from public telephones (but not from in-room phones).

Calling home from the US

You've got several options when calling abroad from the US, the most convenient of which is using your **credit card** – most pay phones now accept them. A cheaper option is using a **prepaid phone card**, sold at most convenience stores in denominations of $5 and $10. You'll find a phone number and special PIN number on the back – just dial the number, enter the PIN, and compose the number you're trying to reach (see box, opposite).

More expensive is using a **telephone charge card** from your phone company back home that will bill the call to your home account. Since most major charge cards are free to obtain, it's certainly worth getting one at least for emergencies, but bear in mind that rates aren't necessarily cheaper than calling from a public phone with a calling card; in fact, they may well be more expensive.

If all else fails, you can call **collect** by dialling ☎0, and then the number you wish to reach; the operator will take it from there. Otherwise, ☎1-800/COLLECT and ☎1-800/CALL-ATT both claim (vehemently) to have the cheapest options.

Mobile phones

If you're from overseas and you want to use your **mobile phone** in Boston, you'll need to check with your phone provider whether it will work abroad and what the call charges are. Unless you have a tri-band phone, it is unlikely that a mobile bought for use outside the US will work inside the States (and vice versa).

Useful telephone numbers

Area code ☎617
Directory assistance ☎411 or 1-800/555-1212 (for toll-free numbers)

Emergencies ☎911 for fire department, police, and ambulance.
Operator ☎0

International calling codes

Calling Boston from abroad international access code + 1 + 617 + seven-digit number.

To make international calls **from the US**, dial **011** followed by the country code (note that if you're calling **Canada**, you simply need to dial a 1, then the area code and number, as though you were making a domestic call):

Australia 61
Ireland 353

New Zealand 64
United Kingdom 44

For codes not listed here, dial the operator or check the front of the local White Pages.

In the UK, for all but the very top-of-the-range packages, you'll have to inform your phone provider before going abroad to get international access switched on. You may get charged extra for this depending on your existing package and **where you are traveling** to. You're also likely to be charged extra for incoming calls while away. If you want to retrieve messages, you'll have to ask your provider for a new access code, as your home one is unlikely to work.

For further information about using your phone abroad, check out ⓦwww.telecomsadvice.org.uk/features/using_your_mobile_abroad.

Email

The best way to check your **email** is to pop into a local university and use one of their free public computers. Harvard's Holyoke Center, at 1350 Massachusetts Ave in Cambridge, has a couple of stations with ten-minute access maximum. The same goes for MIT's Rogers Building, at 77 Massachusetts Ave (also in Cambridge). Boston's main public library, at 700 Boylston St, has free fifteen-minute Internet access on the ground floor of the Johnson building. Cybercafés are limited to *Newbury Open*, at 252 Newbury St (Mon–Fri 9am–8pm, Sat & Sun noon–7pm; $5/hr; ☎617/267-9716, ⓦwww.newburyopen.net; Back Bay **T**), and *Adrenaline Zone*, at 40 Brattle St, lower level (Sun–Thurs 11am–11pm, Fri & Sat 11am–midnight; $5/hr; ☎617/876-1314, ⓦwww.adrenzone.com; Harvard **T**).

If you have a laptop with a wireless card, you'll find **wireless access** plentiful in Boston. Most hotels feature wi-fi hotspots, as does the public library, *Newbury Open*, the CambridgeSide Galleria, in Cambridge, and branches of *Starbucks*. For a list of wi-fi hotspots in and around the city, visit ⓦboston.about.com/b/a/022333.

Mail

Boston's **postal service** is as efficient as most US cities' and has multiple outlets scattered about town. For the quickest service, use the coin-operated machines to buy books of stamps – letters and postcards within the US cost 37¢ and 23¢, respectively.

The biggest post office in Downtown is J.W. McCormack Station in Post Office Square, at 90 Devonshire St (Mon–Fri 7.30am–5pm; ☎617/720-4754); Cambridge's central branch is at 770 Massachusetts Ave, in Central Square (Mon–Fri 7.30am–6pm, Sat 7.30am–3pm; ☎617/876-0620). The General Post Office, 25 Dorchester Ave, behind South Station, is open 24 hours a day (☎617/654-5326). You can receive mail at the latter by having it addressed to you c/o Poste Restante, GPO, 25 Dorchester Ave, Boston MA, 02205. To collect letters, present some form of photo ID at the window between 10am and 1pm Monday–Saturday. Note that non-acquired letters are thrown out after thirty days.

The media

Despite its legacy as the birthplace of America's first newspaper (*Publick Occurences*, published in 1690), Boston hardly ranks among the country's most media-savvy cities. The better media here is intellectual rather than newsy, and you'll certainly be engaged by *The Atlantic Monthly*, one of the US's most venerable magazines, and a slew of leftist weeklies. For all that, though, Boston's real reporting strength is sports-related: a hurricane may have hit Louisiana, but if the Celtics or the Patriots played the same day, that's what will be on the front page of the city's two daily papers (and the top story on television and radio news). It makes for pretty parochial coverage but newspapers from other US cities, as well as foreign newspapers and magazines, can be bought at Out of Town News, at Harvard Square, and major bookstores like Barnes & Noble and Borders.

Newspapers and magazines

While Boston lacks the media flash of nearby New York City, it's no stranger to intrigue: two *Boston Globe* columnists were busted in 1998 for writing fake stories. Though the scandal tarnished the reputation of the city's oldest newspaper, **The Boston Globe** (50¢; ⓦ www.boston.com/globe) remains Boston's best general daily; its fat Sunday edition ($2) includes substantial sections on art, culture, and lifestyle. The **Boston Herald** (50¢; ⓦ www.bostonherald.com) is the *Globe's* tabloid alternative and is best for getting your gossip and local sports coverage fix. The free daily (Mon–Fri) **Metro** paper (ⓦ www.metro .lu) is now also available in the city from bins outside T stations, though those familiar with its London counterpart will find it a slimmer, less comprehensive read.

The rest of the city's print media consists primarily of listings-oriented and **free weekly papers**. To know what's going on, the *Boston Phoenix* (ⓦ www.bostonphoenix .com), available at sidewalk newspaper stands around town, is essential, offering extensive entertainment listings as well as good feature articles. Other freebies like *Improper Bostonian* (ⓦ www.improper.com), the *Phoenix's* biweekly listings magazine, *Stuff@Night*, and *The Boston Event Guide* all have good listings of new and noteworthy happenings about town (though the features are primarily ad-driven). *Bay Windows* (ⓦ www.baywindows.com), a small weekly catering to the gay and lesbian population, is available free at most South End cafés and bars; the cover price is 50¢ otherwise. The *Cambridge TAB* has news articles and listings exclusively about local Cambridge events.

The monthly **Boston Magazine** ($3.95; ⓦ www.bostonmagazine.com) is a glossy lifestyle publication with good restaurant reviews and a yearly "Best of Boston" round-up.

TV and radio

You're likely to see more **television** than you might back home just by having a drink or eating out: televisions are as common as pint glasses in Boston bars and restaurants, and they're usually airing home-team games. Most hotels have cable TV, so you'll be able to catch regular **news** on the four major networks: CBS (channel 4), ABC (channel 5), NBC (channel 7), Fox (channel 25), and CNN, as well as keep abreast of your favorite dramas and sitcoms.

The best **radio stations** are on the FM dial, including WGBH (89.7), which carries National Public Radio (NPR) shows, plus jazz, classical, and world music; WBUR (90.9), earnest, leftist talk radio; WJMN (94.5) for good hip-hop beats; WFNX (101.7) for mainstream alternative hits; and WODS (103.3), an oldies station. To get in on Boston's sports fanaticism, tune into WEEI (850AM) for day-long sports talk.

Opening hours, public holidays, and festivals

The opening hours of specific attractions, monuments, memorials, stores, and offices are given in the relevant accounts throughout the guide. Telephone numbers are provided so that you can check current information with the places themselves.

Opening hours

As a general rule, **museums** are open daily 10am to 5.30pm, though some have extended summer hours; a few art galleries stay open until 9pm or so one night a week. Smaller, private museums close for one day a week, usually Monday or Tuesday. **Federal office buildings** (some of which incorporate museums) are open Monday through Friday 9am to 5.30pm. **Stores** are usually open Monday through Saturday 10am to 7pm and Sunday noon–5pm; some have extended Thursday and Friday night hours. **Malls** tend to be open Monday through Saturday 10am to 7pm (or later) and Sunday noon to 6pm.

In the wake of the terrorist attacks of September 11, 2001 – plus subsequent security scares – some Boston buildings and landmarks have **suspended tours** and **prohibited access** to the general public as they re-evaluate security measures. Throughout the Guide we've noted the places that may be affected by such changes and recommend calling ahead before heading off for a tour at any of these destinations.

Public holidays and festivals

On the **national public holidays** listed in the box opposite, stores, banks, and public and federal offices are liable to be closed all day. The Museum of Fine Arts and Isabella Gardner museums, on the other hand, open on holiday Mondays – but no others – year round. The traditional **summer tourism season**, when many attractions have extended opening hours, runs from **Memorial Day to Labor Day**.

Boston has a huge variety of **annual festivals and events**, many of them historical in scope, like the annual Fourth of July reading of the Declaration of Independence and the mid-June reenactment of the Battle of Bunker Hill. Such is the range of festivals throughout the rest of the year, it's hard to turn up without your trip coinciding with at least one; Boston's full **festival calendar** is detailed in Chapter 21, "Festivals and events."

Do note that during all major festival periods – particularly the Head of the Charles Regatta, Easter, Memorial Day, and the Fourth of July – it can be very difficult to find accommodation in the city. Book well in advance if you plan to visit Boston at any of these times.

National public holidays

The following are public holidays on which banks, post offices, and many (although by no means all) shops and attractions will be closed:

Jan 1 **New Year's Day**

Third Mon in Jan **Martin Luther King, Jr.'s Birthday**

Third Mon in Feb **Presidents' Day**

Last Mon in May **Memorial Day**

July 4 **Independence Day**

First Mon in Sept **Labor Day**

Second Mon in Oct **Columbus Day**

Nov 11 **Veterans' Day**

Fourth Thurs in Nov **Thanksgiving**

Dec 25 **Christmas Day**

Crime and personal safety

Boston is one of the safer American cities, making solo travel, even for women, relatively worry-free. There are, as with anywhere, exceptions; at night-time especially, areas like Dorchester, Roxbury, the Fens, Downtown Crossing, and parts of the South End can feel deserted and sketchy – but you're unlikely to find yourself in many of these neighborhoods after dark, anyway. The **T** is also safe by day and, for the most part, at night; if you stick to the lines that serve the major nightlife areas (especially the Green and Red lines), you're unlikely to have any trouble.

Pickpocketing is less of a problem in Boston than it is elsewhere in the US, but that doesn't mean it never happens; use common sense and keep an eye on your belongings when at the ATM, on the subway, and paying up at corner stores. If you are robbed, call the police at ☏911. Note that **drugs**, including marijuana, are illegal and you will be fined and possibly sentenced to jail time if caught taking or selling them.

Travelers with disabilities

People with disabilities will find Boston fairly easy to negotiate – the city is pretty flat, most curbs have dropped lips, and many restaurants and attractions are wheelchair-accessible. For all its modernization, however, Boston remains a colonial city with the prerequisite cobblestoned streets and winding roads to match – sections around Faneuil Hall, the Financial District, and Beacon Hill, in particular, may require extra planning.

Transportation

It's always a good idea for people with special needs to alert their travel agents of this when booking: things are far simpler for those with disabilities when the various travel operators or carriers you'll be using are expecting you. A **medical certificate** of your fitness to travel, provided by your doctor, is also useful; some airlines or insurance companies may insist on it. Most **airlines** do whatever they can to ease your journey and will usually let attendants of more seriously disabled people accompany them at no extra charge. **Amtrak** has train cars with accommodation for passengers with disabilities, and guide dogs travel free and may accompany blind, deaf, or disabled passengers in the carriage. Be sure to give 24 hours' notice. **Greyhound buses** are not equipped with lifts for wheelchairs, though staff will assist with boarding, and the "Helping Hand" scheme offers two-for-the-price-of-one tickets to passengers unable to travel alone (make sure to carry a doctor's certificate).

The American Automobile Association produces the *Handicapped Driver's Mobility Guide* for **disabled drivers** (available from Quantum-Precision Inc, 225 Broadway, Suite 3404, New York, NY 10007). The larger car rental companies provide cars with hand controls at no extra charge, though only on their full-size (which is to say, most expensive) models; reserve well in advance.

Getting around

For people with mobility impairments, getting around Boston is possible for the simple reason that the city is relatively flat and curb cuts abound. **Public transportation** can also be used: many MBTA buses and **T** stops are wheelchair-accessible; for detailed information, call ☎617/222-5976 or ☎617/222-5123, or visit ⓦwww.mbta .com. In addition, most major **taxi** companies have some vehicles with wheelchair lifts; Metro Cab (☎617/242-8000) comes highly recommended.

Very Special Arts (☎617/350-7713; ⓦwww.accessexpressed.net) has superior information on the accessibility of museums, sights, movie theaters, and other cultural venues in the Boston area. For everything else, contact the **Massachusetts Office on Disability**, a one-stop resource for all accessibility issues whether in Boston or further afield; call ☎617/727-7440 or toll-free on 1-800/322-2020.

Contacts for travelers with disabilities

In the US and Canada

Access-Able ⓦwww.access-able.com. Online resource for travelers with disabilities.
Massachusetts Office on Disability ☎1-800/322-2020, ⓦwww.state.ma.us/mod

Mobility International USA ☎541/343-1284, ⓦwww.miusa.org. Information and referral services, access guides, tours, and exchange programs. Annual membership ($35) includes quarterly newsletter.
Society for the Advancement of Travelers with Handicaps (SATH) ☎212/447-7284, ⓦwww.sath.org. Nonprofit organization comprising travel agents, tour operators, hotels, airlines, and travelers with disabilities.
Wheels Up! ☎1-888/389-4335, ⓦwww .wheelsup.com. Provides discounted airfares and tour prices for disabled travelers; also publishes a free monthly newsletter.

In the UK and Ireland

Disability Action Group Northern Ireland ☎028/9049 1011. Provides information about access for disabled travelers abroad.
Holiday Care UK ☎0845/124-9971 (in UK), +44 208/760-0072 (outside UK) , Minicom ☎0845/124-9976, ⓦwww.holidaycare.org.uk. Provides free lists of accessible accommodation in the US and other destinations.
Irish Wheelchair Association Republic of Ireland ☎01/833 8241. Useful information provided about traveling abroad with a wheelchair.
RADAR (Royal Association for Disability and Rehabilitation) UK ☎020/7250 3222, Minicom ☎020/7250 4119, ⓦwww.radar.org.uk. A good source for information and advice on travel.

In Australia and New Zealand

ACROD (Australian Council for Rehabilitation of the Disabled) Australia ☎02/6282 4333, ⓦwww.acrod.org.au. Provides lists of travel agencies and tour operators for people with disabilities.
Disabled Persons Assembly New Zealand ☎04/801 9100, ⓦwww.dpa.org.nz. Resource center with lists of travel agencies and tour operators.

The City

The City

Downtown Boston

Boston's compact **Downtown** encompasses both the colonial heart and the contemporary core of the city. This assemblage of compressed red-brick buildings tucked in the shadow of modern office towers may seem less glamorous than other American big-city centers, but the sheer concentration of historic sights here more than makes up for whatever's lacking in flash. During the day, there's a constant buzz of commuters and tourists, but come nightfall, the streets thin out considerably. A few notable exceptions are the commercialized Quincy Market area, which has a decent, if somewhat average, bar scene; Chinatown, with its popular late-night restaurants; and the Theater District, which is particularly animated on weekends.

Boston Common (a king-sized version of the tidy greenspaces at the core of innumerable New England villages) is the starting point for the city's popular **Freedom Trail**, a self-guided walking tour that connects an assortment of historic sights by a ribbon of red brick embedded in the pavement. Abutting the Common, several churches and old buildings are worth a peek on your way toward **Washington Street**, where the **Old State House** and **Old South Meeting House** provide high-water marks in pre-Revolution interest. Just east, the **Financial District**'s short streets still follow the tangled patterns of colonial-village lanes, though they are now lined with all manner of tall office buildings. A couple of blocks north stands the ever-popular meeting place of **Faneuil Hall**. East of Boston Common, small but vibrant **Chinatown** and the nearby **Theater District** are primarily of interest after dark; also in the area is the **Leather District**, where empty warehouses and low rents gave rise, in the 1990s, to a series of art galleries. Finally, you can get the flavor of Boston Harbor, once the third-busiest in the world and now enjoying a new vibrancy thanks to its recon-nection to the city with the completion of the Big Dig. Along the waterfront, scenic wharfs jut out into Massachusetts Bay; the most bustling, **Long Wharf**, is the departure point for **whale-watching** excursions and trips to a handful of offshore **islands** that make for relaxing getaways from the center.

Though colonial Downtown boasted numerous hills, they've since been smoothed over, and only the name of a particularly pronounced peak – Tri-mountain – lives on in **Tremont Street**. **King's Chapel**, on Tremont, and the nearby Old State House mark the periphery of Boston's earliest town center, and the colonies' first church, market, newspaper, and prison were all clustered here, though much closer to the shoreline than are the plaques that now mark their former sites. **Spring Lane**, a tiny pedestrian passage off Washington Street, recalls the springs that lured the earliest settlers over to the Shawmut Peninsula from Charlestown. The most evocative streets, however, are those whose essential char-acters have been less diluted over the years – **School Street**, **State Street**, and the eighteenth-century enclave known as **Blackstone Block**, near Faneuil Hall.

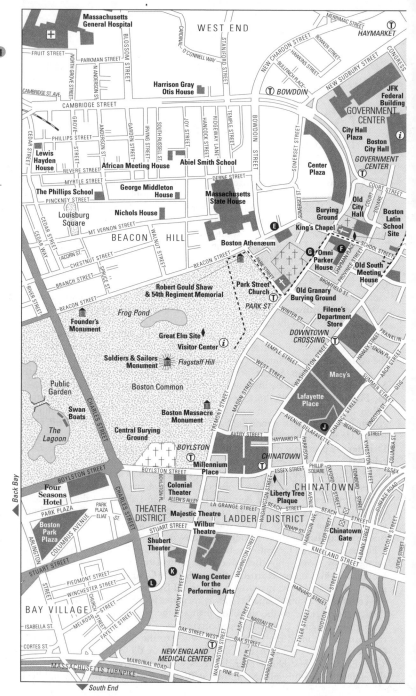

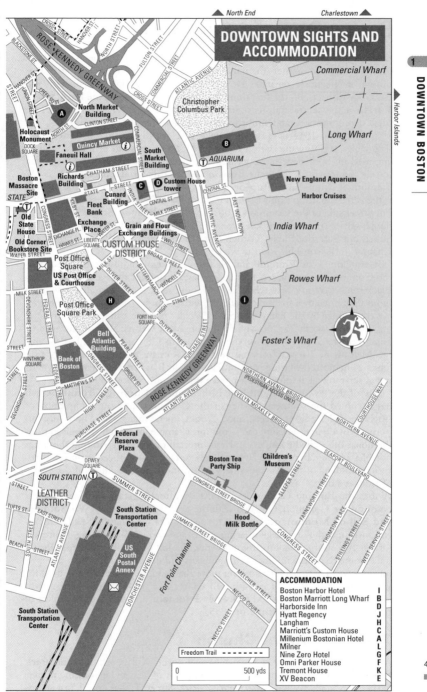

Commercial Wharf

Christopher Columbus Park

Long Wharf

Harbor Islands

A North Market Building

Holocaust Monument

Quincy Market *i*

Faneuil Hall

South Market Building

B

i AQUARIUM

Boston Massacre Site

STATE

Richards Building

Old State House

Old Corner Bookstore Site

WATER STREET

Boston Massacre Site

Fleet Bank

Cunard Building **C** **D** Custom House tower

New England Aquarium

Harbor Cruises

India Wharf

Exchange Place

Grain and Flour Exchange Buildings

CUSTOM HOUSE DISTRICT

Post Office Square

US Post Office & Courthouse

Post Office Square Park

H

Rowes Wharf

Bell Atlantic Building

Bank of Boston

I

N

Foster's Wharf

NORTHERN AVENUE BRIDGE (PEDESTRIAN ACCESS ONLY)

EVELYN MOAKLEY BRIDGE

Federal Reserve Plaza

DEWEY SQUARE

SOUTH STATION *T*

LEATHER DISTRICT

Boston Tea Party Ship

Children's Museum

South Station Transportation Center

Hood Milk Bottle

US South Postal Annex

South Station Transportation Center

Fort Point Channel

Freedom Trail - - - - - - -

0   500 yds

ACCOMMODATION

Boston Harbor Hotel	I
Boston Marriott Long Wharf	B
Harborside Inn	D
Hyatt Regency	J
Langham	H
Marriott's Custom House	C
Millenium Bostonian Hotel	A
Milner	L
Nine Zero Hotel	G
Omni Parker House	F
Tremont House	K
XV Beacon	E

Boston Common and around

Boston's premier greenspace, **Boston Common**, is a fifty-acre chunk of green, which is neither meticulously manicured nor especially attractive, though it effectively separates Downtown from the posher Beacon Hill and Back Bay districts. It's the first thing you'll see emerging from the **Park Street T station**, the central transfer point of America's first subway and a magnet for small demonstrations and, unfortunately, panhandlers.

Established in 1634 as "a trayning field" and "for the feeding of Cattell," as a slate tablet opposite the station recalls, the Common is still primarily utilitarian, used by both pedestrian commuters on their way to Downtown's office towers and tourists seeking the **Boston Visitor Information Pavilion** at 147 Tremont St (Mon–Sat 8.30am–5pm, Sun 10am–6pm; ☏617/536-4100), which is the official starting point of the Freedom Trail. The shabbiness of the Tremont Street side of the Common is offset by lovely **Beacon Street**, which runs the length of the northern side, from the gold-domed State House to Charles Street, opposite the Public Garden (for fuller coverage of Beacon Street, see Chapter 4, Beacon Hill and the West End).

Even before John Winthrop and his fellow Puritan colonists earmarked Boston Common for public use, it served as pasture land for the Reverend William Blackstone, Boston's first white settler. Soon after, it disintegrated into little more than a gallows for pirates, alleged witches, and various religious heretics – a commoner by the name of Rachell Whall was once hanged here for stealing a bonnet worth 75¢. Newly elected president George Washington made a much-celebrated appearance on the Common in 1789, as did his aide-de-camp, the Marquis de Lafayette, several years later. Ornate eighteenth-century iron fencing encircled the entire park until World War II, when it was taken down for use as scrap metal; it's now said to grace the bottom of Boston Harbor.

One of the few actual sights here is the **Central Burying Ground**, which has occupied the southeast corner of the Common, near the intersection of Boylston and Tremont streets, since 1756. Gilbert Stuart, best known for his portraits of George Washington – the most famous of which is replicated on the dollar bill – died penniless and was interred in Tomb 61. Among the other notables are members of the largest family to take part in the Boston Tea Party, various soldiers of the Revolutionary Army, and Redcoats killed in the Battle of Bunker Hill.

From the Burying Ground it's a short walk to **Flagstaff Hill**, the highest point on the Common, crowned with the granite, pillared Civil War **Soldiers and Sailors Monument**, which is topped by a bronze statue of Lady Liberty and surrounded by two cap-wearing sailors and two bayonet-toting infantry. A former repository of colonial gunpowder, the hill overlooks the **Frog Pond**, once home to a large number of amphibians and site of the first water pumped into the city. These days it's nothing more than a kidney-shaped pool, used for wading in summer and ice-skating in winter (see p.243). From here, a path leads to the elegant, two-tiered **Brewer Fountain**, an 1868 bronze replica of one from the Paris Exposition of 1855.

The Park Street Church

An oversized version of a typical New England village church, the **Park Street Church** (July–Aug daily 9am–3pm, rest of year by appointment; free; ☏617/523-3383, ⊛www.parkstreet.org; Park Street **T**) has stood just across from Boston Common since 1809, at the northeast corner of Park and Tremont streets. Though a rather uninteresting mass of bricks and mortar, its ornate 217-foot-tall white telescoping **steeple** is undeniably impressive. To get an idea of the immensity of the building, including the spire, check out the view from tiny Hamilton Place, across Tremont. Ultimately, the structure's reputation rests not on its size but on the scope of events that took place inside: the first Sunday School in the country started here in 1818; the next year, the parish sent the country's first missionaries to Hawaii; a decade later, on July 4, 1829, William Lloyd Garrison delivered his first public address calling for the nationwide abolition of slavery (Massachusetts had already scrapped it in 1783); and on July 4, 1831, the classic patriotic song *America* ("My country 'tis of thee...") was first sung to the church rafters.

△ Boston Common

Park Street itself slopes upward along the edge of Boston Common toward the State House (see p.56). It was once known as **Bulfinch Row**, for its many brick townhouses designed by the architect Charles Bulfinch (see p.89), but today only one remains – the imposing bay-windowed **Amory-Ticknor House** at no. 9, built in 1804 for George Ticknor, the first publisher of the *Atlantic Monthly*; unfortunately, it's not open to the public.

The Old Granary Burying Ground

One of the more peaceful stops on the always-busy Freedom Trail, the **Old Granary Burying Ground** (daily 8am–dusk; free; Park Street **T**) is the resting place of numerous leaders of the American Revolution. Its odd name comes from a grain warehouse that once stood on the site of the adjacent Park Street Church. The two-acre tract, set a few feet above the busy Tremont Street sidewalk, was originally part of Boston Common; today it's hemmed in by buildings on three sides. The fourth, with its Egyptian-Revival arch entrance, fronts Tremont.

From any angle, you can spot the stocky **obelisk** at dead center that marks the grave of Benjamin Franklin's parents, but some of the most famous gravesites can only be properly appreciated from the Tremont sidewalk, at the southern rim of the plot. On the side closest to Park Street Church, a boulder with an attached plaque marks the tomb of revolutionary **James Otis**, known for his articulate tirades against British tyranny. A few tombs down, as you head away from the church, rest the bones of **Samuel Adams**, the charismatic patriot whose sideline in beer brewing has kept him a household name. Next to his tomb is the group grave of the five people killed in the **Boston Massacre** of 1770, an event which fueled anti-Tory feeling in Boston (see p.58).

Somewhat more secure burial vaults and table tombs – semi-submerged sarcophagi – were preferred by wealthier families. **Peter Faneuil**, who gave his money and his name to Boston's most prominent hall, is interred in one of the latter in the left rear corner of the grounds. Midway along the back path is the grave of famed messenger and silversmith **Paul Revere**, opposite that of Judge **Samuel Sewall**, the only Salem Witch Trial magistrate to later admit that he was wrong. Back across from the judge's grave on the Park Street Church side, a white pillar marks the resting spot of Declaration of Independence signer **John Hancock**. Robert Treat Paine, another signatory, lies along the eastern periphery.

The Boston Athenæum

Around the block from the Old Granary Burying Ground, the venerable **Boston Athenæum**, at 10½ Beacon St (Mon 9am–8pm, Tues–Fri 9am–5.30pm, Sat 9am–4pm; free; ☎617/227-0270, ⊛www.bostonathenaeum.org; Park Street **T**), was established in 1807, and stakes its claim as one of the oldest independent research libraries in the country. In naming the building, the Boston Brahmin founders demonstrated not only their high-minded classicism but also their marketing sensibility, as the city was consequently endowed with a lofty sobriquet – the "Athens of America" – that has stuck.

Following extensive renovations in 2002 to "modernize" the edifice (a replica of the Palazzo da Porta Festa in Vicenza, Italy), the most significant change, at least for visitors, is that only the first-floor library is open to nonmembers. Best known are its special collections, including the original library of King's Chapel – which counts the 1666 edition of Sir Walter Raleigh's *History of the*

The Freedom Trail

Boston is so permeated by history that the city often stands accused of living in its past, and tourist-friendly contrivances like the **Freedom Trail** only serve to perpetuate that notion. It originated when, like many American cities, Boston experienced an economic slump in the years after World War II as people migrated to the suburbs; in response, resident William Schofield came up with the idea of a trail highlighting historic Boston sights to lure visitors – and their money – back into town.

Delineated by a 2.5-mile-long red-brick stripe in the sidewalk, the trail stretches from Boston Common to Charlestown, linking sixteen points "significant in their contribution to this country's struggle for freedom." It's a somewhat vague qualifier, resulting in the inclusion of several sights that have little to do with Boston's place in the American Revolution. In the relevant column, there's the Revolution-era **Old North Church**, whose lanterns warned of the British arrival; **Faneuil Hall**, where opposition to the Brits' proposed tea tax was voiced; the **Old South Meeting House**, where the first protests took place; the **Old State House**, which served as the Boston seat of British government; and the site of the **Boston Massacre**.

More dubious stops include the **USS *Constitution***, built fully two decades after the Declaration of Independence (but which failed, notably, to sink under British cannon fire, earning her the nickname "Old Ironsides"); the **Park Street Church**, built another fifteen years later as a Puritan place of worship; and the former **Old Corner Bookstore**, a publishing house for American (and some British) writers. You'll also find two reminders of British dominion – the **Bunker Hill Monument**, an obelisk commemorating, ironically, a British victory, albeit in the guise of a moral one for America, and **King's Chapel**, built to serve the King's men stationed in Boston. Finally, you can check out the digs of the gilt-domed **Massachusetts State House** after visiting the gravesites of the Boston luminaries who fought for it; they lie interred in three separate **cemeteries**.

Unfortunately, some of the touches intended to accentuate the attractions' appeal move closer to tarnishing it. The people in period costume stationed outside some of the sights can't help but grate a little, and the artificially enhanced atmosphere is exaggerated by the bright red-brick trail and pseudo old signage that connects the sights. Still, the Freedom Trail remains the easiest way to orient yourself Downtown, and is especially useful if you'll only be in Boston for a short time, as it does take in many "must-see" sights. For more information and an interactive timeline of Boston's history, visit ⓦ www.thefreedomtrail.org. You can also pick up a detailed National Park Service **map** at the **Visitor Information Pavilion** (see p.50) in Boston Common, from where the trail begins; a combination entrance ticket ($10) is available for three sights – the Old South Meeting House, the Old State House, and the Paul Revere House. It can be purchased from the ticket desk at each attraction.

Freedom Trail sights

World among its holdings – as well as books from the private library of George Washington. There is also an impressive array of paintings by the likes of John Singer Sargent and Gilbert Stuart.

King's Chapel Burying Ground and King's Chapel

Boston's oldest cemetery, the moody **King's Chapel Burying Ground**, located at the northeast corner of Beacon and Tremont streets (10am–4pm; free; Park Street **T**), often goes unnoticed by busy passersby. Coupled with its accompanying church, however, it's well worth a tour despite the din of nearby traffic. There are many beautifully etched gravestones here, with their winged skulls and contemplative seraphim; one of the best examples belongs to an unknown Joseph Tapping near the Tremont Street side. Among the many prominent Bostonians buried here are **John Winthrop**, the first governor of Massachusetts, and **Mary Chilton**, the first Pilgrim to set foot on Plymouth Rock; near the center of the plot is the tomb of **William Dawes**, the unsung patriot who accompanied Paul Revere on his famous "midnight ride" to Lexington. King's Chapel Burying Ground was one of the favorite Boston haunts of author **Nathaniel Hawthorne**, who visited the grave of a certain Elizabeth Pain, the inspiration for the adulterous Hester Prynne in his novel *The Scarlet Letter* (Hawthorne himself is buried in Concord's Sleepy Hollow Cemetery; see p.159).

King's Chapel

The most conspicuous thing about gray, foreboding **King's Chapel**, on the premises of the burying grounds, is its lack of a steeple (there were plans for one, just not enough money). But the belfry does boast the biggest bell ever cast by silversmith Paul Revere, which you can't help but notice if you happen to pass by at chime time. A wooden chapel was built on this site first, amid some controversy in 1686, when King James II revoked the Massachusetts Bay Colony's charter and installed Sir Edmund Andros as governor, giving him orders to found an Anglican parish – a move that for obvious reasons didn't sit too well with Boston's Puritan population. The present chapel, completed in 1754 by Peter Harrison under instructions to create a church "that would be the equal of any in England," is entered through a pillar-fronted portico added in 1789, when it became the country's first Unitarian Church.

While hardly ostentatious, the elegant Georgian interior, done up with wooden Corinthian columns and lit by chandeliers, provides a marked contrast to the minimalist adornments of Boston's other old churches. It also features America's oldest pulpit, which dates from the late 1600s, and many original pews, including a Governor's Pew along the right wall. The best time to enter the building is during one of the weekly **chamber music concerts** (Tues 12.15–12.45pm; $2 suggested donation).

The Washington Street Shopping District

To a Bostonian, Downtown proper comes in two packages: the **Washington Street Shopping District** (namely the School Street area and Downtown Crossing) and the adjacent Financial District (see p.58). The former, situated east of the King's Chapel Burying Ground, has some of the city's most historic sights – the **Old Corner Bookstore**, **Old South Meeting House**, and **Old State House** – but it tends to shut down after business hours, becoming eerily quiet at night. All can be seen in half a day, though you'll obviously need to allow more time if shopping is on your agenda; the stretch around **Downtown Crossing** is decidedly more commercial than historical.

Narrow and heavily trafficked today, in colonial times **Washington Street** connected the Old State House to the city gates at Boston Neck, an isthmus that joined the Shawmut Peninsula to the mainland, thus ensuring its position as the commercial nerve center of Boston. The best way to begin exploring the area is via **School Street**, anchored on its northern edge by the dignified **Omni Parker House**, the city's most venerable hotel, which has a rich history: John F. Kennedy announced his congressional candidacy here in 1946, down the hall from the room in which Charles Dickens first read *A Christmas Carol*, and Ho Chi Minh and Malcolm X both used to wait tables at the hotel's restaurant. If you'd like, pop in and order a slice of Boston cream pie (really a layered cake with custard filling and chocolate frosting all around): it was invented here in 1855, and the hotel reportedly still bakes 25 of them a day.

For the rest of its modest length, School Street offers up some of the best in Old Boston charm, beginning with the antique gaslights that flank the severe west wall of King's Chapel. Just beyond is a grand French Second Empire building that served as Boston City Hall from 1865 to 1969; it's near the site of the original location of the **Boston Latin School**, founded in 1635 (a mosaic embedded in the sidewalk just outside the iron gates marks the exact spot). Benjamin Franklin, a statue of whom graces the courtyard, and John Hancock were among the more illustrious graduates of this, America's first public school.

The Old Corner Bookstore

A few doors down from the Latin School site, where School Street joins Washington, stands the gambrel-roofed, red-brick building that was once the **Old Corner Bookstore** (State Street **T**). In the nineteenth century, Boston's version of London's Fleet Street occupied the stretch of Washington from here to Old South Meeting House, with a convergence of booksellers, newspaper headquarters, and publishers; most celebrated among them was Ticknor & Fields, Boston's hottest-ever literary salon. This highly esteemed publishing house was once located in the bookstore itself and handled the likes of Emerson, Longfellow, Hawthorne, Dickens, and Thackeray. One of America's oldest literary magazines, *Atlantic Monthly*, was published upstairs here for many years; later *The Boston Globe* moved in. It too has since vacated, but it maintained the site as The Globe Corner Bookstore, an atmospheric travel bookstore until its demise here, in 1997 (a second outlet carries on the trade in Harvard Square; see p.231). Currently, at press time, the building is still looking for a tenant.

The Old South Meeting House

A charming brick church building recognizable by its tower, a separate but attached structure that tapers into an octagonal spire, Washington Street's big architectural landmark, the **Old South Meeting House**, faces the Old Corner Bookstore one block south, at no. 310 (9am–5pm $5, kids $1; ☎617/482 -6439, ⓦwww.oldsouthmeetinghouse.org; Downtown Crossing **T**). An earlier cedarwood structure on the spot burned down in 1711, clearing the way for what is now the second-oldest church building in Boston, after Old North Church in the North End (see p.74). Its Congregationalist origins required simplicity inside and out, with no artifice to obstruct closeness to God. This also endowed Old South with a spaciousness that made it a leading venue for anti-imperial rhetoric. The day after the Boston Massacre in 1770, outraged Bostonians assembled here to demand the removal of the troops that were ostensibly guarding the town. Five years later, patriot and doctor Joseph Warren delivered an oration to commemorate the incident; the biggest building in town was so packed that he had to crawl through the window behind the pulpit just to get inside.

More momentously, on the morning of December 16, 1773, over five thousand locals met here, awaiting word from Governor Thomas Hutchinson on whether the Crown would actually impose duty on sixty tons of tea aboard ships in Boston Harbor. When a message was received that it would, Samuel Adams rose and announced, "This meeting can do nothing more to save the country!" His simple declaration triggered the **Boston Tea Party**, perhaps the seminal event leading to the War for Independence.

The Meeting House served as a stable, a British riding school, and even a bar before becoming the **museum** it is today. One of the things lost in the transition was the original high pulpit, which the British tore out during the Revolution and used as firewood; the ornate one currently on view is a replica from 1808. There's not much to see other than the building itself – note the exterior **clock**, installed in 1770, which you can still set your watch by – but if you take the audio tour, included in the admission price, you'll hear campy re-enactments of a Puritan church service and the Boston Tea Party debates, among other more prosaic sound effects.

Old State House and around

Skyscrapers dwarf the graceful three-tiered window tower of the red-brick **Old State House** (daily 9am–5pm; $5, kids $1; ☎617/720-1713, ⊛www.bostonhistory.org; State Street **T**), at the corner of Washington and State streets, amplifying rather than diminishing its colonial-era dignity.

For years, this structure, reminiscent of an old Dutch town hall, was the seat of the Massachusetts Bay Colony and consequently the center of British authority in New England; later it served as Boston's city hall. In 1880 it was nearly demolished so that State Street traffic might flow more freely, and an unsuccessful attempt was also made to move the site to Chicago for the 1893 World Fair. But the building has remained intact, its fate spared by the **Bostonian Society**, the city's official historical society, founded specifically to preserve the building; today the site houses a small but comprehensive **museum**. An impassioned speech in the second-floor Council Chamber by **James Otis**, a Crown appointee who resigned to take up the colonial cause, sparked the quest for independence from Britain fifteen years before it was declared. Otis argued against the Writs of Assistance, which permitted the British to inspect private property at will; legend has it that on certain nights you can still hear him hurling his anti-British barbs, along with the cheers of the crowd he so energized, but museum staff has no comment. The **balcony** overlooking State Street is as famous as Otis's speech, for it was from here on July 18, 1776, that the Declaration of Independence was first read publicly in Boston – a copy having just arrived from Philadelphia. That same night the lion and unicorn figures mounted above the balcony were set ablaze; those currently on display are replicas. Just to show there were no hard feelings, Queen Elizabeth II, the first British monarch to set foot in Boston since the Revolution, read the Declaration of Independence from the balcony as part of the American bicentennial activities in 1976.

As for the historical society's **museum**, the permanent ground-level exhibit, "Colony to Commonwealth," chronicles Boston's role in inciting the Revolutionary War. Dozens of images and artifacts track, to varying degrees of interest, the events that led up to the establishment of the Commonwealth of Massachusetts (though not, curiously, to the events leading up to US independence). Displays include a bit of tea from Boston's most infamous party; the plaque of royal arms that once hung over Province House, official residence of the colonial governors; the flag that the Sons of Liberty draped from the Liberty Tree to announce their meetings; a six-minute underwhelming Boston Massacre "sound and light" show; and the most galvanizing image of the Revolutionary period, Paul Revere's propagandistic **engraving** of the

△ Old State House

Boston Massacre. Upstairs are rotating exhibits on the history of the city and, incongruously, a display on old Boston hotels and restaurants.

The Boston Massacre Site

Directly in front of the Old State House, a circle of cobblestones embedded in a small traffic island marks the site of the **Boston Massacre** (State Street **T**), the tragic outcome of escalating tensions between Bostonians and the British Redcoats who occupied the city. Riots were an increasingly common occurrence in Boston by the time this deadly one broke out on March 5, 1770. It began when a young wigmaker's apprentice heckled an army officer over a barber's bill. The officer sought refuge in the Custom House (then opposite the Old State House), but when a throng of people gathered at the scene, the mob grew violent, hurling snowballs and rocks at arriving soldiers. When someone threw a club that knocked a Redcoat onto the ice, he rose and fired. Five Bostonians were killed in the ensuing riot – including a young black man named Crispus Attucks, considered the first casualty of the Revolution – resulting in Governor Hutchinson's order to relocate occupying troops to Castle Island in Boston Harbor. Two patriots, John Adams and Josiah Quincy, actually defended the eight soldiers in court; six were acquitted, and the two who were found guilty had their thumbs branded.

Downtown Crossing

Centered on the intersection of Washington and Winter streets, **Downtown Crossing** is a busy pedestrian area whose strip of department stores and smaller shops recalls the time before malls.

The recent influx of trendy shops such as H&M alongside bargain hunters' favourite Filene's Basement means Downtown Crossing is losing its image as an area that caters to lower-income shoppers. One could easily spend a half day shopping here but there's little else to see, unless you have the money and inclination to eat at the historic *Locke-Ober* restaurant on Winter Place (see p.197).

The Financial District

Boston's **Financial District**, a small tract of real estate east of Washington Street and bounded by the waterfront, hardly conjures the same interest as those of New York and London, but it continues to wield influence in key

Views of Downtown

Whether local or from out of town, people can't seem to get enough of Boston's **skyline** – its pastiche of brownstone churches and glass-paneled skyscrapers framing Massachusetts Bay ranks it among the country's finest. No wonder, then, that so many buildings have public (and often free) viewing floors. You can check out Boston from every angle by ascending the *Marriott's Custom House* (see p.176), the Prudential Tower (see p.102), and the Bunker Hill Monument (see p.81). The best lay of the land, though, is had from the water; board the Charlestown ferry (see p.77), visit the Harbor Islands (see p.67), or take a ferry to Provincetown (see p.167) for a particularly stunning view.

fields (like mutual funds, invented here in 1925). The area is not entirely devoid of historic interest, though it's generally more manifest in plaques than actual buildings. Like most of America's business districts, it beats to an office hours-only drum, and many of its little eateries and Irish pubs are closed on weekends (some brash new restaurants have begun to make inroads, however).

The mostly immaculate streets follow the same short, winding paths as they did three hundred years ago; only now, thirty- and forty-story skyscrapers have replaced the wooden houses and churches that used to clutter the area. Still, their names are historically evocative: **High Street**, once known as Cow Lane, used to lead to the summit of the now-vanished eighty-foot-tall Fort Hill. **Arch Street** recalls the decorative arch that graced the Tontine Crescent, a block of stately townhouses designed in 1793 by Charles Bulfinch and unfortunately destroyed by the Great Fire of 1872, which began in the heart of the district. Tucked among the relatively generic skyscrapers are several well-preserved nineteenth-century mercantile masterpieces; head down the curve of **Franklin Street** and you'll see rounded greystone Victorian buildings also designed by Bulfinch.

Milk Street and Post Office Square

The most dramatic approach to the Financial District is east from Washington Street via **Milk Street**. A bust of **Benjamin Franklin** surveys the scene from a recessed Gothic niche above the doorway at no. 1; the site marks Franklin's birthplace, though the building itself only dates from 1874.

Further down Milk, the somber, 22-story **John W. McCormack Federal Courthouse** building houses one of Boston's larger post offices, with a section where stamp collectors can pick up special edition sets. An earlier building on this site gave the adjacent **Post Office Square** its name; today its triangular layout and cascading fountains are popular with area professionals during the lunch hour. Though it's not officially open to the public, you might try sneaking up to the glass atrium atop the building at **One Post Office Square** for jaw-dropping views of Boston Harbor and Downtown. The city's skyline encompasses the architectural excesses of the 1980s and a few Art Deco treats, too; the best example of the former is the **First National Bank of Boston** tower at 100 Federal St, with its bulging midsection, nicknamed "Pregnant Alice."

The prime Art Deco specimen, meanwhile, is nearby at 185 Franklin St – now the **Verizon Building**. The step-top building was a 1947 design, while in 2001 the phone booths outside were given a similarly Deco look. If you're here during business hours, check out the fusty nook off the right-hand side of the lobby, home to a replica of the Boston attic room where Alexander Graham Bell first transmitted speech sounds over a wire in 1875; the wooden chamber is a meticulously reassembled version of the original that was installed in 1959 and, with the exception of an evocative diorama of an old Boston cityscape, it looks like nothing's been touched since. Head back to the lobby to see the impressive 360-degree mural that glorifies the exciting world of *Telephone Men and Women at Work*.

Exchange Place, at 53 State St, is a mirrored-glass tower rising from the facade of the old Boston Stock Exchange; the *Bunch of Grapes* tavern, watering hole of choice for many of Boston's Revolutionary rabble-rousers, once stood here. Behind it is tiny **Liberty Square**, formerly the heart of Tory Boston – the British tax office had its address here, in 1765, and was destroyed by angry colonists – and now mostly of note for its improbable bronze sculpture, called *Aspirations for Liberty*; it depicts two rebels holding each other up in honor of the Hungarian anti-Communist uprising of 1956.

Government Center

Tremont Street's major tenant, **Government Center**, lies northwest from Exchange Place along Congress Street. Its sea of towering gray buildings on the former site of Scollay Square – once Boston's most notorious den of porn halls and tattoo parlors – is by far the least interesting section of Downtown Boston. As part of a citywide face-lift, Scollay was razed in the early 1960s, eliminating all traces of its salacious past and, along with it, most of its lively character. Indeed, the only thing that remains from the square's steamier days is the Oriental Tea Company's 227-gallon **Steaming Kettle** advertisement, which has been clouding up the sky across from the Government Center **T** stop since 1873. The area is now overlaid with concrete, thanks to an ambitious plan developed by I.M. Pei, and towered over by two monolithic edifices: **Boston City Hall**, at the east side of the plaza, and the **John F. Kennedy Federal Building**, on the north. Unless the workings of bureaucracy get you going, the only conceivable reason to stop here is to check out the **visitor's center** (Mon–Fri 8.30am–5.30pm) on the fourth floor of City Hall, which has the usual array of travel information and some aberrantly clean public restrooms.

Faneuil Hall Marketplace and around

Popular with locals and tourists alike, the **Faneuil Hall Marketplace** (Faneuil rhymes with "Daniel"), set on a pedestrian zone east of Government Center, is the kind of active, bustling public gathering place that's none too common in Boston nowadays. Built as a market during colonial times to house the city's growing mercantile industry, it declined during the nineteenth century and, like the area around it, was pretty much defunct until the 1960s, when it was successfully redeveloped as a restaurant and shopping mall.

Faneuil Hall

Much-hyped **Faneuil Hall** (Mon–Sat 10am–9pm, Sun noon–6pm; ☎617/523-1300, ⓦwww.faneuilhallmarketplace.com; State Street **T**) itself doesn't appear particularly majestic from the outside; it's simply a small, four-story brick building topped with a Georgian spire – hardly the grandiose auditorium one might imagine would have held the Revolutionary War meetings that earned it its "Cradle of Liberty" nickname.

The structure once housed an open-air market on its first floor and a space for political meetings on its second, a juxtaposition that inspired local poet Francis Hatch to pen the lines, "Here orators in ages past / Have mounted their attacks, / Undaunted by the proximity / Of sausage on the racks." Faneuil Hall was where revolutionary firebrands such as Samuel Adams and

James Otis whipped up popular support for independence by protesting British tax legislation. The first floor now houses a panoply of tourist **shops** that make for a less-than-dignified memorial; you'll also find an information desk, a post office, and a BOSTIX kiosk. The auditorium on the second floor has been preserved to reflect modifications made by Charles Bulfinch in 1805, the focal point being a massive – and rather preposterous – canvas depicting an imagined scene of Daniel Webster speaking here as a range of luminaries from Washington to de Tocqueville look on. More down-to-earth, perhaps, is the story of how Beantown residents suspected of being spies during the War of 1812 were asked what flew atop Faneuil Hall as a weathervane. Those who knew it was a grasshopper were trusted as true Bostonians; those who didn't were regarded with suspicion, and, in extreme cases, decapitated.

Dock Square, Blackstone Street, and the Holocaust Memorial

Immediately in front of Faneuil Hall lies **Dock Square**, so named for its original location directly on Boston's waterfront (carvings in the pavement indicate the shoreline in 1630). The square's center is dominated by a statue of **Samuel Adams**, interesting mostly for its somewhat over-the-top caption: "A Statesman, fearless and incorruptible." A dim, narrow corridor known as Scott's Alley heads north of the market to reach Creek Square, where you enter **Blackstone Street**, the eastern edge of a tiny warren of streets bounded to the west by Union Street. The area has, so far, been bypassed by urban renewal and maintains a reasonably authentic representation of central Boston's original architectural character. Its uneven cobblestoned streets and low brick buildings have remained largely untouched since the 1650s; many of them now house restaurants and pubs.

The one touch of modernity here is nearby on Union Street, where you'll see six tall, hollow, glass pillars erected as a **memorial** to victims of the Holocaust. Built to resemble smokestacks, the columns are etched with quotes and facts about the human tragedy – with an unusual degree of attention to its non-Jewish victims. Steam rises from grates beneath each of the pillars to accentuate their symbolism, an effect that's particularly striking at night.

Quincy Market

The markets just behind Faneuil Hall – three parallel oblong structures and one 1970s concrete mall that house restaurants, shops, and office buildings – were built in the early eighteenth century to contain the trade that had quickly outgrown its space in the hall. The center building, known as **Quincy Market** (Mon–Sat 10am–9pm, Sun noon–6pm; ☎617/523-1300, ⓦwww .faneuilhallmarketplace.com; State Street **T**), features a super-extended corridor lined with stands selling a variety of decent, if pricey, take-out treats; the mother of the city's modern food courts, it was built in 1822 under the direction of Boston's mayor at the time, Josiah Quincy.

To either side of the market are the **North** and **South Markets**, which hold restaurants and popular chain clothing stores. The cobblestone corridors between them host a number of vendor carts offering curios and narrow specializations (one sells only plaid clothing, another nothing but puppets). You'll also find the usual complement of street musicians, fire-jugglers, and mimes, weather permitting. There's not much to distinguish it from any other shopping complex, though there are several good restaurants and a nice concentration of bars (including a replica of the *Cheers* set), which are scarce elsewhere in the Downtown area. Overall, however, sitting on a bench in the carnivalesque heart of it all on a summer day, eating scrod while the mobs of townies and tourists mill about, is a quintessential, if slightly contrived, Boston experience.

The Custom House District

The not-quite-triangular wedge of Downtown between State and Broad streets and what was the Fitzgerald Expressway is the unfairly overlooked, and rather loosely named, **Custom House District**, dotted with some excellent architectural draws, chief among them the **Custom House** itself. Surrounded by 32 huge Doric columns, it was built in 1847, though the thirty-story Greek Revival tower was only added in 1915. Not surprisingly, it is no longer the tallest skyscraper in New England – a status it held for thirty years – and it's dwarfed by the John Hancock Tower (see p.102). That said, despite now being part of a Marriott hotel, it still has plenty of character and terrific views nonetheless; you can check them out from the 360-degree observation deck free of charge (daily 10am & 4pm).

The **Grain and Flour Exchange Building**, a block away at 177 Milk St, is another district landmark. This fortress-like construction recalls the Romanesque-Revival style of prominent local architect H.H. Richardson. Its turreted, conical roof, encircled by a series of pointed dormers, is a bold reminder of the financial stature this district once held. **Broad Street**, which runs perpendicular to Milk Street, was built on filled-in land in 1807 and is still home to several Federal-style mercantile buildings designed by Charles Bulfinch, notably those at numbers 68–70, 72, and 102.

On **State Street**, long a focal point of Boston's maritime prosperity, get a look at the elaborate cast-iron facade of the **Richards Building** at no. 114 (a clipper ship company's office in the 1850s) and the **Cunard Building** at no. 126, its ornamental anchors recalling Boston's status as the North American terminus of the first transatlantic steamship mail service. Trading activity in the nearby harbor brought a thriving banking and insurance industry to the street in the 1850s, along with a collection of rather staid office buildings. A modern exception is the opulent **Fleet Bank** headquarters at no. 75, a medium-sized skyscraper crowned with 3600 square feet of gold leaf and containing a six-story lobby decked out in marble, mahogany, and bronze.

The Theater and Ladder districts

Just south of Boston Common is the slightly seedy **Theater District** – the small area around the intersection of Tremont and Stuart streets. Not surprisingly, you'll have to purchase tickets in order to inspect the grand old interiors of the theaters for which it's named, but it's well worth a quick walk along Tremont Street to admire their facades. At the intersection of Washington and Avery streets you'll find the 1928 Beaux Arts **Opera House**, which reopened

Banned in Boston

Boston's Puritan founders would be horrified to find that an area called the **Theater District** exists. Their ingrained allergy to fun resulted in theatrical performances actually being outlawed in Boston until 1792, and in 1878, the Watch & Ward Society was formed to organize boycotts against indecent books and plays. Still, the shows went on, and in 1894 vaudeville was born at the lavish (now extinct) B.F. Keith Theater. Burlesque soon followed, prompting the city licensing division in 1905 to deny performances that didn't meet their neo-Puritan codes – thus the phrase "Banned in Boston." In fact, as recently as 1970, a production of *Hair* was banned for a month due to its desecration of the American flag.

Despite this censorship, Boston still managed to become the premier theater tryout town that it is today: high production costs on Broadway have dictated that hits be sifted from misses early on, and Boston has long been a cost-efficient testing ground. During the 1920s, the heyday of theater in the city, there were as many as forty playhouses in the Theater District alone. However, the rise of film meant the fall of theater, and after brief stints as movie halls, many of the grand buildings – most notably the Art Deco **Paramount**, the crumbling **Opera House** (formerly the Savoy), and the **Modern Theater**, all on lower Washington Street – slid into disrepair and eventual abandonment, although the Opera House has since been reopened (see below).

its doors in fall 2004 after being closed for more than a decade. The **Colonial** – still the grande dame of Boston theater – is just off **Piano Row**, a section of Boylston Street between Charles and Tremont that was the center of American piano manufacturing and music publishing in the nineteenth and early twentieth centuries. There are still a few piano shops in the area, but the hip restaurants and clubs in the immediate vicinity are of greater interest; many are tucked between Charles and Stuart streets around the mammoth **Massachusetts Transportation Building** and cater to the theater-going crowd.

South along Tremont from the Colonial is the beautifully ornate **Cutler Majestic Theatre**, which has recently been restored. Just down the street you'll also find the porticoed **Wilbur Theatre** (see p.223), the place to go for Broadway shows; when it opened in 1914, it was the first Boston theater to have its own guest lounge, which today is used by the nightclub *Aria* (see p.218). Adjacent to the Wilbur, the old **Metropolitan Theater**, a movie house of palatial proportions, survives as the glittering **Wang Center for the Performing Arts** (see p.223), home of the Boston Ballet. Across the street is the darling **Shubert Theater** (see p.223), the so-called "Little Princess of the Theater District"; its plush, 1600-seat auditorium is home to the Boston Lyric Opera, as well as some Broadway productions.

The tenor around Washington Street between Essex and Kneeland was relatively seedy a decade ago. Designated as an "adult entertainment zone" in the 1960s (when it replaced Scollay Square as the city's Red Light district and known, enigmatically, as "the Combat Zone," the latter-day **Ladder District** was home to a few X-rated theaters and bookshops until trendy restaurants and nightclubs designated it the new "It" spot and pushed the less reputable businesses out. PR hacks successfully renamed the area after its ladder-like layout (Tremont and Washington form the rails; Winter and Avery streets, the top and bottom rungs), but failed to alter its daylight character, which, despite the addition of a *Ritz-Carlton* at the corner of Tremont and Avery streets, remains rather desolate. At night, the place has slightly more energy, as theater-goers come here to dine before or after shows. Other than this, the only real sight of note is the plaque at the corner of Essex and Washington streets that marks where the so-called **Liberty Tree** stood. This oak, planted in 1646, was a favored meeting point of the Sons of Liberty; as such, the British chopped it down in 1775.

Chinatown and the Leather District

Boston's **Chinatown** lies wedged into just a few square blocks between the Financial and Theater districts, but it makes up in activity what it lacks in size. Just lean against a pagoda-topped payphone on the corner of **Beach** and **Tyler streets** – the neighborhood's two most dynamic thoroughfares – and watch the way life here revolves around the food trade at all hours. By day, merchants barter in Mandarin and Cantonese over the going price of produce; by night, Bostonians arrive in droves to eat in the restaurants. Walk down either street and you'll pass most of the bakeries, eateries, and indoor markets, in whose windows you'll see the usual complement of roast ducks hanging from hooks and aquariums filled with future seafood dinners. The area's at its most vibrant during various **festivals** (see Chapter 21, Festivals and events), none more so than **Chinese New Year** (late Jan, early Feb), when frequent parades of papier-mâché dragons fill the streets and the acrid smell of firecrackers permeates the air. During the **Festival of the August Moon**, held, as you may have guessed, in August, there's a bustling street fair. Call the Chinese Merchants' Association for more information (☎617/482-3972).

The prosperity of Boston's Chinatown has increased dramatically since the late 1990s, and consequently is expanding to the north, now bordering Downtown Crossing. Despite this growth, the heart of Chinatown contains little in the way of sights, and the atmosphere is best enjoyed by wandering around with no particular destination in mind. Still, there are a few important landmarks, such as the impressive **Chinatown Gate**, a three-story red-and-gilt monolith guarded by four Fu dogs, located at the intersection of Hudson and Beach streets, a gift from Taiwan in honor of Chinatown's centennial. Adjacent **Tian An Men Park** provides a place to rest, but it's poorly kept, generally littered with trash, and inhabited by fearsomely aggressive pigeons.

Just east of Chinatown, the six square blocks bounded by Kneeland, Atlantic, Essex, and Lincoln streets form the **Leather District** (also known as the **Garment District**), which takes its name from the time when materials were shipped through warehouses here to keep the shoe industry – a mainstay of the New England economy – alive. Since then, the Financial District, with which it is frequently lumped, has taken over as economic hub, and the leather industry has pretty much dried up. The distinction between the Financial and Leather districts is actually quite sharp, and most evident where High Street transitions into **South Street**, the Leather District's main drag. Stout brick warehouses replace gleaming modern skyscrapers, and a melange of merchants and gallery owners take over from the suited bankers. Some of the edifices still have their leather warehouse **signs** on them; check out the Boston Hide & Leather Co at 20 East St – though other than the old sign, don't expect to see much. The nearby **South Street Station**, Boston's main train and bus terminus, has little to recommend it architecturally.

Despite its lack of historical interest, the Leather District's abundance of cheap warehouse space in the 1990s attracted a number of **art galleries** and trendies, making it the capital of Boston's modest contemporary arts scene (though the South End is trying to take over that title). For a list of galleries, see p.235.

The waterfront

Boston's urban renewal program, sparked by the beginning of the Big Dig in the early 1990s, has resulted in a resurgence of its waterfront area. The tearing down of the John Fitzgerald Expressway, which, since the 1950s, had separated the waterfront from the rest of Downtown, has allowed the city to reconnect with the sea through a series of ambitious projects such as the expansion of the New England Aquarium and the conversion of wharf buildings into housing. Landscaping of the space formerly occupied by I-93 is due for completion in November 2005, and the resulting thirty-acre public park could well see the wharves regain some of their glory from the days when Boston was an important port.

There's still no doubt, though, that the waterfront thrives on tourism, with stands, concentrated around **Long Wharf,** selling tacky T-shirts, furry lobsters, and the like. Nevertheless, strolling the atmospheric **Harborwalk** that edges the water affords unbeatable views of Boston, and is a pleasant respite from the masses that can clog Faneuil Hall and the Common. You'll also find plenty of diversion if you've got little ones in tow at the **Children's Museum** and the **New England Aquarium**. Otherwise, you can do some watery exploring on a number of **boat tours**, or escape the city altogether by heading out to the **Harbor Islands**.

Long Wharf

Long Wharf has been the waterfront's main drag since its construction in 1710. Not surprisingly, summer is its busiest season, when the wharf is dotted with stands vending kitschy souvenirs and surprisingly good ice cream. This is also the main point of departure for Boston Harbor Cruises (☎617/227-4321, ⊛www.bostonharborcruises.com), which runs **whale-watching** excursions as well as ferries to the Harbor Islands (see p.68).

Walk out to the end of Long Wharf for an excellent vantage point on **Boston Harbor**. Since the city is surrounded by other land masses, you'll only see a series of peninsulas and islands, which are generally smoky and grinding with industry. The view from Long Wharf is perhaps most enjoyable – and still relatively safe – at night, when even the freighters appear graceful against the moonlit water.

The New England Aquarium

Next door to Long Wharf is the waterfront's major draw, the **New England Aquarium** (July–Aug Mon, Tues & Fri 9am–6pm, Wed & Thurs 9am–8pm, Sat, Sun & holidays 9am–7pm; Sept–Jun Mon–Fri 9am–5pm, Sat & Sun 9am–6pm; $15.95, kids $8.95; City Pass accepted; ☎617/973-5200, ⊛www.neaq.org; Aquarium **T**). Like many of the Boston waterfront attractions, this one is most fun for kids, though engaging enough for anyone whose sights aren't set too high. Over

The Harborwalk

Like the Freedom Trail, the **Harborwalk** was designed to lure tourist dollars with the promise of an historic theme. On this particular trip back in time, blue plaques illustrate the relevance of various points in Boston's role as a major commercial port – a face of the city that seems ever more a thing of the past, especially with the Harbor's recent notoriety for pollution. While the walk's sights don't have the all-star quality of those on the Freedom Trail (some would need spicing up just to pass for mundane), the red-brick waterside promenade does provide a decent excuse to take a picturesque stroll along the water, with any enhanced historical context serving as a bonus.

Visitor center maps can help steer you on the self-guided stroll that starts at the corner of State Street and Merchant's Row and proceeds along the wharves – passing by scads of swanky condominiums, upscale hotels like the *Boston Harbor Hotel* (see Chapter 11, Accommodation), and countless moored sailboats – before ending up on the Congress Street bridge at the Boston Tea Party Ship. The views of the harbor are pretty spectacular, with modern glass buildings reflecting towering boat masts in their facades.

the last decade, a multimillion-dollar expansion program has seen the addition of a West Wing, the Aquarium Medical Center (giving visitors a look at animal care), and an **IMAX theater** (daily 9.30am–9.30pm; $8.95, kids $6.95).

The indoor aquarium has plenty of good exhibits, such as the penguins on the bottom floor. Be sure to play with the special laser device that maneuvers a red point of light around the bottom of their pool; the guileless waterfowl mistake the light for a fish and follow it around obediently. In the center of the aquarium's spiral walkway an impressive collection of marine life thrives: a three-story, 200,000-gallon cylindrical tank packed with moray eels, sharks, stingrays, and a range of other sea exotica that swim by in unsettling proximity. The aquarium also runs excellent **whale-watching** trips into the harbor (early April–late Oct; 3.5–5hr, call for times and specific dates; $29, kids $20; ☎617/973-5281).

The Children's Museum and the Seaport District

It's hard to miss the larger-than-life 1930s-era **Hood Milk Bottle** across the Congress Street bridge from Downtown. This food stand actually serves little dairy produce, however (save for ice cream), and instead does most of its trade in hot dogs and hamburgers.

Behind it, the engaging **Children's Museum**, 300 Congress St (daily 10am–5pm, Fri till 9pm; $9, kids $7, Fri 5–9pm $1; ☎617/426-8855, ⊛www .bostonkids.org; South Station **T**), comprises five floors of deceptively educational exhibits designed to trick kids into learning about a huge array of topics, from kinematics to the history of popular culture. The key here is interactivity: displays are meant to be touched rather than observed, like the climbing maze in the central shaft that no one over 14 could possibly get into. Other exhibits are amusing even for adults, particularly those on Japanese youth culture and the replica of "Grandma's House," replete with authentic 1950s furniture, vintage commercials on the television, and a meat loaf in the oven.

The Children's Museum sits in the **Seaport District**, which loosely refers to the harborside area across the Northern Avenue bridge from Downtown, accessible by a free shuttle from the South Station **T**, where businesses have recently banded together in an attempt to forge a collective identity. The only real draw here, however, is the excellent range of restaurants near Boston's **Fish Pier**. There's also a number of odoriferous **lobster wholesalers** on the pier and along Northern Avenue. If you happen to be in the area and love crustaceans, you'll avoid paying standard market price by braving the harrowing sights and smells of these seafood warehouses.

Boston Tea Party Ship

Moored in the Fort Point Channel alongside the Congress Street bridge is a replica of one of the three notorious ships that launched the Boston Tea Party. The ship, and a neighboring museum (℡617/338-1773, ⊛www.bostonteapartyship .com), was closed after it was hit by lightning in August 2001; plans are afoot for both to be reopened in late 2005. Improvements will include interactive exhibits, a doubling of the museum's size, and the addition of two replica ships. Spirited re-creations of the Tea Party itself are still held on occasion in the area, but don't be taken in: this is not the site of the actual event. The Tea Party took place on what is today dry land, near the intersection of Atlantic and Congress streets. Indeed, at the **Harbor Plaza**, 470 Atlantic St, there's a commemorative plaque engraved with a lively, but silly, patriotic poem expressing outrage at "King George's trivial but tyrannical tax of 3p. per pound."

The Harbor Islands

Extending across Massachusetts Bay from Salem south to Portsmouth, the thirty islands that make up the bucolic **Harbor Islands** originally served as strategic defense points during the American Revolution and Civil War. It took congressional assent to turn them into a national park, in 1996, with the result that six are now easily accessible by ferry from Long Wharf. Even so, they're still lightly trafficked in comparison to most Boston sights, which

The Boston Tea Party

The first major act of rebellion preceding the Revolutionary War, the **Boston Tea Party** was far greater in significance – especially as a popular symbol – than it was in duration. On December 20, 1773, a longstanding dispute between the British government and its colonial subjects, involving a tea tax, came to a dramatic head. At nightfall, an angry mob of about a thousand, which had been whipped into an anti-British frenzy by Samuel Adams at Old South Meeting House, converged on Griffin's Wharf. Around a hundred of them, some dressed in Indian garb, boarded three brigs and threw the cargo of tea overboard. The protestors disposed of 342 chests of tea, each weighing 360 pounds – enough to make 24 million cups, and worth more than one million dollars by today's standards.

While it had the semblance of spontaneity, the event was in fact planned beforehand, and the mob was careful not to damage anything but the offending cargo. In any case, the "party" transformed protest into revolution; even Governor Hutchinson agreed that afterwards, war was the only recourse. The ensuing British sanctions, colloquially referred to as the "Intolerable Acts," along with the colonists' continued resistance, further inflamed the tension between the Crown and its colonies, which eventually exploded at Lexington and Concord several months later.

Island bound

A 45-minute ride connects Long Wharf with central **George's Island** (July–Aug daily on the hour 10am–5pm; May & Sept to mid-Oct daily 10am, noon & 2pm; June daily 10am, noon, 2pm, & 4pm; $10, kids $7; ☎617/222-6999, ⓦwww.harborexpress .com; Aquarium Ⓣ), the hub from which water taxis (free) shuttle visitors to the remaining five. The islands lack a freshwater source, so be sure to bring **bottled water** with you. You should also consider packing a picnic lunch (best arranged through nearby *Sel de la Terre*; see p.198), though if you've come without, you can make do on beachfare from George's **snackbar** or – for a small snack – go **berry-picking** on **Grape** and **Bumpkin** islands. In the interest of preserving island ecology, no bicycles or in-line skates are allowed. You can **camp**, for a nominal fee, on four of the islands (May to mid-Oct; Lovell & Peddock ☎617/727-7676; Bumpkin & Grape 1-877/422-6762); you'll need to bring your own supplies. In all cases, good walking shoes are required as most of the pathways consist of dirt roads. The Harbor Islands **information** kiosk, at the foot of Long Wharf, keeps a detailed shuttle **schedule** and stocks excellent **maps**. Visit ⓦwww.bostonislands.org and ⓦwww.nps.gov/boha for more information.

makes them ideal getaways from the city center, especially on a hot summer day, when their **beaches** and **hiking** trails will easily help you forget urban life altogether. Their wartime legacy has left many of the winding pathways and coastal shores dotted with intriguing fortress **ruins** and **lighthouses**, which makes for attractive scenery; the views of Boston from this distance are simply sublime as well.

The most popular and best serviced of the lot is the skipping-stone-shaped **George's Island**, a heavily used defensive outpost during the Civil War era; the remains of **Fort Warren** (April to mid-Oct daily dawn–dusk; free), a mid-nineteenth-century battle station, covers most of the island. Constructed from hand-hewn granite, and mostly used as a prison for captured Confederate soldiers, its musty barracks and extensive fortress walls are on the eerie side, while the parapets offer some stunning Downtown views. You'll get more out of a visit by taking a Park Ranger tour (free), where you'll learn the legend of the Lady in Black – a prisoner's wife who was hanged while attempting to break her husband out of jail.

The remaining Harbor Islands are hardly must-sees, and you'd need to spend a full day island hopping thanks to the irregularity of the shuttle services from George's Island that take you out there. The densely wooded and sand-duned **Lovell** is probably your best bet after George's, as it hosts the islands' only life -guarded sand beach, near the remains of Fort Standish – an early-twentieth -century military base. The largest of all, the 134-acre **Peddock**, is laced with hiking trails connecting the remains of Fort Andrews, a harbor defense used from 1904 to 1945, with a freshwater pond and wildlife sanctuary. Romantic **Bumpkin** was once the site of a children's hospital whose ruins, along with the casements of an old stone farmhouse, lie along raspberry bush-fringed pathways. More berries grow on **Grape**, an ideal bird-watching spot. Furthest at sea, **Little Brewster Island** hosts the 1716 Boston Light, the country's last man-powered beacon (call ☎617/223-8666 to arrange a visit).

The North End

T he **North End**, a small yet densely populated neighborhood with narrow streets, has a detached quality, but from both the Haymarket and North End **T** stations there's easy access to the area. Once here, you can cover must-see sights like the **Paul Revere House**, **Old North Church**, and **Copp's Hill Burying Ground** fairly quickly, while being sure to experience the vibrant cafés, bakeries, restaurants, and food shops in this, Boston's most authentically **Italian** neighborhood. This Italian flavor is particularly pronounced during the eight annual summer **festas** (see Chapter 21, Festivals and events), during which members of private charity clubs march figurines of their patron saints (usually the same as those of their home towns in Italy) through the streets. The processions, complete with marching bands, stop every few feet to let people pin dollar bills to streamers attached to the statues.

Some history

In colonial times, the North End was actually a peninsula. Because it was occasionally cut off by high tides, a series of short bridges was built to the main part of town, known as the South End (not to be confused with today's South End, covered in Chapter 6). This physical separation bred antagonism, culminating every November 5 in **Pope's Day**, when North and South Enders paraded effigies of the Pope through their neighborhoods to a standoff on Boston Common, where the rival groups attempted to capture each other's pontiff. If the North Enders won, they would burn the South Ender's effigy atop Copp's Hill.

Spiritually, the community was dominated by **Increase Mather**, who ministered at the North Church and whose 1689 *Memorable Providences, Relating to Witchcraft and Possessions* probably fueled the hysteria that led to the Salem Witch Trials (see p.160). But the North End was also the residence of choice for the wealthy merchant class; Massachusetts Bay Colony governors Hutchinson and Phips owned spacious homes here. Following the Revolutionary War, however, many British loyalists fled to Nova Scotia, and, as the North End declined, it became a magnet for free blacks known as the **New Guinea Community**, as well as immigrant groups.

The **Irish** were the first immigrants to flock to the area, putting down roots from 1840 onwards (John F. Fitzgerald, JFK's grandfather and mayor of Boston, was born on Ferry Street in 1863, and the late president's mother, Rose, on nearby Garden Court in 1890). With the onset of the potato famine in 1845, the trickle became a flood – in 1847 alone, some 13,000 new arrivals settled here. Employment opportunities for the Irish were limited, however: "No Irish Need Apply" signs were common, and a decade after their arrival the community began to disperse throughout the Greater Boston area. The Irish were succeeded in the North End by Eastern European Jews, who were in turn edged out by **southern Italians** in the early twentieth century. The Italians have, for the most part, stayed put.

Though **landfill**, which began in the 1820s, temporarily ended the district's physical isolation, it became a place apart once more when the elevated I-93 (or John Fitzgerald Expressway) tore through the city in 1954. But Boston's massive urban regeneration, through the Big Dig, means that, as with the waterfront, the North End has again been rejoined with the city. Not all of the construction is complete, however – landscaping of the space formerly occupied by the elevated freeway isn't scheduled to end until November 2005 – but even just getting here is now so much simpler.

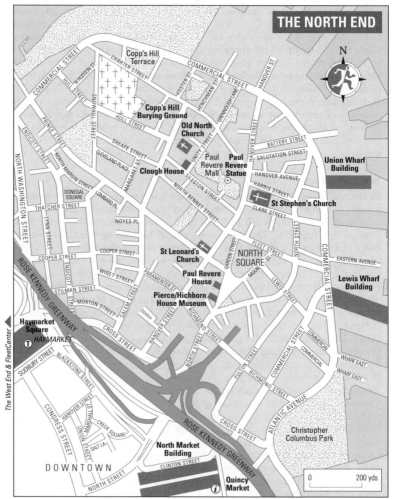

THE NORTH END

Downtown & The Waterfront ▼

Over the years, local Mafia types ensured that crime (of the unorganized kind) was virtually nonexistent here, and helped make the neighborhood one of the safest in the city. This, combined with comparatively low rents, made the area attractive to yuppies, who gentrified the waterfront and rehabilitated tenements in the heart of the district. However, despite this more recent influx of outsiders, life in the North End continues much as it has for decades – complete with laundry dangling from upper-story windows, grandmothers gossiping in Italian in front of their apartment buildings, and folks whiling away the hours in local cafés and bars.

Hanover Street

Long the main connection between the North End and the rest of Boston, **Hanover Street** – especially where it meets Parmenter and Richmond – is the scene of many of the area's trattorias, cafés, and bakeries, giving the street a distinctly European flavor (albeit now somewhat diluted by chain stores). However, traditional Italian spots remain, including *Mike's Pastry*, at no. 300 (see p.234), and the quieter side of the neighborhood reasserts itself on the short blocks north of the Paul Revere Mall (not a "mall" in the modern sense, but a cobblestoned park). But even this area is home to an increasing number of restaurants, geared as much to locals as to tourists.

North Square and around

The triangular wedge of cobblestones and gaslights known as **North Square**, found one block east of Hanover between Fleet and Richmond streets, is one of the most historic and appealing pockets of Boston. Here the eateries recede in deference to the **Paul Revere House**, the oldest residential address in the city, at 19 North Square (mid-April to Oct daily 9.30am–5.15pm; Nov to mid-April 9.30am–4.15pm; closed Mon in Jan, Feb, and March $3; ☎617/523-2338, ⊛www.paulreverehouse.org). A North Ender for most of his life, Revere lived here from 1770 to 1800 (except for much of 1775, when he hid out from the British in Watertown), and during these thirty years he sired a brood of sixteen. Before being restored to its seventeenth-century appearance in 1908, the small Tudor-style, post-and-beam structure, which dates from about 1680, had served in turn as a grocery store, tenement, and cigar factory. It stands on what once was the site of the considerably grander home of Puritan heavyweight Increase Mather (father of Cotton), which burned down in the Great Fire of 1676.

Though the building is more impressive for its longevity than its appearance, the second-story overhang and leaded windows provide quite a contrast to the red-brick buildings around it. The inside is a letdown, as none of the artifacts are original to the house, and the first-floor "hall," or living room, is curious, as it resembles a hunting lodge, complete with low ceiling and enormous fire-place. Later examples of Revere's self-made silverwares are found upstairs, as is a small but evocative exhibit about the mythologizing of Revere's horseback ride to warn patriots that the British were coming.

The Pierce/Hichborn House and North Street

A small courtyard, whose centerpiece is a glass-encased 900-pound bell that Revere cast, separates the Paul Revere House from the **Pierce/Hichborn House** (tours by appointment only; $3; ☎617/523-2338). A simple Georgian-style

Paul Revere

It wasn't until decades after his death that **Paul Revere** achieved fame for his night-time journey to Lexington to warn John Hancock and Sam Adams of the impending British march inland to seize colonial munitions. When he did, it was thanks to a fanciful 1863 poem by Henry Wadsworth Longfellow called *Paul Revere's Ride,* which failed to note that another patriot, **William Dawes**, made the trip as well. Its opening line, "Listen, my children, and you shall hear / Of the midnight ride of Paul Revere," is perhaps as familiar to American schoolchildren as the Pledge of Allegiance, but during his lifetime, this jack-of-all-trades was principally known for his abilities as a **silversmith** (with a side business in false teeth) and a **propagandist** for the patriot cause – not so much as a legendary messenger.

Revere's engraving of the Boston Massacre, on display in the Bostonian Society's museum (see p.56), did much to turn public opinion against the Tories, and he even went so far as to stage an exhibition of more patriotic engravings at his North End home on the first anniversary of the incident. He also rode on horseback to carry news of the Boston Tea Party to New York and Philadelphia – only hours after participating in the event. After the Revolution, Revere engraved the first American currency, though a more profitable venture was his bell-and-cannon foundry in the present-day town that bears his name, located just north of Boston. He died in 1818 at the age of 83, and rests among his Revolutionary peers in the Old Granary Burying Ground (see p.52).

residence – and the oldest brick house in Boston – it was built in 1710 by glazier Moses Pierce, and later owned by Paul Revere's cousin, Nathaniel Hichborn, who was considerably wealthier than his more famous relative. As such, the sparsely furnished interior of the prosperous shipbuilder's modest home, with its unremarkable period tables and chairs, along with a few decorative lamps and pieces of cabinetry, speaks volumes about Yankee thrift. Also worth noting are **Baker's Alley**, which runs between the Pierce/Hichborn House and the *Limoncello* restaurant, and **Quincy Court** across the street – both prime examples of how narrow the surrounding streets would have been in colonial times.

South from North Square, Garden Court Street (on which the Revere House and the Pierce/Hichborn House are located) runs into **North Street**, which was somewhat of a red-light district in the early nineteenth century, but today is only an average residential side street. Its one distinguishing feature, the **oldest sign** in Boston, is affixed to the third floor of a building at the corner of Richmond Street – the initials "W, T, S" refer to the owners of an inn that stood here in 1694.

St Stephen's Church and Paul Revere Mall

Further north, at Hanover's intersection with Clark Street, you'll find the striking, three-story, recessed-brick arch entrance to **St Stephen's Church**. The church was built on this site in 1714 and replaced by a Charles Bulfinch design in 1804. A fire ravaged the building in 1929, but in 1964 it was restored according to Bulfinch's plan; its interior is a great example of the architect's austere Federal style. A more recent claim to fame is that the funeral ceremony for JFK's mother, Rose Kennedy, was held in the understated apse, in 1995.

Originally called New North Church, St Stephen's received its current name in 1862, in order to keep up with the increasingly Catholic population of the North End. Though it seems firmly planted today, the whole building was actually moved back sixteen feet when Hanover Street was widened in 1870.

△ Paul Revere Statue in Paul Revere Mall

Just across Hanover, the famous bronze **statue** of Paul Revere astride his borrowed horse marks the edge of the **Paul Revere Mall**, a tree-lined, cobblestoned park also known as the Prado. This much-needed open space was carved out of a chunk of apartment blocks in 1933 and runs back to tiny **Unity Street** – home of the small 1712 red-brick **Clough House**, at no. 21; this private residence is of little interest, other than that it was built by a mason who lay the brick of the nearby Old North Church.

Old North Church

Rising unobstructed above the surrounding homogeneous blocks of red-brick apartments, the simple yet noble **Old North Church** at 93 Salem St (daily June–Oct 9am–6pm, Nov–May 9am–5pm; ⓦwww.oldnorth.com) is one of the most emblematic sights in Boston. Built in 1723, and inspired by St Andrew's-by-the-Wardrobe in Blackfriars, London, it's the oldest church in Boston, easily recognized by its gleaming 191-foot **steeple**. The weathervane perched on top is the colonial original, though the steeple itself is a replica – hurricanes toppled both its first, in 1804, and its replacement, in 1954.

It was a pair of lanterns that secured the structure's place in history, though. The church sexton, Robert Newman, is said to have hung both of them inside ("One if by land, two if by sea") on the night of April 18, 1775, to signal the movement of British forces from Boston Common, which then bordered the Charles River, to Paul Revere and William Dawes. However, some historians speculate that the lanterns were actually hung from another church, also called Old North, which occupied the North Square spot where the Sacred Heart Italian Church now stands, at no. 12; the fact that irate Tories burned it for firewood in 1776 adds credence to the theory. What is certain is that Revere had already learned of the impending British advance and was riding to Lexington by the time the lanterns were in place – he simply needed Newman's help to alert Charlestown in case his mission was thwarted. As it turned out, both he and Dawes were detained by British patrols, but each managed to continue his ride.

The **interior** of the church is spotlessly white and well lit, thanks to the Palladian windows behind the pulpit. Other details include twelve bricks, set into the vestibule wall, from a prison cell in Boston, England, where an early group of Pilgrims were incarcerated, and the four eighteenth-century cherubim near the organ that were looted from a French vessel. You can also check your watch by the **clock** at the rear; made in 1726, it's the oldest one still ticking in an American public building. Have a wander, too, among the high box pews: no. 62 belonged to General Thomas Gage, commander-in-chief of the British army in North America, while descendants of Paul Revere still lay claim to no. 54. Beneath your feet, the timber on which the pews rest is supported by 37 basement-level brick crypts; one of the 1100 bodies encased therein is that of John Pitcairn, the British major killed in the Battle of Bunker Hill. His remains were tagged for Westminster Abbey, but they never made it home to England. The eight bells inside the belfry – which is unfortunately not open to the public – were the first cast for the British Empire in North America and have since tolled the death of every US president.

Some of Old North's greatest charms are actually outside the church itself, notably the diminutive **Washington Memorial Garden**, the brick walls of which are bedecked with commemorative plaques honoring past church members, and the inviting **eighteenth-century garden**, its terraces packed with lilies and roses, as well as some curious umbrella-shaped flowers known, appropriately, as archangels.

Salem and Prince streets

While the Old North Church is certainly its star attraction, **Salem Street**, especially the lower blocks between Prince and Cross, is arguably the North End's most colorful artery. The actual street – whose name is a bastardization of "Shalom Street," as it was known to the earlier Eastern European Jewish settlers – is so narrow that the red-brick buildings seem to lean into one another, and light traffic makes it a common practice to walk right down the middle of the road. Traveling south, an agreeable onslaught of Italian grocers, aromatic *pasticcerias*, and cafés begins rather abruptly at Salem's intersection with Prince, starting with *Bova's Bakery* at no. 134 (see p.233); above this point the street is primarily residential. At the southern part, as soon as you traverse Cross Street, the Neapolitan bustle ends; continuing on under what's left of the expressway will lead you to the commercialized Quincy Market and bland Government Center in Downtown.

Perpendicular to Salem Street is bustling **Prince Street**, a narrow road cutting through the heart of the North End on an east–west axis. Like most streets in the neighborhood, it's also lined with *salumerias* and restaurants, but tends to be more social – locals typically while away the day along the pavement here on folding chairs brought from home.

At the corner of Hanover Street and parallel to Prince Street, **St Leonard's of Port Maurice Church**, 14 N Bennet St, was the first Italian-Catholic church in New England when it was founded in 1873. The ornate interior is a marked contrast to Boston's stark Protestant churches, while the so-called "Peace Garden" in front, with its prosaic plantings and tacky statuary, is, in a sense, vintage North End.

Copp's Hill Burying Ground and Copp's Hill Terrace

Up Hull Street from Old North Church, **Copp's Hill Burying Ground** (daily dawn–dusk) displays eerily tilting slate tombstones, stunning harbor views, and the graves of some significant sons of the North End. The first burial here, on the highest ground in the North End, took place in 1659. Among the ten thousand interred are nearly a thousand men from the "New Guinea Community" – including Prince Hall, who founded the first Black Masons lodge and played an important role in the 1783 act that abolished slavery in Massachusetts. The most famous gravesite here is that of the **Mather family**, just inside the wrought-iron gates on the northern Charter Street side. Increase Mather and his son Cotton – the latter a Salem Witch Trial judge – were big players in Boston's early days of Puritan theocracy, a fact not at all reflected in the rather diminutive, if appropriately plain, brick vault tomb. As for other noteworthy graves, **Robert Newman**, who hung Paul Revere's lanterns in the Old North Church, is buried near the western rim of the plot, as is **Edmund Hartt**, the builder of the famous ship the USS *Constitution* ("Old Ironsides"; see p.79).

You'll notice, too, that many gravestones have significant chunks missing – a consequence of British soldiers using them for target practice during the 1775 Siege of Boston. The grave of one Captain Daniel Malcolm, toward the left end of the third row of gravestones as you enter the grounds, bears particularly strong evidence of the English maneuvers: three musketball marks scar his epitaph, which hails him as a "true son of liberty" and an "enemy of oppression".

The granite **Copp's Hill Terrace**, a plateau separated from the burial ground on the northern side by Charter Street, was the place from which British cannon bombarded Charlestown during the Battle of Bunker Hill. On a sweltering day in 1919, a 2.3-million-gallon steel storage tank of molasses – used in the production of alcoholic beverages – exploded nearby, creating a syrupy tidal wave fifteen feet high that engulfed entire buildings and drowned 21 people along with a score of horses. Old North Enders – the kind you'll see playing bocci in the little park at the bottom of the terrace – claim you can still catch a whiff of the stuff on an exceptionally hot day.

Charlestown

Across Boston Harbor from the North End (see Chapter 2), a largely Irish working-class neighborhood stands quite isolated from the city, despite its annexation more than a century ago. The Big Dig has dramatically reshaped the landscape for the better, and the new Leonard P. Zakim Bridge, with its towering, obelisk-style suspension poles, pays architectural homage to the local Bunker Mill Monument.

There are two main ways to get to **Charlestown**: one is to take the T to North Station and walk over the Charlestown Bridge – which affords great views of both Boston Harbor and the Zakim Bridge. The other is to take the short $1.50 ferry trip from the waterfront's Long Wharf, which deposits you on the eastern outskirts of the Charlestown Navy Yard, where the area's big draw, the **USS Constitution**, is berthed.

Just a few minutes' walk northwest from the Navy Yard, Charlestown's center, **City Square**, is the point from which most notable streets in the area radiate out. Directly north is the neighborhood's only other major sight, the **Bunker Hill Monument**, as well as the last stop on the Freedom Trail, which runs across the Charlestown Bridge from the North End. Otherwise, the rest of the district is fairly nondescript and could even be described as dodgy on its outskirts – though this shouldn't cause much worry: if you stick to the USS *Constitution* and the monument, you needn't spend more than a morning in Charlestown. A relative lack of appealing restaurants or bars, save the renowned *Olives* and its offshoot, *Figs* (see Chapter 13, Restaurants), makes it unlikely you'll be coming back in the evening.

Some history

The earliest **Puritan settlers** had high hopes for developing Charlestown when they arrived in 1629, but an unsuitable water supply pushed them over to the Shawmut Peninsula, which they promptly renamed Boston. Charlestown grew slowly after that, and had to be completely rebuilt after the British burned it down in 1775; almost as many houses were lost in that blaze as had been torched in the entire Revolutionary War.

The mid-1800s witnessed the arrival of the so-called "lace-curtain Irish" (those who were somewhat better off than their North End compatriots), and the district remains an **Irish** one at heart. The neighborhood was long a haven for criminals, too: if a bank was robbed in Boston, the story goes, police would simply wait on the Charlestown Bridge for their quarry to come home. Today, though, the criminal element has all but disappeared from the area, since urban professionals took over many of the Federal- and Colonial-style townhouses south of the Bunker Hill Monument. The resulting mood in Charlestown is one of amiable neighborliness imbued with an

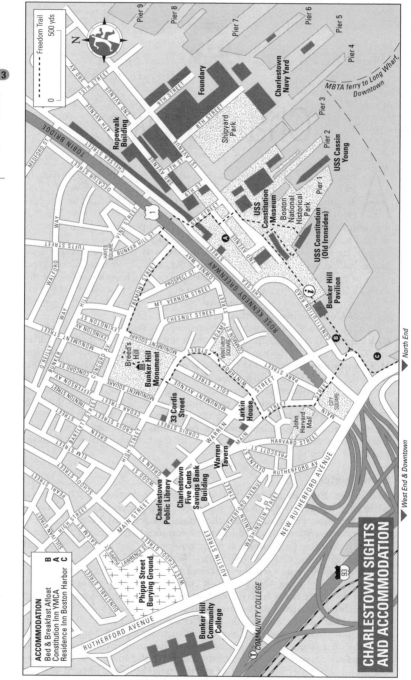

CHARLESTOWN SIGHTS AND ACCOMMODATION

ACCOMMODATION
Bed & Breakfast Afloat   B
Constitution Inn YMCA   A
Residence Inn Boston Harbor C

------ Freedom Trail
0   500 yds

N

Pier 9
Pier 8
Pier 7
Pier 6
Pier 5
Pier 4
Pier 3

MBTA ferry to Long Wharf, Downtown

Charlestown Navy Yard
Shipyard Park
Foundary
Ropewalk Building
TOBIN BRIDGE
DECATUR STREET
CHELSEA STREET
MEDFORD ST
3RD AVENUE
2ND AVENUE
4TH AVENUE
5TH AVENUE
HILL STREET
8TH STREET
9TH STREET
1ST ST
5TH ST
3RD ST

USS Cassin Young
Pier 2
Pier 1
USS Constitution Museum
Boston National Historical Park
USS Constitution (Old Ironsides)
Bunker Hill Pavilion

VINE STREET
TUFTS STREET
HAYES SQUARE
BUNKER HILL ST
HILL STREET
WALLFORD
WAY
WAY
PROSPECT STREET
TREMONT STREET
MT. VERNON STREET
CHESNUT STREET
LEXINGTON AV
MONUMENT SQUARE
CONCORD ST
CORDIS STREET
ADAMS STREET
WINTHROP SQUARE
SOLEY STREET
WINTHROP STREET

2ND AVENUE
1ST AVENUE
ROSE KENNEDY GREENWAY
CHELSEA GREENWAY
CONSTITUTION ROAD
LOWNEY WAY

i

B
C
North End

Breed's Hill
Bunker Hill Monument
33 Cordis Street
Larkin House
Warren Tavern
Charlestown Five Cents Savings Bank Building
Charlestown Public Library
Phipps Street Burying Ground
Bunker Hill Community College

MONUMENT STREET
O'REILLY
WAY
BUNKER HILL ST
CONCORD ST
JEFFERSON AV
CEDAR STREET
TRENTON STREET
BARTLETT STREET
GREEN STREET
HIGH STREET
ELM STREET
CROSS STREET
WOOD ST
GREEN ST
SCHOOL STREET
PEARL STREET
SALEM STREET
MAIN STREET
AUSTIN STREET
LAWRENCE ST
TUFTS ST
WALKER ST
DUNSTABLE STREET
SULLIVAN STREET
WEST SCHOOL STREET
PARK STREET
WARREN AVENUE
MONUMENT AVENUE
WARREN STREET
MAIN STREET
HARVARD STREET
DEVENS ST
PRESCOTT ST
OLVENS ST
WASHINGTON STREET
UNION STREET
RUTHERFORD STREET
RUTHERFORD AVENUE
NEW RUTHERFORD AVENUE
RUTHERFORD AVENUE

John Harvard Mall
CITY SQUARE

West End & Downtown

93
COMMUNITY COLLEGE
T

air of quiet affluence, especially along the southern blocks of Main Street, where the better restaurants are found.

The Charlestown Navy Yard and the USS Constitution Museum

Opened in 1800, the sprawling **Charlestown Navy Yard** was one of the first and busiest US naval shipyards – riveting together an astounding 46 destroyer escorts in 1943 alone – though it owes most of its present-day liveliness to its grandest tenant, the frigate USS *Constitution* at Constitution Wharf. Today, under the aegis of the Boston National Historical Park, an umbrella association preserving Boston sights deemed nationally significant, the yard has largely been repurposed to house marinas, upscale condos, and offices.

What's worth checking out here, though, is the **USS Constitution Museum** (daily May–Oct 9am–6pm, Nov–April 10am–5pm; free; ☎617/426-1812, ⓦwww.ussconstitutionmuseum.org), located in a substantial granite structure a short walk from the *Constitution* and across from Pier 1. It's a good idea to visit the museum before you board the ship itself, as its excellent exhibits help contextualize the vessel and her unparalleled role in American maritime history. One especially evocative display consists of curios which sailors acquired during a two-year, round-the-world diplomatic mission begun in 1844, creatively arranged under a forest of faux palm fronds. Among the souvenirs are wooden carved toys from Zanzibar, a chameleon from Madagascar preserved in a glass jar, and a Malaysian model ship made of cloves. Upstairs you'll find temporary exhibits, as well as replicas of the sailors' hammock-style bunks.

The USS Constitution ("Old Ironsides")

As tall as a twenty-story building and three hundred feet long from bowsprit to back end, the **USS Constitution** (daily 10am–4pm; free; ⓦwww .ussconstitution.navy.mil) is impressive from any angle. Launched in 1797 to safeguard American merchant vessels from Barbary pirates and, later on, the French and British navies, the ship earned her nickname during the War of 1812; cannonballs fired from the British HMS *Guerrière* bounced off the hull (the "iron" sides were actually hewn from live oak, a particularly sturdy wood from the southeastern US), leading to the first and most dramatic American naval conquest of that war. The *Constitution* went on to win more than forty battles before she was retired from active service in the 1830s; stints as flagship with Mediterranean and African squadrons were followed by use as a training ship until her full naval commission was returned in 1940, making her the oldest commissioned warship afloat in the world. When, in 1997, the *Constitution* went on her first unassisted voyage in 116 years, news coverage was international in scale, a measure of the worldwide respect for the symbolic flagship of the US Navy.

Though authentic enough in appearance, the *Constitution* has certainly taken its hits (roughly ninety percent of the ship has been reconstructed). Even after extensive renovations, Old Ironsides is still too frail to support sails for extended periods of time, and the only regular trips she makes are annual Fourth of July turnarounds in Boston Harbor. There's often a line to visit the ship, especially in the summer, and access has been further slowed by increased security checks, but it's nonetheless worth the wait to get a close-up view of the elaborate rigging that can support some three dozen sails totaling almost an acre in area.

After ambling about the main deck, you can scuttle down nearly vertical stairways to the lower deck, where there's an impressive array of cannon, many of them christened with fighting names like Raging Eagle and Jumping Billy, arranged in two long rows. Most of the ship's 54 cannon are actually replicas – when Old Ironsides ceased to be a fighting vessel, its munitions were removed for use in battle-worthy ships – but two functional models face downtown from the bow of the main deck. They still get a daily workout, too, shooting off explosive powder to mark mast-raising and -lowering (dawn and dusk, respectively); were they to fire the 24-pound balls for which they were originally outfitted, they'd topple the Customs House tower across the bay in downtown Boston.

The rest of the Navy Yard

Berthed in between Old Ironsides and the museum is the hulking gray mass of the World War II destroyer **USS Cassin Young** (daily June–Oct 10am–5pm, Nov–May 10am–4pm; free). While several similar destroyers were made in Charlestown, the *Cassin Young* was built in San Pedro, California, and served primarily in the Atlantic and Mediterranean before eventually being transferred to the National Park Service for use as a museum ship in 1978. There's not much of interest to see here, though, aside from the expansive main deck's depth chargers and tiny infirmary. The cramped chambers below – the Captain's rooms and "head," or restroom, among them – are mostly of interest to World War II buffs, who can inspect them by taking a 45-minute guided tour (June–Oct hourly 10am–5pm, Nov–May 11am, 2pm, & 3pm; free).

At the northern perimeter of the Navy Yard, there's not much to recommend a visit to the quarter-mile-long, two-story, granite **Ropewalk Building**, where most of the cordage used by the US Navy was made after 1837. Though it is closed to the public, Navy aficionados may be interested to know that the narrow building is the last remaining complete structure devoted to rope-making in the country. At the opposite end of the Yard, near the point where you access the Charlestown Bridge, the **Charlestown Navy Yard Historical Center** offers information and screens a rather dated, twenty-minute program entitled *The Whites of Their Eyes* (daily 9.30am–4.30pm; $4; ☎617/241-7575), which attempts to recreate the Battle of Bunker Hill with blinking lights and voiceovers passing for multimedia.

City Square and around

Charlestown's center is a few minutes' walk northwest of the Navy Yard. At the end of a scenic, if barren, harborfront walk is **City Square** – a park space that doubles as a traffic circle. The square is anchored at its northern tip by *Olives*, one of Boston's most popular restaurants, and the 1913 yellow-brick three-story Charlestown Municipal Building on its east side.

Harvard Street, which runs off the square's northwest side, was posthumously named for John Harvard, the young Charlestown-based minister whose library and funds launched the country's first university, in Cambridge. The street curves through the small **Town Hill** district, site of the neighborhood's first settled community. Here you'll also find John Harvard Mall and Harvard Square (not to be confused with the celebrated one in Cambridge), both lined with well-preserved homes.

Main, Devens, and Cordis streets

Main Street extends north from the square; at no. 55 you'll find the wooden 1795 house of **Deacon John Larkin**, who lent Paul Revere his horse for the ride to Lexington and never got it back. You can't go inside, so press on to the quaint **Warren Tavern**, at no. 105, a small three-story wooden structure. Both Larkin's house and the Warren Tavern were built soon after the British burned Charlestown in the Battle of Bunker Hill. The tavern, named for doctor Joseph Warren, personal physician to the Adams family (as in President John Adams) before he was killed in the Battle of Bunker Hill, still functions as a popular watering hole today (see Chapter 14, Drinking).

West of the tavern, the monumental 1876 **Charlestown Five Cents Savings Bank Building**, at 1 Thompson Square, boasts a steep mansard roof and Victorian Gothic ornamentation, even though it now houses street-level convenience stores; the modest external vault belonging to its original tenants still protrudes from the eastern wall. A good ten minutes' walk further west takes you to the **Phipps Street Burying Ground**, dating from 1630, which has an unusual layout allegedly corresponding to that of Charlestown itself, and quirky gravestones like that of Prince Bradstreet, memorialized as "an honest man of color." While many Revolutionary soldiers are buried here, it lacks the historical resonance of some other burying grounds in the city, and you need not go out of your way to visit.

Retrace your steps to the Warren Tavern and head down crooked **Devens Street** to the south (called Crooked Lane in 1640) and **Cordis Street** to the north, which are packed with historic, private houses, many of which are lovely to look at, though they don't offer anything in the way of tours. Of these, the worn Revival mansion at 33 Cordis St is the most striking, with its white Ionic columns standing tall amidst its quaint New England neighbors.

Monument Avenue and Winthrop Square

North from Main Street toward the Bunker Hill Monument, the red-brick townhouses along **Monument Avenue** – long the dividing line between the moneyed and blue-collar classes in Charlestown – are some of Boston's most exclusive residences. Though no house really stands out, strolling past the medley of Federal and Revival structures en route to the Bunker Hill monument holds low-key appeal. Nearby along Winthrop Street, **Winthrop Square** is Charlestown's unofficial common; the prim rowhouses overlooking it form another upscale enclave. Appropriately enough, considering its proximity to Bunker Hill, the common started out as a military training field; a series of bronze tablets at its northeastern edge list the men killed just up the slope in the Battle of Bunker Hill.

The Bunker Hill Monument

Atop a butte confusingly known as Breed's Hill (see box, p.83), a gray obelisk that's visible from just about anywhere in Charlestown serves as a **monument** (daily 9am–4.30pm; free) commemorating the **Battle of Bunker Hill**. It was here that colonial troops positioned themselves on the night of June 16, 1775, to wage what was ultimately a losing battle, despite its recasting by US historians as a great moral victory in the fight for independence. The obelisk is notable for being both the country's first monument funded entirely by public donations, and the first to popularize the dagger-like style epitomized by the Washington Monument in DC. Centrally positioned in Monument Square and fronted by a strident, sword-bearing statue of Colonel William Prescott, a lodge

△ Bunker Hill Monument

The Battle of Bunker Hill

The Revolutionary War was at its bloodiest on the hot June day in 1775 when British and colonial forces clashed in Charlestown. In the wake of the battles at Lexington and Concord two months earlier, the British had assumed full control of Boston, while the patriots had the upper hand in the surrounding areas. The British, under the command of generals Thomas Gage and "Gentleman Johnny" Burgoyne, intended to sweep the countryside clean of "rebellious rascals." Colonials intercepted the plans and moved to fortify **Bunker Hill**, the dominant hill in Charlestown. However, when Colonel William Prescott arrived on the scene, he chose to occupy **Breed's Hill** instead, either due to a mix-up – the two hills were often confused on colonial-era maps – or tactical foresight, based on the proximity of Breed's Hill to the harbor. Whatever the motivation, more than a thousand citizen-soldiers arrived during the night of June 16, 1775, and fortified the hill with a 160-foot-long earthen redoubt by morning.

The next day, spotting a Yankee fort on what they took to be Bunker Hill, the redcoats, each carrying 125 pounds of food and supplies in preparation for a three-day military foray into the country, rowed across the harbor to take the rebel-held town. On the patriots' side, Colonel Prescott issued an order to his troops not to fire "'til you see the whites of their eyes," such was their limited store of gunpowder. Though vastly outnumbered, the colonials successfully repelled two full-fledged assaults, the even rows of underprepared and overburdened redcoats making easy targets. Some British units lost more than ninety percent of their men, and what few officers survived had to push their troops forward with their swords to make them fight on. However, the tide began to turn by the third British assault, as the redcoats shed their gear and reinforcements arrived. The colonials' supply of gunpowder was dwindling, too, though they continued to fight with stones and musket butts; meanwhile, British cannon fire from Copp's Hill in the North End had turned Charlestown into an inferno. Despite the eventual loss for the patriots, the battle did much to persuade them – and the British, who lost nearly half their men who fought in this battle – that continued armed resistance made independence inevitable.

at its base houses dioramas of the battle, while inside, 294 steps ascend to the top of the 221-foot granite shaft. Hardy climbers will be rewarded with sweeping views of Boston, the Harbor, surrounding towns, and, to the northwest, the stone spire of the **St Francis de Sales Church**, which stands atop the real Bunker Hill, but is too out of the way to warrant a visit.

Beacon Hill and the West End

A dignified stack of red brick rising over the north side of Boston Common, **Beacon Hill** is Boston at its most traditional. Once home to numerous historical and literary figures – including John Hancock, John Quincy Adams, Louisa May Alcott, Oliver Wendell Holmes, and Nathaniel Hawthorne – the area has remained the address of choice for the city's elite, and, looking around, it's not hard to fathom why. The narrow, hilly byways are lit with **gaslamps** that burn 24/7 (historically it was cheaper to leave them on than to snuff them out and relight them on a daily basis) and lined with quaint, nineteenth-century **townhouses**, all part of an enforced preservation that prohibits modern buildings, architectural innovations, or anything else from disturbing the carefully cultivated atmosphere of urban gentility. (Even Starbucks has been forced to adopt the neighborhood's distinctive signage in order to reside here.)

In colonial times, Beacon Hill was the most prominent of three peaks, known as the Trimountain, which formed Boston's geological backbone. The sunny south slope was developed into prime real estate and quickly settled by the city's political and economic powers, but the north slope was traditionally closer in spirit to the **West End**, a tumbledown port district populated by free blacks and immigrants. The north slope was home to so much salacious activity, in fact, that outraged Brahmins – Beacon Hill's moneyed elite – termed it "Mount Whoredom."

During the twentieth century, this social divide was largely eradicated and clever real estate agents and developers have been quick to bracket the West End with Beacon Hill. Condominiums have recently been built on Bowdoin Street – one of the arteries that joins the two neighborhoods – and businesses up to ten blocks from the Hill itself have taken on a "Beacon Hill" prefix as part of their names. The result is that Beacon Hill is fast losing its exclusionary feel (though members of polite society still refer to the south slope as "the good side"). Both sides, in fact, have much to offer: on the south slope, there's the grandiose **Massachusetts State House**, residences of past and present luminaries, and attractive boulevards like **Charles Street** and **Beacon Street**, the former full of quaint antiques shops and cafés, the latter snugly crowded with prim townhouses; this is the Boston of popular image, and an integral part of most any visit. More down-to-earth, the north slope, around Cambridge Street, has its share of atmospheric blocks as well, plus some signature sights of the **Black Heritage Trail** (see box, p.91) – a walking tour that explores the history of Boston's nineteenth-century African-American community and includes the **African Meeting House**, the warren of alleyways used by fleeing slaves to escape arrest, and the superb **Robert Gould Shaw/54th Regiment Memorial**.

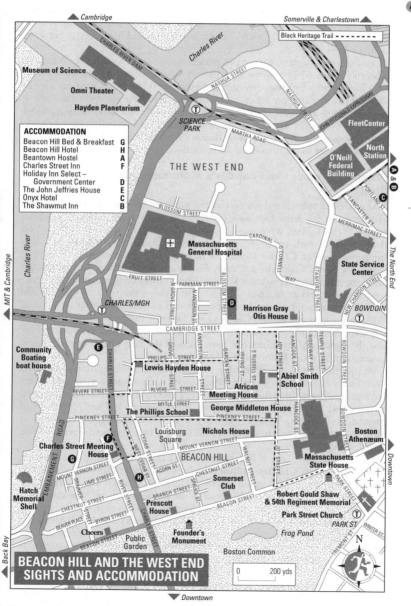

▲ Cambridge

Somerville & Charlestown ▲

Black Heritage Trail - - - - - - - -

Charles River

CHARLES RIVER DAM

NASHUA STREET

JOHN FITZGERALD EXPRESSWAY

Museum of Science

Omni Theater

Hayden Planetarium

SCIENCE PARK

MARTHA ROAD

NASHUA STREET

FleetCenter

North Station

O'Neill Federal Building

A & B

THE WEST END

PORTLAND ST.

C

LANCASTER ST.

MERRIMAC STREET

BLOSSOM STREET

CARDINAL O'CONNELL WAY

ACCOMMODATION
Beacon Hill Bed & Breakfast ... G
Beacon Hill Hotel ... H
Beantown Hostel ... A
Charles Street Inn ... F
Holiday Inn Select –
  Government Center ... D
The John Jeffries House ... E
Onyx Hotel ... C
The Shawmut Inn ... B

✚ **Massachusetts General Hospital**

STANIFORD STREET

NEW CHARDON STREET

State Service Center

BOWDOIN

Charles River

MIT & Cambridge ▲

FRUIT STREET

PARKMAN STREET

BLOSSOM STREET

N GROVE STREET

CHARLES/MGH

D

Harrison Gray Otis House

CAMBRIDGE STREET

Community Boating boat house

CHARLES STREET

E

PHILLIPS STREET

GROVE STREET

ANDERSON STREET

GARDEN STREET

IRVING ST.

S RUSSELL ST.

HANCOCK ST.

RIDGEWAY AVE.

TEMPLE STREET

BOWDOIN STREET

BOWDOIN

The North End ▶

REVERE STREET

Lewis Hayden House

REVERE STREET

MYTLE STREET

The Phillips School

African Meeting House

Abiel Smith School

JOY STREET

HANCOCK ST.

George Middleton House

PINCKNEY STREET

PINCKNEY STREET

Boston Athenæum

Downtown ▶

CHARLES STREET

CEDAR STREET

WEST CEDAR STREET

Charles Street Meeting House

F

G

MOUNT VERNON STREET

Louisburg Square

Nichols House

MOUNT VERNON STREET

WALNUT STREET

JOY ST.

Massachusetts State House

BEACON HILL

H

ACORN ST.

CHESTNUT STREET

SPRUCE ST.

Somerset Club

PARK STREET

🏛

Robert Gould Shaw & 54th Regiment Memorial

EMBANKMENT ROAD

Hatch Memorial Shell

MOUNT VERNON STREET

LIME STREET

CHESTNUT STREET

BRANCH STREET

BEACON STREET

RIVER STREET

Prescott House

Park Street Church

PARK ST.

T

WINTER ST.

Back Bay ▲

BEAVER PLACE

BYRON STREET

BEACON STREET

CHARLES STREET

Cheers

Public Garden

🏛 **Founder's Monument**

Frog Pond

Boston Common

N

**BEACON HILL AND THE WEST END
SIGHTS AND ACCOMMODATION**

0 ——— 200 yds

▼ Downtown

Beacon Street

Running along the south slope of Beacon Hill above the Common, **Beacon Street** was described by Oliver Wendell Holmes in the late nineteenth century as Boston's "sunny street for the sifted few." Its lofty character remains today: a row of stately brick townhouses, fronted by ornate iron grillwork, presides regally over the area. The ground level of one of these homes holds what might be the most famous address on the block, that of the **Cheers Pub** (see p.210). Formerly known as *Bull & Finch*, the bar that inspired the hit TV series unabashedly trades on the association and has added a gift store at street level.

Continuing along, look for **purple panes** in some of the townhouses' windows, especially at nos. 63 and 64; the story behind this odd coloring evinces the street's long association with Boston wealth and privilege. When panes were installed in some of the first Beacon Street mansions, they turned purple upon exposure to the sun, due to an excess of manganese in the glass. At first an irritating accident, they were eventually regarded as the definitive Beacon Hill status symbol due to their prevalence in the windows of Boston's most prestigious homes; some residents have gone so far as to shade their windows purple in imitation.

Prescott House, the Founder's Monument, and Somerset Club

It may lack purple-tinted panes, but the elegant bowfronted 1808 **Prescott House**, at no. 55 (May–Oct Wed, Thurs, & Sat noon–4pm, tours every 30min; $4; ☎617/742-3190, ⊛www.nscda.org/ma; Park St **T**), is the only house on Beacon Street with public access to its inner chambers. Designed by Asher Benjamin, one of Charles Bulfinch's most prolific understudies, for Boston merchant James Colburn, its most distinguished inhabitant was renowned historian and Harvard professor William Hickling Prescott, whose family occupied its five floors from 1845 to 1859. Hung above the pastiche of Federalist and Victorian furniture inside are two crossed swords belonging to Colonel William Prescott and British Captain John Linzee – the professor and his wife's respective grandfathers. The men fought against each other at Bunker Hill, and the sight of their munitions here inspired William Thackeray, a frequent houseguest, to write his novel, *The Virginians*.

Across the street, the **Founder's Monument** commemorates Boston's first European settler, William Blackstone, a Cambridge-educated loner who moved from England with his entire library to a piece of wilderness he acquired for next to nothing from the Shawmut Indians – the site of present-day Boston. A stone bas-relief depicts the apocryphal moment in 1630 when Blackstone sold most of his acreage to a group of Puritans from Charlestown.

Back on the north side of Beacon Street, and a few steps past Spruce Court, is the last of a trio of **Charles Bulfinch houses** (see box, p.89) commissioned by lawyer and future Boston mayor Harrison Gray Otis over a ten-year period; the four-story Neoclassical house has been home to the American Meteorological Society since 1958. Just east of here, it's hard to miss the twin-swelled granite building at nos. 42–43, built for Colonel David Sears's family by Alexander Parris of Quincy Market fame (see p.61). Its stern Greek Revival facade has welcomed members of the exclusive **Somerset Club** since 1872, an organization so elitist that when a fire broke out in the kitchen in 1945, firemen who arrived were ordered to come in via the cumbersome servants' entrance, a heavy iron-studded portal.

Purveyors of Fine Wines, Food & Spirits

△ Emmet's Pub, on Beacon Street

Robert Gould Shaw/54th Regiment Memorial

Further up Beacon Street, a majestic monument honors **Robert Gould Shaw** and the **54th Massachusetts Regiment**, America's first all-black company (except for its commander) to fight in the Civil War. Led by Shaw, scion of a moneyed Boston Brahmin clan, the regiment performed its service bravely, though it was isolated from the rest of the Union army, given the worst of the military's resources, and saddled alternately with menial and dangerous assignments. Most of its members, including Shaw, were killed in a failed attempt to take Fort Wagner from the Confederates in 1863. Augustus Saint-Gaudens's outstanding 1897 high-relief bronze sculpture depicts the 54th marching with the Angel of Death flying above them. The names of the soldiers who died in action were belatedly added in 1982 in a list on its reverse side. Robert Lowell won a Pulitzer Prize in 1964 for his poem about the monument, "For the Union Dead," and the regiment's story was depicted in the 1989 film *Glory*. The monument is also the starting point of the excellent National Park Ranger-led walking tour of the **Black Heritage Trail** (see box, p.91).

The Massachusetts State House

Across from the memorial, at the confluence of Park and Beacon streets, rises the large gilt dome of the **Massachusetts State House** (Mon–Fri 10am–4pm, last tour at 3.15pm; free; Park Street **T**), the scale and grandeur of which recalls the heady spirit of the newly independent America in which Charles Bulfinch designed it. The original 1795 design actually makes up only a small portion of the existing structure – the huge wings jutting out on either side, as well as the extension in the rear, were added much later. An all-star team of Revolution-era luminaries contributed to the original construction. Built on land donated by John Hancock, its cornerstone was laid by Samuel Adams, and the copper for its dome was rolled in Paul Revere's foundry in 1802 (though it was covered over with 23-karat gold leaf in the 1870s). Its front lawn is dotted with statuary honoring favorite sons such as Henry Cabot Lodge and JFK; to the right of the State House is a statue of Civil War General Joseph Hooker, whose name was given to prostitutes thanks to him frequently procuring them for his troops. There is also a statue of Mary Dyer, who became a symbol for religious freedom when she was put to death in 1660 for adhering to her Quaker faith. The statue overlooks the spot on Boston Common where she was hanged.

Once inside the labyrinthine interior, make your way up a flight to the second floor, where 45-minute tours start from **Doric Hall** – though you'd do as well to grab a free map and show yourself around. Littered with statues and murals celebrating even the most obscure Massachusetts historical events and the statesmen who shaped them, the floor's central hallway leads to the impressively sober **Hall of Flags**, a circular room surrounded by tall columns of Siena marble, lit by a vaulted stained-glass window bearing the state seal and hung with the original flags carried by Massachusetts soldiers into battle. On the third floor, a carved wooden fish known as the **Sacred Cod** hangs above the Senate chambers. The state senators took this symbol of maritime prosperity so seriously that when Harvard pranksters stole it in the 1930s, they shut down the government until it was recovered.

Behind the State House, on Bowdoin Street, lies pleasant, grassy **Ashburton Park**, centered on a pillar (a replica of a 1789 Bulfinch work) indicating the hill's original summit, which was sixty feet higher. Beacon Hill got its name from the makeshift warning light to ships in the night that once stood in the pillar's place; an iron skillet filled with combustibles and dangled from a 65-foot iron post.

The architecture of Charles Bulfinch

America's foremost architect of the late eighteenth and early nineteenth centuries, **Charles Bulfinch** (1763–1844) developed a distinctive style somewhere between Federal and Classical that remains Boston's most recognizable architectural motif. Mixing Neoclassical training with New England practicality, Bulfinch built residences characterized by their rectilinear brick structure and pillared porticoes; examples remain throughout Beacon Hill, most notably at **87 Mount Vernon St** and **45 Beacon St**. While most of his work was residential, Bulfinch, in fact, made his name with the design of various government buildings, such as the 1805 renovation of **Faneuil Hall** and, more significantly, the **Massachusetts State House**, whose dome influenced the design of state capitols nationwide.

Bulfinch's talents also extended to urban planning. He designed the layout of Boston's **South End**, as well as the now demolished **Tontine Crescent**, a half-ellipse crescent planned around a small park that won Bulfinch praise but ruined him financially; what vestiges remain are found around the Financial District's **Franklin** and **Arch streets**. Bulfinch was also adept at designing massive greystone mercantile warehouses in both Victorian and Federal styles, examples of which can be seen at **68–70 Broad St**, and churches – the North End owes **St Stephen's** to Bulfinch. Furthermore, his wide-ranging skill caught the attention of President James Monroe, who in 1818 commissioned Bulfinch to serve as the architect of Washington DC's **US Capitol**.

Louisburg Square and around

Farther down the street, between Mount Vernon and Pinckney streets, **Louisburg Square** (which will have a silent "s" or not, depending on whom you ask) forms the gilded geographic heart of Beacon Hill. An oblong green space flanked on either side by rows of stately brick townhouses, it's the city's only private park, owned by the surrounding residents. Encompassed by wrought-iron fencing to keep out nonresident plebeians, and featuring statues of Columbus and Aristides the Just, the square owes its distinction less to its architectural character than to a history of illustrious residents, among them novelist Louisa May Alcott and members of the Vanderbilt family. Today, a sense of elite civic parochialism makes this Boston's most coveted address for a select few: the 2004 Democratic presidential candidate, Senator John Kerry, and his wife, ketchup heiress Teresa Heinz, are among those who call the square home.

Pinckney Street

North of Louisburg Square runs **Pinckney Street**, once the sharp division between the opulent south and ramshackle north sections of Beacon Hill – original developers planned it as such, arranging their stables and estates so that only the back entrances fringed the street. In the 1920s, resident Robert Lowell expressed shock at the proximity of his home at 91 Revere St to these shadier environs, claiming that while he lived only fifty yards from Louisburg Square, he was nevertheless "perched on the outer rim of the hub of decency." The distinction is no longer so sharp, and now Pinckney is yet another picturesque Beacon Hill street, all the more worth a stroll thanks to its location at the crest of the hill; on a clear day, its intersection with Anderson Street affords views of the West End and across the Charles River to Cambridge – not the prettiest vista, but good for getting the lay of the land.

Two historically important if aesthetically modest sights on the Black Heritage Trail (see box, opposite) can also be found on Pinckney: the 1797 clapboard **George Middleton House,** Beacon Hill's first African-American-built private dwelling, is at 5-7, while the red-brick **Phillips School**, the first integrated school in Boston, is at the street's intersection with Anderson.

Mount Vernon Street

A walk on **Mount Vernon Street** along the flat of the hill brings you past some of Beacon Hill's most beautiful buildings. At no. 55, the neighborhood's only residence open year-round to the public, the **Nichols House** (May–Oct Tues–Sat 12.15–4.15pm; Nov–Dec & Feb–April Mon & Thurs–Sat noon–4.15pm, tours start fifteen minutes past the hour; $5; ☎617/227-6993, ⓦwww.nicholshousemuseum.org; Park Street **T**), is yet another Bulfinch design. The building was most recently the home of eccentric spinster and accomplished landscape gardener Rose Standish Nichols, who counted among her allegiances Fabian Socialism and the International Society of Pen Pals. Miss Rose, as she is known to posterity, lived in the house until her death in the early 1960s – though the faint odor of roses permeating the air here today is supposed to imply that she may still be haunting the hallways. While the detailed thirty-minute tour by the curator may be gripping only for those with an abiding interest in antique furnishings and decorations (there are some striking Asian tapestries, Federal-period furniture, and an original self-portrait by John Singleton Copley), it does give a brief glimpse of the overstuffed life of leisure once led by Beacon Hill's moneyed elite.

The Federal-style **Charles Street Meeting House**, with its set-back, cupolaed roof, stands on the corner of Mount Vernon and Charles Street, the commercial center of Beacon Hill, lined with scores of restaurants, antiques shops, and pricey specialty boutiques (see Restaurants and Shopping chapters). A hotbed of political activity in the nineteenth century, the Meeting House has been repurposed as an office building with a basement café. At Mount Vernon's intersection with Brimmer Street, you'll find the vine-covered **Church of the Advent**; with its pointed arches and starkly contrasting stone and red-brick facade, it's a striking example of High Victorian Gothic. If you poke your head in during one of their frequent weekly masses, you can check out the decadent gold altar and detailed grillwork along the apse.

Acorn and Chestnut streets

A block south of Mount Vernon Street, narrow **Acorn Street** still has its original early nineteenth-century cobblestones. Barely wide enough for a car to pass through, it was originally built as a minor byway to be lined with servants' residences. Locals have always clung to it as the epitome of Beacon Hill quaint; in the 1960s, residents permitted the city to tear up the street to install sewer pipes only after exacting the promise that every cobblestone would be replaced in its original location. One block further south, **Chestnut Street** features some of the most intricate facades in Boston, notably Bulfinch's **Swan Houses**, at nos. 13, 15, and 17, with their recessed arches and marble columns, and delicate touches like scrolled door knockers and wrought-iron lace balconies.

The Esplanade

Spanning nine miles along the Charles River, the **Esplanade** is yet another of Boston's well-manicured public spaces, complete with requisite playgrounds, landscaped hills, lakes, and bridges. The nicest stretch runs alongside Beacon Hill and continues into Back Bay, providing a unique, scenic way to appreciate the Hill from a distance, as well as being a leading hotspot for the city's young and attractive. On summer days the Esplanade is swarming with well-toned joggers and rollerbladers, many of them seemingly on the prowl for a partner. Just below the Longfellow Bridge (which connects to Cambridge, across the river; see Chapter 9) is the Community Boating Boathouse, the point of departure for sailing, kayaking, and windsurfing outings on the Charles (April–Oct daily 9am–5pm; two-day visitor's pass $50; ☎617/523-1038, ⊛www.community -boating.org). The two-day pass gets you unlimited use of their equipment.

The white half-dome rising from the riverbank along the Esplanade is the **Hatch Shell** (☎617/626-1250, ⊛www.mass.gov/dcr; Charles **T**), a public performance space best known for its Fourth of July celebration (see p.252), which features a free concert by the Boston Pops, a pared-down version of the Boston Symphony Orchestra that performs popular, rather than classical, music. This event is always terribly overcrowded, but the other summer happenings at the Shell, such as free movies and jazz concerts, occur almost nightly and can be far more accessible.

The African Meeting House and around

Back along Pinckney Street from the Esplanade, **Smith Court** was the center of Boston's substantial pre-Civil War black community, back when the north slope was still a low-rent district; now it's home to a few crucial stops on Boston's **Black Heritage Trail** (see box below).

The Black Heritage Trail

In 1783, Massachusetts became the first state to declare slavery illegal, partly in recognition of black participation in the Revolutionary War. Subsequently, large communities of free blacks and escaped slaves swiftly sprang up in the North End and Beacon Hill. The neighborhoods' proximity to the shipyards was convenient to the men, while the nearby upper-class houses meant domestic work for the women. Very few blacks live in either place nowadays, but the **Black Heritage Trail** traces Beacon Hill's key role in local and national black history and is the most important historical site in America devoted to pre-Civil War African-American history and culture.

The 1.6-mile loop takes in fourteen historical sights, which are detailed in a useful **guide** available at the African Meeting House (and the information center in Boston Common; see p.50). Much of what there is to see, however, is quite ho-hum on its own; the best way to experience the trail is by taking a National Park Service **walking tour** (late May to early Sept Mon–Sat 10am, noon, & 2pm, Sept–June call a day in advance to reserve; free; ☎617/742-5415, ⊛www.nps.gov/boaf; Park St **T**). The two-hour tour superbly puts the history of Boston's black community into context.

Starting from the **Robert Gould Shaw Memorial** (see p.88), the tour passes the **George Middleton House**, the **Phillips School**, and the cupola-topped **Charles Street Meeting House**, which housed the First African Methodist Episcopal Church until it left Beacon Hill (the last black institution to do so) in 1939. Near the end of the walk, you'll find the superficially unremarkable, but historically significant, **Lewis and Harriet Hayden House** at 66 Phillips St, whose owner, a former escaped slave himself, regularly opened his door to fugitive slaves and abolitionists alike as part of the Underground Railroad, and **Smith Court**, home to the **African Meeting House** and **Abiel Smith School** at the end of **Holmes Alley**, a common escape route used by runaway slaves.

Free blacks who were denied participation in Boston's civic and religious life until well into the nineteenth century worshiped and held political meetings in what became known as the **African Meeting House**, at 8 Smith Court. Informally called the Black Faneuil Hall, it was a hotbed for abolitionist activity in the mid-1800s; indeed, William Lloyd Garrison founded the New England Anti-Slavery Society in the building's simple, second-floor auditorium, in 1832.

Today, the sober former church is home to the **Museum of Afro-American History** (Mon–Sat 10am–4pm; donation suggested; ⓦwww.afroammuseum .org; Park Street T), which, considering the importance of the site it occupies, is rather a disappointment. You won't find much in the way of displays, only a rotating exhibit on the first floor – usually contemporary African-American art – and the meeting house on the second, which has been restored to look like the most basic of churches it once was. Well-informed docents lead **free tours** and add much to contextualize what little you actually see.

At the end of Smith Court, walk along part of the old Underground Railroad used to protect escaped slaves, who once ducked into the doors along narrow **Holmes Alley** that were left open by sympathizers to the abolitionist cause. The **Abiel Smith School**, at 46 Joy St (same hours as above), built in 1834, was the first public educational institution established for black schoolchildren in Boston. It now showcases exhibits for the Museum of Afro-American History; check out "Separate Schools, Unequal Education," which traces, as the name indicates, the history of racial inequality in the American school system. There's also a **gift shop** with a wide range of literature related to the African-American experience.

The West End

North of Cambridge Street, the tidy rows of townhouses are replaced by a more urban spread of office buildings and old brick structures, signaling the start of the **West End**. Boston's main port of entry for immigrants in post-Colonial times, this area was populated by a broad mix of ethnic groups as well as transient sailors who brought a rough-and-tumble sex-and-tattoo industry with them. However, the eventual drift of Boston's ethnic populations to the southern districts, along with 1960s urban renewal, has effaced the district's once-lively character with sterile, modern facades.

That said, a vestige of the old West End remains in the small tangle of byways – namely Friend, Portland, and Canal streets – behind the high-rise buildings of Massachusetts General Hospital, where you'll see urban warehouses interspersed with numerous Irish bars. Every bar swells to a fever pitch after Celtics basketball and Bruin hockey games at the nearby **FleetCenter**, the slick, corporate-named arena on top of North Station at 150 Causeway St (tours daily at 11am, 1pm, & 3pm; $5; ⓦwww.fleetcenter.com). For anyone wanting to see the remnants of I-93 and the subsequent landscaping of the area the elevated expressway used to occupy, Causeway Street, which runs in front of the Fleet-Center, is the place to do so.

The Harrison Gray Otis House

Back along Cambridge Street at no. 141, the brick **Harrison Gray Otis House** (Wed–Sun 11am–4.30pm, tours hourly; $8; ☎617/227-3956, ⓦwww.historicnewengland.org; Charles T), originally built for the wealthy Otis family in 1796 by Bulfinch, sits incongruously among mini-malls and office buildings (another of the family's houses can be seen on Beacon

Street; see p.86). In the 1830s, this building served as a Turkish bath before its transformation into a medicine shop and later a boarding house. In the 1920s, the structure was literally rolled back from the present-day median strip to make way for the highway. Its unadorned exterior gives no hint of the painstaking 1970s restoration that returned the house's interior to its original, eye-numbing Federal-style colors. Tours offer a glimpse into the lifestyle of Boston's elite following the American Revolution.

The Museum of Science

Situated on the Charles River Bridge, at the northernmost part of the Esplanade, Boston's **Museum of Science** (July to early Sept daily 9am–7pm, Fri till 9pm, Sept–June daily 9am–5pm, Fri till 9pm; $14, kids $11; CityPass accepted; ☎617/723-2500, ⓦwww.mos.org; Science Park **T**) consists of several floors of interactive – if patchy and often well-worn – exhibits illustrating basic principles of natural and physical science. There's enough here to entertain kids for most of a day, though that doesn't make it off-limits to fun-loving adults, too.

The best exhibit is the **Theater of Electricity** in the Blue Wing, a darkened room full of optical illusions and glowing displays on the presence of electricity in everyday life; the world's largest Van de Graaf generator gives daily electricity shows in which simulated lightning bolts flash and crackle. You can also play virtual volleyball here: the outline of your body appears on a wall-sized screen, then you attempt to hit a virtual ball with your virtual shadow. More cerebral is Mathematica, in which randomly dropped balls fall neatly into a bell curve to demonstrate the notion of probability, and Virtual Fish Tank, a trippy underwater exhibit that encourages visitors to create and care for their own virtual sea-life. Be sure to check out the Big Dig exhibit on the lower level, where videos and interactive displays provide an engaging chronicle of Boston's Sisyphean attempt to put the unsightly elevated I-93 underground.

The museum also holds the **Charles Hayden Planetarium** and the **Mugar Omni Theater** ($8.50, kids $6.50; ☎617/723-2500, ⓦwww.mos.org), though neither has too much to recommend it. The planetarium hosts talks and presentations throughout the day – free with museum admission – but it's better known for its laser shows, usually set to a soundtrack of classic rock and shown before an audience of precocious children and teenagers. In a similarly flashy vein, the Omni Theater's enormous domed IMAX screen and state-of-the-art sound system provide plenty of stunning sensory input (though not the most hard-and-fast actual information).

Back Bay

M eticulously planned **Back Bay** – where elegant tree-lined streets form a pedestrian-friendly neighborhood that looks much as it did in the nineteenth century, right down to the original gaslights and brick sidewalks – exudes a far more cosmopolitan air than similarly affluent Beacon Hill, with which it inevitably draws comparisons. A youthful population helps offset stodginess and keeps the district, which begins at the **Public Garden**, buzzing with chic eateries, trendy shops, and the aura of entitlement that goes with both. Aside from the trust-fund vibe, the other main draw here is a trove of exquisite Gilded Age rowhouses; walking around, it seems as if there's no end to the fanciful bay windows and ornamental turrets. With a few exceptions, the brownstones get fancier the farther from the garden you go (the order in which they were built), a result of one-upmanship on the part of architects and those who employed them.

Running parallel to the Charles River in neat rows, Back Bay's east–west thoroughfares – **Beacon**, **Marlborough**, **Newbury**, and **Boylston streets**, with **Commonwealth Avenue** in between – are transsected by eight shorter streets. These latter roads have been so fastidiously laid out that not only are their names in alphabetical order, but trisyllables are deliberately intercut by disyllables: Arlington, Berkeley, Clarendon, Dartmouth, Exeter, Fairfield, Gloucester, and Hereford (though Gloucester, purists protest, only looks trisyllabic) – until Massachusetts Avenue breaks the pattern at the western border of the neighborhood. The grandest rowhouses are to be found on Beacon Street and Commonwealth Avenue, while Marlborough, with its tree-lined blocks, is more atmospheric, and Boylston and Newbury are the main commercial drags; the latter has become so trendy that it's now known as Boston's Rodeo Drive. In the midst of it all is a small greenspace, **Copley Square**, surrounded by the area's main sights: **Trinity Church**, the imposing **Boston Central Library,** and the city's skyline-defining **John Hancock Tower**.

Some history

Back Bay was fashioned (as was its neighbor, the South End; see Chapter 6) in response to a shortage of living space in Boston, a problem still somewhat unresolved. An increasingly cramped Beacon Hill prompted developers to revisit a failed dam project on the Charles River that had made a swamp of much of this area. With visionary architect and urban planner **Arthur Gilman** at the helm of a huge landfill job (earth for the landfill came from an area called Needham Heights, now known colloquially as Needham Flats), the sludge began to be reclaimed in 1857.

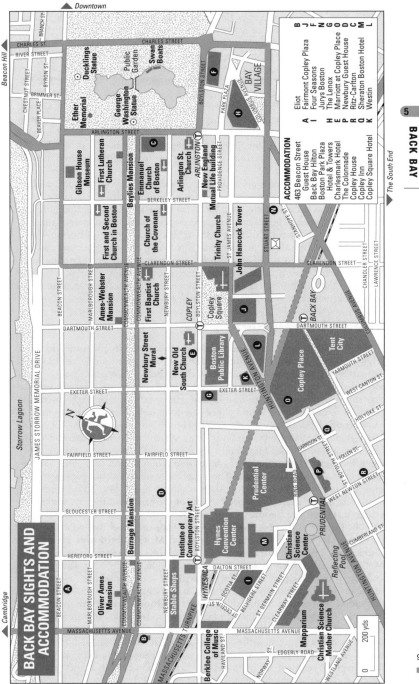

BACK BAY SIGHTS AND ACCOMMODATION

Downtown

Beacon Hill

Cambridge

Kenmore Square

Storrow Lagoon

JAMES STORROW MEMORIAL DRIVE

The South End

BAY VILLAGE

Public Garden
- Ether Memorial
- Ducklings Statue
- George Washington Statue
- Public Garden
- Swan Boats

Gibson House Museum
First Lutheran Church
Baylies Mansion
Emmanuel Church of Boston
Arlington St. Church
New England Mutual Life building
First and Second Church in Boston
Church of the Covenant
Ames-Webster Mansion
First Baptist Church
Trinity Church
John Hancock Tower
Copley Square
Newbury Street Mural
New Old South Church
Boston Public Library
Oliver Ames Mansion
Burrage Mansion
Institute of Contemporary Art
Stable Shops
Hynes Convention Center
Prudential Center
Christian Science Center
Christian Science Mother Church
Mapparium
Berklee College of Music

Copley Place
Tent City

Reflecting Pool

Streets
CHARLES STREET · BRANCH ST · RIVER STREET · BYRON ST · CHESTNUT STREET · BEAVER PLACE · BRIMMER ST · ARLINGTON STREET · BOYLSTON STREET · PARK PLAZA · COLUMBUS AVENUE · STANHOPE ST · BEACON STREET · MARLBOROUGH STREET · COMMONWEALTH AVENUE · NEWBURY STREET · BERKELEY STREET · CLARENDON STREET · ST JAMES AVENUE · PROVIDENCE STREET · STUART STREET · CHANDLER STREET · LAWRENCE STREET · DARTMOUTH STREET · EXETER STREET · FAIRFIELD STREET · GLOUCESTER STREET · HEREFORD STREET · MASSACHUSETTS AVENUE · MASSACHUSETTS TURNPIKE · HUNTINGTON AVENUE · YARMOUTH STREET · WEST CANTON ST · HOLYOKE ST · GARRISON ST · FOLLEN ST · ST BOTOLPH STREET · WEST NEWTON STREET · CUMBERLAND ST · DALTON STREET · SCOTIA ST · BELVIDERE STREET · ST GERMAIN STREET · CLEARWAY STREET · ST CECILIA ST · HAVILAND ST · EDGERLY ROAD · NORWAY ST · WESTLAND AVENUE

ACCOMMODATION

463 Beacon Street Guest House	A
Back Bay Hilton	I
Boston Park Plaza Hotel & Towers	H
Charlesmark Hotel	E
The Colonnade	P
Copley House	D
Copley Inn	C
Copley Square Hotel	M
Eliot	B
Fairmont Copley Plaza	J
Four Seasons	F
Jurys Boston	N
The Lenox	G
Marriott at Copley Place	O
Newbury Guest House	Q
Ritz-Carlton	R
Sheraton Boston Hotel	S
Westin	L

0   200 yds

N

Taking his cue from Georges Eugène Haussmann's new wide boulevards in Paris, Gilman decided on an orderly street pattern extending east to west from the Public Garden, which itself had been sculpted from swampland only two decades before. By 1890, the cramped peninsula of old Boston could claim 450 new acres, on which stood a range of churches, townhouses, and schools.

Not surprisingly, Back Bay quickly became one of the city's most sought-after addresses, although its popularity subsided somewhat during the Great Depression, when single families were unable to afford such opulence. During this period, developers converted many of the spaces into apartments, often gutting the interiors in the process; other properties were purchased by colleges and universities. In the 1990s, however, gentrification and the demand for entire houses led to developers knocking out many of the apartment walls their predecessors erected.

Despite what may have happened on the inside, the exteriors of most buildings remain unaltered, due largely to landmark preservation laws, and many retain their old wood ornamentation and Victorian embellishments. All this authentic charm contributes to high rents which feed, in turn, the consumer-driven culture on Newbury Street – a far cry from the traditional image of Boston – with its hundreds of upscale shops, high-end hair salons, and tiny gourmet eateries. Back Bay has its share of urban problems, too, from a shortage of parking space and bad traffic jams to homeless people trawling for designer garbage. But the pervasive grace of the bowfronts and wrought-iron terraces masks these issues and proffers an air of well-heeled serenity.

The Public Garden

The value of property in Boston increases the closer its proximity to Back Bay's lovingly maintained **Public Garden**, a 24-acre park founded in 1837 and earmarked for public use since 1859. Of the garden's 125 types of trees – many identified by little brass placards – most impressive are the weeping willows that ring the picturesque artificial lagoon. Here you can take a fifteen-minute ride in one of six **Swan Boats** (April–late June daily 10am–4pm; late-June to early Sept daily 10am–5pm; early to mid-Sept Mon–Fri noon–4pm, Sat & Sun 10am–4pm; $2.50; ⊛www.swanboats.com), which trace gracious figure-eights in the oversized puddle. The campy, pedal-powered conveyances, inspired by a scene in Wagner's opera *Lohengrin*, have been around since 1877, long enough to become a Boston institution. The boats carry up to twenty passengers at a time, and in the height of summer there is often a line to hop on board; instead of waiting, you can get just as good a view of the park from the tiny suspension bridge that spans the lagoon.

Public Garden's other big family draw also happens to be fowl-related: a cluster of popular bronze birds collectively called **Mrs Mallard and Her Eight Ducklings**. The sculptures were installed in 1987 to commemorate Robert McClosky's 1941 *Make Way for Ducklings*, a children's tale set in the park (it's unlikely you'll ever pass the sculptures without seeing someone "riding" one of the ducks). Of the many other statues and monuments throughout the park, the oldest and oddest is the thirty-foot-tall **Good Samaritan** monument along the Arlington Street side; the granite and red-marble column is a tribute to, of all things, the anesthetic qualities of ether. Controversy as to which of two Boston men invented the wonder drug led Oliver Wendell Holmes to dub it the "Either Monument." Finally, a dignified equestrian statue of **George Washington**, installed in 1869 and the first of him astride a horse, watches over the garden's Commonwealth Avenue entrance.

Beacon Street

As a continuation of Beacon Hill's stately main thoroughfare, **Beacon Street** was long the province of blueblood Bostonians. Despite being so close to the Charles River, however, its buildings turn their back to it, principally because in the nineteenth century the river was a stinking mess. One such building, the Italian Renaissance townhouse at no. 137, holds the remarkable **Gibson House Museum** (Wed–Sun 1–3pm, tours hourly, ring bell on hour for entry; $5; ☎617/267-6338, ⊛www. thegibsonhouse.org), which preserves the home built for Catherine Hammond Gibson in 1860, twenty years after the death of her well-to-do husband. In the somber interior, there's a curious host of Victoriana, including a still-functioning dumbwaiter, antique globes, and writing paraphernalia (one of the Gibsons was a noted travel writer), and gilt-framed photos of Catherine's relatives. Notable among the various chinoiserie is the stunning gold-embossed "Japanese Leather" wallpaper that covers a good portion of the abode, and a sequined pink velvet cat house or, if you prefer the Gibsons' term, "pet pagoda." Near the museum, at no. 84, you'll find *Cheers* (see p.210) – the inspiration for the hit TV series – which, until 2002, was known as the *Bull & Finch Pub.*

Things get less interesting at the far end of Beacon Street (furthest from the Public Garden); the one structure of note is the turreted **Charlesgate Building** at no. 535, a former hotel that's been nicknamed "The Witch's Castle," for obvious reasons, by the Emerson College students who now call it home.

Marlborough Street

Sandwiched between Beacon Street and Commonwealth Avenue, quiet **Marlborough Street** is one of the most prized residential locales in Boston – with its brick sidewalks and vintage gaslights – after Beacon Hill's Louisburg Square and the first few blocks of Commonwealth Avenue. Even though the townhouses here tend to be smaller than elsewhere in Back Bay, they display a surprising range of styles when it comes to ornamentation, especially along the blocks between Clarendon and Fairfield streets; check out **no. 362**, for starters, with its elegant windows topped by trompe l'oeil arches.

Back at the crossroad with Berkeley Street, no. 66 is one of Boston's more bizarre buildings: a Gothic-Modern hybrid that houses the **First and Second Church in Boston** (opening times vary, ☎617/267-6730, ⊛www.fscboston .org). As its name suggests, the church represents the first and second churches in Boston, which have been amalgamated since 1870. The First Church's covenant was signed on July 30, 1630 by prominent members of the Massachusetts Bay Colony, and the Second Church was founded in the North End in 1649. A fire in 1968 destroyed much of the original church, designed by renowned Boston architects William Ware and Henry Van Brunt. The present edifice – added to the old facade in 1972 – is the work of Paul Rudolph; the two very different styles clash in the most eye-jarring way.

Commonwealth Avenue

Commonwealth Avenue, Back Bay's 220-foot-wide showcase street, was modeled after the grand boulevards of Paris, and its tree-lined, 100-foot-wide median forms the first link in Frederick Law Olmsted's so-called **Emerald Necklace**, which begins at Boston Common and extends all the way to the Arnold Arboretum in Jamaica Plain. The flagship *Ritz-Carlton* hotel on Arlington

Street forms a fittingly upscale backdrop to the promenade, itself peppered with several elegantly placed **statues**, though with the exception of a particularly dashing likeness of Revolutionary War soldier **John Glover** (who helped Washington cross the Delaware in 1776) between Berkeley and Clarendon streets, few of these hold any interest. "Comm Ave," as locals irreverently call it, is at its prettiest in early May, when the magnolia and dogwood trees are in full bloom, showering the brownstone steps with their fragrant pink buds.

One set of these steps – the first as you walk along the avenue – belongs to the **Baylies Mansion**, at no. 5, which has housed the Boston Center for Adult Education since 1941. Feel free to slip inside for a look at the opulent Louis XV ballroom built expressly for Baylies's daughter's coming-out party (in the old-fashioned sense). You'll have to be content to see the Queen Anne-style **Ames–Webster Mansion**, a few blocks down at the corner of Dartmouth Street, from the outside. Built in 1872 for railroad tycoon, Massachusetts governor, and US congressman Frederick Ames, it features a two-story conservatory, central tower, and imposing chimney. Down the street is the **Burrage Mansion**, at no. 314, a fanciful synthesis of a Vanderbilt-style mansion and the French château of *Chenonceaux*. The exterior of this 1899 urban palace is a riot of gargoyles and sundry carved cherubim; inside, it's less boisterous, currently serving as a retirement home. Further on, the Beaux Arts chateau at no. 355 is the **Oliver Ames Mansion** (no relation to the railroad tycoon), topped by multiple chimneys and dormer windows; its interior now comprises offices and, as such, is not open to the public.

The First Baptist Church of Boston

Rising above the south side of the avenue at no. 110 is the landmark belfry of the **First Baptist Church of Boston** (Mon–Fri 10am–4pm; ⓦwww .firstbaptistchurchofboston.org), designed by architect H.H. Richardson in 1872 for a Unitarian congregation – though at bill-paying time only a Baptist group was able to pony up the necessary funds, hence the name. The puddingstone exterior is topped off by a 176-foot **bell tower**, which is covered by four gorgeous friezes by Frédéric-Auguste Bartholdi, who designed the Statue of Liberty; Bartholdi and Richardson became friends when the two studied together at the École des Beaux Arts in Paris. More interesting than what the tableaux depict (baptism, communion, marriage, and death) are some of the illustrious stone-etched visages, particularly those of Emerson, Longfellow, Hawthorne, and Lincoln. Trumpeting angels protrude from each corner, inspiring its inglorious nickname, "Church of the Holy Bean Blowers."

The interior is exceedingly plain in comparison to the detailed facade, but its high ceiling, exposed timbers, and Norman-style rose windows are still worth a peek if you happen by when someone's in the church office. If you've a mind to visit, ring the bell on the Commonwealth Avenue side and hope for the best.

Newbury and Boylston streets

Take a walk down **Newbury Street** and it's hard to imagine this was once considered one of Back Bay's least fashionable addresses. Thought of as a poor relation to nearby Commonwealth Avenue, just to the north, Newbury was almost exclusively residential when the earliest buildings were constructed in 1857, and its first retail shop didn't open until 1905. Today the street comprises eight atmospheric blocks of Victorian-era brownstones housing more than three hundred alternately traditional and eclectic boutiques, art galleries, and restaurants, plus ubiquitous chain stores like the Gap and NikeTown. Fashion victims, wannabe models, and wealthy foreign students have colonized cafés like *29 Newbury* and *Café Armani* (see Chapter 12), but despite the occasional nod to pretentiousness, the strip's overall mood is surprisingly inviting. And not all is shopping or dining: Newbury and the somewhat less commercially oriented **Boylston Street** are home to most of the old schools and churches built in the Back Bay area.

The Emmanuel Church of Boston and Church of the Covenant

On the first block of Newbury Street, sandwiched between fancy hair salons and upscale retail stores, is the **Emmanuel Church of Boston**, an unassuming rural Gothic Revival building. Of greater interest is the full-blown Gothic Revival **Church of the Covenant**, further down the street on the same side. Most passersby are too intent on window shopping to notice the soaring steeple, so look up before checking out the interior, famous – like its neighbor, the Arlington Street Church – for its Tiffany stained-glass windows, some of which are thirty feet high. The **Gallery NAGA** (Newbury Associated Guild of Artists), in the chapel (Tues–Sat 10am–5.30pm; ☎617/267-9060, ⓦwww .gallerynaga.com) is one of Boston's biggest contemporary art spaces, and stages new exhibits of works by artists from Boston and New England; it's also a nice setting for chamber music performances – the Boston Pro Arte Chamber Orchestra was founded here.

The rest of Newbury Street

Designed as an architect's house, the medieval flight-of-fancy at **109 Newbury St** is arguably more arresting for its two fortress-like brownstone turrets than the Cole Haan footwear inside. A block down and across the street, at **no. 144**, is the Rodier Paris boutique, but again the burnt sienna-colored building with mock battlements hunkered over it steals the show. Originally the Hotel Victoria in 1886, it looks like a combination Venetian-Moorish castle, and isn't a bad place to have a condo, which is how it serves the neighborhood today. A block further along, on the exposed side of no. 159, is the **Newbury Street Mural**, a fanciful tribute to a hodgepodge of Boston notables, from Sam Adams to Sammy Davis Jr; a key to who's who is affixed to the parking attendant's booth in the lot next to it.

Newbury gets progressively funkier west of Exeter Street; the shoppers are more often students and locals than wealthy types venturing in from the suburbs. This is where you'll find Boston's most original fashion boutiques and alternative record stores, in addition to several decent restaurants with popular summer sidewalk terraces. On the final block, between Hereford Street and Massachusetts Avenue, a span of nineteenth-century **stables** has been converted to commercial space; check out the cavernous Patagonia clothing shop at no. 346 for the best example.

Arlington Street Church and the New England Financial building

Right on the corner of Boylston and Arlington streets, Back Bay's first building, the **Arlington Street Church** (Mon–Fri 10am–5pm, ☎617/536-7050, ⓦwww.ascboston.org), is a minor Italianesque masterpiece whose construction in 1861 started a trend that resulted in many Downtown congregations relocating to posher quarters in Back Bay. Arthur Gilman, chief planner of

Back Bay, designed the clay-colored, squat structure, marked by a host of Tiffany stained-glass windows, added from 1895 to 1930. A history of progressive rhetoric has also earned it some note: abolitionist minister William Ellery Channing intoned against slavery here just a year before the Civil War erupted, and the church was a favored venue of peace activists during the Vietnam War; nowadays there's an active gay congregation. A block down is the prison-like **New England Financial building**, with some national chain stores on the first floor that do little for its character. It's worth nipping inside, though, for a look at the **murals**, which depict such historic regional events as John Winthrop sailing from Old to New England aboard the *Arbella*, Paul Revere sounding his famous alarm ("The British are coming! The British are coming!"), and the Declaration of Independence being read in Boston for the first time, from the balcony of the Old State House.

The New Old South Church

On the corner of Boylston and Dartmouth streets stands one of Boston's most attractive buildings, the **New Old South Church** (Mon–Fri 9am–5pm). There's actually some logic to the name: the congregation in residence at Downtown's Old South Meeting House outgrew it and decamped here in 1875. You need not be a student of architecture to be won over by the Italian Gothic design, most pronounced in the ornate, 220-foot bell tower – rebuilt in 1940 after the original started leaning – and copper-roof lantern, replete with metallic gargoyles in the shape of dragons. The dramatic zebra-striped archways on the Dartmouth Street side are, unfortunately, partially obscured by the entrance to the Copley **T** station. The church isn't just to be admired from the outside, either: its interior is an alluring assemblage of dark woods set against a forest green backdrop, coupled with fifteenth-century, English-style stained-glass windows.

The Institute of Contemporary Art

Well down Boylston Street nearer Massachusetts Avenue, the **Institute of Contemporary Art**, at no. 955 (Tues, Wed, & Fri noon–5pm, Thurs till 9pm, Sat & Sun 11am–5pm $7, free Thurs 5–9pm; ☎617/266-5152, ⊛www.icaboston.org), is Boston's main modern art venue, though it has no permanent collection to speak of. Housed in half of an odd Romanesque-style police and fire station built in 1886 – the other half of which is still home base for Back Bay's firefighters – the ICA hosts about four exhibits and installations a year, but many of them meet with mixed success. Its small size (with just two floors plus a basement theatre; see p.223) is ideal for showcasing solo artists, but its thematic exhibits are vastly more accessible. In 2006 the ICA will move to a new venue, three times the size of the present one, at Fan Pier on the waterfront.

Copley Square and around

Bounded by Boylston, Clarendon, Dartmouth, and St James streets, **Copley Square** is the busy commercial center of Back Bay. Various design schemes have come and gone since the square was first filled in the 1870s; the present one is a remnant from 1984, a nondescript grassy expanse and a heavy, slab-like fountain anchored by two stone obelisks on the Boylston Street side. A farmers' market materializes opposite the *Fairmont Copley Plaza Hotel* on Fridays in the spring and summer. Fortunately, the square's periphery holds more interest than the space it surrounds.

Trinity Church

In his meticulous attention to detail – from the polychromatic masonry on the outside to the rather generic stained-glass windows within – Boston architect H.H. Richardson seemed to overlook the big picture of his 1877 **Trinity Church**, at 206 Clarendon St (daily 8am–6pm; $4; ⍟www.trinityboston.org), which, as one 1923 guidebook averred, "is not beautiful." Critics in Richardson's time disagreed, dubbing it a masterpiece of the Romanesque Revival style, which Richardson initially attempted with his First Baptist Church (see p.98). The hulking exterior is a bit easier on the eyes when approached from Clarendon instead of Dartmouth, where you'll get the classic, dead-on view; gazing up at the chunky centered tower from behind affords an unusual, even dizzying, perspective. From here, you'll also have an easier time of finding the church's cloister and hidden garden, one of Back Bay's more enchanting quiet spots. Skip the rather spartan interior, which feels more empty than awe-inspiring – unless, of course, you happen to be there on Friday at 12.15pm, in which case there are often **free organ recitals**. Indeed, the most interesting aspect of Trinity Church is probably its juxtaposition to the John Hancock Tower, in whose mirrored panes it's reflected; a shot of them together is a classic Boston image. Interesting, too, is the fact that the church rests rather precariously on 4500 submerged wood pilings – before the advent of modern construction techniques this was the only way for buildings to stay put in the very moist depths of Back Bay.

The Central Library

A decidedly secular building anchoring the end of Copley Square opposite Trinity Church, the **Central Library** (Mon–Thurs 9am–9pm, Fri–Sat 9am–5pm; ☎617/536-5400, ⍟www.bpl.org) is the largest public research library in New England and the first one in America to permit the borrowing of books. McKim, Mead & White, the leading architectural firm of its day, built the Italian Renaissance Revival structure in 1852. The Copley Square facade, with its sloping red tile roof, green copper cresting, and huge arched windows, is quite magnificent, while the visibility of the entrance is heightened by the presence of the spiky yet sinuous lanterns overhanging it. The massive inner bronze doors were designed by Daniel Chester French (sculptor of the Lincoln Memorial in Washington DC); beyond them, a musketeer-like statue of Sir Henry Vane stands guard. This early governor of the Massachusetts Bay Colony believed, or so the inscription relates, that "God, law and parliament" were superior to the king, which apparently didn't do much for his case in 1662, when his freethinking head got the chop.

Beyond the marble grand staircase and beneath the extensively coffered ceilings are a series of **murals**, most impressive of which is a diaphanous depiction of the nine Muses. Nearby stands a statue of a smiling, naked woman holding a baby in one hand and a bunch of grapes in the other, a replica of an original bacchante that, due to neo-Puritan prudishness, never graced the library's inner courtyard as intended. Just to the right is the gloomy **Abbey Room**, named for Edwin Abbey's murals depicting the Holy Grail legend, and where Bostonians once took delivery of their books. Most of these were kept in the imposing **Bates Reading Room**, which, with its 218-foot-long sweep, 50-foot-high barrel-vaulted ceiling, dark oak paneling, and incomparable calm, hasn't changed much since its debut more than a century ago. The library's most interesting feature is tucked away on the top floor, however, where the darkly lit **Sargent Hall** is covered with more than fifteen astonishing murals painted by John Singer Sargent between 1890 and 1916. Entitled the *Triumph of Religion*, the works are a mastery of detail incorporating appliquéd metal, paper, and jewels – most striking in the north end's stunning twin *Pagan Gods* ceiling vaults – and plaster relief, evident in Moses' twin tablets which project from the east wall. First-time visitors should pick up a floor plan and explanatory pamphlet at the top of the stairs to guide you through the works; they're quite overwhelming without. Afterwards, you can take a breather in the library's open-air central **courtyard**, modeled after that of the Palazzo della Chancelleria in Rome.

The John Hancock Tower

At 62 stories, the **John Hancock Tower**, at 200 Clarendon St, is the tallest building in America north of New York City and, in a way, Boston's signature sky-scraper – first loathed, now loved, and taking on startlingly different appearances depending on your vantage point. In Back Bay, the characteristically angular edi-fice is often barely noticeable, due to deft understatement and wafer-thin design in deference to adjacent Trinity Church and the old brownstones nearby. This modern subtlety in the face of historic landmarks is a signature quality of architect I.M. Pei (of the Louvre Pyramid and Bank of China, Hong Kong fame). From Beacon Hill, the tower appears broad-shouldered and stocky; from the South End, taller than it actually is; from across the Charles River, like a crisp metallic wafer. One of the best views is from the **Harvard Bridge**, which connects the western edge of Back Bay and Massachusetts Avenue with MIT in Cambridge; from there, you'll be able to see clouds reflected in the tower's lofty, fully mirrored coat. With such a seamless facade, you'd never guess that soon after its 1976 construction, dozens of windowpanes popped out, showering Copley Square with glass, due to a design flaw that prompted the replacement of over 10,000 panes.

Today, most of the building is given over to offices, and its main attraction, the sixtieth-floor **observatory**, which afforded some of the most stunning views around, is permanently closed due to security concerns arising after the events of September 11, 2001. (You'll have to head instead to the Prudential Skywalk for deluxe Boston vistas.) Next door is the old Hancock Tower, which cuts a distinguished profile in the skyline with its truncated step-top pyramid roof. It's locally famous for the neon weather beacon on top, which can be decoded with the help of the jingle, "Solid blue, clear view; flashing blue, clouds are due; solid red, rain ahead; flashing red, snow instead" (except in summer when red signifies the cancellation of a Red Sox game).

Copley Place

On the corner of Huntington Avenue and Dartmouth Street, **Copley Place** (☏617/369-5000, ⓦwww.simon.com) isn't a spot to venture into without a credit card. Not only is this mall home to the *Westin* and *Boston Marriott* hotels (see Chapter 11, Accommodation), but it also contains numerous high-end stores. The 9.5-acre site is slightly garish – all indoor waterfalls and potted trees – but its two floors are packed with ladies who lunch shopping at designer outlets like Tiffany, Armani Exchange, and Christian Dior. The mall is linked to the more generic shops at the Prudential Tower (see below) via a series of enclosed skywalks.

The Prudential Tower

Not even the darkest winter night can cloak the ugliness of the **Prudential Tower** ("The Pru"), at 800 Boylston St, just west of Copley Square. The 52-story gray intruder to the Back Bay skyline is one of the more unfortunate by-products of the urban renewal craze that gripped Boston and most other American cities in the 1960s – though it did succeed in replacing the Boston & Albany rail yards, a blighted border between Back Bay and the South End.

Apart from being the starting point for Duck Tours (see p.37), its chief selling point is its fiftieth-floor **Skywalk** (daily 10am–10pm; $9; ☎617/859-0648, ⓦwww.prudentialcenter.com), which, at 700 feet, is not quite as high as the nearby John Hancock Observatory, but it does offer the only 360-degree aerial view of Boston. On a clear day you can make out Cape Cod across the waters of Massachusetts Bay and New Hampshire to the north. If you're hungry (or just thirsty) you can avoid the admission charge by ascending two more floors to the *Top of the Hub* restaurant (see p.204); your bill may well equal the money you just saved, even if you just get coffee or a drink, but during most daytime hours it's fairly relaxed, and you can linger over your order. Well below, the crowded first-floor **Shops at Prudential Center** is a generic yet lively shopping mall, adjoining the hulking mass of the bland **Hynes Convention Center**.

The Christian Science buildings

People gazing down at Boston from the top of the Prudential Tower are often surprised to see a 224-foot-tall Renaissance Revival basilica vying for attention amidst the urban outcroppings lapping at its base. This rather artificial-looking structure is the central feature of the world headquarters of the sprawling **First Church of Christ, Scientist**, 175 Huntington Ave (Mon–Sat 10am–4pm; free; ☎617/450-2000, ⓦwww.tfccs.com; Symphony **T**), which was founded by Mary Baker Eddy in 1879. With seating for 3000 (and an enormous pipe organ), it dwarfs the earlier, prettier Romanesque **Christian Science Mother Church** just behind it, built in 1894 and decked out with spectacular opalescent stained-glass windows. The nice thing about exploring the central plaza, a huge concrete block hammered out around the two churches by I.M. Pei in the early 1970s, is that no one tries to convert you. In fact there may be no better place in Boston to contemplate the excesses of religion than around the center's 670-foot-long, red-granite-trimmed **reflecting pool**, which, through some high-tech miracle, manages to cool water for the complex's air-conditioning system.

The highlights of a visit here, though, are on the ground floor of the **Mary Baker Eddy Library**, at 200 Massachusetts Ave (Tues & Wed, Sat & Sun 10am–5pm, Thurs & Fri 10am–9pm, closed Mon; $5; ☎1-888/222-3711, ⓦwww.marybakereddylibrary.org; Symphony). The entrance foyer alone is worth a peek, as trippy glass and a bronze fountain that appears to cascade with words rather than water was added to the grand Art Deco lobby in a four-year restoration project completed in 2002; the sayings – mostly to do with peace and humanity – are projected from the ceiling for an effect that verges on holographic. Another unique marvel is the **Mapparium** tucked behind the lobby. You can walk across the thirty-foot diameter of this curious stained-glass globe on a glass bridge. The technicolor hues of the six hundred-plus glass panels, illuminated from behind, reveal the geopolitical reality of the world in 1935, when the globe was constructed, as evidenced by country names such as Siam, Baluchistan, and Transjordan. Intended to symbolize the worldwide reach of the Christian Science movement, the Mapparium has perhaps a more immediate payoff: thanks to the spherical glass surface, which absorbs no sound, you can whisper, "What's Tanganyika called today?" at one end of the bridge and someone on the opposite end will hear it clear as a bell – and perhaps proffer the answer.

△ Christian Science Center

Less interesting is the upstairs **library**, which is primarily concerned with amassing every piece of writing, videotape, and audio ever produced by or involving Mary Baker Eddy; unless you're a devotee, you can easily give it a miss.

Bay Village

Back near the Public Garden, one of the oldest sections of Boston, **Bay Village**, bounded by Arlington, Church, Fayette, and Stuart streets, functions as a small atmospheric satellite of Back Bay. This warren of gaslights and tiny brick houses has managed to escape the trolley tours that can make other parts of the city feel like a theme park; of course, that's in part because there's not all that much to see. The area is, however, popular with Boston's gay population, who colonized it back in the late 1980s before the current vogue for nearby South End.

The neighborhood's overall resemblance to a miniature Beacon Hill is no accident, as many of the artisans who pieced that district together built their own, smaller houses here throughout the 1820s and 1830s. A few decades later, water displaced from the filling in of Back Bay threatened to turn the area back into a swamp, but Yankee practicality resulted in the lifting of hundreds of houses and shops onto wooden pilings fully eighteen feet above the water level. Backyards were raised only twelve feet, and when the water receded many building owners designed **sunken gardens**. One of the most unusual remnants from the nineteenth century is the **fortress** at the intersection of Arlington and Stuart streets at Columbus Avenue. Complete with drawbridge and fake moat, it was built as an armory for the First Corps of Cadets (a private military organization), and, until recently, had been relegated for use as a convention center by the *Boston Park Plaza Hotel* (see p.178); today it houses Boston's branch of the upscale New York steakhouse *Smith & Wollensky* (see p.198).

The obvious streets to explore are **Piedmont**, **Winchester**, and **Church**, which radiate out from the *Park Plaza* anchoring the neighborhood. Footsteps beyond, lightly trafficked **Melrose and Fayette streets** are also worth inspection: it's here you'll find the neighborhood's last remaining sunken gardens – tiny, and often gated, private lawns lying just below street level. There's little else to see here by day: Bay Village really wakes up after the sun sets, when men of all ages zero in on places like the *Luxor*, one of the more popular gay clubs in Boston. For reviews of the hotspots, see chapters 14 (Nightlife) and 16 (Gay Boston).

The South End

O ver the last decade, **the South End**, which extends below Back Bay from Huntington Avenue to where I-93 emerges above ground, has gone from being a predominantly residential neighborhood to one of Boston's most happening areas. Quaint and trendy in equal measure, the rise to prominence of a number of hip restaurants and art galleries in the South End coupled with a vibrant multicultural population has made it *the* place to live in the city.

The neighborhood's heart, nicknamed the **Golden Triangle** by South End realtors, is bounded by Tremont Street, Dartmouth Street, and Columbus Avenue. This posh enclave boasts a spectacular concentration of Victorian architecture, unmatched anywhere in the US. In fact, the sheer number of such houses earned the South End a **National Landmark District** designation in 1983, making the 500-acre area the largest historical neighborhood of its kind in the country. In addition to its architecture, the South End is also known for its well-preserved ironwork – a French botanical motif known as Rinceau adorns many of the houses' stairways and windows (see box, p.110). Unsurprisingly, details like these made the area quite popular with upwardly mobile Bostonians (among them a strong gay and lesbian contingent), who moved in and gentrified the neighborhood in the mid-1990s. The upshot has been some of the most happening streetlife in town, while the South End has become the breeding ground for chefs looking to push the boundaries of haute cuisine. The activity is most visible on **Tremont Street** and on pockets of **Washington Street**, a few blocks below the Back Bay **T**, the neighborhood's only subway stop.

A couple of as yet ungentrified areas do exist, namely in a small quadrant below Tremont Street, which is home to most of Boston's Puerto Rican community, and a patch along Dartmouth Street near Copley Place, where the low-income housing co-op of Tent City presides. As well, surrounding areas such as Roxbury are some of the poorest in the city. Along the outer reaches of the neighborhood, the tension can be palpable, and appropriate caution should be taken, especially at night.

Some history

Like Back Bay, the South End was originally a marshland that now sits on land-fill. Though the mud-to-mansion process kicked off in 1834 – predating Back Bay by more than twenty years – the neighborhood really took shape between 1850 and 1875, when it was laid out according to plans designed by **Charles Bulfinch** some fifty years earlier; its similarity to Beacon Hill, completed just two years prior to development here, is striking, though the South End "look"

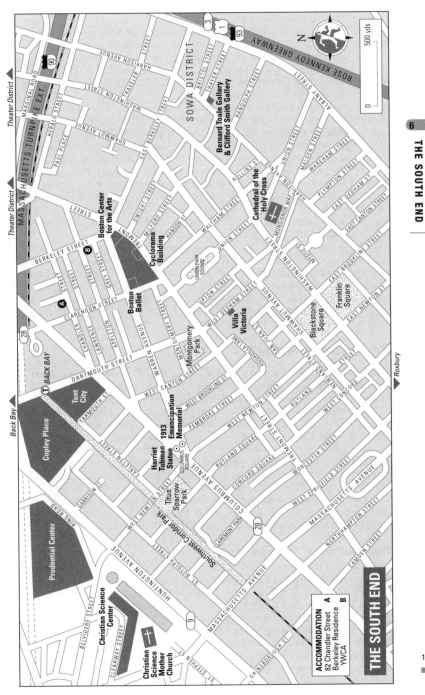

THE SOUTH END

ACCOMMODATION
82 Chandler Street   A
Berkeley Residence YWCA   B

Theater District

Theater District

Back Bay

Roxbury

MASSACHUSETTS TURNPIKE EXT

ROSE KENNEDY GREENWAY

SOWA DISTRICT

N

500 yds
0

Bernard Toale Gallery & Clifford Smith Gallery

Cathedral of the Holy Cross

Boston Center for the Arts

Cyclorama Building

Boston Ballet

Villa Victoria

Franklin Square

Blackstone Square

Union Park Square

Montgomery Park

Tent City

Copley Place

Prudential Center

Christian Science Center

Christian Science Mother Church

1913 Emancipation Memorial

Harriet Tubman Statue

Titus Sparrow Park

Southwest Corridor Park

BACK BAY

HARRISON AVENUE

WASHINGTON STREET

TRAVELER STREET

SHAWMUT AVENUE

HERALD STREET

MARGINAL ROAD

PAUL PLACE

BERKELEY STREET

TREMONT STREET

MILFORD STREET

DWIGHT STREET

HANSON STREET

WALTHAM STREET

UNION STREET

ROLLINS ST

MONSIGNOR WAY

HARRISON AVENUE

WASHINGTON STREET

MYSTIC ST

EAST BERKELEY STREET

THEATER STREET

BRISTOL STREET

RANDOLPH STREET

ALBANY STREET

MALDEN STREET

WAREHAM STREET

PLYMPTON STREET

EAST DEDHAM ST

EAST CANTON STREET

EAST BROOKLINE STREET

EAST NEWTON ST

CLARENDON STREET

CHANDLER STREET

LAWRENCE STREET

APPLETON STREET

GREY STREET

MONTGOMERY STREET

WARREN AVENUE

DARTMOUTH STREET

WEST CANTON STREET

WEST BROOKLINE ST

PEMBROKE STREET

WEST NEWTON STREET

RUTLAND SQUARE

CONCORD SQUARE

WORCESTER STREET

WEST SPRINGFIELD STREET

MASSACHUSETTS AVENUE

NORTHAMPTON STREET

CAMDEN STREET

COLUMBUS AVENUE

CLAREMONT PARK

RUTLAND STREET

WEST CONCORD STREET

TREMONT STREET

SAN JUAN ST

AGUADILLA LANE

SHAWMUT AVENUE

WASHINGTON STREET

UPTON STREET

WEST DEDHAM STREET

CARLETON STREET

YARMOUTH ST

GARRISON ST

RING ROAD

BELVIDERE STREET

CLEARWAY STREET

HUNTINGTON AVENUE

ST BOTOLPH STREET

ST STEPHEN ST

GAINSBOROUGH ST

HEMENWAY ST

WEST NEWTON STREET

COLUMBUS SQUARE

3

1

93

90

28

9

28

107

is more homogeneous and streamlined, dominated by red-brick bowfront townhouses that are modestly taller than their Beacon Hill predecessors. As for greenspace, quaint slivers like Union Park Square were created to attract wealthy buyers who had progressively been moving to the Boston country-side; the marketing campaign to draw them southward included, among other schemes, naming neighborhood arteries like Appleton and Chandler streets after well-to-do merchant families.

This initial success began to flag, however, when many of these families experienced financial decline after the **Panic of 1873**. Following the Panic, what nouveau riche were left headed for the recently created Back Bay, while waves of immigrants moved in to take their place, turning numerous South End townhouses into boarding homes, or razing them altogether to make room for low-income living space. The lure of affordable housing attracted large numbers of the city's **African-American population**, too, at the turn of the twentieth century, who left expensive Beacon Hill digs to install themselves here; consequently, Sammy Davis Jr grew up in the neighborhood, and Dr Martin Luther King Jr and his wife, Coretta Scott King, rented an apartment here while the future civil rights leader attended Boston University.

In the 1970s, the African-American population was in turn pushed out to Roxbury, being replaced by **Puerto Ricans and Dominicans**, who initiated local community housing projects like Villa Victoria. Two decades later, **gentrification** commenced in earnest, leading to, among other things, the opening of several art galleries in the streets south of Washington Street, a geographical concentration latterly going by the name of SoWa (South of Washington), recalling New York's über-trendy SoHo.

Dartmouth Street

The South End's main access point, the Back Bay **T**, opens up onto **Dartmouth Street**, which becomes increasingly upscale the closer it gets to Tremont Street, a few blocks southeast. To the north is Copley Place (see p.102), a shopping mall that's on the cusp of Back Bay and the South End. Immediately below Copley Place, at no. 130, is Dartmouth's most important occupant, **Tent City** – a mixed-income housing co-op that owes its name to the 1968 sit-in protest (tents included) staged on the formerly vacant lot by residents concerned about the neighborhood's dwindling low-income housing. This activism thwarted plans for a parking garage to be built here, and the result is a terrific example of environmental planning. Built in 1988, the section of the co-op closest to Copley Place blends seamlessly with the mall's modern facade, while the part closer to Columbus Avenue incorporates a series of Victorian houses for which the neighborhood is known.

The Southwest Corridor Park

The pocket of land separating Tent City from Copley Place marks the start of the five-mile **Southwest Corridor Park**, a grassy 4.7-mile promenade that connects the Back Bay **T** with the Forest Hill **T** station near the beautiful Arnold Arboretum in Jamaica Plain (see p.136). The park runs parallel to the Orange MBTA line and was designed with low shrubs to increase visibility and give an "open" feeling. Around Forest Hill, the park includes recreational facilities such as tennis and basketball courts, but here it serves mainly as the start of a biking and walking path. Part of another creative urban project, the park expertly covers the tracks of a long-gone nineteenth-century railroad corridor.

Columbus Avenue

Defining the northern edge of the Golden Triangle, **Columbus Avenue** is lined with handsome Victorian houses; the main interest, however, is a tiny wedge of parkland known, obviously enough, as **Columbus Square**. The square, more or less the outer boundary of the triangle, contains two bronze relief sculptures, commemorating Boston's role as part of the Underground Railroad. The nine-foot-tall **Harriet Tubman "Step on Board" Memorial**, by Boston sculptor Fern Cunningham, depicts the strident abolitionist leading several weary slaves to safety, while the nearby 1913 **Emancipation Memorial** is a more harrowing portrait of the slaves' plight: the foursome here are achingly thin and barely clothed. More African-American history is found behind the park, along Warren Avenue; the Gothic red-brick **Concord Baptist Church**, at no. 190, welcomed Martin Luther King Jr as a guest minister during his Boston University days.

Appleton and Chandler streets

Cobblestoned **Appleton Street** and quiet **Chandler Street**, which jut off to the northeast from Dartmouth, are the most sought-after South End addresses. The appeal is obvious: the tree-lined streets are graced with refurbished flat- and bowfronted rowhouses that would easily be at home in London's Mayfair. In addition, unlike many of their neighbors, the houses here have an extra (fourth) story, and are capped off by mansard roofs. Keep an eye out for the Frisbee-sized bronze discs embedded in the sidewalk in front of the houses, too – they're remnants of coal-heating days, when the stuff was delivered through the portals and straight into the basement.

The best way to see the houses in this area is to take the South End Historical Society's annual October **house tour** (price varies; ☎617/536-4445, ⊛www .southendhistoricalsociety.org), in which residents open their doors to the public. The rest of the year, you can still enjoy the ambience by grabbing a pastry from the *Appleton Bakery* (see p.185), at 123 Appleton St, and watching the streetlife from its sidewalk benches.

Clarendon and Tremont streets

South End's architecture is more working-class along **Clarendon Street**, one block northeast of Dartmouth Street. There's little to see here until you reach Warren Street, anchored by a 1991 arch-windowed red-brick building used as a practice space by the renowned **Boston Ballet** (call ☎617/695-6950 to schedule a studio tour). The building gets some of its architectural inspiration from the substantial red-brick **Second Baptist Church** across the way, with its late-1860 Gothic facade. It no longer serves as a church, however, since the interior was razed by fire and its surviving walls were incorporated into a condominium in 1991.

The heart of the South End, and the linchpin of the Golden Triangle, is at the intersection of Clarendon and **Tremont** streets, where an upmarket pseudo-square is flanked by some of the trendiest restaurants in Boston; the acclaimed *Hamersley's Bistro* (see p.204), at 553 Tremont St, holds fort at the square's southern corner. The only real sight is smack in the middle: the domed **Cyclorama Building**, built in 1884 to house an enormous, 360-degree painting of the Battle of Gettysburg (since moved to Gettysburg itself). It was later used as a carousel space, a boxing ring, and even the site of the Boston Floral Exchange in 1923, and repurposing here continued until 1972, when its current tenants, the **Boston Center for the Arts** (☎617/426-7700, ⊛www.bcaonline.com), moved in and created three basement theaters devoted to modern performances (see Chapter 16, Performing arts and film); the old "Gettysburg" space now showcases temporary art exhibits. If the ornate kiosk in front of the building looks somewhat oversized, that's because it originally served as the cupola of an 1850s Roxbury orphanage; it was moved here in 1975, when the orphanage was demolished.

The rest of Tremont Street carries on the high-end restaurant theme set by *Hamersley's*, especially at luxurious eateries like *Aquitaine* and *Truc* (see Chapter 13, Restaurants). Worth a quick peek en route to gastronomic heaven is the old **St Cloud Hotel**, at 567 Tremont St, a French Second Empire building dating from 1872 that still boasts a facade of white marble and green bay windows; most of the building now houses real-estate offices.

Union Park Square

Charming **Union Park Square**, east of Tremont along Union Park Street, is a tiny decorative park which, in typical English fashion, you can walk around but not through – an elegant wrought-iron fence encircles it to make sure you keep off the grass. The ovalesque park is framed by about twenty refined brownstone rowhouses, representing a pastiche of styles from Italianate to Greek Revival, all of them with bigger windows and more elaborate cornice-work than houses on surrounding streets. Of these, the residence at **14 Union Park St**, with its overhanging portico and rounded bay windows, is worth a nod – it's among the few single-family homes to escape condo-conversion in this deluxe area.

Just past the square along Union Park Street is the whitewashed **St John the Baptist Church** (open for Sunday mass only); a pretty blue-hued Nativity mosaic on its facade adds the only splash of color. Edward Everett Hale, author of *Man without a Country*, a short story about a self-exiled man sentenced to a lifetime alone at sea (made into a film in 1973), was minister here from 1856 to 1909; a statue of him can be seen in the Public Garden (see p.96).

Washington Street and around

The South End's other major artery (along with Tremont), **Washington Street**, intersects with Union Park Street and extends southwest to Roxbury. Though intended to resemble a French grand boulevard, the only real similar-

---

Know your irons

As you walk around the South End, you'll notice a slew of brownstones adorned with curlicued **cast iron** on everything from stairway railings and flower boxes to windowsills and balconies. A distinctive South End feature, the fancy ironwork was, like the area's street-naming convention, intended as a perk to attract upwardly mobile residents back from the suburbs. The arboreal-themed lacing is known as the **Rinceau style** (from the French, and meaning "small branch"), and the neighborhood boasts around seven variations on the serpentine scroll, ranging from a simple run of acanthus leaves to elaborate arabesques sprouting off from a central rosette. Some of the best can be seen on **West Canton Street** (a few blocks southwest along Tremont St), where a series of sandstone stairways are trimmed with a wavy version inset with garden roses. Don't let their intricacy fool you, though – by the mid-1850s, technological innovations meant that scrolls such as these were about as easy to stamp out as notebook paper.

△ Union Park Square

ity is its width; the street itself is worn and devoid of the bustle of Tremont Street. What activity exists tends to focus on its major tenant, the 1875 **Cathedral of the Holy Cross**, at no. 1400, which in 2002 unfortunately found itself at the center of the Catholic priest sex abuse scandal. Distinguished by uneven and truncated twin towers – intended as steeples until the parish ran out of money – the vast neo-Gothic interior seats two thousand and boasts some fine stained-glass work, including a multicolored rose window depicting the Bible's King David.

The only other sight nearby is a few blocks southwest, at the corner of West Brookline Street, where the charmless **Blackstone Square**, named for Boston's original settler William Blackstone, occupies a city block. Like much in the neighborhood, it, too, is laid out in English fashion, with diagonal spokes leading to a central fountain. This public space, with equally ramshackle **Franklin Square** across the street, was once the official entry-point to Boston, but nowadays is rather seedy, and really not worth your time.

Villa Victoria and around

North from Blackstone and Franklin squares, a rather bland bronze **plaque** at the corner of Washington and West Dedham streets commemorates the 56th infantry of World War II, a largely Puerto Rican regiment, and serves as an unofficial marker of the community's southern frontier.

The real heart of the enclave, though, is two blocks up West Dedham at **Villa Victoria**, a housing project serving 3000 members of the community. This place, like Tent City, was also the result of late-1960s public activism. And, though the buildings suffer from 1970s architectural aesthetics, their coral hues and setting around a central square, **Plaza Betances**, suggest a Hispanic influence that sets them apart from the rest of the South End's Victoriana. The main draw here is in the square itself, where the **Ramón Betances Mural** occupies wall space measuring a whopping 45 feet long by 14 feet high. Created in 1977 by 300 local children, the brightly colored mosaic has less to do with its namesake (a leader in Puerto Rico's fight for independence from Spain) than simple childlike hope and optimism, as demonstrated by myriad cartoonish faces and flowers that surround a massive sun; it may be Boston's best piece of public art.

Harrison and Thayer streets

Around the intersection of **Harrison** and **Thayer** streets, near the eastern edge of the South End, a handful of **art galleries** have showrooms in cavernous loft spaces. Wandering around the self-styled **SoWa** district could easily distract you for an hour or so. Certainly, the **Bernard Toale Gallery**, at 450 Harrison St (Tues–Sat 10.30am–5.30pm, ☎617/482-2477, ⊛www.bernardtoalegallery.com), is worth a peek; when its namesake and owner, one of Boston's foremost art connoisseurs, moved here from his tony Newbury Street digs in 1998, he effectively sanctified the area as the new arts hotspot. Another happening art space, **Clifford-Smith Gallery** (Tues-Fri 11am–5pm, ☎617/695-0255, ⊛www.cliffordsmithgallery.com), is upstairs; it showcases tech-savvy installations along with more traditional media like painting and photography. For a more complete list of galleries, see Chapter 18, Shopping.

Kenmore Square, the Fenway, and west

At the western edge of Back Bay (see Chapter 5), the decorous brown-stones and smart shops fade into the more casual **Kenmore Square** and **Fenway** districts. While both areas are somewhat removed from the historical-sights-of-Boston circuit, they're good fun nonetheless, exuding a youthful vibe and, perhaps surprisingly, some of the city's more notable cultural landmarks. The Fenway spreads out beneath Kenmore Square like an elongated kite, taking in a disparate array of sights ranging from **Fenway Park**, where baseball's 2004 World Series Champions, the Red Sox, play, to some of Boston's finest high-culture institutions, like **Symphony Hall**, the **Museum of Fine Arts**, and the **Isabella Stewart Gardner Museum**. Further west, and more residential, are the communities of **Allston–Brighton** and **Brookline**; the former is home to a young, hip crowd of students, thanks to its proximity to Boston University, and the latter boasts the birthplace of JFK, though in truth visitors will not find all that much to do in either.

Kenmore Square and around

Kenmore Square, at the junction of Commonwealth Avenue and Beacon Street, is the unofficial playground for the students of Boston University, as most of its buildings can be found here. Back Bay's Commonwealth Avenue Mall leads right into this lively stretch of youth-oriented bars, record stores, and casual restaurants that cater to the late-night cravings of local students; as such, the square is considerably more alive when school is in session. Many of the buildings on its north side have been snapped up by BU, such as the bustling six-story Barnes & Noble bookstore at 660 Beacon St, on top of which is perched the monumental **Citgo Sign**, Kenmore's most noticeable landmark. This huge neon advertisement, a pulsing red triangle that is the oil company's logo, has been a popular symbol of Boston since it was placed here in 1965.

Southwest along Brookline Avenue from the square, you can cross over the Massachusetts Turnpike (via a bridge) to the block-long **Lansdowne Street**,

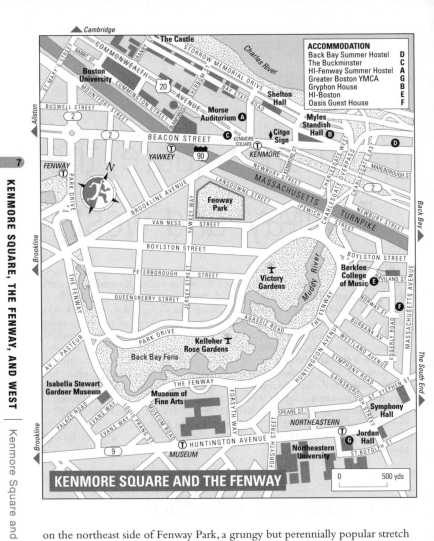

KENMORE SQUARE AND THE FENWAY

ACCOMMODATION
Back Bay Summer Hostel   D
The Buckminster   C
HI-Fenway Summer Hostel   A
Greater Boston YMCA   G
Gryphon House   B
HI-Boston   E
Oasis Guest House   F

on the northeast side of Fenway Park, a grungy but perennially popular stretch of show-your-ID bars and nightclubs (see Nightlife chapter). There's little point in coming here during daylight hours, though, as most of the action takes place after midnight.

Boston University

One of the country's largest private schools, **Boston University**, has its main campus alongside the Charles River on the narrow stretch of land between Commonwealth Avenue and Storrow Drive. Though it boasts a few Nobel Prize winners among its faculty, such as Derek Walcott and Elie Wiesel, the school is more interesting for its creative reuse of old buildings, such as the dormitory **Myles Standish Hall**, at 610 Beacon St, a scaled-down version of New York's Flatiron Building that once was a hotel where notables like Babe

Ruth camped out. One of its rooms also served as the fictional trysting place of Willy Loman in Arthur Miller's *Death of a Salesman*. Behind the building on Bay State Road, many of the turn-of-the-century brownstones serve as BU graduate institutes and smaller residence buildings, such as **Shelton Hall**, also a former hotel with an illustrious past: playwright Eugene O'Neill spent his last days in 1953 in one of the rooms here. The ornate High Georgian Revival mansion at **no. 149**, meanwhile, holds the office of the current university president. Bay State Road ends at **The Castle**, an ivy-covered Tudor mansion now used for university functions. Just beyond is one of BU's few green spaces, the **Warren Alpert Mall**, and its so-called "BU Beach," a sliver of lawn that's been purposefully upswept at the edge to shield busy Storrow Drive from view.

Back on Commonwealth Avenue, the domed **Morse Auditorium**, formerly a synagogue, continues the repurposing theme, nowadays hosting student graduations, lectures, and occasional performances. One long block down is the closest thing the BU campus has to a center, **Marsh Plaza**, with its Gothic Revival chapel and memorial to Martin Luther King Jr, one of the university's more celebrated alumni.

Fenway Park

Considering that baseball is treated with such reverence in Boston, it's appropriate that every Bostonian's – if not every New Englander's – favorite team, the **Red Sox**, plays in one of the country's most fabled ballparks: **Fenway Park**. Constructed in 1912, Fenway, at 24 Yawkey Way, a tiny, asymmetrical wedge just off Brookline Avenue, is one of the few surviving early parks. Free of the uniformity that marks later stadia, it boasts a giant 37-foot-tall leftfield wall (the "Green Monster") and is famous for its awkward dimensions, including an abnormally short rightfield line (302 feet) and a fence that doesn't at all approximate the smooth arc of most outfields. That the leftfield wall was built so high makes up for some of the short distances in the park and can prove maddening to fielders, dealing with the crazy caroms a ball hit off the wall might take.

In the past, it was often rumored that the Red Sox would move from Fenway, as it's one of the few stadia from its era that has not been replaced by a more modern, spacious, and commercially conscious park. Pressure groups opposing a move seem to have been successful, though, and innovations – like building seats atop the Green Monster in 2003 – were implemented by renowned architect Janet Marie Smith. Tours of the park are available (daily 9am–4pm or up to three hours before a game; $10; ☎1/877-RED-SOXX, ⊛www.redsox .com; Kenmore or Fenway **T**), the highlight of which is getting up close with the Green Monster, and visiting the locker room once occupied by Red Sox greats like Ted Williams, Carl Yazstremski, and Babe Ruth, before he became a Yankee (see box, p.116). More so than touring the park, seeing a game is a must for any baseball fan, and a reasonable draw for anyone remotely curious. The season runs from April to October, and tickets are quite affordable, though, unfortunately, difficult to get hold of; the 2004 season was entirely sold out and, given the team's historic win in that year's World Series, demand will likely only grow. Check out Chapter 19, Sports and outdoor activities, for more details on tickets and the team.

When the Boston Red Sox defeated the St Louis Cardinals in Major League Baseball's World Series on October 28, 2004, it brought an end to one of the longest streaks of futility by an American major sports team in history, the infamous **Curse of the Bambino**.

The roots of the curse lie at the turn of the twentieth century, when Boston's baseball team (then called the Pilgrims) became the first to represent the American League in the World Series (played between the winners of the American and National leagues). Financial success allowed them to build a new stadium, **Fenway Park**, in 1912, and Boston won the **World Series** during its first year there, as well as in 1915, 1916, and 1918, led in the latter years by a young pitcher named **George Herman Ruth**, nicknamed "Babe" as well as "the Bambino," who also demonstrated an eye-opening prowess at hitting home runs. The team seemed poised to become a dynasty, until owner **Harry Frazee** turned his finances toward a Broadway play starring his girlfriend and sold off most of the players at bargain prices – including Ruth, who went to the rival **New York Yankees**. The Yankees went on to become the most successful franchise in professional sports history, while Frazee's play, *No, No, Nanette*, flopped, and so did his baseball team. A series of misses, blow-outs, gaffes, and spooky occurrences led to the self-styled team of mavericks' fate to indeed be seen as a curse brought on by the ill-advised sale of Ruth to the Yankees.

One of the more notable instances of the curse occurred in **1978**, when a late-season collapse was capped off with light-hitting Yankees' shortstop **Bucky Dent** slugging a three-run homer to beat the Sox in a one-game playoff series. Perhaps the most talked-about stunner of all, however, occurred in **1986** when, just one strike away from clinching the World Series in game six against the New York Mets, the Sox began a series of miscues that brought about another particularly crushing loss, culminating in first baseman **Bill Buckner** allowing a hit to slip through his legs, letting in the winning run. In June 2001, when asked about the curse, star pitcher **Pedro Martinez** replied: "Wake up the Bambino and let me face him – I'll drill him in the ass;" shoulder problems duly shut him down for two months. More recently, with the Sox leading game seven of the **2003 American League Championship Series**, poor pitching from Martinez allowed the Yankees – who else? – to tie the game in the eighth inning, before **Aaron Boone**, in the 11th, hit a home run to culminate another season of Red Sox heartbreak.

The Sox reached the ALCS again in 2004, and this time, when their opponent would be either the Minnesota Twins or the New York Yankees, the *Boston Globe* taunted the team's archrivals with the front-page splash of "Go Yankees. We want to kick your butt on the way to the World Series." The Yankees obliged, setting up perhaps the most extraordinary chain of events in Major League Baseball history.

Before the ALCS game one at Yankee Stadium, the Sox's new star pitcher, **Curt Schilling**, said: "I'm not sure of any scenario more enjoyable than making 55,000 people from New York shut up." Unbeknownst to the fans, Schilling was injured and pitched like a drain, and the Sox fell behind three games to none, following a humiliating 19-8 loss at Fenway. But a surprising Boston win carved in the bottom of the ninth in game four galvanized the team, and they went on to defeat the Yankees 4-3 – the only time a major league baseball team has reversed a 3-0 score in postseason history. By the time the Sox came up against the Cardinals in the **World Series**, they were a juggernaut: In a **four-game sweep**, the Red Sox ended the 86-year-old curse, which Sox owner John Henry in a massive overstatement called "the biggest thing since the Revolutionary War."

To read more about the Curse of the Bambino being put to the test, pick up local sportswriter Dan Shaughnessy's book of the same name (see Contexts, p.272). More history can be found at ⓦwww.bambinoscurse.com.

The Back Bay Fens

The Fenway's defining element, the snakelike **Back Bay Fens** (daily 7.30am–dusk; ⓦwww.emeraldnecklace.org/fenway), occupies land due east of the stadium, starting where the prim Commonwealth Avenue Mall leaves off. This segment of Frederick Law Olmsted's **Emerald Necklace** was fashioned from marsh and mud in 1879, a fact reflected by frequent vistas of swaying reeds and the name of the waterway that still runs through the park space today – the **Muddy River** – a narrow channel crossed in its northernmost part by an H.H. Richardson-designed medievalesque puddingstone bridge. In the northern portion of the park, local residents maintain small garden plots in the wonderfully unmanicured **Victory Garden**, the oldest community garden in the US. Nearby, below Agassiz Road, the more formally laid out **Kelleher Rose Garden** boasts colorful hybrid species bearing exotic names like Voodoo, Midas Touch, and Sweet Surrender. The area also makes an agreeable backdrop for some of Boston's smaller colleges, such as Simmons and Emmanuel, as well as the Harvard Medical School.

△ Muddy River in the Back Bay Fens

The Berklee College of Music and Symphony Hall

The renowned **Berklee College of Music** makes its home east of the Fens near Back Bay, its campus buildings concentrated mostly on the busy stretch of Massachusetts Avenue south of Boylston Street, an area with several appropriately budget-friendly eateries. Looming a few short blocks south, **Symphony Hall**, home to the **Boston Symphony Orchestra** (see p.221), anchors the corner of Massachusetts and Huntington avenues. The inside of the 1900 McKim, Mead and White design, modeled after the no longer extant Gewandhaus in Leipzig, Germany, resembles an oversized cube, apparently just the right shape to lend it its perfect acoustics. The big English Baroque-style building across the street is **Horticultural Hall** (☎617/933-4900, ⓦwww.masshort.org), headquarters of the Massachusetts Horticultural Society, which occasionally stages herbaceous events on site but is better known for hosting the annual New England Spring Flower Show (see p.251). **Jordan Hall**, venue for the **New England Conservatory of Music**'s chamber music concerts (see p.221), is a few blocks down on Huntington, at nos. 290–294. The modern campus of **Northeastern University** spreads out on both sides of the avenue about a half-mile further south. There's not much to see here, though; it's largely a commuter campus, and as such lacks the collegiate atmosphere of Boston's more happening universities.

The Museum of Fine Arts

Rather inconveniently located in south Fenway – but well worth the trip – the **Museum of Fine Arts**, at 465 Huntington Ave (Mon & Tues, Sat & Sun 10am–4.45pm, Wed–Fri 10am–9.45pm, Thurs & Fri West Wing and selected galleries only after 5pm; $15, $13 Thurs & Fri after 5pm, by contribution Wed after 4pm; CityPass accepted; ☎617/267-9300, ⓦwww.mfa.org; Museum Ⓣ), is New England's premier art space. Founded in the 1850s as an adjunct of the Boston Athenæum when that organization decided to focus more exclusively on local history rather than art, the collection was given public imprimatur and funding by the Massachusetts Legislature in 1870. After moving around at the end of the nineteenth century, it found its permanent home here in 1906.

Most recently, the sprawling three-floor granite complex has proven too small for its **extensive collection**, despite measuring almost 550,000 square feet, and is in the throes of a remedial five-year expansion period – the ninth such enlargement since the museum's 1909 opening. While one projected goal is the improvement of museum "wayfinding" – navigating the labyrinthine corridors and galleries, as they are now utterly bewildering, even with the museum map in hand – the better layout promises more inconvenience in the interim, with gallery closures and relocations scheduled well into 2007. Consequently, if you're looking for a particular piece, be sure to ask where it is; well-informed staffers maintain ground-floor **booths** near the Huntington Avenue and West Wing entrances and float around the galleries as well.

Trying to see all of the massive collection in one day is a daunting prospect at best; conveniently, though, the **entrance fee** entitles you to visit the museum

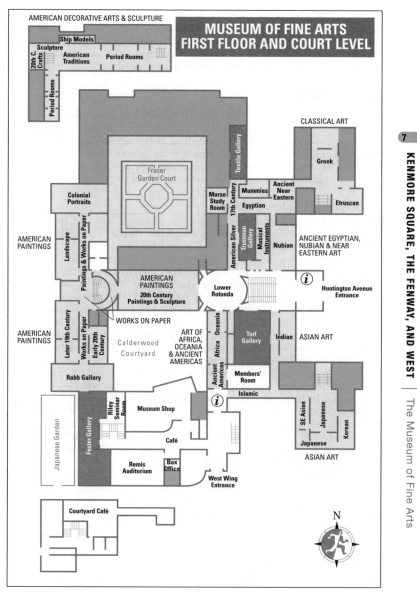

AMERICAN DECORATIVE ARTS & SCULPTURE

**MUSEUM OF FINE ARTS
FIRST FLOOR AND COURT LEVEL**

Ship Models

Sculpture

20th C. Crafts

American Traditions

Period Rooms

Period Rooms

CLASSICAL ART

Greek

Textile Gallery

Fraser Garden Court

Colonial Portraits

Morse Study Room

17th Century

Mummies

Ancient Near Eastern

Egyptian

Etruscan

AMERICAN PAINTINGS

Landscape

Paintings & Works on Paper

American Silver

Trustman Gallery

Musical Instruments

Nubian

ANCIENT EGYPTIAN, NUBIAN & NEAR EASTERN ART

AMERICAN PAINTINGS

20th Century Paintings & Sculpture

Lower Rotunda

(i)

Huntington Avenue Entrance

WORKS ON PAPER

Later 19th Century

Works on Paper

Early 20th Century

Calderwood Courtyard

ART OF AFRICA, OCEANIA & ANCIENT AMERICAS

Oceania

Africa

Ancient Americas

Torf Gallery

Indian

ASIAN ART

AMERICAN PAINTINGS

Rabb Gallery

Members' Room

Islamic

SE Asian

Japanese

Korean

Japanese Garden

Foster Gallery

Riley Seminar Room

Museum Shop

Café

(i)

Japanese

ASIAN ART

Remis Auditorium

Box Office

West Wing Entrance

N

Courtyard Café

twice in a ten-day period on presentation of your original ticket. Perhaps the easiest way to stay focused is by concentrating on one particular main building: the **West Wing** holds the marvelously dense American painting collection, substantial Impressionist art, and blockbuster **special exhibits**, while the adjoining **Huntington Building** contains one of the best collections of arts of the ancient world and Asia. The two buildings are joined by interconnecting galleries, which culminate in the Huntington Avenue-side **rotunda**, the second floor of which is a must-see for the outstanding John Singer Sargent **murals** decorating its walls and ceilings. Completing the current layout are several smaller wings with an emphasis on decorative arts.

West Wing

The modern, graystone, I.M. Pei–designed **West Wing** lacks a bit of personality, but it draws the bigger crowds of the two MFA buildings thanks to its important collection of American paintings, Impressionist works, and stellar temporary exhibits. The first takes up most of the ground floor starting chronologically, but annoyingly, layout-wise, near the rear, in the Colonial Portraits gallery; the latter two are housed on the second floor.

American art collections

The **American** gallery features important paintings from the two major figures of the Colonial period – **John Singleton Copley** and **Gilbert Stuart**. Copley, one of Boston's favorite sons and after whom Copley Square is named, is mainly represented 'by portraits of revolutionary figures like Paul Revere, John Hancock, and Sam Adams. His other works include likenesses of Boston notables such as Nicholas Boylston, the Boston merchant after whom the town's prominent street is named, and Massachusetts Solicitor General Samuel Quincy. One of Copley's most celebrated works, the gruesome narrative *Watson and the Shark*, is also on display here (though it's a full-scale replica made by the artist of the original, which is on permanent display at the National Gallery of Art in Washington DC). The dramatically vivid piece was an immediate success when first exhibited at London's Royal Academy in 1778 and is notable for two reasons: no other American artist had yet attempted "reportage-style" painting, and this was Copley's first work to not include a person of note (though Brook Watson did survive his encounter with the shark and go on to become Lord Mayor of London). Gilbert Stuart is represented by the nationalistic *Washington at Dorchester Heights,* which is displayed along with his portrait of the first US president that graces the one-dollar bill, and portraits of wives of Revolutionary figures, such as those of Mrs Paul Revere, Mrs Samuel Smith, and Martha (Mrs George) Washington.

The works lining the long hallway that leads back to the front entrance are of lesser interest than what's in the adjoining rooms, such as the Romantic naturalist **landscapes** from the first half of the nineteenth century. **Albert Bierstadt**'s quietly majestic *Lake Tahoe, California,* a particular standout, mingles with Neoclassical representations of sea battles, such as **Thomas Birch**'s jubilant *The Constitution and the Guerrière*, which depicts the engagement from whence the USS *Constitution*'s nickname, "Old Ironsides," originates.

From the latter half of the century are **James Abbott McNeill Whistler**'s moody *Nocturne in Blue and Silver: the Lagoon* and several works from the Boston School, notably **Childe Hassam**'s evocative *Boston Common at Twilight* and several works by **John Singer Sargent**. Sargent's work, on display here with that of other American Impressionists, is from early in his career, before he decided that murals, and not portraiture, were the way forward (see Shapiro Rotunda, p.123). Included in the collection are the provocatively spare *Daughters of Edward Darley Boit,* in which the Boston painter's daughters are pictured in their father's Paris residence; the touching *Mrs Fiske Warren and Her Daughter,* with the Boston socialite pictured in Fenway Court (now the Isabella Stewart Gardner Museum); and the simple *Nude Study of Thomas E McKeller*, a Boston hotel bellman and Sargent's favorite model. Also on display are various studies for Sargent's Boston Public Library murals, such as *Frieze of the Prophets*.

The era's highlights, a trio of haunting seascapes painted by **Winslow Homer** shortly before his death, hang midway along the corridor, by the stairway to the upper galleries. Early twentieth-century American work is displayed in the last room on the left, where **Edward Hopper**'s dour *Drugstore* hangs beside his uncharacteristically upbeat *Room in Brooklyn*; check out as well **Maurice Prendergast**'s sentimental renderings of genteel life, *Sunset* and *Eight Bathers*.

Rounding out the wing, the **Lane Gallery**, tucked behind the stairs to the second floor and extending to the ground floor of the Huntington Building, is particularly strong on early to mid-twentieth century American works. The standout, **Jackson Pollock**'s tense, semi-abstracted *Troubled Queen*, pre-dates his famous splatter-painting style and overlooks **Alexander Calder**'s wire *Cow* stabile. The gallery's far walls count **Georgia O'Keefe**'s majestically antlered *Deer's Skull with Pedernal* hanging catercorner to **Charles Sheeler**'s ironically titled *View of New York* – which you'll have to see for yourself to appreciate the joke. The exit between these last two works puts you in the Lower Rotunda of the Huntington Avenue Building, face-to-face with underwhelming Boston School works; the most intriguing, **William McGregor Paxton**'s oriental-themed *The New Necklace*, plays nicely with themes of light and shadow in its depiction of a well-to-do young woman disinterestedly receiving the gift of a necklace.

European art collections

The stairs leading from within the American galleries to the second-floor **European** galleries put you smack in the middle of the collection. Like the first floor, it actually begins chronologically to the far right, in a room showcasing Dutch paintings from the Northern Renaissance, including two outstanding **Rembrandt** works, which emphasize his mastery of light and shadow, *Artist in his Studio* and *Old Man in Prayer*. A gruesome work by **David Teniers the Younger**, *Butcher's Shop*, hangs nearby. Several rooms of grandiose Rococo and Romantic work from the eighteenth and early nineteenth centuries lead off to the right of the central hallway; most interesting are **Pannini**'s self-referential *Picture Gallery with Views of Modern Rome*, Jean-Baptiste Greuze's erotic *Young Woman in White Hat*, **Tiepolo**'s complex allegory *Time Unveiling Truth*, and **Turner**'s renowned fire and brimstone *Slave Ship*. The rooms across the hall contain a good survey of European modern art, among them **Henri Matisse**'s resplendent *Vase of Flowers*, **Max Beckman**'s morbid *Still-Life with Three Skulls* – declared degenerate by the Nazis – and **Braque**'s autumnal *Still Life with Peaches, Pears and Grapes*.

The culmination of the wing is the late-nineteenth-century collection, which begins with works by early Impressionists: **Manet**'s *Execution of Emperor Maximilian* and **Degas**'s *Edmond and Thérèse Morbilli* exhibit the stark use of color and interest in common subjects that went on to influence other French artists. The subsequent Impressionist room contains **Monet**'s heavily abstracted *Grainstack (Snow Effect)* and *Rouen Cathedral (Morning Effect)*, though his tongue-in-cheek *La Japonaise*, a riff on Parisian fashion trends, steals the show. Degas figures prominently here again with his agitated *Pagans and Degas' Father* and a bronze cast of the famous *Little Fourteen-Year-Old Dancer*, as does **Renoir**, whose radiant *Dance at Bougival* looks onto *Psyche*, a delicate Rodin marble. The room's highlight, however, is its selection of Post-Impressionist art, best of which is **Picasso**'s coldly cubist *Portrait of a Woman*, **Van Gogh**'s richly hued *Enclosed Field with Ploughman* and *Houses at Auvers*, and **Gauguin**'s

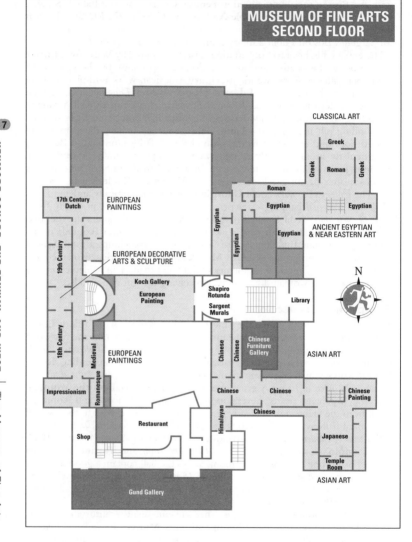

bizarre relief wood sculpture, *Be in Love and you will be Happy*, in which the artist casts himself seizing a woman's outstretched hand and ordering her to do as the title instructs.

The Koch Gallery

Halfway back along the main corridor, the **Koch Gallery**, which connects the West Wing with the second floor of the Huntington Building's rotunda, ranks among the museum's more spectacular showings. Designed to resemble a

European palace hallway, its wood-inlaid ceilings cap walls hung two-high with dozens of portraits and landscapes of varying sizes. The southern wall finds largely **religious** pieces, three of which belong to **El Greco**, whose sparse *Fray Hortensio Felix Paravicino* contrasts sharply with **Francesco del Cairo**'s *Herodias with the Head of St John the Baptist*, a macabre depiction that'll have you thinking twice about tongue-piercing.

The opposite wall showcases predominantly **portraits** and **landscapes**, most emblematic of which is **Velazquez**'s austere *Philip IV, King of Spain*, dating from the artist's time as court painter. Another standout is **Poussin**'s harmonious *Mars and Venus*, which provides an uplifting counterpoint to the nearby **Rubens** piece *Head of Cyrus Brought to Queen Tomyris*, an epic story of retribution in which the artist's sons served as models for the Queen's pages. The doors at the far end put you in the upper Rotunda, under John Singer Sargent's superb murals (see below).

Huntington Avenue Building

Connected to the West Wing by both the Lane and Koch galleries, the 500-foot granite-faced **Huntington Avenue Building** was the first MFA structure to open on this site in 1909. It's significantly gloomier than the West Wing addition, due to a lack of natural light but here you'll find the museum's impressive – and often overwhelming – collection of **ancient world** and **Asian** arts.

Ancient world galleries

A series of MFA-sponsored digs at Giza have made its **Egyptian collection** not only the standout of the museum's **ancient world** holdings, but also one of the finest and most extensive of its kind in the world. Eight galleries over two floors feature some 40,000 objects, including sculpture, pottery, and sarcophagi ranging from prehistoric times to the Roman period. Best among the first-floor findings is the small gallery on **Egyptian Funerary Arts**, with gorgeous blue canopic jars, pristine shrouds, and mummies – including one for a baby crocodile that likely served as a well-to-do family's pet.

While rather modest by comparison, the **Nubian collection** preceding the Funerary Arts gallery is nevertheless the largest of its kind outside Africa. Most of the pieces, such as the *Granite Stela of King Tanyidamani*, are also funerary and actually quite similar to their Egyptian contemporaries. Upstairs are several imposing statues of King Mercerinus and Queen Kha-Merer-Nebty – notable for their strongly defined features – a colossal head of Ramses II, a strident King Anlamani from the Great Temple of Amen, and two fully reconstructed burial chambers of Old Kingdom royalty, one of which features a sixteen-ton sarcophagus made of granite.

Not nearly as well represented, the **Classical** section is worth a glance mostly for its numerous Grecian urns, a fine Cycladic *Female Figure*, and several Etruscan sarcophagi with elaborately wrought narrative bas-reliefs.

The Shapiro Rotunda

Between the second-floor Egyptian and Asian galleries is the outstanding **Shapiro Rotunda**, its dome and en-suite colonnade inset with twenty **murals** and fourteen **bas reliefs** by John Singer Sargent, who undertook the commission following his Boston Public Library work (see p.101). Operating under the belief that mural painting – not portraiture – was the key to "artistic immortality," this installation certainly guaranteed the artist a lasting place in the MFA and some controversy to boot: when the ten-year project was completed shortly before Sargent's death in 1925, his Classical theme was falling out of vogue and his efforts were considered the "frivolous works of a failing master." Today, after a 1999 refurbishment that revitalized the works – much of which depict debates between Classical and Roman Art using figures from Greek mythology – it's clear that what many had described as a confused set of subjects (art, theater, philosophy, mythology, and architecture) is actually a perfect representation of the museum's collections, portrayed through a visual feast of fluid lines and color schemes.

Asian galleries

South of the rotunda, the **Asian galleries** – though they're among the best of their kind in the world – don't get nearly the attention they deserve, in all likelihood due to their awkward layout and hard-to-find galleries. Two in particular are worth ferreting out, and none more so than the magnificent recreation of Japan's oldest surviving **Buddhist temple**, complete with gray stone floors, tapered wooden columns, and coffered ceiling. Seven Buddhas dating to the ninth century recline inside the darkened temple; two of them represent the Buddha of Infinite Illumination. The antechambers contain a marvelous array of Japanese scrolls and screens, including ornamental munitions – such as Samurai swords – that date back to the thirteenth century. The woodblock print cityscapes of Ando Hiroshige, with their sharply delineated chromatic schemes, influenced Van Gogh, Gauguin, and Whistler. Changes in twentieth-century Japanese culture are depicted through wonderful displays of Meissen kimonos, the advent of which heralded the first time the lower classes were allowed to wear silk.

The Emerald Necklace

The string of vegetation that stretches through Boston's southern districts, known as the **Emerald Necklace**, grew out of a project conceived in the 1870s, when landscape architect **Frederick Law Olmsted** was commissioned to create for Boston a series of urban parks, as he had done in New York and Chicago. A Romantic naturalist in the tradition of Rousseau and Wordsworth, Olmsted conceived of nature as a way to escape the ills wrought by society, and considered his parks a means for city-dwellers to escape the clamor of their everyday life. He converted much of Boston's remaining open space, which was often disease-ridden marshland, into a sequence of meticulously manicured outdoor spaces beginning with the **Back Bay Fens**, including the **Riverway** along the Boston–Brookline border, and proceeding through **Jamaica Pond** and the **Arnold Arboretum** to Roxbury's **Franklin Park**. While Olmsted's original skein of parks was limited to these, further development linked the Fens, via the Commonwealth Avenue Mall, to the Public Garden and Boston Common, all of which now function as part of the Necklace, and which make it all the more impressive in scale. By November 2005, when the landscaping over the Big Dig construction project is complete, a thirty-acre park will be added to the Necklace around Quincy Market in Downtown. The Necklace's sense of pristine natural wonder has slipped in the century since its creation – the more southerly links in the chain, starting with the Fens, have grown shaggy and are unsafe at night.

The **Boston Park Rangers** organize free walking tours (daily 9am–5pm; ☎617/635-7383, ⓦwww.cityofboston.gov/parks/ParkRangers) that cover each of the Necklace's segments, and Olmsted fans won't want to miss the **Frederick Law Olmsted National Historic Site** at 99 Warren St (see p.127).

The **Chinese** section is equally superb, with scrolls decorated with spare naturalist abstractions as well as finely detailed graphic narratives, and several life-size statues; that of *Guanyin, Bodhisattva of Compassion* is one of the best-preserved pieces from the twelfth-century Jin Dynasty. Don't leave before checking out the remarkable **Chinese Furniture Gallery**, a dull name for what is in fact a life-size staging of an upper-class Chinese house. Arranged beneath its pagoda-style roof are ornate examples of sixteenth- and seventeenth-century Chinese furniture, such as handsomely carved teak day beds, lacquered tables inlaid with birds and flowers, and household items like the strategy game Wiegi, in which the goal is to surround other players' pieces.

The Isabella Stewart Gardner Museum

Less broad in its collection, but more distinctive and idiosyncratic than the MFA, is its neighbor, the **Isabella Stewart Gardner Museum**, at 280 The Fenway (Tues–Sun 11am–5pm; $10, $11 on weekends; Citypass accepted; ☏617/566-1401, ⊛www.gardnermuseum.org; Museum **T**). Eccentric Boston socialite Gardner (1840–1924) collected and arranged more than 2500 objects in the four-story Fenway Court building she designed herself – right down to the marbleized paint technique she demonstrated to her workers atop a ladder – making this the country's only major museum that is entirely the creation of a single individual. A hodgepodge of works from around the globe, the collection is presented without much attention to period or style; Gardner's goal was to foster the love of art rather than its study, and she wanted the setting of her pieces to "fire the imagination." Your imagination does get quite a workout: there's art everywhere you look, with most of the objects unlabeled, placed in corners or above doorways, for an effect that is occasionally chaotic, but always striking, and at times quite effective. Gardner's will stipulated that every piece in the collection stay put, or else the entire kit and kaboodle was to be shipped to Paris for auction and the proceeds given to Harvard.

To get the most out of a visit, aim to join the hour-long Friday **tours** (free; 2.30pm), but get there early as only twenty people are allowed at a time, and places are allocated on a first-come-first-served basis. Alternatively, the **gift**

Heist at the Gardner

In possibly the most famous unsolved **art theft** of all time, the Isabella Stewart Gardner Museum was robbed on March 18, 1990. At around 1.30am, as the city's St Patrick's Day celebrations were coming to a close, two men dressed as police officers knocked on the side door of the museum and were allowed to enter by security guards. Within minutes, the guards were overpowered and the men pillaged some $300 million worth of art, including three Rembrandts and a Manet. The paintings were crudely cut from their frames, and the ragged edges are still on display. Despite the lure of a $5 million reward and numerous leads that have implicated everyone from the IRA to the Mafia to a notorious art thief, the paintings have yet to be recovered. Adding insult to injury, the museum wasn't insured, and if the thieves were captured today they possibly wouldn't face prosecution, owing to the Massachusetts statute of limitations on robberies.

shop sells a worthwhile **guide** ($5) detailing the location and ownership history of every piece on display, while self-guided audio-tour equipment can be rented for $4.

The first floor

The Gardner is best known for its spectacular central **courtyard** styled after a fifteenth-century Venetian palace; the second-century Roman mosaic of Medusa at its center is fittingly surrounded by stone-faced statuary and fountains, and brightened up, year round, by flowering plants and trees. However, the museum's greatest success is the **Spanish Cloister** flanking the courtyard, a long, narrow corridor just through the main entrance that perfectly frames **John Singer Sargent**'s ecstatic representation of Spanish dance, *El Jaleo*, and also contains fine seventeenth-century Mexican tiles, as well as Roman statuary and sarcophagi. A door nearby leads discreetly to the **Monks Garden**, a Mediterranean outdoor space bursting with palms and bougainvillaea.

The first floor's remaining side-rooms hold Gardner's small collection of European modern art: **Degas**'s tiny and austere portrait of a Parisian actress called *Madame Gaujelin* and **Matisse**'s sunstreaked *The Terrace, St Tropez*, are in the **Yellow Room**, while **Manet**'s stern portrait of his mother, *Madame Auguste Manet*, is in the appropriately dim **Blue Room**. The floor's final room, the **Macknight**, was Gardner's writing room when she was in residence and frequently doubled as Sargent's guestroom; atop one of the bookshelves is a poignant late-life portrait of his hostess, *Mrs Gardner in White*, which reveals the closeness of their friendship.

The second floor

Up one level, what was once a first-rate display of **seventeenth-century Northern European** works was debilitated by a 1990 **art heist** in which two Rembrandts and a Vermeer were among ten canvases stolen (see box, p.125). You can spot the missing artworks by their empty frames.

Even with these glaring absences the second-floor **Dutch Room** retains **Rembrandt**'s early *Self-Portrait* across from **Rubens**'s heavily ornamented *Thomas Howard, Earl of Arundel*.

Next door, the magnificent **Tapestry Room** is hung with rich mid-sixteenth-century Brussels tapestries, including the *Abraham Series*, illustrating the life of the prominent Bible figure; it's a sumptuous backdrop for the weekend chamber orchestra concerts held here from September to May (☎617/566-1401). The **Short Gallery** extending north from the Tapestry Room is devoted primarily to **etchings**, many of which hang on hinged wooden panels; one bears a sign noting the theft of four Degas works from its spot – his chalk *Racehorse* remains at the bottom of the rear panel. Rounding out the floor, the colorful **Raphael Room** finds its namesake's officious *Portrait of Tommaso Inghirami*, the Vatican's rotund chief librarian, above his early *Lamentation over the Death of Christ*, which sits, unassumingly, on the desk below. The nearby walls find a couple of **Botticelli**s as well, most notably his highly stylized *Tragedy of Lucretia*.

The third floor

Gardner had an affinity for **altars**, and her collection contains several, cobbled together from various religious artifacts. A dramatic concentration of these surrounds the third-floor stairwell and includes a medieval stone carving of the beheading of John the Baptist, a particularly agonized twelfth-century wood carving of *Christ from a Deposition Group* from Spain, and **Giovanni Minelli**'s maudlin painting, *Entombment of Christ*. Perhaps the most notable sacred art on display is in the **chapel**, also on the third floor, which incorporates sixteenth-century Italian choirstalls and stained glass from Milan and Soissons cathedrals, as well as assorted religious figurines, candlesticks, and crucifixes, all surrounding **Paul-César Helleu**'s moody representation of the *Interior of the Abbey Church of Saint-Denis*.

Between the stairwell and the chapel is the **Gothic Room**, a somberly decorated chamber whose chief attraction is **John Singer Sargent**'s controversial life-size *Portrait of Isabella Gardner* that prompted the public to rename her "Saint Isabella," thanks to the halo effect of the background. The portrait was considered so "provocative" by Gardner's husband that he asked that it not be displayed until after her death. Completing the third floor, the **Titian** and **Veronese rooms** comprise a strong showing of Italian Renaissance and Baroque work, including Titian's famous *Europa* (which was voted Boston's most important work of art by other museum directors in 2002) and **Crivelli**'s Mannerist *St George and the Dragon*. Also in the **Veronese Room** are four minute **Whistler**s, including *Little Note in Yellow and Gold*, yet another portrait of the museum's doyenne, albeit a softer and more feminine version.

Allston-Brighton and Brookline

There's little doing west of the Fenway – just a few largely residential areas, accessible on the Green Line, that seem more or less extensions of Boston and Cambridge. In fact, **Allston-Brighton**, a triangular community that spreads south from the Charles River down to Beacon Street, was originally conceived as a Cambridge adjunct. Nowadays, it's a funkier community than its neighbor across the river, with laid-back restaurants, a plethora of Jewish delis and bakeries (hit up *Kupel's*, at 421 Harvard St, for exceptional bagels) and innovative shops crammed into a couple of blocks along Harvard Street. It hardly ranks as a destination in its own right, however.

Marginally more interesting is the affluent town of **Brookline**, where much of the activity is focused around bustling **Coolidge Corner**, at Beacon and Harvard streets. Of note in these parts is the **Coolidge Corner Theater**, at 290 Harvard St, a refurbished arthouse cinema sustained by the many students living in the area. The main draw, though, is the nearby **John F. Kennedy National Historic Site**, at 83 Beals St (Mid-May to late October, Wed–Sun 10am–4.30pm, closed winter; $3; ☎617/566-7937, ⓦwww.nps .gov/jofi), which preserves the unremarkable home where JFK was born on May 29, 1917. Inside, a narrated voiceover by the late president's mother, Rose, adds some spice to the plain, roped-off rooms. To get to the heart of Brookline, take the Green Line's C branch to Coolidge Corner or D branch to Brookline Village.

It's a bit of a hike to the last of Brookline's attractions; along the suburb's southern fringe is the **Frederick Law Olmsted National Historic Site**, at 99 Warren St (Fri–Sun 10am–4.30pm; free; ☎617/566-1689 ⓦwww.nps .gov/frla). Known as Fairsted, this expansive house doubled as Olmsted's family home and office. Though almost one million landscape schemes are archived here, ranging from his work on Yosemite Valley to New York's Central Park, it's a dry retrospective that will appeal mostly to Olmsted buffs. That said, the surrounding grounds are (unsurprisingly) quite idyllic; you could hardly ask for better strolling territory.

The southern districts

The parts of Boston most visitors see – Downtown, Beacon Hill, Back Bay, and the North End – only comprise a small portion of the city. To the south of the city center lies a vast spread of residential neighborhoods known collectively as the **southern districts**, including **South Boston**, **Dorchester**, **Roxbury**, and **Jamaica Plain**, whose oft-downtrodden character can come as quite a shock after Boston's polished colonial core. Though they do offer a more complete picture of urban life, these areas are unlikely to divert your interest for long (or at all), especially if you're short on time. Nevertheless, JFK-junkies will be rewarded by Dorchester's worthwhile **John F. Kennedy Library and Museum**, and no one should miss Jamaica Plain's superb **Arnold Arboretum**, with its world-renowned array of bonsai trees; the two combine to make a terrific half-day outing, and are easily accessible by the **T**.

Once rural areas dotted with the swank summer homes of Boston's elite, in the late nineteenth century the southern districts became populated by middle- and working-class families pushed from increasingly crowded Downtown. Three-story rowhouses soon replaced mansions, and the moniker "streetcar suburbs" – after the trolley that debuted in 1899 and connected these once remote areas with Downtown – was coined as a catchall for the newly redefined neighborhoods. Following World War II, each was hit to varying degrees by economic decline, and the middle class moved farther afield, leaving the districts to the mostly immigrant and blue-collar communities that remain today. Personal safety is an issue in these parts, and the streets can feel desolate by day and dodgier still by night. The exception, Jamaica Plain, has become more gentrified in recent years, and its main drag, Centre Street, has a pleasant, laid-back vibe and some good lunch options.

South Boston

Across Fort Point Channel from Downtown and east into Boston Harbor lies **South Boston**, affectionately referred to as "Southie" by its large Irish-American population. Originally a peninsula separated from Boston proper by waterways, it was connected to the city by bridge in 1805, and throughout the nineteenth century it grew in size, augmented by landfills, and in population, thanks to a steady influx of immigrants. South Boston remained solidly blue-collar and Irish until just after World War II, when it was particularly hard hit by recession, and its makeup began to change. Despite some economic revival

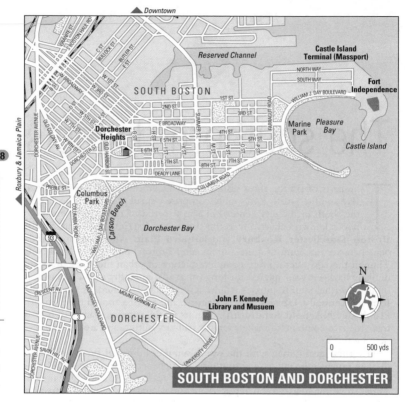

SOUTH BOSTON AND DORCHESTER

– especially in the shipbuilding industry – and some gentrification over the last decade, the area is still tainted by the reputation of being Boston's hotbed of racial tension, owing to friction between its old timers and the newer communities of African-Americans, Hispanics, and gays. Indeed, during the 2004 Democratic Convention, held in Boston, an attempt to promote the city's outlying neighborhoods was almost scuppered when New York Democrats expressed concern about their welcoming party being held in Southie. New York State Democratic Committee Chairman Herman "Denny" Farrell Jr went so far as to say: "For those of us who were on the frontlines of that struggle [for civil rights], the prospect of celebrating in a neighborhood that so fiercely opposed integration is very troubling." Fortunately, however, the residents of Southie put on a great party, and Farrell Jr apologised for "putting his foot in his mouth."

The area's Celtic heritage is quite evident on the main commercial boulevard, **Broadway**, where seemingly every laundry, convenience store, and even Chinese restaurant has a sign plastered with shamrocks. You'll also find an unsurprising profusion of Irish bars along West Broadway that make up in enthusiasm for the mother country what they lack in authenticity.

Castle Island

South Boston narrows to an end in Boston Harbor on a 22-acre strip of land called **Castle Island**. The island was once only connected to the mainland via a causeway bridge, but landfill projects in the nineteenth century fashioned it into a peninsula. Castle Island lies just off the terminus of William J. Day Boulevard, and is a favorite leisure spot for Southie residents and, in fact, for many Bostonians. Park and beaches cover the spit, though you wouldn't want to swim offshore, since Boston Harbor's waters, while cleaner than in the past, are far from non-toxic – and they're freezing, to boot. However, the views of Downtown and the harbor are spectacular, best appreciated via the walkway that, thanks to its circular shape, is known as the "Sugar Bowl." The walkway follows along a narrow peninsula that curls out into the water. Closer to the mainland, the island's lone snack bar, *Sullivan's*, founded in 1951, is a local institution. Here a seasonal army of young employees serves tasty portions of seafood and grilled fare, while the 50¢ hot dogs are said to be the best in New England.

Fort Independence

Fort Independence (Sat & Sun noon–3.30pm; free; Broadway **T**, then bus #9 or #11), a stout granite edifice just north of Castle Island, was one of the earliest redoubts in the Americas, originally established in 1634, though it has been rebuilt several times since. Today, what remains is a skeleton of its 1801 version, and its slate-gray walls aren't much to look at from the outside. However, free ranger-led weekend tours provide some decent history and folklore about the dank interior corridors. For instance, one legend has it that friends of an officer shot dead in a duel sealed his killer alive in a chamber in the fort's dungeons. Ten years later, Edgar Allan Poe, while assigned to duty here as an officer in the US Army, heard the tale and used it as the basis for his story, *The Cask of Amontillado*.

△ Fort Independence

Dorchester

Occupying the southeast corner of the city, **Dorchester** lies beneath South Boston, below Columbia Road. Originally built on the narrow strip that connected Boston to the mainland, it's now a fairly unlovely and uninteresting lower- and middle-class residential neighborhood. North Dorchester was from its earliest days a center of trade and is still a largely industrial area. South Dorchester has seen more turbulence over the years – once a coveted spot for upper-class country homes, it followed the streetcar suburb pattern of the southern districts and remained relatively affluent until after World War II, when the middle class left; property values soon plummeted, and crime and unemployment rose. Today, both parts of Dorchester are home to a broad ethnic mix, notably Irish, Haitians, Vietnamese, Caribbeans, and African-Americans. Save for the **John F. Kennedy Library and Museum** (JFK's mother lived in Dorchester as a girl), there's not much to see, and parts – especially in South Dorchester – are downright unsafe.

John F. Kennedy Library and Museum

As with all presidential museums, the **John F. Kennedy Library and Museum**, at Columbia Point (daily 9am–5pm; $10, CityPass accepted; ☎1-866/JFK-1960, ⓦwww.jfklibrary.org; JFK/UMass **T**; free shuttle every twenty minutes), is faced with the difficult job of extolling a president and icon's virtues while maintaining a veneer of scholarly objectivity. Though it performs the task with mixed results, the **museum** stands out by providing a fascinating glimpse into the culture of a recent, storied, era, while being spectacularly situated in a stunning, glass-fronted, curvilinear I.M. Pei-designed building – allegedly the architect's favorite commission – offering panoramic views over Boston Harbor. The **library**, however, is not open to the public, only to researchers with specific requests, and holds JFK's papers (some 8.4 million pages in all) from his curtailed term in the Oval Office. The museum is also the repository for Ernest Hemingway's original manuscripts; Kennedy helped Hemingway's wife get the papers out of Cuba following her husband's 1961 suicide (call ☎1-866/JFK-1960 for an appointment to see them).

The museum opens with a well-done eighteen-minute **film** covering Kennedy's political career up until the 1960 Democratic National Convention, and is peppered with soundbites from Kennedy himself. On leaving the auditorium and entering the exhibition space, other displays cover the presidential campaign of 1960 and highlights of the truncated Kennedy administration against a backdrop of stylized recreations of his campaign headquarters, the CBS studio that hosted the first televised presidential debate between him and Richard Nixon, and the main White House corridor. The campaign exhibits are most interesting for their TV and radio ads, which illustrate the squeaky-clean self-image America possessed at that time. Several features on JFK and the media unabashedly play up the contrast between Kennedy's telegenic charisma and Nixon's jowly surliness, citing it as a key factor in JFK's victory over Tricky Dick. The section covering the Kennedy administration is more serious, animated by a 22-minute film on the Cuban Missile Crisis that evokes the tension of the event, while possibly exaggerating Kennedy's heroics. Most sobering is the darkened hallway towards the end where a televised announcement of the president's assassination plays in a continuous loop. Lighter fare is on display in the **Jackie O. exhibits**, which trace her evolution from young debutante to First Lady-cum-popular icon; items on display include her outfits, her camera, and her baby brush.

The best part of the museum is actually outside of the exhibition chambers: a 115-foot-high **atrium** overlooking the harbor, with a gigantic American flag suspended above modest inscriptions bearing some of Kennedy's more memorable quotations – affecting enough to move even the most jaded JFK critic.

Dorchester Heights Monument

At the convergence of South Boston and Dorchester rises **Dorchester Heights** (Broadway **T** to bus #11 to G St stop), a neighborhood of three-story rowhouses whose northernmost point, Thomas Park, is crowned by a 70ft tall square marble Georgian revival **monument** commemorating George Washington's bloodless purge of the Brits from Boston. After the Continental Army had held the British under siege here for just over a year, Washington wanted to put an end to the whole thing. On March 4, 1776, the general amassed all the artillery around and placed it on the towering peak of Dorchester Heights, so the tired redcoats could get a good look at the patriots' firepower. Intimidated, they swiftly left Boston – for good.

Thomas Park, generally empty and pristinely kept, still commands the same sweeping views of Boston and its southern communities that it did during the Revolutionary War. The best vista is from the top of the monument itself, though it's only open sporadically (July & Aug Wed 4–8pm, Sat & Sun 10am–4pm; free) and is quite a bit out of the way from any major points of interest.

Roxbury

One of the city's most maligned neighborhoods, **Roxbury** occupies much of south central Boston below the South End, between Dorchester and Jamaica Plain. This formerly pastoral region was one of the city's most coveted addresses in the seventeenth and eighteenth centuries, when wealthy families built sumptuous country homes here. It wasn't really until the 1950s that the area hit hard times, and the urban blight has left its scars, despite an ongoing attempt to restore some of the impressive, if neglected, properties and attract former South Enders who've been pushed out by that neighborhood's skyrocketing real estate prices. While it's nowhere as dangerous as the rougher sections of bigger cities like LA, visitors still may feel unwelcome or unsafe in parts, especially at night. For exploring by day, the area holds some historical interest around **Dudley Square**, where a couple of African-American institutions have been preserved, but the main attraction here, especially if you have children in tow, is the **Franklin Park Zoo**, in yet another of Frederick Law Olmsted's greenspaces.

Dudley Square and around

Roxbury's commercial center is **Dudley Square** – the intersection of Dudley and Warren streets – which is little more than the usual mix of shops and convenience stores. If you're in the area, check out the **Dillaway Thomas House**, at 183 Roxbury St between Dudley Square and the Roxbury Crossing **T** stop (Wed–Fri 10am–4pm, Sat & Sun noon–5pm; donation requested), a structure built in 1750 as a parsonage and subsequently used as a fort in the Revolutionary War. Its first floor is remarkably well-preserved, featuring many details of its original construction, such as exposed beams, while the upstairs has rotating exhibits of African- and African-American-themed art; the best part, though, may be the serene apple orchard surrounding it.

Further south, the **Museum of the National Center for Afro-American Artists**, at 300 Walnut Ave (Tues–Sun 1–5pm; $4; ☎617/442-8614, ⊛www .ncaaa.org), housed in the Victorian Gothic "Oak Bend" mansion, has a decent collection of African-American visual art from throughout the twentieth century, highlighted by some richly textured woodcuts by Wilmer Jennings and Hale Woodruff, as well as Edward McCluney's painting *Nine American Masters*, depicting authors Toni Morrison and Alice Walker, and jazz great Ella Fitzgerald, among others.

Franklin Park and the zoo

The southernmost link in the Emerald Necklace (see box, p.124), **Franklin Park** was one of Olmsted's proudest accomplishments when it was completed, owing to the sheer size of the place, and its scale is indeed astounding: 527 acres of greenspace, with countless trails for hikers, bikers, and walkers leading through the hills and thickly forested areas. That's about it, though, as much of the park has unfortunately become overgrown from years of halfhearted upkeep. It's quite easy to get lost among all the greenery and forget that you're still in the city, though this is perhaps not such a hot idea – the park borders some of Boston's more dangerous areas, and the place can feel quite threatening, especially at night.

The **Franklin Park Zoo**, on the far eastern edge of Franklin Park (April–Sept Mon–Fri 10am–5pm, Sat & Sun 10am–6pm, Oct–March daily 10am–4pm; $9.50, kids $5; ☎617/541-LION, ⊛www.zoonewengland.com; Forest Hills **T**) is much like any other zoo, and is really only essential if you're traveling with kids, who'll definitely get a kick out of the Children's Zoo, where they're allowed to pet and feed rhinos and the like. Adults may enjoy the decent array of exotic fauna, much of which is contained in the African Tropical Forest, an impressively recreated savanna that's the largest indoor zoo design in North America, housing gorillas, monkeys, and pygmy hippos. More fun is had at Bird's World, a charming relic from the days of Edwardian zoo design; there's a huge, ornate wrought-iron cage you can walk through while birds fly overhead.

Jamaica Plain

Diminutive **Jamaica Plain** – "JP" in local parlance – is one of Boston's more successfully integrated neighborhoods, with a good mix of students, immigrants, and working-class families crowded into its relatively cheap apartments. Located between Roxbury and the section of the Emerald Necklace known as the Muddy River Improvement, the area's activity centers on, appropriately, **Centre Street**, which holds some inventive, and remarkably inexpensive, cafés and restaurants (see chapters 12 and 13). While you might call in at the historic estate just off the street or indulge at one of those eating establishments, the

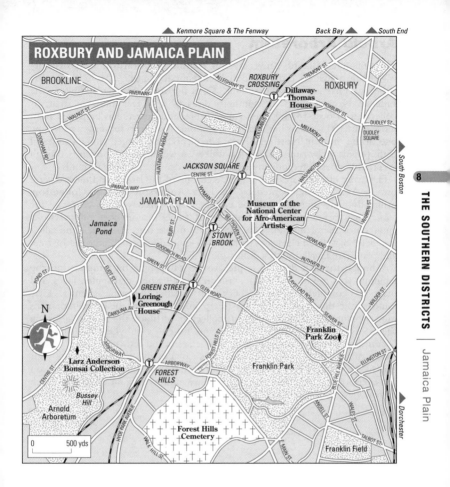

ROXBURY AND JAMAICA PLAIN

BROOKLINE

ROXBURY CROSSING

ROXBURY

Dillaway-Thomas House

JACKSON SQUARE

JAMAICA PLAIN

Jamaica Pond

Museum of the National Center for Afro-American Artists

STONY BROOK

GREEN STREET

Loring-Greenough House

Franklin Park Zoo

Larz Anderson Bonsai Collection

FOREST HILLS

Franklin Park

Bussey Hill

Arnold Arboretum

Forest Hills Cemetery

Franklin Field

N

0   500 yds

more likely bet is to head straight for the neighborhood's star attraction, the **Arnold Arboretum**, on its southwestern edge.

Loring-Greenough House

At Centre Street's foot stands the fusty **Loring-Greenough House**, at 12 South St (June–Aug Tues & Sat 10am–noon, Sun noon–2pm, Sept–May Tues & Sat 10am–noon; $3 donation requested; ☎617/524-3158, ⓦwww.lghouse .org; Forest Hills **T** or Back Bay **T** to bus #39), built in 1760 for Loyalist Commodore Joshua Loring and confiscated by colonial troops in 1775 for use as a Revolutionary War hospital. Restored to private use in 1780, the mid-Georgian mansion house was occupied by lawyer David Stoddard Greenough's family until 1926, when it was designated a historic site. The house's significance – as the last of JP's country estates from that period – does more for it than its refurbished chambers, whose highlights are unrelated exhibits of jeweled handbags and ornate calling-card cases collected by the women of the Tuesday Club, the organization that manages the house.

Arnold Arboretum

The 265-acre Harvard University-run **Arnold Arboretum**, at 125 Arbor-way (daily dawn to dusk; $1 donation requested; ☎617/524-1718, ⊕www .arboretum.harvard.edu; Forest Hills **T**), is the most spectacular link in the Emerald Necklace and the southern districts' only real must-see sight. Its collection of over 14,000 trees, vines, shrubs, and flowers has benefited from more than 100 years of both careful grooming and ample funding, and is now one of the finest in North America. The plants are arranged along a series of paths populated by runners and dog-walkers as well as serious botanists, though it certainly doesn't require any expert knowledge to enjoy the grounds.

The array of Asian species – considered one of the largest and most diverse outside Asia – is highlighted by the **Larz Anderson Bonsai Collection**, brilliantly concentrated along the Chinese Path walkway at the center of the park. The arboretum also has more than 700 trees that are over 100 years old; eighteen of them (including an 1881 silver maple that, at 120ft, is the tallest tree here) have been chosen as part of a self-guided Centenarian tour (the trees and plants are labeled with a gold tag).

Although the staff does an impressive job of keeping the grounds looking fabulous year-round, it's best to visit in spring, when crabapples, lilacs, and magnolias complement the greenery with dazzling chromatic schemes. "Lilac Sunday," the third Sunday in May (see p.252), celebrates the arboretum at its most vibrant (and busiest), when its collection of **lilacs**, the second largest in the US, is in full bloom. **Fall** is also a good time to visit, when the arboretum becomes a glorious mass of blazing oranges, reds, and browns.

One of the best ways to appreciate the scope of the place is to make your way to the top of 198-foot **Bussey Hill** in the arboretum's center, where you can overlook the grounds in their impressive entirety and, on a clear day, catch a great view of Downtown Boston as well.

9

Cambridge

Just across the Charles River from Boston, **Cambridge** is altogether more unbuttoned and laid-back than its big city counterpart, and populated by a younger, more bohemian type of resident. Highlighted by two of the most illustrious institutions of higher learning in the country, its denizens, including clean-cut college students, grungy punks, starched, standoffish business people, and street artists performing magic tricks, manage to support a buzzing streetlife and café culture that can either be seen as a refreshing change from provincial Boston or just a continuation of it.

A walk down Cambridge's colonial-era brick sidewalks and narrow, crooked roads takes you past some plaques and monuments honoring literati and revolutionaries who lived and worked in the area – some hailing from as early as the seventeenth century. As in most modern towns, you'll also find idiosyncratic neighborhoods, congestion, a growing homeless population, and numerous meeting points where busloads of visitors get dropped off for a quick poke around. Nevertheless, Cambridge manages – perhaps even better than Boston itself – an exhilarating mix of colonial past and urban present; the extensive range of residents and activities, and the sheer energy that pervades its classrooms and coffeehouses, make it an essential stopover while traveling in the area.

Cambridge resembles a bow tie, with Harvard Square forming the knot. On its southern border is the sinuous Charles River, with Boston on the opposite bank, while the concave northern side is shared with the large, mostly residential town of **Somerville**, popular with locals for its restaurant and café scene centering on the alternative vibe of **Davis Square**. Cambridge proper, meanwhile, is loosely organized around a series of squares – actually confluences of streets that are the focus of each area's commercial activity. By far the most important of these is **Harvard Square**, which radiates out from the **T** stop along Massachusetts Avenue, JFK Street, and Brattle Street. Roughly coterminous with Harvard Square is **Harvard University**; together, these two areas make up the cultural and academic heart of Cambridge. This is where people converge to check out the famous Ivy League institution, historical monuments, a lively coffeehouse-and-bookstore scene, and a disgruntled counterculture. Its total area – only a single square mile – is small in comparison with the entirety of Cambridge, but the density of attractions here make it one part of town not to be missed.

Old Cambridge, the clean, impeccably kept colonial heart of the city, is easily accessible from Harvard Square; sights here include impressive mansions – most notably the **Longfellow House** – and peaceful **Mount Auburn Cemetery**. East from here, on the other side of the university,

Central and **Inman squares** represent the core of **Central Cambridge**, a working-class neighborhood far more down-to-earth than its collegiate counterpart but rapidly catching up on the rails as urban regeneration and subsequent gentrification take place. A similar atmosphere pervades in **East Cambridge**, as well; both areas grew up around industry rather than academia, but their proximity to Downtown Boston has led to increasing real estate prices and an "upscaling" of residents. East Cambridge draws most of its modern-day interest from the **Massachusetts Institute of Technology**, one of the world's premier science and research institutions. Home to some innovative – if at times peculiar – architecture and an excellent museum, MIT spreads out below **Kendall Square**, which itself is home to a cluster of stalwart high-tech companies. Finally, above Harvard, **Northwest Cambridge** is an ill-defined corner of the city, a catchall term for some of the places not identified with its more happening districts – and as such is easily overlooked. Despite some good shopping and decent restaurants, especially along **Huron Avenue** and around **Porter Square**, the area is more of interest to residents than to travelers.

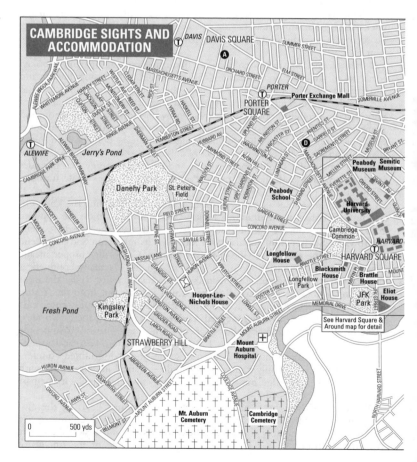

Some history

Cambridge began inauspiciously in 1630, when a group of English immigrants from Charlestown founded **New Towne** (actually a village) on the narrow, swampy banks of the Charles River. These Puritans hoped New Towne would become an ideal religious community; to that end, they founded a college in 1636 for the purpose of training clergy. Two years later, the college took its name in honor of a local minister, **John Harvard**, who bequeathed his library and half his estate to the nascent institution. New Towne was eventually renamed **Cambridge** after the English university where many of its founders were educated, and became one of the largest publishing centers in the New World after the arrival of the printing press in the seventeenth century. Its university and printing industry established Cambridge as an important center of intellectual activity and political thought, and during the late eighteenth century its population became sharply divided between the many artisan and farmer sympathizers of the revolution and the moneyed Tory minority; when fighting began, the Tories were driven from their mansions on modern-day Brattle Street (then called "Tory Row").

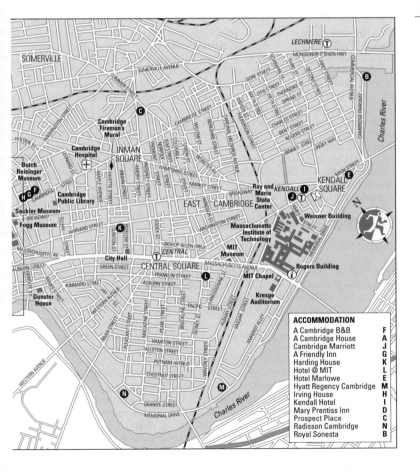

ACCOMMODATION	
A Cambridge B&B	F
A Cambridge House	A
Cambridge Marriott	J
A Friendly Inn	G
Harding House	K
Hotel @ MIT	L
Hotel Marlowe	E
Hyatt Regency Cambridge	M
Irving House	H
Kendall Hotel	I
Mary Prentiss Inn	D
Prospect Place	C
Radisson Cambridge	N
Royal Sonesta	B

The area remained unincorporated until 1846, when the Massachusetts Legislature granted a city charter linking Old Cambridge (the Harvard Square area) and industrial East Cambridge as a single municipality. Initially, there was friction between these two very different neighborhoods; in 1855, citizens from each area unsuccessfully petitioned for them to be granted separate civic status. Even today each area retains a distinctive character. The late nineteenth and early twentieth centuries brought substantial growth to the town. A large, mainly Irish immigrant population was drawn to opportunity in the industrial and commercial sectors of East Cambridge, while academics increasingly sought out Harvard, whose reputation continued to swell, and the **Massachusetts Institute of Technology**, which moved here from Boston in 1916. Today, with roughly half of its near-100,000 residents affiliated with universities, Cambridge is one of America's intellectual strongholds.

Harvard Square and around

The Harvard **T** station marks Cambridge's epicenter, opening up onto **Harvard Square**, where a moody youth brigade stews in the shadow of the Harvard Yard buildings. A small **tourism kiosk** run by the Cambridge Tourism Office (daily 9am–5pm; ☎617/441-2884 or 1-800/862-5678, ⬤www .cambridge-usa.com) faces the station exit, but more of the action is in the adjacent sunken area known as **The Pit**, a triage center for fashion victims of alternative culture. Teens spend entire days sitting here admiring each other's green hair and body piercings while the homeless (and some of the teens) hustle for change and other handouts. This is also the focal point of the **street music scene**, where folk diva Tracy Chapman (a graduate of Tufts University, in nearby Somerville) and country maven Bonnie Raitt (a Radcliffe alumna) both got their starts. The square reaches its most frenetic state on Friday and Saturday nights and Sunday afternoons, when all the elements converge – crowds mill about, evangelical demonstrators engage in shouting matches with angry youths, and magicians, acrobats, and bands perform on every corner.

The Old Burying Ground

Facing Harvard Square to the north along Massachusetts Avenue is one of Cambridge's first cemeteries, the **Old Burying Ground**, whose style and grounds have scarcely changed since the seventeenth century. You're supposed to apply to the sexton of nearby **Christ Church** for entry, but if the gate at the path beside the simple, graywashed, eighteenth-century church is open (as it frequently is), you can enter so long as you're respectful of the grounds.

The epitaphs have an archaic ring to them ("Here lyes..."), and the stone grave markers are adorned in a style blending Puritan austerity and medieval superstition: inscriptions praise the simple piety of the staunchly Christian deceased, but are surrounded by death's-heads carved to ward off evil spirits. Its most famous occupants include several of Harvard's first presidents as well as two black veterans of the Revolutionary War, Cato Stedman and Neptune Frost. Be sure to check out the **milestone** at the northeast corner of the cemetery, found just inside the gate, whose 250-year-old inscription is still readily visible. Originally set to mark the then-daunting distance of eight miles to Boston, the letters A.I. identify the stone's maker, Abraham Ireland.

Dawes Island

A triangular traffic island squeezed into the intersection of Massachusetts Avenue, Garden Street, and Peabody Street, **Dawes Island** is anything but bucolic – the wedge of concrete serves as Harvard Square's central bus stop. The island is named after the patriot who rode to alert residents that the British were marching to Lexington and Concord on April 19, 1775 – the *other* patriot, that is, William Dawes (see box, p.72). While Longfellow opted to commemorate Paul Revere's midnight ride instead, Cantabrigians must have appreciated poor Dawes's contribution just as much. Bronze hoofmarks in the sidewalk mark the event, and several placards provide information on the history of the Harvard Square/Old Cambridge area.

△ Harvard Square

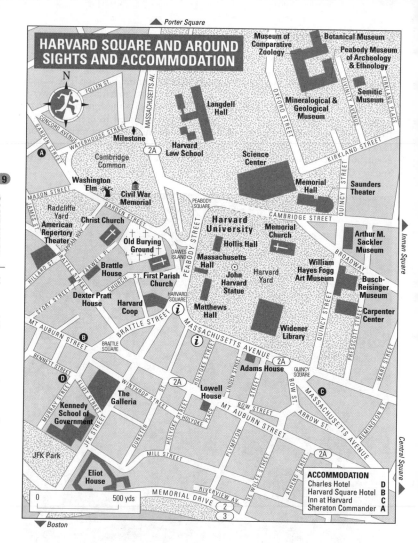

HARVARD SQUARE AND AROUND SIGHTS AND ACCOMMODATION

Porter Square

N

Museum of Comparative Zoology
Botanical Museum
Peabody Museum of Archeology & Ethnology
Semitic Museum
Mineralogical & Geological Museum
Langdell Hall
Milestone
Harvard Law School
Science Center
Memorial Hall
Saunders Theater
Cambridge Common
Washington Elm
Civil War Memorial
Radcliffe Yard
American Repertory Theater
Christ Church
Old Burying Ground
Harvard University
Hollis Hall
Memorial Church
Arthur M. Sackler Museum
Brattle House
First Parish Church
Massachusetts Hall
John Harvard Statue
Harvard Yard
William Hayes Fogg Art Museum
Busch-Reisinger Museum
Dexter Pratt House
Harvard Coop
Matthews Hall
Carpenter Center
Widener Library
Adams House
The Galleria
Lowell House
Kennedy School of Government
JFK Park
Eliot House

0   500 yds

MEMORIAL DRIVE

Boston

Inman Square

Central Square

ACCOMMODATION
Charles Hotel   D
Harvard Square Hotel   B
Inn at Harvard   C
Sheraton Commander   A

Cambridge Common and Radcliffe Yard

A trapezoidal patch of green between Massachusetts Avenue, Garden Street, and Waterhouse Street, **Cambridge Common** has been a site for recreation and community events since the area's earliest settlers used it as a cow pasture. Visitors flock here for its historical interest, but locals congregate for Frisbee and sunbathing – although after dusk it can be an altogether lonelier, and somewhat dodgier, place.

Early Harvard commencements took place here, as did public debates and training exercises for the local militia. You can retrace a portion of the old **Charlestown–Watertown path**, along which the British Redcoats beat a sheepish retreat to Watertown during the Revolutionary War, and which still transects the park from east to west. A broad range of **statuary** dots the southeast corner of the park, and you can't miss the towering monument to Lincoln and the Civil War dead, which all but overshadows the recently added tableau of two emaciated figures nearby, wrought as an unsettling memorial to the Irish Potato Famine.

Just across Garden Street from Cambridge Common is a less crowded park, **Radcliffe Yard**, originally the center of Radcliffe College, established in 1878 to give women access to (then exclusively male) Harvard; the two colleges merged in the 1970s. The yard itself is a picturesque, impeccably preserved quadrangle; enclosed by brick buildings and Ionic columns, it's dotted with fountains and pathways, making it a great place for a summer picnic or stroll.

Along JFK Street

The stretch of **JFK Street** below Harvard Square holds more of the city's many public spaces, certainly the least of which is **Winthrop Square**, site of the original New Towne marketplace and since converted into a lackluster park. Cross the park and walk down Winthrop Street to the right to get a sense of the sloping topography and narrow street design of early Cambridge. Here you'll see a **stone wall** that was built along the original shoreline of the Charles River.

John F. Kennedy Park, located where JFK Street meets Memorial Drive, was only finished in the late 1980s. Though certainly not the first pious shrine to Boston's favorite modern son, this one is cleaner and more spacious than most other parks in the area. The **memorial** to Kennedy in its center lacks the usual grandeur; it's a low, pink-granite pyramid surrounded by a moat, covered constantly but imperceptibly by a thin film of flowing water.

Harvard Yard and the university

The transition from Harvard Square to **Harvard Yard** – the proper center of the university – is dramatic: in a matter of only several feet, the buzz of car

The Washington Elm

The most prominent feature on Cambridge Common is the revered **Washington Elm**, under which it's claimed George Washington took command of the Continental Army. The tree is at the southern side of the park, almost facing the intersection of Garden Street and Appian Way, and is predictably accompanied by a wealth of commemorative objects: a cannon captured from the British when they evacuated Boston, a statue of Washington standing in the shade of the elm, and monuments to two Polish army captains hired to lead revolutionary forces – excessive rewards, really, for mercenaries. What the memorials don't tell you is that the city of Cambridge cut down the original Washington Elm in 1946 when it began to obstruct traffic; it stood at the common's southwest corner, near the intersection of Mason and Garden streets. The present tree is actually the offspring of that tree, raised from one of its branches. To further confuse the issue, the Daughters of the American Revolution erected a monument commemorating the southeast corner of the park as the spot where Washington did his historic thing. And recently, American historians have adduced evidence strongly suggesting that Washington never commissioned the troops on the common at all, but rather in Wadsworth House at Harvard Yard.

traffic and urban life gives way to grassy lawns and towering oaks, pervaded by an aura of Ivy League academia. Unfortunately, this aura is often broken by the sound of clicking cameras from tour groups, who can make the place seem more like an amusement park than a staid university campus. You can join the hullabaloo by taking a free one-hour student-guided walking tour from the Harvard Events & Information Center in the Holyoke Center, 1350 Massachusetts Ave (June–Aug Mon–Sat 10am, 11.15am, 2pm, & 3.15pm; Sept–May Mon–Fri 10am & 2pm, Sat 2pm; no tours during breaks in the academic calendar; ☎617/495-1551, ⊛www.news.harvard.edu/guide), where you can also pick up maps and brochures detailing everything Harvard-related.

The Old Yard

The most common entrance to Harvard Yard is the one directly across from Harvard Square proper, which leads by **Massachusetts Hall** (holding the office of the university president) to the **Old Yard**, a large, rectangular area dating from 1636, when it was created as a grazing field for university livestock. In front of stark, symmetrical, slate-gray **University Hall** is the yard's icon, the **John Harvard statue**, source of the oft-told story of the "three lies" (it misdates the college's founding; erroneously identifies John Harvard as the college's founder; and isn't really a likeness of the man at all). While it's a popular spot for visitors to take pictures, male college students prize the statue as a prime spot to urinate in public; anyone managing to pull off the feat is granted a certain honorary status among students on campus – as a result, there are now about twenty surveillance cameras trained on the site, acting as a deterrent.

Along the northwest border of the yard, stout **Hollis Hall** is the dormitory where Henry David Thoreau lived as an undergraduate. The architectural contrast between modest Hollis, which dates from 1763, and its grandiose southern neighbor, **Matthews Hall**, built around a hundred years later, reflects Harvard's transition from a quiet training ground for ministers to a wealthy, cosmopolitan university. The **indentations** in Hollis's front steps were caused by students who used to warm their rooms by heating cannonballs; come time to leave their quarters for the summer, they would dispose of the cannonballs by dropping them from their windows rather than having to carry them down the stairs. Harvard's first chapel, the charming 1744 **Holden Chapel** to the rear, is also worth a quick peek for its attractive Georgian architecture and provincial blue-and-white pediment.

The New Yard

To the east of the Old Yard lie the grander buildings of the Tercentenary Theatre, colloquially known as the **New Yard**, where a vast set of steps leads up to the enormous pillars of **Widener Library**. Named after Harvard grad and *Titanic* victim Harry Elkins Widener, whose mother paid for the project, it's the center of the largest private library collection in the US, boasting a first folio of Shakespeare and a Gutenberg Bible among its holdings (you'll need Harvard student ID to see them). At the opposite side of the New Yard is **Memorial Church** (☎617/495-5508, ⊛www.memorialchurch.harvard.edu), whose narrow, white spire strikes a balancing note to the heavy pillared front of Widener; its 172-foot-high steeple, topped by a medieval pennant-shaped **weathervane**, is a classic postcard image of Harvard Yard. Inside the church, the nave bears the names of alumni who've died at war; the organ at the rear is a much fancier affair, adorned with gilded carvings of starfish, kelp, cod, and crab.

The Science Center and Law School

The immense structure facing the New Yard is Harvard's **Science Center**. The big lecture halls on the first floor are home to some of Harvard's most popular classes; one celebrity professor who taught here was the late evolutionary biologist Stephen Jay Gould. A popular myth has it that the center was designed to look like a camera, since one of its main benefactors was Polaroid magnate Edwin Land, but any likeness is purely accidental.

Up Massachusetts Avenue, on the east side of Cambridge Common, lies the main quad of the famed **Harvard Law School**, founded in 1817. The campus focuses on the stern gray pillars of **Langdell Hall**, an imposing edifice on its western border, whose entrance bears the inscription "*Non sub homine, sed sub deo et lege*" ("Not under man, but under God and law"). In 1997 the hall underwent a $35 million renovation project and now mainly serves as home to the **Harvard Law Library**, where you can practically smell the stress in the air. You can apply for visitor's privileges at the front desk, though the process is expedited if you download and complete the application form from ⓦwww .law.harvard.edu.

Memorial Hall and the Carpenter Center

The rest of the campus lies east of the Science Center, starting with the pointed arches and flying buttresses of **Memorial Hall**, built to commemorate the Harvard students who died during the Civil War. While it resembles a church, right down to its central vaulted **narthex**, which is bathed in filtered sunlight through Tiffany and LaFarge stained-glass windows, the space actually serves as **Sanders Theater**, undoubtedly Harvard's most impressive public lecture space.

The modern **Carpenter Center** is hard to miss as you continue past Memorial Hall and look down Quincy Street: the slate-gray granite slab stands out amidst Harvard's ever-present brick motif. Completed in 1963 as a center for the study of visual art at Harvard, the Carpenter Center is the only building in America designed by modernist French architect Le Corbusier (known for Zurich's Centre Le Corbusier and avant-garde furniture design), and its jarring difference from its surroundings has drawn a great deal of criticism from staunch Harvard traditionalists. Still, it's a striking and reasonably functional space; be sure to traverse its trademark feature, a **walkway** that leads through the middle of the building, meant to reflect the path worn by students on the lot on which the center was constructed. The modest **Sert Gallery**, on the third floor (Mon–Sat 10am–5pm, Sun 1–5pm; free; no phone, ⓦwww.artmuseums.harvard.edu/sert), puts on rotating contemporary art exhibits culled from Harvard's collections, while the lower floors of the building frequently display student art exhibits.

Harvard University art museums

Harvard's three art museums – the **William Hayes Fogg**, the **Busch–Reisinger**, and the **Sackler** (Mon–Sat 10am–5pm, Sun 1–5pm; $6.50; free Sat 10am–noon; ☏617/495-9400, ⓦwww.artmuseums.harvard.edu) – have benefited from years of scholarly attention and donors' financial generosity. Largely

The **Harvard Hot Ticket** is a pass scheme that allows entrance into six of the university's museums – the Fogg, the Bush-Reisinger, the Sackler, the Natural History, the Peabody, and the Semetic – for just $10, saving you $4. You can purchase the pass at any of the museum box offices, or at the Harvard Events and Information Center in the Holyoke Center, at 1350 Massachusetts Ave.

underappreciated and underattended by most visitors – not to mention the students themselves – the collections are easily some of the finest in New England; certainly the Fogg has the most important collection of Picassos around.

The William Hayes Fogg Art Museum

Housed on two floors surrounding a lovely mock sixteenth-century Italian Renaissance courtyard, the **William Hayes Fogg Art Museum**, at 32 Quincy St, showcases the highlights of Harvard's substantial collection of Western art. Much of the first floor is devoted to **medieval** and **Renaissance** material, mainly religious art with the usual complement of suffering Christs, mainly housed in the far room to the right, below a marvelous circa-1540 oak ceiling carved with scrolls and arabesques. This part of the collection is best for a series of capitals salvaged from the French cathedral of Moutiers-Saint-Jean, which combine a Romanesque predilection for classical design with medieval didactic narrative. Additional first-floor chambers are devoted to **portraiture** of the seventeenth and eighteenth centuries, featuring two Rubens, a Rembrandt, and three Poussins, among them the startling *Hannibal Crossing the Alps*, which depicts the great Carthaginian instructing his troops from atop a massive tusked elephant. The remainder is rather stale, though the work of local John Singleton Copley figures prominently.

The second floor includes spaces for rotating exhibits, as well as smaller rooms displaying the museum's well-chosen **Impressionist**, **Post-Impressionist**, and **Modernist** works. There's an especially strong showing from the late-nineteenth-century French contingent of Dégas, Monet, Manet, Pissarro, and Cézanne. You'll also see Picasso's *Mother and Child*, famously exemplary of his blue period, a sickly *Self-Portrait, dedicated to Paul Gauguin* by Van Gogh, and Toulouse-Lautrec's queasy *The Hangover (Suzanne Valadon)*. But it's the focus on American counterparts to European late-nineteenth- and early-twentieth-century artists that truly distinguishes the collection, from the fine range of John Singer Sargent portraits, his solitary *The Breakfast Table* among them, to an ethereal Whistler *Nocturne* in blue and silver tints. Modernism is represented by, among others, Jackson Pollock's narrow beige and black *No. 2*, and Charles Sheeler's outstanding *Upper Deck*, a representation of technology that ingeniously combines realism with abstraction. Fine examples of lesser-known nineteenth-century sensualist works are also displayed throughout the museum; look for Rodin's downright sexy *Eternal Idol* marble, and Gustave Moreau's highly eroticized *Apparition*.

The Busch-Reisinger Museum

Secreted away at the rear of the Fogg's second floor is the entrance to Werner Otto Hall, home of the rich – though somewhat jarring – collection of the **Busch–Reisinger Museum**. Despite its small size, it's one of the finest collections of German Expressionists and Bauhaus works in the world. Its six rooms contain *fin de siècle* art, including Klimt's *Pear Tree*, a dappled meditation on the natural environment, and several Bauhaus standouts like Feininger's angular *Bird Cloud* and Moholy-Nagy's *Light-Space Modulator* – a quirky sculpture-machine set in motion for ten-minutes just once a week (Wed 1.45pm) due to its fragility. The gallery is strongest in Expressionist portraiture, notably, Kirchner's sardonic *Self-Portrait with a Cat* and Beckmann's garish *The Actors*, a narcissistic triptych that features a self-portrait as its centrepiece.

The Arthur M. Sackler Museum

Right out of the Fogg and dead ahead, the Arthur M. Sackler Building, 485 Broadway, houses three floors that make up the **Sackler Museum**, dedicated to the art of **classical**, **Asian,** and **Islamic** cultures. The museum's holdings have far outgrown its available space, which is why the first floor is devoted to rotating exhibits based on permanent collection holdings. Islamic and Asian art are featured in the second floor and show illustrations from Muslim texts, Chinese landscapes from the past several centuries, and an outstanding collection of Japanese woodblock prints. The third floor is best known for its excellent array of sensuous **Buddhist sculptures** from ancient China, India, and Southeast Asia; one of them is housed in an ornate gilt and bronze portable shrine. You'll also see a strong display of classical work – standing out from the usual Greek vases and sculpture are **coins** from the reign of Alexander the Great and **seals** from ancient Babylonia.

Harvard Museum of Natural History and Peabody Museum of Archeology and Ethnology

North of the Sackler, Divinity Avenue holds another series of galleries, three of which (the Harvard University Herbaria, Mineralogical and Geological Museum, and Museum of Comparative Zoology) are grouped together in a consortium called the **Harvard Museum of Natural History** (ⓦwww .hmnh.harvard.edu). A separate entity, the **Peabody Museum of Archeology and Ethnology**, is linked to the HMNH via a walkway. Entry to both is via a common ticket (daily 9am–5pm; $7.50, free Sun 9am–noon year round and Wed 3–5pm Sept–May).

The result is a pretty specialized collection of academic odds and ends; still, even the most dispassionate observer will find something of interest here, especially so in the Peabody and the Herbaria, which, in certain cases, succeed at rendering the arcane almost enthralling. The Mineralogical and Geological Museum, on the other hand, along with the Museum of Comparative Zoology, is less compelling.

The Peabody Museum of Archeology and Ethnology

Although considered a separate body, the best of Harvard's natural history museums, the **Peabody Museum of Archeology and Ethnology**, 11 Divinity Ave (ⓣ617/495-2269, ⓦwww.peabody.harvard.edu), displays materials culled from the university's anthropological and archeological expeditions. The strength of the museum lies in its collection of pieces from **Mesoamerica**, ranging from digs in the pueblos of southwestern United States to artifacts from Incan civilizations. The ground-floor anthropological material centers mainly on indigenous cultures of North America, with colorful kachina dolls crafted by Arizona Hopi for their children, and stupendous examples of Northwest Coast ceremonial masks with pronounced bird beaks. In addition, there is a detailed presentation on the Ju/wa bushmen of the Kalahari Desert. The displays are extensive and informative, covering the history, art, traditions, and lifestyles of native peoples from around the world – though the wax dummies in traditional garb and the miniature dioramas can't help but seem hokey and out of place.

Mineralogical and Geological Museum

A second-floor passageway connects the Peabody with Harvard's **Mineralogical and Geological Museum**, at 24 Oxford St (☎617/495-3045,⊛www.peabody .harvard.edu/museum_mineral), the thrust of whose collection is, basically, a bunch of rocks with a stunning 1600-pound amethyst-encrusted cavity serving as their centerpiece. As such, if you don't know anything about geology, this probably won't do too much for you, as the only easily accessible display (to the layperson, anyway) concerns birthstones. On the other hand, it's reputed to be one of the world's finest mineral collections, and most of the gems are truly gorgeous.

The Harvard University Herbaria

Right next door, and similarly narrow in scope, the **Harvard University Herbaria**, at 26 Oxford St (☎617/495-2365, ⊛www.huh.harvard.edu /collections/botanical), is also connected by walkway to the former two. While much of the collection is only of interest to botanists, it's definitely worth a look for the stunning **Ware Collection of Glass Models of Plants**. This project, the work of a father-and-son team from Dresden, Germany, began in 1887 and terminated almost fifty years later in 1936, leaving the museum with an absolutely unique and visually stunning collection of flower models constructed to the last detail, entirely from glass.

The Museum of Comparative Zoology

Housed in the same building as the Botanical Museum, but lacking a knockout attraction like the Ware Collection, the **Museum of Comparative Zoology** (☎617/495-3045, ⊛www.mcz.harvard.edu) is really just the tip of the iceberg of the university's collection of zoological materials. Most of the collection is inaccessible to visitors; what is on display consists of rote presentations of stuffed dead animals with some fascinating amber-preserved insects and impressive fossils thrown in.

The Harvard Semitic Museum

Facing the Peabody is the **Harvard Semitic Museum**, at 6 Divinity Ave (Mon–Fri 10am–4pm, Sun 1–4pm; free; ☎617/495-4631, ⊛www.fas.harvard .edu/~semitic), whose informative, if somewhat unfocused, displays chronicle excavations made by Harvard's Department of Near Eastern Languages and Civilizations. Pieces range from Egyptian tombs to Babylonian cuneiform, and include a particularly appealing collection of tiny stone-cut votive figurines from ancient Cyprus. What distinguishes the collection, though, is its focus on the process and methodology of the digs, with concomitant examples of charts, infrared devices, and dusting tools, in addition to their results.

Harvard houses

Harvard's upperclassmen residences, most of which are nested in the quad east of JFK Street and south of Massachusetts Avenue, are a visible – and sometimes ostentatious – reminder of the university's legacy. Nearest the Yard, at 46 Plympton St, **Adams House** has the most rebellious history of the lot, having been used as a revolutionary prison for General "Gentleman Johnny" Burgoyne, and later serving as a speakeasy during Prohibition. Just south of Adams juts the graceful, blue-topped bell tower of **Lowell House**, at 2 Holyoke Place, which boasts one of Harvard's most beautiful courtyards, surrounded by a compound of sober brick dormitories and fastidiously manicured grounds. Further southwest, along the banks of the Charles, rises the purple spire of **Eliot House**, at 101 Dunster St, a community that remains a bastion of social privilege and can count David Rockefeller and Leonard Bernstein as former residents. To the east, at 945 Memorial Drive, lies **Dunster House**, whose red Georgian tower top is a favorite subject of Cambridge's tourist brochures; it was modeled after Christ Church College's Big Tom in Oxford. Alongside Adams, Dunster has long been considered a center for radical culture – at least by Cambridge's very proper standards: while the other residences were often praised for their building of a "house spirit," Dunster had no rules or regulations, but rather a reputation for "extreme informality."

Old Cambridge: Upper Brattle Street

After the outbreak of the American Revolution, Cambridge's bourgeois majority ran the Tories out of town, seizing their sumptuous houses as quarters for the Continental Army. What was then called Tory Row is modern-day **Brattle Street**, the main drag of the **Old Cambridge** district. Extending west from Eliot Street and Harvard Square, Brattle runs through a tree-lined neighborhood of expansive, impeccably kept lawns foregrounding stately mansions, many of which have been labeled with blue oval plaques commemorating their former owners.

The Brattle House and Farwell Place

The first of several noteworthy residences along Brattle Street, the **Brattle House**, at no. 42, doesn't reflect the unabashedly extravagant lifestyle of its former resident, the Revolutionary War commander General William Brattle. The plain facade doesn't appear nearly as grand as it once did, dwarfed as it is by surrounding office buildings, nor is it open to the public – no great loss since it now only houses offices.

Down the street and to the right, tiny **Farwell Place** features several modest Federal-style houses dating to the early nineteenth century and is the best (and only remaining) example of the square's residential character before it became a teeming center of activity. The recently restored house at no. 17 is one of the best examples of the genre; it now houses Christ Church's thrift shop (Tues & Thurs 10am–4pm, Sat 11.30am–2.30pm; ☎617/492-3335).

The Dexter Pratt House

A sign on the corner of Brattle and Story streets marks the site of a tree that once stood near the **Dexter Pratt House**, at 56 Brattle St, home of the village blacksmith celebrated by Longfellow in a popular poem that began, "Under a spreading chestnut tree / The village smithy stands, / The smith a mighty man is he, / With large and sinewy hands; / And the muscles of his brawny arms / Are strong as iron bands." In 1876, the chestnut was cut down, despite Longfellow's vigorous opposition, because it was spreading into the path of passing traffic. The city of Cambridge fashioned a chair out of the felled tree and presented it as a birthday present to Longfellow, who then composed a mawkish poem about the whole affair ("From My Easy Chair"), and all was forgiven. These days the Federal-style building has the humdrum role of home to the Hi-Rise Bread Company, producers of some of the finest baked treats in greater Boston. Beyond the house, at the intersection of **Mason** and **Brattle streets**, a neighborhood of elite mansions signals the edge of Old Cambridge proper.

The Longfellow House

One house on Brattle Street you can visit is the recently renovated **Longfellow House** at 105 Brattle St (May–Oct; Wed–Sun 10am–4.30pm, tours hourly 10.30–11.30am & 1–4pm; $3; ☎617/876-4491, ⊛www.nps.gov/long; Harvard **T**). Erected for Royalist John Vassal in 1759, who promptly vacated it on the eve of the Revolutionary War, and used by George Washington as headquarters during the siege of Boston, it later became home to Longfellow, who moved in as a boarder in 1843. When he married the wealthy Fanny Appleton, her father purchased the house for them as a wedding gift, and Longfellow lived here until his death in 1882.

Preserved to recall the styles of the era, the result is a solid, if somewhat strenuously presented, example of Brattle Street opulence during the nineteenth century. The halls and walls are festooned with Longfellow's furniture and art collection, including etchings of fellow writers like Ralph Waldo Emerson and Nathaniel Hawthorne. Most surprising is the wealth of nineteenth-century pieces from the Far East amassed by Longfellow's renegade son, Charlie, on his world travels; four of his Japanese screens are included, the best of which, a two-panel example depicting geishas in spring and winter costumes, is in an upstairs bedroom. His other son, Ernie, stayed at home, trying – and failing – to make a name for himself as a landscape painter; a number of his unremarkable works adorn the walls of the house.

The Hooper-Lee-Nichols House

Another of the Brattle Street mansions open to the public is the bluewashed **Hooper-Lee-Nichols House** at no. 159 (Tues & Thurs 2–4pm, tours every hour; $5; ☎617/547-4252, ⊛www.cambridgehistory.org), half a mile west of the Longfellow House. While a bit out-of-the-way – one of the area's oldest residences – does give an intimate sense of colonial Cambridge life. It's particularly unusual for its various architectural incarnations: it began as a stout, post-medieval farmhouse and underwent several renovations until it became the Georgian mansion it is today. Rooms have been predictably restored with period writing tables, canopy beds, and rag dolls, but knowledgeable tour guides spice things up a bit, opening secret panels to reveal centuries-old wallpaper and original foundations. Its sporadic hours don't lend themselves to impromptu visits, and you'll have to knock vigorously on the front door to gain entry.

The Mount Auburn Cemetery

Past the Hooper-Lee-Nichols House, at the intersection of Brattle and Mount Auburn streets, is the **Mount Auburn Cemetery**

(@www.mountauburn.org). When founded in 1831, it was America's first landscaped cemetery; today its 170 acres of grounds are more like a beautifully kept municipal park than a necropolis, with as many joggers as there are mourners. The best way to get a sense of the cemetery's scope is to ascend the **tower** that lies smack in its center atop a grassy bluff – from here, you can see not only the entire grounds but, on a clear day, all of Downtown Boston and its environs. Of course, like most cemeteries in the Boston area, Mount Auburn also has its share of deceased luminaries, most notably Winslow Homer and Isabella Stewart Gardner; ask the folks in the main office for a map of famous graves if you're interested.

Central Square

A mile east of Brattle Street, **Central Square**, bordered by Massachusetts Avenue, Prospect Street, and Western Avenue, is roughly in the geographical center of Cambridge, and is the city's civic center as well. The square is an interesting mix of cultural and industrial Cambridge – a working-class area that's steadily being gentrified, with an ethnically diverse population and little of the hype that surrounds other parts of town. There's nothing much to see, but this is a good place to shop and eat, and home to some of the best **nightlife** in Cambridge. Indeed, you'll find substantially more activity here after dark, especially along Massachusetts Avenue, as denizens flock to hear live music.

The Gothic quarters of **City Hall**, at 795 Massachusetts Ave (Mon–Fri 8.30am–5pm), house Cambridge's municipal bureaucracy and act as an occasional venue for town meetings or public events, and the imposing marble **Clifton Merriman Building** across the street, at 770 Massachusetts Ave, houses a post office (Mon–Fri 7.30am–6.45pm, Sat 7.30am–2pm; ☎617/575-8700, @www.usps.com), but little else stands out here.

Inman Square

Overshadowed by Cambridge's busier districts, **Inman Square** marks a quiet stretch directly north of Central Square that's centered on the confluence of Cambridge, Beacon, and Prospect streets. There's not much of note here, either – just a pleasant, mostly residential neighborhood where much of Cambridge's working-class, Portuguese-speaking population resides. What does make Inman worth a visit, though, along with its ethnic markets, is its broad range of excellent restaurants, where you can enjoy some of the town's finest food without breaking the bank. If you're in the area, check out Inman's lone landmark, the charmingly inexpert **Cambridge Firemen's Mural**, on the front of the Inman Square Firehouse at 1384 Cambridge St. This piece of public art was painted by a young local artist named Ellary Eddy in 1976 and depicts then-members of Engine No. 5; it also includes images of Benjamin Franklin, who founded the country's first volunteer fire department, and George Washington, who stayed in Cambridge during the Siege of Boston.

East Cambridge

East Cambridge is split into two main areas of activity, though neither has especially much to recommend it unless you're into checking out the corporate headquarters of numerous biotech and software companies that survived the dot-com bust. In the northernmost region, there's the **CambridgeSide Galleria** (see p.235), a gargantuan shopping multiplex where mall rats mingle in the neon-lit food court. A couple of blocks southwest, and adjacent to the Massachusetts Institute of Technology, **Kendall Square** grew from the ashes of the post-industrial desolation of East Cambridge in the 1960s and 1970s to become a glittering testament to the economic revival that sparked Massachusetts in the 1980s. Technology and its profits built the square, and it shows. By day, Kendall bustles with tech students and programmers lunching in chic eateries; at night, the business crowd goes home and the place becomes largely deserted. The exception to this is the Kendall Square Cinema (see p.224), which draws large crowds to see some of the best arthouse and second-run movies in the area.

The Massachusetts Institute of Technology

Occupying more than 150 acres alongside the Charles River, the **Massachusetts Institute of Technology** (**MIT**) provides an intellectual counterweight to the otherwise working-class character of East Cambridge. Originally established in Allston (see p.127) in 1865, MIT moved to this more auspicious campus across the river in 1916 and has since risen to international prominence as a major center for theoretical and practical research in the sciences. Both NASA and the Department of Defense pour funds into MIT in exchange for research and development assistance from the university's best minds. The nerdy character of MIT is reflected in the fact that everything is obsessively numbered and coded: students can, for example, go to 1-290 (the Rogers Building) for a lecture in 1.050 (Solid Mechanics), which gets you closer to a minor in 1 (Civil and Environmental Engineering).

Architecturally speaking, the campus buildings and their layout also reflect this quirky character, emphasizing function and peppering it with a peculiar notion of form. MIT is also undergoing a major expansion project that's so ambitious, there's no scheduled completion date; details of the latest additions can be found at ⓦweb.mit.edu/evolving.

The Rogers Building

Behind the massive pillars that guard the entrance of MIT's main building, the **Rogers Building**, at 77 Massachusetts Ave, you'll find a labyrinth of corridors – known to Techies as the **Infinite Corridor** – through which students can traverse the entire east campus without ever going outside. Atop the Rogers Building is MIT's best-known architectural icon, a massive gilt hemisphere called the **Great Dome**. Just inside the entrance to Rogers, you'll find the **MIT Information Center** (Mon–Fri 9am–5pm), which dispenses free campus maps and advice.

The Ray and Maria Stata Center

Despite looking like a set of egg timers designed by Salvador Dalí, the **Ray and Maria Stata Center**, which houses the Computer, Information, and Intelligence Sciences departments, is the $200 million work of renowned architect Frank Gehry and was partly funded by Bill Gates of Microsoft. Opened in May 2004, this was the newest addition to the MIT campus at the time of writing; self-guided tours of the public spaces on the first and third floors are possible Mon–Fri 9am–5pm. There are several entrances to the building, all of which lead to Student Street, bizarrely located *in* the building. An information desk is conspicuous by its location under a huge question mark hanging from the ceiling.

△ The Ray and Maria Stata Center at MIT

The Kresge Auditorium and MIT Chapel

MIT has drawn the attention of some of the major architects of the twentieth century, who have used the university's progressiveness as a testing ground for their more experimental ideas. Two of these works can be found in the courtyard across Massachusetts Avenue from the Rogers Building. The **Kresge Auditorium**, designed by Finnish architect Eero Saarinen, features an impressive rounded roof – though its real claim to fame is that it amazingly rests on three, rather than four, corners; Saarinen designed the structure over breakfast, using his grapefruit as a model. In the same courtyard is his red-brick **MIT Chapel**, shaped like a stocky cylinder with an abstract sculpture crafted from paper-thin metals serving as a rather unconventional spire; inside, a delicate metal screen scatters light patterns across the floor.

A couple of blocks back toward Kendall Square, the I.M. Pei-designed **Weisner Building** hosts the **List Visual Art Center** (Tues–Sun noon–6pm; free), which displays student works; heavily influenced by science and relying on a great deal of computer design, they're often more technologically impressive than visually appealing.

The MIT Museum

Of much greater interest than the Art Center is the **MIT Museum**, near Central Square at 265 Massachusetts Ave (Tues–Fri 10am–5pm, Sat & Sun noon–5pm; $5; ☎617/253-4444, ⊛web.mit.edu/museum). The museum has several permanent displays, of which the holography exhibit, a collection of seriously cool eye-trickery, and the Metafield Maze, a virtual reality labyrinth projected onto the floor, are both sure to delight. Another chamber hosts Mind and Hand, a dry retrospective on 150 years of MIT; the highlight is a small retrospective on some of the pranks ("hacks") pulled by Techies, which details how the madcap funsters wreaked havoc at the annual Harvard–Yale football game, once landing a massive weather balloon in the middle of the gridiron.

Northwest Cambridge and Somerville

Off any university-oriented or colonial heritage sightseeing circuit, **Northwest Cambridge** has more mundane charms on offer. If the amorphous area has a center, it's **Porter Square**, a mile north of Harvard Square along Massachusetts Avenue. The walk from Harvard will take you past some of Cambridge's most chic lounges and boutiques, while Porter Square itself is hard to miss – look for the 46-foot red kinetic sculpture *Gift of the Wind*, by Susumu Shingu; it's right outside the subway stop. Just before this gargantuan mobile is the **Porter Exchange**, a mall of mostly unimpressive shops, save for an obscure hallway lined with tiny Japanese food outlets – cramped bar-style restaurants where, unless you speak Japanese, you'll have to point to the menu to order.

Strawberry Hill

In the lowest corner of Northwest Cambridge, just to the east of the Fresh Pond reservoir, slopes the gentle grade of **Strawberry Hill**, whose main street, **Huron Avenue**, runs up and around it. This slice of upper-middle-class suburbia is serene and arboreal, one with a charming array of apothecaries and specialty shops. *Formaggio Kitchen*, at no. 244, has some of the best cheeses in town, and the bookshelves at Bryn Mawr Book Shop, 373 Huron Ave, still open onto the street. Places like these make for a lovely promenade, but needn't be major stops on your itinerary – the area is predominantly local, and there are no sights to speak of.

Davis Square

Beyond Porter Square, sleepy **Somerville**'s ongoing "discovery" by young residents is reflected in the gentrification of the area's central plaza, **Davis Square**, a former working–class stronghold. You're unlikely to make it this far out, however, unless you're angling to jump on the scenic **Minuteman Bike Trail**, which begins nearby, at the Alewife **T** stop, and continues through Arlington and Lexington to Bedford (☎651/542-BIKE, ☻www.massbike .org). Still, if you've got the time to spare, the square itself is a fun place to kick around for an afternoon. Homey coffee shops face the square's central plaza, which, on weekends, is typically occupied by folksy musicians and street performers.

Out of the city

While there's enough of interest in Boston itself to keep you going for several days at the very least, the city lies at the center of a region concentrated with historic sights, and there's plenty to see and do within a relatively short distance, though most of it merits little more than a half-day visit. Perhaps the best inland day trip you (or history buffs, at least) can make within a 25-mile radius of Boston is to the revolutionary battle-grounds of **Lexington** and **Concord**, but the city also makes an excellent base for visiting the numerous quaint and historic towns that line the North Shore of the Massachusetts coast. With its gruesome witch trials, **Salem,** around thirty minutes by train from North Station, is often travelers' first place of interest, and there's much more there besides, notably sights highlighting its prosperous days as a major port. Nearby **Marblehead** is pretty enough to merit a wander, too, if lacking any real must-sees; after a short stop there, you can continue on to the more rustic **Gloucester**, the setting of Sebastian Junger's book *The Perfect Storm*, and **Rockport**, worthwhile if you have the time and are captivated by the faded glories of the New England fishing trade. Route 1 is the quickest way up the coast, though coastal Route 1A is more scenic. **Buses** run up this direction as well, operated both by the MBTA and by independent tour companies (see p.37) as does the MBTA commuter rail, with **trains** leaving regularly from Boston's North Station, on the Orange and Green lines.

On the South Shore, the 1627 Pilgrim village of **Plymouth** is the main tourist draw, though it has little to offer other than recreations of Pilgrim settlements and the vessel that brought them here, the *Mayflower II*. **Provincetown** on Cape Cod, which is reachable by ferry in summer and by air in winter, is the one must-see spot within the Boston vicinity. New England's, and possibly North America's, premier gay and lesbian destination has happening street life, fantastic seafood, and stunning beaches capped by huge sand dunes.

Lexington and Concord

The sedate towns of **Lexington** and **Concord**, almost always mentioned in the same breath, trade on their notoriety as the locations of the first armed confrontation with the British during the time of the American Revolution. Lexington is mostly suburban, while Concord, five miles west, is even sleepier, though it has a bit more character. Most of the towns' historical quarters have been incorporated into the **Minute Man National Park**, which takes in the Lexington Battle Green, North Bridge, and much of Battle Road, the route the

British followed on their retreat from Concord to Boston. These famous battles are evoked in a piecemeal but relentless fashion throughout the park, with scale models, remnant musketry, and the odd preserved bullet hole. The Old Manse and The Wayside, two rambling old Concord houses with bookish pasts, are also situated on the park's grounds, while other literary sights, like **Walden Pond** in Concord, lie just beyond its boundaries. It's worth noting that, despite being accessible from Boston by train, a car is really necessary here, due to the distances between sites and the lack of decent public transport.

Lexington

The main thing to see in **Lexington** is the wide-open space called **Battle Green**. The land serves as the town's common and is fronted by Henry Kitson's iconic *Minute Man* statue. This imposing bronze figure of Captain John Parker bearing a musket, built in 1900, stands on boulders dislodged from the stone walls behind which the colonial militia fired at their British opponents on April 19, 1775.

On the eastern periphery of the green, the **visitor's center** (daily: April–Nov 9am–5pm; Dec–March 9am–4pm, free; ☎781/862-7753, ⊛www.nps .gov/mima) has a diorama that shows the detail of the battle and a host of revolutionary regalia belonging to both sides. Facing the green, the **Buckman Tavern** (April–mid-Nov Mon–Sat 10am–5pm, Sun noon–5pm; 30–45min guided tour; $5; ☎781/862-5598, ⊛www.lexingtonhistory.org/buckman_ 2002), an eighteenth-century bar and hostelry that served as the Minute Men's headquarters while awaiting news of British incursion, looks like a typical pub, right down to its seven-foot-wide fireplace and lengthy tap bar on the first floor. The tour includes a visit to the spare, upper chambers, but the only bonafide vestige of revolutionary activity is the hole from a British bullet that's been preserved in an inner door near the taproom.

A couple of blocks north, at 36 Hancock St, a plaque affixed to the brown, two-story **Hancock–Clarke House** (mid-March to late Oct Mon–Sat 11.30am–4.30pm, Sun 1–4.30pm; 30–45min guided tour $5; ☎781/862-1703) solemnly reminds that this is where "Samuel Adams and John Hancock were sleeping when aroused by Paul Revere"; the latter was the grandson of Reverend John Hancock, the man for whom the house was built in 1698. Exhibits on the free-admission first floor include the drum on which William Diamond beat the signal for the Minute Men to converge and the pistols that British Major John Pitcairn lost on the retreat from Concord. Less interesting is the small wooden **Munroe Tavern**, somewhat removed from the town center at 1332 Massachusetts Ave (April–late Oct Mon–Sat 11.30am–4.30pm, Sun 1–4.30pm; 30–45min guided tour; $5; ☎781/862-2016), which served as a field hospital for British soldiers, though only for a mere hour and a half. If you intend to visit all three sights, you'll save a bit by getting a combination ticket ($10), available at any of the three.

If you're looking to have a **meal**, you might want to try *Via Lago*, at 1845 Massachusetts Ave (☎781/861-6174), a casual counter-service spot that's good on fresh, tasty pastas, sandwiches, and salads; or you can head to *Vinny Testa's*, 20 Waltham St (☎781/860-5200), for heaping portions of reliable Italian fare like fennel sausage lasagna and spaghetti bolognese.

Concord

One of the few sizable inland towns of New England at the time of the Revolution, **Concord**, a fifteen-minute drive on Route 2 west of Lexington, and

△ *Minute Man* statue in Lexington's Battle Green

a forty-minute train ride ($5 one way) from Boston's North Station, retains a pleasant country atmosphere despite its reputation as just another wealthy western suburb. Trains arrive at Concord Station, about half a mile from the city center, and within walking distance of the rambling **Colonial Inn** (☎1-800/370-9200, ⊛www.concordscolonialinn.com), near the corner of Main and Monument streets. An old hostelry with a traditional dining room and a tavern that served as a makeshift revolutionary hospital during the war, the inn is also a good place to stop for a pint or a hearty lunch.

From the top of **Hill Burying Ground** to the west, you can survey Concord, as did Major Pitcairn when the Americans amassed on the far side of North Bridge. A few blocks behind it on Route 62 is **Sleepy Hollow Cemetery** – though not the one of headless horsemen fame that is located far from here in the Hudson River Valley. You will, however, find eminent Concord literati Emerson, Hawthorne, Thoreau, and Louisa May Alcott buried atop the graveyard's "Author's Ridge," as signs clearly indicate.

North Bridge and Old Manse

The most hyped spot in Concord, **North Bridge** is the site of the first effective armed resistance to British rule in America. If you take the traditional approach from Monument Street, you'll be following the route the British took. Just before crossing the bridge, an inscription on the mass grave of some British regulars reads, "They came 3000 miles and died to keep the past upon its throne." The bridge itself, however, looks a bit too well-preserved to provoke much sentiment, and no wonder – it's actually a 1954 replica of yet another replica of the original structure.

A stone's throw from North Bridge, the gray-clapboard **Old Manse**, at 269 Monument St (mid-April to Oct Mon–Sat 10am–5pm, Sun noon–5pm; $8; ☎978/369-3909, ⊛www.concord.org/town/manse/old_manse), was built for Ralph Waldo Emerson's grandfather, the Reverend William Emerson, in 1770. The younger Emerson lived here on and off, and, in 1834, penned *Nature* here, the book that signaled the beginning of the Transcendentalist movement. Of the numerous rooms in the house, all with period furnishings intact, the most interesting is the small upstairs study, where Nathaniel Hawthorne, a resident of the house in the early 1840s, wrote *Mosses from an Old Manse*, a rather obscure book that gave the place its name. Hawthorne passed three happy years here shortly after getting married to his wife, Sophia, who, following a miscarriage, used her diamond wedding ring to etch the words "Man's accidents are God's purposes" into a window pane in the study. Another point of interest can be found on the first floor, where there's a framed swath of original English-made wallpaper with the British "paper tax" mark stamped on the back.

The Wayside and Concord Museum

Another literary landmark, **The Wayside**, is east of the town center at 455 Lexington Rd (April–Oct Tues, Wed, Fri 2pm and 4pm, Sat & Sun 11am, 1.30pm, 3pm, 4.30pm; $4; ☎978/318-7825, ⊛www.nps.gov/mima/wayside). The 300-year-old yellow wooden house was once home to both the Alcotts and the Hawthornes, though at different times. Louisa May Alcott's girlhood experiences here formed the basis for *Little Women* (though she actually penned the novel next door at the Orchard House, where the family lived from 1858 to 1867 and her father, Bronson, founded his School of Philosophy). Among the antique furnishings, the most unusual is the slanted writing desk at which Hawthorne toiled standing up, in the fourth-floor "tower" he added on for that purpose. If you don't feel like taking a guided tour, the small but very well-presented **museum** (free) at the admissions area provides a brief overview of the home.

Just down the road at no. 200 stands the excellent **Concord Museum** (Jan–March Mon–Sat 11am–4pm, Sun 1–4pm; April–Dec Mon–Sat 9am–5pm, Sun noon–5pm; $8; ☎978/369-9763, ⊛www.concordmuseum.org). Located on the site of Emerson's apple orchard, it has more than a dozen galleries displaying period furnishings from eighteenth- and nineteenth-century Concord, including a sizable collection of Thoreau's personal effects, such as the bed from his Walden Pond hut (see below). More interesting, however, are the Revolutionary War artifacts throughout, such as one of the signal lanterns hung from the Old North Church in Boston, to warn of the British march.

When hunger strikes, you can try the *Cheese Shop*, at 29 Walden St (☎978/369-5778), a great place to stop for deluxe picnic fixings from pâté and jellies to, of course, all manner of cheeses. If you favor a sit-down meal, head to *Walden Grille*, 24 Walden St (☎978/371-2233), a refurbished nineteenth-century firehouse, for chicken quesadillas, baby spinach with sliced pear salad, or crisp fried oysters. Main courses start at $8.

Walden Pond

Though the tranquility that Thoreau sought and savored at **Walden Pond**, just two miles south of Concord proper off Route 126 (daily dawn–dusk; $5 parking; ☎978/369-3254, ⊛www.mass.gov/dem/parks/wldn), is for the most part gone – thanks mainly to the masses of tourists who pour in to retrace his footsteps – the place itself has remained much the same since the author's famed two-year exercise in self-sufficiency began in 1845. "I did not feel crowded or confined in the least," he wrote of his life in the simple log cabin; and, though his semi-fictionalized account of the experience might have you believing otherwise, Thoreau hardly roughed it, taking regular walks into town to stock up on amenities and receiving frequent visitors at his single-room hut.

The reconstructed **cabin**, complete with a journal open on its rustic desk, is situated near the parking lot (you'll have to content yourself with peering through the windows), while the site of the original structure, closer to the shores of the pond, is marked out with stones. The pond itself, which spans about a quarter-mile across (and is only half a mile long), is quite the popular swimming hole. The water looks best at dawn, when the pond still "throws off its nightly clothing of mist"; late-risers should plan an off-season visit to maximize their transcendental experience of it all.

Salem

If you arrive in **Salem** on the commuter rail from Boston's North Station ($3.50 one-way), the first thing you'll see when disembarking is a wrecking yard – but don't let that put you off. Salem, just sixteen miles from Boston on I-95, is a quaint little town with an unusual history that's more than worth discovering on an overnight stay. This is where Puritan self-righteousness reached its apogee in the horrific **witch trials** of 1692, and the place uses the stigma to its advantage by hyping up the correlating spookiness, especially around **Halloween**, which, despite some of the cheesiness on offer, is a great time to

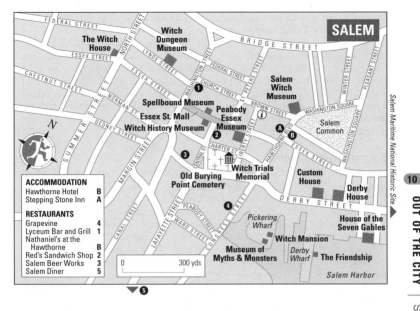

visit. Around the holiday, sites are open longer, myriad special events, talks, and walking tours are held, and you get the chance to do some leaf-peeping during New England's spectacular fall season (ⓦwww.hauntedhappenings.org).

To gather **information**, head to the helpful Salem National Visitor's Center, at 2 New Liberty St (daily 9am–5pm; ☎978/740-1650, ⓦwww.salemweb .com), which also serves as the Salem Heritage Trail's unofficial starting point (see overleaf). The **Salem Trolley** (April–Oct 10am–5pm; $10; ☎978/744 5469, ⓦwww.salemtrolley.com), just one way to see the town, is an hour-long tour run by entertaining guides and allows you to hop on and off at leisure.

Accommodation

While there are around a dozen hotels in Salem and its immediate surrounds, most of them are of the chain motel variety. Visitors wishing to stay overnight will find just a couple of places that stand out.

Hawthorne Hotel 18 Washington Square West ☎978/744-4080, ⓦwww.hawthornehotel .com. Built in 1920, this restored hotel, furnished with eighteenth-century reproduction furnishings, is the place to stay in Salem. Rooms are smart and comfortable, and wireless Internet access is available. An adjoining B&B is also on the property. Rates start from $80 per night.

Stepping Stone Inn 19 Washington Square ☎978/741-8900, ⓦwww.thesteppingstoneinn .com. This B&B, located next to the Salem Witch Museum, has eight rooms. Closed Dec–March. Rooms start from $95 and include full breakfast.

The town

Less known than its witch-trials past were the many years Salem spent as a flourishing seaport (in 1790 it was the sixth biggest city in the country), and the remnants from this era only add to the unsettling aura, with abandoned wharves, rows of stately sea captains' homes, and an astounding display of riches at the **Peabody Essex Museum**.

Today, the 1.7-mile **Salem Heritage Trail** (modeled after Boston's Freedom Trail, red-brick and all) links the town's principal historic sights, the majority of which are tied to the town's gruesome witch-hanging days. In an even more ironic twist of history, a sizable (around 5000 at the last count) and highly visible contingent of **Wiccans** now live proudly in modern Salem. These latter-day sorceresses are more than willing to accept modest fees for their fortune-telling services; keep in mind they're as much a part of the tourist industry as everything else in Salem.

Salem's witch sights

The **Salem Witch Museum**, at 19½ Washington Square (daily: July–Aug 10am–7pm; Sept–June 10am–5pm; $6.50; ☎978/744-1692 or 1-800/544-1692, ⊛www.salemwitchmuseum.com), is the hokiest of all Salem's sites involving the trials. Its self-billing as a multimedia sound-and-light show makes it sound grander than it actually is: wax figures are used to depict the hysteria, and, thanks to the museum's circular seating arrangement, there are significant portions of the show where you can't actually see what's happening. Nonetheless, that it's housed in a suitably spooky former Romanesque church enhances the atmosphere, and the show offers a decent orientation on the events of 1692. In front of the museum is the imposing statue of a caped **Roger Conant**, founder of the town's original 1626 Puritan settlement, which was called Naumkeag after the eponymous river; the name was changed to Salem – a bastardization of "shalom" (meaning peace) – in 1629.

Salem's downtown thoroughfare, Essex Street Pedestrian Mall, is littered with museums and stores selling witch-related paraphernalia with varying degrees of tact and taste. The **Spellbound Museum**, at 190 Essex St (April–Oct 10am–5pm; Nov–March call for hours; $10; ☎978/745-0138, ⊛www.spellboundtours.com), is one of the best museums in town and displays a range of curios from around the world, like shrunken heads, vampire hunting kits, and tools used by practitioners of voodoo. The museum also hosts an entertaining evening ghost-hunting tour (daily at 8pm; $12) around the town's supposedly haunted sights; visitors are encouraged to take as many pictures as possible in the hope of capturing light anomalies called "orbs" – supposedly the first manifestations of spirits – on camera. At the **Witch History Museum**, 197-201 Essex St (daily 10am–5pm; $6; ☎978/741-7770, ⊛www.witchhistorymuseum.com), you can catch an impressive live presentation of the witch trials and tour a slightly hokey recreation of "Old Salem" village. On the west side of town, the **Witch Dungeon Museum**, at 16 Lynde St (April–Nov daily 10am–5pm; $6; ☎978/741-3570, ⊛www.witchdungeon.com), occupies a nineteenth-century clapboard church and treats visitors to farcical re-enactments of key witch trial-related events. Upstairs, it's the trial of Sarah Good – a pipe-smoking beggar woman falsely accused of witchcraft – based on actual court transcripts; after the show, actors escort you below ground to a re-created dungeon with prison cells no bigger than telephone booths. Dank and supremely eerie, it's not hard to believe claims that the place is haunted.

On a less sensationalistic note, two blocks further west, at 310 Essex, is Salem's only surviving house with an actual link to the trials. The misleadingly named **Witch House** (May–Nov 10am–5pm; $6; ☎978/744-8815, ⊛www.salemweb.com/witchhouse) is the former home of judge Jonathan Corwin. Furnished with antiques, the museum focuses more on Purtian life than on the trials themselves, which are only mentioned toward the end of the half-hour tour.

Wedged into a corner of the **Old Burying Point Cemetery** at Charter and Liberty streets, the **Witch Trials Memorial** is a simple series of stone blocks etched with the names of the hanged. One of the judges, John Hathorne, is also buried here.

The last two of Salem's major spooky exhibits are on the waterfront and linked through the Fright Pass combination ticket: the **Museum of Myths and Monsters** and the **Witch Mansion** (April–Nov 10am–midnight; $15; ☎978/745-7283, ⊛www.halloweeninsalem.com). The former has high-tech animation displays that depict various tales of monsters from around the world, while cleverly hidden actors set out to startle visitors; the latter hosts 3-D presentations that feature an unsavory character called Professor Nightmare, which will at least have the kids jumping from their seats.

The Peabody Essex Museum

Right up Liberty Street from the Witch Trials Memorial is a mix of red-brick and glass buildings that make up the **Peabody Essex Museum**, at East India Square on the Essex Street Mall (daily 10am–5pm; $13; ☎978/745-9500 or 1-866/745-1876, ⊛www.pem.org), the oldest continuously operating museum in the US. Fresh from a 2003 facelift and expansion by Canadian architect Moishe Safdie, whose trademark is the use of atrium entranceways, the museum's vast space incorporates more than thirty galleries exhibiting art and artifacts from around the world, illustrating Salem's one-time importance as a major point of trade between the Eastern and Western worlds. Founded by ship captains in 1799 to display their exotic items obtained while overseas, the museum also boasts the biggest collection of nautical paintings in the world. Other galleries hold Chinese and Japanese export art, Asian, Oceanic, and African ethnological artifacts, American decorative arts, and, in a preserved house that the museum administers, court documents from the Salem Witch Trials.

On the ground level, creatively curated whaling exhibits feature not only the requisite scrimshaw but Ambrose Garneray's gruesome 1835 painting, *Attacking the Right Whale* (which depicts five sailors killing a whale, blood and all), and the gaping lower jaw of a sperm whale. A cavernous central gallery on the second floor features fanciful figureheads from now-demolished Salem ships hung from the walls, plus the reconstructed salon from America's first yacht, *Cleopatra's Barge*, which took to the seas in 1816. Special exhibitions are found on the third floor.

The Salem Maritime National Historic Site

Little of Salem's original waterfront remains, although the 2000-foot-long **Derby Wharf** is still standing, fronted by the imposing Federalist-style **Custom House** at its head. These two, and ten other mainly residential buildings once belonging to sea captains and craftsmen, make up the **Salem Maritime National Historic Site**, which maintains a **visitor's center** at 174 Derby St (daily 9am–5pm; ☎978/740-1650, ⊛www.nps.gov/sama). The Custom House is where Nathaniel Hawthorne worked as chief executive officer for three years, a stint which he later described as "slavery." The office-like interior is rather bland, as is the warehouse in the rear, with displays of tea chests and such. Park rangers (guides, really) also give free tours of the adjacent **Derby House** (daily 9am–5pm), whose millionaire owner had it built here, overlooking the harbor, to monitor his shipping empire more closely. Next door, the **West India Goods Store** sells things like sugar and molasses and nautical knick-knacks like fishhooks common to Salem's nineteenth-century shops, including "gunpowder tea," a tightly rolled, high-grade Chinese green tea. On the water you'll find the **Friendship**, a reconstruction of a 171-foot, three-masted Salem East Indiaman that was built in 1797 and has been moored here since 1998. Daily self-guided tours are available from 9am to 5pm.

The House of the Seven Gables

The most famous sight in the waterfront area is undoubtedly the **House of the Seven Gables**, at 54 Turner St (daily: Jan–June and Nov–Dec 10am–5pm; July–Oct 10am–7pm; $11; ☎978/744-0991, ⊕www.7gables.org), a rambling old mansion by the sea that served as inspiration for Hawthorne's novel of that name. Forever the "rusty wooden house with seven acutely peaked gables" that Hawthorne described, this 1688 three-story dwelling has some other notable features, such as the bricked-off "Secret Stairway" that leads to a small room. The house was inhabited in the 1840s by Susan Ingersoll, a cousin of Hawthorne whom he often visited. The author's birthplace, a small, undistinguished house built before 1750, has been moved to the grounds, which also feature a wishing well amidst lovely surrounding gardens.

Eating and drinking

While Salem has a couple of decent restaurants, much of the fare on offer is bog standard and aimed primarily at the hordes of tourists.

Grapevine 26 Congress St ☎978/745-9335. Top-notch bistro with exotic dishes like Cambodian mussels and roasted red snapper with Thai sauce, plus good vegetarian options.

Lyceum Bar and Grill 43 Church St ☎978/745-7665. Popular spot for Yankee cooking with modern updates like dill-infused clam chowder and lobster stuffed with shrimp, scallions, ginger, and breadcrumbs.

Nathaniel's at the Hawthorne 18 Washington Square ☎978/744-4080. Upscale comfort food, featuring such items as roasted scrod and grilled pork tenderloin.

Red's Sandwich Shop 15 Central St ☎978/745-3527. Hearty breakfast and brunch fare from anything with eggs, salads and grilled sandwiches served in a stone house built in 1700.

Salem Beer Works 278 Derby St ☎978/745-2337. You can try innovative microbrews, such as Bluebeery (blueberry beer), or nouveau pub food like boneless chicken wings and smoked salmon.

Salem Diner 70 Loring Ave ☎978/741-7918. Basic diner fare in an original Sterling Streamliner diner car.

Marblehead

Adjacent to Salem, the maritime town of **Marblehead**, about a thirty-minute drive on I-95 northeast of Boston, is filled with winding streets made up of small but well-preserved private sea captains' homes that lead down to the harbor. Once the domain of Revolutionary War heroes – it was Marblehead boatmen who rowed Washington's assault force across the Delaware River to attack Trenton – it's now mainly home to Boston commuters. One thing that hasn't changed over the years is the town's dramatic setting on a series of rocky ledges overlooking the wide natural harbor, which makes it one of the East Coast's biggest **yachting centers**. The annual Race Week, the highlight of the Marblehead regatta established in 1889, takes place at the end of July.

Settled in 1629, Marblehead has largely escaped commercialism thanks to its occupants' affluence and, oddly, a severe shortage of parking. The latter should not deter you from visiting, however, as this is one of the most picturesque ports in New England. You can get a good look at it from **Fort Sewall**, which juts into the harbor at the end of Front Street; these are the remnants of fortifications the British originally built in 1644, which later protected the USS *Constitution* (on view in the Charlestown Navy Yard; see p.79) in the War of 1812. Closer to the center of town is **Old Burial Hill**, which holds the graves of more than six hundred Revolutionary War soldiers and has similarly sweeping views. **Abbot Hall**, on Washington Street (Mon, Tues, Thurs, & Fri 8am–5pm, Wed 7.30am–7pm, Sat 9am–6pm, Sun 11am–6pm), an attractive 1876 town hall which can be seen from far out at sea, houses Archibald Willard's famous patriotic painting *The Spirit of '76*, created for the Philadelphia Centennial Exposition of 1876, and the 1684 town deed signed by Nanapashemet Indians.

Given Marblehead's waterfront location, seafood headlines the town's few dining options. If you're looking for a **snack**, try *Flynnie's at the Beach*, on Devereaux Beach (☎781/639-3035; summers only), for inexpensive fish and chips. Alternatively, *The Landing*, 81 Front St (☎781/639-1266, ⊛www.thelandingrestaurant.com), serves fresh seafood in a room overlooking the harbor; you can also tuck into a steak at *The Barnacle*, 141 Front St (☎781/631-4236), while sitting on an outdoor terrace overlooking the water.

Gloucester

Founded in 1623, **Gloucester**, just forty miles north of Boston up Route 1 to 127, is the oldest fishing and trading port in Massachusetts – though years of overfishing the once cod-rich waters have robbed the town of any aura of affluence it may have had in the past. Indeed, what little fame remains stems from the tragedy of the *Andrea Gale*, a local fishing boat caught, and lost, in the worst storm in (recorded) history, when three simultaneous storms merged off the coast in October 1991 and produced 100-foot-high waves; its story is told in Sebastian Junger's *The Perfect Storm* (see "Books," p.271). The fate of all the sailors (some 100,000 total) who have perished offshore is commemorated by a 1923 bronze statue, *Man at the Wheel*, overlooking the harbor. There is little contemporary action besides – the once-ballyhooed **Rocky Neck Art Colony** is not much of a colony anymore – though a number of local artists do show their work in area galleries. Unfortunately, most of these are undistinguished, and others are downright tacky.

Gloucester's only really compelling attraction is found a short drive south along the rocky coast of Route 127: the imposing **Hammond Castle Museum**, at 80 Hesperus Ave (June–Aug daily 10am–5pm; Sept–May Sat & Sun 10am–3pm; $8; ☎978/283-7673, ⊛www.hammondcastle.org), whose builder, the eccentric financier and amateur inventor John Hays Hammond Jr, wanted to bring medieval European relics to the US. The austere fortress, which overlooks the ocean from the spot that inspired Longfellow's poem *The Wreck of the Hesperus*, is loaded with treasures, from armor and tapestries to, strangely enough, an elaborately carved wooden facade of a fifteenth-century French bakery, and the partially crushed skull of one of Columbus's shipmates. The ultimate flight-of-fancy, however, is the 30,000-gallon pool whose contents can be changed from fresh to salt water at the switch of a lever – Hammond allegedly liked to dive into it from his balcony.

Should you fancy a **meal**, stop by the *Blackburn Tavern*, at 2 Main St (☎978/282-1919), for the usual pub grub, or sit seaside at *The Studio*, 51 Rocky Neck Ave (☎978/283-4123), for steak or fresh seafood.

Rockport and around

About five miles north of Gloucester, **Rockport** is a coastal hamlet that's more self-consciously quaint than its southern neighbor – though only oppressively so on summer weekends, when it becomes tourist central. Its main drag is a thin peninsula called **Bearskin Neck**, lined with old salt-box fishermen's cottages transformed into art galleries and restaurants. The Neck rises as it reaches the sea, and there's a nice view of the rocky harbor from the end of it. Otherwise, aside from some decent antique shopping and strolling around **Dock Square** at the town's center, there isn't much doing here.

Inside the aptly named **Paper House** (daily April–Oct 10am–5pm; suggested donation), a few miles north of here in the small residential neighborhood of **Pigeon Cove**, everything is made of paper, from chairs and a piano (keys excepted) to a desk made from copies of the *Christian Science Monitor*. It's the end result of a twenty-year project undertaken in 1922 by a local mechanical engineer who "always resented the daily waste of newspaper." Decide for yourself if you think he's helped the cause.

For **food** in Rockport, the *Greenery Restaurant*, at 15 Dock Square (☎978/546-9593), has a pleasant atmosphere, with a light seafood and vegetarian menu. More upscale, *My Place by the Sea*, on Bearskin Neck (☎978/546-9667), has a stupendous seaside setting to match its delicious lobster. If you want wine with your meal, you'll have to bring your own, however, as there's none sold here; Rockport is a "dry town."

Plymouth

Though the South Shore makes a clean sweep of the coast from suburban Quincy to the former whaling port of New Bedford, really the only place of interest is tiny **Plymouth**, America's so-called "hometown," forty miles south of Boston. It's mostly given over to commemorating the landing of the 102 Pilgrims here in December of 1620 and need only be visited by people with a real interest in the story.

The famous **Plymouth Rock**, where the Pilgrims are said to have touched land, is enclosed by a solemn, pseudo-Greek temple by the sea. As is typical with most sites of this ilk, the rock is of symbolic importance only – the Pilgrims had already spent several weeks on Cape Cod before landing here, and no one can be sure where they actually did land. On the hill behind the venerable stone, the **Plymouth National Wax Museum**, at 15 Carver St (daily: March–May & Oct–Nov 9am–7pm; June–Sept 9am–9pm; closed Dec–Feb; $5; ☎508/746-6468), has a kitschy sound-and-light tableau of the early days of settlement. Down the street is the unconvincing **Pilgrim Hall Museum**, at 75 Court St (Feb–Dec daily 9.30am–4.30pm; $5; ☎508/746-1620, ⓦwww .pilgrimhall.org), where you enter a room filled with furniture that may or may not have come over on the *Mayflower*, along with numerous pairs of shoes that the Pilgrims may or may not have worn.

A more authentic attraction, and a better way to spend your time, is the replica of the *Mayflower*, called the **Mayflower II** (April–Nov daily 9am–5pm; $8; ☎508/746-1622), which was restored in 2000. The ship is berthed on the State Pier in Plymouth Harbor, but before entering the ship you'll encounter a tacky display of carboard cutouts telling the story of America's forbears. Built in Britain by English craftsmen following the detailed and historically accurate plans of an American naval architect at MIT, the *Mayflower II* was ceremoniously docked in Plymouth in 1957 and given to America as a gesture of goodwill. You're free to wander the

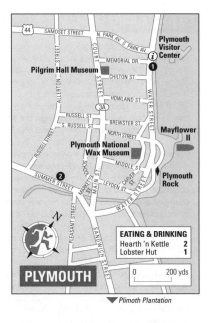

Plimoth Plantation

ship at leisure, and there are trained staff members – in contemporary clothing – available to answer any questions. Others in period costume will put on a well-presented pretence of ignorance of current events.

Similar in approach and authenticity is the **Plimoth Plantation**, three miles south of town off Route 3 (April–Nov daily 9am–5pm; $20; ☎508/746-1622, ✉www.plimoth.org). Everything you see in the plantation, such as the Pilgrim Village of 1627 and the Wampanoag Indian Settlement, has been created using traditional techniques; even the farm animals were "backbred" to resemble their seventeenth-century counterparts. Again, actors dressed in period garb try to bring you back in time; depending on your level of resistance, it can be quite enjoyable. If you intend to see both the Plantation and the *Mayflower II*, you'd do better to buy a combo ticket ($22) from the admissions desk.

If you so desire, you can slake your thirst at the *John Carver Inn*, at 25 Summer St (☎1-800/274-1620, ✉www.johncarverinn.com), which has a tavern and a **restaurant**, the *Hearth 'n Kettle*, that's an excellent setting for a very American meal, such as prime rib or meat loaf, or a drink; as far as other eating options go, the *Lobster Hut*, on the waterfront (☎508/746-2270), has good, reasonably priced seafood.

Provincetown

The brash fishing burgh of **Provincetown**, at the northeastern tip of Cape Cod, is a popular summer destination for bohemians, artists, and fun-seekers lured by the excellent beaches, art galleries, and welcoming, liberal atmosphere.

Massachusetts pilgrimage

The band of English **Pilgrims** that spurred Britain's attempt to colonize New England were way off course when their vessel, the *Mayflower*, arrived in Cape Cod harbor on November 21, 1620 – they had actually been aiming for the Hudson Valley, where the Virginia Company had granted them a parcel of land. Instead of recharting their path, however, the 102 Church of England Separatists decided to claim for themselves the land they surveyed before them. The decision prompted the 41 men aboard to draft and sign the **Mayflower Compact**, self-proclaimed as the "first written constitution in the world," which the group agreed to uphold with "all due submission and obedience"; the document became the foundation for all subsequent American governmental legalese.

After going ashore in **Provincetown**, the land party returned with reports of bleak and extreme conditions, and the lot sailed on to rocky shore a few miles west, where they disembarked during a brutal winter storm, on December 16, 1620. The group that came ashore christened the new land **Plymouth**, after their English starting point, and strove to establish a life free of the religious persecution they had known back home. In doing so, however, the Pilgrims encountered such harsh conditions that within the first year of their arrival, almost half of their number had died. Even so, when the *Mayflower* sailed once more for England the following spring, not a single Pilgrim returned with her.

The emigrants' lot changed for the better in the fall of 1621, when the harvest, which they had sown with the help of resident **Wampanoag Indians**, a local Algonquin tribe, proved bountiful. To celebrate, the Pilgrims invited the natives to join them in a three-day feast that's considered the genesis of the modern-day American **Thanksgiving**, a yearly November celebration decreed by Abraham Lincoln more than two centuries later, on October 3, 1863.

A ninety-minute ferry ride from Boston (see box, p.170), P-town, as the coastal community of some 5000 year-round residents is known, is one of America's premier gay and lesbian resorts – complete with frequent festivals and theme weekends. It also offers excellent people-watching and could well be called "Pooch Town," thanks to the number of pampered pups on parade; you may want to catch the annual Dog Olympics (in October), stop into a doggy boutique for items like sunglasses and fleeces, or pick up a treat for your pet at a dog bakery.

Thanks to a smallish population of fishermen that began settling here in the mid-1800s, P-town also has a detectable **Portuguese** culture; this legacy is now celebrated in an annual June festival with a parade, a blessing of the fleet, Portuguese food, and traditional dances.

Visitor information can be gathered at the Town Hall, 260 Commercial St (daily 9am–5pm; ☎508/487-7000, ⊛www.provincetowngov.org). You can also visit ⊛www.provincetown.com before making your trip; gay men and lesbians should check ⊛www.gayprovincetown.com.

Accommodation

P-Town's **accommodation** options run the gamut from full-scale resorts to motels, with a few B&Bs and rental villas rounding out the package. Provincetown Reservations (☎1-800/648-0364, ⊛www.ptownres.com) and Intown Reservations (☎1-800/677-8696, ⊛www.intownreservations.com) can usually rustle up lodgings at busy times. The prices below reflect the lowest rate for a standard double room throughout most of the year.

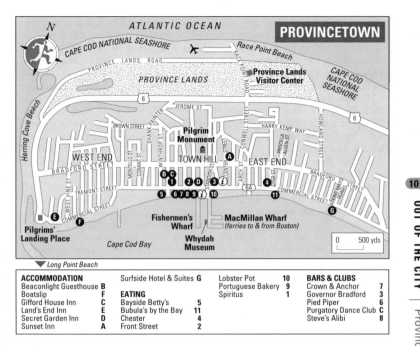

ACCOMMODATION		Surfside Hotel & Suites	**G**	Lobster Pot	**10**	BARS & CLUBS	
Beaconlight Guesthouse	**B**			Portuguese Bakery	**9**	Crown & Anchor	**7**
Boatslip	**F**	EATING		Spiritus	**1**	Governor Bradford	**3**
Gifford House Inn	**C**	Bayside Betty's	**5**			Pied Piper	**6**
Land's End Inn	**E**	Bubula's by the Bay	**11**			Purgatory Dance Club	**C**
Secret Garden Inn	**D**	Chester	**4**			Steve's Alibi	**8**
Sunset Inn	**A**	Front Street	**2**				

Beaconlight Guesthouse 12 Winthrop St ☎1-800/696 9603, ⓦ www.beaconlightguesthouse .com Stylish ten-room guest house with individually appointed rooms, equipped with air conditioning, TV, and VCR. $100.

Boatslip 161 Commercial St ☎508/487-1669, ⓦ www.glresorts.com A fun-packed resort-syle atmosphere that caters to the gay and lesbian market. Rooms equipped with refrigerators and data ports. $110.

Gifford House Inn 9–11 Carver St ☎1-800/434-0130, ⓦ www.giffordhouse.com Popular gay resort with lobby piano bar, restaurant, and the Purgatory Dance Club (see p.172); continental breakfast included in rates. $100.

Land's End Inn 22 Commercial St ☎1-800/276-7088, ⓦ www.landsendinn.com Lovingly decorated rooms and suites, many with sweeping ocean views, in a fanciful

turreted house; continental breakfast included. $110.

Secret Garden Inn 300a Commercial St ☎866/786-9646, ⓦ www.provincetown .com/secretgardeninn Four quaint rooms in a house with a veranda, done up in country furnishings, and with modern touches like TVs and air conditioning; country breakfast included. $100.

Sunset Inn 142 Bradford St ☎508/487-9810, ⓦ www.sunsetinnptown.com Clean, quiet rooms in an 1850 captain's house with double or queen beds and private or shared bath. $80.

Surfside Hotel & Suites 543 Commercial St ☎1-800/421-1726, ⓦ www.surfsideinn .cc Located at the far east end of town, this clean, recently refurbished hotel offers excellent vistas over the bay. Its location also makes it quieter than many other hotels in town. Wi-fi access available. Prices start from $100.

The town and beaches

Provincetown's center is essentially two three-mile long streets connected by nearly forty tiny lanes of no more than two short blocks each, making for a pretty compact place that's easy to get around on foot. The first of these two main strips, the aptly named **Commercial Street**, is where the action is, loaded with restaurants, cafés, art galleries, and trendy shops. Jutting right into the middle of Provincetown Harbor, just off Commercial Street, **MacMillan Wharf** is busy as well, though with whale-watching boats, yachts, and colorful old Portuguese fishing vessels. It also houses the engaging **Whydah Museum**, at 16 Macmillan Wharf (June–Aug daily 10am–7pm; May & Sept–Oct daily 10am–5pm; Nov–Dec Sat & Sun 10am–5pm; $8, free with Boston Harbor Cruises ticket; ☎508/487-8899, ⊛www.whydah.com), which displays some of the bounty from the *Whydah*, a pirate ship commandeered by "Black Sam" Bellamy that shipwrecked off the coast of Wellfleet in April 1717. The collection ranges from odds-and-ends like silver shoe buckles and flintlock pistols to rare African gold jewelry attributed to West Africa's Akan people that was likely en route to England, where it would have been melted to make guineas.

Two blocks north of the wharf, on Town Hill, is the 252-foot granite tower of the **Pilgrim Monument**, named for the Puritans who actually first landed near here before moving on to Plymouth. From the observation deck of the Florentine-style bell tower (daily May–June & Sept–Nov 9am–4.15pm; July–Aug 9am–7pm; $6; ☎508/487-1310, ⊛www.pilgrim-monument.org), accessible by stairs and ramps, the whole Cape (and sometimes Boston) can be seen. At the bottom of the hill on **Bradford Street**, the second of the two main roadways, is a bas-relief monument to the Pilgrims' **Mayflower Compact**.

In the quiet **West End** of P-Town, many of the weathered clapboard houses are decorated with colored blinds, white picket fences, and wildflowers spilling out of every possible crevice. A modest bronze **plaque** on a boulder at the western end of Commercial Street commemorates the Pilgrims' actual landing place. West of town, along Route 6A, **Herring Cove Beach** is justly famous for its sunsets, while at the Cape's northern tip, off Route 6, **Race Point Beach**, a wide strip of white sand backed by tall dunes, is the archetypal Cape Cod beach. It abuts the ethereal **Province Lands**, where vast sweeping moors and bushy dunes are threatened by a deadly sea, site of some 3000 known shipwrecks.

One of the best things to do around Provincetown is to take an organized, but unusual, tour: choose to either ramble about the dunes in a four-wheel-

Provincetown by ferry

Two companies make the trip across Massachusetts Bay to Provincetown: **Boston Harbor Cruises** departs from **Long Wharf** (daily late May to mid–June departing 9am, returning 4pm; late June to early Sept Mon–Wed departing 9am and 2pm, returning 11am and 4pm; Thurs–Sun departing 9am, 2pm, & 6.30pm, returning 11am, 4pm, & 8.30pm; early Sept to early Oct Mon departing 9am and 2pm, returning 11am and 4pm; Tues and Wed departing 9am returning 4pm; Thurs departing 9am and 6.30pm returning 4pm and 8.30pm; Fri–Sun departing 9am, 2pm, and 6.30pm and returning 11am, 4pm, and 8.30pm; $58 return; ☎617/227-4321, ⊛www.bostonharborcruises .com; Aquarium Ⓣ), while **Bay State Cruises** leaves, somewhat inconveniently, from the west side of the **World Trade Center pier** (daily late May to early Oct departing 8am, 1pm, & 5.30pm, returning 2hr later; $58 return; ☎617/748-1428, ⊛boston -ptown.com). The latter has an excellent **excursion fare** for weekend day-tripping as well: $29 will get you to P-town and back with a three-hour window to tool around in – keep in mind, though, that the boats take three hours each way (late May to early Sept Fri–Sun departing 9.30am, returning 3.30pm).

drive vehicle with **Art's Dune Tours**, at 9 Washington Ave (April–Oct 10am–dusk; $12; ☎508/487-1950 or 1-800/894-1951, ⊛www.artsdunetours .com), or fly over them in a replica 1938 biplane ($60; ☎1-888/BIPLANE or 508/428-8732; advance reservations required). Twenty-minute flights take off from the Cape Cod Airport, near the intersection of Race Lane and Route 149; if you wish, you and two friends can also opt to board a Cessna ($69; same phone) instead.

Another, simpler, way of seeing P-Town is to rent a **bike**. Arnold's, at 329 Commercial St (June–Aug 9am–7pm; Sept–May 9am–5pm; ☎508/487-0844) offers mountain bikes for four hours ($12) – ample time to cycle the excellent paths that run through the huge dunes and out to Race Point beach. If you prefer, Venture Athletics, at 220A Commercial St (☎508/487-2395), rents **kayaks** out for $3.50 an hour, allowing you to paddle your way around the harbor.

Eating

Restaurants in Provincetown range from the expected lobster-joints to those serving high-end gourmet fare.

Bayside Betty's 177 Commercial St ☎508/487-6566. Funky waterfront eatery with hearty breakfasts and seafood dinners; it's also a popular spot to grab a martini. Main courses from $13.

Bubulas by the Bay 183-185 Commercial St ☎508/487-0773, ⊛www.bubulas.com. Gaudy multicolored restaurant on the main drag that's excellent for people-watching. Service can be slow, but the focaccias ($6) and salads ($8–12) at lunchtime are well worth the wait.

Chester 404 Commercial St ☎508/487-8200, ⊛www.chesterrestaurant.com. Sophisticated pillar-fronted eatery with stellar New American menu featuring dishes like wild mushroom risotto and seared sea scallops, plus a well-chosen wine list. Expensive (most entrees are around $30) but worth it.

Front Street 230 Commercial St ☎508/487-9715, ⊛www.frontstreetrestaurant .com. Popular Italian and Continental restaurant located in a Victorian house; menu changes weekly, but you might find dishes like potato-crusted salmon with raspberry butter, and chickpea and artichoke flan.

Lobster Pot 321 Commercial St ☎508/487-0842, ⊛www.ptownlobsterpot.com. Let the landmark neon lobster sign lead you to ultrafresh and affordable crustaceans. The excellent clambake (chowder, mussels, lobster, corn-on-the-cob, and red potato) costs $26.

Portuguese Bakery 299 Commercial St ☎508/487-1803. A great stop for baked goods, particularly the fried rabanada (similar to french toast).

Spiritus 190 Commercial St ☎508/487-2808. One of the cheapest places to fill up on fabulous pizza and gourmet coffee. Open late.

Drinking and nightlife

P-town's **nightlife** is heavily geared towards a gay clientele, resulting in ubiquitous tea dances, drag shows, and video bars; some spots have terrific waterfront locations and terraces to match, making them ideal locations to sit out with a drink at sunset.

Boatslip 161 Commercial St ☎800/451-SLIP, ⊛www.glresorts.com. The Sunday tea dances at this resort are legendary; you can either dance away on a long wooden deck overlooking the water, or cruise inside under a disco ball and flashing lights.

Crown and Anchor 247 Commercial St ☎508/487-1430, ⊛onlyatthecrown.com. A massive complex housing several bars, including The Vault, P-Town's only leather bar, Wave, a video-karaoke bar, and Paramount, a cabaret with nightly acts.

Governor Bradford 312 Commercial St
℡508/487-9618. Dining on one side and a
Crow's Nest-style bar on the other. In the
bar you can play anything from backgam-
mon to the state lottery, and the spirit servings are the most generous in town.
Pied Piper 193 Commercial St ℡508/487-1527,
ⓦwww.thepied.com. Though predominantly
a lesbian club (it's the oldest one in the
country), the outdoor deck and inside
dance floor at this trendy waterfront space
attract men, too, for their longstanding

After Tea T-Dance (Sun 6.30–9pm). Thurs
is Classic Disco night; Friday and Saturday
are house nights.
Purgatory Dance Club in the *Gifford House Inn*
9–11 Carver St ℡1-800/434-0130, ⓦwww
.giffordhouse.com. P-Town's main leather
club is the place to cruise; Sunday's the
main night it all happens.
Steve's Alibi 291 Commercial St ℡508/487-
2890, ⓦwww.stevesalibi.com. Campy bar
with four daily drag shows (4pm, 7pm,
9pm, & 11pm).

Listings

Listings

Accommodation

Despite the opening of some new hotels and B&Bs over the last few years, for such a popular travel destination Boston has a surprisingly limited range of reasonably priced **accommodation**. Though there are still bargains to be found, prices at many formerly moderate hotels have inched into the expense-account range: you're looking at spending upwards of $200 just to stay the night during **high season** – which, while not unanimously agreed upon, is often late summer and early fall.

Your best bet to save money is to make your booking online: most hotels offer discounted rates on their websites, as do discount **booking agencies** like Orbitz (Ⓦhotels.orbitz.com). If you call, be sure to inquire about special packages when reserving a room. Additional discounts can often be had with an AAA membership, which usually knocks around ten percent off the rate. Your other option, if you don't mind braving the sharp East Coast winter, is to come in the **off-season**, usually November through April, when many hotels not only have more vacancies but also offer weekend package discounts. At any other time of year, be sure to make reservations well in advance. September (start of the school year) and May through June (graduation) are particularly busy months, due to the large student population here. October, when leaf-peeping season starts, is also expensive.

In response to the hotel crunch, some visitors turn to less-expensive **bed and breakfasts**, many of which are tucked into renovated brownstones in Back Bay; other good B&B choices can be found outside the city center, in Brookline and Cambridge. Short-term **furnished apartments**, spread throughout the city, are another option, though most have two-week minimums. There are also a handful of decent **hostels** if you're looking for truly budget accommodation.

Throughout this chapter we give a price for hotels, B&Bs, and hostels. It reflects the lowest price for a standard double room for most of the year – although, depending on availability and season, you may end up paying up to two or three times more.

Finally, all accommodations are **keyed** to the relevant **chapter map** in the Guide portion of this book; see the index for page numbers.

Hotels

Boston and Cambridge combined have an underwhelming fifty or so hotels between them, a shortage that helps, somewhat, to explain their exorbitant prices.

While Boston hotels are not suited to every traveler's budget, they do cater to most tastes and range from the usual assortment of chains to some excellent independently run hotels, the highest concentration of which – including some of the best – are in **Back Bay**. Most of the business hotels are located in or around the **Financial District**.

Modestly cheaper rates can be found at **Cambridge**'s hotels, though rates at these, too, go sky-high around college commencement and during the fall. A handful of gay-friendly hotels, mostly in the **South End**, are listed in the Gay Boston chapter on p.226.

Downtown

Boston Harbor Hotel 70 Rowes Wharf ☏617/439-7000 or 1-800/752-7077, ⊛www .bhh.com; Aquarium T. Opulent accommodation in an atmosphere of studied corporate elegance. There's a health club, pool, gracious concierge staff, and rooms with harbor and city views; the former are substantially pricier. $210.

△ Boston Harbor Hotel

Boston Marriott Long Wharf 296 State St ☏617/227-0800 or 1-888/236-2427, ⊛www .marriott.com; Aquarium T. All the rooms here boast harbor views, but the stunning vaulted lobby is what really makes this *Marriott* stand out. The rooms themselves are standard business-class affairs, with the expected high-speed Internet access, in-room movies, and generic furnishings. $199.

Harborside Inn 185 State St ☏617/723-7500, ⊛www.hagopianhotels.com; State T. This small hotel is housed in a renovated 1890s mercantile warehouse across from Quincy Market. The (relatively) reasonably priced rooms – with exposed brick, hardwood floors, and cherry furniture – are a welcome surprise for this part of town. $155.

Hyatt Regency 1 Avenue de Lafayette; ☏617/912-1234, ⊛bostonfinancial.hyatt.com; Downtown Crossing T. The *Hyatt* is just one of the reasons for Downtown Crossing's regeneration over the past years. The plush hotel is beautifully furnished with antiques, and there's a fantastic array of services. Wi-fi Internet access available. $169.

Langham Hotel 250 Franklin St ☏617/451-1900, ⊛www.langhamhotels.com; State T. This stern granite building in the heart of the Financial District is the former Federal Reserve Bank of Boston and was, until 2004, the home of Boston's Le Meridien. The hotel's spacious rooms are decorated in a contemporary French style, and each one features cable TV, high-speed Internet access, Italian marble bathrooms, and more. $245.

Marriott's Custom House 3 McKinley Sq ☏617/310-6300 or 1-888/236-2427, ⊛www.marriott.com; Aquarium T. All the rooms at this Downtown landmark-turned-hotel are high-end, one-bedroom suites with spectacular Boston Harbor and city views; there's also a great gym on the top floor. $169.

Millennium Bostonian Hotel Faneuil Hall Mar-ketplace ☏617/523-3600 or 1-866/866-8086, ⊛www.millenniumhotels.com; State T. Right in the heart of Downtown, the *Millennium Bostonian* has splendid quarters, some with fireplaces and – unusual for Boston – balconies. The rooms and lobby are festooned with portraits of famous colonial-era figures; common areas have wi-fi access. $139.

Milner 78 Charles St South ☏617/426-6220 or 1-877/MILNERS, ⊛www.milner-hotels.com; Boylston T. An uninspiring but afford-able hotel, the *Milner* is convenient to the Theater District, Bay Village, and the Public Garden. All room rates include a continental breakfast, served in a European-style nook in the lobby. $89.

Nine Zero Hotel 90 Tremont St ☏617/772-5800 or 1-800/434-7347, ⊛www.ninezerohotel.com;

Park St T. Executive-class boutique hotel with 190 polished quarters equipped with high-speed Internet access, wi-fi, CD players, and VCRs, as well as cushy linens. $229.

Omni Parker House 60 School St ⊤617/227-8600 or 1-800/843-6664, ⓦ www .omniparkerhouse.com; **Park T.** Though the present building only dates from 1927, the *Omni Parker House* is the oldest continuously operating hotel in the US. The lobby, decorated in dark oak with carved gilt moldings, recalls the splendor of the original nineteenth-century building. The rooms, which have free high-speed Internet access, are small, however, and a bit dowdy. $129.

Tremont House 275 Tremont St ⊤617/426-1400, ⓦ www.marriott.com; **NE Medical Center T.** The opulent lobby of this *Marriott*-managed 1925 hotel, the former national headquarters of the Elks Lodge, somewhat compensates for its rather small rooms; and if you want to be in the thick of the Theater District you can't do better. $120.

XV Beacon 15 Beacon St ⊤617/670-1500 or 1-877/XVBEACON, ⓦ www.xvbeacon.com; **Park St T.** Ultra-decadent boutique hotel across from the Boston Athenaeum, with 61 spectacular rooms equipped with marble bathrooms, Kiehl toiletries, CD player, beautiful upholstery, and working gas fireplaces; some rooms even have four-poster beds. All rates include access to your own chauffered Mercedes for the length of your stay. $295.

Charlestown

Constitution Inn YMCA 150 Second Ave ⊤617/241-8400 or 1-800/495-9622, ⓦ www .constitutioninn.com. Despite its billing as a YMCA, this inn, which is easily connected to Downtown by ferry, has 150 private rooms equipped with cable TV, air conditioning, and private baths; there's also an on-site weight room, sauna, and pool. Though predominantly servicing military personnel, civilians are more than welcome. $109.

Residence Inn Boston Harbor 34-44 Charles River Ave ⊤617/242-9000, ⓦ www.marriott .com. One of Boston's newest hotels, the Marriott's *Residence Inn* is an all-suiter close to some of the main sights along the Freedom Trail. The amazing views of Boston's skyline over the river more than make up for the slightly sterile atmosphere. Wi-fi Internet access available. $99.

Beacon Hill and the West End

Beacon Hill Hotel 25 Charles St ⊤617/723-7575 or 1-888/959-BHHB, ⓦ www .beaconhillhotel.com; **Charles T.** A luxurious boutique hotel occupying two mid-1800s brownstones. Its twelve sleek chambers are decked out with flat-screen televisions, mahogany fireplaces, and louvered windows. Internet access is available in all rooms. $199.

Charles Street Inn 94 Charles St ⊤617/314-8900, ⓦ www.charlesstreetinn.com; **Charles T.** This intimate nine-room inn features lavish rooms styled after the (presumed) tastes of various Boston luminaries; the Isabella Stewart Gardner room features a Rococo chandelier, while Oliver Wendell Holmes's chamber boasts a king-sized sleigh bed. All rooms come with working fireplaces, too. $250.

Holiday Inn Select – Government Center 5 Blossom St ⊤617/742-7630 or 1-800/HOLIDAY, ⓦ www.holiday-inn.com; **Bowdoin T.** Somewhat misleadingly named – it's located in the West End and more convenient to Beacon Hill than Government Center – this Holiday Inn-standard property has all the modern accoutrements, including a weight room and pool. $170.

The John Jeffries House 14 David G Mugar Way ⊤617/367-1866, ⓦ www.johnjeffrieshouse .com; **Charles T.** Mid-scale, recently renovated hotel at the foot of Beacon Hill, with a cozy lounge and rooms done up in Victorian style, with cable TV and air conditioning; single-occupancy studios include kitchenettes. And, though it's wedged in between a busy highway and the local T stop, multipaned windows keep most of the sound out. $95.

Onyx Hotel 155 Portland St ⊤617/557-0005, ⓦ www.onyxhotel.com; **North Station T.** The stark, glass-paneled front of this small luxury hotel belies an opulent interior.The Ruby Room bar is great for a nightcap. $189.

The Shawmut Inn 280 Friend St ⊤617/720-5544 or 1-800/350-7784, ⓦ www.shawmutinn .com; **North Station T.** Located in the old West End near the FleetCenter, the *Shawmut Inn* has 66 comfortable, modern rooms, all of which come equipped with kitchenettes and include continental breakfast. Nothing special, but not bad at all for the price. $90.

Back Bay

Back Bay Hilton 40 Dalton St ☎617/236-1100 or 1-800/874-0663, ⓦwww.hilton.com; Hynes **T**. Though this chain hotel is fairly charmless, it does have good weekend packages, a fitness room and pool, as well as a guaranteed good American-style breakfast at the hotel's informal restaurant, *Boodle's* (see review p.201). It's actually a bit away from Back Bay, closer to the bohemian area of the Berklee College of Music than the shops of Newbury Street – a plus in some folks' eyes. $130.

Boston Park Plaza Hotel & Towers 64 Arlington St ☎617/426-2000 or 1-800/225-2008, ⓦwww.bostonparkplaza.com; Arlington **T**. The *Park Plaza* is practically its own neighborhood, housing the original *Legal Seafoods* restaurant (see p.203) and three other eateries, plus offices for American, United, and Delta airlines. Its old-school elegance and hospitality – plus its central location – make it stand out; the high-ceilinged rooms are comfortable, too. $109.

Charlesmark Hotel 655 Boylston St ☎617/247-1212, ⓦwww.thecharlesmark.com; Copley **T**. A European-style hotel with 33 cozy, smallish rooms featuring beechwood furnishings and modern accoutrements, such as CD players, VCRs, and dataports. $119.

The Colonnade 120 Huntington Ave ☎617/424-7000 or 1-800/962-3030, ⓦwww .colonnadehotel.com; Prudential **T**. With its beige poured-concrete shell, the *Colonnade* is barely distinguishable from the Church of Christ buildings directly across the street. Still, there are spacious rooms (if at a price) and, in summer, a rooftop pool – the only one in Boston. $350.

Copley Square Hotel 47 Huntington Ave ☎617/536-9000 or 1-800/225-7062, ⓦwww .copleysquarehotel.com; Copley **T**. Situated on the eastern fringe of Copley Square, this family-run, low-key hotel is popular with a predominantly European crowd. The rooms won't win any style awards, given their dowdy linens, but they're spacious enough and equipped with modem hook-ups, cable TV, coffeemakers, and the like. $180.

Eliot 370 Commonwealth Ave ☎617/267-1607 or 1-800/442-5468, ⓦwww.eliothotel.com; Hynes **T**. West Back Bay's answer to the

Ritz-Carlton, this plush, nine-floor suite hotel has sizable rooms with kitchenettes, luxurious Italian marble baths, huge beds with Egyptian cotton sheets, and wi-fi access. $215.

Fairmont Copley Plaza 138 St James Ave ☎617/267-5300 or 1-800/795-3906, ⓦwww.fairmont.com; Copley **T**. Built in 1912, the *Fairmont* has long boasted Boston's most elegant lobby, with its glittering chandeliers, mirrored walls, and trompe l'oeil sky. Most rooms are decorated in a French Neoclassical style and have high-speed Internet access (wi-fi is available in the lounge). Even if you don't stay here, be sure to have a martini in the fabulous *Oak Bar* (see p.211), with its high-coffered ceilings and mahogany chairs. $199.

Four Seasons 200 Boylston St ☎617/338-4400 or 1-800/332-3442, ⓦwww.fourseasons.com; Arlington **T**. The tops in city accommodation, with 288 large rooms. The penthouse-level health spa has an indoor pool that seems to float over the Public Garden, and the superlative *Aujourd'hui* restaurant (see p.201) is housed here, too. $350.

Jurys Boston Hotel 350 Stuart St ☎617/226-7200, ⓦwww.jurysdoyle.com; Copley Square **T**. Set in a 1920s building that used to be Boston Police headquarters, the 220 smallish rooms in this lavishly furnished hotel have huge beds, marble bathrooms, multi-head showers, and heated towel racks. The function rooms are named after the celebrated Irish writers Shaw, Yeats, Beckett, Joyce, and Wilde; displays in the lobby show old police memorabilia. $165.

The Lenox 710 Boylston St ☎617/536-5300 or 1-800/225-7676, ⓦwww.lenoxhotel.com; Copley **T**. Billed as Boston's version of the New York's *Waldorf-Astoria* when its doors first opened in 1900, the *Lenox* – after a recent renovation – is still one of the most upscale hotels in the city, with 212 rooms featuring high ceilings, walk-in closets, and, in some, working fireplaces. $308.

Marriott at Copley Place Copley Place ☎617/236-5800 or 1-800/228-9290; ⓦwww .marriott.com; Copley **T**. There's not a whole lot of character here but it's modern, clean, and well-located, with an indoor pool. Ask about lower weekend rates that include full breakfast. $179.

Ritz-Carlton 15 Arlington St ☏617/536-5700 or 1-800/241-3333, ⓦwww.ritzcarlton.com; **Arlington T.** This is the *Ritz-Carlton* flagship, and even if the rooms are a bit cramped, the hotel retains a certain air of refinement, especially after a multimillion-dollar refurbishment to celebrate the hotel's 75th anniversary in 2004. There are excellent views of the Public Garden from the second-floor dining room or street-level *Ritz Bar.* $345.

Sheraton Boston Hotel 39 Dalton St ☏617/236-2000 or 1-800/325-3535; ⓦwww.sheraton.com/boston Hynes **T.** After a major renovation, the Sheraton is looking less like a chain and more like a Back Bay boutique. Featuring sleigh beds with pillow-top mattresses and an expanded in-room work area, the *Sheraton* mostly plays host to convention-goers – the Hynes Convention Center and Prudential Center are both connected to the hotel. $129.

Westin Copley Place ☏617/262-9600 or 1-800/228-3000, ⓦwww.westin.com; **Copley T.** Rooms are modern and spacious at this well-located hotel. Always hopping with convention-goers, it's a lively place to hole up in winter. Be sure to request a room facing the Charles River. $289.

Kenmore Square and the Fenway

The Buckminster 645 Beacon St ☏617/236-7050 or 1-800/727-2825, ⓦwww.bostonhotelbuckminster.com; **Kenmore T.** Though renovated not so long ago, the 1905 *Buckminster*, with its antique furnishings, retains the feel of an old Boston hotel. Its Kenmore Square location also puts it within easy walking distance of Fenway Park and Boston University. Great rates, too. $80.

Gryphon House 9 Bay State Rd ☏617/375-9003 or 1-877/375-9003, ⓦgryphonhouseboston.com; **Kenmore T.** This hotel-cum-B&B around the corner from Fenway has eight wonderfully appointed suites equipped with working gas fireplaces, cable TV, VCR, CD player, high-speed Internet connection, continental breakfast, and free parking (a big plus in Boston). You won't want to leave your room. $149.

Hotel Commonwealth 500 Commonwealth Ave ☏617/933-5000, ⓦwww

.hotelcommonwealth.com; **Kenmore T.** Old-world charm mixed with modern decor makes this a welcome addition to Boston's luxury hotel scene. $269.

Cambridge

Cambridge Marriott 2 Cambridge Center ☏617/494-6600 or 1-800/228-9290, ⓦwww.marriott.com; **Kendall T.** Stately, well-appointed rooms with a minimum of pretension. Many have views of the river, while the rest look out onto industrial Kendall Square. Some weekend packages include a sumptuous brunch. $210.

Charles Hotel 1 Bennett St ☏617/864-1200 or 1-800/882-1818, ⓦwww.charleshotel.com; **Harvard T.** Clean, bright rooms – some overlooking the Charles – with a good array of amenities: cable TV, Shaker furniture, and access to the adjacent WellBridge Health Spa. There's also an excellent jazz club, *Regattabar*, and restaurant, *Henrietta's Table*, on the premises – see p.217 and p.206 for reviews. $199.

Harvard Square Hotel 110 Mt Auburn St ☏617/864-5200 or 1-800/222-8733, ⓦwww.theinnatharvard.com; **Harvard T.** While its rooms aren't as elegant as its sister hotel, the *Inn at Harvard* (see overleaf), they do have a pleasant enough oak-and-burgundy decor and amenities like minifridges; great location in the midst of Harvard Square. $129.

Hotel Marlowe 25 Edwin H Land Blvd ☏1-800/825-7140, ⓦwww.hotelmarlowe.com; **Kendall Square T.** Cambridge's plushest hotel is as funky as they come, with bright, boutiquey designs in the rooms. High-speed Internet access available. $149.

Hotel @ MIT 20 Sidney St ☏617/577-0200 or 1-800/524-2538, ⓦwww.hotelatmit.com; **Kendall Square T.** Contemporary hotel anchoring an office tower near MIT, with a lobby festooned with AI robots created by the university's tech-savvy students. The modern rooms have nice touches like louvered window shades and muted color schemes, and come with high-speed Internet access, both wired and wi-fi. $129.

Hyatt Regency Cambridge 575 Memorial Drive ☏617/492-1234 or 1-800/233-1234, ⓦwww.cambridge.hyatt.com; **Kendall T.** This brick ziggurat-like monolith, with luxurious rooms, pool, health club, and a patio with a gazebo, has a picturesque location on the Charles, but it's a hike from Cambridge's major points of interest. $180.

Inn at Harvard 1201 Massachusetts Ave ☏617/491-2222 or 1-800/222-8733, ⓦwww .theinnatharvard.com; **Harvard T.** Harvard University owns this red-brick, European-influenced hotel, set directly on its campus. Its four-story atrium was inspired by a Venetian piazza, and its rooms, while small, have huge writing desks and look out onto Harvard Square. $125.

Kendall Hotel 350 Main St ☏617/577-1300, ⓦwww.kendallhotel.com; **Kendall Square T.** This hotel near MIT occupies a former 1893 fire station. Its 65 rooms are country-chic, with quilts and reproduction antiques; modern furnishings include high-speed Internet access. $119.

Radisson Cambridge 777 Memorial Drive ☏617/492-7777 or 1-800/333-3333, ⓦwww .radisson.com; **Central or Harvard T.** The business-class rooms at this chain hotel,

located between Harvard and MIT, are nothing extraordinary, but many come with terrific views of the Charles and Back Bay; also, there's an indoor pool and gym. Wi-fi Internet access available. $139.

Royal Sonesta Cambridge Parkway ☏617/491-3600 or 1-800/SONESTA, ⓦwww.sonesta .com; **Kendall Square T.** Luxury quarters with good views of the Boston skyline. The fancy rooms have big, sparkling bathrooms, though the vast lobby is festooned with strikingly bad art. $239.

Sheraton Commander 16 Garden St ☏617/547-4800 or 1-800/535-5007, ⓦwww .sheratoncommander.com; **Harvard T.** The hotel's name refers to George Washington, who, legend has it, took command of the Continental Army on nearby Cambridge Common. Rooms tend to be rather dark and small, though there are some cute frills, such as terrycloth robes, nightlights, and even an umbrella service (should you have forgotton to pack yours). $125.

Bed and breakfasts

The **bed and breakfast** industry in Boston is thriving, for the most part because it is so difficult to find accommodation here for under $200 a night – and some B&Bs offer just that, at least in the off-season. On the other hand, many B&Bs cash in on the popularity of their old–world charm, meaning their prices may hover near those of the swankier hotels.

Some of the best B&Bs are outside the city, in either **Cambridge** or **Brookline**, though there are nice in-town options as well. You can make reservations directly with the places we've listed; there are also numerous B&B **agencies** that can do the booking for you and find you a room in an unlisted house (see box, opposite).

Charlestown

Bed & Breakfast Afloat 28 Constitution Rd ☏617/241-9640, ⓦwww.bostonharbor .com/bb; **Community College T.** Guests at this unusual B&B get to hole up on their own personal houseboat, sailboat, or yacht, right in Boston Harbor; the fancier vessels come with DVD players and deck-top Jacuzzis. All come with continental breakfast and access to the marina pool. $99.

Beacon Hill

Beacon Hill Bed & Breakfast 27 Brimmer St ☏617/523-7376, ⓦwww.lanierbb.com; **Charles T.** Only three spacious rooms with fireplaces are available in this well-situated 1869 brick townhouse. There

are sumptuous full breakfasts; two-night minimum stay, three on holiday weekends. $200.

Back Bay

463 Beacon Street Guest House 463 Beacon St ☏617/536-1302, ⓦwww.463beacon.com; **Hynes T.** The good-sized rooms in this renovated brownstone, in the heart of Back Bay, are available by the night, week, and month, and come equipped with kitchenettes, cable TV, and various hotel amenities (though no maid service); some have a/c, hardwood floors, and ornamental fireplaces. Ask for the top-floor room. $69.

Copley House 239 W Newton St ☏617/236-8300 or 1-800/331-1318, ⓦwww.copleyhouse .com; **Prudential T.** Furnished studios and

B&Bs and short-term rental agencies

Bed & Breakfast Agency of Boston 47 Commercial Wharf, Boston, MA 02110 ☎617/720-3540 or 1-800/248-9262, UK ☎0800/895 128, ⓦwww.boston-bnbagency .com. Can book you a room in a brownstone, a waterfront loft, or even aboard a yacht.

Bed & Breakfast Associates Bay Colony Ltd PO Box 57166 Babson Park Branch, Boston, MA 02157 ☎781/647-4949 or 1-888/486-6018, ⓦwww.bnbboston.com. Features some real finds in Back Bay, the South End, and Cambridge. Friendly and helpful staff.

Bed & Breakfast Reservations PO Box 590264 Newtown Center, MA 02459 ☎617//964-1606 or 1-800/832-2632,

ⓦwww.bbreserve.com. Lists B&Bs in Greater Boston, North Shore, and Cape Cod.

Boston Reservations/Boston Bed & Breakfast, Inc ☎617//332-4199, ⓦwww .bostonreservations.com. Competitive rates at B&Bs as well as at leading hotels. Reservation packs include maps and directions from Logan airport and to local sights. Will also book rooms in many other cities worldwide.

Greater Boston Hospitality PO Box 1142 Brookline, MA 02446 ☎617//277-5430, ⓦwww.bostonbedandbreakfast.com. Rentals in homes, inns, and condominiums. Good for booking out-of-town accommodation.

one-bedroom apartments on an attractive edge of Back Bay, across from the Copley Plaza shopping center; rented by the week or month. $80.

Copley Inn 19 Garrison St ☎617/236-0300 or 1-800/232-0306, ⓦwww.copleyinn.com; **Prudential T.** Comfortable rooms with full kitchens, friendly staff, and a great location make this an ideal place to stay in Back Bay. Visitors get one night free with a week's stay. $85.

Newbury Guest House 261 Newbury St ☎617/437-7666, ⓦwww.newburyguesthouse .com; **Copley T.** Big Victorian brownstone that still fills up whenever there's a big convention in town, so be sure to call ahead. The 32 rooms range from cramped chambers with overstuffed chairs to spacious bay-windowed quarters with hardwood floors and sleighbeds. Continental breakfast included, and all rooms have high-speed Internet access. $100.

The South End

82 Chandler Street 82 Chandler St ☎617/482-0408 or 1-888/482-0408, ⓦwww.channel1.com /82chandler; **Back Bay T.** Basic rooms with minimal service in a restored, 1863 brownstone that sits on one of the most up-and-coming streets of the South End. Breakfast is served on the sunny top floor – where you'll also find the best room in the house, with a working fireplace and great views.

Wi-fi Internet access is available throughout the hotel. $95.

Kenmore Square and the Fenway

Oasis Guest House 22 Edgerly Rd ☎617/267-2262, ⓦwww.oasisgh.com; **Symphony T.** Sixteen comfortable, very affordable rooms, some with shared baths, in a renovated brownstone near Symphony Hall. They feature a continental breakfast and a meet-and-greet soiree at 8pm – they supply the hors d'oeuvres, you bring the booze. $69.

Brookline

Beacon Inn 1087 and 1750 Beacon St ☎617/566-0088 or 1-888/575-0088, ⓦwww .beaconinn.com; **Hawes T.** Fireplaces in the lobbies and original woodwork contribute to the relaxed atmosphere in these two nineteenth-century brownstones, part of the same guest house. The rooms here would be well-suited to a country inn, with their patterned wallpaper, hardwood floors, and window sconces; some have working fireplaces. $99.

Beacon Townhouse Inns 1047 Beacon St ☎1-800/872-7211; 1023 Beacon St ☎1-888-714-7779, ⓦwww.beacontownhouseinn.com; **Saint Mary T.** Two National Register historic brownstones within walking distance of the Fenway and Boston University; the rooms are perfectly ordinary, but come with private bath and cable TV; some have kitchenettes. $89.

Brookline Manor Inn 32 Centre St
☏617/232-0003 or 1-800/535-5325, ⓦwww
.brooklinemanorinn.com; Coolidge Corner **T**.
This small guest house, with private and
shared baths, is located on a pleasant
stretch off Beacon Street, just a short subway ride from Kenmore Square. The same
management also runs the *Beacon Townhouse Inns*. $99.

Cambridge

A Cambridge B&B 1657 Cambridge St
☏617/868-7082 or 1-877/994-0844, ⓦwww
.cambridgebnb.com; Harvard **T**. This homely
colonial revival house has three pleasant
rooms outfitted with canopy beds, and
a common room furnished with overstuffed chairs and plenty of lace. Shared
bath. $75.

A Cambridge House 2218 Massachusetts Ave
☏617/491-6300 or 1-800/232-9989, ⓦwww
.acambridgehouse.com; Davis **T**. Though a
bit far out from any points of interest, this
classy B&B with gorgeous rooms decked
out in canopy beds and period pieces is
worth the trek for its full breakfasts plus
evening wine-and-cheese in the parlor
$109.

A Friendly Inn 1673 Cambridge St ☏617/547-
7851, ⓦwww.spacewarptechnology.com/afi/;
Harvard **T**. A good deal, and just a few
minutes' walk from Harvard Square. The

rooms are nothing special and the service
doesn't exactly live up to the name, but
there are private baths, cable TV, and laundry. $77.

Harding House 288 Harvard St ☏617/876-2888,
ⓦwww.irvinghouse.com; Harvard **T**. This cozy
Victorian home has fourteen bright rooms
with hardwood floors, throw rugs, TV, and
air-conditioning; includes breakfast. Shared
or private bath. $75.

Irving House 24 Irving St ☏617/547-4600,
ⓦwww.irvinghouse.com; Harvard **T**. A quaint
option near Harvard Square sharing the
same management as the *Harding House*,
with laundry and kitchen facilities; both
shared and private baths are available.
$85.

Mary Prentiss Inn 6 Prentiss St ☏617/661-
2929, ⓦwww.maryprentissinn.com; Harvard
T. Eighteen clean, comfortable rooms in an
impressively refurbished mid-nineteenth-
century Greek Revival building. Full breakfast and snacks are served in the living
room, or, weather permitting, on a pleasant
outdoor deck. $129.

Prospect Place 112 Prospect St ☏617/864-7500
or 1-800/769-5303, ⓦwww.prospectpl.com; Central **T**. This Italianate edifice holds a restored
parlor, along with nineteenth-century period
antiques – including two grand pianos
– and recently renovated, floral-decor
rooms. $75.

Hostels

There are a fairly limited number of **hostel** accommodations in Boston, and
if you want to get in on them, you should definitely book ahead, especially in
the summertime.

Beantown Hostel 222 Friend St ☏617/723-
0800; North Station **T**. This former bowling
alley has several co-ed and single-sex dorm
rooms, plus a comfy lounge with TV and
Internet access. Curfew 1.45am. $22/dorm
bed.

Berkeley Residence YWCA 40 Berkeley St
☏617/375-2524, ⓦwww.ywcaboston.org
/berkeley; Back Bay **T**. Clean and simple
rooms for women only in a safe location
– next door to a police station. All rates
include breakfast; dinner is an additional
$6.50. Singles are $56, doubles $86, and
triples $99, plus a $2 membership fee.

Greater Boston YMCA 316 Huntington Ave
☏617/927-8040, ⓦwww.ymcaboston.org;

Symphony **T**. Good budget rooms, and
access to the Y's health facilities (including
a pool and weight room). Singles are $46–
66, but you can get a four-person room for
$96. Co-ed facilities are available from late
June until early September; the rest of the
year it's men only. Ten days maximum stay.

**HI–Back Bay Summer Hostel 519 Beacon
St** ☏617/353-3294, ⓦwww.usahostels.org;
Kenmore **T**. This converted BU dorm has
63 beds, and a handful of basic single and
double rooms. The perks, such as free linen
service, self-serve laundry, and TV room
make it popular with visiting international
students. Open mid-June to late August
only. $24–54.

HI–Boston 12 Hemenway St ☎617/536-1027, ⊛www.bostonhostel.org; **Hynes T.** Around the Back Bay–Fenway border, this hotel features standard dorm accommodation with three or four beds per room. Members $29, nonmembers $32.

HI–Fenway Summer Hostel 575 Commonwealth Ave ☎617/267-8599, ⊛www.bostonhostel.org; **Kenmore T.** Another converted BU residence with private rooms and a handful of three-bed dorms with en-suite baths and air conditioning; there's also laundry and Internet access on-site. Open mid-May to late Aug. $35.

Cafés and light meals

U nlike Boston's accommodation options, its choices for quick bites are numerous. The city is packed with all manner of cafés, diners, delis, pizzerias, and other places where you can warm up with a coffee, grab a hefty sandwich or salad, and generally refuel yourself in this city that demands much energy for walking about and exploring.

We've broken down the listings below into two categories: **cafés** and **light meals**. Obviously there will be some crossover between the two, as most cafés offer more than just a good cup of coffee and a relaxing atmosphere. Also, you may find some of the spots serve full meals; however, we've tried to categorize more dinner-oriented options in Chapter 13, Restaurants.

Cafés

Boston's status as a university town is reflected in its well-established **café** scene. The toniest spots are those that line Back Bay's **Newbury Street**, where you pay as much for the fancy environs as for the quality of the coffee. Value is much better in the **North End**, where Italian cafés serve excellent beverages and desserts, plus provide the liveliest atmosphere in town. The most laid-back cafés are across the river in **Cambridge**, catering to the large student population.

Downtown

Boston Coffee Exchange 101 Arch St ☏617/737-3199; **Downtown Crossing T.** Cramped spot with a good selection of pastries and sweets to nosh while sipping some of the best coffee in town. The decaf is so delicious, you'll be surprised it's not the real thing.

The North End

Caffè dello Sport 308 Hanover St ☏617/523-5063; **Haymarket T.** A continuous stream of

Eating and drinking maps

Within this chapter, as well as Chapter 13, Restaurants, and Chapter 14, Drinking, you'll find maps where we've keyed the eating and drinking options for the major Boston neighborhoods. These maps can be found on the following pages:

Rai Uno soccer matches is broadcast from the ceiling-mounted TV sets, pleasing the very local crowd. Opens at 6am.

Caffé Paradiso 255 Hanover St ☎617/742-1768; **Haymarket T**. Not much on atmosphere, but the pastries – such as torta rustica and spinach pie – are, hands-down, the best in the North End. The superb gelato is the only home-made stuff around.

Caffé Vittoria 296 Hanover St ☎617/227-7606; **Haymarket T**. A Boston institution, the Vittoria is one of the city's most authentic Italian cafés. Its dark wood paneling, pressed tin ceilings, murals of the Old Country, and Sinatra-blaring Wurlitzer are all vintage North End. The café is only open at night, though a street-level addition next door is open by day for excellent cappuccinos.

Beacon Hill

Panificio 144 Charles St ☎617/227-4340; **Charles T**. Fine cups o' joe, fresh tasty pastries (biscotti is the standout), and some of the best home-baked bread in the city. Table service available in the evening.

Back Bay

Ben & Jerry's 174 Newbury St ☎617/536-5456; **Hynes T**. This Newbury Street branch of Vermont's finest has a host of flavors to pile on the pounds – and a few that don't, like low-carb blueberry. Other stores are located at 20 Park Plaza (☎617/426-0890) and the Prudential Center (☎617/266 0767).

JP Licks 352 Newbury St ☎617/236-1666; **Hynes T**. A sister ice cream bar of the locally famous Jamaica Plain establishment reviewed below. Try the white-russian flavor.

The Other Side Cosmic Café 407 Newbury St ☎617/536-9477; **Hynes T**. This ultracasual spot on "the other side" of Massachusetts Avenue, cut off from the trendy part of Newbury Street, offers gourmet sandwiches, creative green salads, and fresh juices. Local band videos and short art films are shown Monday nights; there's a jazz/ambient brunch on weekends.

Romano's Bakery & Coffee Shop 33 Newbury St ☎617/266-0770; **Arlington T**. Affordable pastries, sandwiches, and coffee drinks on the poshest block of Newbury Street. Rotating exhibits of contemporary paintings hang on the walls. Cash only.

Trident Booksellers & Café 338 Newbury St ☎617/267-8688; **Copley T**. A window seat at this bookstore café (see p.230 for store review) is the ideal vantage point from which to observe the flood of young passersby outside. Try the Momos Tibetan dumplings, which are steamed with a deliciously spicy meat filling.

The South End

Appleton Bakery 123 Appleton St ☎617/859-822; **Back Bay T**. Excellent pastry shop and place to people-watch.

Charlie's Sandwich Shoppe 429 Columbus Ave ☎617/536-7669; **Back Bay T**. A little diner-style hole-in-the-wall that offers some of the best breakfasts in Boston, such as the decadent banana and pecan griddlecakes; the coffee ain't too bad either, but beware – no customer toilets.

Flour Bakery + Café 1595 Washington St ☎617/267-4300; **Back Bay T**. Quite possibly the best café in town, this stylish South End spot has a drool-worthy array of brioche au chocolat, old-fashioned sour cream coffee cake, gooey caramel nut tarts, rich cakes, savory sandwiches, home-made breads, and thirst-quenching drinks. Choosing just one can be torture.

▽ Flour Bakery + Café

CAFÉS AND LIGHT MEALS | Cafés

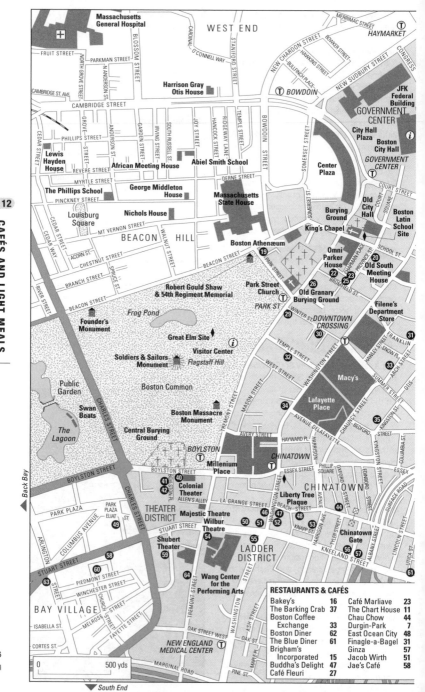

RESTAURANTS & CAFÉS

Bakey's	16	Café Marliave	23
The Barking Crab	37	The Chart House	11
Boston Coffee		Chau Chow	44
Exchange	33	Durgin-Park	7
Boston Diner	62	East Ocean City	48
The Blue Diner	61	Finagle-a-Bagel	31
Brigham's		Ginza	57
Incorporated	15	Jacob Wirth	51
Buddha's Delight	47	Jae's Café	58
Café Fleuri	27		

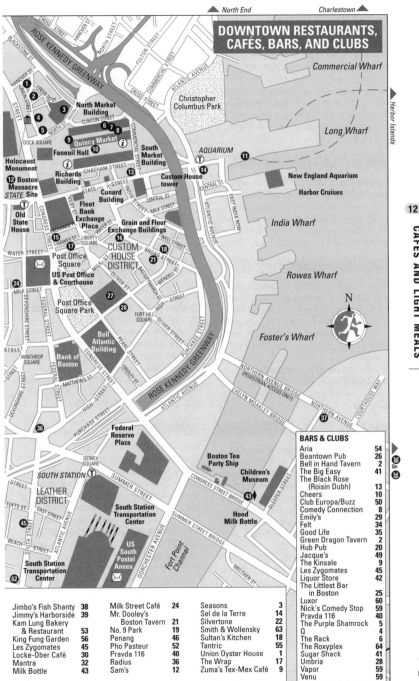

DOWNTOWN RESTAURANTS, CAFÉS, BARS, AND CLUBS

Commercial Wharf

Christopher Columbus Park

Long Wharf

Harbor Islands

North Market Building

Quincy Market

Faneuil Hall

South Market Building

AQUARIUM

New England Aquarium

Harbor Cruises

Holocaust Monument

Boston Massacre STATE Site

Richards Building

Custom House tower

Old State House

Cunard Building

Fleet Bank Exchange Place

Grain and Flour Exchange Buildings

India Wharf

Rowes Wharf

Post Office Square

US Post Office & Courthouse

CUSTOM HOUSE DISTRICT

Post Office Square Park

Foster's Wharf

N

Bell Atlantic Building

Bank of Boston

ROSE KENNEDY GREENWAY

NORTHERN AVENUE BRIDGE (PEDESTRIAN ACCESS ONLY)

NORTHERN AVENUE

Federal Reserve Plaza

SOUTH STATION

LEATHER DISTRICT

South Station Transportation Center

US South Postal Annex

Boston Tea Party Ship

Children's Museum

Hood Milk Bottle

South Station Transportation Center

Fort Point Channel

BARS & CLUBS

Aria	54
Beantown Pub	26
Bell in Hand Tavern	2
The Big Easy	41
The Black Rose (Roisin Dubh)	13
Cheers	10
Club Europa/Buzz	50
Comedy Connection	8
Emily's	29
Felt	34
Good Life	35
Green Dragon Tavern	2
Hub Pub	20
Jacque's	49
The Kinsale	9
Les Zygomates	45
Liquor Store	42
The Littlest Bar in Boston	25
Luxor	60
Nick's Comedy Stop	59
Pravda 116	40
The Purple Shamrock	5
Q	4
The Rack	6
The Roxyplex	64
Sugar Shack	41
Umbria	28
Vapor	59
Venu	59

Jimbo's Fish Shanty	38	Milk Street Café	24	Seasons	3
Jimmy's Harborside	39	Mr. Dooley's		Sel de la Terre	14
Kam Lung Bakery		Boston Tavern	21	Silvertone	22
& Restaurant	53	No. 9 Park	19	Smith & Wollensky	63
King Fung Garden	56	Penang	46	Sultan's Kitchen	18
Les Zygomates	45	Pho Pasteur	52	Tantric	55
Locke-Ober Café	30	Pravda 116	40	Union Oyster House	1
Mantra	32	Radius	36	The Wrap	17
Milk Bottle	43	Sam's	12	Zuma's Tex-Mex Café	9

Garden of Eden Café 571 Tremont St ☎617/247-8377; Back Bay **T**. The doyen of the South End café scene has a prime streetside terrace, perfect espressos, and delectable morsels like orange- and pistachio-encrusted pâté de canard and chocolate and raspberry mousse cakes. You can also stock up on outstanding cheeses and pastries from the adjoining gourmet shop, or try the salad lunch boxes, which start around $3.

Kenmore Square and the Fenway

Espresso Royale Caffe 736 Commonwealth Ave ☎617/277-8737; Kenmore **T**. Funky little coffeeshop serving traditional cups of java alongside original blends like a zesty orange cappuccino; the cheerful decor is enhanced by abstract wall paintings and cozy seats.

The southern districts

Coffee Cantata 605 Center St, Jamaica Plain ☎617/522-2223; Heath St **T**. Inviting local café with good coffee and delicious cupcakes, complemented by more substantial offerings like frittatas and asparagus ravioli. The service sometimes leaves a little to be desired.
JP Licks 659 Center St, Jamaica Plain ☎617/524-6740; Heath St **T**. Luscious ice cream, hearty bagels, and more at this funky Jersey cow-themed café.

Cambridge

1369 Coffee House 757 Massachusetts Ave ☎617/576-4600; Central **T**. The *1369* mixes earnest thirty-something leftists with youthful hipsters in a relaxed environment. Your best bets are the standard array of caffeinated beverages and particularly exquisite desserts. A second location, also cozy and laid-back, is at 1369 Cambridge St (☎617/576-1369; #69 bus).
Algiers 40 Brattle St ☎617/492-1557; Harvard **T**. A fashionable North African café popular with the artsy set. While the food is so-so and the service slow, the coffee is first-rate. The

cozy nooks are usually populated by Harvard bookworms taking advantage of the restorative powers of the signature mint coffee.
Bookcellar Café 1971 Massachusetts Ave ☎617/864-9625; Porter **T**. Relaxed basement coffeehouse with a few old sofas and some folding chairs on the concrete floor – but the java is good (and cheap) and you can peruse the wide range of magazines and used books while you chill.
Café Pamplona 12 Bow St ☎617/547-2763; Harvard **T**. Eurochic hits its pretentious peak in this tiny basement café. The coffee is average, and the waitstaff a bit snooty. On balmy evenings, the patio seating provides refuge from thick blue clouds of clove cigarette smoke.
Caffé Paradiso 1 Eliot St ☎617/868-3240; Harvard **T**. This glossy Italian café strikes a bright, comfortable contrast to the dimness of most Harvard Square coffeehouses. The coffee is good (and reasonably priced); the service is swift, and the setting free of pretension.
Tealuxe 0 Brattle St ☎617/441-0077; Harvard **T**. A former curiosity shop that's reincarnated itself as the only teahouse in Harvard Square, Tealuxe manages to stock over 100 varieties of the beverage – though the place is smaller than a teacup. Art Deco trimmings help you "skip the java in flavor of tea" in style. Another branch is at 108 Newbury St (☎617/927-0400), in Boston.

Somerville

Diesel 257 Elm St ☎617/629-8717; Davis **T**. They take their caffeine seriously at this trendy, garage-like coffee shop where patrons get revved on High Octane (double shots), Vietnamese blends, or just plain black java. Purists might be disappointed to learn they do serve herbal teas, as well.
Someday Café 51 Davis Sq ☎617/623-3323; Davis **T**. This ultra laid-back café is as close an approximation to a university common room as you'll find outside of a dormitory – mismatched sofas and resident couch potatoes included.

Light meals

In most neighborhoods in Boston you won't have a problem finding somewhere to grab **breakfast** or a **light meal**, whether it's from a diner, deli, or take-out stand. But be warned that if you ask for a sub or hoagie here, people may not know what you're talking about – in Boston, deep-filled sandwiches, and especially hot or toasted ones, are known as grinders. Many of the pubs in Chapter 14, Drinking, and the cafés above also offer food all day.

Downtown

Bakey's 45 Broad St ☎617/426-1710; **State T.** Easily recognizable from its decorative sign depicting a man slumped over an ironing board, *Bakey's* was one of the first after-hours Irish pubs to surface in the Financial District. Though it can be pricey ($10.50 for a turkey sandwich), it's a safe bet if you're caught hungry while wandering around this part of town.

Brigham's Incorporated 50 Congress St ☎617/523-9822; **State T.** Wholesome *Brigham's* features burgers and "MegaMelt" sandwiches, plus an excellent soda fountain. Great ice cream, too; stick to basic flavors – chocolate chip, vanilla – and you'll be happiest.

Café Fleuri 250 Franklin St in the Langham Hotel ☎617/451-1900; **State, Aquarium, or Downtown Crossing T.** Though this restaurant does standard upscale meals all day, it's mainly worth checking out on Saturday afternoons (Sept–May), when its $18 all-you-can-eat Chocolate Bar Buffet entitles you to sample everything from chocolate Grand Marnier ravioli to chocolate-croissant bread pudding. Truly decadent.

Finagle-a-Bagel 70 Franklin St ☎617/261-1900; **Downtown Crossing T.** A small Boston chain with more than fifteen varieties of bagels, from pumpkin raisin to triple chocolate chip, that are always served fresh. A Back Bay branch is at 535 Boylston St (☎617/266-2500; **Copley T**).

Kam Lung Bakery and Restaurant 77 Harrison St ☎617/542-2229; **Chinatown T.** Tiny take-out joint that peddles dim sum, bakery treats (sweet rolls, sugary moon pies), and more exotic delicacies like pork buns and meat pies.

Milk Bottle 300 Congress St ☎617/482-3343; **South Station T.** This Boston landmark in front of the Children's Museum dishes out bagels, hot dogs, ice cream, and coffee from its tiny kiosk window; patrons content themselves

by sitting at nearby picnic tables. Open May–Oct.

Milk Street Café 50 Milk St ☎617/542-3663; **State T; Post Office Square Park** ☎617/350-7273; **Downtown Crossing T.** Kosher and quick are the key words at these two Downtown eateries, popular with suits and vegetarians for the large designer sandwiches and salads. Entree-and-salad combos start at $5.95.

Sultan's Kitchen 72 Broad St ☎617//338-7819; **Aquarium T.** The best Turkish food in Boston, this lunch spot is favored by businessmen who line up for the agreeably spicy Ottoman classics. Take a table in the casual upstairs room and you'll feel a million miles away from nearby tourist-laden Quincy Market.

Tantric 123 Stuart St ☎617/367 8742; **Boylston T.** This Eastern-themed café offers great wraps and salads (try the Five Spice for $5.95), plus it's one of the only lunch options in the Theatre District.

The Wrap 82 Water St ☎617/357-9013; **State T.** Sandwiches rolled in tortillas, fruit smoothies, and other lunchtime treats – all quick, easy, and cheap.

The North End

Café Pompeii 280 Hanover St ☎617/227-1562; **Haymarket T.** Though you may not enjoy the garish murals or mediocre pizza, this is the only local joint that's open really late (until 4am).

Ernesto's 69 Salem St ☎617/523-1373; **Haymarket T.** The cheap, oversized slices of thin-crust pizza served here can't be beat for a quick lunch.

Galleria Umberto 289 Hanover St ☎617/227-5709; **Haymarket T.** When a place is only open daily from 11am to 2pm and there's a line out the door during that time, you know something good is cooking. Here, that something is pizza, cut into greasy, delicious squares.

Rabia's 73 Salem St ☎617/227-6637; **Haymarket T.** The best thing about this small restaurant is the "Express Lunch" special: a heaping plate of pasta, chicken parmigiana, or the like is yours to savor for a mere $5 from noon until 2pm daily.

Theo's Cozy Corner 162 Salem St ☎617/241-0202; Haymarket Ⓣ. This inexpensive Italian eatery is worth visiting on the weekends for breakfast. Try the pancakes.

Sorelle Bakery and Café 1 Monument Ave ☎617/242-2125. Enjoy phenomenal muffins, cookies, and orange and poppy scones ($1.50 each), plus pasta salads and other

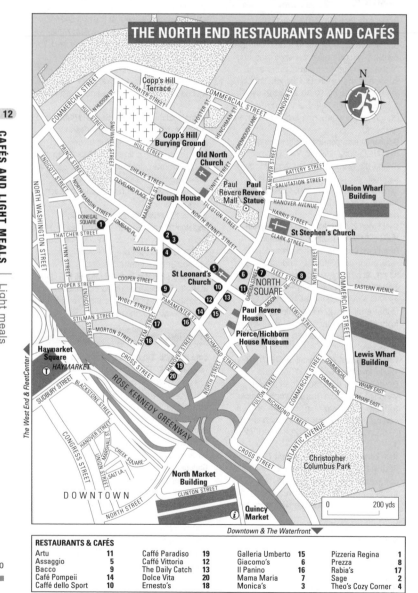

THE NORTH END RESTAURANTS AND CAFÉS

The West End & FleetCenter ◀

Downtown & The Waterfront ▼

RESTAURANTS & CAFÉS

Artu	**11**	Caffé Paradiso	**19**	Galleria Umberto	**15**	Pizzeria Regina	**1**
Assaggio	**5**	Caffé Vittoria	**12**	Giacomo's	**6**	Prezza	**8**
Bacco	**9**	The Daily Catch	**13**	Il Panino	**16**	Rabia's	**17**
Café Pompeii	**14**	Dolce Vita	**20**	Mama Maria	**7**	Sage	**2**
Caffé dello Sport	**10**	Ernesto's	**18**	Monica's	**3**	Theo's Cozy Corner	**4**

lunch fare on *Sorelle's* delightful hidden patio.

Beacon Hill and the West End

Paramount 44 Charles St ℡617/720-1152; **Charles T.** The Hill's neighborhood diner serves Belgian waffles and frittatas to the brunch regulars by day, and decent American standards like hamburgers and meat loaf by night. Expect long waits on weekends.

Ruby's Diner 280 Cambridge St ℡617/367-3224; **Charles T.** Very basic breakfast chow (like eggs and such) done cheaply and well. Open all night Thurs–Sat.

Back Bay

29 Newbury 29 Newbury St ℡617/536-0290; **Arlington T.** A small, upscale café/bar and eatery with good salads ($7) and the like. In warmer weather, the self-consciously hip crowd migrates to the sidewalk terrace. Don't miss the 29 Smooch, the signature dessert made with brownies and caramel ice cream. Open until 1.30am.

Armani Café 214 Newbury St ℡617/437-0909; **Copley T.** People-watching is the mot du jour at this fashionista hotspot where patrons seem to enjoy wearing black and talking on their cellphones from behind dark sunglasses; the good contemporary Italian fare (entrees $12–20), like saffron shrimp risotto and veal scaloppine, shouldn't be overlooked, mind you.

Café Jaffa 48 Gloucester St ℡617/536-0230; **Hynes T.** Boston's best falafel and other Middle Eastern staples are served in this cool, inviting space with polished wood floors.

Emack & Bolio's 290 Newbury St ℡617/247-8772; **Copley T.** Pint-sized ice-cream parlor named for a long-defunct rock band. Try a scoop each of Chocolate Moose and Vanilla Bean Speck in a chocolate-dipped waffle cone to get hooked.

Steve's Greek-American Cuisine 316 Newbury St ℡617/267-1817; **Hynes T.** Excellent Greek food makes this one of Boston's classic cheap eats (most dishes cost $3–6). Steve's Greek Salad is a favorite among the Newbury Street lunch crowd, and the Grilled Chicken Sandwich could convert a vegetarian.

The South End

Bertucci's Brick Oven Pizzeria 43 Stanhope St ℡617//247-6161; **Back Bay T.** Though it may not be the best pizza in Boston, this funky spot's inexpensive slices more than do the trick, and the free garlic bread is great. Lunch pasta specials are available for $7.95.

Finale 1 Columbus Ave ℡617/423-3184; **Boylston or Arlington T.** Devilishly good desserts are the mainstay at this extremely cushy sweet-tooth emporium; the top-notch wines and cordials that go with them are a treat, too.

Garden of Eden 57 Tremont St ℡617/247-8377; **Boylston T.** Pleasant and friendly staff make this café, with mainly vegetarian fare ($5–8) and great desserts, a joy.

Geoffrey's 578 Tremont St ℡617/266-1122; **Back Bay T.** This cheerful, affordable eatery serves a range of salads and sandwiches, as well as more substantial fare like seven-vegetable couscous, asparagus mousse ravioli, and huge portions of cake.

Mike's City Diner 1714 Washington St ℡617/267-9393; **Back Bay T.** Classic diner breakfasts and lunches – both greasy but good – in an out-of-the way setting. How can you resist a breakfast that includes two eggs, two pancakes, choice of meat, home fries, or grits and toast and is called "the emergency room"?

Kenmore Square and the Fenway

Anna's Taqueria 1412 Beacon St ℡617/739-7300; **Coolidge Corner T.** Exceptional tacos, burritos, and quesadillas are the only things on the menu at this bright, extremely cheap Mexican eatery – but they're so good, branches had to be opened around the corner at 446 Harvard St (℡617/277-7111; Coolidge Corner T) and in Cambridge at 8222 Somerville Ave (℡617/661-8500; Porter T) to accommodate its legions of devotees.

The Elephant Walk 900 Beacon St ℡617/247-1500; **Fenway T.** Top-notch Cambodian/French resturant with great sampler menus from $15. A sister branch is in Cambridge, at 2067 Massachusetts Ave (℡617/492-6900; Porter Square T).

Cambridge

C'est Bon 1432 Massachusetts Ave ℡617/661-0610; **110 Mt Auburn St** ℡617/492-6465;

Harvard T (both locations). Small, centrally located shop, in two branches, both of which serve excellent coffee, freshly baked goods, and the best falafel in Cambridge at inexpensive prices. Open late.

Darwin's Ltd 148 Mt Auburn St ☎617/354-5233; Harvard T. The rough-hewn exterior conceals a delightful deli serving the best sandwiches on Harvard Square – inventive combinations include roast beef, sprouts, and apple slices served on freshly baked bread.

Frescos Cafe 134 Massachusetts Ave ☎617/491-8866; Kendall T. A favorite haunt of MIT students, this bohemian café has excellent breakfasts that start at $5. Lunch-time specials include hearty soups and sandwiches.

Herrell's Ice Cream 15 Dunster St ☎617/497-2179; Harvard T. Both the long lines and the profusion of "Best of Boston" awards that adorn the walls attest to the well-deserved popularity of this local ice-cream parlor. The chocolate pudding flavor is a particular delight, especially combined with "smoosh-ins," such as Junior Mints or crushed Oreo cookies. Open until midnight.

Kendall House of Pizza 201 Third St ☎617/547-1790; Kendall T. This Greek-family owned restaurant wins no prizes for decor, but the hearty pizzas, subs, and souvlaki are cheap ($5) and tasty.

Leo's Place 35 JFK St ☎617/354-9192; Harvard T. Until it received Ben Affleck's patronage (he considers it home to the best burger in America), Leo's red-walled retro diner was the best-kept secret in Cambridge. Despite the crowds, the breakfasts ($5) and burgers (from $6) are still a must.

Pinnochio's 74 Winthrop St, no phone; Harvard T. Serves huge Neapolitan slices and the best meatball sub in town. Open until 1am.

Porter Square Café and Diner 1933 Massa-chusetts Ave ☎617/354-3898; Porter T. This combination coffeehouse/diner spot is best for good, cheap American breakfast fare. Specials are served all day, and there's a make-your-own omelette option, too.

Toscanini's 1310 Massachusetts Ave ☎617/354-9350; Harvard T. An ever-chang-ing ice-cream list includes original flavors like Khulfee – a concoction of pistachios, almonds, and cardamom. Another branch is at 899 Main St (☎617/491-587; Kendall T).

Restaurants

H istorically, weather-beaten Yankees have tended to favor hot and hearty meals made from native ingredients without a lot of fuss. Today, though, while outsiders may see menu items like broiled scrod, clam chowder, and Yankee pot roast as quintessentially New England, most Bostonians consider such dishes as little more than part of the tourist package.

Indeed, the city's current dining scene mirrors the increasing diversity of Boston's population itself, with innovative restaurants taking root everywhere – most recently, in the South End, where French and fusion cuisine (in a fashionable setting, of course) are the catch of the day. Happily, too, there is no shortage of places to eat in Boston: the city is packed with bars and pubs that double as restaurants, cafés that serve full and affordable meals (for these, see p.184), plus plenty of higher-end, dinner-only options.

As for Boston's culinary landscape, there are ever-popular **Italian** restaurants – both traditional southern and fancier northern – that cluster in the **North End**, mainly on Hanover and Salem streets. The city's tiny **Chinatown** packs in not only a fair number of Chinese spots, but **Japanese**, **Vietnamese**, and **Malaysian**, too. Dim sum, where you choose selections from carts wheeled past your table, is especially big at lunchtime.

On the other end of the spectrum, Boston's trendiest restaurants, many serving voguish **New American** fusion cuisine, tend to cluster in **Back Bay** and the **South End**. Meanwhile, across the Charles, **Cambridge**'s eating options, mostly laid out along Massachusetts Avenue between Central, Harvard, and Porter squares, run the gamut from budget Mexican eateries to high-end American cuisine. Funky (if slightly out-of-the-way) Inman Square, just below Cambridge's border with **Somerville**, has a few good spots as well, many of them specializing in contemporary twists on New England classics.

Eating and drinking maps

Within this chapter, as well as Chapter 12 Cafés and light meals, and Chapter 14, Drinking, you'll find maps where we've keyed the eating and drinking options for the major Boston neighborhoods. These maps can be found on the following pages:

Restaurants by cuisine

American
Amrheins p.205
Anthem p.199
Audubon Circle p.204
Aujourd'hui p.201
Bartley's Burger Cottage p.205
Blackfin Chophouse and Raw Bar
  p.201
The Blue Cat Café p.201
The Blue Diner p.196
The Boston Diner p.196
Bob the Chef p.205
Boodles p.201
Cambridge Common p.206
Charlie's Kitchen p.206
Claremont Café p.204
Cottonwood Restaurant & Café p.201
Durgin-Park p.196
Grill 23 p.203
Hamersley's Bistro p.204
Harvard Gardens p.201
Henrietta's Table p.206
The Hungry I p.201
Locke-Ober Café p.197
Mr Dooley's Boston Tavern p.197
Redbones p.207
The Rosebud Diner p.207
Silvertone p.198
Smith & Wollensky p.198
Top of the Hub p.204
Washington Square Tavern p.205

Brazilian
Buteco p.205

Chinese
Betty's Wok & Noodle Diner p.201
Chau Chow p.196
East Ocean City p.196
King Fung Garden p.197

French
Aquitane p.204
Central Kitchen p.206
Chez Henri p.206
Hamersley's Bistro p.204
L'Espalier p.203
Les Zygomates p.197
Mistral p.204
No. 9 Park p.197
On the Park p.204
Radius p.197
Sel de la Terre p.198

German
Jacob Wirth p.196

Indian
Bombay Café p.201
Café of India p.206
Diva p.207
Kashmir p.203
Rangoli p.205
Royal India p.206
Tandoor House p.207

Irish
Doyle's Café p.205
Matt Murphy's p.205

Italian
Artu p.199
Assaggio p.198
Bacco p.198
Bella Luna p.205
Café Marliave p.196
Croma p.201
Dolce Vita p.198
Giacomo's p.198
Il Panino p.198
Mama Maria p.198
Monica's Trettoria p.198
No. 9 Park p.197
Papa Razzi p.203
Pizzeria Regina p.199
Prezza p.199
Ristorante Toscano
  p.201

In the following pages, we've divided our listings up by neighborhood; you'll also find a complete cross-referenced list by cuisine in the box above. Note that it's always a good idea to make reservations ahead of time, especially at the more upscale places.

Downtown

The Barking Crab 88 Sleeper St (at the Northern Avenue Bridge) ☎617/426-CRAB; **South Station T.** This endearing seafood shack aims to please with its homey atmosphere, friendly service, and unpretentious, inexpensive menu – centered around anything they can pull from the ocean and fry, sauté, marinate, or grill. Located right on the Boston Harbor with a view of the city skyline from the patio. Prices start at $5 for appetizers, $8 for entrees.

The Blue Diner 150 Kneeland St ☎617/695-0087; South Station T. Campy bar and restaurant that's a popular spot for a late-night nosh. The excellent cheeseburgers are $7.25, and a steak dinner will set you back $15. Open until 4am on weekends.

The Boston Diner 178 Kneeland St ☎617/350-0028; South Station T. Occupying the small freestanding 1920 structure once owned by *The Blue Diner*, the *Boston Diner* has a more authentic atmosphere thanks to its wooden booths and all-night clientele (it's open 24hours). Huge homemade hamburgers cost $5.

Buddha's Delight 5 Beach St ☎617/451-2395; Chinatown T. The "beef" and "chicken" at this vegetarian Vietnamese place are actually made from tofu, but, while the ersatz meats don't exactly taste like the real thing, they're still good. Prices are $5–13. *Buddha's Delight Too* is at 404 Harvard St, Brookline (☎617/739-8830; Coolidge Corner T).

Café Marliave 10 Bosworth St ☎617/423-6340; Park T. This Italian-American hideaway is one of Boston's oldest restaurants; it's located in the former Province House, where the British governor lived in pre-Revolution times. Visit for the first-rate ravioli and unmistakeably Bostonian ambience; located behind the *Omni Parker House Hotel*.

The Chart House 60 Long Wharf ☎617/227-1576; Aquarium T. Three-floor restaurant with rich food for the rich, though worth the price if you can afford it; the lobster ($36) and swordfish ($24) are particularly good. For a less highbrow experience, try eating on the first floor – while you lose the view for which this chain is also known, you'll also feel more casual.

Chau Chow 52 Beach St ☎617/426-6266; Chinatown T. One of the first Chinatown restaurants to specialize in seafood, and still one of the best. The setting is stripped-down so there's nothing to distract you from delicious salt-and-pepper shrimp or, if you're in a more adventurous mood, sea cucumber. *The Grand Chau Chow*, just across Beach Street, serves basically the same food at somewhat higher prices and with fancier accoutrements such as tablecloths and linen napkins. Main courses at *Grand* are $8–15.

Durgin-Park 340 Faneuil Hall Marketplace ☎617/227-2038, @www.durgin-park.com; Government Center T. A Boston landmark in operation since 1827 (their slogan is "established before you were born"), *Durgin-Park* has a no-frills atmosphere and a somewhat surly waitstaff. But that doesn't stop folks from coming for the sizable, pot roast ($8.95) and roast beef dinners in the upstairs dining room. The downstairs raw bar is considerably livelier.

East Ocean City 25–29 Beach St ☎617/542-2504; Chinatown T. Another seafood specialist that's full of aquariums, letting you greet your dinner before it appears on your plate. The soft-shell crabs are especially good. Entrees are $8–12.

Ginza 16 Hudson St ☎617/338-2261; Chinatown T. Open until 3am on weekends, *Ginza* is a popular after-hours spot serving perhaps the best sushi in the city. Any of the vast number of options goes well with a pitcher of warm house sake. There's another location in Brookline at 1002 Beacon St (☎617/566-9688; St Mary's T).

Jacob Wirth 31 Stuart St ☎617/338-8586; Arlington T. A German-themed Boston landmark, around since 1868. Even if you don't like bratwurst washed down with a hearty lager, something is sure to please. A Boston must-visit.

Jae's Café 212 Stuart St ☎617/451-7788; Arlington T. A popular chain restaurant, the first floor of this branch has a sushi bar (around $3 per piece) and jazz room while the third floor hosts a Korean barbecue where chefs slice and dice at your table. In between lies the main café, with an emphasis on Korean seafood, though you can also create your own noodle dish. Another location is at 520 Columbus Ave (Prudential T).

Jimbo's Fish Shanty 245 Northern Ave ☎617/542-5600, @www.jimmysharborside .com; South Station T. Operated by the proprietor's of *Jimmy's Harborside* (see below), serving basically the same food at lower prices ($8–12 for mains) in a more casual atmosphere, and without the picturesque views.

Jimmy's Harborside 242 Northern Ave ☎617/423-1000, @www.jimmysharborside .com; South Station T. Totally tacky, but

RESTAURANTS | Downtown

the harbor views and seafood are beyond reproach. House specialties include the sizable king lobsters ($29) and New England Fisherman's Platter ($21), featuring scallops, shrimp, clams, and calamari.

King Fung Garden 74 Kneeland St ☎617/357-5262; Chinatown T. The interior won't impress with its size or style, but the authentic Shangdong province food served here will. Inexpensive and delicious, the *King* is best on classics like pot stickers, scallion pancakes, and (if you let them know ahead of time) Peking duck. This is the place where other Chinatown chefs eat, so rest assured you're in good hands.

Les Zygomates 129 South St ☎617/542-5108, ⓦwww.leszygomates.com; South Station T. An eclectic crowd ranging from bankers to black-clad artists gathers for the inventive contemporary French cuisine and the prime selection of wines (more than a hundred international varieties) at this restaurant, which takes its name from the French term for the facial muscles that make you smile. Try the sole filet with salmon mousse for $23.

Locke-Ober Café 3 Winter Place ☎617/542-1340; Park T. Don't be fooled by the name: *Locke-Ober Café* is very much a restaurant, and one of the most blueblooded in Boston. The fare ($25 for entrees) consists of stuff like steak tartare and oysters on the half shell, and the setting is dark, ornate, and stuffy. The dress code includes jacket and tie for men.

Mantra 52 Temple Place ☎617/542-8111, ⓦwww.mantrarestaurant.com; Park St T. A snazzy hookah den completes the over-the-top atmosphere at this chi-chi Indian-French restaurant, where you can dine on grilled filet mignon and caramelized sweetbreads, or treat yourself to a chocolate "degustation" – four rich, cocoa-infused desserts.

Mr Dooley's Boston Tavern 77 Broad St ☎617/338-5656; State T. One of the many Irish pubs downtown, though with a quieter, more laid-back feel than the rest. Known for its live music acts and Traditional Irish Breakfast Sundays (bacon, eggs, black pudding, and baked beans), which is good because finding anything open around here on Sunday is a challenge. Bar closes at 2am.

No. 9 Park 9 Park St ☎617/742-9991, ⓦwww.no9park.com; Park St T. Highly recommended restaurant whose plates are busy with southern French and Italian entrees ranging from crispy duck with quince ($35) to bison ribeye ($41). A seven-course tasting menu ($85; with wine, $135) allows you to try almost everything.

Penang 685 Washington St ☎617/451-6373; Chinatown T. The painfully overdone interior of this restaurant, named for an island off the northwest coast of Malaysia, is countered by consistently good food: try the roti canai appetizer or the copious yam pot dinner ($8.95).

Pho Pasteur 682 Washington St and 8 Kneeland St ☎617/482-7467; Chinatown T. Both branches of this restaurant offer numerous variations on pho, a Vietnamese noodle dish. The Kneeland location serves only pho, while the one on Washington has other Vietnamese specialties as well – and it's all incredibly cheap.

Pravda 116 116 Boylston St ☎617/482-7799, ⓦwww.pravda116.com; Arlington T. Known more for its faux-hip scene than its Mediterranean-American entrees and reasonably priced tapas. There's a small, popular dance club in the rear (see p.210).

Radius 8 High St ☎617/426-1234, ⓦwww.radiusrestaurant.com; South Station T. Housed in a former bank, this ultramodern French restaurant tries to inject a dose of minimalist industrial chic to the cautious Financial District with über cool decor and innovative rotating menu. New Yorker Michael Schlow's tasty nouvelle cuisine is complemented by an extensive wine list.

Sam's 100 City Hall Plaza ☎617/227-0022; Government Center T. Specializing in "modern comfort food," Sam's fabulously fresh offerings range from scallops served on mashed potatoes and tropical salsa to pasta tossed with garlic, basil, chicken, green beans, and (wait for it) grapes.

Seasons North and Blackstone sts (in the Millennium Bostonian Hotel) ☎617/523-4119; Government Center or State T. With inventive, truly excellent Modern American fare, such as stone crab with smoked corn minestrone, *Seasons* has a knack for attracting up-and-coming chefs before sending them on their way to culinary stardom. Expect to pay about $30 (plus tip) per head for two courses.

RESTAURANTS | Downtown

Sel de la Terre 255 State St ☎617/720-1300; Aquarium T. The less-expensive sister to upscale *L'Espalier* (see p.203), *Sel de la Terre* honors its name (salt of the earth) with rustic Provençal fare like hearty bouillabaisse, lamb and eggplant, and perhaps the best french fries in Boston. Conveniently, you can acquire the fixings for a waterfront picnic here, too, by calling ahead to order a hamper ($15, minus the basket), and picking it up on your way to the ferry.

Silvertone 69 Bromfield St ☎617/338-7887; Downtown Crossing T. Though cocktails are the big draw at this Downtown Crossing basement bar and eatery, its Caesar salads and roasted salmon with homemade potato chips are excellent and surprisingly inexpensive.

Smith & Wollensky 101 Arlington St ☎617/423-1112, ⓦwww.smithandwollensky .com; Arlington T. New York's famous steakhouse opened its Boston doors in late 2004, in an 1891 recreation of a medieval castle. The excellent dry-aged steaks begin around $30.

Union Oyster House 41 Union St ☎617/227-2750, ⓦwww.unionoysterhouse.com; Government Center or State T. The oldest continuously operating restaurant in America has two big claims to fame: King Louis-Philippe lived over the tavern during his youth, and, perhaps apocryphally, the toothpick was first used here. The food is good, too: fresh, well-prepared seafood, plus one of Boston's best raw bars – six oysters will set you back around $10.

Zuma's Tex-Mex Café 7 N Market St ☎617/367-9114; State T. Tex-Mex is a long way from home in Boston, but *Zuma's* comes up with a close approximation, complemented by a garish interior and sassy waitstaff. The fajitas, which come to your table billowing with smoke, are especially good and ably complemented by the salty, tangy margaritas.

The North End

Assaggio 29 Prince St ☎617/227-7380; Haymarket T. An extensive wine list allows *Assaggio* to stand on its own as a wine bar, but it's also reliable for classic Italian fare with contemporary touches, such as penne in vodka sauce, The main dining room, with its ceiling mural of the zodiac

and steady stream of opera music, is calm and relaxing.

Bacco 107 Salem St ☎617/624-0454, ⓦwww .baccoboston.com; Haymarket T. Restaurateuer Patrick Buben's addition to the North End scene serves contemporay Italian fare in a laid-back atmosphere with modern furnishings. Try the lemon swordfish with the pasta of the day ($20).

The Daily Catch 323 Hanover St ☎617/523-8567; Haymarket T; 261 Northern Ave ☎617/338-3093; South Station T. Ocean-fresh seafood – notably calamari and shellfish (Sicilian-style, with megadoses of garlic) – draws big lines to this tiny storefront restaurant. The downtown location offers a solid alternative to the touristy Yankee scrod-and-chips thing.

Dolce Vita 237 Hanover St ☎617/720-0422, ⓦwww.dolcevitaristorante.com; Haymarket T. Sit in the quiet upstairs dining room of this longstanding North End spot to savor their famous "Ravioli Rose," served in a tomato cream sauce ($12.95). Don't come here if you're in a hurry, though – service can be very slow.

Giacomo's 355 Hanover St ☎617/523-9026; Haymarket T. This small eatery, with its menu written on a chalkboard attached to a brick wall, serves fresh, flavorful seafood and pasta specialties; try the pumpkin tortellini in sage butter sauce. There's a South End location, too, at 431 Columbus Ave (t617/536-5723; Back Bay T). Dinner only, closed Mondays.

Il Panino Express 11 Parmenter St ☎617/720-1336, ⓦwww.ilpanino.com; Aquarium T. A bona-fide Boston best, with incredible pasta specials at lunch; a bit more formal by night, when prices are $6–16.

Mama Maria 3 North Square ☎617/523-0077; Haymarket T. A favorite special-occasion restaurant, and considered by some to be the best the district has to offer; in any case its location, on historic North Square, is as good a reason as any to come. Though the service can be slow, the northern Italian fare is of consistently impeccable quality. Dinner only.

Monica's Tratorria 67 Prince St ☎617/720-5472; Haymarket T. Some of the most intensely flavored Italian fare around, prepared and served by Monica's three sons, one of whom drew the cartoons plastered over the walls. They do a brisk takeout (sandwiches and such) at lunch, though the best dishes are reserved for dinner. Monica herself has a gourmet shop around the corner, at 130 Salem St.

Pizzeria Regina 11 1/2 Thatcher St ☎617/227-0765, ⊛www.polcaris.com; Haymarket **T**. This North End legend is a great spot for tasty, cheap pizza, served in a neighborhood feed station, where the wooden booths haven't budged since the 1940s. A second branch is in the Faneuil Hall Marketplace, and further openings are scheduled in the Prudential Center and South Station in 2005.

Prezza 24 Fleet St ☎617/227-1577; Haymarket **T**. New, minimalist Italian hotspot offering decadent dishes like sweet rock shrimp and risotto with shaved black truffles. A two-course meal will cost around $45.

Sage 69 Prince St ☎617/248-8814, ⊛www.sageboston.com; Haymarket **T**. Diminutive Italian restaurant that doesn't scrimp on flavor. The refreshing seasonal menu finds dishes like creamy spinach agnolotti in truffle butter; perfect fodder for an intimate tête-à-tête.

Charlestown

Figs 67 Main St ☎617/242-2229, ⊛toddenglish.com; Community College **T**. This noisy, popular offshoot of *Olives* (see below) has excellent thin-crust pizzas, topped with such savory items as figs and prosciutto or caramelized onions and arugula. Another location is at 42 Charles St in Beacon Hill (☎617/242-3447; Charles T).

Meze 100 City Square ☎617/242-MEZE, ⊛www.mezeboston.com; Community College **T**. A recent and welcome addition to the Charlestown dining scene, *Meze* has collected awards by the bucketful. And it's no surprise why: the food at this traditional Greek taverna is as authentic as it comes. Take a very big appetite – the dishes are huge.

Olives 10 City Square ☎617/242-1999, ⊛toddenglish.com; Community College **T**. *Olives* is consistently rated among Boston's best restaurants, and justifiably so. Chef Todd English turns out (very expensive) New Mediterranean food, such as pork Milanese with an apple, sausage, and cheddar calzonette of unforgettable flavor in sizable portions. No reservations save for parties of six or more. Closed Sun and Mon.

Beacon Hill and the West End

Anthem 138 Portland St ☎617/523-1037, ⊛anthemboston.com; North Station **T**. A glitzy modern American bistro with some interesting takes on Yankee staples. Try the Figgy Piggy (pork shank with braised figs, $19) or the superb meatloaf with italian sausage ($14).

Artu 89 Charles St ☎617/227-9023; Charles **T**. Though squeezed into a tiny storefront on Charles Street, *Artu* keeps things fresh, flavorful, and affordable. The authentic Italian menu focuses on soups, risottos, roast meats, and panini (entrees are around $8). The other location in the North End, at 6 Prince St (☎617/742-4336; North Station T) is larger, but equally charming.

Beacon Hill Bistro 25 Charles St (in the Beacon Hill Hotel) ☎617/723-1133; Charles **T**. Sleek New American and French bistro with an upscale feel. Short ribs with prunes ($9) share counter space with cod with capers and tomatoes ($18.50); breakfast is traditional American.

The Federalist 15 Beacon St (in the XV Beacon hotel) ☎617/670-1500; Park St **T**. The lofty, chandeliered dining room verges on sterile, but the seafood is anything but. The

▽ Olives

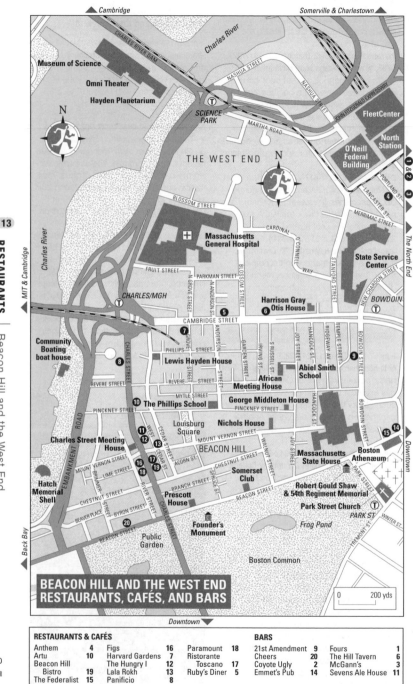

BEACON HILL AND THE WEST END RESTAURANTS, CAFÉS, AND BARS

0   200 yds

RESTAURANTS & CAFÉS

Anthem	4	Figs	16	Paramount	18
Artu	10	Harvard Gardens	7	Ristorante	
Beacon Hill		The Hungry I	12	Toscano	17
Bistro	19	Lala Rokh	13	Ruby's Diner	5
The Federalist	15	Panificio	8		

BARS

21st Amendment	9	Fours	1
Cheers	20	The Hill Tavern	6
Coyote Ugly	2	McGann's	3
Emmet's Pub	14	Sevens Ale House	11

swordfish ($36) and halibut ($35) are out of this world.

Harvard Gardens 316 Cambridge St ☎617/523-2727, ⓦwww.harvardgardens.com; **Charles T.** Candle-lit romance is on the menu here, where a happening singles' scene goes on in the bar area. A great spot for brunch, too – try the pastrami hash, "perfect for curing last night's indulgence" ($9.50).

The Hungry I 71 Charles St ☎617/227-3524; **Charles T.** Don't sweat the pricey menu and hyped-up, romantic surroundings – the food here is delectable and features a changing menu of classic American fare with creative twists. If you come on a night when the signature venison with poivre noir (black pepper) is served, prepare for food heaven.

Lala Rokh 97 Mount Vernon St ☎617/720-5511, ⓦwww.lalarokh.com; **Park T.** Have the waitstaff help you with the inscrutable menu at this exotically plush Azerbaijani restaurant, where you can fill up on the appetizers (such as roasted eggplant kashk-e-bademjan) and torshi (condiments) alone. Main courses are $14–19.

Ristorante Toscano 47 Charles St ☎617/723-4090; **Charles T.** In the midst of the 1990s' New Italian craze, *Toscano* stayed traditional, and survived. It serves particularly good southern Italian food, made with flair and fresh ingredients.

Back Bay

Azure 65 Exeter St (in The Lenox) ☎617/933-4800; **Copley T.** Modern American fusion is the order of the day in this classy restaurant. The golden trout with apple-smoked bacon ($19) and filet mignon with Hawaiian blue prawns ($29) are amazing.

Aujourd'hui 200 Boylston St (in the Four Seasons) ☎617/338-4400 or 1-800/332-3442; **Arlington T.** Near the top of everyone's list of Boston's best restaurants, this is a good place to splurge. Nibble roasted Maine lobster (at market price) – accompanied by crabmeat wontons, pineapple compote, and fenugreek broth – served on antique china while enjoying the view of the Public Garden.

Betty's Wok & Noodle Diner 250 Huntington Ave ☎617/424-1950, ⓦbettyswokandnoodle.citysearch.com; **Symphony T.** Mix and match from a list of rice, noodles, sauces (from Asian Pesto to Cuban Chipotle-Citrus),

vegetables, and meats and, minutes later, you'll be enjoying a piping-hot plateful of tasty Chino-Latino food, for around $15. Open everyday until 11pm.

Blackfin Chophouse and Raw Bar 116 Huntington Ave ☎617/247-2400; **Prudential or Copley T.** The *Blackfin* is a nautically themed addition to the Back Bay restaurant scene. A great sushi bar is complemented with dry aged chops (from $15) and some unusual sides such as bourbon whipped sweet potatoes.

The Blue Cat Café 94 Massachusetts Ave ☎617/247-9922; **Hynes T.** This cavernous restaurant/bar has gone back to basics with a rustic, exposed-brick decor and tasty, all-American staples like pizzas, pastas, and steaks. Popular with an after-work crowd, who guzzle martinis while chowing down. Entrees range $12–19.

Bombay Café 175 Massachusetts Ave ☎617/247-0555; **Hynes T.** The chicken tikka and stuffed naan are good bets – as is anything with seafood – at this casual Indian restaurant. Main dishes cost $12–15.

Boodles 40 Dalton St (in the Back Bay Hilton) ☎617/236-1100 or 1-800/874-0663; **Hynes T.** English-style steakhouse serving the usual grill fare and some eighty microbrews to a predominantly older crowd of theater-goers. The food's not terribly adventurous, but certain standbys, like the Caesar salad and smoked clam chowder, are good, if unextraordinary. Buffet-style all-you-can-eat Sunday brunch is also a good option.

Cactus Club 939 Boylston St ☎617/236-0200; **Hynes T.** Cavernous Tex-Mex restaurant with funky decor and surprisingly tasty nibbles (including great quesadillas); the *Cactus* is equally sought out for its popular bar.

Cottonwood Restaurant & Café 222 Berkeley St ☎617/247-2225, ⓦwww.cottonwoodboston.com; **Arlington T.** Creative, tasty Southwestern fare served in a bright setting on the first floor of the 22-story Houghton Mifflin Building. Locally (and justly) famous for its margaritas, this is one of Back Bay's best bets for lunch or Sunday brunch with a twist. Try the Cottonwood Mixed Grill: chicken breast, pork loin, and steak grilled to order with achiote rice, ranch beans, sautéed peppers, onions, and warm flour tortillas ($17).

Croma 269 Newbury St ☎617/247-3200, ⓦwww.cromaboston; **Hynes T.** Much of

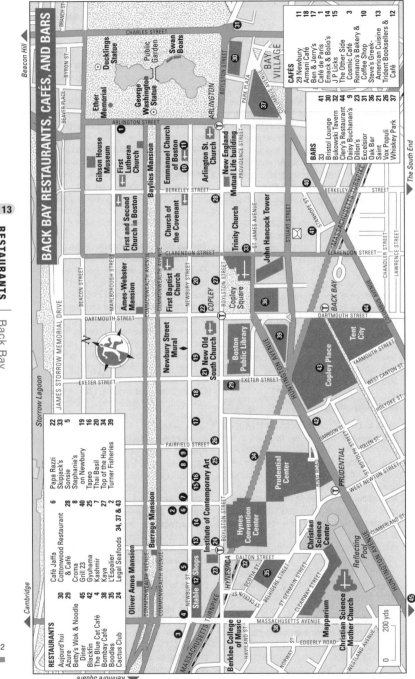

BACK BAY RESTAURANTS, CAFÉS, AND BARS

RESTAURANTS

Aujourd'hui	30
Azure	29
Betty's Wok & Noodle Diner	45
Blackfin	42
The Blue Cat Café	4
Bombay Café	38
Boodles	35
Cactus Club	24
Café Jaffa	6
Cottonwood Restaurant & Café	28
Croma	8
Grill 23	40
Gyuhama	25
Kashmir	7
Kaya	27
L'Espalier	36
Legal Seafoods	34, 37 & 43
Papa Razzi	22
Skipjack's	33
Sonsie	5
Stephanie's on Newbury	19
Tapeo	16
Thai Basil	20
Top of the Hub	34
Turner Fisheries	39

CAFÉS

29 Newbury	11
Armani Café	18
Ben & Jerry's	17
Café de Paris	1
Emack & Bolio's	14
J P Licks	15
The Other Side Cosmic Café	3
Romano's Bakery & Coffee Shop	10
Steve's Greek-American Cuisine	13
Trident Booksellers & Café	12

BARS

33	41
Bristol Lounge	30
Bukowski Tavern	32
Clery's Restaurant	44
Daisy Buchanan's	9
Dillon's	23
Excelsior	31
Oak Bar	36
Saint	21
Vox Populi	26
Whiskey Park	37

Croma's menu is standard Italian fare. Avoid the salads, which are average, and stick with the stone-oven baked pizzas with a twist, such as the Peking Duck ($11.99), Greek (olives, feta, red onion, and peppers; $11.75) and Inglese (bacon, egg, and imported sausage; $11.50).

Grill 23 & Bar 161 Berkeley St ☎617/542-2225, @www.grill23.com; **Arlington T.** This carnivore-fest is as clubby as Boston gets: the steaks are aged in-house and accompanied by myriad wines, and the atmosphere is buzzy despite the requirement of formal dress. Expect to pay around $20 for a steak.

Gyuhama 827 Boylston St ☎617/437-0188; **Hynes T.** A very noisy basement-level sushi bar, favored by many college students for late-night eating. Listen to Japanese rock music as nigiri sushi, spicy maki rolls, and grilled shrimp are cooked at your table.

Kashmir 279 Newbury St ☎617/536-1695; **Hynes T.** The food and decor are equally inviting at Newbury Street's only Indian restaurant. Good choices include shrimp samosas, tandoori rack of lamb, and vegetarian curries, all of which go well with the excellent naan bread. There's a good lunch buffet for $9 on weekdays and $12 on the weekend.

Kaya 581 Boylston St ☎617/236-5858, @www.kayausa.com; **Copley T.** This is the place to go when the craving for Japanese-Korean food kicks in; try the teriyaki salmon or steaming shabu shabu (which means "swish swish") beef. *Kaya* now has two sister restaurants, one at 1924 Massachusetts Ave in Cambridge (☎617/497-5656; Porter Square T), and the other at 1366 Beacon St in Brookline (☎617/738-2244; Washington St T).

Legal Seafoods 27 Park Square (in the Park Plaza Hotel) ☎617/426-4444, @www.legalseafoods.com; **Arlington T; 255 State St** ☎617/227-3115; **Aquarium T; 100 Huntington Ave, Level Two, Copley Place** ☎617/266-7775; **Copley T; 800 Boylston St, Prudential Center** ☎617/266-6800; **Prudential T; 5 Cambridge Center** ☎617/864-3400; **Kendall T; 20 University Rd** ☎617/491-9400; **Harvard T.** This local chain is probably the best-known seafood restaurant in America, and for many, it's the best as well. Its trademark is freshness: the clam chowder ($3.95 a cup), Boston scrod ($9.95), and lobster are all top quality. There are some New Asian offerings on the menu,

too. Go early to avoid long lines, which can be expected no matter the location or day of the week.

L'Espalier 30 Gloucester St ☎617/262-3023, @www.lespalier.com; **Hynes T.** A ravishing French restaurant with first-rate food in a Back Bay brownstone. The minimalist portions at lofty prices, however, suggest that ambience is factored (generously) into your bill.

Papa Razzi 271 Dartmouth St ☎617/536-9200; **Copley T.** Though this urbane, basement-level eatery doesn't look like a chain restaurant, it is – a fact that's reflected in the menu of standard-issue bruschetta ($7.50), salads (from $5), and pastas ($8–13). It's all good, but for more authentic fare, head to the North End. Another branch is at 100 Cambridgeside Place (☎617/577-0009; Kendall T).

Skipjack's 199 Clarendon St ☎617/536-3500, @www.skipjacks.com; **Arlington T.** Cool, South Beach-style decor and a bold menu distinguish this seafood spot from its rival, the always-busy *Legal Seafoods*. Look for the gingered sea bass ($24.95) or fried scrod with tartar sauce ($16.95). The Sunday jazz brunch is popular.

Sonsie 327 Newbury St ☎617/351-2500, @www.sonsieboston.com; **Hynes T.** The pretension factor is high at this scenester hangout, where the ultra-trendy meet over strange marriages of French and Asian food. Dishes include tuna sashimi rice paper rolls with avocado and spicy mayonnaise ($15), and grilled swordfish with saffron polenta, Tuscan kale, and charred squid vinaigrette ($24). Worth braving the scene if only for the warm chocolate bread pudding ($8).

Stephanie's on Newbury 190 Newbury St ☎617/236-0990, @www.stephaniesonnewbury.com; **Copley T.** Though they pride themselves on their smoked salmon potato pancake, what sets Stephanie's apart is their sidewalk dining in the prime people-watching territory of Newbury Street. Open until midnight.

Tapeo 266 Newbury St ☎617/267-4799, @www.tapeo.com; **Copley T.** An authentic Spanish addition to the Newbury Street dining scene, *Tapeo* has a cool vibe and great tapas such as boneless pheasant with mushrooms and sausage with fig sauce. Dishes start from $5.

Thai Basil 132 Newbury St ℡617/424-8424;
Copley **T**. Excellent and affordable seafood, vegetarian, and pad thai dishes,
plus a cool, soothing decor in which to
enjoy it; parties of six can get the full
experience by reserving an entire bam-
boo-matted room.

Top of the Hub 800 Boylston St ℡617/536-
1775, ⊛www.selectrestaurants.com; Prudential
T. There are several benefits of dining atop
the 50th floor of the Prudential Tower, not
the least of which is enjoying the excellent
city views from the big, bright dining space.
There's also surprisingly inventive New England fare, such as spicy clam broth instead
of chowder.

Turner Fisheries 10 Huntington Ave ℡617/424-
7425, ⊛www.turnersboston.com; Prudential **T**.
At this cheerful spot, the traditional
New England seafood – scrod, Boston
clam chowder, lobster bisque – is as
good as any in the city. Try the"power
lunch," where you get two seafood
dishes for $15. Most nights feature live
jazz performances.

The South End

Aquitaine 569 Tremont St ℡617/424-8577;
Back Bay **T**. This swanky French brasserie
is the place to be and be seen; settle into
a marvelous leather banquette, gape at the
astonishing array of wines, and feast on the
best steak frites and foie gras in town.

B&G Oyster 550 Tremont St ℡617/423-0550;
Back Bay **T**. If you can manage to get a
table at this tiny restaurant, you're in luck.
The oysters (from $2 each) are simply the
best Boston has to offer.

Claremont Café 535 Columbus Ave ℡617/247-
9001; Back Bay **T**. Diverse appetizers (like
cornmeal-fried oysters with jicama slaw),
imaginatively garnished entrees and
particularly flavorful desserts, including a
stellar banana creme pie. Closed Mon.

Delux Café & Lounge 100 Chandler St
℡617/338-5258; Back Bay **T**. The South
End's cool spot of the moment is this retro
hideaway boîte. The menu is loosely American fusion (try the Mediterranean chicken,
$8.95), but it doesn't matter, as most go for
the buzz more than the food.

Franklin Café 278 Shawmut Ave ℡617/350-
0010; Back Bay **T**. Very popular in the gay
and lesbian scene, this upscale diner has
earned local fame for its tasty renditions of

Yankee comfort food like turkey meatloaf
with spicy fig sauce ($12).

Hamersley's Bistro 553 Tremont St ℡617/423-
2700, ⊛www.hamersleysbistro.com; Back Bay
T. *Hamersley's* is widely regarded as one
of the best restaurants in Boston, and with
good cause. Every night star chef (and
owner) Gordon Hamersley dons a baseball
cap and takes to the open kitchen, where
he dishes out unusual – and unforgettable
– French-American fare that changes with
the season, such as pan-roasted lobster
with leeks, roasted chestnuts, and black
truffles ($38).

Mistral 221 Columbus Ave ℡617/867-9300,
⊛www.mistralbistro.com; Arlington **T**. Still
one of *the* places to go in Boston, *Mistral*
serves pricey modern Provençal food in
a bright, airy space. Despite the raves,
the food doesn't live up to the cost (some
entrees are almost $50). Dinner only.

On the Park One Union Park ℡617/426-0862;
Back Bay **T**. Its secluded setting on the
quiet south side of Union Park is as much
of a draw as the French bistro fare at this
neighborhood restaurant. The vegetarian
cassoulet is a winner, and there's an intimate brunch on weekends. Expect to pay
around $15 a head for two courses.

Pho Republique 1415 Washington St
℡617/262-0005, ⊛www.phorepublique.net;
Back Bay **T**. Funky Vietnamese restaurant
that attracts a young, stylish clientele who
dine on hearty servings of pho ($15) and
sip divine lychee martinis ($9); an in-house
DJ keeps patrons nodding their heads long
after their meal is done.

Prairie Star 111 Dartmouth St ℡617/262-7575,
⊛www.prairiestargrillandbar.com; Back Bay **T**.
While the name of this Tex-Mex eatery has
changed (it used to be the *Baja Mexican
Cantina*), the quality of the food has not.
Free tacos at 5–7pm make it popular with
the after-work crowd.

Kenmore Square and the Fenway

Audubon Circle 838 Beacon St ℡617/421-
1910; Kenmore **T**. The seemingly endless
bar is what grabs your attention first, but
it's the food that's worth staying for. Any of
the appetizers are good bets, as is anything
grilled – from burgers with chipotle ketchup
to tuna steak with banana salsa and fufu
(fried plantains mashed with coconut milk).
Expect to pay around $8 per dish. There's

a limited selection of homemade desserts, as well.

Buteco 130 Jersey St ☎617/247-9508; **Kenmore T**. The setting's not much, but the downright tasty Brazilian home-cooking served at this no-frills joint more than compensates. The feijoada – a sausage, dried beef, and black bean stew – is utterly authentic (and only served on Sat & Sun). A live Brazilian band often plays.

Great Bay 500 Commonwealth Ave (in *Hotel Commonwealth*) ☎617/933-5000 @www .hotelcommonwealth.com; **Kenmore T**. This top seafood restaurant more than lives up to its reputation. Pancetta-wrapped swordfish ($27), Block Island swordfish with shitake mushrooms ($32), and wolffish with artichoke ragout $(26) are all sublime.

Allston-Brighton and Brookline

Ducky Wok 122–126 Harvard Ave, Allston-Brighton ☎617/782-8868; **Harvard Ave T**. Despite having the worst restaurant name in Boston, this popular Chinese-Vietnamese place allows you to select your own fish from a giant tank. The lemongrass chicken, stir-fried peapod stems, and avocado smoothies (for dessert) all stand out.

Matt Murphy's 14 Harvard St, Brookline ☎617/232-0188, @www.mattmurphyspub .com; **Coolidge Corner T**. Authentic Irish comfort food such as potato and leek soup with warm brown bread and rabbit pie with Irish soda bread crust. The place is tiny, and you may have to wait, but it's well worth it.

Rangoli 129 Brighton Ave, Allston-Brighton ☎617/562-0200, @www.rangoliboston.com; **Harvard Ave T**. Inexpensive southern Indian fare, favoring spicy vegetarian selections. Be sure to try the dosa: sourdough pancakes rolled like giant cannoli around a variety of savory fillings (from $6.50).

Washington Square Tavern 714 Washington St, Brookline ☎617/232-8989, @www .washingtonsquaretavern.com; **Washington Square T**. Cozy, off-the-beaten-path restaurant/bar with an eclectic fusion menu that turns out inventive meals like pork tenderloin with fig glaze and sweet potatoes ($18). Just hanging out and absorbing the vibe at the bar is worthwhile, too.

Wonder Bar 186 Harvard Ave, Allston-Brighton ☎617/351-2665; **Harvard Ave T**. Popular late-night twenty- and early thirtysomething hangout that scores points with its clay

pot concoctions and tapas snacks, though it really comes alive after dark. The strict dress code (no tennis shoes, ripped jeans, or hats) is a bit over-the-top for the grungy neighborhood, however.

The southern districts

Amrheins 80 W Broadway, South Boston ☎617/268-6189, @www.amrheins.net; **Broadway T**. A Southie landmark and a favorite of local generations for generations. The good-ole' American comfort food won't dazzle your palate, but it's reasonably priced and you get a lot of it. Sunday brunch is a $10.95 all-you-can-eat affair.

Bella Luna 405 Centre St, Jamaica Plain ☎617/524-6060; **Green St T**. Nouvelle pizza with a funky array of fresh toppings – you can order from their list of combinations or design your own; prices start from $4.99. There's a jazz brunch on Sunday mornings and live entertainment on most weekends.

Bob the Chef 604 Columbus Ave, Roxbury ☎617/536-6204, @www.bobthechefs.com; **Mass Ave T**. The best soul food in New England. Good chitlins, black-eyed peas, and collard greens – and don't miss the house specialty, "glori-fried chicken wings" ($5.95). Live jazz on weekends.

Doyle's Cafe 3484 Washington St, Jamaica Plain ☎617/524-2345; **Green St T**. Excellent, inexpensive Irish pub-restaurant, with fish-and-chips, rack of lamb, burgers, clam chowder, and good beers on tap. A friendly neighborhood place that's equally good for a drink or brunch.

Cambridge

Bartley's Burger Cottage 1246 Massachusetts Ave ☎617/354-6559; **Harvard T**. The walls here are decorated with references to political humor and pop culture, while the names of the dishes on the menu poke fun at celebrities of the hour. The food itself is loaded with cholesterol, but a burger (from $6) and "frappé" (milkshake) here is a definite experience.

Blue Room 1 Kendall Sq ☎617/494-9034, @www.theblueroom.net; **Kendall T**. Unpretentious restaurant with superlative grilled fusion; pan-seared skate ($21) and braised lamb ($23) are common, but what accompanies them – cumin and basmati yogurt or tomatillos – isn't. The menu changes with what ingredients are available, so the food is always fresh and innovative.

Boca Grande 1728 Massachusetts Ave ⓣ617/354-7400, ⓦwww.bocagrande .citysearch.com; **Porter T.** Somewhere in between a restaurant and a taco stand, crowded *Boca* features delectable, if not quite authentic, Mexican fare at incredibly low prices (no entree is above $5). The overstuffed burritos are excellent meals in themselves. Two more branches are at 149 First St, Cambridge (ⓣ617/354-5550; Kendall T) and 1294 Beacon St (ⓣ617/739-3900; Washington St T).

Border Café 32 Church St ⓣ617/864-6100; **Harvard T.** Cambridge's most popular Tex-Mex place is pretty good, though not nearly enough to justify the massive crowds that form on weekend nights. The margaritas are salty and strong, and the moderately priced food is so pungent you'll carry its aroma with you for hours afterward.

Café of India 52 Brattle St ⓣ617/661-0683; **Harvard T.** This inexpensive Indian spot stands out primarily because of its uplifting, woody interior; in summer, the facade is removed for semi-alfresco dining. Its best dishes are tried-and-true Indian standards – chicken tikka, saag paneer, and particularly light, delectable naan bread.

Cambridge Common 1667 Massachusetts Ave ⓣ617/547-1228; **Harvard or Porter T.** Half bar, half restaurant, Cambridge Common is a popular after-work place for young professionals and graduate students. The "Ultimate Nachos" appetizer could stand as a meal on its own. A downstairs music venue, the *Lizard Lounge* (see p.217), has decent rock and jazz acts almost nightly.

Central Kitchen 567 Massachusetts Ave ⓣ617/491-5599; **Central T.** Hip Central Square bistro with a chalkboard menu offering delightful French classics (moules frites, $12) and New American twists (porcini-dusted half chicken, $18) in an intimate, stylish setting.

Charlie's Kitchen 10 Eliot St ⓣ617/492-9646; **Harvard T.** Marvelous townie hangout in the heart of Harvard Square, with red vinyl booths, sassy waitresses with beehive hairdos, and greasy diner food. Every so often a "lobsterfest menu" is available for $10, allowing even the poorest of us to try the shellfish.

Chez Henri 1 Shepard St ⓣ617/354-8980; **Harvard or Porter T.** If you can get a table (no reservations, and the weekend wait tops one hour, even late at night), you'll enjoy what may well be Cambridge's finest cuisine. Chef Paul O'Connell's experiment in fusion brings Modern French together with Cuban influences, best sampled in the light salads, excellent Cuban ceviche appetizers, and seared monkfish ($24.95).

East Coast Grill 1271 Cambridge St ⓣ617/491-6568, ⓦwww.eastcoastgrill.net; **Harvard or Central Square T.** A festive and funky atmosphere in which to enjoy fresh seafood from the raw bar (six oysters for $10.50, jumbo shrimp $2.50 each) and Caribbean side dishes such as grilled avocado, pineapple salsa, and fried plaintains. The Sunday serve-yourself Bloody Mary bar is reason enough to visit.

Harvest 44 Brattle St ⓣ617/868-2255, ⓦwww .the-harvest.com; **Harvard T.** Upscale, white-tableclothed Harvard Square institution with an oft-changing menu of rich New American cuisine; the smashing outdoor courtyard is another fine feature.

Henrietta's Table 1 Bennett St (in the Charles Hotel) ⓣ617/661-5005; **Harvard T.** One of the only restaurants in Cambridge that serves classic New England fare. Rich entrees such as roasted duck ($15) or pork chops ($15.75) work well with side dishes of wilted greens or mashed potatoes – although some would say a trip to *Henrietta's* is wasted if it's not for their famous brunch, served every Sunday from noon to 3pm; it costs $35 per person but allows unlimited access to a cornucopia of farm-fresh treats from around New England.

Iruña 56 JFK St ⓣ617/868-5633; **Harvard T.** Located in a diminutive, unassuming spot in an alley off JFK Street, this fairly uncrowded spot serves authentic Spanish fare. Lunch specials are incredibly cheap, including paella and a rich arroz con pollo; dinner is more expensive but equally good.

Koreana 154 Prospect St ⓣ617/576-8661, ⓦwww.koreanaboston.com; **Central Square T.** Tables here have a built-in grill allowing you to barbecue your own tasty food (prices start from $16). The sushi bar (from $3 per piece) is also pretty good.

Pho Pasteur 35 Dunster St, in the Garage ⓣ617/864-4100; **Harvard T.** This more upscale Harvard Square incarnation of the successful Chinatown string of Vietnamese joints (see p.197) serves a variety of filling and delicious pho noodle soups beginning at $5.95. The spring rolls ($3.95) are another treat.

Royal India 313 Massachusetts Ave ☎617/491-1988; **Kendall T.** There are only 32 seats in the *Royal India* and there's often a wait as it's a favorite of MIT students, but it's more than worth it. The menu's a blend of Bengali and North Indian cuisine and signature dishes such as the poora roast eggplant ($5.95) and kasha mangsho (spicey goat, $10.95) are top class.

Siam Garden 45 1/2 Mt Auburn St ☎617/354-1718, ⓦ www.siamgarden.com; **Harvard T.** Tasty and cheap Thai food in an atmosphere that tries really hard to invoke images of the exotic East. Try the huge Siam Combo appetizer plate ($11.95) consisting of chicken and beef sate, vegetable rolls, wings, knom jips (seafood wrapped in wonton skin), and golden triangles (fried tofu served with peanut and chili sauces).

Tandoor House 569 Massachusetts Ave ☎617/661-9001; **Central T.** Consistently at the top of the list of Cambridge's many fine Indian restaurants, *Tandoor* has excellent chicken saag and a great mushroom bhaji. Definitely the best Indian spot outside Harvard Square – and perhaps in the whole city.

Trattoria Pulcinella 147 Huron Ave ☎617/491-6336, ⓦ www.trattoriapulcinella.net; **Porter T.** A creative menu blends fresh ingredients with Continental flair. The eggplant-stuffed ravioli with a tomato basil garlic sauce ($20) is a must, as is the perfectly decadent tiramisu. Waitstaff is unusually attentive without being intrusive.

UpStairs on the Square 91 Winthrop St ☎617/864-1933, ⓦ www.upstairsonthesquare.com; **Harvard T.** Born from the ashes of *UpStairs at the Pudding*, when the Harvard favorite had to move, this new restaurant, like its predecesser, serves excellent food. The grilled veal porterhouse chop with

cranberries ($36) is delightful. Reservations are needed.

Somerville

Dalí 415 Washington St ☎617/661-3254, ⓦ www.dalirestaurant.com; **Harvard T.** Waitresses dance the flamenco at this upscale tapas restaurant, which features live, energetic Spanish music, excellent sangria, a good wine list. and superlative tapas (from $4.50). Order the Spanish white asparagus, farm trout with red wine sauce, and the braised rabbit in sweet-and-sour sauce; your taste buds will thank you.

Diva 246 Elm St ☎617/629-4963, ⓦ www.divabistro.com; **Davis T.** This trendy Davis Square spot isn't your typical Indian restaurant: the space is stylishly modern and cushy, the entrees pricey ($11–17), and the northern and southern dishes unusually mild, spice-wise.

Gargoyles on the Square 215 Elm St ☎617/776-5300, ⓦ gargoylesonthesquare.citysearch.com; **Davis T.** The classiest joint in Davis Square combines contemporary American fare with a touch of French; look for the homemade ravioli with apple and brie ($9). There's a $20 minimum on Fri and Sat.

Redbones 55 Chester St ☎617/628-2200, ⓦ www.redbones.com; **Davis T.** All styles of American barbecue ($10–19) are represented in huge portions here, accompanied by delectable sides such as collard greens and Cajun "dirty rice." After eating, you won't likely have room for dessert – but if you do, the pecan pie is top-notch. Long lines form at dinner, so arrive early. No credit cards.

The Rosebud Diner 381 Summer St ☎617/666-6015; **Davis T.** Authentic diner car with red vinyl booths, pink neon sign, and chrome detail, serving the expected burgers, fries, and Boston cream pie along with more contemporary favorites like pasta, grilled chicken, and veggie burgers.

Drinking

D espite – or, perhaps, because of – the lingering Puritan ethic that pervades Boston, people here tend to **drink** more than they do in the rest of the country, with the consequence that few American cities offer as many bars per capita in which to knock back a few beers. Before you start planning a big night out, however, it's worth pointing out that drinking in Boston is not without its headaches – and we don't just mean the morning after.

While the number of watering holes in Boston is high, the range of options is not, and most **stop serving alcohol at 2am**. Another sticking point is that the city's university culture means the US **drinking-age minimum of 21** is strictly enforced; even if you're obviously of-age, you'll still be required to show at least one form of valid photo **identification**, either in the form of a driver's license or passport, to gain entrance to any place serving drinks. Finally, as the T shuts down at 12.30am, it can be difficult to find a taxi due to the mass exodus of drinkers when the bars let out. Also, smokers will find themselves marginalized thanks to the **smoking ban**, which went into effect in June 2003.

As for types of places, it's not surprising that, given the city's Irish heritage, **pubs** make up the majority of Boston's drinking establishments. Especially high concentrations of these are found in the **West End**, **Cambridge**, and **Downtown** around Quincy Market; many are unextraordinary, but several are the real deal, drawing as many Irish expats as they do Irish-American locals.

More upscale are the **bars** and **lounges** of **Back Bay**, especially those along Newbury and Boylston streets, which offer as much scenester attitude as atmosphere. Some of the most popular bars in this area are actually adjuncts of restaurants and hotels; still others cater to the city's gay population (see chapter 17, Gay Boston, for the best).

The rest of the city's neighborhood bars, pick-up joints, and yuppie hotspots are differentiated by their crowds: **Beacon Hill** tends to be older and stuffier;

Eating and drinking maps

Within this chapter, as well as Chapter 12, Cafés and light meals, and Chapter 13, Restaurants, you'll find maps where we've keyed the eating and drinking options for the major Boston neighborhoods. These maps can be found on the following pages:

Downtown, mainly around Quincy Market and the Theater District, draws a healthy mix of tourists, business people, and sporty types; while **Kenmore Square** and **Cambridge** are mainly student-oriented, with a clientele sporting a generic uniform of khakis, university logo T-shirts, and baseball caps.

Downtown

Beantown Pub 100 Tremont St ☎617/426-0111; Park Street T. This centrally located pub has a range of decent beer, a varied jukebox, and is a great place to play pool.

Bell in Hand Tavern 45 Union St ☎617/227-2098; State or Government Center T. The oldest continuously operating tavern in Boston, dating from 1795, draws a fairly exuberant mix of tourists and young professionals.

The Black Rose (Roisin Dubh) 160 State St ☎617/742-2286; State T. Down-home Irish pub specializing in imported beers from the Emerald Isle: Harp, Murphy's, and – especially – Guinness all flow freely. Things get pretty boisterous on weekends.

Cheers Faneuil Hall Marketplace ☎617/227-0150, ⊛www.cheersboston.com; Aquarium T. A replica of the NBC set (the originial inspiration is on Beacon St; see below), this place is little more than an overpriced tacky tourist trap that's good for a photo-op.

Emily's 48 Winter St ☎617/423-3649; Park T. Red-velvet curtains and floor-to-ceiling mirrors give this Downtown spot as much style as any place in Back Bay, but without the accompanying attitude. On weeknights it's mellow, while on weekends a DJ spins Top 40 mixes to overenthusiastic (or overserved) dancers.

Good Life 28 Kingston St ☎617/451-2622; Downtown Crossing T. This trendy, swanky bar generates quite a buzz, owing as much to its potent martinis as its 1970s decor, which features wicked groovy orange vinyl walls; also serves standard bar food, including "east of" Buffalo wings.

Green Dragon Tavern 11 Marshall St ☎617/367-0055; Government Center T. Another tavern that dates to the colonial era, this was a popular meeting place for patriots during the Revolution. There's a standard selection of tap beers, a raw bar, and a full menu rife with twee historical humor ("One if by land, two if by seafood").

Felt 533 Washington St ☎617/350-5555; Downtown Crossing T. *Felt* is an upscale pool hall full of the young and beautiful willing to pay $14 an hour for a table. One of the new places to be seen.

Hub Pub 18 Province St ☎617/227-8952; Downtown Crossing T. Self-billed as the "friendliest pub in the hub," this small bar does indeed have a warm atmosphere and some bizarre decor upstairs where you can sit in booths themed like funfair teacups.

The Kinsale 2 Center Plaza ☎617/742-5577; Government Center T. Shipped brick by brick from Ireland to its current location in the shadow of Government Plaza, this outrageously popular Irish pub is as authentic as it gets; the menu even lists beer-battered fish and hot pastrami on a "bulkie" (Boston slang for a sandwich bun).

Les Zygomates 129 South St ☎617/542-5108; South Station T. This elegant wine bar (also reviewed p.197) has a wide and exceptional selection of varietals. Neophytes might want to get their palates wet at the weekly wine-tasting sessions (Tues 6–8pm; $25).

The Littlest Bar in Boston 47 Province St ☎617/523-9766; Downtown Crossing T. The tiny size of this place – it only admits 38 people in its cramped quarters at any given time – is part of the charm, as are the quality pints of Guinness and free music by bands crammed into an alcove

▽ The Littlest Bar in Boston

– perhaps also the littlest performance space in Boston.

Pravda 116 116 Boylston St ☎617/482-7799; Boylston T. Red curtains, plush seating, and back-lit walls are a fittingly decadent backdrop to the whopping 116 varieties of vodka on tap (whence the digits in the bar's name). Unfortunately, you won't find any mysterious-looking Russians sipping the spirits; the crowd is more suited to an Abercrombie & Fitch catalog.

The Purple Shamrock 1 Union St ☎617/227-2060; State or Government Center T. A lively watering hole that draws a broad cross-section of folks, the *Shamrock* has one of Boston's better straight singles scenes. It gets very crowded on weekends.

The Rack 24 Clinton St ☎617/725-1051; Government Center T. Well-dressed twenty- and thirtysomethings convene at this pool hall to dine, smoke cigars, drink a bewildering variety of cocktails, and, of course, shoot a rack or two. While there are 35 pool tables and a fair share of wannabe hustlers, about half the crowd shows up just to see and be seen.

Umbria 295 Franklin St ☎617/338-1000; Aquarium T. One of the latest additions to the city's bar scene, *Umbria* breaks from the mould by following the current trend for ultralounges – a hybrid of bar, nighclub, and restaurant. Stick by the bar, though, for the fabulous martinis.

Charlestown

Tavern On The Water 1 8th St Pier 6, ☎617/241-242-8040, ⓦ www.tavernonthewater .com; Community College T. Actually a steak restaurant; skip the rather overpriced fare and sip a cocktail here and take in the great views of Boston Harbor.

Warren Tavern 2 Pleasant St ☎617/241-8142; Community College T. Paul Revere and George Washington were both regulars here, and the oldest standing structure in Charlestown is still decent for a drink. Also has a generous menu of good tavern food.

Beacon Hill and the West End

21st Amendment 148 Bowdoin St ☎617/227-7100; Bowdoin T. This dimly lit, down-home watering hole, which gets its name from the amendment that repealed Prohibition, is a favorite haunt of legislators from the adjacent State House and students from nearby Suffolk University.

Cheers 84 Beacon St ☎617/227-9605, ⓦ www .cheersboston.com; Arlington T. Formerly the *Bull & Finch*, the bar that served as the inspiration for the TV series now goes the whole hog when trying to pull in the tourists. The inside bears little resemblance to the set – for that, you have to go to the *Cheers* in Faneuil Hall (see above). The food, though cutely named (eNORMous burgers), is pricey and mediocre. Plus, it's almost certain that nobody will know your name.

Coyote Ugly 234 Friend St ☎617/854-7300; North Station T. When the much-loved Irish Embassy pub closed to make way for this NYC chain bar (on which the movie was based), there was much mourning among Boston's drinking community. Gone was the authentic atmosphere, to be replaced by cute girls dancing on the bar. Packed at weekends but recommended only for the young-at-heart.

Emmet's Pub and Restaurant 6-B Beacon St ☎617/742-8565; Park Street T. Named after the Irish rebel Robert Emmet, this cozy watering hole tucked in the quieter section of Beacon Street is one of the more relaxed places to have a beer in town; the bulk of its business comes from government workers from the nearby State House during happy hour. The kitchen serves decent staples, such as fish and chips.

Fours 166 Canal St ☎617/720-4455, ⓦ www .thefours.com; North Station T. The classiest of the West End's sports bars, with an army of TVs to broadcast games from around the globe, as well as paraphernalia from the Celtics, Bruins, and other local teams.

The Hill Tavern 228 Cambridge St ☎617/742-6192; Charles T. The only centrally located bar in Beacon Hill, this classic yuppie hangout attracts suits who like to tip back a lot of pricey imported beer; there's often a long line to get in on weekend nights.

McGann's 197 Portland St ☎617/227-4059; North Station T. An authentic Irish bar, but with a more upmarket, restauranty feel. There are Irish and British eats like shepherd's pie and pan-seared calf's liver, if you're in the mood.

Sevens Ale House 77 Charles St ☎617/523-9074; **Charles** T. While the tourists pack into nearby *Cheers*, you can drop by this cozy wood-paneled joint to watch a game or shoot darts in an authentic Boston neighborhood bar. Wide selection of draft beers, plus daily specials, substantial food, and a relaxed feel.

Back Bay and the South End

33 33 Stanhope St ☎617/572-3311, ⓦwww.33restaurant.com; **Back Bay** T. Sashay through the discreetly labeled doors and head straight down the smoked-glass stairwell to this restaurant-lounge's intimate basement club. Decked out in a curious pastiche of wire netting and puffy, mushroom-cap footstools, this place is popular with a thirtysomething set who taps its feet to deep house.

Bristol Lounge 200 Boylston St ☎617/351-2053; **Arlington** T. An upmarket lobby-side lounge in the *Four Seasons* where the desserts are as popular as the drinks and a pianist plays smooth jazz that's ideal for the post-theater crowd.

Bukowski's Tavern 50 Dalton St ☎617/437-9999; **Hynes** T. Arguably Boston's best dive bar, this watering hole has views over the Mass Pike and such a vast beer selection that a home-made "wheel of indecision" is spun by waitstaff when patrons can't decide what to drink. Excellent rock 'n' roll jukebox, plus regular poetry and fiction readings, too.

Clery's Restaurant 113 Dartmouth St ☎617/262-9874; **Back Bay** T. Despite a name change (known, until recently, as *The Claddaugh*), and a renovation, this Irish bar and restaurant on the northern edge of the South End remains lackluster in the food department while consistently packing in a lively drinking clientele; head downstairs to the sofa-strewn lounge area and cozy up with a pint by the fire.

Daisy Buchanan's 240A Newbury St ☎617/247-8516; **Copley** T. A real-life beer commercial: young guys wearing baseball caps eye up scantily clad gals, watch sports on TV, and contribute nightly to the bar's pervasive smell of booze.

Dillons 955 Boylston ☎617/421-1818; **Hynes** T. Formerly a trendy restaurant and housed in what used to be a police department building, *Dillons* is an upscale Irish bar/restaurant popular with the post-work crowd.

Excelsior 272 Boylston ☎617/421-1818; **Copley** T. Technically a restaurant offering imaginative modern American cuisine, *Excelsior* is more famous among Bostonians for its happening bar scene and impressive cocktails.

Lucky's 355 Congress St ☎617/357-5825; **South Station** T. Over the water and quite a walk, this subterranean lounge bar is one of Boston's best-kept secrets – mainly because it's off the beaten tourist path. Weekends see Frank Sinatra impersonators get the thirtysomething locals swinging.

Oak Bar 138 St. James Ave in the Fairmont Copley Plaza ☎617/267-5300; **Copley** T. Rich wood paneling, high ceilings, and excellent martinis make this one of the more genteel Back Bay spots to drink.

Saint 90 Exeter St ☎617/236-1134; **Copley** T. Upscale bar/club where the young and beautiful come to dance on weekends. The door staff can be obstructive, though, so being a member helps.

Vox Populi 755 Boylston St ☎617/424-8300; **Copley** T. Trendy post-work spot that's perfect for people-watching in summer. The modern American food is nothing to write home about – better stick to the impressive cocktail list.

Whiskey Park 64 Arlington St (in the Park Plaza) ☎617/542-1482; **Arlington** T. Owned by Rande Gerber (aka Mr Cindy Crawford), this lounge's chic chocolate-brown leather-chair design was conceived by Michael Czysz, the guy behind Lenny Kravitz's swinging Miami pad. The prices match the celebrity name-dropping, but there's hardly a better place in town to grab a cocktail.

Kenmore Square and the Fenway

An Tua Nua 835 Beacon St ☎617/262-2121; **Kenmore** T. A very popular BU pub that's a great spot for "Soex" – by day, catch a pint and a Sox game; by night see all the people on the pull looking for sex in the nightclub. Also offers good (though standard) bar food, plus a great view of Beacon Street.

Audubon Circle 838 Beacon St ☎617/421-1910; **Kenmore** T. Sleek, modern bar, where a well-dressed crowd gathers for cocktails

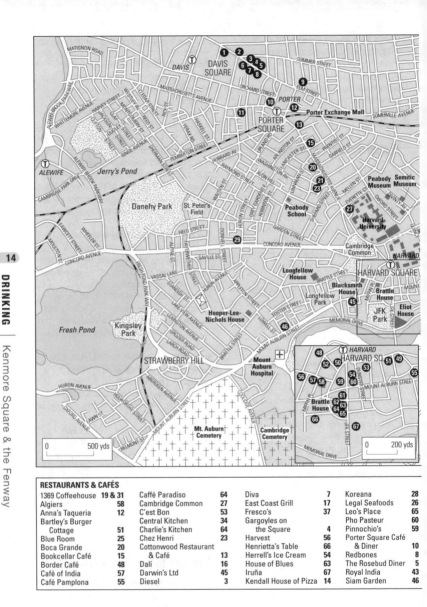

RESTAURANTS & CAFÉS

1369 Coffeehouse	**19 & 31**	Caffé Paradiso	**64**	Diva	**7**	Koreana	**28**
Algiers	**58**	Cambridge Common	**27**	East Coast Grill	**17**	Legal Seafoods	**26**
Anna's Taqueria	**12**	C'est Bon	**53**	Fresco's	**37**	Leo's Place	**65**
Bartley's Burger		Central Kitchen	**34**	Gargoyles on		Pho Pasteur	**60**
Cottage	**51**	Charlie's Kitchen	**64**	the Square	**4**	Pinnochio's	**59**
Blue Room	**25**	Chez Henri	**23**	Harvest	**56**	Porter Square Café	
Boca Grande	**20**	Cottonwood Restaurant		Henrietta's Table	**66**	& Diner	**10**
Bookcellar Café	**15**	& Café	**13**	Herrell's Ice Cream	**54**	Redbones	**8**
Border Café	**48**	Dalí	**16**	House of Blues	**63**	The Rosebud Diner	**5**
Café of India	**57**	Darwin's Ltd	**45**	Iruña	**67**	Royal India	**43**
Café Pamplona	**55**	Diesel	**3**	Kendall House of Pizza	**14**	Siam Garden	**46**

and fancy bar food (see review p.204) before and after games at nearby Fenway Park.

Bill's Bar 5 1/2 Lansdowne St ☎617/421-9678, ⓦwww.billsbar.com; Kenmore T. A fairly relaxed and homey Lansdowne Street spot, with lots of beer, lots of TV screens, and occasional live music – in which case expect a cover charge of $5.

Boston Beer Works 61 Brookline Ave ☎617/536-2337; Kenmore T. A brewery located right by Fenway Park, *Boston Beer Works* is a popular place for the Red Sox faithful to warm up before games and drown their sorrows

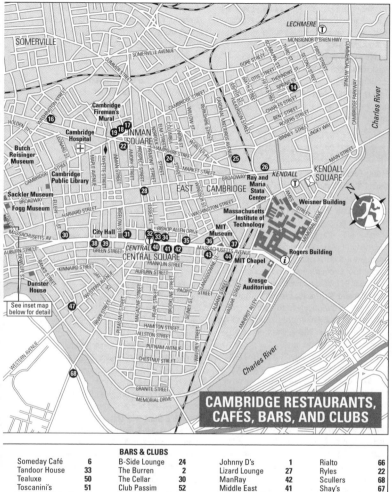

CAMBRIDGE RESTAURANTS, CAFÉS, BARS, AND CLUBS

		BARS & CLUBS					
Someday Café	6	B-Side Lounge	24	Johnny D's	1	Rialto	66
Tandoor House	33	The Burren	2	Lizard Lounge	27	Ryles	22
Tealuxe	50	The Cellar	30	ManRay	42	Scullers	68
Toscanini's	51	Club Passim	52	Middle East	41	Shay's	67
Trattoria Pulcinella	29	The Druid	18	Miracle of Science	36	T.T. the Bear's	41
UpStairs on		Enormous Room	34	Paradise	44	Temple Bar	21
the Square	62	The Field	32	People's		Thirsty Scholar	
		Grafton Street	49	Republik	39	Pub	9
		Grendel's Den	61	Phoenix Landing	40	Tir Na Nog	11
		Hong Kong	51	Plough & Stars	38	Wally's Café	35
		House of Blues	63	Regattabar	66	Western Front	47

after. Their signature ale is the Boston Red, but the seasonal brews are also worth a taste. Decent food, too.

Copperfield's/Down Under 98 Brookline Ave ☏617/247-8605; Kenmore **T**. Two adjoining bars, though the difference between them is minimal: both offer cheap drafts and pool, and are frequented by a raucous collegiate crowd. Cover of $5 on weekends to see loud bands.

The southern districts

Brendan Behan 378 Centre St, Jamaica Plain ☏617/522-5386; Jackson Square **T**. The godfather of Boston's Irish pubs, this dimly lit institution has the usual friendly staff all week long, as well as live music and free buffets available on most weekends.

James's Gate 5–11 McBride St, Jamaica Plain ☎617/983-2000; Forest Hills T. Beat Boston's harsh winter by sipping Guinness beside the blazing fireplace in this cozy pub, or by trying the hearty fare in the restaurant in back. Traditional Irish music on Sundays, open mic on Thursdays.

Cambridge

B-Side Lounge 92 Hampshire St ☎617/354-0766; Central T. Cantabridgians flock to this trendy dive bar to partake of its extensive drinks list and quirky bar food (hard-boiled eggs, anyone?). The en-suite kitchen's tasty soul food offerings are none too shabby either, making this the kind of place where a quick stop for an after-work drink often winds up leading to dinner, too. Great for weekend brunch.

The Cellar 991 Massachusetts Ave ☎617/876-2580; Harvard T. The two floors here, each with a bar, are regularly filled with a crowd of Harvard faculty members, older students, and other locals imbibing fine beers and killer Long Island iced teas.

The Druid 1357 Cambridge St ☎617/497-0965; #69 bus, Central T. Recently refurbished Inman Square favorite that has lost some of its tacky faux Irish decor; a huge Celtic motif has been removed from the wall. The Guinness, however, is as good as ever.

Enormous Room 577 Massachusetts Ave (no phone); Central T. Walking into this comfy lounge tucked above *Central Kitchen* (see p.206) is like entering an opium den minus the pipe smokers. Sundry good-looking types primp and pose on thick-piled futon mattresses and deep leather sofas, while deep house music is piped in over the sound system.

The Field 20 Prospect St ☎617/354-7345; Central T. Although *The Field* is located between Harvard and MIT, this Irish pub attracts an eclectic non-college crowd. You can play pool or darts while you sip one of several varieties of tap beers.

Grafton Street 1280 Massachusetts Ave ☎617/497-0400; Harvard T. Authentic, cozy Irish pub atmosphere, *Grafton Street* is home to an older, well-dressed set that enjoys smooth drafts and equally good food.

Grendel's Den 89 Winthrop St ☎617/491-1160; Harvard T. A favorite spot of locals and grad students for drinking ale. A fantastic happy-hour special includes big plates of appetizers (fried calamari, nachos) for just $1.50 each.

Hong Kong 1236 Massachusetts Ave ☎617/864-5311; Harvard T. The bizarre home-made "Scorpion," a potent concoction served in a dragon boat and loaded with ample straws for communal sharing, makes this bland restaurant-bar definitely worth a visit – once.

Miracle of Science 321 Massachusetts Ave ☎617/868-2866; Central T. Surprisingly hip despite its status as an MIT hangout. Featuring noir decor and a trendy crowd of well-dressed professionals, it can get quite crowded on weekend nights.

People's Republik 880 Massachusetts Ave ☎617/492-8632; Central or Harvard T. Smack dab between MIT and Harvard, *People's Republik* attracts a good mix of technocrats and potential world-leaders as a result. It takes its Communist propaganda seriously – with its posters on the walls, anyway; the range of tap offerings is positively democratic.

Phoenix Landing 512 Massachusetts Ave ☎617/576-6260; Central T. The *Phoenix* is about the only place in Cambridge you'll still catch European sporting events, and the place can be fun despite its surly waitstaff. On weekend nights it turns into a club.

Plough & Stars 912 Massachusetts Ave ☎617/441-3455, ⊛www.ploughandstars.com; Central or Harvard T. Off-the-beaten-path neighborhood hideaway that's very much worth the trek, whether for its animated cribbage games, pub grub, or its nightly live Irish music.

Rialto 1 Bennett St ☎617/661-5050; Harvard T. The bar adjunct to the posh restaurant of the same name caters to a wealthy crowd that matches the plush atmosphere. Dress semi-formal and be prepared to pay big-time for the drinks and cocktails, which are, admittedly, excellent.

Shay's 58 JFK St ☎617/864-9161; Harvard T. Unwind with grad students over wine and quality beer at *Shay's*, a relaxed contrast to the crowded and sweaty student-oriented sports bars of Harvard Square.

Temple Bar 1688 Massachusetts Ave ☎617/547-5055, ⊛www.templebarcambridge .com; Harvard or Porter T. Cambridge's stand-out scenester bar attracts a chi-chi crowd to its smart digs outfitted with attractive touches like fancy floral arrangements and artsy Martini Rosso advertising posters.

Somerville

The Burren 247 Elm St ☎617/776-6896, ⓦwww.burren.com; Davis T. Busy student bar whose overflowing crowds, with the expected baseball caps and cargo pants, spill out onto its outdoor terrace, a prime spot for Davis Square people-watching.

Thirsty Scholar Pub 70 Beacon St ☎617/497-2294, ⓦwww.thirstyscholarpub.com; Harvard T. One of the coziest bars around, *Thirsty's* warm red-brick and burnished-wood interior is matched by a smiling waitstaff and down-home comfort food like shepherd's pie and baked beans. Bring a book to read, or listen up while distinguished writers declaim their own at the bar's oft-hosted readings.

Tir na Nog 366A Somerville Ave ☎617/628-4300, ⓦwww.thenog.com; Washington Square T. Tiny, wonderful pub with a marvelously homey feel, thanks to bookcase-lined walls and friendly barstaff who pour terrific pints behind a gleaming mahogany bar. Live music on weekends.

Nightlife

I n the last decade Boston's **nightlife** has received something of a wake-up call, although for a major American city, its scene still feels small and is geared primarily to a buttoned-down college crowd; you'll find that even at the wildest venues, locals tend to sport the reserved preppy look characteristic of Boston's universities.

A few stylish clubs have sprung up in areas, such as **Downtown Crossing**, that were previously ghost towns by night. Boylston Place – which links Boston Common with the Theater District and is known locally as "The Alley" – is where most of the action is found. Though the city is by no means a 24-hour one, these hotspots have breathed fresh air into a scene that once lived in the shadow of the city's highbrow culture. Elsewhere, the same old clubs reinvent themselves every few years in the hopes of catching up with current trends.

Live music plays a huge role in the city's nightlife arena, with bars and clubs catering to a young crowd, especially around Kenmore and Harvard squares, where you're as likely to hear a squalling rock band as a mellow DJ. Boston has spawned its share of enormous **rock** acts, from the ever-enduring dinosaur rockers Aerosmith to a smattering of post-punk and indie favorites such as the Pixies and Sebadoh. There is a bit less in the way of **jazz** and **blues**, but you can usually find something cheap and to your liking almost any day of the week. If you're interested in hearing classical or opera, check Chapter 16, Performing arts and film.

For **club and music listings**, check Thursday's *Boston Globe* "Calendar," the *Boston Phoenix*, the *Improper Bostonian, Metro*, and *Stuff@night*. You'll also find a number of websites helpful for up-to-date listings; for details on media and websites, see p.30.

Live music

The strength of Boston's **live music** is in the intimacy of its smaller venues, though superstar acts make the city a regular stop on their world tours as well. Two of the biggest **concert halls** are far out of town: the Tweeter Center, south of the city in Mansfield (☎508/339-2333, ⓦwww.tweetercenter.com), and the Worcester Centrum, an hour or so west in Worcester (☎508/755-6800, ⓦwww.centrumcentre.com).

On a more human scale, plenty of **alternative venues** serve up everything from name bands to obscure new acts; if all else fails, there's always street music at "The Pit" in Harvard Square (p.140), where you're bound to hear some free amateur acts – whether you like it or not.

Rock venues

FleetBoston Pavilion Fan Pier, Northern Ave
T617/728-1600, Wwww.fleetbostonpavilion
.com; South Station **T**. Concerts by well-
known performers from Harry Connick Jr
to Deep Purple are held here during the
summer under a huge white tent at Boston
Harbor's edge.

FleetCenter 50 Causeway St T617/624-1000,
Wwww.fleetcenter.com; North Station **T**. This
arena, up in the West End, attracts many of
the big-name acts that pass through New
England – usually at hefty prices.

**Lizard Lounge 1667 Massachusetts Ave, Cam-
bridge** T617/547-0759; Harvard or Porter **T**.
The downstairs portion of the *Cambridge
Common* restaurant (see p.206) is a favorite
among local students. Rock and jazz acts
are onstage almost nightly for a fairly nominal cover charge (usually around $5), while
every Monday there's a stand-up comedy
hour.

Middle East 472 Massachusetts Ave, Cambridge
T617/864-3278, Wwww.mideastclub.com;
Central **T**. Local and regional bands of
every sort – salsa to ska and mambo to
hardcore – stop in regularly at this Cambridge institution. Bigger acts are hosted
downstairs; smaller ones ply their trade in
a tiny upstairs space. A third venue, the
Corner, has free shows every night, with
belly dancing every Sunday and "Punk
Rock Aerobics" on Saturday. The attached
restaurant, *ZuZu*, serves decent Middle
Eastern food.

Orpheum Theater 1 Hamilton Place T617/679-
0810; Park or Downtown Crossing **T**. Housed
in a former movie theater, the *Orpheum*
is now a venue for big-name music
acts. The small space ensures you're
closer to the action, but it sells out quickly
and the cramped seating discourages
dancing.

Paradise Rock Club 967 Commonwealth Ave
T617/562-8800, Wwww.thedise.com;
Kenmore **T**. One of Boston's oldest
venues for live performances by mid-
range acts, the *Paradise* recently
celebrated its 25th anniversary with the
opening of a new venue next door, the
Paradise Lounge, which serves food
and hosts art exhibitions to a rock soundtrack.

T.T. the Bear's 10 Brookline St, Cambridge
T617/492-BEAR, Wwww.ttthebears.com;

Central **T**. A downmarket version of the
Middle East, with less popular acts in a
space with a gritty intimacy its neighbor
lacks. All kinds of bands appear, mostly
punk, rock, and electronica.

Jazz, blues, and folk venues

Club Passim 47 Palmer St, Cambridge
T617/492-7679, Wwww.clubpassim.com; Harvard **T**. Folkie hangout in Harvard Square
where Joan Baez and Suzanne Vega got
their starts. World music and spoken word
performances in windowed basement setting.

Johnny D's 17 Holland St, Somerville
T617/776-2004, Wwww.johnnyds.com; Davis
T. A mixed bag with talent ranging from
the sublime to the ordinary, and a $10
cover charge for most shows. Acts include
garage bands, progressive jazz sextets,
traditional blues artists, and some uncate-
gorizables.

Regattabar 1 Bennett St, Cambridge
T617/661-5000, Wwww.regattabarjazz
.com; Harvard **T**. Despite its location in
the *Charles Hotel*, which leads to a more
sedate crowd, this place draws top acts
and is generally considered the best jazz
bar in the city. Dress nicely and prepare
to pay anything from a $10–25 cover; it's
sometimes necessary to purchase tickets
ahead of time.

Ryles 212 Hampshire St, Cambridge
T617/876-9330, Wwww.rylesjazz.com; Central
T. Two levels of live music – swing and
salsa upstairs, and smooth jazz and blues
downstairs. *Ryles* also does a good jazz
brunch on Sunday, where a plate of corned
beef hash and eggs costs $8.

Scullers 400 Soldiers Field Rd, Cambridge
T617/783-0090, Wwww.scullersjazz.com;
Harvard **T**. Upscale jazz club in the
DoubleTree Guest Suites draws five-star
acts, including some of the stars of the
contemporary jazz scene. You'll need
to hop in a taxi to get here, as the walk
along the river at night can be risky. The
cover charge varies wildly – anywhere
from $12 to $55.

Wally's Café 427 Massachusetts Ave, Roxbury
T617/424-1408, Wwww.wallyscafe.com; Massachusetts **T**. This refreshingly unhewn bar
is Boston's oldest jazz joint, and its A-list
jazz (Thurs, Fri, & Sat), blues (Mon), swing
(Tues), and fusion (Wed & Sun) shows draw

a vibrant crowd. It gets pretty packed on weekends, but that's part of the experience. No cover.

Western Front 343 Western Ave, Cambridge ⊤617/492-7772, @www.thewesternfrontclub

.com; Central **T**. The *Front* puts on rollicking jazz, blues, and reggae shows for a dance-crazy audience. Drinks are cheap, and the Jamaican food served on weekends is delectably authentic.

Nightclubs

Boston's **nightclubs** are mostly clustered around "The Alley" (Boylston Place), the Theater District, and Kenmore Square with a few prominent ones in Back Bay and the South End. Many of the venues in those two neighborhoods are **gay clubs**, often the most happening places in town; for a complete listing, see Chapter 17, Gay Boston.

The music at these clubs changes almost nightly, so to keep apprised of what's on, check the individual club websites, the "Calendar" section in Thursday's *Boston Globe*, or the listings in the weekly *Boston Phoenix* and daily *Metro*. **Cover charges** are generally in the $5–15 range, though sometimes there's no cover at all. Boston's venues tend to be easily entered – no New York–style selection at the door – though there is a tendency for bouncers to frown upon sneakers and jeans in favor of collared shirts and dress pants. On weekends, clubs can be overrun with suburbanites and yuppies; come on a weeknight for the most authentic local scene.

Downtown, Back Bay, and the South End

Aria 246 Tremont St ⊤617/338-7080, @www.ariaboston.com; Boylston **T**. This cushy, upscale club in the basement of the Wilbur Theater is as close as Boston gets to the velvet-rope attitude of New York clubs. The emphasis is more on lounging around in plush seats and posing for the well-dressed Euro crowd than dancing to house music, an activity relegated to a small dancefloor. Cover $7–15.

The Big Easy One Boylston Place ⊤617/351-7000, @www.alleyboston.com; Boylston **T**. Bar and jazz club with a New Orleans theme and a mix of live acts and DJs; open Thursday to Saturday night only. Cover $5–8.

Club Europa/Buzz 67 Stuart St ⊤617/267-8969, @www.buzzboston.com; Boylston **T**. On the edge of the Theater District, this is one of Boston's better dance clubs. Most of the action is on the third floor; the second tends to be louder and more crowded. On Saturday night the club becomes "Buzz," long the most plugged-in gay disco in Boston.

Liquor Store 25 Boylston Place ⊤617/357-6800, @www.liquorstoreboston.com; Boylston **T**. One of the latest additions to "The Alley," in the space formerly occupied by *Envy* and

La Boom, *Liquor Store* looks as though it could be here to stay – as the young and beautiful party hard to current hits, R&B, and house while trying their luck on the mechanical bull.

Q 25 Union St ⊤617/742-2121, @www.somerspubs.com; Government Center **T**. Located above *Hennesey's* in Faneuil Hall, *Q* is a Euro-themed dance club that attracts a mainly touristy crowd.

The Rack 24 Clinton St ⊤617/725-1051, @www.therackboston.com; Boylston **T**. Similar to *Felt* (see p.209), *The Rack* is an upscale club with pool tables, rather than an upscale bar. The strict dress code requires collared shirts for men and forbids hats, T-shirts, ripped jeans, and sandals, among other items. There's a $5 cover on Saturday after 9pm.

The Roxyplex 279 Tremont St ⊤617/338-7699, @www.roxyboston.com; Boylston **T**. The Theater District's biggest club has almost taken over the *Tremont House* hotel and now features the *Roxy* and *Matrix* clubs (one cover – either $15 or $20 – gets you into both), the *Caprice Lounge* for cocktails and dining, and *Encore*, a cabaret venue.

Sugar Shack One Boylston Place ⊤617/351-2510, @www.alleyboston.com; Boylston **T**. This perennial favorite with the collegiate set features a decor of fake broken windows

Comedy central

Boston's **comedy clubs** can be a pleasant alternative to the club scene, especially when you factor in the lack of dress code and the top-notch comics who often headline as part of a cross-country tour.

Comedy Connection, 245 Quincy Market (☏617/248-9700, ⓦwww .comedyconnectionboston.com; Government T), is a high-caliber venue attracting both local and national acts; Thursday nights are popular with the college crowd as Frank Santos, the "R-Rated Hypnotist," takes the stage.

The city's only improv venue, the **Improv Asylum Theater**, 216 Hanover St (☏617/263-6887, ⓦwww.improvasylum.com; North Station T), often brings the house down with off-the-cuff sketches based on audience cues. Boston's comedy mainstay, **Nick's Comedy Stop**, 100 Warrenton St (☏617/482-0930, ⓦwww .nickscomedystop.com; Boylston T), has brought in national acts including the likes of Jay Leno and Jerry Seinfeld during its twenty-year tenure. In all cases, book your tickets ($10–40) ahead of time, as shows often sell out.

and drinks with names like Raspberry Truffle. Dance to hip-hop, R&B, and Top 40 at this cheesy club, and discover what college guys look like without their baseball caps on the sweaty dancefloor. There's a $5 cover on Friday, and $8 cover on Saturday. **Venu** 100 Warrenton St ☏617/338-8061, ⓦwww.venuboston.com; Boylston T. The city's ultimate hotspot, this slick Theater District club with different theme nights throughout the week gives you opulent eye candy for your hefty ($15) cover charge: Art Deco stylings, beautiful patrons, and a laser-lit dancefloor.

Kenmore Square and the Fenway

An Tua Nua 835 Beacon St ☏617/262-2121; Kenmore T. Despite its Gaelic name ("the new beginning"), this popular neighborhood hangout is just as much a dance bar as it is an Irish pub. Thursday's hip-hop nights get especially crowded with BU and Northeastern undergrads, who sweat it out on the dancefloor or check each other out from the many ringside seats.
Avalon 15 Lansdowne St ☏617/262-2424, ⓦwww.avalonboston.com; Kenmore T. Avalon's 1500-person capacity makes it the biggest dance club in Boston, and any weekend night the place is positively jamming, often to the tracks laid down by out-of-town talent like Paul Oakenfold and John Digweed. The cavernous central floor

is flanked on either side by bars. Sunday is gay night, while mid-week often sees live rock performances. On Friday the $20 cover also gets you into three other clubs: Axis, The Modern, and Embassy (see below).
Axis 13 Lansdowne St ☏617/262-2437, ⓦwww.axisboston.com; Kenmore T. Adjacent to Avalon, the Axis leans more toward techno and trance. On Friday, the doors between the two clubs open to form a megaclub.
Bill's Bar 5 1/2 Lansdowne St ☏617/421-9678; Kenmore T. This fairly relaxed Lansdowne Street spot packs it in for its hip-hop nights (Tues & Sat) and nightly live music shows; covers range from $5 to $15, depending on who's in the house.
The Modern 36 Lansdowne St ☏617/351-2581; Kenmore T. A relaxed lounge filled with plush forest-green velvet chairs, and host to various DJ nights. The upstairs part, called Embassy, has a similar but even more laid-back atmosphere.
Sophia's 1270 Boylston St ☏617/354-7001; Kenmore T. Lively dance club with a Latin beat. There's a roof to cool off on, drop-in salsa lessons (Thurs–Sat), plus a stylish downstairs restaurant serving Spanish tapas and full meals. A strictly enforced dress code (no blue jeans or sneakers) keeps the crowd looking posh; when there's a cover, it's $15.

Performing arts and film

Boston has a vibrant cultural scene, and many of its artistic institutions are second to none in the US. Foremost among these is the Boston Symphony Orchestra, which gave its first concert more than a century ago. Indeed, Boston is arguably at its best in the **classical music** department, and there are many smaller but internationally known chamber and choral music groups – from the Boston Symphony Chamber Players to the Handel & Hayden Society – to shore up its reputation. The Boston Ballet is also world-class, though it's probably best known locally for its annual holiday production of *The Nutcracker,* with audience numbers ranking it as the most attended **ballet** in the world.

The **theater** here is quite active, too, even if it is a shadow of its 1920s heyday, when more than forty playhouses were crammed into the **Theater District** on the edge of downtown. The "big four" theaters – the Colonial, the Wilbur, the Charles, and the newly restored Opera House – are operated by Broadway In Boston (Ⓦ www.broadwayinboston.com), an organization that brings Broadway hits up north. Many of the other theaters are used as "try-out" venues for shows that will later hit New York. For current productions, check the listings in the *Boston Globe's* Thursday "Calendar" section, the *Boston Phoenix,* or the *Improper Bostonian.*

There is the usual big-city glut of multiplexes showing first-run **films**. For foreign, independent, classic, or cult cinema, you'll have to look mainly to other municipalities – Cambridge is best in this respect, though Brookline and Somerville also have their own art-movie and rerun houses.

Classical music

Boston prides itself on being a sophisticated city of high culture, and nowhere does that show up more than in its proliferation of **orchestras** and **choral groups** and the venues that house them. This is helped in no small part by the presence of four of the premier music academies in the nation: the Peabody Conservatory, the New England Conservatory, the Berklee College of Music, and, across the river in Cambridge, the Longy School of Music.

Most of the companies listed below perform at regular venues, which we've reviewed right after (and those performance spaces do put on additional concerts as well). Check the usual listings sources for concert information, or call the groups directly.

Chamber music ensembles

Alea III and Boston Musica Viva ☎617/353-3340, ⓦ www.aleaiii.com (Alea III) and ☎617/354-6910, ⓦ www.bmv.org (Boston Musica Viva). Two regulars at BU's Tsai Performance Center.

Boston Baroque ☎617/484-9200, ⓦ www .bostonbaroque.org. The first permanent Baroque orchestra in the country (it was founded in 1973) performs at Jordan Hall and Harvard's Sanders Theatre.

Boston Camerata ☎617/262-2092, ⓦ www .bostoncamerata.com. Regular performances of choral and chamber concerts, from medieval to early American, at various locations in and around Boston.

Boston Chamber Music Society ☎617/349-0086, ⓦ www.bostonchambermusic.org. This society has soloists of international renown who perform twice a month and four times in August at various venues through the city.

Boston Symphony Chamber Players ☎617/638-9289 or 1-888/266-1200, ⓦ www .bso.org. The only permanent chamber group sponsored by a major symphony orchestra and made up of its members; they perform at Jordan Hall.

The Cantata Singers & Ensemble ☎617/267-6502, ⓦ www.cantatasingers.org. Boston's premier choral group, which also performs at Jordan Hall.

Handel & Haydn Society ☎617/266-3605, ⓦ www.handelandhaydn.org. Performing chamber and choral music since 1815; can be heard at Symphony Hall.

Masterworks Chorale ☎617/781/235-6210, ⓦ www.masterworkschorale.org. A state-wide society dedicated to choral performances; concerts are held in Harvard's Sanders Theatre.

Pro Arte Chamber Orchestra ☎617/661-7067, ⓦ www.proarte.org. Cooperatively run chamber orchestra in which musicians have full control. Gives Sunday afternoon performances in Harvard's Sanders Theatre.

Performance venues

Berklee Performance Center 136 Massachusetts Ave ☎617/747-2261 for scheduling information or ☎617/931-2000 for tickets, ⓦ www.berkleebpc.com; Symphony **T**. Berklee College of Music's main performance center, known for its quality contemporary repertoire.

Isabella Stewart Gardner Museum 280 The Fenway ☎617/278-5150, ⓦ www .gardnermuseum.org; Museum **T**. Chamber and classical concerts, including many debuts, are held regularly at 1.30pm on weekends Sept–May in the museum's ornate Tapestry Room. The $20 ticket (available at the door or online from ⓦ www .ticketweb.com) includes museum admission.

Jordan Hall 30 Gainsborough St ☎617/536-2412, ⓦ www.newenglandconservatory.edu; Symphony **T**. The impressive concert hall of the New England Conservatory, one block west from Symphony Hall, is the venue for many chamber music performances, as well as those by the Boston Philharmonic (☎617/868-6696, ⓦ www.bostonphil.org).

Museum of Fine Arts 465 Huntington Ave ☎617/369-3770/3306, ⓦ www.mfa.org; Museum **T**. During the summer, the MFA's jazz, folk, and world music "Concerts in the Courtyard" take place each Wednesday at 7.30pm; a variety of indoor performances – from tango to opera recitals – are also scheduled for the rest of the year.

Sanders Theatre 45 Quincy St ☎617/496-4594, ⓦ www.fas.harvard.edu/~memhall/sanders .html; Harvard **T**. Inspired by Christopher Wren's Sheldonian Theatre in Oxford, England, the Sanders is known for its 180-degree design. The Boston Philharmonic, the Boston Chamber Music Society, Masterworks Chorale, and the Boston Baroque all perform here.

Symphony Hall 301 Massachusetts Ave ☎617/266-1492 for concert information, ☎617/638-9289 or 1-888/266-1200 for tickets, ⓦ www.bso.org; Symphony **T**. This is the regal, acoustically perfect venue for the Boston Symphony Orchestra, currently under the direction of James Levine; the famous Boston Pops concerts happen in May and June, and in July and August, the BSO retreats to Tanglewood, in the Berkshires.

Tsai Performance Center 685 Commonwealth Ave ☎617/353-TSAI for event information or ☎617/353-8725 for box office, ⓦ www.bu.edu /tsai; Boston University **T**. Improbably tucked

PERFORMING ARTS AND FILM | Classical music

into Boston University's School of Management, this mid-sized hall is a frequent venue for chamber music performances, prominent lecturers, and plays; events are often affiliated with BU and either free or very inexpensive.

Dance

The city's longest-running **dance** company is the world-class **Boston Ballet** (☎617/695-6950 or 1-800/447-7400, ⓦwww.bostonballet.org); their biggest blockbuster, the yearly performance of the *The Nutcracker*, has an audience attendance of more than 140,000. The troupe performs at the Wang Theatre and the Colonial Theatre (see "Major venues" in Theater, below).

In addition, smaller but still prominent troupes, like **World Music** (ⓦwww.worldmusic.org), put on music and dance performances that are a bit less traditional and staid, in venues like the Berklee, the Shubert, and the Orpheum Theater (also below in "Major venues").

Theater

It's quite possible to pay dearly for a night at the **theater**. Tickets to the bigger shows range from $25 to $75 depending on the seat, and there is, of course, the potential of a pre- or post-theater meal (see p.195 for restaurants in the Theater District). Your best option is to pay a visit to **BosTix** (☎617/482-BTIX) – a half-price, day-of-show ticket booth with two outlets: in Copley Square, at the corner of Dartmouth and Boylston streets, and Faneuil Hall, by Abercrombie & Fitch (Mon–Sat 10am–6pm, Sun 11am–4pm; ☎617/482-2849) – tickets go on sale at 11am, and only cash is accepted.

Full-price tickets can be had via **Ticketmaster** (☎617/931-2000, ⓦwww.ticketmaster.com) or by contacting the individual theater directly in advance of the performance. The **smaller venues** tend to showcase more offbeat and affordable productions; shows can be under $10 – though you shouldn't bank on that.

Major venues

American Repertory Theater 64 Brattle St, at the Loeb Drama Center, Cambridge ☎617/547-8300, ⓦwww.amrep.org; Harvard **T**. Excellent theater near Harvard Square known for staging plays by big names like Shaw and Wilde as well as postmodern heavyweights like Ionesco and Stoppard.

Charles Playhouse 74 Warrenton St ☎617/426-6912, ⓦwww.broadwayinboston.com; Boylston **T**. The Charles has two stages, one of which is more or less the permanent home of *Shear Madness*, a participatory, comic murder mystery that's now become the longest-running non-musical in American theater (ⓦwww.shearmadness.com; $34). The other is currently permanent home to the Blue Man Group, creative, alternative performance artists (ⓦwww.blueman.com; $28–56).

Colonial Theatre 106 Boylston St ☎617/426-9366, ⓦwww.broadwayinboston.com; Boylston **T**. Built in 1900 and since refurbished, this is the glittering *grande dame* of Boston theaters, known primarily for its Broadway-scale productions.

Cutler Majestic Theatre 219 Tremont St ☎617/824-8725, ⓦwww.maj.org; Boylston **T**. Emerson College, a communications and arts school, took stewardship of this 1903 Beaux Arts beauty in 1983. The lavish venue, with soaring Rococo ceiling and Neo-classical friezes, reopened in 2003 following extensive renovations, and has resumed hosting productions of the Emerson Stage company and the Boston Lyric Opera.

Huntington Theatre Company 264 Huntington Ave ☎617/266-8488, ⓦwww.bu.edu/huntington; Symphony **T**. Productions at this small playhouse, the official theater of

Boston University, range from the classic to the contemporary, but they are consistently well staged.

Opera House 539 Washington Street ☎617/259-3400, ⓦwww.broadwayinboston .com; Boylston **T**. New England's premier performing arts venue, a 1928 Beaux Arts building, reopened in summer 2004 after an extensive refurbish.

Shubert Theatre 265 Tremont St ☎617/482-9393 or 800/447-7400, ⓦwww.wangcenter .org; Boylston **T**. Stars from Sir Laurence Olivier to Kathleen Turner have played at the city's "Little Princess," which is one of the two venues at the Wang Center for the Performing Arts. An extensive renovation has restored the 1680-seat theater to its prettier early 1900s appearance, with white walls and gold-leaf accents replacing the previous gaudy brown tones.

Wang Theatre 270 Tremont St ☎617/482-9393 or 800/447-7400, ⓦwww.wangcenter .org; Boylston **T**. The second theater in the Wang Center for the Performing Arts and Boston's biggest performance center, this venue opened in 1925 as the Metropolitan Theater, a movie house of palatial proportions. Its original Italian marble, gold-leaf ornamentation, crystal chandeliers, and 3800 seats all remain. The Boston Ballet is headquartered here; when their season ends, Broadway musicals often take center stage.

Wilbur Theatre 246 Tremont St ☎617/423-4008, ⓦwww.broadwayinboston.com; Boylston **T**. *A Streetcar Named Desire*, starring Marlon Brando and Jessica Tandy, debuted in this small Colonial Revival theater before

going to Broadway, and the Wilbur has been working on trying to live up to that production ever since. In winter, avoid the seats toward the back, where the loud, old heating system may leave you straining to hear.

Smaller venues

Boston Center for the Arts 539 Tremont St ☎617/426-2787, ⓦwww.bcaonline.org. Back Bay **T**. Several theater troupes – many experimental – stage productions at the BCA, which incorporates a series of small venues on a single South End property. One of these is the Cyclorama Building, originally built to house a monumental painting called *The Battle of Gettysburg* (see p.109).

Hasty Pudding Theatre 12 Holyoke St, Cam-bridge ☎617/495-5205, ⓦwww.hastypudding .org. Harvard **T**. Harvard University's Hasty Pudding Theatricals troupe, one of the country's oldest, mounts one show per year (usually a musical comedy; Feb & March) at its eponymous theater, then hits the road – after which the Cambridge Theatre Com-pany moves in.

Institute of Contemporary Art Theatre 955 Boyl-ston St ☎617/927-6620, ⓦwww.icaboston.org; Hynes **T**. Count on the unconventional at the theater of the ICA, Boston's leading venue for all things postmodern and cutting-edge.

Lyric Stage 140 Clarendon St ☎617/437-7172, ⓦwww.lyricstage.com; Copley **T**. Both pre-mieres and modern adaptations of classic and lesser-known American plays are held at this small theater within the big YWCA building.

PERFORMING ARTS AND FILM | Film

Film

In Boston, as in any other large American city, it's easy enough to catch general-release **films** – the usual listings sources carry all the details you need. If you're looking for out-of-the-ordinary film fare, however, you'll have to venture out a bit from the center. Whatever you're going to see, admission will cost you about $9, though matinees before 6pm can be considerably cheaper. You can call ☎617/333-FILM for automated film listings; online listings can be found at ⓦwww.bostonmovietimes.com.

AMC Fenway 13 401 Park Drive ☎617/424-6266; Fenway **T**. Multiplex showing usual blockbuster fare for popcorn munchers with the occasional off-beat flick thrown in.

Boston Museum of Science, Mugar Omni Theatre ☎617/723-2500, www.mos.org;

Science Park **T**. Daytime-only showings of mainly documentaries dealing with the natural world and science.

Brattle Theater 40 Brattle St, Cambridge ☎617/876-6837, ⓦwww.brattlefilm.org; Harvard **T**. An historic basement indie cinema that looks its age. Hosts a thematic film series plus occasional author appearances and readings.

Coolidge Corner Moviehouse 290 Harvard St, Brookline ☎617/734-2500, ⊛www.coolidge.org; **Coolidge Corner** T. Film buffs flock to this classic theater for foreign and independent movies. The interior has balconies and is adorned with Art Deco murals.

Harvard Film Archive Carpenter Center, 24 Quincy St, Cambridge ☎617/495-4700, ⊛www.harvardfilmarchive.org; **Harvard** T. A mixed bag of artsy, foreign, and experimental films are shown here.

Kendall Square Cinema One Kendall Square, East Cambridge ☎617/494-9800, ⊛www.landmarktheatres.com; **Kendall** T. All the neon decoration, cramped seating, and small screens of your average multiplex, but this one has the area's widest selection of first-rate foreign and independent films. It's actually located on Binney St, near Cardinal Medieros Ave.

Museum of Fine Arts Theater 465 Huntington Ave ☎617/267-9300, www.mfa.org/film; **Museum** T. Offbeat art films and documentaries, mostly by locals, often accompanied by lectures from the filmmaker. Also hosts several showcases like the Boston Jewish Film Festival and the Boston French Film Festival.

Somerville Theatre 55 Davis Square, Somerville ☎617/625-5700, ⊛www.somervilletheatreonline.com; **Davis** T. Wacky home for camp, classic, cult, independent, foreign, and first-run pictures. Also doubles as a venue for live music. It's way out there – in more ways than one – past Cambridge, but well worth the trip.

Sony Nickelodeon 606 Commonwealth Ave ☎617/424-1500; **Kenmore** T. Originally an art-flick place, now taken over by the Sony group; it shows the better of the first-run features.

Gay Boston

For a town with a Puritan heritage and long-entrenched Blue Laws, it may come as some surprise that Boston is one of the more gay-friendly cities on the East Coast. Much of the action centers around the **South End**, a largely residential area whose gay businesses (primarily restaurants, galleries, and cafés) are concentrated on a short stretch of Tremont Street above Union Park. It's not unusual here to see a gay pride flag flying openly and same-sex couples sitting together on their stoops, enjoying summer nights along with the rest of the neighborhood's diverse community.

Adjacent to the South End, on the other side of Arlington Street, is tiny **Bay Village**, a smaller gay enclave with a couple of good bars and clubs. Largely leftist **Cambridge**, at least around Harvard Square, is also gay-friendly, with a few established gay nights to show for it, while **Jamaica Plain**, a neighborhood south of Boston proper, is quietly establishing itself as a lesbian-friendly community.

Although the city's **gay nightlife** ranges from leathermen at the *Ramrod* to cocktail-swilling guppies at *Club Café*, it remains small and fairly concentrated; the lesbian club scene, meanwhile, despite gaining more of a foothold in recent years, is still vastly under-represented in comparison.

In the summer, the **Back Bay Fens** and the **Charles River Esplanade**, between Dartmouth and Fairfield streets, at the northern perimeter of Back Bay, is a popular spot for cruising. Footbridges lead from the end of both streets over Storrow Drive to a narrow urban beach alongside the river. You can't swim in the Charles, but it's more than acceptable to sun yourself in a bathing suit here. The area can get a bit dicey at night, though, as can the rest of the Esplanade.

Information and resources

Boston's two free **gay newspapers** are *in newsweekly* (Ⓦwww.innewsweekly .com) and *Bay Windows* (Ⓦwww.baywindows.com). The latter is one of two good sources for **club information** – the other being the gay-friendly alternative paper *The Boston Phoenix*. All can be found in various venues and bookstores, notably Cuttyhunk, Calamnus, and New Words (see p.228). The latter two's vestibules also have gay and lesbian community **bulletin boards**, with postings for apartment rentals, club happenings, and so forth.

General resources and support groups	

Boston Alliance of Gay, Lesbian, Bisexual, and Transgender Youth (BAGLY) Ⓦwww.bagly.org.

Hosts events, discussion groups, and much more.

Boston Glass Community Center 93 Massachusetts Ave ☎617/266-3349,

ⓦwww.bostonglass.org; Hynes **T**. Drop-in center for people aged 13–25.
Fenway Community Health Center 7 Haviland St ⓣ617/267-0900 or 1-888/242-0900, ⓦwww .fenwayhealth.org. All manner of health care for the gay community.
Gay and Lesbian Helpline ⓣ617/267-9001. General information source.

Butch Dyke Boy ⓦwww.butchdykeboy.com. Thorough resource for the lesbian community, with local message boards, event listings, columns, and more.
Link Pink ⓦwww.linkpink.com. Definitive "pink pages" for businesses, hotels, shops, and services catering to the New England GLBT community.

The List ⓦwww.queeragenda.org. Sign up to receive free weekly emails about upcoming gay and lesbian events in the Boston area.

Sports and travel

The Metropolitan Health Club 209 Columbus Ave ⓣ617/536-3006. One of the most gay-friendly gyms in the city.
Pride Sports Boston ⓦwww.geocities.com /pridesportsboston. An alliance of gay- and lesbian-friendly gyms that organizes, among other events, Boston's team in the Gay Games.
Travel Alternatives Group ⓣ1-800/464-2987, ⓦwww.gaytravelnews.com. They'll route your call to your nearest gay-friendly travel agent.

Accommodation

All of Boston's **accommodations** are gay-friendly but none endorse a strict gay–only clientele policy. That said, you're likely to find more gay visitors than straight ones sleeping in the city's few gay-run hotels. Most are situated in **Back Bay** and the **South End**, putting you within walking distance of the city's best gay bars and cafés; a quieter option in **Jamaica Plain** may appeal to members of the lesbian community, given its proximity to dyke-friendly spots like the *Midway Café*. The **rates** below refer to the lowest cost of a standard double room throughout most of the year; taxes are not included.

463 Beacon Street Guest House 463 Beacon St ⓣ617/536-1302, ⓦwww.463beacon.com; Hynes **T**. The good-sized rooms in this renovated brownstone, in the heart of Back Bay, are available by the night, week, and month, and come equipped with kitchenettes, cable TV, and various amenities (though no maid service); some have air conditioning, hardwood floors, and ornamental fireplaces. Ask for the top-floor room. $69
Chandler Inn 26 Chandler St ⓣ617/482-3450 or 1-800/842-3450, ⓦwww.chandlerinn.com; Back Bay **T**. Comfortable, 56-room, European-style hotel above the popular *Fritz* bar (see opposite); perks like satellite TV, in-room Internet hook-up, and continental breakfast are included in the rates. $90
Oasis Guest House 22 Edgerly Rd ⓣ617/267-2262, ⓦwww.oasisgh.com; Symphony **T**.

Sixteen comfortable, affordable rooms, some with shared baths, in a renovated brownstone near Symphony Hall. Complimentary continental breakfast is served every morning, and there's a nightly meet-and-greet at 8pm – they supply the hors d'oeuvres, you bring the booze. $69
Taylor House 50 Burroughs St, Jamaica Plain ⓣ617/888/228-2956, ⓦwww.taylorhouse .com; Green Street **T**. This delightful B&B, with two beautiful golden-retriever mascots, is a bit out of the way, but its three charming rooms, tucked away on the second floor of an 1855 Italianate house, feature queen-sized beds, TV with VCR, and Internet access. Complimentary continental breakfast, which includes fresh baked bread, is served daily. $119

Bars, clubs, and cafés

Only one **club** in Boston maintains its gay banner seven days a week, the long-standing *Vapor* (formerly *Chaps*); to pick up the slack, some of Boston's more popular clubs designate one or two nights a week as gay nights. The best ones, *ManRay* (Thurs), *Buzz* (Sat), and *Avalon* (Sun) draw a good mix; see Chapter 15, Nightlife, for further details on these and other venues.

The hottest lesbian ticket around is Thursday night at *Toast Lounge*, in Somerville. For those night owls who haven't gotten their fill of dancing after the clubs close, ask around for an invite to Boston's hush-hush, after-hours private party at *Rise* (306 Stuart St); the members-only stomping ground for gays and straights only gets going at 2am.

Aria 246 Tremont St ☎617/338-7080, ⓦwww .ariaboston.com; Boylston **T**. *Aria*, one of the city's plushest venues, in the basement of the Wilbur Theatre, hosts a Wednesday night dance party called Signs of Life. Glamourous, energetic, and very housey.

Avalon 15 Lansdowne St ☎617/262-2424, ⓦwww.avalonboston.com; Kenmore **T**. With a 1500-person capacity, *Avalon* is the biggest dance club in Boston, and any weekend night the place is positively jamming, often to the tracks laid down by out-of-town talent like Paul Oakenfold and John Digweed. The cavernous central floor is flanked on either side by bars. Sunday is the grand-daddy of Boston gay nights.

Axis 13 Lansdowne St ☎617/262-2437, ⓦwww.axisboston.com; Kenmore **T**. On Mondays, Boston's gay crowd heads to this hippest of venues, which is edgier than most other clubs in the city. Excellent cruising.

Buzz 51 Stuart St ☎617/267-8669, ⓦwww .buzzboston.com; New England Medical **T**. Resident DJs Michael Sheehan and Mary-Alice lay down dance and house tracks at this two-floor dance club, where the drinks are poured by pumped and shirtless bartenders. $10 cover.

Club Café 209 Columbus Ave ☎617/536-0966, ⓦwww.clubcafe.com; Back Bay **T**. This combination restaurant/video bar popular among South End guppies has two back lounges, *Moonshine* and *Satellite*, showing the latest videos and making a wide selection of martinis with fey names like Pouty Princess and Dirty Birdie. Thursday nights are an institution on the gay scene.

Club Hollywood 41 Essex St ☎617/417-0186, ⓦwww.shuttavac.com/hollywood; Chinatown **T**. *Club Hollywood's* Saturday night dance party vies with *Toast Lounge's* Thursday celebration as the city's premier lesbian

event. DJ Mix Mistress takes to the decks on the club's second floor, while rotating guests are featured on the first.

Eagle 520 Tremont St ☎617/542-4494; Back Bay **T**. Neighborhood bar whose eagle-bedecked interior has the looks of a biker hangout, and attracts an outgoing crowd that gets busiest around last call. A live DJ spins house and Top 40 on the weekends; his recorded sessions are played back on weeknights. No cover.

Francesca's Espresso Bar 565 Tremont St ☎617/482-9026; Back Bay **T**. A great place to check out the Tremont Street crowd passing by the plate-glass windows, this coffee shop gets packed in the evenings before clubs open, with a largely gay clientele caffeinating itself for a night out.

Fritz 26 Chandler St ☎617/482-4428; Back Bay **T**. This South End sports bar below *Chandler Inn* (see Accommodation above) is often considered the gay version of *Cheers*, thanks to its mix of casually attired locals and visitors, plus the convivial staff. Good for Sunday brunch.

Jacque's 79 Broadway ☎617/338-7472; Boylston **T**. Priscilla, Queen of the Desert, invades New England at this drag dream where past-it divas lip-synch "I Love the Nightlife" while youngsters explore gender issues and transvestite/transexual prostitutes peddle their wares. Showtime is 10.30pm Tues–Sun, but beware – the festivities end at midnight, Cinderella.

Luxor 69 Church St ☎617/423-6969; Arlington **T**. Not as popular as it once was, but still a good place to drink and cruise, either in the upstairs gay video bar with a modern finish or downstairs at the sports bar.

Machine 1254 Boylston St ☎617/266-2986; Kenmore **T**. A favorite with the gay crowd on Fridays and Saturdays when the club's large dancefloor and top-notch music has

Boston Pride (June) A nine-day festival that culminates in a parade starting at Boston Common. ⓦ www.bostonpride.org.

Boston Indoor Tennis Classic (end July) Tennis tournament organized by G&L group, Tennis 4 All. ⓦ www.tennis4all.org.

Fantasia Fair (Oct) The US's longest running continuous transgender event has been in Provincetown since 1975. ⓦ www.fantasiafair.org.

Out on the Edge (Oct) Held at the Boston Center for Arts, this is one of the world's premier queer theater fests. ⓦ www.thetheateroffensive.org.

Holly Folly (Dec) Provincetown's big gay Yuletide fest draws the crowds back to the Cape Cod seaside town. ⓦ www.hollyfolly.com.

the place pumping. The pool tables, video screens, Internet terminals, and bar near the dancefloor let you take a breather and soak up the scene.

ManRay 21 Brookline St, Cambridge ☎617/864-0400, ⓦ www.manrayclub.com; Central **T**. One massive space with five bars, two dancefloors, and four very different theme nights. Campus (Thurs & Sat) is relatively wholesome, with J Crew types and plenty of straights. The scene is altogether different on Fridays, when a fetish-and-bondage fest, replete with leather and dominatrixes galore, takes over.

Midway Café 3496 Washington St, Jamaica Plain, ☎617/524-9038, ⓦ www.midwaycafe.com; Green Street **T**. Neighborhood hangout with a popular Thursday Dyke Night; there's free pool 8–10pm, $2 drink specials 9–10.30pm, and dancing till 2am. $5 cover.

Paradise 180 Massachusetts Ave, Cambridge ☎617/494-0700, ⓦ www.paradisecambridge.com; Central **T**. Upstairs, male dancers (almost) bare it all; those who want to keep some clothes on stay downstairs where

a smallish dancefloor rocks out to Top 40 tunes. Open till 1am Sun–Thurs and 2am Fri & Sat.

Ramrod 1254 Boylston St ☎617/266-2986, ⓦ www.ramrodboston.com; Kenmore **T**. This Fenway meat market attracts a pretty hungry crowd with its strictly enforced Levi/leather dress code (Fri & Sat) – no shirts or cologne allowed. Not quite as hardcore as it sounds, as it's directly upstairs from the harmless *Machine* (see p.227).

Toast Lounge 70 Union Sq (in the Holiday Inn) ☎617/623-9211, ⓦ www.toastlounge.com; Porter Sq **T**. New in 2003, *Toast*'s buzzy atmosphere has become a firm favorite on the lesbian scene, with a popular Thursday night dance party. On Saturday, it's straight couples' turn to hit the floor.

Vapor 100 Warrenton St ☎617/695-9500; Arlington **T**. *Vapor* hosts a piano bar with open mic sessions on Monday and retro night on Tuesday, but things heat up with Latin on Wednesday, R&B and soul at Mocca on Thursday, and House on Friday and Saturday. DJ Danae spins on Sunday.

Bookstores

Calamus Bookstore 92B South St ☎617/338-1931, ⓦ www.calamusbooks.com; South Station **T**. Born from the ashes of the much-lamented Glad Day bookstore, Calamus is owned by former Glad Day manager John Mitzel and is easily recognized by the Rainbow flag outside.

Cuttyhunk 540 Tremont St ☎617/423-1965, ⓦ www.wethinktheworldofyou.com; Back Bay **T**. The name has changed (because so many people couldn't remember We Think

the World of You), but Cuttyhunk is still one of the best resources for gay and lesbian literature in Boston. Also sells DVDs and a good selection of international magazines, plus distributes free gay newspapers.

New Words 186 Hampshire St, Cambridge ☎617/876-5310, ⓦ www.centerfornewwords.org; Central Square **T**. This lesbian bookstore caters to all aspects of the literary scene with reading rooms, a host of workshops, and slam poetry events.

Shopping

T hough Boston has its share of chain stores and typical mall fare, there are plenty of unusual and funky places to **shop** here. The city is perhaps best loved for its bookstores, having established a reputation as a literary haven and academic center; on a more modern – and fashionable – note, it has also become known for its small, exclusive boutiques that feature the work of local designers.

No matter what you're looking for, Boston is an extremely pleasant place in which to shop for it, with unique, high-quality stores clustered on charming avenues like Beacon Hill's Charles Street and Back Bay's Newbury Street. The former has a dense concentration of **antiques shops**, while the latter is an eight-block stretch that starts off trendily, with all manner of clothes and crafts, then begins to cater to more of a student population as it moves west past Exeter Street; here, **record stores** and **novelty shops** take over, a theme continued out to Kenmore Square. This span also has its fair share of big **bookstores** – though the best are clustered in and around Harvard Square, across the Charles River in Cambridge.

The rest of the action takes place in various downtown quarters, first and foremost at **Faneuil Hall Marketplace**. This area has become more commercialized over the years, but enough homespun boutiques remain to make a trip here worthwhile, not to mention the many food stalls of **Quincy Market**. To the south, **Downtown Crossing**, at Washington and Summer streets, is centered on **Filene's Basement**, a bargain-hunter's delight for marked-down brand-name clothing. Stores are generally open 9.30 or 10am to 6 or 7pm Monday through Saturday (sometimes later on Tuesday and Wednesday) and on Sunday from noon to 6pm.

Antiques

Abodeon **1731 Massachusetts Ave, Cambridge** ☏617/497-0137; Porter T. A terrific trove of classic twentieth-century design, with furniture by top modern designers as well as assorted new bric-a-brac. Pretty expensive, but most things are cheaper than they would be in New York or LA.

Cambridge Antique Market **201 Monsignor O'Brien Hwy** ☏617/868-9655, ⓦwww .marketantique.com: Lechmere T. Slightly off-the-beaten-track, but the 150 dealers at this five-floor cooperative-style market have everything from nineteenth-century furniture to vintage clothing.

Cunha, St John and Vining **131 Charles St** ☏617/720-7808, Charles T. Tucked away on the first floor of a recessed building, this shop is easy to miss, but inside is a varied array of Continental antiques – eighteenth- and nineteenth-century English, Italian, and French, plus nineteenth-century Chinese formal pieces.

Judith Dowling Asian Art 133 Charles St
☏617/523-5211; Charles **T**. A first-rate selection of Asian pieces from all periods, though at prices that encourage browsing rather than buying.

Marcoz Antiques 177 Newbury St ☏617/262-0780; Arlington **T**. Boutique with eighteenth- and nineteenth-century French, English, and American furniture and accessories.

Twentieth Century Limited 73 Charles St
☏617/742-1031; Charles **T**. Antique pieces from the early twentieth century, with a focus on American Art Deco and works from the Roaring Twenties; good costume jewelry, too.

Bookstores

Boston has a rich history as a literary city, enhanced by its numerous universities as well as the many traces of authors and publishing houses that have at one time called the town home. This legacy is well reflected in the quality and diversity of **bookstores** found both in Boston and neighboring Cambridge. For books with a Boston connection, along with a history of literature in nineteenth-century Boston, see Contexts.

New

Barnes & Noble Downtown Crossing
☏617/426-5502; Downtown Crossing **T**; Prudential Center, 800 Boylston St ☏617/247-6959; Prudential **T**; 660 Beacon St ☏617/267-8484; Kenmore **T**; 325 Harvard St, Brookline ☏617/232-0594; Coolidge Corner **T**. Four large outposts of the national bookstore chain, with decent newsstands and good selections of bargain books and calendars. The one on Beacon Street is topped off by the neon Citgo sign (see p.113).

Brookline Booksmith 279 Harvard St, Brookline ☏617/566-6660, ⓦ www.brooklinebooksmith .com; Coolidge Corner **T**. This cozy shop with hardwood floors doesn't have a particular strength, but its friendly staff makes it perfect for browsing; holds a good author reading series, too.

Harvard Book Store 1256 Massachusetts Ave, Cambridge ☏617/661-1515, ⓦ www.harvard .com; Harvard **T**. Three huge rooms of new books upstairs, with a basement for used volumes and remainders downstairs. Academic and critical work in the humanities and social sciences dominate, with a healthy dose of fiction thrown in.

Harvard Cooperative Society 1400 Massachusetts Ave, Cambridge ☏617/499-2000, ⓦ harvard.bkstore.com; Harvard **T**. Founded in 1882 by a group of students, the Coop carries an extensive range of college textbooks, but it's also the best place to buy Harvard and MIT insignia sportswear and clothing.

MIT Press Bookstore 292 Main St, Cambridge ☏617/253-5249, ⓦ www.mitpress.mit.edu

/bookstore; Kendall Square **T**. Lots of fascinating science and tech stuff, much of it surprisingly accessible, and racks of discounted and remaindered books as well. Also organizes the authors@MIT series of talks, usually held in the Kirsch Auditorium at the Stata Center (32 Vassar St).

Trident Booksellers & Café 338 Newbury St
☏617/267-8688, www.tridentbookscafe.com; Copley **T**. A preferred lair of Back Bay's New Agers. If the aroma of one too many essential oils doesn't deter you, buy an obscure magazine and have a flip-through over coffee in the café (see p.185).

▽ Trident Booksellers & Café

Used

Brattle Book Shop 9 West St ☎617/542-0210, ⓦwww.brattlebookshop.com; **Downtown Crossing T.** In these fairly dingy digs is one of the oldest antiquarian bookstores in the country. Has a good selection of yellowing travel guides and wonderful sets of old copies of *Life* magazine.

Bryn Mawr Book 373 Huron Ave, Cambridge ☎617/661-1770, ⓦwww.brynmawrbookstore .com; **Porter T.** This Cambridge bookstore vends used titles in a friendly, relaxed setting. Weather permitting, there are sidewalk displays for pedestrian browsers.

House of Sarah 1309 Cambridge St, Cambridge ☎617/547-3447; **Central T.** A wacky Inman Square spot in which to peruse used fiction and scholarly work; sit in one of the chunky red couches and look up at the various stuffed creatures hanging from the ceiling. It's possible here to find a 25¢ copy of a Danielle Steele novel or some remaindered Foucault, plus coffee and snacks are often served, compliments of the proprietors.

Travel

Globe Corner Bookstore 28 Church St, Cambridge ☎617/497-6277, ⓦwww.globecorner .com; **Harvard T.** These travel specialists are well stocked with maps, travel literature, and guidebooks, with an especially strong New England section.

Willowbee & Kent 519 Boylston St ☎617/437-6700; **Copley T.** The first floor of this roomy store has a good range of travel guidebooks and gear; the second is given over to a travel agency.

Specialty

Kate's Mystery Bookstore 2211 Massachusetts Ave ☎617/491-2660, ⓦwww .katesmysterybooks.com; **Davis T.** Mystery-only bookstore selling both old and new titles; you'll know the place from the faux gravestones in the front yard.

Lucy Parsons Center 549 Columbus Ave ☎617/267-6272, ⓦwww.tao.ca/~lucyparsons; **Mass Ave T.** The far left lives on in this shrine to socialism, with a particular bent toward women's issues, labor issues, and radical economics. They also have free pamphlets on local demonstrations, plus occasional readings and lectures.

New England Comics 14a Eliot St ☎617/354-5352, ⓦwww.newenglandcomics.com; **Harvard T.** Back issues of classic comics, new editions, and graphic novels fill this Cambridge stalwart. There are six other locations in New England, including Allston (131 Harvard Ave ☎617/783-1848; Harvard Ave T) and Brookline (316 Harvard St ☎617/566-0115; Coolidge Corner T).

Nini's Corner/Out of Town News Harvard Square, Cambridge; Harvard T. Few published magazines cannot be found at one of these two good, old-fashioned newsstands that lie directly across from each other in the heart of Harvard Square.

Schoenhof's 76A Mount Auburn St, Cambridge ☎617/547-8855, ⓦwww .schoenhofs.com; **Harvard T.** Well-stocked foreign language bookstore that's sure to have that volume of Proust you're looking for, as well as any children's books you might want.

Clothes

It's unlikely you'd consider Boston a center for cutting-edge fashions – more the type of place to buy tweedy suits and conservative wear; still, there's enough variety among local designers to make browsing a fun way to pass the time. Newbury Street (ⓦwww.newbury-st.com) is your most likely target, where you'll find big-name but generic designer stores like Armani, Chanel, and Ralph Lauren.

Designer stores

Alan Bilzerian 34 Newbury St ☎617/536-1001; **Arlington T.** Tri-level store with international haute couture from Jean-Paul Gaultier and Comme des Garçons alongside the owner's own label. Menswear and accessories occupy the first floor and womenswear the second; clubwear roosts in a small basement section.

Allston Beat 348 Newbury St ☏617/421-9555, ⓦwww.allstonbeat.com; Hynes **T**. This small but dense fashion den may exceed the vinyl per square foot limit. Cutting-edge designer wear is ogled by teenagers too young to afford it and others too old to wear it.

Gypsy Moon 1780 Massachusetts Ave ☏617/876-7095, ⓦwww.gypsymoon.com; Porter **T**. For the well-dressed Wiccan, eccentric women's wear is sold by a staff that can help you look your best at the next coven meeting.

House of Culture 286 Newbury St ☏617/236-1090; Copley **T**. Local designer Patrick Petty was wardrobe stylist to Mark Wahlberg and Boys II Men, and even if you're not in the market for his creations, nip in to browse and pick up clubbing flyers.

Jasmine/Sola 344 Newbury St ☏617/867-4636, ⓦwww.jasminesola.com; Arlington **T**; 37a Brattle St, Harvard Square ☏617/354-6043; Harvard **T**; Prudential Center ☏617/578-0550; Prudential **T**. Trendy shop retailing streetwear labels like Miss Sixty, Diesel, Juicy Couture, and Bloom, as well as shoes and accessories; menswear shop at the Harvard location.

J. Press 82 Mt Auburn St ☏617/547-9886; Harvard **T**. Old Harvard lives on in J. Press's sober collection of high-quality men's suits; rates are mid-level ($400–1000 per suit) for the store's genteel clientele.

Louisboston 234 Berkeley St ☏617/262-6100, ⓦwww.louisboston.com; Arlington **T**. Occupying a stately, freestanding building from 1863 that once housed Boston's Museum of Natural History (which became the Museum of Science), this is the city's classiest and most expensive clothes emporium. Though mostly geared toward men, the top floor is reserved for designer womenswear.

Riccardi 116 Newbury St ☏617/266-3158; Arlington **T**. This, the hippest designer schmatta shop in Boston, could hold its own just fine in Paris or New York. A few of the labels on parade are Dolce & Gabbana, Romeo Gigli, and Jean-Paul Gaultier.

Serenella 134 Newbury St ☏617/266-5568; Arlington **T**. High-end women's boutique selling Euro labels like Pucci and Balenciaga to a well-heeled clientele.

Suzanne 81 Newbury St ☏617/266-4146; Arlington **T**. Women's special occasion apparel by leading international designers such as Montana and Thierry Mugler.

Wish 49 Charles St ☏617/227-4441, ⓦwww.wishstyle.com; Charles **T**. This gem of a boutique offers pretty dresses and ensembles by Nanatte Lepore, Theory, and Velvet that'll put you in good stead for either a Nantucket getaway or a Sunday stroll on Charles Street.

Chain stores

Armani 22 Newbury St ☏617/267-3200, ⓦwww.emporioarmani.com; Arlington **T**. The Italian workaholic's Boston store displays the typical no-fuss classical designs that go down well in this city. The *Armani Café* (214 Newbury St; see p.191) is next to the sportswear-brand Emporio Armani store (210-212 Newbury St ☏617/262-7300).

Burberry 2 Newbury St ☏617/236-1000; Arlington **T**. The famously conservative British clothier seems right at home in its four-story Newbury Street digs, across from the *Ritz-Carlton*. Excellent quality stuff; pricey, too.

Chanel 5 Newbury St ☏617/859-0055; Arlington **T**. Located in the lobby of the *Ritz-Carlton*, this branch sells everything Chanel, from Karl Lagerfeld's ready-to-wear collections to cosmetics.

Express 80 Newbury St ☏617/437-1377, ⓦwww.expressfashion.com; Arlington **T**; 321 Washington St ☏617/227-8264: State **T**; Copley Place, 100 Huntington Ave ☏617/536-9751: Back Bay **T**; Cambridgeside, 100 Cambridge Place ☏617/494-8408; Kendall **T**. The New York young men and women's low-cost fashion brand has four branches in the city.

Lucky 229 Newbury St ☏617/236-0102; ⓦwww.luckybrandjeans.com; Hynes **T**. Currently one of America's hottest jeans brands, thanks to the "Lucky you" message on the inside of the fly.

Patagonia 346 Newbury St ☏617/424-1776; Hynes **T**. Patagonia invented the soft, synthetic fleece called "Synchilla," and there's still no better way to fend off a Boston winter than in a jacket or vest lined with the colorful stuff.

Quicksilver Boardriders Club 326 Newbury St ☏617/850-0874; Hynes **T**. Quicksilver is perfectly suited to Boston, thanks to its beachwear in summer and warm fleeces for those cold New England winters.

SHOPPING | Clothes

Ralph Lauren 95 Newbury St ☏617/424-1124; **Arlington T.** The preppy Polo brand much loved by Ivy Leaguers sits well in the home of MIT and Harvard.

Urban Outfitters 361 Newbury St ☏617/236-0088, ⓦ www.urbanoutfitters.com; **Hynes T; 11 JFK St, Cambridge** ☏617/864-0070; **Harvard T.** Youth fashion labels from Diesel to Stussy, plus funky home furnishings and irreverent gift items.

Used and thrift

Bobby from Boston 19 Thayer St ☏617/423-9299; **NE Medical or Broadway T.** Long adored by local rockers and movie wardrobe professionals, Bobby's South End loft is, hands-down, the best place to find men's vintage clothing from the 1920s through the 1960s.

The Garment District/Dollar-a-Pound 200 Broadway, Cambridge ☏617/876-5230, ⓦwww.garment-district.com; **Kendall T.** Warehouse full of bins crammed with used togs. If you have the time to sift through the leftovers of twentieth-century fashion, you'll happen upon some great bargains – all at the rate of $1.50 per pound of clothing. And on Fridays, it's reduced to 75¢ per pound.

Mass Army & Navy Store 895 Boylston St ☏617/267-1559; **Hynes T.** You can stock up on camouflage and combat boots at this military surplus store, plus there's a good and inexpensive range of (mostly men's) pants, shirts, and shoes worth inspecting.

Oona's 1210 Massachusetts Ave, Cambridge ☏617/491-2654; **Harvard T.** Since 1972, Oona's has been the place to find vintage "experienced clothing" – in this case kimonos, flapper dresses, leather jackets, and various accessories.

Second Time Around 176 Newbury St ☏617/247-3504, ⓦwww.secondtimearound .net; **Arlington T; 8 Eliot St** ☏617/491-7185; **Harvard T.** Great prices on barely worn, albeit conservative, clothing, predominantly from Banana Republic, the Gap, Anne Taylor, and Abercrombie & Fitch.

Crafts

Beadworks 349 Newbury St ☏617/247-7227, ⓦwww.beadworksboston.com; **Hynes T.** With so many kinds of beads, it's a good thing the sales staff can assist you in creating a "distinctly personal adornment."

The Cambridge Artists' Cooperative 59A Church St ☏617/868-4434, ⓦwww.cambridgeartistscoop .com; **Harvard T.** Three floors fill this Harvard Square shop with all kinds of crafts, from woodcarvings and glass sculptures to wearable art and beaded bags.

Rugg Road Paper Co. 105 Charles St ☏617/742-0002; **Charles T.** They've got fancy paper products of all kinds, including lovely cards, stationery, and wrapping paper.

Simon Pearce 115 Newbury St ☏617/450-8388 or 1-877/452-7763, ⓦwww .simonpearce.com; **Arlington T.** Hand-blown glassware from this Irish-born, Vermont-based craftsman.

Food and drink

Look no further than the North End for all manner of tasty pastry; for gourmet-style take-home eats, Cambridge is especially strong in variety.

Bakeries

Bova's Bakery 76 Prince St ☏617/523-5601, ⓦwww.northendboston.com/bovabakery; **Haymarket T.** An all-night bakery in the North End, selling delights like plain and chocolate cannolis, oven-fresh cakes, and whoopie pies; famously cheap, too, with most items around $5.

LMNOP Bakery 79 Park Plaza ☏617/338-4220; **Arlington T.** Purveyor of bread to neighboring restaurants, this hideaway is the best gourmet bakery in Boston. Besides those breads, they also have pastries and cookies, plus great sandwiches and pasta specials at lunchtime.

Maria's Pastry Shop 46 Cross St ☏ 617/523-1196 or 1-888/688-2889, ⓦwww

.northendboston.com/marias; **North Station T**. The place doesn't look like much, but Maria's has the best Neapolitan treats in town; her custard-filled *sfogliatelle* and *ossa di morti* (bones of the dead) cookies are to die for.

Mike's Pastry 300 Hanover St ☎617/742-3050; **Haymarket T**. The famed North End bakery is one part Italian and two parts American, meaning in addition to cannoli and tiramisu, you'll find counters full of brownies and cookies. The homemade ice cream is not to be missed – but expect to wait in line for it.

Panini 406 Washington St ☎617/666-2770; **#86 bus.** Baguettes and bruschetta, desserts and danishes – Panini offers a diverse array of baked goods, all created on the premises. So popular it's hard to find a place to sit on weekends.

Rosie's Bakery 243 Hampshire St ☎617/491-9488, ⓦwww.rosiesbakery.com; **#69 bus; 2 South Station** ☎617/239-4684. This bakery offers the richest, most decadent desserts in Cambridge. Their specialty is a fudge brownie called the "Chocolate Orgasm" (though the less provocatively named lemon squares are just as good). A second outlet is in South Station, while visitors to Lexington, MA, can check out the branch at 32 Waltham St (☎781/862-1991).

Gourmet food and wine shops

Barsamian's 1030 Massachusetts Ave, Cambridge ☎617/661-9300; **Harvard or Central T**. Gourmet meats, cheeses, coffee, and bread, plus a great range of desserts – including the best tart in Cambridge.

Cardullo's 6 Brattle St, Cambridge ☎491-8888, ⓦwww.cardullos.com; **Harvard T**. Gourmet products from just about anywhere are available at this well-stocked Harvard Square store; if nothing else, be sure to stop in for a sample. Depending on the weather, you can sit at one of the sidewalk tables and watch the people go by.

Dairy Fresh Candies 57 Salem St ☎617/742-2639 or 1-800/336-5536, ⓦwww.dairyfreshcandies.com; **North Station T**. Mouth-watering array of confections, from chocolates and hard candies to dried fruits and nuts; the perfect pick-me-ups for a Little Italy stroll.

Formaggio Kitchen 244 Huron Ave, Cambridge ☎617/354-4750, ⓦwww.formaggiokitchen.com; **Harvard Square T**; **268 Shawmut Ave**, ☎617/350-6996; **Back Bay T**. One of the best cheese shops in Boston; the gourmet meats, salads, sandwiches, and baked goods are also worth sampling.

Monica's Salumeria 130 Salem St ☎617/742-4101; **Haymarket T**. Lots of imported Italian cheeses, cooked meats, cookies, and pastas.

Polcari's Coffee 105 Salem St ☎617/227-0786, ⓦwww.northendboston.com/polcaricoffee; **Haymarket T**. Old and fusty, but brimming with coffees, as well as every spice you could think of. Worth going inside for the aroma alone.

Salumeria Italiana 151 Richmond St ☎617/523-8743 or 1-800/400-5916, ⓦwww.salumeriaitaliana.com; **North Station T**. Arguably the best Italian grocer this side of Rome. Stocks only the finest cheeses, meats, balsamic vinegars, and more.

Savenor's 160 Charles St ☎617/723-6328; **Charles T**. Known for its meats, this small gourmet food shop in Beacon Hill also has a better-than-average produce selection, in addition to prepared foods – ideal for taking to the nearby Charles River Esplanade for a picnic.

See Sun Co. 19 Harrison St ☎617/426-0954; **Chinatown T**. The most accessible of Chinatown's markets. Has all the basics, like huge bags of rice and a dizzying range of See Sun soy sauces, plus more exotic delicacies like duck's feet.

V. Cirace & Sons 173 North St ☎617/227-3193; **North Station T**. A great liquor store, with the expected range of Italian wines – it's in the North End, after all – and much more.

Health food

Bread & Circus 15 Westland Ave ☎617/375-1010; **Symphony T**. The Boston branch of this New England whole-foods chain, near Symphony Hall, has all the alternative foodstuffs you'd expect, plus one of Boston's best salad bars.

Nature Food Centers GNC 545 Boylston St ☎617/536-1226; **Copley T**. If you're looking for vitamin-enriched fruit juices, organic produce, and other healthful items, this small store in Copley Square is bound to have it.

SHOPPING | Crafts • Food and drink

Galleries

Dozens of Boston's major **art galleries** can be found on Newbury Street; most are generally browser-friendly. South Street, in downtown's so-called Leather District, tends to feature the most contemporary work, as does the SoWa district in the South End.

Alianza 154 Newbury St ☎617/262-2385; **Arlington T.** An artsy American crafts gallery whose strength is creative ceramics, glass work, and jewelry, with funky sculptural clocks and picture frames as well.

Arden Gallery 129 Newbury St ☎617/247-0610, @www.ardengallery.com; **Arlington T.** Arden's focus is on abstractionist contemporary paintings, vivid examples of which are displayed in the oversized second-story bowfront window.

Barbara Krakow Gallery 10 Newbury St, 5th floor ☎617/262-4490, @www.barbarakrakowgallery.com; **Arlington T.** This A-list multimedia gallery attracts the hottest artists from New York City and around the globe; Kiki Smith and Annette Lemieux are but two of the stars that have shown here in recent years.

Bernard Toale Gallery 450 Harrison St ☎617/482-2477; **Back Bay T.** Curator Bernard Toale officially sanctified the burgeoning SoWa district when he moved his Newbury Street gallery here in 1998. Painting, photography, drawing, sculpture, video, and prints are all featured.

Clifford-Smith Gallery 450 Harrison St, 3rd floor ☎617/695-0255, @www.cliffordsmithgallery.com; **Back Bay T.** Hip gallery with large-scale multimedia installations and some photography.

Gallery NAGA 67 Newbury St ☎617/267-9060, @www.gallerynaga.com; **Arlington T.** Contemporary painting, sculpture, studio furniture, and photography from Boston and New England artists, located in the Gothic Revival Church of the Covenant.

International Poster Gallery 205 Newbury St ☎617/375-0076, @www.internationalposter.com; **Copley T.** More than 6000 posters on display from 1895 through World War II.

Nielsen Gallery 179 Newbury St ☎617/266-4835, @www.nielsengallery.com; **Copley T.** Back Bay's oldest gallery puts the accent on contemporary painting and drawing, and, occasionally, sculpture.

The Society of Arts and Crafts 175 Newbury St ☎617/266-1810, @www.societyofcrafts.org; **Arlington T.** The oldest non-profit crafts group in America has two floors here. The first is its commercial outpost, with a wide range of ceramics, glass, and jewelry; the second floor is reserved for themed (and free) special exhibitions.

Malls and department stores

The major **malls** quite obviously cobble together all your needs in one convenient location; none here particularly stand out save perhaps the marketplace at Faneuil Hall, for atmosphere alone. For **department stores**, the idiosyncratic Filene's Basement, in Downtown Crossing, is an institution.

Malls

CambridgeSide Galleria 100 Cambridgeside Place ☎617/621-8666, @www.cambridgeside-galleria.com; **Kendall T.** Not too different from any other large American shopping mall. The haze of neon and packs of teens can be draining, but there's no similarly dense and convenient conglomeration of shops in Cambridge.

Copley Place 100 Huntington Ave ☎617/375-4400, @www.shopcopleyplace.com; **Copley T.** This ambitious, upscale office-retail-residential complex features more than a hundred stores and an eleven-screen multiplex. The best of the shops are a Rizzoli bookshop, a Neiman Marcus department store, the gift shop for the Museum of Fine Arts, and the Artful Hand Gallery, representing solely American artists; the rest is pretty generic.

Faneuil Hall Marketplace Faneuil Hall ☎617/523-1300, @www.faneuilhallmarketplace.com; **Government Center T.** The city's most famous market, with a hundred or so shops, plus next door's Quincy Market. It's a bit tourist-oriented, but still worth a trip.

The Heritage on the Garden 300 Boylston St ☎617/423-0002; **Arlington T.** Not so much a mall as a very upscale mixed-use complex across from the Public Garden, consisting of condos, restaurants, and boutiques. The latter include Arche Shoes, Escada, Sonia Rykiel, Villeroy Boch, and Hermès.

The Shops at Prudential Center 800 Boylston St ☎617/267-1002; **Prudential T.** This conglomeration of a hundred or so mid-market shops is heavily patronized by local residents and conventioneers from the adjacent Hynes Convention Center, who seem to genuinely enjoy buying commemorative T-shirts and ties from the center-atrium pushcarts.

Department stores

Filene's 426 Washington St ☎617/357-2100, ⓦwww.filenes.com; **Downtown Crossing T.** The merchandise inside downtown Boston's oldest department store is standard issue; the stunning 1912 Beaux Arts facade is not. You'll have better luck downstairs, in Filene's Basement.

Filene's Basement 426 Washington St ☎617/542-2011, ⓦwww.filenesbasement.com; **Downtown Crossing T.** Established in 1908, Filene's Basement is a separate business from Filene's; the discounted merchandise comes here not only from upstairs, but from other big-name department stores and a few Boston boutiques. The markdown system works like this: after 14 days, merchandise is discounted 25 percent, after 21 days, 50 percent, and after 28 days, 75 percent. Anything that lasts more than 35 days goes to charity. Be warned: dressing rooms are communal.

Lord & Taylor 760 Boylston St ☎617/262-6000, ⓦwww.lordandtaylor.com; **Copley T.** Excellent place to stock up on high-end basics, from sweaters and suits to jewelry and cosmetics.

Macy's East 450 Washington St ☎617/357-3000, ⓦwww.macys.com; **Downtown Crossing T.** Much the generic urban department store, with all the basics covered, including a better-than-average cosmetics section and a men's department that outshines that of next-door neighbor Filene's.

Neiman Marcus 5 Copley Place ☎617/536-3660, ⓦwww.neimanmarcus.com; **Copley T.** Boston's most luxurious department store, with prices to match. Three levels, with an impressive menswear collection on the first.

Music

Boston Beat 279 Newbury St ☎617/247-2428, ⓦwww.bostonbeat.com; **Hynes T.** A first-floor store stocking lots of independent dance and techno labels.

Disc Diggers 401 Highland Ave, Somerville ☎617/776-7560, ⓦwww.discdiggers.com; **Davis T.** The largest selection of used CDs in New England, though higher in quantity than quality. Forgotten albums by one-hit wonders abound.

Looney Tunes 1106 Boylston St ☎617/247-2238; **Back Bay T**; **1001 Massachusetts Ave** ☎617/876-5624; **Harvard T.** Rare classical and jazz CDs are the strength at this extremely cramped music store; the sidewalk bargain cassette bin usually yields some good finds, too.

Mojo Music 904 Massachussets Ave ☎617/547-9976; **Central T.** Grotty grotto-style store with a mountain of used LPs, CDs, books, and DVDs to search through.

Newbury Comics 332 Newbury St ☎617/236-4930, ⓦwww.newbury.com; **Hynes T.** Boston's biggest alternative record store carries lots of independent labels you won't find at the national chains, along with a substantial array of vinyl, posters, zines, and kitschy t-shirts. It's also a good place to pick up flyers on local club happenings.

Nuggets 486 Commonwealth Ave ☎617/536-0679, ⓦwww.nuggetsrecords.com; **Kenmore T.** American jazz, rock, and R&B are the strong suits at this venerable new and used record store.

Pipeline 257 Washington St ☎617/591-0590; **#63 bus.** This alluringly bizarre store defies categorization. Mainly used CDs and vinyl, particularly deep on indie and imports. Also new music, kitsch Americana, and videos of the Russ Meyer film ilk.

Planet Records 54B JFK St ☎617/492-0693, ⓦwww.planet-records.com; **Harvard T; 536**

Commonwealth Ave ☎617/353-0693; Kenmore **T**. To buy that old Duran Duran or Styx LP missing from your collection – or to sell one you've listened to a tad too much – head to this basement secondhand music shop in Harvard Square. Buys and sells CDs, too.
Satellite 49 Massachusetts Ave ☎617/536-5482, ⓦwww.satelliterecords.com; Hynes **T**. This storefront hideaway has a great selection of imported techno and trance, in both CD and vinyl format.
Skippy White's 538 Massachusetts Ave ☎617/491-3345; Central **T**. Excellent collection of jazz, blues, R&B, gospel, funk, and hip-hop. Hum a few bars and the knowledgeable salesfolk will guide you to the right section.
Smash City Records 304 Newbury St ☎617/536-0216, ⓦwww.smashcityrecords.com; Arlington **T**. Aside from its velvet Elvis collection, what distinguishes this record store from the others is its massive stock of vinyl for $1; there's even a free bin.

Stereo Jack's 1686 Massachusetts Ave ☎617/497-9447, ⓦwww.stereojacks.com; Porter **T**. Jazz and blues specialists selling mostly used, but some new stuff, too. CDs, tapes, and vinyl.
Tower Records 1249 Boylston St ☎617/247-5900, ⓦwww.towerrecords.com; Hynes **T**. Typically vast representative of this music superstore chain, with a standard selection of popular music, as well as jazz, classical, world beat, and the like.
Twisted Village 12 Eliot St ☎617/354-6898, ⓦwww.twistedvillage.com; Harvard **T**. A really weird mix of fringe styles, among them avant-garde, beat, spoken word, and psychedelic rock.
Virgin Megastore 360 Newbury St ☎617/896-0950, ⓦwww.virginmegamagazine.com; Hynes **T**. Multinational chain featuring every kind of music. Particularly good for rare imports.

Specialty shops

Aunt Sadie's 18 Union Park St ☎617/357-7117; Back Bay **T**. General store-themed South End shop with delightfully campy items like vintage Hawaiian postcards and fun, scented candles with original odors like beach (coconut oil) and amusement park (popcorn).
Black Ink 101 Charles St ☎617/723-3883; Charles **T**; 5 Brattle St, Cambridge ☎617/497-1221; Harvard **T**. Eclectic assortment of things you don't really need but are cool anyway: rubber stamps, a smattering of clothes, amusing refrigerator magnets, and a wide assortment of vintage postcards.
Condom World 332 Newbury St ☎617/267-7233; Arlington **T**. Every style, shape, and flavor of condom you can imagine.
Fi-Dough 103 Charles St ☎617/723-3266, ⓦwww.fidough.com; Charles **T**. Terrific gourmet dog food and salon – stop in for a gift for the furry one you left back home, or bring your pet with you to nosh on free samples.
Fresh 121 Newbury St ☎617/421-1212; Arlington **T**. Pear Chocolate and Fig Apricot are only two varieties of the several sweet-sounding soaps you'll find in this chic bath and body store. They carry over three hundred varieties of French milled soaps,

lotions, oils, and makeup, packaged so exquisitely you won't want to open them.
Fresh Eggs 58 Clarendon St ☎617/247-8150, ⓦwww.fresheggsinc.com; Back Bay **T**. Small boutique featuring exceptionally stylish home furnishings and tchotchkes, from pillow cases to bookends; conveniently, most of it is small enough to carry home in your bag.
Justin Tyme Emporium 91 River St, Cambridge ☎617/491-1088; Central **T**. Justin's is all about pop culture artifacts, featuring boffo American detritus like lava lamps, Donny and Marie Osmond pin-ups, and campy T-shirts with iron-ons.
Kitty House 223 Newbury St ☎617/262-0362, ⓦwww.kittyhouse.net; Arlington **T**. Pretty much every Hello Kitty product ever made can be found at this small basement store devoted to the Japanese collectible. Kind of scary.
Koo de Kir 65 Chestnut St ☎617/723-8111, ⓦwww.koodekir.com; Charles **T**. The goal at this stylish, modern spot is to make even the most everyday objects artistic and beautiful. For a pretty penny, you can buy such beautified home furnishings and accessories here.
Leavitt and Pierce 1316 Massachusetts Ave, Cambridge ☎617/547-0576; Harvard **T**.

Old-school tobacconists that have been around almost as long as Harvard. An outstanding selection of cigars, imported cigarettes, and smoking paraphernalia (lighters, rolling papers, ashtrays), plus an upstairs smoking loft right out of the carefree past. **The London Harness Company 60 Franklin St** ⊤617/542-9234, ⓦwww.londonharness.com; **Downtown Crossing T.** Chiefly known for its high-quality luggage, this place reeks of traditional Boston – indeed, Ben Franklin used to shop here. They also sell items like chess sets, clocks, candlesticks, and inlaid decorative boxes.

Loulou's Lost & Found 121 Newbury St ⊤617/859-8593; **Arlington T.** It's said that Loulou scours the globe in search of such essentials as tableware embossed with French cruise ship logos and silverware from long-gone five-star restaurants. A fine place to indulge your inner Martha Stewart. **Marquis De Sade 73 Berkeley St** ⊤617/426-2120; **Back Bay T.** Proffering a wide range of leather items and hardcore sexual paraphernalia, this South End shop leaves little to the imagination.

Matsu 259 Newbury St ⊤617/266-9707; **Copley T.** A hip little shop featuring a medium-sized range of sleek Japanese clothing, knickknacks (desk clocks, stationery, funky pens), and contemporary home decor items.

Million-Year Picnic 99 Mt Auburn St, Cambridge ⊤617/492-6763; **Harvard T.** For the comic-obsessed. Features Japanese anime, *Superman*, *Tank Girl*, *Dilbert*, and more, and is stronger on current stuff than old material. The staff has encyclopedic knowledge, and is tolerant of browsers.

Sherman's 26 Province St ⊤617/482-9610; **Downtown Crossing T.** Forget those overpriced travel boutiques in the malls; this cavernous Downtown Crossing emporium stocks not only an impressive range of luggage, but just about every travel gadget imaginable.

Sugar Heaven 218 Newbury St ⊤617/266-6969, ⓦwww.sugarheaven.us; **Hynes T.** Pick up a bucket on your way in and fill it to the brim with candy from all over the world, including ones you may have thought were extinct (such as Pop Rocks).

Women's Union Shop 1 Washington Mall ⊤617/536-5651, ⓦwww.weiu.org; **Arlington T.** The retail outpost of this long-established private social services organization features quality handmade household knickknacks, toys, wrapping paper, stationery, and a range of antiques.

SHOPPING | Specialty shops

19

Sports and outdoor activities

Bostonians have an acute love-hate relationship with their professional **sports** teams, obsessing over the four major franchises – baseball's Red Sox, football's Patriots, basketball's Celtics, and hockey's Bruins – with evangelical fervor. After years of watching their teams narrowly miss championship bids, all their Christmases came at once with the Red Sox finally ending 86 years of hurt by taking the 2004 World Series and the Patriots earning their third title in four seasons just a few months later.

Local sports fans have an admirable tenacity, following their teams closely through good seasons and bad; indeed, supporters seem to love bemoaning their teams' woes nearly as much as they do celebrating their victories. This lively, vocal fan base makes attending a game a great way to get a feel for the city, though fans of an opposing team who might be inclined to root against Boston, be warned: you're in store for censure from the local faithful.

While the Patriots' **Foxboro Stadium** is located out of town and has little to recommend it, the **FleetCenter**, where the Celtics and Bruins play, is at least conveniently accessible by **T**, even if it lacks the history of the classic Boston Garden that it replaced (the Garden was demolished in 1997). For fans of baseball, there is no more essential pilgrimage than the one to the Red Sox' idiosyncratic Fenway Park, accessed by the Green Line's Kendall **T**.

Boston isn't a city where **participatory sports** thrive particularly well, due mostly to the area's often dreary weather. There are, however, more than a number of good areas for jogging, biking, rollerblading, and the like, especially around the Esplanade, not to mention the possibility of getting out on the water that surrounds the city. The **Department of Conservation and Recreation** (**DCR**), 251 Causeway Street (☎617/626-1250, ⓦwww.mass.gov/dcr), oversees most facilities.

Baseball

The Boston **Red Sox** finally stopped tormenting fans when they won the 2004 World Series against the St Louis Cardinals, so breaking the infamous "Curse of the Bambino" – the uncanny string of bad luck and near-misses that had plagued them since selling off Babe (hence Bambino) Ruth to the hated New York Yankees. The ongoing rivalry between the Sox and Yankees is legendary, though Boston's need to define themselves relative to the Yankees' success may ease a bit thanks to their recent breakthrough. The self-styled team of mavericks should stay competitive for the coming years, remaining full of talent despite losing star pitcher Pedro Martinez to the New York Mets at the end of 2004.

Venue and tickets

Even when the Red Sox aren't performing so well, it's worth going to a game just to see **Fenway Park**, at 24 Yawkey Way, one of America's sports treasures. Dating from 1912, it's the oldest baseball stadium in the country, much more intimate than most, and one of bizarre dimensions, best represented by the abnormally tall (37-foot) left-field wall, dubbed the "Green Monster." Grandstand tickets can cost upwards of $45, but bleacher seats start from $12 and put you amid the raucous fans; there are few better ways to spend a Sunday summer afternoon in Boston. The stadium is near the Kenmore **T** stop; for ticket information, call ☏617/482-4SOX or visit ⓦwww .redsox.com. Best to get tickets well in advance of games. The season runs from April through September, with playoffs in October.

Basketball

While Boston's other sports franchises once had a reputation for falling short of victory, basketball's **Celtics** have won sixteen NBA championships – more than any other US professional sports teams except baseball's New York Yankees and hockey's Montréal Canadiens. But while they enjoyed dynastic success in the 1960s and 1980s, when they played on the buckling parquet floors of the beloved Boston Garden, the Celts fell on hard times in the 1990s, and have not won a title since 1986. The team did make three consecutive playoff spots in 2002–04, and it is hoped that a new victorious era may be just around the corner.

Venue and tickets

The Celtics play in the sleek if soulless **FleetCenter**, 150 Causeway St (☏617/624-1000, ⓦwww.nba.com /celtics), located near the North Station **T** stop in the West End. Most tickets are pricey – good seats run between $50 and $150 – but you can sometimes snag some in the rafters for as little as $10; for those, show up in front of the stadium on game day and hope for the best. The season begins in late October and continues all the way through June, playoffs included.

Football

For years, the New England **Patriots** were saddled with the nickname "Patsies," and generally considered to be a laughingstock. Recently, they've been more like a dynasty, having won Super Bowls in 2002, 2004, and 2005. Led by quarterback Tom Brady and the top coach in the business, Bill Belichick, the team conducted a 21-game winning streak from 2003 to 2004, setting an all-time standard.

Even before they won the three Super Bowls, going to a game wasn't a reasonable goal unless you had connections or were willing to pay a scalper upwards of $100 – tickets sell out far in advance. If you can get your hands on a pair the old-fashioned way, expect to pay $49–99 a head. The stadium is located in distant Foxboro, just north of the Massachusetts–Rhode Island border (for information, call ☎1-800/543-1776; for tickets, dial ☎617/931-2222 or visit ⓦwww.patriots.com). Better to drop by a sports bar on a Sunday afternoon during the fall season (Sept–Dec); the best ones are located in the West End (see Chapter 14, Drinking).

Ice hockey

Until a decade ago, ice hockey's Boston **Bruins** were a consistently successful franchise, at one point running up a streak of 26 straight winning seasons – the longest in professional sports, including appearances in the Stanley Cup finals on two occasions, 1988 and 1990, both of which they barely lost. A series of retirements, injuries, and bad luck turned things around and by the mid-90s they were posting the worst records in the National Hockey League. The team did qualify for the playoffs in 2003 and 2004.

An equally entertaining, and cheaper, alternative to the Bruins is **college hockey**. The biggest event is the "Beanpot," an annual competition that takes place on the first two Mondays in February, in which the four big local teams – **Boston University Terriers**, **Harvard Crimson**, **Boston College Eagles**, and **Northeastern Huskies** – compete for city bragging rights.

You can catch the Bruins at the **Fleet-Center**, 150 Causeway St (North Station **T**; ☎617/624-1000, ⓦwww.bostonbruins.com), where tickets are expensive ($19–99), especially if a good opponent is in town. The long regular season begins in October and continues, with playoffs, into June.

Meanwhile, BU plays at Walter Brown Arena, 285 Babcock St (☎617/353-3838, ⓦwww.bu.edu/athletics); Harvard at Bright Hockey Center, N Harvard St, Allston (☎617/495-2211 or 1-877/GO-HARVARD, ⓦwww.fas.harvard.edu/~athletic); BC at the Conte Forum, Chestnut Hill (☎617/552-GoBC, ⓦbceagles.ocsn.com); and Northeastern at Matthews Arena, St Botolph St (☎617/373-GoNU, ⓦwww.gonu.com). Beanpot tickets ($15–25; ☎617/931-2000, also available from team websites) are hard to come by, but regular-season seats go for around $5; the games are quite fun.

Running, rollerblading, and cycling

On the rare days that Boston is visited by pleasant weather, residents take full advantage of it, turning up in droves to engage in **outdoor activities**. The most popular of these are **running**, **rollerblading**, and **cycling**, and they all pretty much take place along the banks of the Charles River, where the Esplanade provides eighteen miles of well-kept, picturesque trails stretching from the Museum of Science all the way down to Watertown and Newton.

On the Cambridge side of the Charles is Memorial Drive, closed off to traffic between Western Avenue and Eliot Bridge (May to mid-Nov Sun 11am–7pm); it's a prime place for blading and tanning.

Two of the most popular **bike trails** in the area are the Dr Paul Dudley White Bike Path (really just another name for the Esplanade loop) and the Minuteman Bikeway, which runs 10.5 miles from Alewife **T** station on the Red Line in Cambridge through Lexington to Bedford.

You can take your bike on the T's Red, Orange, and Blue lines (Mon–Fri 10am–2pm & 7pm–close, Sat & Sun all day), except on Patriots' Day, St Patrick's Day, Independence Day, and at 8.30–11pm whenever there's a Red Sox game or an event at the FleetCenter. MBTA buses and the Green Line do not allow bicycles on board at any time. When taking your bicycle on the subway, always follow the conductor's directions.

△ Runners in the Boston Marathon

Blade rentals generally start at around $15/day; bike rentals around $25/day.

Back Bay Bicycles 333 Newbury St ☎617/247-2336, ⓦwww.backbaybicycles.com; Hynes **T**.

Beacon Hill Skate Shop 135 S Charles St ☎617/482-7400; Charles **T**.

Blades, Boards and Skates 349 Newbury St ☎617/437-6300, ⓦwww.blades.com; Hynes **T**.

Community Bicycle Supply 496 Tremont St ☎617/542-8623, ⓦwww.communitybicycle .com; Copley **T**.

Wheelworks Bicycle Workshop 259 Massachusetts Ave, Cambridge ☎617/876-6555; Central **T**.

The DCR (see p.239) has information about bike trails as well.

Charles River Wheelmen ☎617/332-8546 or 325-BIKE, ⓦwww.crw.org. Organize regular, and usually free, bike tours on weekends from April through November.

InLine Club of Boston ☎617/781/932-5457, ⓦwww.sk8net.com. Organizes community skates and other in-line events.

Massachusetts Bicycle Coalition, 44 Bromfield St, room 207 ☎617/542-2453, ⓦwww .massbikeboston.org; 214A Broadway, Cambridge ☎617/491-7433. Information about bike trails, and sells a Boston bike map ($4.50).

Ice skating

The DCR operates several **ice-skating rinks** in the Boston area between mid-November and mid-March, of which the best-kept and most convenient to downtown is the **Steriti Memorial Rink**, at 550 Commercial St (☎617/523-9327) in the North End. When it's cold enough, the lagoon in the Public Garden offers free skating, while the **Frog Pond** in Boston Common (Mon 10am–5pm, Tues–Thurs & Sun 10am–9pm, Fri–Sat 10am–10pm; $3; ☎617/635-4505; Park St **T**) charges for the sport but does rent skates on-site (adults $5, children $3). To find out dates and times and keep tabs on skating conditions throughout the city, visit the DCR website (see p.239).

Water sports

The image of white sails dotting the Charles River Basin and Boston Harbor may be inviting; alas, you'll be stuck watching them from shore unless you have recognized **sailing** credentials or are willing to take a class. Should you have the former, present them to the Boston Harbor Sailing Club on Rowes Wharf (☎617/720-0049, ⓦwww.bostonharborsailing.com; Aquarium **T**) and you can rent yourself a variety of boats from a daysailer ($25/hr–$75/day) to a cruiser ($139/hr–$417/day).

Classes are available through a number of outfits, the best being Community Boating (April–Oct; learn to sail class $75; ☎617/523-1038, ⓦwww.community -boating.org) and Piers Park Sailing Center, 95 Marginal St (April–Oct; ☎617/561-6677, ⓦwww.piersparksailing.org; Maverick **T**), which does a 21-hour course for $495. Children sailors get the best deal of all, though, through Community Boating (see Chapter 20, Kids' Boston).

Possibly an easier way to get on the water is renting a **canoe** or **kayak** from the Charles River Canoe and Kayak Center, Sailor's Road (May–Oct Fri 1pm–dusk, Sat–Sun 10am–dusk; ☎617/462-2513, ⓦwww.ski-paddle.com; Harvard **T**), which maintains a green-roofed kiosk 200 yards from the Eliot Bridge on the Boston side of the Charles. Equipment is rented by the day or hour (canoes and kayaks $14–56); lessons are also available, but certainly not required.

Fitness centers

If you're staying at a hotel without a gym and are in need of a workout, a number of **health clubs** and **fitness centers** offer one-time daily memberships for out-of-towners. The Beacon Hill Athletic Clubs (ⓦwww .beaconhillathleticclubs.com), with locations at 261 Friend St (Ⓣ617/720-2422; North Station T), 3 Hancock St (Ⓣ617/367-2422; Park St T), and 85 Atlantic Ave (Ⓣ617/742-0055; State St T), offers free day passes through its website. The City Gym and Aerobic Center, at 542 Commonwealth Ave (Ⓣ617/536-4008; Hynes T), offers day passes for $10. The Boston Athletic Club, 653 Summer St (Ⓣ617/269-4300, ⓦwww.bostonathleticclub.com; Downtown Crossing T), charges $25 a day for full use of their facilities, which include a sauna and pool, on presentation of your hotel key.

Otherwise, women can pay $12 to take advantage of Boston Fitness for Women, 27 School St (Ⓣ617/523-3098; Government Center T), a gym with a relaxed female-only environment. Both sexes can practice their downward dogs at the drop-in **yoga** classes led by Baron Baptiste Power Yoga Institute (Ⓣ617/661-YOGA, ⓦwww.baronbaptiste.com); its two locations, at 139 Columbus Ave, Boston ($12 per class $3 for showers; Back Bay T), and 2000 Massachusetts Ave, Cambridge ($12; Porter T), also rent mats ($1).

Bowling

Massachusetts's variation on tenpin bowling is **candlepin bowling**, in which the ball is smaller, the pins narrower and lighter, and you have three rather than two chances to knock the pins down. It's somewhat of a local institution that is sadly on the wane in the city itself. The best places to find it in the Greater Boston area are Lanes and Games, 195 Concord Turnpike, Somerville (daily 9am–midnight; Ⓣ617/876-5533, ⓦwww.lanesgames.com; Alewife T) and Milky Way, 403-405 Centre St, Jamaica Plain (Mon–Thurs 6pm–midnight, Fri–Sat 5pm–12.45am, Sun 5–11pm; Ⓣ617/524-3740, ⓦwww .milkywayjp.com; Heath St T). Suburban and regional venues still abound; visit ⓦwww.masscandlepin.com for a list of venues.

The local demise of candlepin bowling has been countered by a renaissance of the more conventional form of the game. Kings at 10 Scotia St in Back Bay (Mon–Wed 5pm–2am, Thurs–Sun 11.30am–2am, Ⓣ617/266-BOWL, ⓦkingsbackbay.com; Hynes T) is an upscale 16-lane bowling alley/bar usually packed to the rafters.

Paintball

Among all the miscellaneous forms of sports(like) entertainment in the city, perhaps the oddest (and most fun, if you're into this type of thing) is **paintball** – a kind of simulated warfare where you shoot paintballs rather than bullets (and they do sting) at members of the opposing team, all while scampering around an area full of bunkers and obstacles. The proceedings take place in Somerville at Boston Paintball, 43 Foley St (reservations Ⓣ617/941-0123, ⓦwww.bostonpaintball.com; $29.95; Sullivan Sq T).

Pool

There are plenty of places to shoot **pool** in the Boston area, and not just of the divey variety you'll invariably find in some of the city's more down-and-out bars. One of the best is *Boston Billiard Club*, 126 Brookline Ave (℡617/536-7665, Ⓦwww.bostonbilliardclub.com; Kenmore Ⓣ), a classy and serious pool hall that also has a nice bar. *Flat Top Johnny's*, at One Kendall Square in Cambridge (℡617/494-9565, Ⓦwww.flattopjohnnys.com; Kendall Ⓣ), draws a diverse young clientele to its smoky environment. *The Rack* at 24 Clinton St across from Faneuil Hall (℡617/725-1051; Government Center Ⓣ) and *Felt* at 533 Washington St (℡617/350-5555; Downtown Crossing Ⓣ) both draw well-heeled yuppies and ardent pool players. The best pub to play is the *Beantown Pub*, 100 Tremont St (℡617/426-0111; Park Street Ⓣ).

Kids' Boston

O ne of the best aspects of **traveling with kids** in Boston is the feeling that you're conducting an ongoing history lesson. While that may grow a bit tiresome for teens, younger children tend to eat up the colonial-period costumes, cannons, and the like. Various points on the Freedom Trail are, of course, best for this, though getting out of the city to Lexington and Concord (see Chapter 10, Out of the city) will lead you along a similar path.

The city's **parks**, notably Boston Common, Franklin Park, and the Public Garden – where you can ride the Swan Boats in the lagoon during summer or climb on the sculpture *Mrs Mallard and Her Eight Ducklings* – make nice settings for an afternoon with the children, too. The best outdoor option, however, may be a Red Sox game at Fenway Park, as the country's oldest baseball stadium is easily reached by the **T** and games here are affordable (see p.239) – if you can get tickets. **Harbor cruises** are also a fairly popular and unique way to see Boston, as is ascending to the top of one of the city's skyscrapers. There are, as well, a number of **museums** aimed at the younger set, most of them located along one waterfront or another.

Museums and sights

Though kids might not have **historical attractions** at the top of their list of favorite places, most of Boston's major **museums** manage to make the city's history palatable to youngsters. This is true at the *USS Constitution*, the old warship moored in the Charlestown Navy Yard (see p.79), and the **USS Constitution Museum**, where a video game on the top floor allows kids to test their battle skills.

The **Children's Museum**, the **Museum of Science**, and the **MIT Museum** (p.66, p.93, & p.154, respectively) are three other places to let the little ones loose for a while; all provide a lot of interactive fun that's as easy for adults to get lost in as it is kids, plus the Children's Museum sits behind the 40-foot **Hood Milk Bottle**, a food stand that serves ice cream, hamburgers, and the like. For animal sightings, the **Franklin Park Zoo** and the **New England Aquarium** (p.134 & p.65, respectively) can't be beat. Finally, views from the dizzying heights of the Back Bay's **Prudential Tower** (p.102) are always sure to thrill.

△ Hood Milk Bottle

Activities

For a different kind of education, America's oldest public boating set-up, Community Boating, 21 Embankment Rd (☎617/523-1038, @www.community-boating.org), between the Hatch Shell and Longfellow Bridge, offers youngsters aged 10 to 18 who can swim 75 yards the cheapest **sailing lessons** around, for just $1. The fee also allows summer-long access to the boathouse and entry to a number of one- to five-day classes, including kayaking and windsurfing.

If that seems like too much work, your children can learn things sitting down at the Museum of Science's **Charles Hayden Planetarium** and **Mugar Omni Theater** (adults $8.50, kids $6.50; ☎617/723-2500, @www.mos.org; Science Park **T**), which feature IMAX movies, laser shows set to the music of various rock and pop bands, and documentaries about the solar system.

Afterwards, the kids can check out the **Gilliland Observatory**, which, weather permitting, opens its roof and points its telescopes heavenwards on Friday nights (8.30–10pm; free; ☏617/589-0267 extension 1; Science Park **T**).

Another event that makes learning fun is the Museum of Fine Arts' free "Drop In Drawing" (Sun 11am–4pm, ☏617/267-9300, ⓦwww.mfa.org; Museum **T**), which offers **drawing classes** and **readings** in a number of galleries. Check the website or call the museum directly for additional goings-on throughout the year.

Shops

If and when the history starts to wear thin, there's always the failsafe of Boston's **malls** to divert the kids' attention (see p.235). To combine history with your shopping, you could head to Faneuil Hall and Quincy Market, which are both hundreds of years old. The latter is home to the Chocolate Dipper (☏617/439-0190; Government Center **T**), where strawberries, pineapple slices, cookies, brownies, and more get a quick bath in dark or milk **chocolate**. Red pops, warheads, and other delightful **candies** can be had at Irving's Toy and Candy Shop, 371 Harvard St, Brookline (☏617/566-9327; Coolidge Crossing **T**), while candy from all over the world can be bought at Newbury Street's Sugar Heaven (see p.238). If the kids are screaming for **ice cream**, load them up with homemade scoops of maple cream and cookie dough at *Herrell's*, 15 Dunster St (☏617/497-2179; Harvard **T**), while you indulge in boozy flavors like peach schnapps and Kentucky bourbon.

Few kids can resist FAO Schwarz, 440 Boylston St (☏617/262-5900, ⓦwww .fao.com; Arlington **T**), and whether or not you're turned off by **toys**, the huge bronze teddy bear plunked on the sidewalk in front of this colorful emporium is worth a glance. Inside is a two-level childrens' paradise of enormous stuffed animals, a Barbie boutique, the latest home video games, and many other useless but fun pieces of molded plastic.

Kids' tours

Boston is a great place for kids to see on a **tour**, in part due to the atypical means of public transportation: mostly trolleys and ships. Some of the best and most unusual options follow:

Boston Duck Tours ☏617/723-3825, ⓦwww.bostonducktours.com. See p.37.

Boston Harbor Cruises ☏617/227-4321, ⓦwww.bostonharborcruises.com.

Boston by Little Feet May–Oct Mon & Sat 10am, Sun 2pm; $8; ☏617/367-2345 or 617/367-3766 for recorded info, ⓦwww.bostonbyfoot.com; State St **T**. One-hour Freedom Trail walk for ages 6 to 12. Tours begin in front of the statue of Samuel Adams at Faneuil Hall and include a free map and kids' *Explorer's Guide*.

Freedom Trail Players July–Aug Sat & Sun 11am & 1pm; adults $12, kids $6; ☏617/227-8800, ⓦwww.thefreedomtrail.org. This troupe dresses in colonial garb and acts out Revolutionary historiana along the trail; tours last ninety minutes.

Liberty schooner June–Sept noon, 3pm & 6pm; adults $30, kids $18; ☏617/742-0333, ⓦwww.libertyfleet.com. This boat departs from Long Wharf and sails for two hours around Boston's Harbor Islands.

New England Aquarium April–Oct daily, times vary; adults $29, kids $20; ☏617/973-5277, ⓦwww.neaq.org. Three- to five-hour whale-watching excursions into the harbor.

There's no shortage of **bookstores** catering to children in Boston either; the Children's Book Shop, 237 Washington St (☎617/734-7323, ⓦusers.erols .com/childrensbookshop; Coolidge Crossing ⓣ), and Curious George Goes to Wordsworth, 1 JFK St (☎617/498-0062 or 1-800/899-2202, ⓦwww .curiousg.com; Harvard ⓣ), are sure to have the latest titles, and others you didn't know existed. Near the latter is an excellent **novelty** store, Animal, Vegetable, Mineral, at 2400 Massachusetts Ave (☎617/547-2404; Porter ⓣ), with goldfish bowls full of plastic dinosaurs, rubber eyeballs, and the like.

Theater and puppet shows

If you want to get the tots some (kindergarten) culture, try the Boston Children's Theatre, 321 Columbus Ave (☎617/424-6634, ⓦwww.bostonchildrenstheatre .org), where productions of kids' classics are performed at the C. Walsh Theater, on the Beacon Hill campus of Suffolk University, and the McCormack Theatre, at UMASS Boston. Otherwise, head out to Brookline for the Puppet Showplace Theatre, 32 Station St (Wed and Thurs 10.30am, Sat & Sun 1pm and 3pm; ☎617/731-6400, ⓦwww.puppetshowplace.org); tickets are $8.50 a head – big or small.

Festivals and events

I t's always good to know ahead of time what **festivals** or **annual events** are scheduled to coincide with your trip to Boston – though even if you don't plan it, there's likely to be some sort of parade, public celebration, or seasonal shindig going on. For detailed information, call the Boston Convention and Visitors Bureau (☎1–888/SEE-BOSTON, ⓦwww.bostonusa .com); for a look at public holidays in Boston, see the "Opening hours, public holidays, and festivals" section in Basics.

The schedule below picks out some of the more fun and notable events happening throughout the year, and is not meant to be exhaustive. If you are looking for specific highlights, note that a few nationwide events more or less reach their apotheosis here, such as St Patrick's Day (March) and Independence Day (July); tops in Boston-only happenings include the Head of the Charles Regatta (August) and the Boston Tea Party Re-enactment (December).

January

First Night The New Year's celebration begins on New Year's Eve but carries into the first few days of the year; see events under December, below.

Chinese New Year Usually late month ☎1-888/ SEE-BOSTON Dragon parades and firecrackers punctuate the festivities throughout Chinatown. The New Year can fall in February, too, depending on the Chinese lunar calendar.

February

The Beanpot First two Mondays ⓦwww .fleetcenter.com Popular college hockey tournament, played between Boston University, Harvard, Boston College, and Northeastern. Visit the individual colleges' websites for more information.

March

St Patrick's Day Parade and Festival March 17 ☎1-888/SEE-BOSTON Boston's substantial Irish-American community, along with much of the rest of the city, turns out for this parade through South Boston (see Chapter 8, The southern districts), which culminates in Irish folk music, dance, and food at Faneuil Hall. This also happens to be "Evacuation Day," or the anniversary of the day that George Washington drove the British out of Boston during the Revolutionary War, which gives Bostonians another historical excuse to party

New England Spring Flower Show **Second or third week in March** ☎ 617/933-4984, ⓦ www.masshort.org Winter-weary Bostonians turn out in droves to gawk at hothouse greenery in this week-long horticultural fest, which takes place in Dorchester's Bayside Expo Center. Tickets cost $20.

April

Boston Marathon **Third Monday** ☎ 617/236-1652, ⓦ www.bostonmarathon.org Runners from all over the world gather for this 26.2-mile affair, one of America's premier athletic events. It crosses all over Boston, ending in Back Bay's Copley Square.

Patriot's Day **Third Monday** ☎ 1-888/SEE-BOSTON A celebration and re-creation of Paul Revere's and William Dawes's famous ride from the North End to Lexington that alerted locals that the British army had been deployed against the rebel threat.

△ St Patrick's Day festivities

May

Dulcimer Festival First weekend ☎617/547-6789, ⓦwww.jonweinberg.com/dulcifest Workshops and performances by experts of both mountain and hammer dulcimers are held in Cambridge.

Greater Boston Kite Festival Mid-May ☎617/635-4505 Franklin Park gets taken over by kite-lovers during this celebration, which features kite-making, flying clinics, and music.

Lilac Sunday Third Sunday ☎617/524-1718, ⓦwww.arboretum.harvard.edu/plants/lilac_sunday.html You can view more than three hundred lilac varieties in full bloom at the Arnold Arboretum during this early summer event – a Boston institution.

June

Scooper Bowl/Boston Dairy Festival First week ☎1-888/SEE-BOSTON Cows and other animals are brought back to Boston Common to graze, and, for a modest donation of around $5, you're allowed unlimited samples of the city's best ice creams.

Dragon Boat Festival Variable weekend in early June ☎617/426-6500 ext 778, ⓦwww.bostondragonboat.org A colorful Chinese festival whose highlight, dragon boat racing on the Charles River, is accompanied by the thundering sound of Taiko drums.

Bunker Hill Weekend Sunday nearest June 17 ☎617/242-5601 The highlight of this three-day festival in Charlestown is the parade celebrating the Battle of Bunker Hill (even though the bout was lost by the Americans).

Boston Early Music Festival Every odd-numbered year ☎617/661-1812, ⓦwww.bemf.org This huge, week-long Renaissance fair with a strong music theme includes concerts and exhibitions throughout town.

Boston Globe Jazz Festival Mid to late June ☎617/929-2000 or 1-800/SEE-BOSTON, ⓦbostonglobe.com/promotions/jazzfest The city's leading newspaper sponsors a week-long series of jazz events at various venues; some are free, though shows by big names can be pricey.

July

Harborfest Late June–weekend nearest July 4 ☎617/227-1528, ⓦwww.bostonharborfest.com Includes a series of concerts on the waterfront (mostly jazz, blues, and rock), plus, on July 4th weekend, lots of fireworks and the highly competitive "Chowderfest," where restaurants from the area compete for the "Boston's Best Chowder" crown.

Boston Pops Concert and Fireworks July 4 ☎1-888-4th-POPS, ⓦwww.july4th.org The Boston Pops' wildly popular annual evening concert in the Oval area, in front of the Hatch Shell, is followed by thirty minutes of flashy pyrotechnics; people sometimes line up at dawn in order to get good seats.

Reading of the Declaration of Independence July 4 ☎1-888/SEE-BOSTON Pretend it's July 4th, 1776, by attending the annual reading of the nation's founding document from the Balcony of Old State House.

USS Constitution Turn-Around July 4 Old Ironsides pulls up anchor and sails out (briefly) into Boston Harbor in this annual event that's a salute to the country's independence.

August

August Moon Festival Near the end of the month ☎1-888/SEE-BOSTON During this festival, Chinatown's merchants and restaurateurs hawk their wares on the street amid dragon parades and firecrackers.

Italian Festas Last two weekends in August ☎1-888/SEE-BOSTON Features music, dancing, and games throughout the North End; during the parades, locals pin dollar bills to the floats and statues of the Virgin Mary are borne through the streets.

September

Arts Festival of Boston Around Labor Day weekend ☎617/451-ARTS, ⓦwww.cityofboston.gov/arts Boston is transformed into a giant gallery, with five days of exhibits, arts and crafts pavilions, fashion shows, evening galas, receptions, and outdoor musical performances at various locations.

Boston Film Festival Two weeks in early to mid-September ☎1-888/SEE-BOSTON Boston theaters screen independent films, with frequent discussions by directors and screenwriters.

Cambridge River Festival Mid-September ☎617/349-4380, ⓦwww.cambridgema.gov/~CAC/ Memorial Drive is closed off from JFK Street to Western Avenue for music shows, dancing, and eclectic food offerings, all along the Charles River.

Boston Blues Festival Late September ⓦwww.bluestrust.com This festival brings blues to the shores of the Charles River for two cool, "my-baby-done-left-me" days.

October

Oktoberfest Early October ☎617/491-3434, ⓦwww.harvardsquare.com The usual beer, sauerkraut, and live entertainment in Harvard Square, done Boston style – meaning the hops-fueled shenanigans end at 6pm.

Columbus Day Parade Second Monday ☎1-888/SEE-BOSTON Kicked off by a ceremony at City Hall at 1pm, the raucous, Italian-flavored parade continues into the heart of the North End.

Boston Fasion Week Mid-October ⓦwww.bostonfashion.com Nothing on London, Paris, New York, or Milan, but there are some fun events celebrating local designers.

Head of the Charles Regatta Next-to-last weekend ☎617/868-6200, ⓦwww.hocr.org Hordes of college students descend on the banks of the Charles River between Central and Harvard squares, ostensibly to watch the crew races, but really more to pal around with their cronies and get loaded.

Salem Haunted Happenings/Halloween ☎1-800/777-6848, ⓦwww.salemweb.com Two-week Salem festival, up to and including the 31st, featuring seances and the like and ending with Halloween celebrations.

Open studios

Each fall, the **Boston Open Studios Coalition** arranges for local artists to showcase their paintings, pottery, photographs, and other works of art to the public, on a neighborhood-by-neighborhood basis. Exhibitors include the United South End Artists (☎617/267-8862), the Jamaica Plain Artists (☎617/524-3816), ACT Roxbury (☎617/445-1061 extension 222), the Mission Hill Art Association (☎617/427-7399), and the Fort Point Channel Arts Community (☎617/423-4299). Check newspapers for listings.

November

Annual Lighting Ceremony Late November
℡1-888/SEE-BOSTON Faneuil Hall Marketplace kickstarts the holiday season with
the annual lighting of some 300,000 festive
bulbs.

Thanksgiving Last Thursday ℡1-800/USA-
1620, ⊛www.visit-plymouth.com In Plymouth,
the first Thanksgiving ever is commemorated with tours of old houses and traditional feasts.

December

**Boston Tea Party Re-enactment Sunday nearest
Dec 16** ℡617/338-1773 or 1-888/SEE-BOSTON
A lusty re-enactment of the march from Old
South Meeting House to the harbor, and
the subsequent tea-dumping that helped
spark the American Revolution.
First Night Dec 31–Jan 2 ℡617/542-1399,
⊛www.firstnight.org A family-friendly

festival to ring in the New Year, featuring
parades, ice sculptures, art shows,
plays, and music throughout
Downtown and Back Bay; culminates
in a spectacular fireworks display over
Boston Harbor. A button, granting
admission to all events, tends to run
around $15.

Directory

Airlines Most airlines are represented at Boston's Logan International Airport. Domestic flights typically arrive and depart from terminals B and C, and international flights arrive and depart from Terminal E. For airline contact information, see "Getting there" in Basics.

Babysitting Try Nanny Poppins ($10–18/hr; ☏979/927-1811, ⓦwww.nannypoppins .com).

Banks and ATMs Fleet Financial Group and the Bank of Boston together make up the biggest bank – Fleet Boston – with branches and ATMs throughout the city (☏1-800/841-4000, ⓦwww.fleet.com). Citizens Bank also has branches scattered about town (☏1-800/922-9999, ⓦwww .citizensbank.com). See "Costs, money, and banks" in Basics for more.

Bicycles A copy of Boston's Bike Map ($4.50; ☏1-800/358-6013, ⓦwww .bikemaps.com) will help you find all the trails and bike-friendly roads in the area; pick one up in person at Cambridge's Globe Corner Bookstore, 28 Church St (☏617/497-6277, ⓦwww.globecorner.com; Harvard **T**). For information on rentals, along with the best spots to bike, see both Basics (p.36) and Chapter 19, Sports and outdoor activities (p.241).

Car rentals Local branches: Avis, 3 Center Plaza ☏617/534-1400 or 1-800/331-1212, ⓦwww.avis.com, 41 Westland Ave ☏617/534-1400, 1 Bennett St, Cambridge ☏617/534-1430, and Logan Airport ☏617/561-3500; Hertz, 30 Park Plaza ☏617/338-1500, ⓦwww.hertz.com, Logan Airport ☏617/569-7272, 145 Dartmouth St ☏617/338-1500, 164 Northern Ave ☏617/204-1165, 240 Prescott St ☏617/204-1165, Summer St and Atlantic Ave ☏617/338-1503, 10 Huntington Ave

☏617/338-1506; Enterprise, 800 Boylston St ☏617/262-9215 or 1-800/RENT-A-CAR, ⓦwww.enterprise.com and 839 Albany St ☏617/442-7500; Thrifty, 125 Summer St ☏617/330-5011 or 1-800/367-2277, ⓦwww.thrifty.com and Logan Airport ☏617/634-7350. For nationwide information, see p.36 in Basics.

Consulates Canada, 3 Copley Place, suite 400 ☏617/262-3760, ⓦwww.can-am.gc .ca/boston; France, 31 St James Ave ☏617/542-7374, ⓦwww.consulfrance -boston.org; Germany, 3 Copley Place ☏617/536-4414, ⓦwww.germanconsulate .org/boston; Ireland, 535 Boylston St ☏617/267-9330; Japan, 600 Atlantic Ave ☏617/973-9772, ⓦwww.boston.us.emb -japan.go.jp; UK, 1 Memorial Dr, suite 1600, Cambridge ☏617/245-4500, ⓦwww .britainusa.com/boston.

Emergencies Dial ☏911 for emergency assistance.

Exchange There are currency exchange counters at Logan Airport's Terminal E (International). In the city, there's Thomas Cook, 399 Boylston St ☏1-800/287-7362; Arlington **T** and American Express, 39 JFK St ☏617/868-2600; Harvard **T**.

Film and photography Moto Photo has one-hour developing services and locations in the Financial District, 101 Summer St (☏617/423-6848); Back Bay, 657 Boylston St (☏617/266-6560); and Harvard Square, 36 JFK St, Cambridge (☏617/497-0731).

Health Inn-House Doctor, 839 Beacon St, suite B ☏617/267-9407 or 859-1776; ⓦwww.inn-housedoctor.net. Make 24hr house calls; rates are $150–250; prescriptions cost extra.

Internet Harvard's Holyoke Center, 1350 Massachusetts Ave; MIT's Rogers Building, 77 Massachusetts Ave; and the Boston

Public Library, 700 Boylston St, have free Internet access with ten-to-fifteen minute sessions.

Laundry Back Bay Laundry Emporium, 409A Marlborough St (daily 7.30am–11pm, last wash at 9pm; ☎617/236-4552), is a good, clean bet; drop-off service is $1 per pound.

Parking lots The cheapest downtown options are Center Plaza Garage, at the corner of Cambridge and New Sudbury streets ($9/hr–$25/max; ☎617/742-7807) and Garage at Post Office Square ($3.50/30min–$29/max; ☎617/423-1430).

Pharmacies The CVS drugstore chain has locations all over the city, though not all have pharmacies. For those, try the branches at 155–157 Charles St, in Beacon Hill (open 24 hours; ☎617/227-0437, pharmacy ☎617/523-1028), and 35 White St, in Cambridge's Porter Square (open 24 hours; ☎617/876-4037, pharmacy ☎617/876-5519).

Police Dial ☎911 for emergencies; for non-emergency situations, contact the Boston Police, headquartered at One Schroeder Plaza, in Roxbury (☎617/343-4200, Ruggles St **T**).

Public toilets There aren't too many of these around. The cleanest ones are in the visitors' center on the fourth floor of the City Hall building in Government Center, and in the National Park Service visitors' center across from the Old State House. If desperate, you can always try ducking into a restaurant, bar, or hotel; of the latter, the Fairmont Copley Plaza is tops.

Taxis Boston Cab ☎617/536-5010; Cambridge Taxi ☎617/868-9690; Checker Cab ☎617/536-7000; City Cab ☎617/536-5100; Metro Cab ☎617/782-5500; Town Taxi ☎617/536–5000. If you lose something in a taxi, call ☎617/536-TAXI.

Telephones Local calls made from payphones cost 35¢; all local numbers are ten digits long, starting with the area code (☎617 in Boston, except where specified otherwise) + the seven-digit number. Phonecards, which greatly reduce the cost of a long-distance call, are available at most convenience stores and newsstands.

Time Boston is on Eastern Standard Time, which is five hours behind Greenwich Mean Time. Daylight Savings Time runs from April to October.

Tourist offices Boston National Historical Park, Charlestown Navy Yard ☎617/242-5642, ⓦwww.nps.gov/bost; Boston Parks and Recreation, 1010 Massachusetts Ave ☎617/635-4505, ⓦwww.cityofboston .com/parks; Cambridge Office of Tourism, 4 Brattle St ☎617/441-2884 or 1-800/862-5678, ⓦwww.cambridge-usa.org; Greater Boston Convention & Visitors Bureau, 2 Copley Place, suite 105 ☎1-888/SEE-BOSTON, ⓦwww.boston-usa.com; Massachusetts Office of Travel and Tourism, 100 Cambridge St, 13th floor ☎617/727-3201 or 1-800/447-MASS, ⓦwww.mass -vacation.com.

Travel agents STA (ⓦwww.statravel.com), 297 Newbury St ☎617/266-6014; Arlington **T**; and 12 Eliot St, 2nd floor, Cambridge ☎617/497-1497; Harvard **T**. American Express Travel (ⓦwww.americanexpress .com/travel), 170 Federal St, 1st floor ☎617/439-4400; Downtown Crossing **T**; and 39 JFK St, Cambridge ☎617/868-2600; Harvard **T**.

Wire transfers Western Union has agents at multiple locations, including Store Apple Three, 144 Tremont St (☎617/375-8021), and Stop and Shop, 181 Cambridge St (☎617/742-6094).

DIRECTORY

Contexts

Contexts

A brief history of Boston

B
oston has been an important city since its colonial days, even if it's been usurped in East Coast pre-eminence by New York and Washington DC as the centuries have gone by. Numerous crucial and decisive events, especially as they related to America's struggle for independence, have taken place here; it's also been fertile ground for various intellectual, literary, and religious movements throughout the years. What follows is a very short overview of the city's development, with an emphasis on the key happenings and figures behind them; for a more in-depth look, check out some of the volumes listed in "Books," p.271.

Early exploration and founding

The first indications of explorers "discovering" the Boston area are the journal entries of Giovanni da Verrazano and Estevan Gomez, who – in 1524 and 1525, respectively – passed by Massachusetts Bay while traveling the coast of North America. The first permanent European settlement in the Boston area was undertaken by a group of 102 British colonists, around half of them Separatists – better known now as Pilgrims – chased out of England for having disassociated themselves entirely from the Anglican Church. They had tried to settle in Holland, but the Dutch didn't want them either, so they boarded the Mayflower ship to try the forbidding, rugged coast of North America, where they landed in 1620 near Plymouth Bay – after a short stopover at the tip of Cape Cod – and founded Plimoth Plantation. Within the first decade, one of them, a disillusioned scholarly loner by the name of William Blackstone, began searching for land on which to make a new start; he found it on a peninsula at the mouth of the Charles River known as Shawmut by the local Indians. Blackstone thus became Boston's first white settler, living at the foot of modern-day Beacon Hill with a few hundred books and a Brahma bull.

In 1630, close to one thousand Puritans, led by John Winthrop, settled just across the river to create Charlestown, named after the king of England. Unlike the Pilgrims, the Puritans didn't necessarily plan to disconnect themselves completely from the Anglican Church, but merely hoped to purify themselves by avoiding what they considered to be its showy excesses. Blackstone eventually lured them to his side of the river with the promise of a better water supply, then sold them the entire Shawmut Peninsula, keeping only six acres for himself. The Puritans subsequently renamed the area after the town in England from which many of their company hailed: Boston.

The colonial period

Early Bostonians enjoyed almost total political autonomy from England and created a remarkably democratic system of government, whose primary body was the town meeting, in which white male church members debated over and voted on all kind of matters. This liberal approach was counterbalanced, however, by religious intolerance: four Quakers and Baptists were hanged for their non-Puritan beliefs between 1649 and 1651.

As well during these times, Boston and neighboring Cambridge were making great strides in culture and education: Boston Latin, the (not yet) nation's first secondary school, was established in 1635; Harvard, its first university, a year later; and the first printing press in America was set up in Cambridge in 1639, where the Bay Psalm Book, New England Primer, and freeman's oath of loyalty to Massachusetts were among the first published works.

With the restoration of the British monarchy in 1660, the crown tried to exert more control over the increasingly prosperous and freethinking Massachusetts Bay Colony, appointing a series of governors, notably the despotic Sir Edmund Andros, who was chased from the colony by locals in 1689, only to be reinstalled by the monarchy the following year. Britain's relentless mercantilist policies, designed to increase the nation's monopolistic hold on the new colonies, resulted in a decrease in trade that both plunged Boston into a depression and fanned the anti-British resentment which would eventually reach a boiling point during the mid-1700s. The Molasses Act of 1733, for example, taxed all sugar purchased outside the British Empire, dealing a stiff economic blow to the colonies, who were dependent upon foreign sources for their sugar supply.

The American Revolution

At the outset of the 1760s, governor Francis Bernard informed the colonists that their success was a result of "their subjugation to Great Britain," before green-lighting the Writs of Assistance, which gave British soldiers the right to enter colonists' shops and homes to search for evidence of their avoiding duties. The colonists reacted with outrage at this violation of their civil liberties, and a young Boston lawyer named James Otis persuaded a panel of judges headed by lieutenant governor Thomas Hutchinson to repeal the acts. After listening to his four-hour oration, many were convinced that revolution was justified, including future US president John Adams, who wrote of Otis's speech: "Then and there the child Liberty was born."

Nevertheless, in 1765 the British introduced the Stamp Act, which required stamps to be placed on all published material (the revenue on the stamps would go to the Imperial coffers), and the Quartering Act, which stipulated that colonists had to house British soldiers on demand. These acts galvanized the opposition to the English government, a resistance based in Boston, where a group of revolutionary firebrands headed by Samuel Adams and known as the "Sons of Liberty" teamed up with more level-headed folks like John Hancock and John Adams to organize protest marches and petition the king to repeal the offending legislation. Though Parliament repealed the Stamp Act, in 1766 it issued the Declaratory Acts, which asserted the Crown's right to bind the colonists by any legislation it saw fit, and, in 1767, with the Townshend Acts, which prescribed more tariffs on imports to the North American colonies. This was followed by a troop increase in Boston; by 1768, there was one British soldier in the city for every four colonists.

The tension erupted on March 5, 1770, when a group of British soldiers fired into a crowd of townspeople who'd been taunting them. The Boston Massacre, as it came to be known, was hardly a massacre – only five people were killed, and the accused soldiers were actually defended in court by John Adams and

Josiah Quincy – but the occupying troops were forced to relocate to Castle Island, at the tip of South Boston. The coming crisis was postponed for a few years following the Massacre, until December 16, 1773, when Samuel Adams led a mob from the Old South Meeting House to Boston Harbor as part of a protest against a British tax on imported tea. A segment of the crowd boarded the brig Beaver and two other ships and dumped their entire cargo overboard in an act that's become known as the Boston Tea Party; Parliament responded by closing the port of Boston and passing the so-called Coercive Acts, which deprived Massachusetts of any self-government. England also sent in more troops and cut off the Dorchester Neck, the only land entrance to Boston. Soon after, the colonies convened the first Continental Congress in Philadelphia, with the idea of creating an independent government.

Two months after the province of Massachusetts was declared to be in a state of rebellion by the British government, the "shot heard 'round the world" was fired at Lexington on April 18, 1775, when a group of American militiamen skirmished with a company of British regulars; they lost that fight, but defeated the Redcoats in a subsequent incident at Concord Bridge, and the Revolutionary War had begun. The British troops left in Boston were held under siege, and the city itself was largely evacuated by its citizens.

The first major engagement of the war was the Battle of Bunker Hill, in which the British stormed what was actually Breed's Hill, in Charlestown, on three separate occasions before finally dislodging American battlements. Despite the loss, the conflict, in which the outnumbered Americans suffered fewer casualties than the British, bolstered the patriots' spirits and confidence.

George Washington took over the Continental troops in a ceremony on Cambridge Common on July 2, 1775; however, his first major coup didn't even require bloodshed. On March 16, 1776, under cover of darkness, Washington ordered much of the troops' heavy artillery to be moved to the top of Dorchester Heights, in view of the Redcoats. The British awoke to see battlements sufficient to destroy their entire fleet of warships; on March 17, they evacuated the city, never to return.

This was largely the end of Boston's involvement in the war; the focus soon turned inland and southward. After the Americans won the Battle of Saratoga in 1778, the French joined the war as their allies; on October 19, 1781, Cornwallis surrendered to Washington at Yorktown. Two years later, the United States of America became an independent nation with 1783's Treaty of Paris.

Economic swings and the "Athens of America"

Boston quickly emerged from the damage wrought by British occupation. By 1790, the economy was already booming, due primarily to the maritime industry. A merchant elite – popularly known as the "cod millionaires" – developed and settled on the sunny south slope of Beacon Hill. These were the original Boston Brahmins – though that name would not be coined until seventy years later – infamous for their stuffed-shirt elitism and fiscal conservatism. Indeed, the trust fund was invented in Boston at this time as a way for families to protect their fortunes over the course of generations.

The outset of the nineteenth century was less auspicious. Severe restrictions on international trade, notably Jefferson's Embargo Act in 1807, plunged the port of Boston into recession. When the War of 1812 began, pro-British Bostonian Federalists derided the conflict as "Mr. Madison's War" and, as such, met in Hartford in 1814 with party members from around New England to consider seceding from the Union – a measure that was wisely, though narrowly, rejected. America's victory in the war shamed Bostonians back into their patriotic ways, and they reacted to further trade restrictions by developing manufacturing industries; the city soon became prominent in textiles and shoe production.

This industrial revival and subsequent economic growth shook the region from its recession. By 1820, Boston's population had grown to 43,000 – more than double its total from the census of 1790. The city stood at the forefront of American intellectual and political life, as well, earning Boston the moniker "Athens of America."

One of these intellectual movements had its roots back in the late eighteenth century, when a controversial sect of Christianity known as Unitarianism – premised on the rational study of the Bible, voluntary ethical behavior, and (in Boston only) a rejection of the idea of a Holy Trinity – became the city's dominant religion (and one still practiced at King's Chapel), led by Reverend Ellery Channing. His teachings were the basis for transcendentalism, a philosophy propounded in the writings of Ralph Waldo Emerson and rooted in the idea that there existed an entity known as the "over-soul," to which man and nature existed in identical relation. Emerson's theory, emphasizing intuitive (a priori) knowledge – particularly in contemplation of nature – was put into practice by his fellow Harvard alumnus, Henry David Thoreau, who, in 1845, took to the woods just northwest of the city at Walden Pond in an attempt to "live deliberately."

Boston was also a center of literary activity at this time: historical novels by Nathaniel Hawthorne, such as *The Scarlet Letter*, tweaked the sensibilities and mores of New England society, and poet Henry Wadsworth Longfellow gained international renown during his tenure at Harvard. For more on these developments throughout the nineteenth century, see "Literary Boston in the 1800s," p.268.

This intellectual flowering was complemented by a variety of social movements. Foremost among them was the abolitionist movement, spearheaded by the fiery William Lloyd Garrison, who, besides speechmaking, published the anti-slavery newspaper *The Liberator*. Beacon Hill resident Harriet Beecher Stowe's seminal 1852 novel, *Uncle Tom's Cabin*, turned the sentiments of much of the nation against slavery. Other Bostonians who made key contributions to social issues were Horace Mann, who reformed public education; Dorothea Dix, an advocate of improved care for the mentally ill; Margaret Fuller, one of America's first feminists as well the editor of *The Dial*, a journal founded by Emerson; and William James, a Harvard professor who pioneered new methods in psychology, coining the phrase "stream of consciousness."

Social transformation and decline

The success of Boston's maritime and manufacturing industries attracted a great number of immigrants; the Irish, especially, poured in following Ireland's Potato Famine of the 1840s. By 1860, the city was marked by massive social divide, with overcrowded slums abutting beautiful mansions. The elite that had ruled for the first half of the century tried to ensure that the lower classes were kept in place: "No Irish Need Apply" notices accompanied job listings throughout Boston. Denied entry into "polite" society, the lower classes conspired to grab power in another way: the popular vote.

To the chagrin of Boston's WASP elite, Hugh O'Brien was elected mayor in 1885. His three-term stay in office was followed by that of John "Honey Fitz" Fitzgerald, and in the 1920s, the long reign of James Michael Curley began. Curley was to serve several terms as mayor, and one each as governor and congressional representative. These men enjoyed tremendous popularity among their supporters, despite the fact that their tenures were often characterized by rampant corruption: Curley was elected to his last term in office while serving time in a Federal prison for fraud. Still, while these mayors increased the visibility and political clout of otherwise disenfranchised ethnic groups, they did little to improve the lot of their constituents, which was steadily worsening – along with the city's economy.

Following the Civil War, competition with the railroads crippled the shipping industry, and with it, Boston's prosperous waterfront. Soon after, the manufacturing industry as well felt the impact of bigger, more efficient factories in the rest of the nation. The shoe and textile industries had largely disappeared by the 1920s; many companies had started to move south, where costs were much lower, and industrial production statewide fell by more than $1 billion during that decade. The Great Depression of the 1930s made a bad state of affairs even worse, as there were few natural resources the city provided that could keep it as an economic powerhouse.

On the heels of the depression, World War II turned Boston's moribund shipbuilding industry around almost overnight, but this economic upturn still wasn't enough to prevent a massive exodus from the urban center.

From the 1950s to the 1980s

In the 1950s, a more long-lasting turnaround began under the mayoral leadership of John Collins, who undertook a massive plan to reshape the face of Boston. Many of the city's oldest neighborhoods and landmarks were razed, though it's questionable whether these changes beautified the city. Still, the project created jobs and economic growth, while making the Downtown area more attractive to businesses and residents. By the end of the 1960s, a steady economic resurgence had begun. Peripheral areas of Boston, however, did not share in this prosperity. Collins' program paid little attention to the poverty that afflicted outlying areas, particularly the city's southern districts, or to the city's growing racial tensions. The demographic redistribution that followed the "white flight" of the 1940s and 1950s made Boston one of the most racially segregated cities in America by the mid-1970s: Charlestown's population was almost entirely white, while Roxbury was almost entirely black.

Along with other cities nationwide, Boston was ordered by the US Supreme Court to implement busing – sending students from one neighborhood to another and vice-versa in an attempt to achieve racial balance. More than two hundred area schools were involved, and not all reacted kindly: many Charlestown parents, for their part, staged hostile demonstrations and boycotted the public school system, which was especially embarrassing for Boston considering its history of racial tolerance. City officials finally scrapped their plan for desegregation after only a few years. The racial scars it left began to heal, thanks, in part, to the policies of Ray Flynn, Boston's mayor during the upbeat 1980s, helping to make the decade one of the city's healthiest in recent memory, both economically and socially.

The 1990s and into the twenty-first century

That resurgence spilled over into the 1990s, a decade that saw the job market explode and rents spiral upward in reaction to it. The increase in housing prices was further augmented by the 1996 state vote to abolish rent control in the city, a decision that pushed much of the lower-paid working class out to neighborhoods like Roxbury, and kick-started a condominium boom, especially in the South End, which was radically transformed from a near slum into the trendy hotspot it is today. In any case, it seems that anyone who can afford a posh apartment these days works for some biotech company – Boston's strength in this market spared most of its citizens from the dot-com crash that injured other major US cities' economies.

Indeed, the city has encountered little strife in the last decade – the most notable, and notorious, hubbub occurring in 2002, when the archdiocese of the local Catholic church, the Church of the Holy Cross, found itself at the center of a sex abuse scandal that prompted calls for an overhaul of the procedures concerning the handling of errant priests. While reforms remain undecided at the time of writing, the protesters who took up residency in front of the church doors during the heat of the scandal quieted down in short order, and the church quickly returned to business as usual – though with a tarnished reputation.

Yet of far greater impact on Bostonian life, Downtown's Big Dig project (see box, p.10) was, at over $1.6 billion per mile, the most expensive highway construction project in US history. It was also one of the most protracted and is not due to be officially completed before November 2005 – fourteen years after the first jackhammer sounded in Charlestown. In the meantime, the cleanup of Boston Harbor has had a great effect in reclaiming abandoned beaches and reinvigorating species of long disappeared fauna, many of which are making their homes on the Boston Harbor Islands, a group of idyllic offshore isles originally used as defense posts, but declared a national park in 1996 and subsequently opened to the public, accessible via regular ferries from Long Wharf.

The city's positive economic growth by the end of the twentieth century endowed a number of cultural institutions with funds to spruce up their digs; two of Boston's most intriguing libraries – the staid Boston Athenæum and the eccentric Mary Eddy Baker Library – reopened to the public in 2002, following substantial renovations. The most significant facelift, however, is taking place at the Museum of Fine Arts, where a recently inaugurated multimillion-dollar expansion project designed by renowned British architect Sir Norman Foster is slated for partial completion by 2007. Ironically, the one institution still denied a monetary infusion is one that's been most touted for radical transformation: Fenway Park, the country's oldest ballpark and home to the beloved Boston Red Sox, continues to pack baseball fans into its seats despite the ongoing promise – or threat, depending on your outlook – of a new stadium.

Architecture and urban planning

The land to which William Blackstone invited John Winthrop and his Puritans in 1630 bore almost no resemblance to the contemporary city of Boston. It was virtually an island, spanning a mere 785 acres, surrounded on all sides by murky swamps and connected to the mainland only by a narrow isthmus, "the Neck," that was almost entirely submerged at high tide. It was also very hilly: three peaks formed its geological backbone and gave it the name that Puritans used before they chose Boston – the Trimountain – echoed today in the name of Downtown's Tremont Street.

Colonial development

The first century and a half of Boston's existence saw this sleepy Puritan village slowly expand into one of the biggest shipping centers in the North American colonies. Narrow, crooked footpaths became busy commercial boulevards, though they retained their sinuous design, and the pasture land of Boston Common became the place for public gatherings. By the end of the eighteenth century, Boston was faced with the dilemma of how to accommodate its growing population and thriving industry on a tiny geographical center; part of the answer was to create more land. This had been accomplished in Boston's early years almost accidentally, by means of a process known as wharving out. Owners of shoreside properties with wharves found that rocks and debris collected around the pilings, until eventually the wharves were on dry land, necessitating the building of more wharves further out to sea. In this way, Boston's shoreline moved slowly but inexorably outward.

Post-revolution development

Boston's first great building boom began in earnest following the American Revolution. Harrison Gray Otis's company, the Mount Vernon Proprietors, razed Boston's three peaks to create tracts for new townhouses. The land from the tops of these hills was placed where Boston Common and the Charles River met to form a swamp, extending the shoreline out even farther to create what is now known as "the flat of the hill." Leftover land was used to fill some of the city's other coves and ponds, most significantly Mill Pond, near present-day North End. The completion of the Mount Vernon Proprietors' plans made the resulting area, Beacon Hill, the uncontested site for Boston's wealthy and elite to build their ideal home – as such, it holds the best examples of American architecture of the late eighteenth and early nineteenth centuries, ranging in styles from Georgian to early Victorian.

This period also ushered in the first purely American architectural movement, the Federal style. Prime examples of its flat, dressed-down facades are prevalent in townhouses throughout Downtown and in Beacon Hill. Charles Bulfinch was its leading practitioner; his most famous work was the 1797 gold-domed Massachusetts State House looming over Boston Common, a prototype for state capitols to come. For more information on Bulfinch, see the box on p.89.

The expansion of the city

Boston continued to grow throughout the 1800s. Mayor Josiah Quincy oversaw the construction of a large marketplace, Quincy Market, behind the overcrowded Faneuil Hall building. These three oblong Greek Revival buildings pushed the Boston waterfront back several hundred yards, and the new surface area was used as the site for a symbol of Boston's maritime prosperity, the US Custom House. While Boston had codes prohibiting overly tall buildings, the Federal Government was not obligated to obey them, and the Custom House building, completed in 1847, rose a then-impressive sixteen stories.

Meanwhile, the city was trying to create enough land to match the demand for housing, in part by transforming its swampy backwaters into useable property. Back Bay, for example, was originally just that: a marsh along the banks of the Charles. In 1814, however, Boston began to dam the Charles, filling the resulting area with debris. When the project was completed in 1883, Back Bay quickly became one of Boston's choicest addresses, drawing some prominent families from their dwellings on Beacon Hill. The layout followed a highly ordered French model of city planning: gridded streets, with those running perpendicular to the Charles arranged alphabetically. The district's main boulevard, Commonwealth Avenue, surrounded a strip of greenery that terminated to the east in the Public Garden, a lush park completed by George Meachum in 1859, with ponds, statuary, weeping willows, and winding pathways that is the jewel of Back Bay, if not all Boston.

As if this weren't enough, Back Bay's Copley Square was also the site of numerous high-minded civic institutions built in the mid- and late 1800s, foremost among which were H.H. Richardson's Romanesque Trinity Church and the Public Library, a High Victorian creation of Charles McKim, of the noted firm McKim, Mead and White. But the most impressive accomplishment of the century was certainly Frederick Law Olmsted's Emerald Necklace, a system of parks that connected Boston Common, the Public Garden, and the Commonwealth Avenue Mall to his own creations a bit further afield, such as the Back Bay Fens, Arnold Arboretum, and Franklin Park.

While Boston's civic expansion made life better for its upper classes, the middle and lower classes were crammed into the tiny Downtown area. The city's solution was to annex the surrounding districts, beginning with South Boston in 1807 and ending with Charlestown in 1873 – with the exception of Brookline, which remained a separate entity. Toward the end of the century, Boston's growing middle class moved to these surrounding areas, particularly the southern districts, which soon became known as the "streetcar suburbs." These areas, once the site of summer estates for the wealthy, were built over with one of Boston's least attractive architectural motifs: the three-decker. Also known as the "triple-decker," these clapboard rowhouses held a family on each floor – models of unattractive efficiency.

Modernization and preservation

New construction waned with the economic decline of the early 1900s, reaching its lowest point during the Great Depression. The streetcar suburbs were hardest hit – the white middle class migrated to Boston's nearby towns in the 1940s and 1950s, and the southern districts became run-down, low-rent areas. Urban renewal began in the late 1950s, with the idea of creating a visibly modern city, and while it provided Boston with an economic shot in the arm, the drastic changes erased some of the city's most distinctive architectural features. The porn halls and dive bars of Scollay Square were demolished to make way for the dull gray bureaucracy complexes of Government Center, while the West End, once one of Boston's liveliest ethnic neighborhoods, was flattened and covered over with high-rise office buildings. Worst of all, the new elevated John F. Fitzgerald Expressway (I-93) tore through Downtown, cutting off the North End and waterfront from the rest of the city. (At least today this eyesore – thanks to the Big Dig – is underground.)

Following this period, the fury of displaced and disgruntled residents forced planners to create structures that either reused or integrated extant features of the city. The John Hancock Tower, designed by I.M. Pei and completed in 1975, originally outraged preservationists, as this Copley Square high-rise was being built right by some of the city's most treasured cultural landmarks; however, the tower managed a delicate balance – while it rises sixty stories smack in the middle of Back Bay, its narrow wedge shape renders it quite unobtrusive, and its mirrored walls literally reflect its stately surroundings. Quincy Market was also redeveloped and, by 1978, what had been a decaying, nearly defunct series of fishmongering stalls was transformed into a thriving tourist attraction. Subsequent development has, for the most part, kept up this theme, preserving the city's four thousand acres – and most crucially its Downtown – as a virtual library of American architecture.

Literary Boston in the 1800s

America's literary center has not always been New York; indeed, for much of the nineteenth century, Boston wore that mantle, and since then it has retained a somewhat bookish reputation despite no longer quite having the influence it once did on American publishing.

Puritanism and religious influence

The origins for that period actually go back to colonial times and the establishment of Puritanism. John Winthrop and his fellow colonists who settled here had a vision of a theocratic, utopian "City on a Hill." The Puritans were erudite and fairly well-off intellectuals, but religion always came first, even when writing: in fact, Winthrop himself penned *A Model of Christian Charity* while crossing the Atlantic. Religious sermons were the real literature of the day – those and the now-forgotten explorations of Reverend Cotton Mather such as *The Wonders of the Invisible World*, a look at the supernatural that helped foment the Salem Witch Trials.

In the years leading up to the Revolutionary War, Bostonians began to pour their energy into a different kind of sermon – that of anti-British sentiment, such as rants in radical newspapers like the *Boston Gazette*. Post-revolution, the stifling atmosphere of Puritanism remained to some extent – the city's first theater, for example, built in 1794, had to be billed as a "school of virtue" in order to remain open. But writers began to shake off Puritan restraints and explore their newfound freedom; in certain instances, they drew upon the repressiveness of the religion as a source of inspiration.

The transcendentalist movement

Ironically enough, Boston's deliverance from parochialism began in the countryside, specifically Concord, scene of the first battle of the Revolutionary War. The transcendentalist movement of the 1830s and 1840s, spearheaded by Ralph Waldo Emerson, was born of a passion for rural life, intellectual freedom, and belief in intuitive knowledge and experience as a way to enhance the relationship between man, nature, and the "over-soul." The free thinking the movement unleashed put local writers at the vanguard of American literary expression; articles by Emerson, Henry David Thoreau, Louisa May Alcott, Bronson Alcott (Louisa's father), and other members of the Concord coterie filled the pages of *The Dial*, the transcendentalist literary review, founded by Emerson around 1840 and edited by Margaret Fuller. Fuller, an early feminist, also wrote essays prodigiously; while Alcott penned the classic *Little Women*, and Thoreau authored his famous study in solitude, *Walden*. Meanwhile, a writer by the name of Nathaniel Hawthorne, known mainly for short stories like "Young Goodman Brown," published *The Scarlet Letter*, in 1850, a true schism with the past that examined the effects of the repressive Puritan lifestyle and legacy.

The abolitionist movement and literary salons

The abolitionist movement also helped push Boston into the literary limelight. Slavery had been outlawed in Massachusetts since 1783, and Boston attracted the likes of activist William Lloyd Garrison, who published his firebrand newspaper, *The Liberator*, in a small office Downtown beginning in 1831. Years later, in 1852, Harriet Beecher Stowe's slave narrative *Uncle Tom's Cabin* hit the printing press in Boston and sold more than 300,000 copies in its first year of publication. It, perhaps more than anything else, turned national public opinion against slavery, despite the fact that its writer was a New Englander with little first-hand knowledge of the South or the slave trade.

Another Bostonian involved with the abolitionist cause was John Greenleaf Whittier, who also happened to be among the founding members of Emerson's famed "Saturday Club," the name given to a series of informal literary gatherings that took place at the *Parker House Hotel* beginning in 1855. Oliver Wendell Holmes and poet Henry Wadsworth Longfellow were among the moneyed regulars at these salons, which metamorphosed two years later into *The Atlantic Monthly*, from its inception a respected literary and political journal. One of its more accomplished editors, William Dean Howells, wrote *The Rise of Silas Lapham*, in 1878, a novel on the culture of commerce that set the stage for American Realism. Around the same time, more literary salons were being held at the Old Corner Bookstore, down the street from the Parker House, where leading publisher Ticknor & Fields had their headquarters. Regulars included not only the likes of Emerson and Longfellow, but visiting British authors like William Thackeray and Charles Dickens, who were not only published by the house as well, but also friends with its charismatic leader, Jamie T. Fields. Meanwhile, Longfellow was well on his way to becoming America's most popular poet, writing "The Midnight Ride of Paul Revere," among much other verse, while a professor at Harvard University.

The end of an era

In the last burst of Boston's literary high tide, sometimes resident Henry James recorded the sedate lives of the moneyed – and miserable – elite in his books *Watch and Ward* (1871) and *The Bostonians* (1886). His renunciation of hedonism was well-suited to the stifling atmosphere of Brahmin Boston, where well-appointed homes were heavily curtained so as to avoid exposure to sunlight; however, his look at the emerging battle of the sexes was in fact fueled by the liberty-loving principles of Emerson and colleagues in Concord thirty years before.

The fact that Boston's literary society was largely a members-only club contributed to its eventual undoing. Edgar Allen Poe slammed his hometown as "Frogpondium," in reference to the Saturday Club-style chumminess of its literati. Provincialism reared its head in the Watch & Ward Society, which as late as 1878 instigated boycotts of books and plays it deemed out of the bounds of common decency, spawning the phrase "Banned in Boston." To many observers, Howells's departure from The Atlantic Monthly in 1885 to write for Harper's in New York signaled the end of Boston's literary golden age.

Books

In the reviews below, publishers are listed in the format US/UK, unless the title is only available in one country, in which case the country has been specified. Highly recommended titles are signified by ⊠ . Out-of-print titles are indicated by o/p.

History and biography

Cleveland Amory *The Proper Bostonians* (Parnassus Imprints US). First published in 1947, this surprisingly upbeat volume remains the definitive social history of Boston's old-money aristocracy.

Jack Beatty *The Rascal King: The Life and Times of James Michael Curley, 1874–1958* (Addison Wesley US o/p). A thick and thoroughly researched biography of the charismatic Boston mayor and Bay State governor; valuable too for its depiction of big-city politics in America.

David Hackett Fischer *Paul Revere's Ride* (University of Massachusetts Press/Oxford University Press US/UK). An exhaustive account of the patriot's legendary ride to Lexington, related as a historical narrative.

Jonathan Harr *A Civil Action* (Vintage Books US). The story of eight families in the community of Woburn, just north of Boston, who took a major chemical company to court in 1981, after a spate of leukemia cases raised suspicion about the purity of the area's water supply; made into a movie starring John Travolta in 1998.

Sebastian Junger *The Perfect Storm* (HarperCollins US). A nail-biting account of the fate of the *Andrea Gail*, a six-man swordfishing boat from Gloucester caught in the worst storm in recorded history; later turned into a movie starring George Clooney in 2000.

⊠ **Jonathan Kozol** *Death at an Early Age: The Destruction of the Hearts and Minds of Negro Children in the Boston Public Schools* (Penguin US). Winner of the National Book Award, this is an intense portrait of prejudice and corruption in Boston's 1964 educational system.

⊠ **J. Anthony Lukas** *Common Ground: A Turbulent Decade in the Lives of Three American Families* (Vintage US). A Pulitzer Prize-winning account of three Boston families – one Irish-American, one black, one white middle-class – against the backdrop of the 1974 race riots sparked by court-ordered busing to desegregate public schools.

Michael Patrick MacDonald *All Souls: A Family Story from Southie* (Beacon Press US). A moving memoir of growing up in South Boston in the 1970s among the sometimes life-threatening racial, ethnic, class, and political tensions of the time.

⊠ **Louis Menand** *Metaphysical Club* (Farrar, Strauss & Giroux US). Arguably the most engaging study of Boston heavyweights Oliver Wendell Holmes, William James, Charles Sanders Pierce, and John Dewey ever written, this Pulitzer Prize-winning biography links the foursome through a short-lived 1872 Cambridge salon (the book's title), and extols the effect of their pragmatic idealism on American intellectual thought.

Mary Beth Norton *In the Devil's Snare: The Salem Witchcraft Crisis of 1692* (Knopf US). Analysis of the witchcraft accusations and executions in and around Salem in 1692; collecting newly available trial evidence, correspondence, and papers, Norton argues that the crisis must be understood in the context of the horrors of the Second Indian War, which was being waged at the time in the area around Salem.

Douglass Shand-Tucci *The Art of Scandal: The Life and Times of Isabella Stewart Gardner* (HarperCollins US). Astute biography of this doyenne of Boston society, who served as the inspiration for Isabel Archer in Henry James's *Portrait of a Lady*. The book includes evocative photos of Fenway Courtyard in Gardner's

Venetian-style palace – which is now the Gardner Museum.

Dan Shaughnessy *The Curse of the Bambino* (Penguin US). Shaughnessy, a Boston sportswriter, gives an entertaining look at the Red Sox's "curse" – no championships for 86 years – that began after they sold Babe Ruth to the Yankees. His *At Fenway: Dispatches from Red Sox Nation* (Crown Publishing US) is another memoir of a Red Sox fan.

Hiller B. Zobel *The Boston Massacre* (W.W. Norton US). A painstaking account of the circumstances that precipitated one of the most highly propagandized pre-Revolution events – the slaying of five Bostonians outside the Old State House.

Guidebooks

Charles Bahne *The Complete Guide to Boston's Freedom Trail* (Newtowne Publishing US). Unlike most souvenir guides of the Freedom Trail, which have lots of pictures but little substance, this one is chock full of engaging historical tidbits on the stories behind the sights.

John Harris *Historic Walks in Old Boston* (Globe Pequot US). In most cases, you'll be walking in the footsteps of long-gone luminaries, but Harris infuses his accounts with enough lively history to keep things moving along at an interesting clip.

Walt Kelley *What They Never Told*

You About Boston (Or What They Did Were Lies) (Down East Books US). Who would have guessed that in 1632, Puritans passed the world's first law against smoking in public? This slim book is full of such engaging Boston trivia.

⭐ **Thomas H. O'Connor** *Boston A to Z* (Harvard University Press US). This terrific, often irreverent, guide to the Hub will give you the lowdown on local hotshots from John Adams to "Honey Fitz," institutions like the Holy Cross Cathedral and the L Street Bathhouse, and local lore on everything from baked beans to the Steaming Kettle.

Architecture, urban planning, and photography

⭐ **Philip Bergen** *Old Boston in Early Photographs 1850–1918* (Dover Publications US). Fascinating stuff, including a photographic record of Back Bay's transition from swampland to swanky residential neighborhood.

Robert Campbell and Peter Vanderwarker *Cityscapes of Boston: An American City Through Time* (Houghton Mifflin US). An informative pictorial tome with some excellent photos of old and new Boston.

Mona Domosh *Invented Cities: The Creation of Landscape in Nineteenth Century New York and Boston* (Yale University Press US). Intriguing historical account of how these very different cities were shaped according to the values, beliefs, and fears of the people and society who built them.

Matthew W. Granade and Joshua H. Simon (eds) *50 Successful Harvard Application Essays* (St Martin's Press US). Just in case you want to know who they actually let into this hallowed university anyhow.

Charles Haglund *Inventing The Charles River* (MIT Press US). The past, present, and future of this artificially created river.

Jane Holtz Kay *Lost Boston* (Houghton Mifflin US). A photographic essay of long-gone architectural treasures.

Lawrence W. Kennedy *Planning the City Upon a Hill: Boston Since 1630* (University of Massachusetts Press US). This is the book to read if you want to delve deeper into how Boston's distinct neighborhoods took shape over the centuries.

Alex Krieger, David Cobb, Amy Turner, and Norman B. Leventhal (eds) *Mapping Boston* (MIT Press US). Irresistible to any map-lover, this thoughtfully compiled book combines essays with all manner of historical maps to help trace Boston's conception and development.

Barbara Moore and Gail Weesner *Back Bay: A Living Portrait* (Century Hill Press US). If you're dying to know what Back Bay's brownstones look – and looked – like inside, this book of hard-to-find photos is for you. They do a similar book on Beacon Hill.

Nancy Seasholes *Gaining Ground* (MIT Press US). A wonderful piece explaining just why Boston is 75 percent landfill. Marvel at how much was done in post-Puritan times to radically change the city's landscape.

★ **Susan and Michael Southworth** *AIA Guide to Boston* (Globe Pequot US). The definitive guide to Boston architecture, organized by neighborhood. City landmarks and dozens of notable buildings are given exhaustive but readable coverage.

Walter Muir Whitehill *Boston: A Topographical History* (Harvard University Press US). How Boston went from a tiny seaport on the Shawmut Peninsula to the city it is today, with detailed descriptions of the city's many land-reclaiming projects.

Fiction and drama

Margaret Atwood *The Handmaid's Tale* (Anchor Books US). Cambridge's Ivy League setting inspired the mythical Republic of Gilead, the post-nuclear fallout backdrop for this harrowing tale about women whose lives' purpose is solely reproduction.

James Carroll *The City Below* (Houghton Mifflin US). Gripping historical novel of later-twentieth-century Boston, centered on two Irish brothers from Charlestown.

Michael Crichton *A Case of Need* (Signet US). Written long before Crichton conceived of "ER" or even *Jurassic Park*, this gripping whodunnit opens with a woman nearly bleeding to death on the operating table of a Boston hospital; she goes on to accuse her physician of attempted murder, and finds a trusty colleague trying to get at the truth of the affair.

★ **Nathaniel Hawthorne** *The Scarlet Letter* (Signet Classic US). Puritan New England comes to life, in all its mirthless repressiveness, starring the adulterous Hester Prynne.

William Dean Howells *The Rise of Silas Lapham* (Viking Press US). This 1878 novel was the forerunner to American Realism. Howells's less-than-enthralling tale of a well-off Vermont businessman's failed entry into Boston's old-moneyed Brahmin caste gives a good early portrait of a uniquely American hero: the self-made man.

Henry James *The Bostonians* (Viking Press US). James's soporific satire traces the relationship of Olive Chancellor and Verena Tarrant, two fictional feminists in the 1870s.

★ **Dennis Lehane** *Darkness Take My Hand* (Avon Books US). Perhaps the best in Lehane's Boston-set mystery series; two private investigators tackle a serial killer, the Boston Mafia, and their Dorchester upbringing in this atmospheric thriller.

Michael Lowenthal *The Same Embrace* (Plume US). A young man comes out to his Jewish, Bostonian parents after his twin brother disowns him for his homosexuality; courageous and complex.

John Marquand *The Late George Appley* (Buccaneer Books US o/p). Winner of the 1937 Pulitzer Prize, this novel satirizes a New England gentry on the wane.

Carole Maso *Defiance* (Plume US). A Harvard professor sits on death row after having murdered a pair of her own star students, in this fragmentary, moving confessional.

Arthur Miller *The Crucible* (Penguin US). This compelling play about the 1692 Salem witch trials is peppered with quotes from actual court transcripts and loaded with appropriate levels of hysteria and fervor – a must for witch fanatics everywhere.

Sue Miller *While I Was Gone* (Ballantine US). An emotional psycho-drama centered on a middle-aged woman who spends time under an assumed name in a Cambridge commune, while on the run from her husband.

Susan Minot *Folly* (Washington Square Press US). This obvious nod to Edith Wharton's *Age of Innocence* is set in 1917 Boston instead of New York, and details the proclivities of the Brahmin era, in which women were expected to marry well, and the heartbreak that ensues from making the wrong choice.

★ **Edwin O'Connor** *The Last Hurrah* (Little, Brown US o/p). Fictionalized account of Boston mayor James Michael Curley, starring a 1950s corrupt politician; the book was so popular that the bar at the *Omni Parker House* hotel was named after it.

Sylvia Plath *The Bell Jar* (Harper Perennial USA). Angst-ridden, dark, cynical – everything a teenaged girl wants out of a book. The second half of this brilliant (if disturbing) autobiographical novel about Esther Greenwood's mental breakdown is set in the Boston suburbs, where she ends up institutionalized.

★ **George Santayana** *The Last Puritan* (MIT Press US). The philosopher's brilliant "memoir in the form of a novel," set around Boston, chronicles the short life and education of protagonist Oliver Alden coming to grips with Puritanism.

Erich Segal *Love Story* (Avon US). This sappy story about the love affair between Oliver Barrett IV, a successful Harvard student born with a silver spoon in his mouth, and Jenny

Boston on film

Boston has served as the setting for surprisingly few major **films** despite its historic importance and cultural status. If you want to see how it's been depicted thus far, here are some introductory titles.

Two Sisters from Boston (Henry Koster, 1946)
Walk East on Beacon (Alfred L. Werker, 1952)
The Actress (George Cukor, 1953)
The Boston Strangler (Richard Fleischer, 1968)
Love Story (Arthur Hiller, 1970)
Between the Lines (Joan Micklin Silver, 1977)
Starting Over (Alan J. Pakula, 1979)
The Bostonians (James Ivory, 1984)
Tough Guys Don't Dance (Norman Mailer, 1987)
Good Will Hunting (Gus Van Sant, 1997)
A Civil Action (Steve Zaillian, 1998)
Next Stop Wonderland (Ben Anderson, 1998)
Legally Blonde (Robert Luketic, 2001)
Mona Lisa Smile (Mike Newell, 2003)
Mystic River (Clint Eastwood, 2003)
Spartan (David Mamet, 2004)

Cavilleri, a Radcliffe music student who's had to struggle for everything, has the uncanny ability to captivate even the most jaded reader; made into a movie in 1970.

Jean Stafford *Boston Adventure* (Harcourt Brace US). Narrated by a poverty-stricken young girl who gets taken in by a wealthy elderly woman, this long – but rewarding – novel portrays upper-class Boston in all its magnificence and malevolence.

⭐ **David Foster Wallace** *Infinite Jest* (Little, Brown US).

Sprawling magnum opus concerning a video that eliminates all viewers' desire to do anything but watch said video. Many of the book's best passages take place at Enfield, a fictional tennis academy set outside Boston; another plot line involves a Canadian terrorist separatist cell in Cambridge.

William F. Weld *Mackerel by Moonlight* (Pocket Books US). The former federal prosecutor and governor of Massachusetts turns his hand to writing, in this uneven – though not unworthy – political mystery.

Local accent and jargon

Boston has a language all its own, plus a truly unmistakable regional accent. One of Boston's most recognizable cultural idiosyncrasies is its strain of American English, distinguished by a tendency to drop one's "r"s, as on the ubiquitous T-shirts that exhort you to "Pahk the cah in Havvid Yahd" ("Park the car in Harvard Yard"). Listen, too, for the greeting "How ah ya?" ("How are you?") or the genial assent, "shuah" ("Sure").

These lost "r"s crop up elsewhere, usually when words that end in "a" are followed by words that begin in a vowel – as in "I've got no idear about that." When the nasal "a" (as in "cat") is not followed by an "r", it can take on a soft, almost British tenor: "after" becomes "ahfta." And the "aw" sound (as in "body") is inverted, like "wa": "god" becomes "gwad."

If in doubt, the surest way to fit in with the locals is to use the word "wicked" as an adverb at every opportunity: "Joo guys see the Celts game lahst night? Theah gonna be wicked wasome this yeah!" What follows is a glossary of sorts for proper terms, slang, and jargon in and around Boston.

Terms and acronyms

BC Boston College

Beantown Nickname for Boston – a reference to the local specialty, Boston baked beans – that no one uses any longer.

The Big Dig The project to put the elevated highway I-93 underground.

Brahmin An old-money Beacon Hill aristocrat.

Brownstone Originally a nineteenth-century terraced house with a facade of brown stone; now, any row- or townhouse.

BU Boston University.

Bubbler Water fountain.

C-town/Chuck-town Nickname for Charlestown.

The Cape Shorthand for Cape Cod.

The Central Artery The stretch of I-93 that runs through Downtown, separating the North End and the waterfront from the rest of the city.

Colonial Style of Neoclassical architecture popular in the seventeenth and eighteenth centuries.

Comm Ave Commonwealth Avenue.

Dot Ave Dorchester Avenue.

Federal Hybrid of French and Roman architecture popular in the late eighteenth and early nineteenth centuries.

Frappe Milkshake (meaning milk, ice cream, and syrup) – the "e" is silent. Order a *milkshake* in Boston and you'll likely get milk flavored with syrup – distinctly devoid of ice cream.

Georgian Architectural style popular during the late colonial period; highly ornamental and rigidly symmetrical.

Greek Revival Style of architecture that mimicked that of classical Greece. Popular for banks and larger houses in the early nineteenth century.

Grinder A sandwich made of deli meats, cheese, and condiments on a long roll or bun. Less used now as the more ubiquitous "sub" takes over.

Hamburg Ground beef *sans* bun. Add an "–er" at the end for the classic American sandwich.

Hub Like Beantown, a nickname for Boston not really used anymore.

JP Jamaica Plain.

Ladder District (formerly the Combat Zone). Just north of Chinatown, the once-busy strip of Washington Street designated for adult entertainment has been renamed the Ladder District, after its street grid's resemblance to a multi-runged ladder.

Mass Ave Massachusetts Avenue.

MBTA (Massachusetts Bay Transportation Authority) The agency in charge of all public transit – buses, subways, commuter trains, and ferries.

MGH Massachusetts General Hospital; also, "Mass General."

Packie Liquor store (many signs say "Package Store").

The People's Republic Another name for Cambridge, thanks to the liberal attitude of its residents.

The Pike The Massachusetts Turnpike (I-90); also, "Mass Pike."

Pissa Bostonian for "cool." Sometimes used with "wicked" (see below), ie "wicked pissa," meaning double good.

The Pit Sunken area next to Harvard Square where skaters hang out.

P-town Provincetown.

Scrod Somewhat of a distasteful generic name for cod or haddock. Almost always served breaded and sold cheap.

Southie South Boston.

Spa An independently owned convenience store – not a pampering salon.

The T Catch-all for Boston's subway system.

Three-decker Three-story house, with each floor a separate apartment. Also called a "triple-decker."

Townie Originally a term for residents of Charlestown, it now refers to wicked long-term residents of Boston and its outlying suburbs, most readily identified by their heavy accents.

Victorian Style of architecture from the mid- to late 1800s that is highly eclectic and ornamental.

Wicked The definitive word in the Bostonian patois, still used to intensify adjectives, as in "wicked good."

Rough
Guides
advertiser

Rough Guides travel...

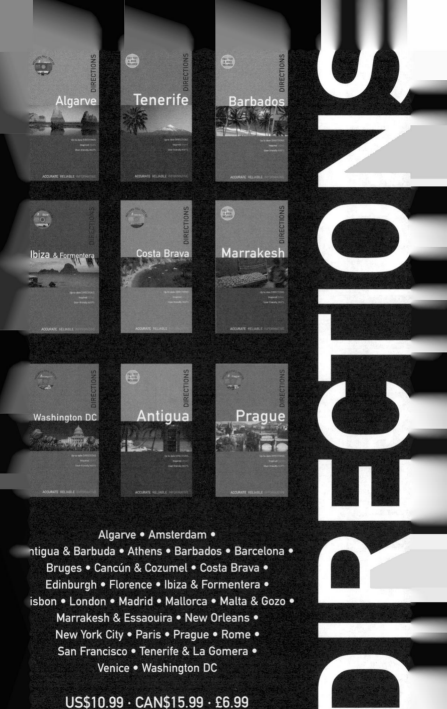

Algarve • Amsterdam •
Antigua & Barbuda • Athens • Barbados • Barcelona •
Bruges • Cancún & Cozumel • Costa Brava •
Edinburgh • Florence • Ibiza & Formentera •
Lisbon • London • Madrid • Mallorca • Malta & Gozo •
Marrakesh & Essaouira • New Orleans •
New York City • Paris • Prague • Rome •
San Francisco • Tenerife & La Gomera •
Venice • Washington DC

US$10.99 · CAN$15.99 · £6.99
www.roughguides.com

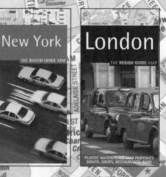

small print and

Index

A Rough Guide to Rough Guides

In the summer of 1981, Mark Ellingham, a recent graduate from Bristol University, was traveling round Greece and couldn't find a guidebook that really met his needs. On the one hand there were the student guides, insistent on saving every last cent, and on the other the heavyweight cultural tomes whose authors seemed to have spent more time in a research library than lounging away the afternoon at a taverna or on the beach.

In a bid to avoid getting a job, Mark and a small group of writers set about creating their own guidebook. It was a guide to Greece that aimed to combine a journalistic approach to description with a thoroughly practical approach to travelers' needs – a guide that would incorporate culture, history, and contemporary insights with a critical edge, together with up-to-date, value-for-money listings. Back in London, Mark and the team finished their Rough Guide, as they called it, and talked Routledge into publishing the book.

That first *Rough Guide to Greece*, published in 1982, was a student scheme that became a publishing phenomenon. The immediate success of the book – with numerous reprints and a Thomas Cook Prize shortlisting – spawned a series that rapidly covered dozens of destinations. Rough Guides had a ready market among low-budget backpackers, but soon also acquired a much broader and older readership that relished Rough Guides' wit and inquisitiveness as much as their enthusiastic, critical approach. Everyone wants value for money, but not at any price.

Rough Guides soon began supplementing the "rougher" information about hostels and low-budget listings with the kind of detail on restaurants and quality hotels that independent-minded visitors on any budget might expect, whether on business in New York or trekking in Thailand.

These days the guides – distributed worldwide by the Penguin group – offer recommendations from shoestring to luxury and cover more than 200 destinations around the globe, including almost every country in the Americas and Europe, more than half of Africa and most of Asia and Australasia. Our ever-growing team of authors and photographers is spread all over the world, particularly in Europe, the USA and Australia.

In 1994, we published the *Rough Guide to World Music* and *Rough Guide to Classical Music*; and a year later the *Rough Guide to the Internet*. All three books have become benchmark titles in their fields – which encouraged us to expand into other areas of publishing, mainly around popular culture. Rough Guides now publish:

- Travel guides to more than 200 worldwide destinations
- Dictionary phrasebooks to 22 major languages
- History guides ranging from Ireland to Islam
- Maps printed on rip-proof and waterproof Polyart™ paper
- Music guides running the gamut from Opera to Elvis
- Restaurant guides to London, New York and San Francisco
- Reference books on topics as diverse as the Weather and Shakespeare
- Sports guides from Formula 1 to Man Utd
- Pop culture books from *Lord of the Rings* to Cult TV
- World Music CDs in association with World Music Network

Visit **www.roughguides.com** to see our latest publications.

Rough Guide credits

Text editor: Amy Hegarty
Layout: Amit Verma
Cartography: Melissa Baker, Katie Lloyd-Jones
Picture research: Jj Luck
Proofreader: Margaret Doyle
Editorial: **London** Martin Dunford, Kate Berens, Claire Saunders, Geoff Howard, Ruth Blackmore, Gavin Thomas, Polly Thomas, Richard Lim, Clifton Wilkinson, Alison Murchie, Sally Schafer, Karoline Densley, Andy Turner, Ella O'Donnell, Keith Drew, Edward Aves, Andrew Lockett, Joe Staines, Duncan Clark, Peter Buckley, Matthew Milton, Daniel Crewe, Nikki Birrell, Chloë Thomson; **New York** Andrew Rosenberg, Richard Koss, Chris Barsanti, Steven Horak, AnneLise Sorensen, Amy Hegarty
Design & Pictures: **London** Simon Bracken, Dan May, Diana Jarvis, Mark Thomas, Jj Luck, Harriet Mills, Chloë Roberts; **Delhi** Madhulita Mohapatra, Umesh Aggarwal, Ajay Verma, Jessica Subramanian, Amit Verma

Production: Julia Bovis, Sophie Hewat, Katherine Owers
Cartography: **London** Maxine Repath, Ed Wright, Katie Lloyd-Jones **Delhi** Manish Chandra, Rajesh Chhibber, Jai Prakash Mishra, Ashutosh Bharti, Rajesh Mishra, Animesh Pathak, Jasbir Sandhu, Karobi Gogoi
Online: **New York** Jennifer Gold, Suzanne Welles, Benjamin Ross; **Delhi** Manik Chauhan, Narender Kumar, Shekhar Jha, Rakesh Kumar, Lalit Sharma
Marketing & Publicity: **London** Richard Trillo, Niki Hanmer, David Wearn, Demelza Dallow; **New York** Geoff Colquitt, Megan Kennedy, Milena Perez; **Delhi**: Reem Khokhar
Custom publishing and foreign rights: Philippa Hopkins
Finance: Gary Singh
Manager India: Punita Singh
Series editor: Mark Ellingham
PA to Managing Director: Megan McIntyre
Managing Director: Kevin Fitzgerald

Publishing information

This fourth edition published July 2005 by
Rough Guides Ltd,
80 Strand, London WC2R 0RL.
345 Hudson St, 4th Floor,
New York, NY 10014, USA.
14 Local Shopping Centre, Panchsheel Park,
New Delhi 110017, India
Distributed by the Penguin Group
Penguin Books Ltd,
80 Strand, London WC2R 0RL
Penguin Putnam, Inc.
375 Hudson Street, NY 10014, USA
Penguin Group (Australia)
250 Camberwell Road, Camberwell
Victoria 3124, Australia
Penguin Books Canada Ltd,
10 Alcorn Avenue, Toronto, Ontario,
Canada M4V 1E4
Penguin Group (New Zealand)
Cnr Rosedale and Airborne Roads
Albany, Auckland, New Zealand

Typeset in Bembo and Helvetica to an original design by Henry Iles.

Printed and bound in China

© Rough Guides Ltd 2005

304pp includes index
A catalogue record for this book is available from the British Library

ISBN 1-84353-443-6

The publishers and authors have done their best to ensure the accuracy and currency of all the information in **The Rough Guide to Boston**, however, they can accept no responsibility for any loss, injury, or inconvenience sustained by any traveler as a result of information or advice contained in the guide.

1   3   5   7   9   8   6   4   2

Help us update

We've gone to a lot of effort to ensure that the fourth edition of **The Rough Guide to Boston** is accurate and up-to-date. However, things change – places get "discovered," opening hours are notoriously fickle, restaurants and rooms raise prices or lower standards. If you feel we've got it wrong or left something out, we'd like to know, and if you can remember the address, the price, the time, the phone number, so much the better.

We'll credit all contributions, and send a copy of the next edition (or any other Rough Guide if you prefer) for the best letters. Everyone who writes to us and isn't already a subscriber will receive a copy of our full-color thrice-yearly newsletter. Please mark letters: "**Rough Guide Boston Update**" and send to: Rough Guides, 80 Strand, London WC2R 0RL, or Rough Guides, 4th Floor, 345 Hudson St, New York, NY 10014. Or send an email to **mail@roughguides.com**

Have your questions answered and tell others about your trip at **www.roughguides.atinfopop.com**

SMALL PRINT

Acknowledgments

James Ellis Tonnes of thanks to my fabulous editor Amy Hegarty who kept me on the straight and narrow copy and deadline wise; my muses Maureen O'Neil, Jennifer Oprie, Amanda Read, Sara Amiro, Sarita Rogers and Randace Moore for showing me all the very best places to go; fellow Leeds fan Mike Bellwood of LUSCNA for showing me his 'rough guide' to Boston; my pal David Bone for coming and keeping me company early on and, finally, to the staff of The Field for letting me use the bar as an office.

The editor wishes to thank James Ellis for his great work throughout, Amit Verma for layout, Melissa Baker and Katie Lloyd-Jones for cartography, Jj Luck for photo research, Margaret Doyle for proofreading, Dan May for clarifications, Nikki Birrell for support, and Richard Koss and Andrew Rosenberg for much-appreciated guidance and feedback.

Readers' letters

Thanks to all the readers who took the trouble to write in with their comments and suggestions (and apologies to anyone whose name we've misspelt or omitted):

Janice Black, P.M. Draper, David Masterton

SMALL PRINT

Photo credits

Cover credits

Main picture Leafy lane, Beacon Hill
© Superstock

Small front top picture Lobster weather vane
© Corbis

Small front lower picture Boston baked
beans © Corbis

Back top picture Old State House Tower
© Corbis

Back lower picture Detail of Beacon Hill
© Corbis

Color introduction

Panoramic Images © Getty Images

Copley Square, Back Bay, with the John
Hancock Tower and Trinity Church
© Island Road Images/Alamy

Red Sox paraphernalia
© Rough Guides

Marlborough Street townhouses
© Rough Guides

Close-up of lobster/seafood dish
© Rough Guides

Freedom Trail signage © Rough Guides

Holocaust Memorial and Downtown skyline
© Richard Cummins/Corbis

Duck tour boats © Rough Guides

People eating at Quincy Market
© Rough Guides

Leonard P. Zakim Bunker Hill Bridge
© Rough Guides

Things not to miss

01 Isabella Stewart Gardner Museum
© Rough Guides

02 Newbury Street shopping © Steve Edson

03 Marble staircase leading to Shapiro
Rotunda and Sargent murals at Museum
of Fine Arts © Chuck Pefley/Alamy

04 Omni Parker House © courtesy of the
Omni Parker House

05 Fenway Park's "Green Monster" left-field
scoreboard © Jim Bourg/Corbis

06 Sevens Ale House © Rough Guides

07 USS Constitution © Taxi/Getty Images

08 Bonsai collection at Arnold Arboretum
© Rough Guides

09 Interior shot of Caffé Vittoria
© Rough Guides

10 Union Oyster House © Rough Guides

11 Ware Collection of Glass Models of Plants
© Rough Guides

12 Competitors row in the Head of the
Charles Regatta © Kevin Fleming/Corbis

13 Old Granary Burying Ground
© Rough Guides

14 Beacon Hill townhouses with gaslamp in
front © Rough Guides

15 Beach houses near Provincetown
© Chris Coe/Axiom

16 Public Garden © Rough Guides

17 Faneuil Hall © Rough Guides

18 Gibson House Museum © Rough Guides

19 Old North Church © Rough Guides

20 Massachusetts State House
© Rough Guides

21 Robert Gould Shaw Memorial on The
Black Heritage Trail © Rough Guides

22 The Boston Symphony performing at
Symphony Hall © Kevin Fleming/Corbis

Black and white photos

Boston Common © Rough Guides, p.51

Old State House © Rough Guides, p.57

Paul Revere Statue in Paul Revere Mall
© Rough Guides, p.73

Bunker Hill Monument © Rough Guides, p.82

Emmet's Pub © Rough Guides, p.87

Christian Science Center
© Rough Guides, p.104

Union Park Square © Rough Guides, p.111

Muddy River, in Back Bay Fens
© Rough Guides, p.117

Fort Independence © Rough Guides, p.131

Harvard Square © Rough Guides, p.141

New State Center at MIT
© Rough Guides, p.153

Henry Kitson's Minute Man statue in
Lexington's Battle Green
© Rough Guides, p.158

Boston Harbor Hotel © Rough Guides, p.176

Flour Bakery + Café © Rough Guides, p.185

Olives © Rough Guides, p.199

The Littlest Bar in Boston
© Rough Guides, p.209

Window seat at Trident Booksellers & Café
© Rough Guides, p.230

Boston Marathon
© Sean Dougherty/Corbis, p.242

Hood Milk Bottle at Children's Museum
© Rough Guides, p.247

St Patrick's Day Parade
© Ted Spiegel/Corbis, p.251

Index

Map entries are in color.

C

D

R

S

T

U

V

W

Y

Z

Map symbols

maps are listed in the full index using colored text

	State boundary		⊙	Statue
	Expressway		🏛 Gardens	Gardens
	Main road		Ⓣ	T system station
	Minor road		ⓘ	Information office
	Pedestrianized road		⊞	Hospital
	Railway		⊠	Post office
	Ferry route		↕	Church
	Waterway			Building
✈	International airport			Church (town maps)
◆	Point of interest			Park
🏛	Monument			Beach
♦	Museum			Cemetery

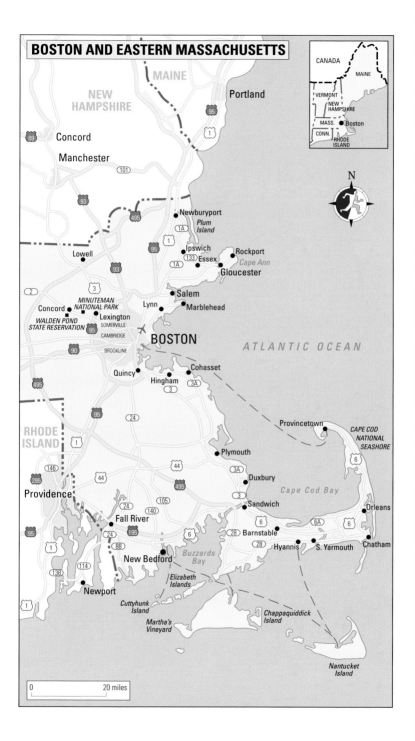

Dedicated to

My Wife Patty
&
My Parents Paul and Doris Griffiths

INTRODUCTION

I was a shy and dull child until I was 8. I was the younger of the Griffiths twins, with a peculiar first name, which demanded explanation. I was the one who got car sick when we borrowed my Uncle Don's 1938 Pontiac and went anywhere. We stopped the car too often to let me get out to upchuck my breakfast.

My shyness made it painful to start kindergarten at the school on the hill in Polk City.

It all seemed to change in 1954, a few months after Grandpa Griffiths died eating popcorn and watching the Saturday night boxing matches on TV. My parents were freed to leave my uncle's farm and free to depart our four-room house and settle on the farm in Grundy County, which my parents had bought in 1940. The farm family who had rented our 196-acre farm moved on, and we moved in. At 42, my father was finally on his own with two farms – including one next door that Mother inherited.

The move would change everything for me.

I stepped into the large empty bedroom upstairs. There on the west wall was a large stack of books, many of them the textbooks the Bohlen kids used for their country school classes up the road.

It was a treasure for the taking. I was quickly consumed by the history books especially. In no time, I memorized the names of the presidents of the United States and their years in office, and could recite them in a blaze. I became a voracious reader. In the one-room country school, I read 40 books from the book shelf during third grade and had my name published for the first time in the Grundy County Register. I was a regular to the Parkersburg library where Random House's

Landmark book series especially gave me a wealth of knowledge. Books led me to excel scholastically and even become class valedictorian.

We took the Des Moines Tribune by mail, so each edition came a day late. On frigid days, when we got it out of the mailbox, the newspaper's inks emitted that distinctive and unmistakable cold newspaper scent. That mesmerizing odor may have been a factor why I chose newspapers and journalism for a career.

In spelling lessons, I prided myself in surrounding a new word in the most creative sentence. I went on to be editor of the school newspaper in my senior year at Parkersburg High School where our work appeared weekly in the Parkersburg Eclipse, the largest county newspaper. I prided myself with my weekly editorials. Community feedback buoyed my choice to study journalism at Iowa State University where I founded a magazine, Cadence, in my freshman year and wrote for many of the campus publications. Graduating in exactly four years, even with a dizzying array of campus leadership and extracurricular work, I joined the Peace Corps, then spent two years in the U.S. Army and then moved on for a master's degree in journalism from Northwestern University on the G.I. Bill.

I decided to return to Northeast Iowa to start my newspaper career. After a six-month stint as a police and courthouse reporter for the Waterloo Daily Courier (now the Waterloo-Cedar Falls Courier), I was named assistant state editor and the farm editor in December 1972. I inherited a job given up by Richard Whitt who six years later won a Pulitzer Prize for local reporting at the Louisville Courier-Journal. Rich had done a weekly farm column called "Rural at Random," which I inherited. I was tasked with producing a commentary each Sunday in the farm section.

I frequently devoted the column to written images of my experiences growing up on our Grundy County farms, one of which has been in our family since 1855, an Iowa "Century Farm." It was where my Grandfather Horace Bawn (from which my first name is derived) and my mother were born. During my eight years as farm editor, I produced 401 columns about farming, farm issues and the distinct adventures of rural life.

In what turned out to be exactly 40 years working for daily newspapers in Iowa and Arizona, I fostered a keen skill of observation and discernment. On the endless hunt for feature stories as assistant

state editor and then state editor for 15 counties of Northeast Iowa, I prided myself in driving into the small towns and letting my curiosity radar lead me to compelling stories about people. Each interview was a moment I was being taught.

"Batting Rocks Over the Barn" draws from many of my columns on rural life – some of which can easily be seen as a time now past and gone. Rural America has been as transformed by science and technology as other sectors of our nation.

I was blessed by hard-working parents who were married for nearly 56 years. They were devoted to the soil and the land. Besides working us kids incessantly on the farm and teaching us an extraordinary work ethic, they were robust storytellers.

They certainly fostered that in this journalist.

In the end, it is the land that tells its stories.

THE REACHES OF SPRING

RIDING THE WILD CREEK

Winter's cold chemistry works gently to change the land in subtle ways.

When the coldest season has grudgingly loosened its grip on the countryside and lifted its ice pack, the trampled land is there again to cultivate and, in many ways, to re-civilize. Once the snows have receded and their moisture has either crept into the spongy earth or has found a stream to take it racing toward Keokuk, a patch of the planet lies covered by a dry glaze.

Walk behind a shed, stroll through a back grove, hike along fences or pasture creeks, or drive into a field for the first time in the spring. It's evident that nature has delicately erased much of last year's remains of man and his work there.

Last year's leaves, weeds and foliage lie pasted together like papier-mâché, held together by nature's glues and still pressed against the ground, even though gone is the icy weight that crushed it against the wet earth.

The scars on the lanes, the marks that steel-toothed machines left in the fields last year are washed smooth. The cornstalks, fractured by pickers that ran them down in harvest, do not appear as raggedly broken once spring arrives. Fence gates and wire and latches have a tarnished feel, what with man's having stopped handling them while winter kept him out of fields. Then it won't be long until sagging field gates stand tall again, till the winter-packed crust on fields is pulverized, till the farmer has reasserted his stewardship of the land.

One of the barometers of spring on our farm was the creek. In some years, fast thaws provoked fascinating dramas. Sometimes spring floods and rapid run-offs showed blatant disregard for property and the soil. But the cataclysmic rush of melted snow and early spring rains into swelling streams were exciting to my brother and me on that Grundy County, Iowa, farm where we grew up in the 1950s and early 1960s.

Rarely did the spring melt make the creek overflow to spill into the pasture and adjacent fields. However, summer downpours triggered flash floods that could send water surging out of the creek banks in an hour.

Like most boys, we were enchanted by water. The abrupt and mad rise of the usually lazy creek attracted us to its banks. We were stirred by the kinetics, the bolting force, its turbulent waters, trampling our "bottom" land, carrying debris from other farms and adding more from ours.

We were simply spellbound by a channel of swift, energized, murky water. Its abnormal velocity charmed us, triggered our adrenaline.

My twin brother, Lincoln, never could leave water alone. He had a fixation about it. He had to do something to any body of water he encountered – splash in it or sail a boat across it, heave something into it to cause a splattering plop or somehow harness it for his diversion.

We must have been 12 years old that Saturday morning in early spring when the creek was rolling full force within the rim of the banks. Lincoln was in a frenzy. He was wildly fascinated by the mystique of the rushing current.

He made up his mind. No one could dissuade him. Lincoln was going to ride the current. He had no canoe, no boat of any kind. But that didn't diminish his notion to travel atop the wild waters.

The closest thing to a boat on the farm was the 4-foot long, galvanized steel bathtub in the cellar. My brother had it down onto the creek bank in minutes. To give it stability, he decided to tie its handles down to a wooden hog pasture gate, which was only a foot longer and a bit wider than the tub.

It was folly, the rest of us said. It was stupid and dangerous. Besides, how far was he going to go in it? Three miles to where the stream dumped into the bigger Beaver Creek? Or on to the giant Cedar River? How would he get back?

His adrenalin flowing strong, Lincoln climbed into his crude craft, clutched an old board for a paddle and shoved off. The current grabbed the rudderless vessel and pulled it, in jerks, downstream at 8 to 10 knots.

Dad was vocally aware of the foolishness of the venture headed for misadventure, so he chose to run along the muddy shore and stay close to the bathtub boat. From the outset, it was evident Lincoln was riding more creek than he had reckoned. Cruising without a rudder and maneuvering himself with just a crude paddle, the novice boatman's square, unstable vessel twisted side to side as it was pulled along.

It wasn't long before Lincoln had had enough. He would have liked to pull over to a bank and disembark, but the creek controlled his fate.

He probably went no farther than 500 yards before the entire unseaworthy craft capsized, tossing him out near a low, flat bank jutting out into the black, chilly water. Our father, who had been running along the overflowing bank was right there to help haul out the floundering, defeated captain whose ship had abandoned him. The bathtub and wooden panel were easily retrieved later downstream, lodged in a fence.

Wet and cold and irritated by everyone's I-told-you-sos, my dejected brother trudged home with new respect for the wild ways of a creek in spring.

BEHIND STRAW DEFENSES

With spring, we could withdraw from behind the fortifications of straw that hugged the foundation of our farmhouse. Those bales of last summer's oat straw were banked up against our rock and concrete foundation to keep winter's cold from creeping into the basement or into the dead space under the main floor or our house where the cellar had not extended. That cellar was under only about a third of the house built in the 1890s. The cold air that reached under the rest of the house could penetrate our living quarters.

Many neighbors and people in town ringed their homes with cheap, available material that has historically bedded livestock and has kept man warm, too.

It was usually well into November – occasionally December – before we began to construct our straw stronghold. By that time, blasts of cold air had made entry into our house, turning it into a drafty enclosure.

The strong winds pushed through cracks and openings in the foundation, relentlessly forcing air up through the floorboards in the downstairs of our farm home. The living room carpet sometimes would lift off the floor and float on a cushion of air when winds outdoors were strong.

Thus, came the weeks before winter's official start. It was time to get a hayrack of straw out of the haymow to build our winter defense. The job was always scheduled for a Saturday morning when we three kids were home from school to help.

First we took tarpaper, or corrugated boxes torn apart, and tacked it all the way around the foundation to a height of about three feet. We fastened it down with nails and laths, or, more often, chunks of wood from corncrib slats.

Then we carried the bales of straw from the rack and stacked them two bales high snugly against the foundation. And there that ring of straw remained through the winter. Our house sat snug in a kind of nest.

Snows and drifts would bury the straw. When the snows eventually melted, the bales soaked up the water. The melting icicles on the roof fed more water to the straw below. By winter's end, the straw had lost its bright yellow and was a water-soaked brown.

When winter retreated and someone had given the call to do yardwork, the bales were assigned first to go. Some had gotten so fat with absorbed water that they could hardly be lifted and moved. The twine on some of them snapped as soon as we tried to lift them. Other twines had rotted. What we then had was wet, loose straw to be loaded by "cakes" into a wheelbarrow to haul away. It usually ended up in a hog house where sows made final good use of it. Never mind the straw's dampness and its starting to rot. The sows still pulled it apart and spread it as their bedding, even when some of the straw may have had ice clinging to it.

In moving the bales away from the foundation, we found recesses where farm cats had made nests, even where one of the tame mallard ducks had been nesting. Spiders, black bugs and other insects would flee once the tarpaper or cardboard was removed.

Finally, there were plenty remnants of the straw to be raked up. Having that straw gone was like putting our winter coats away or like

being able to again leave the dairy cows outdoors all night and spare us from having to clean the manure from the gutters every day.

They talk about "straw dogs" and "straw houses." It all suggests weakness. Certainly winter is a formidable foe, but straw on the farm proved itself to be a strong defense down to our very foundation.

FARMING GUIDED BY PAST CALENDARS

It was time to plant. The pace of the planting art quickened as man mixed seed with earth, laying it to rest with a few morsels of commercial nutrients and pesticides in a bit of the same tradition as Squanto when he buried a fish in the hill of corn for the Pilgrims.

By April, the cadence of agriculture was nothing short of spellbinding. Keeping track of the unfolding year was important on our farm. The cycle of events marking each season was, of course, to be repeated year after year.

And it was only writing down the dates of the first oat seeding or corn planting or first cutting of hay that had a way of knowing where each year we stood in the race to keep pace with the seasons.

On the kitchen wall between the refrigerator and a window hung an over-sized wall calendar. Big Gain Feed Company of West Union issued the same kind of calendar each year. The days and months were blocked off each in two-inch red squares. Ample space was provided to write down the notable events of the days on the farm.

Mother started recording farm happenings to avoid – and sometimes settle – disputes arising from lapses of memory over how early or late the corn was "laid by" (cultivated for a last time) the year before. So she began the task of keeping track of a host of goings-on on our farm, which, in time, led to including more than just agriculturally related events, such as when she put cucumbers on to soak, when the dog caught a rabbit or when some out-of-state company came to call.

But the most important job was keeping track of when each kind of field work was started and finished. Oat seeding dates ranged from April 7 to 24. Planting dates for the garden were dutifully recorded. The old calendars showed our garden went in as early as April 9 and as late as June 11.

Entries included when the baby chicks arrived and how many there were; when the first violet was found in a roadside ditch; when one of us brought home the first pussy willows; when the creek overflowed; or when the dairy calves were driven to spring and summer pasture.

As the season marched on, Mother recorded, in the appropriate box on the calendar, "corn planting finished," "first cutting of hay," "finished up alfalfa baling" or "corn laid by."

Came July and duly recorded was the wind-rowing of oats, subsequently the combining and baling of the straw. Following close behind was the "second cutting of hay." By August, the attention turned to walking the lush cornfields to uproot button weeds and cockleburs, hauling manure from sheds and the barn lot, or handling assorted jobs before school started again. Not all such activities were recorded because their timing wasn't important in future years.

The fall events – last hay baling, first corn picking and silo filling – were all mentioned on the calendar.

At the end of the year, Mother took the calendar down to replace it with a new one from Big Gain. She then copied off the information into a notebook. Invariably, it would be consulted the next year when my father fretted over too much May rain delaying planting. Mother would check the record to show him that things weren't so bad after all.

MECHANIZED FERTILITY RITES

The soil is the soul of the farm. Each spring, man must begin again the burdensome set of agrarian rites required in order to receive its gifts in the fall.

These are the times men try their soils.

It's more than slipping certified seed into the soil's blackness.

As farmers try their soils, the times try their souls. It's a time of anxiety and concern – concern not that the soil will fail, but that they will fail because of the possible imbalance of weather and cultivation on that soil. They are ever mindful of the calendar as they yearn for sunshine, drying breezes and smooth-running equipment, free of breakdowns.

They want no foul-ups in the ritual of wedding seed to soil.

It's time of the year when urban dwellers seem to take the greatest notice of farmers and beam approvingly of their efforts. It's a time when they are inclined to speak glowingly of those midnight field maneuvers, of farmers' shrewd strategy for planning their work between spring showers, and of their display of a green thumb on a grand scale.

The countryside on spring nights is dotted by steadily moving lights on behemoth tractors charging over the earth through the night blackness.

When they drive between cities through the rural countryside, urban laborers whose hours may be 9 to 5 are understandably impressed by such devotion to work – perhaps not realizing that it is done out of necessity, rather than out of zeal.

Out on those machines ride what farmwives call "crazy men." With the coming of favorable weather in April and May, farmers are obsessed with getting that seed into the ground. They well know what that entrails. Most have been through it many times before, although each year they are a little more sophisticated because of newer farm equipment or tillage techniques.

These crazy men become dropouts from other rural activities. They don't go to as many livestock sales or linger at the feed store to chat or go so willingly to meetings of the County Extension or Farm Bureau. In fact, they lose some interest in the rhetoric of the winter – the politics surrounding meat prices or free-trade negotiations.

They slight themselves on sleep, will hardly read and won't talk to their wives about otherwise normal topics. Their eating habits change drastically as their hunger drives are overpowered by greater drives to complete the planting. Some willingly skip a meal or grab a bite while plowing. They prefer being absent from the dinner table than off from nature's timetable. There is no compromise.

Farmyard chores are turned over to others in the family. Farmers don't want to stop to be bothered by anything. They'll forget to pat their own farm dog on the head. Only the weather can halt them. A farmer isn't at peace until the last harrow has crossed the last field because he knows the only predictable thing about weather is that it's unpredictable when he's carrying out his mechanized fertility rites.

FLAILING OATS TO THE WIND

Damp earth yawns in early spring and catches a stinging gust of oats, flailed from a spinning seeder. A yellow blur sprays relentlessly from the clattering rear of the wagon lumbering over cold soil.

The tiny seeds whiz out of the seeder's flywheel at a dazzling speed, flung in all directions like a blaze of tiny bugs escaping from a bottle. The spinning grains flit onto the ground with a hiss, then tumble and roll to a stop beside a clod to await interment.

Oat seeding is probably the easiest, most elementary of the planting arts. Traditionally, it give cause for the first plunge into spring field work. It's a task gotten out of the way quickly, if possible, to make way for the serious duties of planting corn and soybeans. In April, oat seeding toughens tractors' muscles, getting them in shape for what later will be truly hard work.

Some farmers "plant a little oats" out of a primal instinct that it's one of the formalities of spring farming. All in all, there aren't many oat fields anymore on the Iowa landscape.

When we got ready to seed oats, it was kind of a scavenger hunt. Several tanks or fuel drums had to be found, cleaned and loaded into a grain wagon to accommodate the grasses, clover and alfalfa seed that were to be sown with the oats. Some whiskbrooms, a kitchen broom, and some pots and pans from the house were requisitioned on the promise they'd be returned. The utensils were used to carry the loose seed from a tank on the wagon to the seeder itself in back.

Once all the paraphernalia were assembled, the wagon was backed up to the granary where the auger drew oats from the bowels of a grain bin and dumped a stream of seed oats all around the sides of the tanks. The oats climbed the side of the wagon like a drift of sand. Then it was off to the disked field beyond the creek where corn met the sky last year.

After one of us had the seeder's hopper filled with oats and the smaller seed chamber filled with a blend of grass and alfalfa seeds, the fellow on the tractor was told to proceed forward. The sprockets locked on the seeder, the tractor growled, and oat seeding had commenced. The driver tried to steer straight across the field to make even swaths so the seed would be broadcast uniformly throughout the field.

Back and forth, back and forth. We couldn't drive too near to the fence at the end of the field, or we would be seeding the neighbor's field, too.

Those wee seeds cast a colorful blaze of reds and yellows, and the colors were more spectacular when one grabbed a handful of seed and examined them in his palm.

Soon the wagon's combination of seeds vanished into the wind, leaving only empty cloth and paper seed sacks in the bottom of the wagon. Then it was back to the bin for more oats.

When the seeding was done, a disk or harrow churned over the scene, flinging dirt snugly against the seed to finish spring's first agrarian exercise in the fields ready to rear another season of crops.

STALKING MUSHROOMS

The season was so short that there wasn't time to waste – or some other hunters might get there first. So we stole furtively into the deep woods of that Tama County park in pursuit of that wild spring delicacy, the morel mushroom.

We were bound for the wilds to gather a free and untamed fruit, the pitted and, some would say, ugly mushroom. I had already made three treks through those woods that spring to make certain nature hadn't tried to "spring" a fast one by pushing up mushrooms earlier than it was scheduled to do. The mild spring, I feared, had accelerated the growth of the edible, non-flowering plants.

We tramped over a series of hills and through underbrush where terrain and conditions suggested mushrooms should have been growing, but they weren't. It wasn't disappointing to find no mushrooms there. We never had in the past. The terrain had to be passed over en route to where we knew they grew.

The woods were oozing bright greens of a new leafing season. The Dutchman's-breeches had nearly completed their production of tiny underclothing. May apples and jack-in-the-pulpits unwrapped their canopies of foliage so thickly in places that they shrouded the ground, impeding the search for flesh-colored morels.

It wasn't until my wife, Patty, and I clambered over dead trees and stumps and through waterless creeks that we found our Magic Kingdom of the Morel. They were growing everywhere.

I looked around the woods in every direction before I fell to my knees and began to pluck my spring fruit. I wanted no one to see us amid our mushroom garden. Sure enough, we were alone.

Recent rains had nourished the morels, which need ample moisture. We stuffed the mushrooms into plastic buckets and a garbage can liner. Wild flowers and undergrowth had gotten a faster than normal start and were shading and hiding the mushrooms more than in previous years. So we found crooked sticks to waft through the foliage to unveil the mushrooms for gathering.

We gradually searched an ever-wider perimeter around our little field until our pickings became slim to none.

Being stooped over for so long like a ditch digger left me with a cramp in my back. I straightened up to look around and found my wife had disappeared. She didn't respond to my calls. My first thought was that she had taken the pickings and skipped out. But then I saw her sitting on a log far up the hill. She was just waiting for me to say I'd had enough bending and stooping and crawling for one afternoon.

We left the woods, looking back into its heart and recalling that line by Robert Frost, "The woods are lovely, dark and deep."

And now I had mushrooms to eat before I'd sleep.

THROUGH A SPRING GALE FOR ASPARAGUS

It's never certain there will be morel mushrooms next year where they were found this year. Not so with my other spring pursuit — wild asparagus. Those green spears are as likely to be coming up in old spots year after year as rhubarb in the backyard.

One rainy Sunday afternoon when both mushrooms and asparagus were in season, I had a difficult time deciding which to go after. I could have stomped over rotting logs and scrambled up slippery, weed-covered hills in the rain in search of those shy morels.

Instead, I braced myself against the gale out of the northwest and stalked through the familiar railroad right-of-way of our farm for stalks of wild asparagus.

BATTING ROCKS OVER THE BARN

No sooner had I climbed out of the car, than the fierce wind yanked the piece of newspaper from the bottom of the plastic bucket, which, many uses earlier, had contained a commercial powdered milk for baby calves. I had lined the black bucket with paper to cover up grease clinging to it.

The rubberized coat and trousers I had put over my army fatigue shirt and blue jeans were a poor match for the dousing rain.

For more than 20 years, I had tromped through the lush spring grasses in the right-of-way that crossed our farm in quest of asparagus. I'd come to know at what points along the weedy route I could expect to find the slender shoots.

It wasn't long before I had found the first asparagus. Stalks rose through wet grass at that traditional first stop by the telephone pole that no longer carried wires. I snapped off the visible stalks first, then ferreted others from the grass. There was evidence another asparagus hunter had been there since my last time through because of the brown stubs that were left.

Although I had pulled down the bill of my seed-corn-promoting cap to deflect the rain from my glasses, I was futile to keep the wind-driven drops off them. At first, I dried them off on the cuffs of my gloves every few hundred feet. When they were too damp for wiping, I reached into my rubberized trousers and pulled out a shirttail to use to dry my lenses.

I hadn't gotten a third of the way when my bucket was full of the long stems. Fearing my bucket, filled to overload, would begin losing stems as I traipsed along on the rest of the route, I decided to leave the full bucket and trudge the rest of the way into the drenching rain without that burden.

The wind's strong force served one useful purpose. It causes the grasses and more pliant plant growth in the right-of-way to lie down, leaving the turgid asparagus spears to protrude through the growth. They wavered only slightly at the force of the wind and rain.

In time, I clutched an almost unwieldy bunch of asparagus with both hands against my gut. Eventually, I turned around and headed back to my bucket. I tramped down the railroad bed now stripped of the iron rails, spikes and ties – abandoned as a freight-hauling route more than a year before. The railroad company soon after dismantled the track. Many times, I had hauled my asparagus pickings back, walking on one rail in a balancing act.

When I arrived at the bucket, I jostled the just-picked stalks around and pushed and shaved them into it. But it was so full that I had to carry it up under my chin like a pile of books. I wrapped one arm around the front of the bucket as I walked back to the car.

From the old railroad track bed, I looked across our field planted to corn. There in the ditches along the gravel road were urban asparagus hunters searching for stalks of the wild delicacy. They tramped over ground searched moments earlier by other weekend hunters. It wasn't likely they were finding much.

Though thoroughly wet, I had a huge picking to take home – enough, in fact, to have three large meals of cooked asparagus for my family. A lot went to friends at the office and next door.

Later that week, under ideal conditions, I pursued the morels and likewise went home with a satisfying bucket of the springtime treat, which, like asparagus, requires only butter and salt to make it worth the miles of walking, stooping, snapping off and reaping the gifts of the Iowa wild.

CHEWING FOXTAILS OR HOW TO EAT FREE

Next time you see a giant foxtail bouncing in the breeze, go ahead. Latch onto it near the top. Pull steadily and gently until the thin stem slides out from the stalk.

Now chomp off that tender, sweet, light-colored end and chew it. It's savory.

Whether it's the tender tip of a foxtail, the deliciously sour leaves of sheep sorrel, or a handful of dry soybean meal in a gunny sack in the granary, in-between-meal snacks can be had anywhere on a farm.

It's almost impossible to grow up in rural areas and not dine occasionally on the numerous tempting nature foods to be found in meadows and sheds, on limbs and in bushes.

I don't mean you have to make a conscious effort to harvest the offbeat, exotic fruits of the wilds as the late Euell Gibbons did, although I've crawled through many brambles in quest of wild raspberries, strawberries, mushrooms, choke cherries, elder berries, asparagus and blackberries.

There is some spice of life at grabbing for something at hand while going about the routine of farming. In how many idle moments at the side of a hay field while waiting for another wagon to arrive have I plucked a spirited red clover blossom and, one by one, eaten the pink, sweet flowers making up the full blossom.

And in passing by tall stems of the grass family, almost by habit, I pull free the long top of the plant and munch on its succulent end. Many of the grasses have hollow, jointed stems – oats, timothy and barley – and they pull apart like Tinker toys to reveal soft, chewable ends.

Watch a group of people sitting outdoors where something is growing. You may well find someone chewing on stems or leaves – most frequently long blades of grasses.

In late spring while I was growing up, we would go out into the roadside ditch in front of our house, then using a pair of scissors, we'd cut the hollow stems of wild grasses for drinking straws. The straws generally didn't last more than a breakfast-sitting because to wash off the sticky milk or orange juice with soap and water caused them to collapse—or they were clogged.

The hungry boy on a farm may not be able to get into the cookie jar at times, but it's hard to keep him out of the garden. My favorite early summer treat were the leaves of the sweet pea. Then when the pods set on the vines, I relished eating the raw pods whole.

In no trip past the garden from May to October should anyone pass up the chance to drop in and find something to slip into his mouth, at least to chew on – whether it be an early onion or the last unharvested carrots or ground cherries in the fall.

When soybeans' pods got fat, I'd fill my pockets with bean pods to have them like candy to be chomped and devoured.

Who hasn't combined oats and popped a few heads of the yellow grain into his mouth and, with his teeth, carefully forced out the soft germ? And through the corn-growing season, who hasn't eaten a raw ear of field corn when it is in the milk stage? And during the harvest itself, it's normal to munch on kernels of the new corn.

Whether one gets a mouthful of warm milk from the udder of a dairy cow in the barn or finds enough gooseberries in a grove to make his pocket bulge, there's plenty of places to get something to eat besides the dinner table.

SUMMER SURVIVAL

LONG DAYS LONG AGO

Each year when spring gives way to summer, I am reminded of what we tried to do on the first day of summer back in the days when I was a working farm boy.

We tried to get the day off from farm work by declaring it a special "Kids' Day," to somehow parallel Father's Day and Mother's Day. We figured if we could get out of chores, field work and the whole parcel of summertime farm jobs that fall to rural kids, we might just as well do it on the longest day of the year so we could get the full benefit of a day off with optimum sunshine.

But because the work on a farmstead falls into patterns in which each person has his individual chores to do, it took some preparing our parents to the notion that their youngsters weren't going to turn a finger on June 21 or 22 or whichever day the longest day fell on that year.

So we gave fair warning and looked forward with a certain amount of expectancy to that day. We hoped it wouldn't be marred by bad weather. And we hoped hay baling didn't have to take place that day or some other urgent farm work that would necessitate the cancellation of our own fun day.

If all went well, we could be permitted to sleep until we awoke on our own or until we felt like getting up – usually long after the sun had risen.

I would be spared milking cows that day. My twin brother, Lincoln, was liberated from hog and henhouse chores. My sister, Linda, was offered a respite from taking care of the pullets.

For several years, we prevailed on our neighbors to let their kids have the day off, too. That way we could really make it a local children's fun day.

But not being old enough to obtain driver's licenses, we were bound to the countryside. Still we'd find things to do – fish for sunfish or chubs under the bridge, take bicycle rides and play never-ending softball games in Mervan Meyer's spacious front yard or out in a pasture where fly balls and cow pies always seem to meet.

The longest day did take on a family holiday flavor when we would have a picnic at noon under the trees around the farm yard. We ate some of the first harvest of our garden – new potatoes and just-shelled peas. Add to that strawberry shortcake. And across the fields, we could see the promise of greater harvests in the fall. There were the recently cultivated shoots of corn in the field, newly headed fields of oats and recently mowed hayfields.

For at noon on the year's longest day, we were somehow at the zenith of contentment with our world, grateful for the gifts that came through nature's will. There in June, we celebrated the arrival of summer, the fulfillment of spring, the promise of autumn and the oneness of a family living with the land.

Then came the afternoon. We day-vacation kids had more time on our hands than we knew what to do with. Sometimes, in fact, we drifted back to work because of sheer boredom or out simple realization that work had to be done – day off or not.

It always seemed, by the end of those magic days when the sun finally completed its lofty arc and set beyond the fence line willow trees that it was great to have a day off once a year, but not every day, as we presumed the city kids had.

Sometimes we ended up doing night chores after all.

As we took on more responsibility on that farm, the summers came and the third week in June passed unnoticed. The three of us almost forgot we had once demanded childhood holidays. Still there was something special about doing nothing we didn't want to do on the longest day of the year.

FLIES VS. DISCONTENTED COWS

With summer came flies.

About the same time every year, the cows' tails began switching in a fury. Their shoulders quivered. They stamped or twitched in their stanchions. The cows heaved their heads backwards, sweeping their outstretched tongues across the hide on their shoulders – incensed by the incessant fly landings.

And the Holsteins headed for the creek to stand in the deepest water they could find. Fly-tortured cows battled each other, butting their heads into each other's sides in an effort to gain access to the place where the creek would come up highest on their flanks to keep the flies off. Above the knot of cows standing in two or three feet of water danced a squadron of flies.

By then, it was time to dig out our Hudson-brand livestock sprayer. The mostly blue-painted device had a wooden handle on one end and a screw-off nozzle on the other. The tank holding the oily spray was barrel-shaped and was welded to the bottom of the cylinder perpendicular to the long tube with its plunger that sucked up the toxic spray and then, in the reverse stroke, sent it through the nozzle as spray.

Twice a day, we sought to relieve the tension, the vexation, the irritation of those flies that made the cows touchy, irritable and discontented. In the dairy barn, their stanchions rattled as the cattle moved and flexed in an upright position in their stalls to fight the flies. They were stressed and milk production was reduced.

Seemingly the same flies that tormented them in the pasture had ridden into the barn on the cows' backs to continue their aggression. When the light in the barn was right, one could look across the collective backs of the cows and see a silhouetted swarm of chaotic flies jockeying for cowhide.

We sprayed the cows before we started washing their udders or putting on the milk straps or surcingles. We went right down the line with the sprayer. It discharged a steady spray as long as the pumping hand continued to work. Heat from the constant pressure was generated at the base of the sprayer.

An oily coating of spray was applied to the Holsteins' backs, shoulders, legs, bellies and tails. The greasy fog settled down on their

hair, clinging to it and making a sheen. The globules of spray were meant to offend the flies, deter their landing and dispatch them elsewhere.

As dairymen, we hoped it would calm the cows, especially stop their zipping tails that swatted us more successfully than they did the flies.

The air in the cow barn, however, was saturated with the pungent mist. It made me sneeze, and the cats either exited the barn or sat on ledges around the barn, washing themselves in an attempt to remove the film from their fur. Surely it couldn't have been environmentally healthy for any creature on hand.

The intently listening ear could hear the sounds of flies buzzing their last on the barn floor or expiring noisily on the window sills.

Getting all 21 cows in the barn sprayed meant a constant fight. The animals had to be asked, goaded or shoved over in their stalls to let us in to spray their flanks. Most of them welcomed the relief coming their way, although they weren't above kicking or swinging their tails at us, as the flies flitted from their backs to escape the deadly mist.

When we were finished, our arms had cramps, our noses were running, our eyes were watering, and I suppose we had jeopardize our health. But there wasn't an Environmental Protection Agency or Occupational Health and Safety Administration then to worry bureaucratically about our safety.

Flies, cows and man fought it out then. At best, it was a draw.

FASTER THAN MOLASSES IN JULY

There's a trite, old phrase about something being "slower than molasses in January." The converse is "faster than molasses in July." I speak from experience. I was a victim of its great speed one sizzling day in July when I was 16.

One of my responsibility with livestock in those days on the Iowa farm focused on our Holstein dairy cows, primarily milking them and keeping them fed.

On summer days, as soon as the cows were driven up from the pasture and into the barn, they would be treated to ground ear corn. But the corn had to be in the mangers ready for them when the crazily hungry cows were allowed through the barn door. So before heading from the pasture, I'd jab the aluminum scoop shovel into the feed bin,

pull out a heaping shovel of the coarsely ground, yellow-white feed, then carry it gently to the manger.

There, in front of each stanchion, I would do a measured jerk with my wrist. With just the right snap, the scoop would plop a third of the contents of the shovel in front of each cow's place. Three equal piles of feed for three cows per each scoop. It took seven shovels from the bin for the 21 stanchions in the barn.

Just as ice cream is better with chocolate syrup, so we figured the ground corn would be that much better a treat with the topping. Anything flavorful was satisfying to the old gals – soybean meal, mineral stock food or even granular molasses.

But then we tried liquid molasses. It was their favorite topping.

That sticky, black, tar-like syrup came to our farm in 50-gallon barrels, much like motor oil barrels. Their tops had two standard holes in them. One was an air vent, and the larger was for the insertion of a pump. To drain out molasses, the feed supply company had provided a yellow, plastic spigot, which was to be screwed into the smaller of the barrel's two holes once the steel plug was removed. Then after the barrel was laid horizontally, a fellow only had to loosen the larger plug to permit a little air to enter the drum and allow molasses to flow through the open spigot.

We had a prolonged hot period that summer. The sun beat down on that black barrel.

As I remember it now, I put my bucket under the spigot that afternoon as I always had and turned it on. The hot molasses came flowing out. But since it always would come out faster when I loosened the top plug, I unscrewed it as a matter of standard procedure.

I apparently unscrewed the plug too far. Suddenly it came off and shot out of my hand, pushed by an explosive gust of torrid air above a barrel of hot molasses. I looked up from the spigot to the air vent hole just in time to catch the sweet-tasting gush of black, hot molasses in my face. It came sweeping like a river down the front of me.

The jet of molasses burned my eyes. I slipped on the slick, slimy ground, fell and floundered in the puddle of molasses.

I shouted for help, and I struggled in the gooey blackness for the steel plug, aware all the time that valuable molasses were pouring out onto the ground in a chuck-a-lug pulse as air moved into the barrel and the black liquid flowed forth. Like the Dutch boy plugging the dam, I

finally got the palm of one hand over the hole and soon relocated the plug to screw back into the opening.

I knew what it was like to be tarred. I felt plastered. The black substance had glued my T-shirt to my body. My cries of distress brought my family coming from all directions. But instead of giving sympathy or aid, they just stood around howling with laughter at the sight.

My mother's first concern was how she would get my shirt white again, and someone else thought the first priority was to get the camera and take some pictures.

Soon the flies had taken notice of the sweet smell and arrived to feast on the black sugar.

Meanwhile, I slurped up the black lake with a scoop shovel and hauled it in to dump on the cows' ground corn – they got far more than normal that day.

Then I took a bath.

Technically, what happened was the hot sun had heated the air inside the barrel to build up pressure. When the cap was opened too far, the pressure blasted the hot molasses out like a fire hydrant abruptly opened. It took a split second and happened faster than molasses in July.

DOWN UNDER THE BRIDGE

For a second grader, that half-mile route to country school seemed like fascinating terrain. It included cross the Chicago & North Western Railroad tracks with so many opportunities to view mile-long freights bolting down the rails.

The route also included a county gravel road bridge with rusting iron railings. It spanned the creek that split our farm.

Both of those two points along our route were major landmarks in our limited world. But the bridge and creek had special meaning. Almost always on our walks to and from the one-room schoolhouse at the top of a hill, we'd pause at the bridge, an undistinguished structure showing evidence of neglect and scars where it had been struck by the county road grader.

We'd lean over the rails, spit into the creek and cast stones into the usually quiet waters. We watched the concentric circles ripple outward. Then with our toes, we'd rake a bit of gravel off the bridge.

The aggregate would plunge into the water like bombs dropped into the China Sea as we saw on the weekly TV program about American at war called "The Big Picture."

Beneath every bridge, there is the setting of a hideaway. I always liked the mood there, that sense of leaving the high road and crawling beneath it, like the trolls of legends. It was a way of slipping away from the thoroughfare of activity, but still being ever so close to it – and out of view.

Under the bridge, I could hear cars, trucks and tractors whiz by or pound noisily overhead, kicking up the dust and rocks, which showered down into the water on both sides.

Our creek made a sharp bend on the upstream side, and during flash flooding, the fury of the water routed out the creek bottom, leaving a deep hole beneath the bridge, a deep spot that offered one a passable place to skinny dip. But the shaded water was usually too cold, even on the hottest of days.

The hole was one of the few places along the creek that supported fish larger than a minnow. Chubs, bullheads and sunfish inhabited the hole during some, but not all, the years I was growing up.

After chores on summer nights, my twin brother, Lincoln, and I would take our crude fishing poles with the smallest hooks and fish under the bridge. A pile of boulders along the creek offered a place to sit. Swallows inhabited the girders supporting the bridge. And some years, a band of pigeons found the bridge's undersurface good enough to serve as home. All birds, however, fled when we arrived to fish under the bridge.

That spot was the coolest site on the farm in summer, and, in evenings, it was a pleasant place to escape to. Only the distant growl of tractors working late in the fields or the lowing of cows, returned to the pasture after milking, broke up the sounds of the creek.

Sure, the fishing was poor. The catches were mere nibbles for the palate. We couldn't get far from home for an accessible fishing hole. Yet our going down under the bridge for a spell gave us farm kids, isolated as we were in the countryside, an appreciation of the solace found at the junction of a gravel road and a lazy stream.

MAKING HAY

Battalions of clattering machines rumble across Iowa fields in three waves each summer. Making their invasions in between rainstorms, the implements methodically cut, chop, pound, toss, pack and lug off that which waved green and lush days before.

Farmers unleash their mowers and crimpers, their rakes, choppers and balers. They command the sun to pelt it with parching rays and beckon the breeze to puff across the dying and drying stalks.

Then they squeeze it all together and bury it deep in the bowels of a barn's attic.

The process comes all so abruptly, just as the fields are in full bloom and the azure sky suggests a long period of fair weather.

First, a mower scampers into a field. Its ragged arm falls rudely to the ground in the corner of the field where the hay meets the corn. A lever is thrown on the tractor and the sickle grates its teeth to test its sharp readiness. Weeds touching the sickle bar nervously vibrate.

Then the tractor is revved. It gives an eager groan and plunges forward. The grating turns to a metallic clatter.

The sickle rhythmically saws down millions of succulent stalks of alfalfa 16 inches high. They are tripped up and felled so smoothly that it's as if a rope were pulled through a crowd, tripping people and neatly laying them down – all facing the same direction.

Butterflies, which are embracing royal purple alfalfa blossoms and sucking forth sweet nectar, are suddenly clambering in mid-air, as the sweet flowers are torn from their grasp and tossed to the ground.

Likewise, bumblebees, which have latched to clover blossoms, suddenly ride the tall stalks to the ground. On impact, they flounder momentarily in the newly fallen greenery before getting their fat, lethargic bodies airborne again.

Larger creatures, rabbits and pheasant, are rustled from the shady cover, often only after the sickle has cut through their legs and bodies. They drag their broken parts into the hay still standing. They go there to await a new assault, as the mower circles the field, shaving the foliage in each round to reduce a place for creatures to hide from the intrusive machine.

The mower makes fancy on-a-dime turns at the corners of the hay field. Despite skillful driving, the mower's operator still leaves wisps of

uncut hay at the corner – telltale signs of his less than total mastery of his machine.

Then all falls silent across the pillaged field where virtually all that had stood tall lies flat. The silence is to last for 30 hours or more as the sun and wind wring out the hay's juices, shrivel its leaves and toughens its stalks.

The farmer occasionally comes out and kicks the hay around. He gather handfuls of hay and feels them, then throws the wads down and mumbles to himself.

In time, a giant, swirling comb comes to the field to scratch the hay together into a long, fibrous, concentric snarl. The hay rake rolls it into a fat row of curing forage as it trips through the field like an egg beater.

Next come more tractors, a baler and a batch of hayracks. They're accompanied by men who sweat and curse the heat and dust. And in one afternoon, they drag a throbbing machine over the field, pulling it astride that series of ever smaller circles of hay. The baler swallows that alfalfa and clover, packing it like square lifesavers into boxlike bundles that fill huge racks.

And then the bundles and wagons and noisy machines withdraw, leaving behind a brown, coarse stubble, seemingly devoid of life.

All that has grown there has been hauled off. Butterflies flitter across the fields finding no place to land lest they move on to the roadside ditches.

It's quiet again in the field. With time, the greenery subtly returns, pushing forth stems, then buds, then flowers, enticing the insects to quaff their nectars. When alfalfa stems and clover blossoms are brandishing their greenery most winsomely again, the men will launch their armor division for the second cutting.

RIDING THE CULTIVATOR

My boyhood was filled with a variety of work experiences and some demanding jobs that didn't seem to be done by my counterparts, the youngsters on the other farms. Besides doing tasks differently, we worked significantly harder – or so it seemed.

My father believed all children had work potential, no matter how young they were. Play was okay for town kids, he'd say, but country

youth had to learn responsibility. More importantly, their labor was genuinely needed. Kids should always find something to do around the farm – or have it found for them.

One task was cultivating corn. Dad would take us to the field in early June to help him plow the weeds in the corn rows. We performed a task that I had never seen done by kids before nor since.

We were not much more than 4 years-old when we went out for the first early summer of "riding the cultivator," as the duty was called.

Government safety officials would have put a stop to it immediately had they been around in the 1950s to see pre-school aged children hanging onto the back of a two-row field cultivator moving through a cornfield.

Those were the years before weed control became the complicated science it is today with a myriad of herbicides and sophisticated machinery. Back then, weed control was by one means – a cultivator mounted onto a tractor that lowered its set of steel shovels into the soil. And the farmer had to start early after the corn sprouts emerged to get a jump on the weeds.

The tractor would have to creep slowly through the field to keep from kicking the loosened dirt and clods onto the tiny corn leaves. If they were buried and pinned to the ground, the plants would be smothered or, at least, it would stunt their development.

Keeping the corn from being covered and left to die or struggle was the reason we rode the cultivator. Our task was that of rescuer.

It must have been 1948 or 1949 that my father decided to fashion a four-foot long board to fit over the relatively horizontal shanks that connected the cultivator shafts to the tractor. The board had holes drilled in it and wires ran through them to attach the board to the cultivator.

Then two of the three of us kids would sit there, clutching the board, facing backwards as the 1941 Massey Harris 44 six-cylinder tractor plodded through the field, plowing out weeds or grass.

Each of us had to look after one row of just-cultivated corn. If we saw a lump of dirt or a rock lying on top of a hill of corn, we were instructed to hop off our moving bench, trot back to the corn, and, with our hands or feet, uncover the corn. With that accomplished, we were to run back toward the moving tractor, all the time looking at the corn in between to see whether clods had landed on top of any of it in the

meantime. Finally when we got back to the moving tractor, we clenched the board and swiveled our behinds around and sat down.

Those were the days when corn was planted in "hills" every 30 inches apart, not in a continuous string as garden peas are planted. As we would watch the corn coming into view from beneath our seats, and a hill showed no vestige of greenery, we would still have to get off. Often we'd run back to kick the dirt from the would-be hill and find no corn at all growing there.

Sometimes our dad would stop when he knowingly dumped a dirt clod onto some corn. That way, we could hop off right there, undo the damage to the tiny stalk and not have to chase down the moving tractor.

We three youngsters worked in shifts. Two would go out in the morning to ride. At noon, the third would replace one of them. The kid who rode all day usually had the next day off – off from cultivating corn, that is. There was always other work assigned at home.

Corn was cultivated three times usually. Sometimes, we'd ride the cultivator for the second trip through the fields, depending on the height of the corn and its vulnerability to be covered up. It was never necessary to ride the cultivator for the third trip because of the corn's gained height.

We were hot out there in the black dirt with the June sun glaring down. The tractor went at a doggedly slow pace through the corn. The tedium would make us drowsy, our dad included. Occasionally, he would have to stop, get off, find the shadow of a rear tractor wheel and lie down to take a nap. As he laid down, he pulled off his wristwatch, handed it to one of us and told us to wake him up in 10 minutes.

Meanwhile, we would find the water jug and get drinks. I was usually as warm as spit. Then we'd just sit in what shade we could find, maybe chew on foxtail stems and watch the summer breezes waft the young corn until it was time to interrupt Dad's snoring and get us all back onto our weed-fighting machine.

When it cooled off later in the day, a flock of blackbirds would land on the black, damp earth turned up by the cultivator's shovels. There, they would snap up earthworms and bugs.

After the sun went down, well after 9 o'clock, the crew headed home, hungry, tired and caked with black dust.

As we got older, we graduated from the cultivator because our time could be better spent on other farm work. As a substitute, Dad got a

long pole or a relatively straight 7-foot tree branch to reach down from the tractor when he saw corn that had been covered up.

To me, the word "cultivating" still means riding the old board through the fields uncovering corn to make sure there were a few more ears of corn going into the crib in the fall.

THE LIGHTER SIDE OF BALING

Except for cleaning out the pit of the outhouse, I dreaded no farm job more than baling hay. Most of my dislike for that hot, back-breaking toil of hay-making stemmed from my generally slight build – 5 feet 6 inches in height and scarcely 125 pounds. Often bales of alfalfa hay weighed more than I did.

But baling straw was a fresh change because those bales were much easier to lift. The second cutting of hay was always baled just before or after oats were combined and the straw baled. Sometimes we were doing both operations in the same day.

The difference in the two kinds of baling was immense. To get done with the straw and head the baler toward the hay field was a dreadful prospect.

Straw bales could be handily pulled out of the baler and tossed into place on the hayrack. We could stack straw bales six to even seven tiers high on a wagon. Only one's height limited how high we stacked the bright yellow packs of oat stems.

But the tougher and damper hay always weighed more. And if rain threatened, we would reluctantly commence baling, even though the hay would have been better left to dry and cure longer in the windrows.

Long experience taught us to always try to make hay whenever we could.

It was just at straw baling time, however, that we most noticed the difference in the two kinds of baling and appreciated the luxury of baling straw because straw bales were always manageable.

The baler itself was less inclined to balk as straw windrows. The baler sheared its flywheel pins less often from oversized straw windrows. The machine's hopper didn't get clogged by straw as often as it did with hay because hay stems are thicker and heavier that the hollow straw stems.

The baler knife had less trouble biting off straw after the baler's own rakes and augers fed the yellow wads into the chamber where a plunger pounded them flat to make fibrous cakes.

And in the haymow, the straw bales could be flung halfway across the huge second floor of the barn to be stacked and stored.

By contrast, bales of hay, hoisted to the haymow by hay fork or elevator, fell to the floor of the mow with a thud that shook the barn. Some bales simply could not be lifted, at least by me. They were the kind of bales I cheated with. I simply dragged, pushed, shoved or somehow got them off to the side. Then I only hoped the next bales up from the hayrack were lighter.

Often they were not, and the disorder in the haymow was the result. Stronger men were usually enlisted to rectify the snarl of back-wrenching bales. Even with gloves, our hands ached and swelled. The next day after baling, our fat fingers barely curled.

Hay baling came three times a summer. Straw baling happened just once. It didn't seem fair.

In July when the weather was the most sweltering, we got a workout doing both types of baling. And perhaps it is because both came about the same time that I viewed the second cutting of hay as such an abominable exercise.

Never mind that straw dust always irritated my nose and caused it to run profusely, I preferred the lighter side of baling – baling up the straw.

AN EDUCATION IN THE CORNFIELD

City kids gain education each summer when they plunge into Iowa fields to pluck tassels from field corn for commercial seed corn companies.

Detasseling is one of the all-too-few means by which urban young persons encounter rural experiences. Their repainted school buses, their lunches, their bandanna headgear, their blue jeans, their muddy tennis shoes, their water jugs and their radios and iPods are, in short, their trademarks. They're a three-week phenomenon.

The frequent summer rains bring mud and misery to many detasselers, especially the younger ones. Some have never before experienced a two-inch thickness of mud clinging to the soles of their

shoes. Some have never had to pull their footgear off in mud to remove parts of tassels and weed seeds, or scrape off the caked-on wet earth. Often the mud build-up yanks the shoes from their feet. And once they've cleaned the mud off with sticks or scraped them over a woven-wire fence, the shoes simply gather new hunks of good, black Iowa cornfield mud.

Detasselers complain of many things: sunburn and cuts on their arms and legs from corn leaves, aching fingers and arms, soggy sandwiches and hot fruit, melted frosting on the cake in their lunch sacks, itchy corn pollen and thistle patches.

Their fingers are stained green, and girls find their fingernails are damaged – and there's dirt under them, too.

Hair bleaches out. Some detasselers are squeamish to see their paths through the corn rows blocked by large black and yellow spiders.

And early in the mornings, the fields are steamy. The new day's sun beats down on heads and shoulders, triggering the sweat glands, while below, the detasselers' legs are wet and cold from the dew on the weeds and corn leaves.

By midday, trousers and shorts are dry, as is the caked-on mud around the cuffs. Some detasselers change into shorts in the natural privacy of the great fields. Cut-offs, bikinis, T-shirts, sun visors and sun glasses are the garb during the hottest part of the day. Getting a tan is part of the summer job, and most detasselers work at it seriously.

Their weeks in the Iowa jungles come to an end. Hundreds of young people have had a hand in the corn reproduction process. The youth particularly look back on the demanding experience as a friend-making adventure where they earned some money on their own, deepened their tans and learned some lessons about how nothing worthwhile comes easily.

PULLING COCKLEBURS

June rains and July heat made Iowa corn and weeds grow equally well. The weeds that survived the rotary hoe, three trips through the fields by the tractor cultivator and herbicide applications were intent on muscling in on as much of the fields as they could.

Well before the advent of truly effective herbicides, it was the practice on farms to walk corn and bean rows in search of noxious

weeds. Our quest focused on cockleburs and button weed, a hardy pest that was also called butter print or velvet weed.

Uprooting them was an annual practice on our farm. The task went on sometimes across a six-week period from about August 1 to well into September, depending on the weather and what other farm demands interrupted the work.

"Pulling cockleburs" as we termed the ambitious task was about the first farm job I think I was involved in, besides riding the cultivator. I don't think I was yet 5 when I was first pointed down two rows of tall corn and instructed to carry out a search-and-destroy mission on cockleburs and button weeds growing between those two rows of corn and the adjacent "alleys."

Well-drilled on what two weeds to look for, I plodded after them betwixt the two parallel rows, fended off sharp corn leaves, tripped on morning glory vines and scratched to relieve the corn pollen itch on my skin.

Mother and Dad and sometimes hired hands accompanied my brother, sister and me in the project. We were assigned to two rows each. The adults tried to stay even with the kids, partly to make sure we didn't get lost or get off our rows, but more to assist us in pulling giant cocklebur plants whose roots clutched the black soil stronger than we were able to counter.

Even the adults occasionally needed help to pull up some of those weeds after they reached unwieldy size. Then it amounted to one person grasping the weed at a low point on the stalk, while another one planted his feet as if he were a tug-of-war, grabbed hold of the stalk higher up, and then pul-l-l-led.

At the end of oats combining, Dad would declare it was time to head for the cornfields to get an early start before the weed seeds could form and mature. Advanced seeds meant one thing: We'd have to carry the plants down the rows to the end of the fields to be stacked and later hauled home to be burned. That would ensure their destruction and their seeds never to get the chance to germinate.

An immature plant could be pulled, its dirt knocked from its roots, and the naked plant hung over a sturdy corn ear – its tap root pointing to the summer sky. There the weed would die and dry, never getting a chance to touch the soil and maybe revive.

For button weeds, we would sometimes carry feed sacks. When we came upon mature plant, we'd strip the ripest seeds from the stalk and put them in the paper sacks. Those sacks would be taken home and thrown into the fire.

It wasn't always easy to walk so many miles through the corn rows. The deep trench dug by the shovels of the cultivator six weeks before was like the gutter of a bowling alley, two sides sloping toward the middle. It was painful to the arches of our feet to walk through the trench.

Strong summer winds always blew some corn over. The stalks would try to recover or straighten up, but there still remained a snarl of stalks. Thus, a cocklebur puller was forced to leave his assigned rows to get around the gnarled cornstalks. The chance was high that he'd get off his own assigned rows and onto those of someone else. Many times, two persons would come to the end of the field traveling down the same two rows. And on occasion, I might have started out on the right of my brother, only to reach the end of the field at his left. There would follow arguments over who wasn't properly paying attention to his rows and who was to blame. Often, it was a case where everyone had gotten off his respective rows because of the field conditions

Arriving at the end of the field first meant getting a rest until all others got there. Sometimes the first person to the end had to go through all the "drill rows" (a "border" of corn rows at the end of fields for machinery to turn around) and backtrack in search of the water jar set there earlier. The container usually was concealed in the shade of fencerow weeds by a post prominent enough to be discovered later.

The one who fetched the water would take a drink, then hauled the jug back into the lush field to water down the rest of us. Never certain where to return to, he shouted until someone responded. He then knew how far to walk to reach the thirsty weed pullers.

We'd rest a bit, wipe away the sweat and get back on our tired feet. We were assigned new pairs of rows, then we'd head off again in the opposite direction.

We would walk until darkness settled on that leafy field.

What I remember most about the work was that smell of my clothes after an August day in the cornfield – an acrid fragrance from the immixing of sweat, corn pollen and the saps of cockleburs and button weed.

Sometimes in my teenage years, we quit walking the fields and put our trust in herbicides, although they weren't a total answer either.

It was my father's belief that the hardy and ungainly weeds, with their propensity to spread, sapped too much water and nutrients from the soil at the expense of the corn. So we spent the last part of many summers pulling them in the hope there would be fewer to pull in the following years.

But we really never saw much difference.

TAKING A LITTLE TRIP

When the tassels uncurl on the cornstalks, when the auger is unbolted from the combine's bin after the oats are in the shed, when the first wave of back-to-school advertisements appear in the papers, a farm family starts to get anxious about getting away from the place for a while. They think about taking that "little trip."

The word "vacation" has never quite rolled off the tongue of a farmer as unabashedly and freely as from out of the mouth of an urban worker, who, given the three-week vacation or more by his contract, would slowly go mad if he had to spend that time at home in the city.

But farm families enjoy taking that little trip, albeit an often quickly planned and sometimes taken vacation.

I knew farmers who could never compromise their work ethic notions by taking a vacation. Such holiday excursions to them had seemed like something for leisure class hedonists, persons who waste money in endless pursuits of good times. It's partly due to the fact they work so hard for so many years they don't know how to relax with a vacation. Having livestock on the farm to care for was the common barrier to being gone a long time.

I knew farmers who had never felt the rituals of the four seasons availed a slack time when they could leave their farmsteads and disappear in the dust down their own gravel roads, roam out onto strange new highways and go to places that have only been exotic names. There are farmers who'll dismiss the idea of a vacation because the barn needs painting, the sows will be farrowing or the three county fairs in the area start at different times in August.

But some of them find that a dependable neighbor can do a find job with the livestock chores and keep track of the number of calves in the back pasture, the farm dog fed and the cows out of the cornfield,

farmers can more and more accept the idea that they too can take a vacation.

The youngsters in my family somehow talked our parents into a vacation when I was 12. It was our first "little trip." Before that, trips were ruled to be impossible because, we were told, "there's just too much that's gotta be done around home."

But after we spent those two days visiting points of interest along the Mississippi River in northeast Iowa in our first vacation, the ice was broken on taking trips. Our parents discovered how much they enjoyed getting away. They realized the farm could get along without them for a few days.

Every year after that we struck out for more distant spots – the Black Hills, Kentucky, the Ozarks, Northern Minnesota and into Canada, Oklahoma and Florida.

Landed, laboring people need to let the corn grow on its own for a while. They should turn the livestock chores over to a dependable neighbor and those work-weary rural people ought to allow themselves a chance to take a little trip to restore their rural spirits.

AUTUMN ABEYANCE

MELON PATCH SKIRMISHES

Almost every fall before the first hard freeze, we could expect a sneaky band of night visitors to invade our cornfield to carry out piracy of our watermelon patch, hidden behind the cornstalks.

A large watermelon patch was laid out and planted every spring on our farm. We would usually plant melons in that odd-shaped chunk of land where the drill and the point rows met. The difficulty we had with cultivating weeds with a tractor in such oblique rows made it simpler for us to just plant the space to melons.

Dad's grand enthusiasm for melons was well-known in the Parkersburg community. He was always happiest with a knife and fork in his hands and a watermelon split open in front of him, its seed-speckled pinkness glowing wet.

When the melons were ripe, no one left our farm until watermelons and muskmelons were put into his car's trunk. Salesmen and neighbors couldn't come onto the place when my father was wolfing down watermelon without also being handed a piece of melon on a plate to eat.

My father thought everybody shared his love for melon and wanted each person to relish it as he did. So he enjoyed giving melons away.

However, he never tolerated anyone heisting them from his patch.

Throughout the summer when I was on the farm, my dad would be asked in town, "How's your watermelons looking this year, Paul?"

Young fellows bantered with him, saying they'd be out some night to help themselves. Dad dared them to try it. I suppose the dare helped to encourage them. My brother and I were repeatedly pumped for

information on the whereabouts of the year's melon patch. Those high school boys boasted they, too, would be out some night to clean out our melons.

One year my brother, who had a pilot's license, took some older town kids up for ride over our farm. Those boys were delighted to get a bird's-eye view of our melon patch and now knew where Dad had supposedly hidden that year's vining crop.

So late summer came, and our melons were at their best. The imminent coming of melon thieves made Dad fretful and jittery. He was constantly alert to the sounds and speed of all cars going past our farm along the gravel road in the night. He watched out the window to see whether they slowed while passing the cornfield concealing the melon patch. His often repeated complaint was "kids oughta have better things to do at night."

Then one foggy night after he had gone to bed, a bunch came.

Dad got up, roused a hired hand from bed, got dressed and climbed into the hired man's car to give chase. Keeping the car's lights off, they headed down the road through a canopy of fog. A somewhat wild chase ensued over several miles, but the melon crooks got away.

I don't know what the two men would have done had they caught the melon marauders. But the next day, my father delivered lovely ripe watermelons to the homes of two of the youths he believed had tramped through his patch the night before. Dad told the boys' parents, "Your boys can have all the watermelons they want if they'll just ask for them. We've got plenty."

Over the years, there were other skirmishes with melon bandits. Looking back, I wonder who had more fun from it all, the thieves or my father.

I think Dad harbored the notion that his melons were so outstanding that men would go to great trouble to have them.

Once my late Uncle Don Griffiths fired a shotgun above some melon-toting pirates, running from his cornfield. The buckshot fell down around them, the sound made louder by the BB shot scattering down onto the leaves. It struck fear in the fugitives. However, they kept running all the way to the edge of the road where they expected to jump into the getaway car. But the car had abandoned them. Moments later, Dad and my uncle caught up with them. The red-faced melon felons were still holding the goods.

Knowing my dad, I suspect they all sat down there by the road and had watermelon together.

AN AFTERNOON DELIGHT

On Saturday afternoons in October on our farm, a delicious scent pervaded the air. It was as much a smell of fall as the pungent chemicals used to spray down the newly cleaned hen houses or the odors of the freshly cut silage.

Though we had plenty of assigned Saturday work around the farm, none of us wanted to drift too far from the farmhouse kitchen.

We all desired to be on hand to wolf down the pumpkin pie as soon as it came out of the oven. That pie was as much a part of my October memories as all the World Series games I watched or all the Iowa and Iowa State football games I listened to on the radio.

Just after lunch, Mother cleared everything from the kitchen table, got her pumpkins cleaned out and quartered, then put on the stove to boil. Then she started rolling her crusts for as many as eight pies.

It wasn't long until the fresh pumpkin, eggs, spices and other mysterious contents of her unique pies were blended together. She mixed a golden batter that made our mouths water. Dad was always the first to get a coffee cup and scoop up the tasty concoction and guzzle it down. But we were always right behind.

Mother never failed to protest, warning us that it would mean fewer pies or less filling for all of them.

But we knew better. She always made an extra amount on the expectation that we'd all get one-cup samples before the pumpkin batter was poured into the pie shells.

At that point, we were temporarily satisfied and were on our way back outdoors to get on with the work.

Often we were picking corn those afternoons, and the fellow, who was hauling loads of corn in from the field and empty wagons back out repeatedly, stopped by the house to check on the pies' progress.

How often I remember halting the tractor and loaded wagon on the driveway, locking the brakes and dashing to the house to gobble down steaming pumpkin pie. Though it burned my tongue, that didn't

matter. It was savory, too gingery, just too good for me to wait a second longer to devour.

The pies were always gone before the weekend was.

And if we begged enough, Mother might get around to making pumpkin pies again the next weekend.

In the years after I left the farm, Mother loyally went on making those pumpkin pies that made my taste buds celebrate. She always managed each fall to somehow send one or two pies to me when I was at college in Ames. And there were times when my rushed weekends home were just to get some of Mother's homemade pumpkin pies.

I don't know how she made them, and made them so good. I only know there were few pleasures greater than biting into a piece of her hot, spicy pumpkin pie on a Saturday afternoon in October.

SILO SO LOW, SO FILL IT

In late summer, my father surveyed his cornfields. The poorest of the fields that still showed some green in their leaves and their stalks were chosen for the silo – selected to be zipped from their roots, then pulverized to make succulent fodder to be packed away in 40- and 60-foot tall salad bowls – or silos.

Silo filling marked the beginning of doing something about harvesting that corn crop.

Cutting silage was the first of the fall harvesting activities where a farmer found himself without his youngsters to help out. School swept them away. That where-did-they-go feeling came over a farmer as he attached the corn head to the chopper, got its knives sharpened, positioned the blower beside the silo and bolted all the silo pipe together.

At the threshold of my memories are the shadowy recollections of walking in a circle on the inside of my Uncle Don's silo on his farm outside Polk City, Iowa, where we lived for seven years. I was there, my 45-pound body trying to pack down the newly ground, bright greet pulp of fresh, unfermented silage. It smelled intoxicatingly sweet.

The shredded cornstalks poured down out of a connected series of tubing suspended from the spout at the top of the silo. My mother grasped the tubing and directed the jet of silage around the ever higher floor of the silo.

A high-pitched hum came from the silo filler as it spun empty. Then it bore down and lowered its roar as chopped corn was fed along the apron of the hopper into the spinning paddles that flailed the fresh corn salad up the pipe, where it hit the semi-circle spout and was shot in an opposite direction to our feet.

The silage shot out in a barrage, pelting our wet boots. The sounds of the corn pounding through the silo pipe reverberated around the circular silo walls.

In many succeeding years of filling silo, I became more directly involved in the activity. Most often, I was stationed at the rear of a mammoth chopping wagon, pulling mounds of chopped corn out of an automatic unloading wagon. I used a special silage fork (made almost like a four-tine pitchfork, but with the tines bent at a 90-degree angle to the handle).

The apron in the bottom of the wagon shoved back its 7-foot high chunk of packed, chopped corn. As the mound passed out and over the conveyor belt hopper below, the protruding chunk collapsed into fodder. The faster-moving apron grabbed the material and sent it on a collision course with the gyrating blower wheel.

Often too much new silage went into the blower at once and plugged the pipes, taking it skyward. The blower had to then be shut off and the wad of chopped cornstalks dug out of the piping. Sometimes, too, the spout at the top of the pipe wasn't properly directed toward the middle of the silo. Instead the silage overshot the silo and came showering down on us below.

One of us then would have to climb up a ladder on the outside of the silo, get into a simple caged platform we called "the crow's nest," then unwire that spout. It had to be twisted into the right position, then wired down again.

There in the crow's nest, I gazed down, down below to the vast, empty silo. It seemed the huge container would require weeks to fill. However, it took only days of steady work. And outside the structure was a silo-sitter's view of the boy-size machines.

The piping to take up the side of the silo was assembled from 4-foot sections laid end to end on the cow lot ground. It was a grand spectacle to watch a rope, pulley and tractor lift the yards of 8-inch pipe into place on the outside of the silo. The rope was hooked to the tractor's front end. The tractor would inch backwards, pulling the long, steel tube,

first stretched on the ground, upwards from a horizontal to a vertical position.

The man on the ground clutched the bottom end of the pipe and walked it around to where the blower was already planted, next to the silo. He then placed it on top of the blower. By then, the pipe was pulled to its full height above. Once the spout was twisted at the top of the silo to face it in the right direction, the clamp was thrown around the collar at the bottom of the pipe, locking the massive tube of steel to the blower.

And we were ready to "fill silo."

CORN'S BITTER END

Drained of their green, now bleached cardboard brown, the stiff cornstalks cling to their yellow fruit, tucked up under their paper leaves.

In rigid silence, the jointed stalks hold fast to that spot where they burst forth from seeds last May. Their long, broomstick-like spines loom up from a tired, toiled soil – from an earth that was eroded, parched and glazed by a crystal frost at points during the growing season.

Tassels, which reveled in symmetric glory atop fields of lush green when summer was celebrated, now hang precariously to pithy stalks.

A wind gust or perhaps blackbirds will rip them loose, hurdling the ragged tassels into the dead dryness at the floor of the cornfield.

The Iowa farmers' grandest gardens appear dead, inert, dry. But the golden grains are not dry. They need an Indian summer's charm to draw forth the moisture that was sought so earnestly in the arid days of July. Moisture once wanted is now moisture unwanted.

Now in the waning days of the crop year, as those ears hang in wait of harvest, the destiny of that corn is unknown. Will it go into a dozen augers and countless bins en route to an overseas buyer to feed to foreign creatures or to feed people on other continents?

Then there's the matter of prices. The golden grain's future sale price is too unknown – as unknown as the weather is uncertain on the day the corn will be picked. What it will sell for will depend on the notions, moods, optimism, insights and economic intelligence of well-dressed men in the pits of the commodity markets. It will depend on the political whims of Washington and Wall Street, the caprice of

commodity barons, the buying temperament of foreign governments, and the judgment of American grain producers.

Meanwhile, the tattered cornstalks clutch their hardening fruit until man's machines wrestle it away from them.

LIKE CHICKEN THIEVES, WE HOUSED PULLETS

Early darkness that descends over the land in November sends chore workers racing to complete the last tasks of the day.

The fading light bleeds into cold opaqueness. The transition spells the start of night farming operations, all done beneath yard lights, flashlights, machinery headlights and naked fly-stained bulbs in scattered sheds and barns.

We used to spend those kinds of nights stomping through the darkness with handfuls of squawking pullets.

Came fall and fowl needed permanent shelter. The impending operation of housing pullets was faced with displeasure. It meant gathering protesting pullets, tearing them from roosts in brooder houses and stumbling through freezing darkness to cages. There we would stuff the pullets headlong into the wire cages arranged in rows on a hayrack. The flat rack would transport them to lighted hen houses several hundred yards away once we had gathered a full load.

These June-hatched pullets would just be starting to lay eggs by November. The young, lean birds expelled crude, misshapen, undersized eggs to start their productive careers. And they were "unhenlike" in where they chose to lay them. Instead of improvising nests, they deposited eggs in the middle of the brooder house floor or in the chicken yard next to the waterer.

We would have as many as 1,800 white pullets on the threshold of henhood. To make room for them in the hen houses, we culled and sold most of the old hens. They were sent off to the butcher for chicken soup.

Once the last feather had fallen during the coops' coup d'état, the manure in the four buildings was hauled out, wooden roots were scraped of dried chicken wastes and walls and equipment were washed down. A lye water disinfectant was used to thoroughly soak the floors and walls to rid the surroundings of mites and other poultry pests that tormented the former boarders.

Straw or ground corn cobs were then spread about the floors for bedding. We were ready to move in a new generation of egg layers.

As many as 200 pullets could be accommodated at one time in the compartmentalized cages that sat in three rows on the wagon.

Like chicken thieves, we stole into the brooder houses just after darkness and began the resettlement project.

Dad usually pulled the birds from the roosts. He then knocked down their flapping wings until they hung upside down, their necks craned upward. The rude interruption of their sleep set off cackles of disbelief and defiance. Our father put together trios or quartets of the vocal protesters to hand off. Their chorus was a cacophony, often led by the old roosters that were being left behind in the sheds for late fall slaughter.

We chicken runners would latch our gloved hands around the collection of bony legs. "I'll take another one," one of us would say occasionally when the handful was light. Then with six or eight pullets, we would walk across the manure-greased chicken yard to the crates. Somebody, usually Mother, would take them from us and shove the birds head-first into the crates. A tractor's light and a flashlight aided the doorkeeper.

Every now and then a chicken would be accidentally dropped. Our dog, Buddy, was artful at running down the fleeing pullets. He'd pin them down by their necks until one of us retrieved them.

The weight of fidgeting chickens and the cold made our hands get cramps. As the night wore on, we kids cut down on the number of pullets we could carry.

We would haul pullets for five hours or longer before we quit. Sometimes, it was as late as midnight when we housed the last pullet.

It would take several nights until all the pullets were transferred. But a number of the young hens remained at large. They strayed off in the days and decided not to go back to the brooder houses at night to roost. Instead, they would roost in the trees or on a piece of farm equipment in the grove.

So we would spend yet another night in the last round-up. We used long wires with hooks on their ends – called chicken catchers – to reach high into trees or shed rafters and pull them down. Often pullets roosted so high in trees that we had to heave rocks, boards or other available projectiles at them to knock them back to earth where a foot

race through the darkness ensued. It was always several weeks before the last fugitive was caught and locked away in the hen house.

Finally, all was ready for the snow to fly. It wasn't long before the chicken yard, which had been picked clean of vegetation, was buried in snow.

And those "spring chickens" were, by that time, locked into a roost-to-feeder-to-nest-to-feeder-to-roost daily pattern. We were carrying baskets of eggs through the night instead of pullets.

WINTER WATCH

FIGHTING OFF THE FIRST FLAKES

The first snowfall, no matter how insignificant, gains notice. For those first flakes, regardless what the calendar says, make it winter. They had to come. Yet, the snow's stay that first time will be brief. The landscape unites to stave off the first flakes with its waning heat.

There on the granary roof, the tumbling flakes alight and turn instantly to dull gray slush, then to dripping wetness, slurring down the shingles.

The silence of the phenomenon is incredible. Millions of ragged slivers of ice slide out of the sky and plummet to earth without making a sound. Dickens described it by saying, "The old lady in the sky is picking her geese pretty hard today."

The snow falls at its own risk. Some flakes dissolve to their liquid form as they settle down onto machinery still warm from use. The fluff sizzles to steam when it collides with a tractor exhaust pipe or the woodburning heater in the livestock tank down by the barn.

Flakes dive into that tank water, sinking in cold silence, each flake's stunning whiteness gone. Instantly the flakes' intricate configurations are snuffed out on contact with the water.

Yet some of the minute scales of ice find toeholds in cold crevices or recesses where they may survive through the fickle winter. Between old boards, along stumps in the grove and on dead grass of a fence line, the flakes find friendly landing.

They alight and gather on the head of a dairy cow, and she shakes her ears, bats her eyes and causes the hide of her shoulders to quiver as if she were trying to drive off summer flies.

First snows aren't welcomed on silage piles exuding their great internal heat from fermenting. In the same way, if the flakes fall onto a pile of rich, undecomposed manure, the subtle heat from it will dissolve the icy fallout. The farm fights off the first flakes of winter.

Snowflakes distribute themselves so arbitrarily. What blankets the deadness at the vegetable garden could have fallen on a Dubuque golf course or a tenement roof in Chicago. Each flake, while ever so unique to the microscopic eye, has no more individuality than a kernel of corn in a grain bin.

Across the pastures, worn paths are erased. All shades of fall's browns are sheathed in white – a white that muffles the sounds of the countryside and has a disquieting effect on the spirit of man, faced again with his annual adversary, winter.

SENDING THE CALVES HOME THROUGH THE DARK

There must be something about snow – the way it erases the details of the landscape and brings the distances into greater focus – that stirs creatures to wander across its expanse in quest of something beyond.

Our herd of Holstein calves and heifers were nomads in the snowy heart of winter, lured by the wild fields of snow to set out into it in search of feed and, perhaps, adventure.

We kept the younger cattle on our north farm, located more than a mile across the largely unfenced fields from the home farm where the regular dairy herd was kept.

As the weeks after corn picking built into months on our farm, winter took over like a lazy polar bear about to relax on a floating mass of ice, burying us in smothering whiteness.

With the snows, the young cattle left the lot. They tramped across the wizened cornstalks where they had recently foraged and made a beeline southeasterly to the fields around our home place.

In an hour, they had integrated our main 25-cow dairy herd. They showed off and behaved as if they belonged there. The cocky calves

sidled up to the hay bunks and jockeyed for room at the silage bunks at the foot of the silo. The same menu, of course, awaited them at the north farm.

Our only means of sorting them was to drive the milk cows into the newly bedded stalls in the barn. If all went well, the calves and heifers stayed outside. They bawled like waifs when the barn door slammed shut. There in the cold twilight stood as many as 60 furry calves, which needed to be herded back to the North Place where they belonged.

By the time I crawled into more layers of clothing to make the march and had located a flashlight that actually worked, it was dark.

The cattle grudgingly turned their heads northward and trudged across the crusty snow. In time, they were stretched out, most of them tramping to a cadence in the paths ground out by the cattle walking point.

The only sound to intrude the chilled stillness was the crunch of hooves and the papery rip of cornstalks being kicked by the calves shuffling across the field.

The snow cover gave ample reflection to the moon's light, enough for me to survey all flanks of the procession.

Eventually the angular route they took led into a fence row, diverting them in a straight north trajectory. The tall, slender remains of last summer's ragweed no longer concealed the woven wire fence.

The dead weeds provided me with long, woody spears. I couldn't resist pulling them out of the ground to heave at the calves trailing at the rear of the string of homebound beasts. But the sting did little to advance them along more quickly.

In time, the fence row abruptly turned 90 degrees to the west, and the string of calves plodded northwesterly across stubble ground.

The cold ground stabbed at my feet, although the layers of clothing kept the rest of me warm.

Eventually, the herd reached the cow lot on the north farm, where they immediately crowded up to the silage and hay bunks for a homecoming meal.

I pulled the old wooden gate shut on the cow yard. That would keep them close to home tonight.

And my dad would be there waiting with the warm car to take me home.

SOWS, SNOW AND SNOOZING

Sows catch up on sleep when the snow flies. It's hard to arouse the old swine when a snowstorm is wailing outside.

I recall how drifts would meet the slanting roofs of the hog houses. Jets of whisked snow shot up the roofs of the sheds like a water skier soaring up a ramp.

But inside the sheds slept the old sows, piled together like a half dozen 100-pound gunny sacks filled with soybean meal stored in a warehouse for delayed delivery. Now and then, the sows would shift their weight, each trying to hang onto – or to increase – her body contact with the other lethargic sows around her. In the shuffle, some old sow stood to lose her warm place in the pack. A warm rump would get pushed out of the pile, and an entire leg of another brood sow gained entry to the cozy hog flesh.

Now and then, an ear would be bitten. There would be an angry snort, and the whole pile of pork would shuffle. In snarling grunts, they would make charges and countercharges. But in no time, the lazy swine would slip back into their group snooze.

And all would be silent, except for the muffled fury of the wind trying to blast away the roof or else grind it off by pelting it with millions of abrasive snowflakes.

Why should an old sow not stay up with a storm and wait for it to blow itself out? Perhaps her unmindful sleep stems from some latent instinct to hibernate, to huddle together with other sows in passive and oblivious sleep until the last snowdrift has been carved.

I've stomped through deep, new snow to liberate batches of sows holed up inside cozy, portable hog houses – when a storm was over. There were times the snow had completely blocked the 3-foot high doors, sealing in the sows and their body heat.

My aluminum scoop shovel would slip easily into the snow. Then when I lifted the bulky, but light, chunks of snow, they would all suddenly crumble. And the powdery snow would be whipped up into my face. It was a zesty sensation.

Snow that reached well into the hog house, but was, nevertheless, part of the drifts, was wilted from the absorption of body heat.

I'd open the walkway to the outdoors for the awakening sows. In an open place in the snow, I'd dump a bushel of ear corn. From the barn, across snow, I would drag bales of straw to heave into their beds.

When the sows returned from eating, they took quick command of the cakes of straw. They latched their jaws to yellow mats of bedding, and then, as if to shake their heads in an emphatic "NO!," they shook the cakes into fluffy bedding. All the sows worked together, tearing each lump into shreds. They set off a dusty, chaffy cloud of oat dust that would send an asthmatic to Arizona for the winter.

So the sows would get their stomachs filled with corn, make a trip to the waterer or eat snow, and then go back to bed for another sow slumber party session. The first one in got in the middle. She was usually on the softest part for the sleep-in. Moreover, the sow getting there first was assured of being blanketed by more warm bodies than any other member of that soporific sow sorority.

WHEN SNOWBALLS HIT THE BARN

Pow! A snowball disintegrated above my head over the milk house door.

Ping! A harder one exploded on an empty 10-gallon milk can, causing a dull ring and leaving the can plastered with a rough blot of compressed snow.

Mervan Meyer grinned at the sheer might of his last two terrorizing hurls. We had been flinging the nuggets of snow for nearly 15 minutes. The snow had been ripe for warfare. And every stationary object in our path was dotted with the huge splotches of snow.

Our farm, like any farm, afforded countless types of fortifications for assault and retreat for snowball fights.

Only exhaustion or a parent demanding we get back to the chores could bring about a pacification of the farmstead.

The battle went on. I retreated behind a stack of milk cans, about eight of them stacked two high. From behind it, I tossed a volley of snowballs. But being in the shade, the snow was somewhat powdery and not ideal for snowballs.

Merv, easily evading my tosses, repeatedly bent down and scooped up handfuls of the cheap armament from the farm driveway. His orange, cotton farm gloves, like mine, were soaked.

I took time to construct a quality snowball, round and firm with a built-in sting. Like a steel spring, I swiftly unwound my arm and flung the ball of snow with Whitey Ford zing at my best friend who lived across the road. All the kinetics were right. It was on target. Merv abandoned his notion to dodge it in a flash and impulsively threw up his right hand and halted the fistful of snow.

The snowball detonated in his wet glove, colliding in a muffled outburst. He let out a howl, shook his stung hand, and, in the next motion, he prepared his retaliation.

I sought refuge behind a silage wagon, hoping he would wastefully dispose of his snowballs, assembled in anger, by blindly tossing them in my direction and wear himself out. That would give me time to plan my next offensive.

How often we had exhausted each other in countless one-on-one sports. The way he fired snowballs wasn't much different from his style in flinging the many baseballs, softballs, rubber balls or even walnuts. A southpaw, or lefty, Merv wielded a good curve. His accuracy carried over to snowballs.

But this wasn't a time to catch snowballs. He unleashed a barrage of quickly squeezed together, poorly designed snowballs and pelted the silage wagon. We moved on to the chicken house. From behind corners of the building, we fired at each other. When one hard ball of snow smacked in thunderous explosion against the side of the hen house, it triggered a fluttering riot inside. In mass hysteria, the frightened hens flew and hurled their clumsy bodies against each other and at the walls.

That was enough. It was getting dark anyway, and farm chores were waiting. We had both gotten hit repeatedly, but our layers of sweatshirts and long johns had cushioned the snowballs. Our sleeves and gloves were sopping wet and cold, our faces rosy, our noses running, and our bodies sweating inside our clothing.

There was no post-skirmish bitterness, as I turned my attention to the dairy cows and told Merv goodbye in the fading light that hung over our snowy battlefield.

KICKING LOOSE THE ICE IN HOG PANS

I don't know how many round hog pans you've had to turn upside down to stomp with your feet to shake loose solid chunks of ice, then refilled them with water for an old sow or chickens in outbuildings on a cold winter day.

And I don't know how many times you have managed to pry loose a long, steel trough full of ice, then struggled to lift it up on one end before shoving it back to the ground in hopes of jolting loose its slab of ice.

Perhaps, your cow tank never produced what for us was always the largest round ice cube on our farm.

In the heart of winter, we used to produce ice in more shapes than the Play-Doh people could count. Wherever at least one head of livestock had to have water, it seemed that hours later, the beast had a lump of ice that needed to be crushed, dumped, melted or pried loose.

And the longer the cold spells lasted, the more the lumps of pounded-free ice served as evidence of the frustrating winter.

To delay the freeze, we started out hauling them pails of hot water.

The cow tank, an 8-foot diameter concrete slab container, was our greatest challenge. The water there seemingly preferred to be a solid rather than a liquid.

The tank heater was nailed securely to parts of railroad ties, thus anchoring it to the floor of the 2 ½-foot deep tank at the edge of the cow lot. Rocks gave extra weight. One of the first chores in the morning was trying to get the heater blazing in an effort to change the iceberg, which encased the heater, back into the drinking water it had been the day before – no small task.

With fuel oil, newspapers and even waste paper from the house, we succeeded in getting a fire started. Cobs, wood and coal kept it going, too.

With any kind of luck and a lot of smoke, a rim of melted water soon appeared around the sides of the heater. It steadily widened.

In time, we turned on the water faucet and let water bathe the top of the huge ice disc, now looking more like a donut. That fresh water helped to melt the ice, too.

When the cows were turned out of the barn where they were kept all night, they rushed to the tank and stretched their necks toward the middle where the heater had made the water most tolerable to drink.

Sometimes we took the axe to the ice to speed up the melting. In blow after blow, we sprinkled our clothing with wet chips of ice. The heater could never convert all the ice to water. The best approach to watering the cattle was to give them plenty of tap water while they were out there drinking. But the tank was not to be left full of water when the cows returned to the barn for the night. Water left was just more water to freeze solid.

Often, even the tank hydrant was frozen and could not send forth water. We then had to water the cows in the barn without turning them out of their stanchions. We simply hooked up a garden hose to the milk house hydrant and stuck its end into a bucket or aluminum bushel basket. We went from cow to cow, giving them their fill of water. They could drink as fast as they water came from the hose.

Those hardships were the best reasons for the development of electrically heated livestock waterers, which guaranteed every farm creature a drink of water at any time.

THE CAT IN WINTER

Where are they now? Where have all those hordes of cats gone? Those happy cats and motley litters of playful kittens that roamed the farmstead last summer?

Where are those kittens this bleak January, this dismal period that is, in every way, the antithesis of the grand summer of their birth?

In June or July, they were surely everywhere. Their mothers chose their birthplaces with care and imagination – obscure hideaways in haymows, feed rooms and sheds. In time the kittens outgrew their sanctuaries and romped in ever-wider territory. If their mothers were nomadic, the kittens were picked up and moved often to new haunts.

An industrious mother cat hauled them fresh birds and mice or cast-off farm kitchen food during their pre-weaning days. As she carried them bird corpses and wiggly mice, her milk-gland swollen belly swayed to and fro.

All too often, the kittens were weaned, set loose to fend for themselves or live off the charity of the farm family.

Many went to begging at the door of the farmhouse where they lived off welfare. They wailed for handouts, wrestled in the dust of the dooryard and slept amid the marigolds.

Eventually their innocent summer came to an end. Then they stiffened with the coming of chilly nights. Days lost their charm. The first raw winds of fall wafted their fur. Rain drove them under cover. They retreated to windbreaks, went under porches, sought buildings warmed by livestock.

Older doorstep loafers knew enough to move permanently to the cow barn. But kittens, bewildered by the turn in the weather, held steadfastly to the front steps, crying in futility to be let in, to be rescued from the cold rain. Like paupers at a castle door, they earnestly desired to live in the elegance afforded within.

Then came distemper and pneumonia. The youngest and weakest crawled off to die first, too unprepared to endure winter. By steady attrition, the numbers continued to decline. They perished like starving pilgrims of the first winter in America.

Darwin's law prevailed. The fittest survived. Often those survivors were the earliest-born kittens that year. Or those that had spent the summer learning self-sufficiency and independence also tended to survive winter's unapologetic assault.

But for most of the kittens, their nine lives were spent before Christmas.

WINTER'S RELENTLESS GRIP

Winter's continuum – its prolonged and erratic way of mingling pleasant days with cheerless weeks – holds farm activities in somber check until that season finally breaks its hold.

The end of winder rarely comes until the end of winter. Nice days can come in mid-winter, but they're only transient and fleeting, mere respites for the winter to relax its muscles in order to get a firmer hold.

The piles of snow can finally melt on the barn roof and drip, drip, drip to the livestock feeding floor, there to wash a straight furrow in the manure along the barn. But icicles form subtly again, and waters

are locked for at least another day on the roof. And what snow had been safely on the roof is now making a treacherous sheath of ice on the ground.

During January's thaw, corn fields reveal fallen ears and cobs with a few grains still intact for beef cattle and hogs. The livestock take to the fields to fend for the morsels of corn that never got into the grain circuit to go to Japan, New Orleans or the local elevator.

The flanks of dairy cattle are stained by innumerable times they have lain in manure in lots and barns. Other cattle, which have spent the full winter in a feedlot, carry pounds of mud and excrement on their thighs. It clings to their long winter coats like an armor.

But no longer do they stand with the backs bent high, braced against the wind, trying to withstand the cold. They stomp and swing their tails and even bolt across the muddy lot. They skid in the ooze and kick up mud.

Dirty snow festers along fence rows and in ditches, shrinking downward each day. Out of the bottom of the snowbank trickles water bound for the nearest stream, though it may freeze several times before it actually reaches it. It surely has to be viewed in January as a wasted melt – a thaw at a time when hopes are needlessly raised. For though the grand earth feels the warmth of the sun for the first time in months, there will be another snow to cover it all shortly.

Lethargic creeks sluggishly move again when a thaw occurs. Snows in fields dissolve, exposing the remains of last year's crop, just a brown stubble stamped flat by winter's ice.

Spring will come a half-dozen times now before spring comes. It will wither each time the weather turns for the worst. Weather at winter's end is eccentric and temperamental. It gives up reluctantly, begrudgingly, deceptively – and only when the season is right.

LESSONS FROM THE LAND

A TRACTOR TRUCE

My country school pals were some great friends, but there were four of us boys who found one subject upon which we could not agree. And we'd argue and debate that issue in our simple logic all the way through recess and pick it up at the next recess.

It had to do with the best makes of tractors.

We came from different farms where three different brands of tractors ruled the fields in the mid-1950s. We were all vocally zealous about the kind of tractors and types of machinery our fathers operated. Nobody could tell us our dads, in all their wisdom, didn't know and use the best kind of tractor on the market. For they were certainly wise men about such things.

Our one-room school, Beaver No. 2, sat on a hill. Like most rural schools, it was at a corner where two county gravel roads intersected. From our school, we had an excellent view of the daily machinery parade, featuring the finest machinery of 1955.

Many tractors would speed by. Some carried our fathers, breezing by on their state-of-the-art, powerful tractors. They flew by in "road gear," slowing down at the corner, only to gun their tractor motors again once they were past the intersection. Our fathers and other farmers gave us school boys idle entertainment and plenty to talk about.

These tractors were often bound for fields. The kinds of machinery they towed or the equipment mounted on them showed what they were about to do in the fields encircling the rural school – four square miles of 640 acres each coming together at four corners at our school.

Some tractors would be bound for the two nearby towns, Stout or Sinclair to buy or sell grain or feed. Later we'd see or hear the tractors on their return trips.

So while today's school students may learn amid the din of cars, trucks and buses on city streets, we heard tractors on the roads and in the fields.

We boys couldn't, and never did, agree on the superiority of any single tractor. Mervan Meyer, who was 7, boasted that an International Farmall Super M was the final version in the development of the tractor. And the "M" was only approached in performance by a Farmall H, Merv would say. Needless to say, his father had both.

Now Leland Heine, also 7, and in the second grade, was the John Deere proponent. He was saying, "Nothing runs like a Deere" long before the company was saying it in its advertising. The John Deere of that period had two cylinders and made a "putt-putt" sound that was characteristically a "Deere." With only half as many cylinders as the rest of ours, a Deere was gasping for breath and was working "half a deck," we contended.

As for my twin brother and me, age 8 and third graders, we were positive the Massey-Harris (forerunner of the Massey-Ferguson) was God's gift to farming. We had three of those incomparable red machines with bright yellow-gold wheels. Our two 44-Specials and a 44-Six Cylinder were certainly outnumbered in the territory by Deeres, Farmalls, Cases, Olivers, Allis-Chalmers and Fords, but we said it was quality and not quantity that counted.

Our arguments focused on brute strength, a kind of "power politics," which included insults, name-calling and even some crying. We always bet our tractors, if individually pitted against theirs in a tug-of-war fashion, would drag their spinning, lurching machines over the horizon. However, our fathers never were convinced to carry out such tractor pulls "so we could show those guys once and for all."

Somewhere along the way, we agreed to a tractor truce. We wouldn't let tractors be driven between us.

In the years that followed, all three farmers crossed the battle lines and bought other makes of tractors. My father alone was to have three Farmalls and a John Deere in addition to his Massey-Harris models.

That spirited competition in agriculture at all levels still goes on. Farm boys still argue the merits of machinery brands or tractor models

on the school bus or in vocational agriculture class. In more subtle ways, perhaps, their fathers carry on their competition, as they try to out-plow or over-harvest their neighbors with different machinery – all of which they firmly stand behind.

And it goes on in all forms of competition: Angus versus Hereford cattle, Pioneer versus Funks seed brand, plastic tiling versus clay tile. It's part of the tremendous beauty of rural choices. No one can tell you what's the best.

BATTING ROCKS OVER THE BARN

No one has batted more stones over the top of the barn roof than I have.

To me, each rock that ever hummed off the end of a flat stick and soared over the barn was a home run.

When spring loosened the earth's hold on the rocks on the farm driveway and America was alive with baseball talk, rock after rock shot over the top of the barn to the terror of pigeons.

It took a special knack to be able to toss up a stone with the left hand, then grasp the flat stick with both hands, then smack the rock on its way downward. Timing was critical. Struck with the right upward swing of the crude bat, the stone would take off with a snap and shoot in a high trajectory over the barn roof. Before it had struck the ground, silo or cow, I had another rock in my hand.

A seasoned veteran of rock batting knows it takes a fine hunk of wood, ideally with a flat side, to slug rocks the farthest. A tapering handle, which can be tightly gripped, also helps the stone stroker get a good cut. Actually all the bats I used when I was a kid were just splintered boards or slats, rarely more than three inches across and usually about 30 to 36 inches long. All were retrieved from the castoff board pile.

During chores and afterwards, I would stand outside on the driveway and slap rocks over the barn. Often I would take a break from milking as I waited for the milking machines to finish squeezing out what the "slow milking" cows gave up leisurely. At other times, I'd slug the rocks down the driveway over electric wires or over fences along

the road. Some rocks buzzed or hummed at different pitches before hitting the ground.

Anything could be my imaginary stadium wall over which I was slamming game-winning home runs. I swatted so many stones without stopping that an ear could note a cadence to my sport.

My cheap bats were first dented by the wallops, then splintered by the constant impact of the ragged rocks against the wood. When the sticks finally disintegrated, I simply retrieved new ones. Good wood like elm or ash held up the longest.

I had to be careful where I'd put down my bat. To other persons, my bat was just another stick. Sometimes they'd grab it, unaware it was my current rock bat. They'd use it to drive livestock or hold a door to a shed open and invariably abandon it somewhere else.

Sure, I broke a few windows and chipped a little paint off machinery – all accidentally, of course. And I suppose the barn roof suffered from being pelted by stones that never made it over the top.

A lot of "foul balls" went awry. Luckily they never hit or hurt anyone. However, more than one cow or duck was unavoidably stung by a rock.

I hit so many driveway rocks over the barn, the cow lot seemed to have a harder surface than the driveway, or so I figured.

A rock that struck the upper half of the roof was considered a triple. Hitting the lower half gave me a double in my fantasies. If it was a line drive that struck the side of the barn, it was just a "close call" with a window.

While getting the cows, I'd bat anything I could find along the way: a cob, a walnut, the head of a bull thistle, a jimson weed pod or a piece of bone. And in my imaginative mind, I was Rocky Colavito or Stan Musial or Jackie Jensen, hammering the home runs that saved the day. I was a one-man "farm team."

Sure, I was sort of a hazard. Batting rocks was dangerous. But the rocks and board bats were free, and that barn, looming up more than a stone's throw away, dared me to bat a rock over it.

MAP ON THE DRIVEWAY DIRT

So often I recall the frustration of my father, vexed by the mistakes, carelessness or poor job of a farmhand who lacked the same zeal my dad had for excellence in the performance of a farm task.

How clearly I remember the times he put a teenager from town to work on a field job. There on the hard dirt of the driveway leading into the field, he got down on his hands and knees to give the youth his instructions.

Dad grasped a stick and used it to draw a rough map of the field lying before them. In his forever hurried impatience, he gave the town kid a logistics lesson on how the rookie was to rake that hay. The youth squatted over the map. With an uncharacteristic reticence, the kid stared at the scratched dirt, trying to imagine it represented that expanse of drying alfalfa in front of them.

Dad's loud, rushed words of instruction danced across the field like the butterflies that flitted about in the heat of the June morning in quest of blossoms to land on.

"Now you've gotta rake twice around the piece this way. Then when ya get to this corner, bring the rake…" His arms waved and his voice raised, as he explained the simple maneuvers. The kid from town nodded politely.

But they were only half communicating – that man who had never lived any of his 50 years off a farm and the teenager whose days on a farm could be counted on one hand.

And my father ground his short stick into the dirt and went round and round in his earlier marked grooves in the hard soil. His motions were to simulate the route of the hay rake. Finally, they got up, abandoned the crude map and went to actually raking.

Somehow the kid from town got onto how the hay was to be raked, although he left plenty of mowed hay on the ground not turned over and put into a windrow. And some windrows were gobbed up into monstrous bunches that would invariably plug up the baler and lead to sheared pins on the baler's fly wheel.

Over the years, more than a hundred men and boys, drifters and hometown stock, some talented and others ne'er-do-wells, worked for periods of hours to years on our farms. Some went on to be professors, chiropractors, social workers, teachers and factory workers. Others went

to prison, died in high-speed crashes, wasted away with alcoholism or vanished from the area when they go itchy feet, filching as much from our farm as they could before they departed.

But what made the most difference was how they did their jobs: how dependable they were at feeding the sows in the farrowing stalls, how conscientious they were in cultivating the corn and not tearing it out, how careful they were in putting an overhauled engine back together, how safety-conscious they were in avoiding a tractor fire while picking corn, how kind they were to dairy cows, how diligent they were when they mowed hay along the fence line and how mindful they were about closing gates on pastures.

We could forgive a lot of their foul talk, their stormy backgrounds, their penchant for the nightlife and cross temperaments the next day. We didn't fret over their inexperience, their moral character or their fussy eating habits.

But we did decry poor job performances, carelessness, ill treatment of livestock and wasting bushels of grain in the field.

Many neighbors avoided hiring outside help as much as possible. Or they paid a premium for those men who had the special diligence and same regard for a good job well done

A fascinating cross-section of mankind mounted our tractors, flung hay bales, unloaded manure spreaders and buried weeds behind the cultivator on our farm. While most were able-bodied, only some showed what they could do or would do, and that's what frustrated my father.

THE RAT RACE WHEN WE MOVED HOG SHEDS

Rearrange the furniture and other trappings of your house, and the old shelter takes on a new look that's refreshing and gives it a new dimension.

Move the buildings around on your farm to make them more accessible, and it not only changes the farming and chore patterns, but it affords a pleasing shift of the scene.

A number of buildings on our farm were erected on 4 by 4-inch or 4 by 6-inch skids. The skids would act like sled runners and made the buildings portable. Small granaries, hog houses and brooder houses all had sets of skids.

Attached to the skids on each end were No. 9 wire or steel loops. We could fasten log chains to the loops and tow the buildings to new sites around the farm.

Most of the rearranging involved poultry and swine sheds. The hog houses were moved about with no regularity, but brooder houses were moved each spring to clean, grassy parts of the pasture. There, the baby chicks would spend the spring, summer and first part of the fall, going through the transition from chick to pullet to hen.

The announcement that a building would be moved generated excitement for us kids and several farm dogs. Moving buildings meant races after rats, as we tried to e-RAT-icate them from the premises.

The wooden floors of the sheds were never sealed well enough to prevent feed from filtering down to the ground. Hog or poultry bedding also worked down through the floors to make an ideal habitat for rats and mice. We could always expect some kind of rodent or an entire family of mice and rats to be living under hog and brooder houses.

At shed-moving time, at least, it was disappointing if we didn't find any of those creatures living under them. Our corncribs were nearby and accessible to the rodents. Thus, the pests had an ideal living environment.

We were their worst enemies.

Once the big tractor was backed up to the shed, we would have to take a pick axe to dig loose the hitching loops and the front of the skids. We might also have to go along the edge of the buildings with a heavy bar and pry loose the skids to get them sliding along.

When the tractor moved forward and the log chain tightened, the machine groaned, the big tires bit into the ground, and the shed began to move from its spot.

By that time, all the rest of us and the dogs were circled around the shed, all in a frenzy of readiness. We were armed with wooden clubs. We shook them around in anticipation. We called out to the cats, and some of them were on the scene, ready for action.

Without warning, terrified rats began darting out in a blind run. They charged in all directions. Yelping dogs got to the first rats. They took great care to latch onto the rats and clench the critters in their mouths without being bitten. The hounds shook the rats over their heads and crushed the rodents' spines.

We ran down other scuttling rats and smashed them with our clubs.

That "rat race" was a cacophony of commotion. Dogs barked. The tractor groaned. We shouted in somewhat squeamish delight. "Here comes another one!" we'd shout, almost in unison. And we gave chase again. We were always afraid a rat would run up our pant legs. We had to watch out that we didn't club a dog, a cat or a brother while swinging at a rat.

And the poor fellow on the tractor had the boring duty of pulling the shed onward to a new spot. He missed the chance to exterminate rats.

Once the band of rodents was either wiped out or the escapees were long gone, we scratched around in the straw and dirt where the shed had rested, searching for any more rats that might have hidden instead of run.

The entire adventure was repeated as we moved other buildings that day. When it was over, we piled up the dead rodents that the cats hadn't already devoured or hadn't dragged away to their kittens. We fed them to the cats in the barn – those cats that hadn't shown up for the massacre.

The same kind of bedlam occurred in the final stages of corn shelling, too. As we shoveled the last few hundred bushels of corn from the cribs into the sheller, mice began fleeing in every direction. It was easy to run them down, and the cats were there in large numbers, killing mice faster than they could wolf them down.

Yes, it all sounds barbaric and gruesome to anyone who hasn't known the no-win situation of rats on a farm. We had rats despite poisons, cats and even guinea hens (fowl that were supposed to scare them off). We felt we gave our rats a setback every time we wiped out a colony under the hog or brooder houses.

LINCOLN TOOK 'EM FLYING

Starting the summer of our 17th year, my twin brother, Lincoln, began what he had wanted to do all his life – learn to fly. That step was preceded by his launching of hundreds of balsa, aluminum, plastic and paper planes – an epic story in itself, marked by countless adventures and misadventures.

That summer, he abandoned farm work and drove several times a week to the Waterloo Municipal Airport to undertake flying instruction. Then, seemingly in no time, they had Lincoln up in the air, first with an instructor, then going solo. He was flying across the wide blue yonder, flying the friendly skies over our farm.

With each solo trip, he became more and more competent and self-confident. Through that summer before our senior year of high school, farm work became fully unappealing to Lincoln. His mind was on flying. Often I'd have to take his place driving the hay mower or doing his hog chores, so he could go for another lesson.

He would drive to Waterloo, and some 15 minutes after his expected arrival there, our sister Linda and I would have our eyes scanning the afternoon skies in search of a speck that would turn into a growling, humming Piper Cherokee. One of us grounded souls would shout to everybody else around the farmstead, "Here he comes! Get out here! Here he comes!" Lincoln's rented plane would become clearly more visible and louder.

Somebody would get the binoculars and try to get a closer sight of him aviating across our farm at 1,000 feet. If we looked through the field glasses more intensely and he was not too high, we'd see him wave back to us. Of course, we waved wildly in great sweeping motions to get his attention – as if he didn't already know we'd be down there.

When Lincoln was 12 years old, he promised Linda that someday she would be the first passenger once he got his wings to fly.

During Christmas vacation about six months after his flying lessons began, my brother was issued his private pilot's license. Keeping his word, Lincoln gave Linda the first ride on New Year's Day 1964. They flew over our farm and our hometown of Parkersburg just three miles away "as the crow flies."

He was then permitted to fly anyone in a Cherokee or Piper Comanche. He took me up for my first flight ever. In spite of the nausea and air sickness, I enjoyed the fascinating, surreal view of the world from above – the farm, its tiny cows, the course of the creek, the layout of the farmsteads and how hills could not be easily made out.

It cost money to fly, and Lincoln wanted to build his hours of flying time. Thus he invited farm neighbors, schoolmates and some high school teachers to go fly with him. They would divide the $15 per

hour fee three ways since the plane had seating for the pilot and three passengers. My brother got the ride, and the experience, at their expense.

Farm families who took rides with him received special attention in the flights over their farms. He would circle their farmsteads several times, tipping the wings to give them a bird's-eye-view of their homes. They'd click their cameras and marvel over how clean their corn rows were of weeds or that the creek in the pasture should be straightened. And, oh, how they liked the neat squareness of their fields. That quilt of lush farmland always enchanted the persons who were bold enough to go flying with Lincoln.

The time would speed by, and before they wanted it to end, they were touching down at the Waterloo airport.

Lincoln was to continue flying persons during that summer after we graduated. But then he went off to college in Florida to study the engineering side of aeronautics. His flying rating, which qualified him to continue flying, was to lapse because he didn't keep it up on a regular basis. He went on to become a successful aeronautical engineer.

Nevertheless, it was an exciting time in those last few years of growing up when my brother took us to the air to do what we had never done before, to see our farm as we had never seen it before, to look down onto our hometown of Parkersburg and marvel how we could see it all at once and to appreciate the quilted countryside as we had never appreciated it before.

FIRST CAMERA COMMENTARY

Let a kid loose on a farm with a camera, and you'll have a valuable, fascinating collection of pictures for years to come.

The summer we three children became shutterbugs was the start of an amusement that resulted in our recording sights and events that otherwise would have been lost with the fading of memories.

The three of us decided to take our allowance that summer of 1957 and invest it in cameras – one for each of us. We chose to spend our small farm earnings on separate cameras to prevent battles over what should be photographed and who should get the camera next.

It was also the summer we took our first family vacation from the farm, and we knew vacations and cameras went together.

We searched in the catalogues and looked at the offerings at Dreyer's Drug in town. We compared features, made our choices, then insisted that our individual picks were superior to what our brother or sister had selected.

I settled on buying a Brownie Star Flash. It cost me $9.95, and I paid cash for it at Dreyers. Lincoln and Linda ordered theirs from a catalogue, and they had to endure the agony of waiting for theirs to arrive by mail.

So there I was, first with a camera, the envy of my siblings. Taking a roll of Verichrome Pan film, which accompanied my new black, hard plastic camera, I carefully loaded the Brownie. Fingers and hands of my brother and sister poked around to help in the exciting new adventure of photography.

But after we got the back plate clamped down and the film advanced to "1," I decided the first picture I took would have to be something very special. I figured I'd just put the camera back into the Kodak black and yellow box and admire my new possession until the "right" picture opportunity came along.

Word spread to the farm across the road that I had gotten my new camera, and we invited Mervan, age 10, to come over to see my photo-making pride. On a chair on the front lawn, I sat down the box containing the camera. I lifted the lid off the box and revealed the handsome camera, loaded with a flashbulb, just as if it were in a store window showcase.

Without hesitation, Merv reached down and pushed the shutter lever, bathing our two faces in a burst of light.

I was stunned, shocked, furious, devastated. My first picture – the one I had wanted to be special – was wasted. I held back from crying.

I said nothing. I just grabbed up the camera, went to the house and left Mervan outdoors to figure out for himself that he should go home. And there in the house I pouted.

Later when the roll of film was developed, it showed parts of our faces in empty expressions. We were both able to laugh about it by then.

The camera snapped many even less significant situations in the succeeding days and years. Numerous cows were photographed, along with snowdrifts, ice-ravaged trees, flat tires, a duck with a tin can caught in its bill, my brother's head sticking through a hole in a tractor umbrella

while he paused from raking straw and other glimpses of those things seemingly eye-catching at the time.

And it all started the day Mervan pressed down the shutter and showed me the only way to have pictures was to take them – not think about taking them.

I don't remember if I had a special moment when I finally snapped photo No. 2.

IRON, STEEL AND THE LAND

TIME TUGS TENACIOUSLY AT FENCES

We could stretch a new pasture fence as if it were a piano string or a woman's nylon stocking. We made the tractor groan as it pulled the barbed wire taut and until it could tug the steel thread no tighter.

We could staple the wire down to the thickest creosoted post well anchored at the corner of the field. We could use the best tempered wire staples to fasten it all down to the posts along the way. And when we were done, we could pluck the wire and hear a dull ping that would please a violinist.

But give that fence time, and it would be down, rusting in the weeds – crumpled so low that a hen pheasant and her chicks would parade across it as if the fence were part of a wild raspberry thicket.

Whether a fence spans across 100 feet or along an entire mile of fields, it eventually surrenders its tension to relentless and stronger forces.

Torrid summer days cause them to expand and maybe even sag a bit, but sub-zero winter weather and ice storms pull wires tight at the same time they are weighed down by ice.

Rust works constantly on steel, including galvanized steel, to turn it brittle. Cattle "work" a fence – threading their heads between wires to snag ears of fresh green corn or wisps of succulent grass on the other side. They press even harder on wires, straining for everything they can reach.

The tension is gradually lost. Any lower woven wire fences are strangled with weeds and brush. Morning glory vines climb the fabric of wire, later to die and leave their brown skeletons.

A common farm expression was, "If you don't have anything else to do, you can fix fence."

Fences are like friendships. They need constant maintenance to keep them up.

Fixing fence is ultimately restoring its tension. Nothing short of disconnecting all the top barbs and stretching them again would bring back the tension.

You can straighten up the steel posts that are bent or slanted from the force of a cow reaching for cornstalks. You can put your two feet into the bottom of a woven wire fence and pull upward with all your might, trying to draw out the crumpled wires, but it will never look as it did the day you built it.

New fences can be built every spring across creeks, but a heavy one-hour rain and a flash flood can rip them out.

The trend toward less livestock production and greater row-crop farming has meant an elimination of fences altogether. Fewer fences are having to be mended. Many are allowed to let nature wear them down to a useless snarl until farmers wanting to farm the fence rows jerk the remains out.

Maybe they should heed the advice of Chesterton, "Don't ever take a fence down until you know the reason it was put up."

MOTHER'S TIN DRINKING CAN AND CLOTHESLINE POLE

For almost 10 years, my mother drank water from that No. 2 tin can. For nearly a quarter century, her No. 9 wire clothesline stretched between two trees and was supported in the middle by that same rough, hardwood pole, found "out in the timber."

The can and the weathered pole underlined the character of my farmwife mother. Like many rural women, she made do with what she had and found the simplest of possessions worked just fine, thank you.

It must have been about 1952, when she surprised us three kids by taking a tin can that probably contained canned peaches and made it

her drinking cup. She tore the paper label off the side, washed it out with soap and water, made certain the edges were smooth, and sat it on the back of the sink to use whenever she was thirsty.

That was to be *her* drinking can. No one else was to use it. As I remember, she had previously had her own glass beside the sink. However, we three youngsters – and especially Dad – grabbed it every time we wanted a drink, instead of getting our own glasses. So she borrowed an idea from an elderly woman she once knew, and she fashioned her own vessel.

We grew up with that can always beside the sink. I'll always remember how Mother would come inside, thirsty from an afternoon in the garden or from doing work around the farm. She'd turn on the water faucet and let it run a while until it ran cold. Then she'd put the 21-oz. can under the faucet and filled it up. The outside of the can sweated as she raised it to her lips.

Mother always said no water tasted as good as the cold drink she got from her tin can.

As the years passed, the outside of the can turned a dull gray, while the inside rusted deeper into the tin-coated steel.

Finally, it started leaking around the bottom seam where the rust had mostly penetrated to the exterior. Then, I guess, the can was tossed. Mother never started another can. Apparently she didn't because we were about grown and wouldn't even consider drinking out of anyone else's glass.

But I'll never forget the times my mother sent me to the house to fill her can with cold water, then bring it to her at the garden. The frigid well water was easily felt through that metal, and my hands were chilled by the time I delivered the cold, deep-well water. "It's so good," she would say with relief.

And what of the clothesline pole?

Its foot had been anchored in the front lawn since 1954. The nearly 4-inch thick, 8-foot long pole leaned at about a 35-degree angle against the wire.

After the clothesline wire was put between that pine tree and the elm – a distance of about 60 feet – it was evident that the wire could never hold the wet denim farm clothes, the baskets of damp towels and other items that went through the washer in the basement.

The wire would likely snap, dumping all the overalls, blue jeans and others threads to the ground. So the pole was found and wedged into place, giving a midway lift to the wire.

A split in the end of the pole widened with age, making a natural groove to hold the wire. On the nob at the end of the pole, Mother commonly hung her cloth bag containing clothespins. One time a bird moved twigs and debris into the bag and had plans of building a nest there.

At the bottom of that pole, dozens of cats and kittens sharpened their claws. The lacerations they made in the wood remained. The cats also enjoyed climbing the pole, and several kittens could often be seen wrestling on it. Usually, one would be clinging upside down, while a kitten on the ground reached upwards with poking jabs, trying to force the other to tumble into its arms to wrestle some more.

Through winters and winds, rains and heaving Monday washes, the pole endured, a kind of "washday miracle," perhaps.

The tin can and the crudely fashioned clothesline pole, in many ways, characterized my mother —practical, unassuming, modest and enduring.

THE DEATH OF OUR BLACKSMITH

When they buried our village blacksmith at Parkersburg that June day in 1973, they laid to rest a massive man whose steel-driving body had shriveled to but 90 pounds at his time of death at the age of 74.

Heye Renken was a giant, though, in the nearly 30 years he operated a blacksmith and welding shop just off the highway in the south part of town.

Peppery, strong-willed, broad-shouldered and tireless, Heye was the only means for many farmers in Butler and Grundy counties to get broken machinery parts repaired and to get back into the field within hours after those breakdowns.

After implement dealers and parts men had locked their doors, Heye continued to weld broken mower sickles, bent plow shares, and twisted power shafts inside his cluttered blacksmith shop in the same building where he lived alone.

On many afternoons, we would have a mechanical breakdown in a field job, and my father would tell me to "take this in to Heye's to get welded." Heye would usually stop everything he was doing and get to it, and we'd be back in the field in short time.

While the 6-foot, 4-inch man often sourly complained and jawed farmers for needlessly overloading machinery and causing the damage he had to repair, Heye would usually promise to "get to it next." Somehow he did just that. He'd do the most pressing job regardless of how many other items awaited repair. His work conjured Longfellow's classic "The Village Blacksmith" poem, especially the lines:

"….Week in, week out, from morn till night,
You can hear his bellows blow;
You can hear him swing his heavy sledge
With measured beat and slow,…"

Farmers took advantage of Heye because of the loose way he kept books and the rock-bottom welding rates he maintained. The same farmers were to later realize the good thing they had going. But they didn't go to Heye's for the bargain.

They patronized his welding shop because he was a master welder who could return the most bent or cracked piece of machinery to its near-original shape. It was superb welding, done in minutes when minutes counted, and it was done for a seeming steal. He'd charge 50 cents for some welding that others would have charged $2 to do. Pocket change could handle payment.

Unwilling to hire a bookkeeper, Heye tried to handle every phase of the demanding business alone. He tried to keep track of much of the work he did in his mind to write down the charges on accounts later. Many of those charges were never recorded, and the dirty, hot job was done at no cost to the farmer.

But when he did get the work recorded on farmers' accounts, time had lagged, recollections of how many items he welded for a certain farmer were poor, and the farmer received the benefit of the doubt.

The heavy traffic in and out of his shop day after day forced him literally to keep his shoulder to the grindstone. He just got further behind in his bookwork. No aggressive attempt was made to collect on unpaid accounts.

Heye welded a 40-foot harrow for a farmer who later came back to pay for the work. "No, you don't owe me for any welding," Heye told the farmer. The blacksmith couldn't find any record of such work either. Still the persistent farmer explained the harrow in some detail in an effort to refresh Heye's memory.

Finally, Heye blurted, "By gosh, I remember that sucker now! It just slipped my mind." Probably a lot of welding jobs slipped the minds of Heye and the farmers he served. His brother, George Renken, said Heye had a "big pile of statements on uncollected accounts" in his shop that day he had a stroke.

I happened while he was operating an arc welder. Then he slumped, searing a hole in his skin. He was able to drag himself to his living quarters where they later found him biting into the rung of a ladder. Thereafter, he was unable to remember much of anything about the blacksmith shop that had been a bustling center of activity in the farming community.

Heye, a veritable artist with steel, was a compulsive worker. He started welding at 4 or 5 o'clock each morning and quit as late as 9 that night. Sometimes he continued to weld long after he had locked the door to his shop.

There was no other car in town like his black 1946 Pontiac with its rounded rear window and the windshield visors always pulled down. Occasionally, I'd search around Parkersburg to find the car and Heye. Then I'd give him a broken shaft that we needed fixed by early the next morning. At daybreak, it'd be ready to take home.

The appearance of the old bachelor was distinctive, too. His awesome frame was attired in soot-stained bib overalls and a black apron. His oily round cap hugged his head, and as often, as not, it was turned backwards so he could wear his welding mask. Heye clenched a pipe in his teeth as he worked. His rough and calloused hands showed all the evidence of the man's labors. He had a prominent wart on his face.

Heye ate all his meals in the town's cafes and went to the Congregational Church and advertised in the high school yearbooks.

He once farmed with his brothers around Parkersburg, but with a bent toward repairing farm equipment, Heye started Renken Implement, which turned out to be a welding shop instead of an outlet for farm equipment.

The blacksmith developed welding into an art, so that he was to become the best around – and he didn't quit until his heart stopped him at the age of 72. Had his health stood up, the stubborn man would have probably gone another decade. Pickups, tractors and cars would have continue to cluster outside his shop for more years with a band of farmers inside talking German and English over the din of Heye's driving sledge.

His tools and shop were later sold. They knocked down his building and eventually put up a convenience store and gas station.

Heye Renken, once a farmer himself, was a man who took it on himself to keep farm machinery functioning out on the land. The countryside around Parkersburg may still be dotted with now rusting machinery carrying a weld or two of the unfailing blacksmith.

He knew the immediate torment of a mechanical breakdown to a farmer, and he would fix it. He never got rich despite his mastery of the craft. So he was really a philanthropist to the area farmers and they did not forget him.

TRAITS AND TRIALS OF TRACTOR SEATS

Careful research and precise human engineering no doubt went into producing my swivel, free-moving, marvelously adjustable, unceasingly comfortable, smartly designed office chair beside my computer.

Those engineering craftsmen of the modern tractor seat have spared no less care in fashioning the throne on which a farmer may find himself perched for the majority of a day in a busy season.

The vinyl, cushioned seats, styled to fit the posteriors of rural workers, are complete with armrests to bear the upper limbs of farmers when they aren't pulling levers or both arms aren't steering their tractors down long corn rows.

And the soft backrests afford pleasurable support. With most tractors now equipped with comfortable cabs, their seats are assured of being inside where they won't get rained on, overheated or plastered by bird droppings.

Each of our tractors had its own uniquely shaped or positioned seat. If we had been blindfolded and instructed to sit in each seat, it wouldn't have been difficult to determine which seat belonged to which tractor.

At one point on our farm while I was growing up, we had seven tractors in use. Certainly the nature of the seats had much to do with my ease or difficulty in mastering the driving of each tractor.

Some tractors had shiny, steel seats. Our less than full-size behinds slide around on the slick seats as we'd stretch our legs to reach the brakes and clutches.

The springs that supported the seats and gave some shock for the rider were geared for much bigger and weightier derrieres. So the seats bounced negligibly over bumps for us lightweights, and our behinds took the full pounding against the steel seats.

Of course, we did what we could to pad the seats. Over the years, Dad brought numerous cushions that snugly fit the seats. However, they took a lot of abuse from backsides and the weather. Their stitching tore, or wrenches, carried in the back pockets of blue jeans, pierced their covers. In a short time, the stuffing – chunks of foam or cotton – came out of them.

Or the soft cushion was left out in the rain, absorbed water readily, and was subsequently jerked off the seat and tossed aside to dry out. But it took a month to dry out and may have never been used again. (How ghastly it is to sit down onto a wet cushion and feel the chilly water soak into the clothing on your backside).

Most all tractor seats were on hinges and could be flipped upside down in event of rain to keep them dry. It seemed ours seldom were inverted when the drops were falling.

The next best protection for a specially made cushion for a behind was a gunny sack, an old coat or other cast-off garments. Really, any padding would do. Often while mowing alfalfa or making hay, we simply gathered up a handful of cut hay and laid it on the tractor seat, then sat down on it. In time, the hay conformed in shape to the seat and was amazingly comfortable.

Corn husks at picking time also worked well.

Often we took our coats or shirts off in the field, put them on the seats and left them when we shut off the tractors at night. (On washday, Mother could survey tractor seats, tool boxes and pickup cabs for a lot of abandoned clothes).

Through the years, hired help determined the original seats of their pet tractors should be removed and replaced by special "comfort" seats they saw in a farm equipment store. Sometimes those new seats

didn't fit correctly, and they made it that much harder for us to reach the clutch, and the poorly positioned seats caused our legs to rub on the steering wheels.

I did a lot of my growing up on tractor seats. I watched whole days come and go while bouncing or sliding on them while the tractor steadfastly plowed, mowed, baled or did any of a host of other farm maneuvers that gave farm people their only opportunities to sit down on the job.

ANYTHING GOES WITH GATES

Some sag from the fatigue of their vigil.

Other lean lazily, their boards warped and rotten.

Some stretch with taut, unyielding strength across the gaps in fence lines.

Still others can be snarls of rusting barbed wire, patched by baling wire. They can be a tarnished mesh of galvanized fencing stapled to flat boards. Or they are strong fabrications of pipe and steel, while others are mere barriers of weathered wooden panels, fastened by wire to stalwart corner posts.

All are inanimate watchdogs.

They are field gates.

They guard and block the entries into cornfields, back 40s and pastures.

Gates can keep cattle in, but they can't keep weeds and pests out.

They can keep a farmer getting on and off his tractor repeatedly to open and close them. But the fellow he has hired to work for him can never remember to close the same gates on his last trips out of the fields. Or that seemed like the way it was on our farms.

Building codes never reached farm gates. Most were of individual design and were randomly thrown together as combinations of wood, wire, staples and posts. They did their job of keeping stray animals and strangers out of fields and livestock and crops inside fields for a limited number of years.

Then gravity, weather, time, use and abuse led to their downfall. They would grow flimsy, warp, rust or just break down. Eventually, they needed to be jerked out and replaced.

In contrast, many gateways in fields are spanned by elegant, pre-assembled structures of aluminum, steel and painted or treated wood. Sturdy, rectilinear, simple, the commercial gate is probably the most functional and long-lasting

Nevertheless, the cheap gate has a beauty in its haphazard simplicity. And constructing it can be considered the practice of an art.

Take note of the varied forms of gates that block field openings along a rural road. In every mile, there are usually more than a half-dozen driveways into fields.

The most common form is the barbed wire gate made by stapling three or four strands of barbed wire to a corner post planted in the ground. The other ends are wrapped around a 2-by-4 or creosote post so that they stretch across a gateway. Both ends of that post are then set top and bottom into wire hoops fastened to the corner posts on the other side of the driveway.

Boards must be stapled vertically on a new barbed wire gate to keep the four strands of wire separated and uniformly taut.

Perhaps the style and condition of the gates going from roads into fields say something about the farmers themselves.

More and more roadside fences are torn out for good, particularly in this age of increased grain farming along with more raising of livestock in confinement and not in open fields and pastures. No longer are livestock commonly turned into harvested fields to clean up corn ears or grains lost in harvest.

And when fences disappear, so gates with all their haphazard designs and stages of disrepair also disappear.

LAST TRAIN TO STOUT

The last train to Stout is only a fading memory. A freight thundered down the old tracks through our farm for the last time in 1975.

But the Chicago & Northwestern Railroad wasn't making any profit operating freights on that 20.8-mile stretch of rail and ties. It obtained Interstate Commerce Commission approval to abandon the line between Dike and Kesley.

It may have been inevitable. Trains had been so infrequent at times in the final years that some might have thought the rails had

already been abandoned. News of abandonment was sobering, the kind of somber reminder of change, the kind of change that takes away something commanding and strong. Freights are robust and mighty. They're pulsating and periodic, and their lumbering roar through the countryside past cornfields and hog lots had long been part of the cadence of a rural day on our farms.

Anyone who has ever struggled to put some words together from his soul has whittled a wistful phrase or two about trains. The mystique and charm surrounding the railroad compare only to that of the river. Residents along either avenue of distant travel have been spellbound by the kinetics, the unceasing force that barrels through the countryside – and then is suddenly gone.

The C&NW took a northeasterly course through our mile section, splitting the farm. Fields were irregularly shaped because of the angle of its layout, and the result was sheer difficulty in maneuvering machinery built for square fields.

Moreover, we had 1 ½ miles of railroad right-of-way fences to look after, even though the railroad company was officially responsible for fence maintenance. At two points along our part of the track, we had rail crossovers and gates to move machinery and livestock from one side to the other. Cattle and hogs stepped warily over the shiny rails every time we would drive them across. Sometimes cows would bolt down the tracks' embankment and run through the right-of-way parallel to the tracks, unalterably refusing to cross the rails.

I crossed those tracks probably 10,000 times on foot, bicycle, tractor, car, school bus and truck. Crossing it going home always meant first a jolt to the right, then a thrust to the left. I was most aware of that when I crossed the tracks with a huge hayrack of baled hay. More times than once, the shock caused bales to tumble from the rack to the ground beside the tracks. I usually came back later to retrieve them.

I heard the trains go through at night. By day, I counted the number of boxcars in mile-long trains. I marveled at the brightly painted new machinery being hauled on boxcars. We liked to wave to the engineer.

Once the railroad pulled out of our farm neighborhood, it offered to sell all the land back to the farmers. It had originally been taken out of farms in 1898-99. Adjacent property owners bought the land from the C&NW, and some quickly had the rail beds bulldozed and leveled

to be in line with adjacent fields, then the old right-of-ways were put into crop production.

The plowing of those few acres of right-of-way meadows—rich with sumac, wild asparagus, wild blackberries, raspberries, pussy willows and numerous other wildflowers – was a disturbing choice for us who wondered why, oh why, must still more land be put into cultivation – land that was such wonderful wildlife habitat. We left it wild until the farm was finally sold. Then they buyers sent in the bulldozers.

Though the tracks, ties and crossing itself have been long removed, my instincts are still to look both ways for a train before I cross that spot on the gravel road where the iron road used to pass through.

CLAWING THROUGH A TRACTOR TOOL BOX

"Go look in the tool box on the manure loader, and if you don't find one there, check the Ford tractor box…."

The search was on for a crescent wrench or ballpeen hammer or 5/8th open-end wrench or whatever was needed at the moment and couldn't be found. It meant clawing patiently through a tangle of paraphernalia stuffed into each tool box on each farm tractor around the place.

And before the pursued tool was found, I might have had to take a zigzag route to each tractor to rifle through its tool box. Our tractor tool boxes were metal bags of tricks. Their designer must have intended them as mere glove boxes capable of holding not much more than a flashlight, screwdriver and pliers. Ours was never so neatly organized, however.

Each of our tractors was designed with its tool box located in a different place on the machine. The Ford, for example, had a thin enclosure underneath the clutch pedal. I remember it as a compartment of rusty washers and nails, dirt and weed seeds. A second tool box was bought for the tractor and mounted on the inside of a rear-wheel fender.

On the other hand, the Farmall "B" featured an old bakery bread pan riveted under the seat as an auxiliary to another tool box that had been purchased elsewhere and hooked to the fender. Other tractors had sliding metal boxes underneath the operator's platform.

The items that found their way into the tool boxes were a scavenger hunter's delight – bent cotter keys, light fuses, livestock marking chalk, cobbled up baling wire, spark plugs, railroad spikes, reflectors, large bent

bolts to use as hay rack hitching pins in an emergency, grease-covered drill bits, a fruit jar lid and a lot of gritty, oily dirt under it all.

Many nights I scratched and dug around the grungy, cold, steely midst of a tool box in search of a screwdriver. I usually was out on the north 47 acres with a weak flashlight cast down onto the knot of tool box trinkets.

None of the tool boxes, either those that came with the tractors originally nor other specifically bought and mounted on them later, was large enough to accommodate pipe wrenches or the 1 ¼-inch wrenches sometimes needed in the field.

Often I would take a jar of water to the field to drink, but lacking a place to leave it along the periphery of the field, I would put it into the tool box. I made sure the jar's lid was tight to keep the water from leaking out onto the items under it.

But sometimes, I'd open the tool box to take a drink and find a pile of broken glass and a tool box full of water. The jar had banged too hard against a clevis, an old solenoid or some pliers. I'd have to lift the box off its brackets, drain the water out and just lick my parched lips.

One way to lose disfavor with Dad was to leave the tool box lid open and to have the box filled with water from a thunderstorm. It invariably added to items rusting over time.

Cans of motor oil, grease guns, wild asparagus and field mice killed in a hayfield to be taken home to the cats also competed for space in tool boxes with baler shear pins, cable clamps and fence post insulators.

In short, tool boxes weren't designed to accommodate the assorted wherewithal of farming. On our farm, no one seemed ever caught up in his work to sort through the tool boxes and get rid of the riffraff. They were comparable to those catch-all "junk drawers" that could be found somewhere in the house, which sometimes collected what farmers emptied from their pockets. While tool boxes were dumping grounds, they often housed just the thing needed at the moment.

FINDING FATHER FOR THE PHONE

Telephone technology has radically changed from the 1950s. Back then, a long distance call meant a cost to someone and no hesitancy to take care of business as quickly as possible.

How many times did a farmwife go to pick up a ringing telephone only to find the party on the other end was calling long distance and wanted to talk to her husband?

She laid down the receiver while her mind rushed through a stream of ideas of where he might be. "What did he say he was going to do?" she silently asked herself as she hurried out the porch.

Her first glance was to see whether the pickup was still there on the driveway. Of course, there was no telling where in the vast outdoors, beyond the back step, he might be. The weather was often foul when she stepped onto the walk that led to the driveway. She didn't take time to put on a sweater or jacket.

The farmwife let out a yell with a "George! George! Telephone!"

It was the simplest phrase she had shouted hundreds of times. She immediately listened for an "Alright, I'm coming" or "I'll be there" or "Who is it?"

But more often than not, she didn't get any response. He had not heard her cry.

Then she followed her hunches. What did he usually do that time of the day? Was he in the silo or taking care of the sows? Were all the tractors still around? Where was the farm dog? Were the cattle eating new feed in the bunk down in the feedlot?

She quickened her pace, knowing Ma Bell was collecting quarters as she hesitated. She shouted again en route to the barn. But from behind her at the machine shed, her husband answered, "Who is it?"

Now, it is his turn to hurry. He didn't know whether it was an answer to his feeder pig ad in the classifieds, whether it was an insurance adjustor calling to get information on the damage to the machine shed caused by the falling limb or whether it was someone who wants to rent some pasture ground in the spring.

The telephone has been both a vexation and a convenience to farm people since it first came to the rural world.

We didn't have a telephone in my farm home until I was 8 years old. Our first telephone number was simply 2298, and one long ring and two short rings were the cue to answer the phone at our house. I was bashful and balked at talking to anyone on the line. I feared the day I would be the only one around the house and would have to answer the phone.

The old black telephone box was so high on the wall in the kitchen that we needed a chair on which to stand to reach it. In those years, the

phone usually brought calls from neighbors. "We're gonna shell corn tomorrow, and we were wondering if you could help out…." "….we've got the hayracks unloaded that you wanted to borrow." "Some of your pigs have gotten out over here …" "It's such a nice day, I just thought I'd call to see what you folks are doin'."

Our party line was probably like all of them. It was hard to get the line free to make a call. The line was populated by harmless, listeners-in, more commonly referred to as "those Butt-in-skis." (They had mastered the techniques of eavesdropping long before the FBI and NSA made it a practice.)

The telephone company was forever changing things, making phone communications more modern and convenient. The telephone wires that were downed so often by ice storms were buried. The receivers became fancier, the phone numbers longer and the phone books thicker. And the party was over on the party line.

GRUDGE AGAINST GREASE GUNS

If grease guns were real guns, I'm afraid things might have been disastrous. The frustrations I had with them would have prompted me long ago to put the gooey nozzle to my temple where I would have squeezed down on the handle for a last time.

Few chores around farm equipment were as unpopular with me as greasing machinery. I had a fit finding fittings to fill with the viscous slime that would keep bearings, rollers, ball joints and shafts turning with a minimum of wear.

"Grease the combine" was a dreaded command to my ears. No other piece of machinery had more hard-to-reach grease fittings – all of them camouflaged by layers of dirt, chaff and Canadian thistle down, clinging to the grease left on the head of a fitting from the greasing of the day before. Some machinery designers must have had many private laughs in thinking of how much trouble people would have finding and reaching the grease fittings.

I virtually had to memorize where all the fittings were located, but it didn't make it any easier to make contortionist bends to reach the greasing points. A fitting was like a round bald head about a half-inch tall with a smaller round knob coming out of the side. It had a hole the

size of a pencil lead. Grease was forced down into it, and it was trapped inside.

We used two kinds of grease guns. One had a nozzle held stable by being on the end of a steel tube. The nozzle of the other kind was on the end of a rubber hose, reinforced by metal ribbing that extended from the greased gun's barrel, holding the grease, to the nozzle. Thus, there was a choice between using the flexible nozzle that could go around a sharper corner to reach a difficult-to-reach fitting and the rigid stem of the other kind to apply pressure to an easily reached fitting.

We often had to have both kinds loaded with grease and at hand to deal with the varied kinds of fittings to be confronted on a piece of farm machinery.

My most common problem was putting the gun's nozzle over the ball end of the fitting only to find the fitting wouldn't take the grease. Instead, it would be forced out of the side of the nozzle and end up on the outside of the fitting. I'd force my body against the back end of the gun, applying the pressure in an effort to open the mouth of the fitting and make it take the grease.

Sometimes there was a stalemate. No amount of pressure could get the handle to go down. The fitting was locked shut and had to be unscrewed and replaced.

If the nozzle on one gun didn't work, I could try the other grease gun.

Too often the grease gun spit out its last glob of grease before I had made a stop at each fitting. Being out of grease meant finding a 5-gallon bucket of lubricant and going through a messy process to refill the barrel of the grease gun. First, I unscrewed the handle and pump mechanism from the barrel. Then the open end was thrust into the jelly-like green or brown grease. The piston plunger end was pulled back, sucking the grease into the barrel. The rod, which pulled the piston back, had to be locked into place at the rear of the barrel until the grease gun was reassembled. Afterwards, the piston rod could be released.

Occasionally, the rod would, by accident, disengage and the quantity of grease would be cast in a menacing glob out of the gun onto the ground wherever the grease gun was casually aimed.

If I were lucky to get the gun filled without getting any air pocket in it, I still had the end of the barrel to clean off with an old rag and to get my hands cleaned up after that.

Eventually cartridge refills came into use and spared us that nuisance.

Sometimes a baler, combine or hay rake was left all night in the field because a job was uncompleted. Early the next day Dad sent me to the field ahead of time to go over all the fittings with a grease gun. I had to be sure the grease guns were filled before I went all the way out there to do the job. I confess there were times when my grease gun gave out before all the fittings were reached, and the machine was to go about its work with some parts unlubricated.

I still have a grudge against those greasy, grimy guns of August farm work.

COW COMPANIONSHIP

A PASTURE IN THE RAIN

Ominous storm clouds pass overhead, ignored by dairy cows grazing on a hillside. In due time, a few sprinkles pelt the earth, moistening, then chilling what earlier was hot dust on cow paths and on pasture lanes.

Gentle and steady, the shower steps up its tempo, halting the cattle's grazing. They regroup, then slink away from the open high ground in pursuit of shelter of a willow copse near a creek.

Like oxen bearing the body of the pharaoh to his tomb in a pyramid, the cows dolefully plod along, their ears drooping and their heads heaving low.

The downpour overtakes the cattle flies as the beasts' most immediate torment. So the pests are given a respite from the deadly tails. Just five minutes before they flailed at flies. Now those tails hang limp as the cows trudge forward, intent only on getting out of the soaking rains.

While dry, the proud Holsteins cast crisp and groomed appearances. But the drenching rain makes them look lean and wretched, and seemingly has dampened their spirits.

Their interlocking patches of blacks and whites tend to run together as the plastered-down hair lies flat on their flanks. Those mostly white cows appear even pink as their fair skins show through the flattened layers of white hair.

When the lead cow finally reaches the canopy of willows, she plunges into the dry asylum. She plants herself at the center of the trees, well in from the leaky edges where the late-comers must jostle for refuge.

Other cows fall in around her. The last animals drive their heads into the compact herd in an effort to gain a drier spot to wait out the storm. They take up swatting flies again.

Each cow whips her head back to her fly-speckled shoulders to lick away the irksome pests.

In due time, the rain-laden leaves dump the water down from the treetops onto the cattle. It runs down the sides of the knotted cattle and onto the ground where stamping hoofs work up a soft mud.

Soon there is a current in the meandering creek bed nearby. It flushes stagnant summer water from holes drilled by hoofs of cattle standing in the water on hot days.

By now, it is late afternoon. Chore time is near. It's almost time to milk. Across the hollow at the barn, the dairy farmer leans out the barn door. He would like to be seeing cows marching through the rain to the barnyard.

But far across the pasture, through the steady downpour, he spots his herd crowded under that clump of trees like a funeral party under an awning at graveside services. He again mutters he ought to bulldoze out that useless snarl of trees.

He pulls on a rubberized jacket with a hood, and, with his dog, he heads out into the cow lot to the pasture lane and off after his cows.

The farmer cups his hands to his mouth and bellows, "Come, boss! Come, bossies! Come, boss!" As expected, they don't respond. Not today. The familiar call does rustle an instinctive impulse inside the cows to respond and head to the barn – but it's raining hard.

Just before the dairyman has trod down to the cattle's retreat, he spies a lone cow up in the corner of the pasture. A shaky new calf trembles at her flank. The cow stands over the calf's placenta, her tongue slurping it into her mouth. Steam comes off the bodies of both animals.

The farmer accosts the duo, both animals undaunted by the invasion of another being into the procreative rite. The dog, however, shrinks away, reluctant to go near, aware the cow will charge him with little provocation.

To the dairyman's delight, it's a female, a heifer calf, a possible cow someday in his milk production herd. He determines both should be taken home, albeit a painstakingly slow and awkward job. For the bewildered calf, it's like a walk to the end of the earth. Somehow, with a lot of light shoving, the farmer gets the fledgling calf down to the

herd under the trees. Several cows perk their ears and come out to give the youngster a quick examination. After sniffing her, they lose interest and turn away.

The farmer plunges into the thicket, goads the cows into moving home and sicks the dog on them. He then turns his attention again to the calf and cow.

The calf slips around the wet grass and muddy cow path. At the creek crossing, the banks are muddy. The rocks over which the farmer usually steps to ford the stream are under water. He wraps his arms around the calf's flanks and clenches her hoofs with his hands. He hikes her onto his hip, then plunges across the creek. His feet stomp through water that rises to the middle of his shins. The cow lets out a bellow, then follows along in guarded alert that nothing ill occurs to her calf.

For the rest of the way, she puts forth token protests. Yet, she lumbers along. Her swollen udders obstruct her stride, forcing her to rumble forward in an exaggerated, tortuous gait.

Eventually, all segments of the procession arrive at the cow lot. No creature is dry, but the rain has stopped. The cows have come home through a summer rain, and in the trek, a new heifer calf has made her first of possibly several thousand trips home.

In the doorway of his barn—the doorjambs polished smooth by the sides of the cows passing through over time – the dairyman stands in private wonderment at the regenerative processes of his herd. He feels smug about the rains that will keep the pasture grass growing and thriving to furnish ample grass for his Holsteins and steady output of milk in his pails.

This and 364 other days like it make his dairy days a year-round celebration.

IN SEARCH OF SURCINGLES

I wonder how many dairymen have chased cows all over the cow lot or down through the pasture in an effort to retrieve the surcingles or milking straps they forgot to take off the cows' backs before the animals were turned out of their barns.

I used to forget to take them off quite often. Out of that, I learned a lot about sneaking up on cows, running freely outdoors and latching

onto surcingle straps before the cows could haul them off to some far end of the pasture to be lost in the hinterlands.

A surcingle is simply a rubberized belt that goes over a cow's back to support a milking machine. Suspended across the bottom from the belt holes to a steel triangle is a crescent-shaped metal piece called a spring. On that spring is hung the bucket milker, which has four rubber and stainless steel cups extended up to the cow's teats for automatic milking. The milk collects in the "bucket" or tank below.

Our surcingles were black, rubber-covered fibrous cloth. They were about 7 feet long with 15 holes into which went a hook for adjusting the spring's height in relation to the variable girths of our Holsteins – cows that came in all sizes, heights and dispositions.

For a time, I was milking two different dairy herds twice daily.

The herds totaling 40 cows were divided on our two farmsteads. It took a keen understanding of the milking habits – and sometimes kicking habits – of all the cows, and that helped me know how to adjust their surcingles.

I learned to cinch up the surcingles higher than normal for some cows, as I did for the cow we called "Reindeer." That wiry, intolerant cow had a penchant for bringing one of her rear feet up high enough to catch the surcingle spring and pull it out of its triangle holder.

That abrupt action caused the milking machine to bang to the floor, where usually the cow's next move was to put her foot down onto the milker and pull her teats free from the inflation cups. In a final motion, she would kick all the milking equipment into the cow gutter. There it typically turned over, dumping the milk into the gutter where it became lost product. The manure-smeared milker had to be pulled out of the mire and hauled to the milk house to be cleaned up.

I trained myself to know the sound of a surcingle spring being tripped or jerked out of the triangle. I was alert to the sound of a milker dropping to the barn's concrete floor. In a moment, I was there, castigating the cow while demanding she stay cool and let me pull the milker off her before she would send it reeling into the gutter or at the feet of a cow in a stanchion next to her.

Fortunately, surcingles are made so that once they are sprung apart (the spring pulled out of the triangle), they can be snapped back together with just a quick jerk of the hand.

The secret of getting a cow milked out quickly is as much in the arrangement of the surcingle on the cow's back as anything else. By pulling the top of the strap, which sits across the cows upper back, in the direction of her shoulders so that the strap crossed her flanks diagonally, the dairyman gets a rhythmic motion that accelerates milking.

I usually used four milking machines and five straps at a time. As I went down the line of cows, the straps were changed in revolving order from the cow that had just had her milker removed to the cow to be milked next.

Sometimes the hook end of the surcingle helped me in prying cows apart so I could get between them. And the belt end sometimes was used to get a cow up on her feet to milk.

At the end of the milking cycle, there were to be five surcingles hanging on a wood peg in the barn. But it was easy to forget to hang up the last one. For those were days of trying to hurry to get chores done in the morning to get ready for school in 10 minutes or to get into the house at night for supper and homework.

If a cow got out of the barn with a strap on her back without our knowledge, we came up short at the next milking cycle. During the winter months when the cows stayed in the barn all night, a surcingle inadvertently left on a cow after milking in the evening was found in the gutter or straw the next morning.

I've combed pastures and found – and failed to find – surcingles that went out the barn door on the backs of cows.

Surcingles were an integral part of my milking experience. I won't forget how the cows' backs bristled slightly at the tickle of the metal part of surcingles sliding across their spines and ribs, how easily they slipped back over a wet cow's back, or the warmth of the rubberized straps' surface when I'd take them off.

COWS LIKE A TUBA

Cows used to relish the sounds I made on my tuba.

When I was a tuba player in the Parkersburg High School Band, I would serenade the old cows down in the pasture. Those were concerts only cows could appreciate.

On mild nights after the chores were done and I had finished milking our cows, I would crawl inside the circles of shiny brass tubing of my sousaphone, then haul the huge, cumbersome instrument down to the pasture to practice.

Often I'd go down there to play the horn because nearby was our vegetable garden where my mother would be working.

It was always a peaceful setting, bucolic and free of the noises permeating the countryside during the day. Dusk was not far off. The cows were grazing. Green hills glowed like limes as the last rays of sun beamed low across the countryside.

Into the serenity came my intruding tuba and its unmelodic oom-pah-pah.

I would play scales or the unmusical bass part for a piece of band music. Then I'd fool around a little by playing taps or parts of pop hits. I suppose I could be heard a mile away, although there were never complaints.

Sometimes, I'd pucker my lips, take a deep breath and let go with a long, low b-flat. That would bring the cows running toward me, for they wanted to meet up with the bull that seemingly was bellowing in such resonant tones.

Of course, they never found him, but they did come up close enough to the source of their curiosity to sniff my shiny horn. Some even slobbered and tried to lick the big round bell at the top of the sousaphone.

Then in orneriness, I'd take a deep breath, put my lips to the mouthpiece and blurt out a loud, splattering and deafening note. The cows stampeded across the pasture. They romped out a ways, their hoofs kicking high, then whirled around and looked back in sheer disbelief.

During our band's marching season in the fall and spring, I would practice marching by going up and down the driveway on our farm. I'd carry my tuba, trying to play the bass notes for marches by composers like John Philip Sousa and Karl King. All alone, I would practice turns, countermarches and maneuvers used for show formations on the school's football field.

Being small, barely 5 feet, 6 inches, I wasn't built to carry a tuba – at least ones made of brass. It weighed 22 pounds and the full weight pressed down on a spot on the left shoulder. The pain was dreadful. But I also had a great deal of trouble with wind currents that would catch

the huge funnel-like bell and force me backwards when I should have been tramping forward.

I always had trouble practicing the tuba at home. My twin brother complained that the tuba caused noise pollution and that it impeded his hearing the television set. Many times he would swipe the mouthpiece off my tuba and hide it, keeping me from my practice. He would retrieve it only after the program he was watching was over or I put an arm hold on him that caused him to reveal where the mouthpiece had been hidden.

It wasn't easy being a tuba player and living in the country. Other band students could haul their saxophones, flutes, cornets and French horns onto the school buses and stash them in the front of the bus beside the driver. It was just so much carry-on baggage. But if I had packed up my tuba (a step requiring considerable disassembly) by putting it into a velvet-lined case the size of an armchair and then lugged it onto the bus, no one could have gotten around the monstrosity to get on or off the bus.

Instead, I was allowed by my band instructor, Gordon Cosner, to keep a battered, tarnished and outmoded tuba at home. The school owned it along with the two other brass tubas regularly used by the band. But when a third tuba player was added to the band, I had to return the old, dented horn and confine my practice to school.

Several days after I first started playing a tuba, I experienced severe chest pains. Neither I nor anyone else even thought to associate the pain with strain to my chest muscles from blowing a tuba for the first time. In our ignorance, we went to two doctors in an attempt to ascertain the cause of my chest pains. I was privately convinced I would be dying early from lung cancer.

The doctors could find nothing wrong, and the pain eventually went away. It was months later that I had the sudden realization that the tuba had, in fact, caused the chest pain.

I had been fooled by the same tangle of brass tubes that had dumbfounded the cows in the pasture.

CATS HAD STRAINER PAD INDIGESTION

Sanitary sewer departments often complain about disposable diapers clogging their systems because they don't decompose as other materials do.

We always had the same kind of trouble with the milk strainer pads from the milk house. What to do with the round, dripping, sticky pads after they had caught the fine sediment in the milk was a genuine problem.

The main concern was the cats. Some of them loved to eat the fibrous cotton pads, soaked with the sweet cow's milk. But when they ate the pads, it meant one thing – constipation.

In our grade B milking operation from which we sold unpasteurized, raw, whole milk in 10-gallon cans, there were fewer restrictions on sanitation than with Grade A set-ups. The cows' udders were washed, the pulsating milking machines were put onto the cows, and the milk was drawn and dumped into a pail.

The bucket of milk was then poured into a funnel-shaped strainer, resting atop a 10-gallon milk can. Ours was a two-piece strainer. One cotton pad was locked into the bottom of the top section by a dome-like collar. In that first straining, all major sediment, such as cow hairs and sometimes telltale bits of mastitis from an inflamed udder, were caught. The milk dripped down through a doubled-up set of cotton pads pressed between two stainless disks with numerous holes in them. A wire collar held them in place.

Finally, the milk dripped into the milk can. And if we were observant enough, the can would not be allowed to fill up higher than the bottom of the neck of the can. But all too often, I would misjudge how much room was left in a can for more milk. On the next trip back, I would find more milk running down the sides of the can and going into the drain on the milk house floor.

The cotton pads in the strainer's top section had to be changed often to keep milk going into the can as clean as possible and to maintain rapid straining. But there were times, particularly in the spring of the year, when the cows waded through a muddy cow yard and their udders were coated with mud when they lumbered into the barn. Even the most thorough washing of the udders, before the milking machines were put on, didn't remove the very fine sediment.

In such situation, the strainer clogged quickly. It meant tipping the strainer on its side and pouring the milk left unfiltered back into a pail, then replacing the sediment-laden pad with a new Johnson & Johnson Rapid Flo milk pad from the blue box inside a special dispenser mounted on the wall of the milk house.

That's when the problem came up. Where should we toss the old strainer pad?

The barn generally had 21 cows in it, all confined by stanchions that kept the cows from pulling their heads backwards. The bovine were often outnumbered by cats – cats sitting around a shallow, but wide metal pan originally used to feed pigs. The cats waited to be fed milk. Other cats sat on top of the stanchion ledges. Still more cats were underfoot. All were overly friendly and begged to be petted and fed.

Though they were well-fed, a milk-enriched strainer pad was something some cats would "cotton to." They had a real taste for them. However, we didn't think it was good for their digestive tracts.

It seemed as if wherever we disposed of the white, soggy pads, some cat would be there retrieving them. They would pull the pungently sweet pads out of trash cans. If we wadded them and heaved them out the barn window into the manure pile, it wouldn't be long before a cat was taking the trouble to go after them, then sit for 20 minutes chewing the tough filters and somehow swallow them.

Our best strategy was to drop a pad into the cow gutter, then using the toe of our shoes, force it into a fresh cow pie or force it to soak up the fluid wastes in the gutter. That way, we figured, the putrid thing would not tempt a cat to fetch it.

But many times, I saw cats gingerly fish pads out of the manure. Then they'd chew on those parts of the pads that hadn't soaked up cow wastes.

The trouble with it all was that the fibrous cotton pads clogged the cats' innards. I suppose some even died of such indigestion. Many times I saw cats squatted and straining, trying to expel undigested milk filter pads. The old pads must have scoured their digestive systems, like running a patch of cloth down a rifle barrel.

But, oh, the trouble they had excreting them.

What had strained milk so easily caused a hard strain for those cats that couldn't pass up eating a flavorful strainer pad. Maybe Milk of Magnesia was needed at a time like that.

PUNCHING CATTLE TO SUMMER PASTURE

A feature of spring on our farm was throwing open the cow yard gates and starting our dairy calf herd out onto the country road for a three-mile walk to summer pasture.

It meant freeing almost 75 Holstein calves from their bleak confinement, a vegetation-bare lot where they must have thought, in bovine wonderment, that winter would never be replaced by spring and silage never replaced by grass.

But with just a bit of caution, they streamed out the gate and onto a straight stretch of Grundy County roadway, lined with succulent grass. With cocky animal eagerness, they headed to pasture, occasionally kicking up their heels to celebrate the new freedom.

Their destination was what for 20 years had been called Pattersons' Pasture, a rolling 80-acre meadow whose varied terrain I had gotten to know intimately in the years I roamed over it. I searched the hills and hollows for cattle to count, trying to find cattle feared killed by lightning – or perhaps stolen. I tramped in the tall grasses for new calves hidden by their mothers.

Our spring cattle drives were as predictable as the coming of asparagus pickers from Parkersburg to tramp through the ditches along our farm.

Once the herd of black and white cattle of all ages took to the road to stretch their legs, extreme care had to be taken to keep them under control. It took more than a casual understanding of cows and their nature to be able to manage a herd of them going down a road on a spring day.

It took a crew of at least four persons to handle the logistics – guarding the front of the formation and keeping cattle at the rear spurred to keep moving. In our set-up, two people walked and two drove vehicles. Usually a pickup, tractor or car went out front to scout for possible trouble spots, to block off open gates into fields and guide the movement of the cattle at intersections.

The rear vehicle acted as sort of a goading noisemaker to keep pokey calves reminded that they weren't on an afternoon field trip to the park. In addition, that vehicle had served as a buffer to prevent cars from suddenly coming onto the scene and striking the livestock.

Similarly, the lead vehicle served to forewarn drivers of cars, swooping over the crests of hills, that cattle in both the right and left lanes of the road lay ahead.

Two of us walked with the cattle. Each worked a side of the road, prodding dawdling calves in "get-along-little-doggie" fashion.

I'd always try to keep the calves out of the side ditches when I was assigned to walking behind the herd. The damp ground of the ditches, still soggy from the winter snow and succeeding rains, slowed the pace of the animals. But despite the loudest threats and the use of a switch, some refused to stay up on the roadway. Instead, they would tramp through the ditches, kicking loose rusty beer cans embedded in dead grass, defiling roadside violets and leaving huge tracks in newly constructed gopher mounds.

The beasts soon stretched out along the road in a beeline, their hoofs producing a steady grind on the gravel – a lumbering cadence of livestock on the march. Here and there, a yearling heifer butted a grazing calf in an attempt to gain frontage on the roadside meadow where she could grab a wholesome swath of lush grass before the pestering auto behind her blared its horn. At the same time, the driver shouted, "Hey! Getta goin' there!"

The absence of fences along fields presented a special problem. Invariably, venturesome cattle at the front of the procession would go bolting off into an open field, dragging their loyal followers. We would have to dash off toward them to put an end to their defection and get them back on course.

Rarely did we make the journey without the calves taking time out to stop and smell the noses of the cattle belonging to farmer Joe Arends whose pasture was at the midway point on our route.

Car drivers who happened on the scene were always tolerant and understanding. They typically were more intrigued than inconvenienced by our multitude of cattle, spread out between them and the drivers' destinations.

But back in the 1940s, Dad and his brothers were driving a herd of Herefords from a pasture south of Norwalk in Warren County to their farm on the southeast side of Des Moines. The animals had spent the entire summer in the pasture, so they tended to be wild and flighty.

Nevertheless, all was going well on the 25-mile drive, even when they were herding the cattle through the streets of Norwalk. But then a

woman who didn't know a thing about cattle walked out onto her front porch with a look of consternation.

When she saw the cattle parading down the street past her house, she grabbed her apron and waved it at the passing cattle, screaming at them to stay away from her petunias. With that, the critters panicked. They stampeded, went all over her yard, and, yes, trampled her petunias.

THE POULTRY ACCOUNT

A FARMYARD CRITIC: THE GUINEA

We first brought guineas to our farm because someone said those raucous, almost neurotic fowl would scare away any rats we had and keep the farm forever rodent-free. But, at times, their insane cacophony was to almost drive us humans off the place.

Early each summer, the tall weeds and grasses at the rim of the farmyard began to rustle with the undercover movement of baby guineas just hatched and in search of the fruits of June.

Those chicks tripped through the weeds, rushing frantically to keep up with their wary guinea hen mothers, which twittered away at the head of the plunge into a tangled wild.

Often I was attacked by a hen, intent on defending her chicks, which closely resembled baby pheasants. A belligerent guinea hen has the finesse of a helicopter to fly into a person's face and almost hover there while repeatedly flapping her wings and thrashing him with her feet.

But for all a guinea's bellicose, motherly defenses, she's a dodo for her taking her procession through weeds. Once she reaches the other side of the jungle, there invariably are fewer chicks to continue on with her. Some are to be trapped in labyrinthine weeds where their cheeps of distress are lost in their siblings' falling-behind cries ahead.

I know, for us, many were also gobbled down by farmyard cats that considered them wild birds.

Our guineas were either concrete-block gray with white polka dots at adulthood or else dark gray with polka dots. Their leathery, bare heads, their single bony horn protruding from their skulls and their general ugliness conjured visions of the bizarre, winged creatures near some brontosaurus in artists' drawings of the prehistoric animal kingdom.

Their fat, red, undersized wattles always reminded me, at least, of the way Chester A. Arthur, the 21st president of the United States, styled his sideburns and beard.

Anything could trigger the guineas into a frenzy. Any annoyance touched off a raspy protest in which every bird in the flock had a say in a strident, honking staccato. It was unceasing. The din and discord were most prolonged when they were safely at roost in the trees at night.

Their clamor could be ignited by anything – from a tractor being started to a dog's bark to the slam of a lid on a hog feeder. Or Dad might shout a command to me across the barnyard, sending the fitful, high-strung fowl into a new pandemonium. The remainder of my family's shouts was lost in the uproar.

Still, they were graceful at running, enviably independent and ideal scavengers. They caused us little work. As baby guineas progressed from down to feathers and began to take on the semblance of their parents, they were fascinating to watch.

Some could even be friendly, particularly those rescued as chicks and nursed along in paper boxes with heat lamps and later set free. Their penchant for roosting began early with the young birds finding something ever higher at night to roost on, as their wings grew stronger. Before they reached the trees, they roosted on fences, on horizontal bars of machinery and rims of water tanks.

Somehow our flock disappeared by attrition – until there was one lonely hen. She stayed around for several years, laying her tan eggs in nests. They never hatched. Then she, too, vanished.

Sure, it became a quieter farmstead. But the farm lost something beside the strident noise. It lost some of its best critics.

THE SPRING CHICKS

The cheeping of chicks has now become a rare sound on Iowa farms. Egg production fell off drastically, and few farm families took the time and trouble to foster the development of a flock from chick to layer.

Poultry production became a specialized field. Both eggs and broilers are produced in huge facilities that suggest none of the trappings, equipment or procedures associated with the traditional way most of us once – and a few still do – raise chickens.

For us, spring always meant chicks had to be ordered from a hatchery to eventually replace those hens laying, to their hearts' delight, in the hen houses.

In spring, the brooder houses had to be rid of manure from the year before, disinfected and sealed where necessary to prevent the loss of heat We put tarpaper on the floors. For bedding, an assortment of litter was used: cotton hulls, ground corn cobs, peanut shells or oat straw.

The six-sided brooder stove or "hover," as we called it, was finally lowered by a rope from the ceiling of the brooder house and set on the floor. A roll of corrugated cardboard was unwound and was stood on end to form a fence around the brooder to keep the chicks close to the stove so they would remain warm.

On egg case dividers, we sprinkled ground corn and grit for the chicks to peck at after they arrived. Jars were filled with water containing a yellow medicine. Then the jars had to be quickly flipped over onto their glass or plastic stands without spilling any water.

The building was warmed to more than 90 degrees before the chicks arrived at our farm.

We took the station wagon after each batch of just-hatched chickens. The hatchery put them into cardboard cartons, each holding 100 chicks. The cartons, divided into four compartments, had fibrous wood shavings for bedding.

For a number of years, our own laying hens provided the eggs we had hatched out for chicks. We shipped the fertile eggs off to Maude Ritter at La Porte City. She would incubate them in her country hatchery. Every week for a month-long period, she hatched a new bunch of chicks. The main problem we had with having our own eggs set and incubated was the subsequent need to have the chicks sexed – the baby roosters separated from the pullets.

We kept some of those roosters to raise as fryers. But if we couldn't give away the rest of the baby roosters, we had to drown them, and that was an agonizing ordeal that I couldn't take part in.

A cheeping shrill pervaded the station wagon as we came home from Mrs. Ritter's hatchery or from other hatcheries in area towns. The car heater had to be put on high for the benefit of the new chicks. That was almost too much for us to stand.

Once the chicks arrived at the farm, everyone gathered inside the brooder houses to lift the fluffy chicks one-by-one from the cartons, dip their beaks into the water for a drink and shoo them under the hovers. Some would scratch for food, and others would sit in a lump, still trying to get used to the world they had entered that day.

In the first days, a small percentage of the chicks would die. That was expected.

Baby chicks required constant vigilance. The trips to the brooder houses day and night were numerous. In adverse weather, chicks were particularly unpredictable. Often the noise of the wind or rain or the presence of the slightest draft would cause them to crowd together and pile onto one another, invariably smothering victims who got too far under the pack.

Many times we had to haul out dozens of flattened, trampled baby chicken carcasses as result of an abrupt and arbitrary change in the mood of the flock, triggering the pile-on.

In time, the chicks lost their down and developed feathers, long legs and a resistance to the environment that threatened them their first few days. And the chicks were soon chickens and then pullets and roosters. They were able to run free outdoors where other sets of dangers confronted them.

EGG WASHING WOES

For many years, we farm families living near Parkersburg, along with many others in a 50-mile radius of the tiny town of Austinville, dutifully gathered, washed and packed away millions of white, beige -- and sometimes manure-stained – eggs to send to that hamlet's egg produce on a weekly and semi-weekly basis.

The egg money for us, at least, was never put away as a nest egg. It went into the general bank account to keep us going in farming. But for many farmers and farmwives, the egg money was an income used for household expenses. We had big hopes in the 1950s that a lot of hens would equal "egg-tensive" profits. But from a farm economic standpoint, they weren't what they were cracked up to be. We had more than 1,500 hens kept in four chicken houses, including a double-story building.

We would haul more than a thousand eggs per day out of those laying houses in plastic-coated wire baskets. With two gatherings daily, the full baskets took up most of the floor space on the back porch, waiting for that endless evening of egg washing in the kitchen.

On fall and winter nights, Mother would begin the egg washing ordeal at about 6 o'clock, well before her main partner in the project – Dad – was done with the chores outdoors. Our school homework was considered a priority, and we kids helped out only if and when that was completed.

We had begun employing what then was considered a rather advanced egg-washing machine. But, in retrospect, it was a monstrous contraption that was tediously slow and impractical. That egg washer was essentially a square metal box a foot or more fall and 2 feet long with two trays extending out the front. Dirty eggs were set on the right tray in a row and on their sides so that they would roll into the washer by gravity. A rubber roller with screw grooves turned along the bottom of the washer to grab the in-rolling eggs and move them along in assembly-line fashion from right to left. The eggs were swatted by spinning brushes that spattered soapy water and scoured the eggs as they moved and revolved to the other end. Finally, they rolled from the second hole and parked in the tray.

While the operator sat feeding dirty eggs into the right side, he or she had to keep putting the just-washed eggs into the egg crate on the left side. Invariably the "clean" eggs would include eggs with dried-on hen excrement or dried egg yolk, a substance that clung to shells like cement.

It meant wiping the eggs with a damp cloth before dropping them, large end up, into the cases that accommodated 360 eggs or 10 layers of 36 eggs per layer. Cleaning up those eggs with special problems took time.

Meanwhile, the eggs coming out continued to line up and wait to be packed. Sometimes the operator fell behind, and the "out tray" became so filled with eggs that eggs rolled out of the machine and onto the floor.

In trying to handle the quantity of eggs that moved through in such mesmerizing rhythm, Dad became weary, then drowsy. No matter how much he tried to stay awake, he couldn't. Soon he'd be picking eggs out of the basket, and, instead of setting them into the intake tray, he would release them in mid-air. The eggs plopped on the floor. That stirred him to consciousness and evoked a stern scolding from Mother, who ordered and pleaded that he stay awake a little longer until the eggs were all put away.

"We've only a couple more baskets to do," she would emphasize.

But Dad begged, "Let me lie down for just a little bit, then I'll get up and help you finish." Translated, that meant, "I'm going to lie down on the davenport and sleep soundly, and you're going to finish the job yourself."

Night after night, Mother put the rest of the eggs away and then toted case after case of eggs to the porch for the egg man, Leonard Lenz, to load onto his truck the next morning when he might pay us a mere 26 cents per dozen – sometimes less. Few persons beyond the farmstead realized the endless tasks involved with producing the one dozen eggs that city dwellers were buying for 55 cents per dozen in those days.

Maybe that's why most families turned to getting their eggs from the supermarket.

Eventually we threw out the box egg washer. We purchased washers that agitated whole baskets of eggs in a back and forth manner like a washing machine. That accelerated the washing portion of the operation, but it still required handling the eggs and putting them away one by one.

When the egg baskets were finally empty and the cases full, a pan of cracked eggs and others with soft shells was left. We could expect them to be breakfast the next morning.

NIGHTS AND THE DAYS
IN BETWEEN

THUMPING OLD FLASHLIGHTS

I saw much of my world of youth and its accompanying work by the light of a flashlight. It was a flickering light on many occasions, and, oh so dim.

It was a luxury to have a strong-beamed flashlight to use to check the farrowing crates at night or to find the right bolt in the tractor tool box.

No group has made greater use of the flashlight invention than the farm family, nor has any put the handy tool to as many uses or has abused it as much as rural persons.

We went through flashlights as quickly as attorneys through legal pads. In my growing up years, we would have as many as five flashlights on hand it that drawer in the pantry, all of them in different stages of useful life. I'd first reach for the one that appeared to be the newest. If my chances were good, it would flick on with a white burst of light.

But more often, I groaned as I stared down onto a weak, yellow glow that would barely illuminate my path as I walked through darkness on some lonely chore. And surely I didn't expect the flashlight I pulled arbitrarily from the drawer to cast an impressive, long beam into the night's heaven – shining a ray that might be seen in 3 million light years by some being in a different realm.

No, when I reached into the drawer by the sink to pull out one of those farm-battered flashlights, I expected to have to take all of them

out, thump each one, and haul off the one that gave the best promise of lighting my way. If all else failed, I'd look around for some new batteries, then unscrew the spring-filled gadget and change the cylinder of new light. When that instrument for night vision was back together, I usually had a new lease on light.

I think back to the summer nights when it was my turn to get a flashlight and trod down to the brooder houses to close their doors. I always hoped I would find a bright, shining flashlight to accompany me through the pasture, a place where, my imagination told me, boogey men lurked and where the bull patiently waited to ambush me in the dark. But carrying that tube of light gave me security.

En route to locking up the chickens, I would swing my arm holding the flashlight and create fascinating patterns of light in motion. Periodically, I would shine it far ahead to make sure any creatures, lying in wait, would be forewarned of my approach and would flee from the vicinity of the brooder houses.

So often, a flashlight accompanied me to the silo where I forked out silage for the cows in the dark of night. Or I'd situate the flashlight in a spot in the hay mow to light up my work area as I dug out hay to throw out the barn door and into the bunk. In both cases, the light would become increasingly dimmer, and, in the end, I would get no more light from it than I would from a lightning bug.

Frequently I needed both hands to work and had to find a way to still hold the flashlight. I'd poke it through my belt, squeeze it into my armpit, stick it into my pocket in a way it would still shine forward, or even hold the barrel in my mouth.

With a flashlight, I searched for cows in cornfields at night, I squinted in an unlighted machine shed to help overhaul a tractor engine and I've found my way across a creek on the way to a field to take someone's turn on a tractor to do some night fieldwork.

Flashlights helped me unload ear corn into an elevator, aided me hunting for hogs that had gotten out onto the road at night and filled the outhouse with light for night visits.

In short, there is no limit to the uses of flashlights on farms – as long as one keeps them supplied with batteries and knows how to thump them whenever they choose to go dim.

SEEING THE NIGHT LIFE

At nightfall, Iowa farms reveal something that is concealed by day – within the walls of farm buildings, production never stops.

At 10 o'clock each evening, the farmhouse lights may go off. Yet blazing in farrowing houses, barns and poultry buildings may be light bulbs and heat lamps to aid birth, feeding and animal warmth. In an earlier age when farmhouse lights were extinguished, a vast darkness extended over the farmstead.

Nowadays, the countryside is aglow with lighted farm places. Radiating through groves are the blue glow of automatic century night lights, keeping silent vigil with farm dogs.

What rural inhabitant has not lain awake at night and heard the clanking lids of pig feeders or a lamb call to its mother or a cow itching her side rhythmically on a metal gate or listened to the cattle clank their registration tags against a steel tank.

The sleeping habits of livestock are a mystery. How can horses and cows sleep standing up?

But there's nothing mystifying about it when a farmer starts to see more profit from encouraging beef cattle to get midnight snacks at the bunks or pigs to go after food at a creep. Man has been modifying the living patterns of his domestic animals in quest of profit through faster gains in weight.

However, the landscape is not brightened only by stationary light bulbs that accompany night animal activity in buildings. Other lights bob in the darkness as farmers with flashlights in hand go about checking buildings where lambing goes on, barns where sows are farrowing and brooder houses to see new chicks.

At other times, an electrical extension cord may be stretched across the farm yard to light a dismantled tractor engine that must be back together by the next day so a farmer can get on with crucial field work.

And off across the dark fields from spring to late fall, farmers break the blackness with lighted machinery – ever mindful of the caprice of weather that could make that night work the only guarantee for crucial field work to be done on schedule.

The night is part of the day on the farm, for it's a quieter period when most of the day's activity is still carried on under the canopy of

darkness. For animals continue to gain, more milk is generated, the crops go right on growing and more livestock come into the world.

POP BOTTLES FROM THE PAST

It was always a delight to get time off from some chore or farm job and take an unscheduled trip with Dad to a distant town to get a tractor part or essential piece of equipment.

We had such a variety of tractors and machinery that we went in every direction – and sometimes 100 miles away – to obtain the right thingamajig: Ackley, Bristow, Waverly, Dike, Clarksville, Grundy Center, Dumont, Waterloo and New Hartford. All were places with implement dealers to service out well-known, as well as obscure brand-name equipment.

Somewhere along the way, we would stop and each one of us kids would get a bottle of pop and maybe a candy bar, courtesy of Dad. We would slip a nickel into the pop refrigerator just inside the filling station (as we called gas stations), press down on a lever and pull free the kind of cold, wet bottle of pop we wanted. There were all kinds of soda, all with their own unique flavors.

The bottles were notably smaller than today's beverage bottles, and we sipped the sweet liquid slowly. Besides, we were always in a hurry to get back home and back to mowing hay or baling it. So we always paid a penny- or two-cent deposit on each bottle and headed home, drinking the rest of our treat along the way.

In time, those bottles collected at home because many of the soft drinks weren't on the shelf at the local grocery store, and we couldn't take them there to get the deposits back.

And we went on vacation, we were to bring back more bottles unintentionally. Along the route, Dad periodically stopped at service stations and treated all of us to bottles of pop. We would say we wanted Coca-Cola or 7-Up or strawberry or orange. Dad did the best he could to fill our orders.

But if the station didn't have our choices or other familiar brands, he would get us the next closest refreshment, then paid the deposit on the bottles and went back to the car. Then we went on down the road – our sodas in hand, in an attempt to discover America.

In short, we hauled home an assortment of bottles of strange-sounding pop brand names.

Years later, we tore down a garage on the farm. Inside it was a cache of old pop bottles. Seeing some possible antique value in them, I took them home and spent a Saturday night cleaning them up so I could read the bottlers' boasts: "Golden Girl Cola, Refreshing as a Cup of Coffee"; "Go-For" brand that "Hits the Spot," a bottle that features the picture of a gopher on one side and a girl on a diving board on the other; and "Double Cola," which claimed "double measure, double pleasure."

There was "Nehi," "Grapette," "Dr. Swett's Early American Root Beer," "Hi-Q," "Bireley's Non-Carbonated," "Rock Spring," bottled by Jacob Ribs Bottling Works Inc. of Shafer, Minn., "Slim Sour," "Life Beverages," "Red Rock Cola," "Northwestern Full Flavored Beverages," "Big Chief," "Sun Rise Beverage," "O-So Grape Soda (Rich in Dextrose for Quick Energy)," "ABC," "The Double Line," "Mahaska Quality Beverage," "Powell's Beverage," "Ice Cold '76," "Kist," "Howell's Root Beer," "Spring Grove Beverage," "The Village Mixer," "Vess Cola" and "Dodger Cola."

We lost the deposits on more than 90 bottles. Now they are reminders of far-away bottles with sweet-sounding names.

HOOK SHOT FROM BEHIND THE COMBINE

Just about every farm kid who ever enjoyed basketball has had a battle finding – and keeping – a place on the farm yard to play basketball.

No matter where he ended up putting the hoop, he would be crowded out of his playing space by the activities and equipment of the farm. His makeshift basketball court with its imaginary base lines would be repeatedly invaded by tractors and machinery, parked directly across the heel-drawn free-throw line.

Hayrack loads of alfalfa would be unhitched in the middle of his court. And occasionally in the fall, it wouldn't be surprising to come home from school to find a pile of corn dumped in the middle of the playing area to be fed over the next two months to the hogs in the pen nearby.

How could anyone play basketball with all that?

For me, it was a constant up-court battle – the kind no city kid with his fancy backboard on the garage or dandy courts in the park or at school could understand.

When my orange-painted basketball hoop and regulation-size basketball came in the mail from Montgomery Ward, it was mounted on the front of the old garage. I quickly found out, however, the hoop was too close to the roof's eaves, and the ball constantly would be deflected off in all directions.

So I looked over the sides of other buildings on the farm, but I wasn't encouraged. Some of the best sides of buildings were in the middle of the hog and cattle lots. That might have been alright for the Arkansas Razorbacks or the Chicago Bulls, but not for me. I settled on a double-bin granary next to a chicken house. The granary had a broad front side, facing west, and a spacious playing area in front of it.

We took the hoop off the old garage and mounted it onto the siding of the granary, but we could only mount it 9 feet above the ground instead of the standard height of 10 feet. Had it been put a foot higher, we might just as well have put it on the roof. The hoop never was equipped with a net. No doubt it would have deteriorated and unraveled from rain and sun.

The location afforded me a wide-open dirt court, starting far out by a yard light pole. But with it being an open area, my basketball court invariably offered ideal parking space for machinery. Tractors were the most frequent intruders. I could usually move them out of the way when I wanted to shoot baskets. But more than once, I couldn't get them started, either because of a dead battery or some other breakdown that put them there for an extended period.

My dirt court was often muddy. Tractor tires and livestock hoofs dug deep into the mud, and when the ground dried or froze, it was left rough and craggy. It caused me to stumble in my basketball play, and the ball itself would hit the lumps and be deflected awry down the driveway.

Then I fought snow that built drifts so high that I could touch the rim of the basket without reaching.

When the arch of my shots from way outside went too high, the ball was abruptly knocked down by the electric wires. If I threw the basketball too high and cleared the roof, the slope of the roof's backside propelled it far beyond.

Chickens went into chaotic flutter and dashed their bodies against the chicken house walls whenever the ball bounced up against a window or the door. But that's not the only time I was in "fowl trouble."

Our flock of tame Mallard ducks always seemed to prefer spending the nights in a tighter cluster under the hoop. And each morning the ground was heavily sprinkled with droppings that would readily cling to my basketball.

Being the only sports-oriented kid in the family, I played many hours by myself. On cold days, I would bundle up to go out and shoot baskets. Sometimes my clothes were so thick, I could only clumsily fire at the basket from close in.

Sometimes my friend, Mervan, would come from across the road or I would go over and shoot at his basket above the family's garage. While he didn't have the same obstacles with his basketball court that I had, his ran sharply downhill away from the basket. When the ball got away, we had to run down the hill to catch up with it.

Being the shortest boy in my school class, I never went out for varsity basketball. I could only vicariously dream about making winning baskets with last-minute layups or stealing the ball from an all-conference guard.

Still I made some of the most sensational 70-foot shots ever attempted – right through the hoop on that granary. Although those shots were never seen by anyone else, those incredible feats live on in the memories and annals of this one-man farm team.

WOES OF KEEPING TOES COVERED

Gaze down on a farmer's shoes, and you'll probably see leather bare from wear, shoes that need polish, but don't get it.

It has never mattered that once black or brown sheen has been permanently wiped from his footwear. It certainly goes unnoticed by the fellows at the co-op or the guys at the sale barn or a well-dressed bank vice president about to extend a loan to a farmer.

Like blue jeans, more fashionable after they've faded, a farmer's shoes contribute to casting him as a person of active living whose shoes slide across a clutch as easily as they climb over a barn stall or kick a frozen door free. Shoes rubbed down to the leather by work are much

like barns long stripped of their paint by the elements and taking on a weathered appearance.

No doubt any father, rural or urban, is aghast at the number of shoes it takes to shod a family. On our farms, it seemed we were off to visit one of the stores in Parkesburg almost every season. There we were with one shoe off, getting a sweaty foot measured, then stuffed into a cool, new-smelling work shoe.

In a corner of the porch in summer or behind the fuel oil-burning stove in winter, there huddled a collection of shoes, overshoes, black rubberized chore boots, insulated winter shoes and sneakers. No right or left shoe was ever with its pair partner. They were stirred up and scrambled each time one of us went after a pair of shoes. My twin brother and I usually bought shoes alike. His shoes were indistinguishably larger than mine. Thus we had to take note of more distinctive characteristics of the shoes to find our own. The toes of mine always curled upwards more, so the creases across the top were more noticeable.

And because I did more of the chores in the cow barn, my shoes always carried more remnants of the barn. Moreover, my work shoes tramped through much more water, especially in the milk house, and the leather reflected the effects.

Not long after we bought new buckle overshoes or black chore boots that reached up to our knees, they would be punctured. They were often pierced by a silage fork in the course of tossing feed from a silo or cleaning manure from a cow gutter or while walking into the point of a fork in a dark corner of the barn.

When my boots leaked, it was easy to "borrow" my brother's. That simply meant getting his put on before he got to them. But when mine leaked, I had to carefully maneuver my feet while crossing the creek. It meant keeping the leaky boot out of the water. Dad was diligent at getting out his patching kit and slapping a round patch on the boots. But the patches lasted for only a while – and our feet quickly knew when the seals had given out.

The most exasperating problem with boots was to be separated from them abruptly and unexpectedly in a muddy cow lot. So often, I chased a wayward cow through the quagmire of spring rain mixed with mud and manure. Suddenly my boot got locked in the deep, thick muck, while my momentum pulled my leg from the immobile boot.

And in the next movement, my stocking foot plunged down into the cold, sticky, putrid mire. If I was lucky, I could reach back from an awkward position and tug loose the embedded boot, then pull my mud-covered lower leg, strip off the sock and finally stick the bare foot back into the boot.

But usually it meant gingerly stepping around the cold ooze until the boot could be grasped and pulled free. Then it was off to the house to get dry socks and clean trousers.

Footgear took a lot of abuse on farms, even from the sure-footed.

PASSING ON THE PAST

Each one of us carries his own baggage, the baggage of his past, the record of his experiences and deeds, his foibles and his minor triumphs. It's all there in the ever-heavier baggage we bear through life.

But each of us is also an heir of his or her parents' pasts. So many of their experiences, possessions and tales come down to us as legacy. It's our heritage. And it's particularly a rich one if it's a rural legacy. Our parents' verbal accounts of the events of their lives are the folk legends we hear and ought to hear time and again. Some of it we keep and pass on to our children. Some of the tales and accounts are sifted out of our minds and lost forever.

So it is that we who have roots in the land are heirs to a colorful and special inheritance, teeming with stories of a wholesome lifestyle.

We're familiar with the simple, bittersweet feelings we have when we visit places of our own pasts. There's something self-renewing about returning to the farms, fields, woods and creeks that made up the backdrops of our fleeting youth.

Visiting places that mean something to our parents and grandparents adds an extra dimension. The trips there give form and meaning to the stories they have told and retold to us.

One of those places for me is a farm nine miles south of Eagle Grove, Iowa, where the hills along the Boone River smooth out to table-flat countryside.

That Wright County farm was home for my mother's Uncle Newton Bawn back in 1920 where she, her sister Mabel and their father, Horace Bawn, went after the world-wide influenza epidemic took the life of my

grandmother, Dora Bawn. She died on the farm in Grundy County. Understandably, my grandfather wanted to get away. He rented his farm out and took his daughters to the farm near Eagle Grove.

It had a huge barn that could be seen from far.

For my mother, it was home during some transition years in her life and the source of many stories.

There's the story, for example, how she used to run from an ill-tempered ram sheep that foraged on the yard. At night before going to bed, Mother made her walk to the outhouse at the back of the house. She tried to time her trip so the ram would be far from her route.

One night, Mother made her usual rush for the little shed, but the old ram saw her and gave chase. My mother got to the privy just in time to yank the door open, scramble inside and slam the door shut. At that moment, the ram crashed head-down into the outhouse door.

The determined ram then parked himself outside the door to wait for her to attempt her retreat to the house. Time passed, and it was an hour before her cousin Nellie realized that my mother had not come back into the house from her trip out back.

Only then did she go out to rescue the hostage.

That's just one of the tales passed down from the past worth hanging onto.

SPILLS ON THE FARM KITCHEN TABLE

My father took pride in farming his fields of rolling hills carved by creeks. It was termed Grade A soil, commonly touted as the "best in the world."

It took paid hired help to cultivate the land and care for our livestock, and some of them lived with us and ate all their meals at our kitchen table. At night, they smoked in the sitting room by the TV, while we did our homework across the room.

The old farmhouse, erected in the 1890s, had no dining room. The kitchen contained the electric stove next to a wood-burning stove for heat, plus a refrigerator, upright freezer and coat rack. A small pantry with the sink came off the kitchen, and a small back room had storage and another large freezer to accommodate all the meat we devoured from our farm-raised hogs, cattle and poultry. The house had

no bathroom, and we washed our hands and faces in the sink in the pantry. In the tiny cellar, there was a steel bathtub.

My sister Linda, twin brother Lincoln and I shared the dinner table with my mother and father and almost always with at least two hired men who slept in the big bedroom upstairs in a large bed next to two single beds for my brother and me. For many years, my dad employed Floyd and Charles, two bachelor brothers and paid them $25 each a week.

The seven of us sat around a typical 1950s retro dinette set with the table and chairs supported by silver chrome legs that curved sleekly to the floor. The vinyl seats, some worn to the fabric, and the backs were fixed by screws into the metal framework. The table top was a light gray laminate or Formica. We always had the leaf in the table to accommodate the seven or more who ate there. It never had a tablecloth. Just above the table was the clock shelf with room for a black wind-up clock and a radio set to WHO, the 50,000-watt "Voice of the Middle West" radio station (1040 AM) from Des Moines. (Jack Shelley broadcast the noon news, and a few years later, he would be my radio journalism professor at Iowa State University.)

My dad's real estate license was in a frame on the wall behind us. Our dog Buddy was under the table to catch scraps.

Decades earlier, the house had settled, so the floor was lower toward the north window. Whenever a glass of water or Kool-Aid spilled, a stream rapidly rolled "downhill" into the lap of Floyd who was a fixture at the end of the table. Then it dripped onto the floor.

In those days on the farm, the meal at noon was called "dinner," while the night meal was "supper."

My mother sat at the other end of the table, closest to the stove. My father was next to her toward the middle of the tiny kitchen. (Understandably, we never called it the "dining room.") Lincoln sat in the middle next to Charles. I was across from him in the middle of the table between Floyd and Linda, along the wall.

We kids always took turns saying a rote prayer before eating, "Come, Lord Jesus, be our guest and bless this food before us. In Jesus' name, amen" or "God is great and God is good and we thank him for our food. Amen."

My farmwife and registered nurse mother never claimed to be a good cook. She spent most of her time outdoors tending the large

garden, handling her part of the livestock chores, especially looking after baby chickens, taking care of her many flower beds or gathering eggs.

Often we three kids teased her mercilessly with a song I made up, with an up-and-down sing-song rhythm. While she was dishing up food, we chanted, "Potatoes and meat, potatoes and meat, that's all we have for dinner. Potatoes and meat, potatoes and meat, that's all we have for dinner!" Month after month and year after year, she had to listen to it.

Alas, the beef and pork we consumed daily came out of the pressure cooker or frying pan ---essentially leather-like with the life cooked out of it. (Years later, while living in South America, I was treated to *real* meat -- beef and lamb via an "asado," or fire-barbecued and prepared rare).

So much of our mother's cooking was over-cooked, but we didn't realize, at the time, food came any other way. There was such a sameness to our meals, but we never got tired of the bounty from our garden in the growing season. It was enormous – beans, peas, tomatoes, radishes, onions, sweet corn and carrots. Wild raspberries, gooseberries and choke cherries came off non-cultivated areas along fence lines or in groves. There was always dessert, sometimes day-old bakery items that my father brought home for the grocery store owned by a second cousin. Tapioca pudding and pumpkin pies were my dessert favorites.

The table conversation was lively, animated and robust. My parents, who were superb storytellers each, couldn't stop talking about their experiences growing up -- about their brothers, sisters, parents and farm neighbors. The stories were authentic. They were rich in detail, and we begged to hear the same stories over and over, like how one hired man and my mother got lost in a small town three miles away as she went to visit her sister. Or the time Uncle Don got bitten in the rear by a boar and freely pulled down his overalls to show anybody his wound. Or how Mother and Aunt Lillian made ladies' dresses out of feed sacks intentionally made for seamstresses. Or how Uncle Don nearly died when his team of horse got spooked coming down the driveway and raced toward a corncrib, only to be stopped by a pole. Or how my dad agreed to dress up like a young bride at the school for a fund-raiser and could never live it down.

My father had a habit of laughing wildly about the story just told. With a roaring guffaw, he would bring his fist crashing downward on the table, rattling dishes and tableware.

Over the years, my parents took a chance by hiring so many drifters, ne'er-do-wells, men escaping from family strife or from getting a girl pregnant. There were alcoholics, old cusses, some with severe mental disabilities and some parolees.

Most never stayed around long at our place, except Floyd and Charles, who grew up poor along the West Fork River and never got through high school. They never had much to say at the table, largely because their spheres were so small and their experiences limited. They went to town on Saturday night with their $25-checks.

Many workers were hired from town for hay baling or oats combining for several days. Sometimes they were added to the table, or they ate in the shade outdoors. Hired men commonly swore like sailors and could tell the most ribald jokes. Their troubled lives were such a contrast to our prosaic and stable existence, but we listened intently to their commentaries and grew up quicker by that exposure to the "real world."

At the table, I was so much the "smart kid who constantly tested and quizzed everybody to see who knew who was president in 1884, or the capital of India.

Farm prices were desperately low during most of my formative years. Though my dad complained about virtually giving away his pigs at the sale barn, or how far behind planting was because of incessant spring rains or how one of his hardest working tractor had a bearing that needed replacing and baling hay was delayed, our daily table talk never suffered. It flourished on our tribal stories, the misadventure tales retold and our rural rhythm of life.

There's no count as to how many "Dinner is ready!" shouts were hurled across the farmstead for family and farm hands to head to the house to share a down-home meal and talk away.

We usually never had left-overs. Floyd's lap would dry from the overturned water glasses.

Mother kept on turning good steak into petrified meat, and we put our dishes in the sink. And we went outside to the land that had fed us and to the demanding tasks and chores that would steel us and temper us for lives and careers far from that farmhouse — eventually a vacant home that a vandal would burn down, a farmhouse steeped in laughter and retold stories.

CLOSER TO HOME

DISCOVERING HOME

If you ever were a farm youngster who moved with your family to a new farm, you know the thrill of discovery, the exhilaration of exploring a strange farmstead that has suddenly been designated "home."

Because it *was* officially home now, it was wholly within your limits as a young scout, and you were a happy wanderer on the landscape. It was as if you trespassed onto an unfamiliar and secret-filled estate without risk of being caught snooping and scolded. You weren't denied entry anywhere because it was now where you would be living.

Your curiosity ran away with you as you bounded around the buildings, pulled open doors, poked your head into foreign structures and caught strange new odors.

I was just such a boy when I was 8. I was old enough to realize the significance of pulling up roots outside of Polk City in the hill country along the Des Moines River north of Des Moines, then resettling in Grundy County where my mother's family roots run deep.

I had visited that farm several times. I had earlier accompanied Dad to the farm near Parkersburg where he would go to look over his investment, negotiate with tenants and ready the place for the day when he could move his family there and be, at last, owner-operator of that farm bought in 1940, along with the adjacent farm that had continually been in my mother's family since 1855.

That bright and sunny Saturday morning in March gave all portents that winter was receding. In rural Iowa, March was commonly a time

when farm renters/tenants collected their goods, took their children out of schools and moved to other farms just in time to get set up for oat seeding and the crop work to follow.

The driveway of our "new farm" was torn up by trucks – the trucks that had come and gone, some having taken the tenants' assets off the farm in time for our truck to bring a different collection of modest belongings that made farming and living easier in the early 1950s. The front lawn was streaked with tracks caused by trucks biting into the wet, thawing soil.

In one corner of the front yard was a spot where my father had buried my day-old puppy after its death several months before at the farm we lives on near Polk City.

I cried relentlessly as the puppy was losing – and after it lost – its grip on life. Amid my sobs, I demanded it get a burial at a place where I could always be able to visit. So on one of the dozens of truck trips he was to make in the ensuing weeks to the farm in Grundy County, Dad took the body of the Shepherd pup and buried it in the front yard. Later we planted a forsythia bush on that spot. Its yellow brilliance each spring was to be a reminder of what that squirming puppy, born in a wet ditch, had done toward teaching me about love for an animal – albeit his life amazingly brief.

On that morning when we had permanently moved 100 miles northeast, I wasted no time in a reconnaissance of the farm. I set my eyes for the first time on countless spots, buildings and fields where I would learn the arts of work. I didn't know it then, but for every second I peered into a chicken house, a milk house or at the stanchions in the cow barn, I was to spend a hundred of hours there in chores and perfunctory work.

In that nearly empty haymow, I would sweat to exhaustion and harden my muscles that I would carry off to a career where they would rarely be strained. Silent chicken houses would soon be inhabited by laying hens to which I would haul bucket after bucket of ground mash before and after school.

The exploration never ended till I had been through every building and had scanned and scouted the fields and grove.

As new occupants usually do, we imposed our character on that farm. We rerouted fences, tore down buildings and altered the emphasis of the farm operation.

But on Saturday, March 6, 1954, before we had interfered too much with the farmstead, before we began honing it to reflect our agricultural preferences, an 8-year-old boy delighted in exploring the farm where his parents decided to raise him to manhood. It was where they went on to fulfill their dreams until my mother died in 1997 and my father's health required taking him to Arizona to spend his last seven years. He died at the age of 92 – some 50 years to the month that we first arrived on that farm that so framed my formative years.

A PITCHFORK AND A RADIO

It had rounded corners. Its pastel-colored plastic was too fancy for the dairy barn. And its grooved knobs carried the grime of working hands trying to find satisfaction for hungry ears. Dust, chaff, fly specks and cob webs clung to and humbled the Motorola, but its sounds came through, nevertheless.

Still that old barn radio, which played to me and all the other creatures of the barn, was one of the enduring elements of my year on the farm.

Ours sat in a shallow wooden box nailed to a brace on the south wall of the barn – too high for a milk cow to back into when she shifted into reverse to exit the stall and leave the barn. Hooked up to the light switch by the barn door, it automatically came on whenever the switch was turned on.

During the summer months when lights were not needed, we unscrewed the fly-specked, 100-watt light bulbs in the sockets around the barn, so we could turn on the radio immediately when we stepped inside and hit the switch.

That radio, however, was regularly disconnected and taken elsewhere on the farm. If we could get electricity to the jobsite, that radio was there, too. Sometimes we had to string together numerous extension cords of all lengths to reach the shed where we were working. Most often, we wanted the radio to give background rock 'n roll music for our tedious jobs. Usually the job was pitching manure from a chicken house, hog house or cattle shed.

Sometimes we had to disconnect Mother's sewing machine, wall clock or other appliances to round up enough power cords to get the

radio energized near our places of work. And the cords didn't always go back to the house smelling as good as they did when they were borrowed.

We made heavy use of the car radio, too. Sometimes, we would drive the car near where we were working and turn the radio on. We had to be certain we wouldn't run the battery down.

To this day, I associate specific songs to a certain summer when they were popular, almost down to the tasks we were doing while listening to them. Whenever I hear Johnny Horton's hit from 1959 called "The Battle of New Orleans," I clearly remember cleaning out rich-smelling calf manure – countless spreader loads – from a pen in the old barn on the north farm.

The song "Chanson d'Amour," popular about 1958, reminds me always of the twice daily 1 1/2-mile trips to Harold Becker's cornfield with the milk cows. There they'd fend for downed corn ears. But while driving them down the road, the fellow walking in front of the car required the car radio be played at full volume so he could hear it while goading the cows along on the roadside.

Most of the time, we were tuned to KWMT Radio from Fort Dodge. Often, however, it was WHO (1040 A.M.) from Des Moines where we listened to talk radio or to Iowa Hawkeye basketball and football games, with Jim Zabel calling the play-by-play. We never did any work in the barn without the radio as our constant companion. Thousands of now forgotten singers and songs, almost as many commercials and newscasts, entertained and informed us while we were chore-bound.

The durable plastic radio, hauled to all parts of the farmstead, gave a leisurely dimension to our farm work, making us oblivious to the tedium of out tasks.

THE SOUNDS OF PROM

It was handy to have youth from the country work on committees when it came to engineering major productions at school such as junior-senior proms, providing floats for the homecoming parade or materials for the harvest ball staged on the gymnasium floor.

Rural kids made a lot of valuable resources available to school projects like their fathers' give-away lumber, any carpenter tools and hayracks

for constructing parade floats. But rural youth also provided a broad range of practical know-how, gained from experience on construction projects around the farm like building hog stalls or welding together useful farm implements.

At prom-planning time each spring, bands of 16- and 17-year-old juniors tried to turn ambitious prom themes they'd chosen into imaginative, gala and elaborate decorations that would make a movie set director take notice.

When my junior class selected the prom theme of "Moon River," our small class set out to create an idyllic riverside world, complete with pristine scenery surrounding a quaint river filled with crystal clear water passing under a wooden footbridge.

We planned an enchanting world of lush greens and airy blues. A huge silver moon was to hang from the ceiling in the middle of the decorated gym that had housed such an innumerable assortment of events of our school days.

As class president, I assigned juniors to various prom work committees. I put my twin brother, Lincoln, in charge of constructing the giant waterfall, which was to feed our Moon River and make it "wider than a mile."

His task was designing and constructing an authentic-looking waterfall standing 10 feet tall. He and his committee somehow devised a way to make it look real by using a revolving cardboard cylinder about 7 feet tall with a light inside it. By cutting out diagonal strips in the cylinder, a candy-cane effect was created, suggesting running water.

The falls themselves were largely made of paper and crepe in blues and whites. Silver streamers and a fan gave it a rippling illusion.

Lincoln also needed the sounds of a waterfall, but he couldn't find any waterfalls in Northeast Iowa. What to do? He chose to make do with what he had. He borrowed the school's tape recorder, took it home to the farm, hauled it down to the cow tank, pulled up the hydrant handle to run water at full force and recorded an hour's worth of authentic cow tank sounds.

On prom night, the fine-dressed juniors and seniors of the school, their dates and special guests crossed Moon River just like the song says, "in style." They beheld the beautiful, rippling rapids. The spilling splashes of the falls seeming amazingly genuine.

Few knew it was our cow tank providing gurgling accompaniment to the elegance of the evening.

RETURN TO A TINY FARM CEMETERY

They would have been main branches on our family tree had they lived and multiplied. But they died in their youth and thus remained mere nodules on the trunk of that tree.

Nevertheless, for more than 160 years, our family farm on which they lie buried has nurtured the family tree itself. Just as it served the early Bawn settlers, so it serves descendants in a sixth generation.

But three humble graves in the dirt of that farm are, in a sense, a grim legacy handed down from the first generation of the hardship they endured in founding the farm.

The bodies of three youngsters rest in an obscure and little known cemetery, occupying a tiny patch of land in the far southwest corner of the weed-choked backyard of that, the original portion of the farm bought from the government in 1855.

The first Bawn child was buried there in 1859. The other two were interred in 1880. They were the brothers and sister of my grandfather, my mother's father.

Two months after I was married in 1973, I took my young wife Patty to that simple cemetery. In the process, she got a family history lessons.

We went to restore the neglected burial grounds for persons no one still alive had ever met. The cemetery holds three of my great-grandfather's eight children. England-born Francis Bawn came to the United States in 1844, put his coal-mining past behind him, and headed for Iowa after a brief stay in Illinois.

He sought land and found what he wanted just inside of Grundy County, but bordering on the Grundy-Butler county line. The farm was just two miles southeast of Parkersburg, a city founded the same year Francis Bawn settled on that farm.

One of Francis and Lydia Bawn's first children was Earl, who was born on October 4, 1857, precisely 100 years to the day that the Soviets launched the Sputnik satellite, which opened the Space Age. Less than two years later, the youngster died of what my great aunt used to call

"cholera morbidness," an intestinal infection the aunt used to say came from "failing to soak cucumbers overnight." Earl was buried there in the backyard about 50 yards from where the frame house had been.

More sons and daughters were born, including my grandfather, Horace Bawn (derisively called "Horse Barn" when a boy), who was born in 1862.

In March 1880, two children in the family were stricken with diphtheria. A daughter, Ena, 14, and a son, Judd, 10, died four days apart. My grandfather, then 17, was spared.

Because of danger that the disease might spread, the bodies of the two youngsters were not taken by wagon to Parkersburg for burial. Instead, they were put into two crude wooden caskets and buried side by side to the rear of Earl's grave there on the farm.

However, three cenotaphs were placed in the Bawn burial plot in Oak Hill Cemetery in Parkersburg cemetery next to the main Bawn monument, a 15-foot obelisk. To this day, it remains the tallest marker in the cemetery.

My grandfather later took over the 144-acre farm and owned a couple others in the neighborhood, as did his brothers and sisters.

Shortly before he died in 1936, Grampa Bawn replaced the wooden grave markers previously planted at the heads of the graves in the backyard on the farm. He reset the markers with concrete slabs on which he engraved his siblings' names and the raw data of their short lives.

In the intervening years, tenants and hired men lived on that home place, while our family lived on an adjacent farm that merged with the original land. Thus, the cemetery and the backyard grew up to weeds.

When my brother and I were both home from college one summer and, in a moment of reverence for our ancestry, we erected a picket fence around the 8 by 12-foot burial plot. We painted the corncrib slatting white, then took a small paint brush and painted the inset impressions on the markers so they could be read better.

Years had passed, and "perpetual care" was arbitrarily carried out in the little cemetery. So it was that my wife and I found the cemetery as we expected it -- shaded by 7-foot high rag weed. It was barren of sod or other vegetation.

We proceeded to do something about nature's effort to erase all signs of the children's early existence. I chopped weeds while Patty tossed

them over a fence to hogs. We cleaned away other debris, straightened up the picket fence, then painted the wooden slats white. Just the year before, a second section of corncrib slatting had been stretched around the outside of the first fence to reinforce it and give added protection from any possible invasion by livestock.

The slats, rough and thin, resisted the paint brush. What's more, it was difficult painting the two layers of co-existing rolls of slatting.

As we worked, the sun shifted, moving behind the locust and mammoth oak trees, bathing us in shade. But that gave rise to an air force of gnats and mosquitos, which sought our company. Later, I chopped tall weeds outside the fence, felling tall thistles, burdock and pigweed. When we finished, we still had a cemetery in a clearing encircled by weeds forced to retreat a mere five paces.

Yet somehow, we came to realize there's something hallow about having one's ancestors buried in the land he owns.

CHRISTMAS EXPECTATIONS

When we grabbed hold of school bus driver Jack Perry's Christmas presents, a pack of Mars candy bars for each of us, and we stepped down to the icy gravel road, our thoughts turned with great expectations to that long fortnight of Christmas vacation.

I dragged home a couple school books with the best intentions of getting ready for those crucial January exams, but I knew they'd be impossible to find when I needed them that Sunday night after New Year's.

Dad had been talking about what he wanted to get done around the farm with our help during the Christmas break. For him, it was like having us home for a dozen consecutive Saturdays to sort hogs, clean manure from chicken houses or help him overhaul a tractor in the cold machine shed.

Christmas vacation always had a timelessness, marked only by the craving for time to pass quickly on Christmas morning so we could open our presents.

At our house, Mother made dozens of Christmas cookies with chocolate chips, nuts and maraschino cherries and packed them away in large flour cans between layers of waxed paper. The cans were then

stashed away in the cool back pantry. We would surely have cookies through January. A batch of cookies was left in the mailbox out on the gravel road for our rural mail carrier, Harley Hartman, who was also mayor of Parkersburg.

Out of the freezer came packages of beef and pork to be given to Leonard Lenz who twice weekly came to our farm to pick up the cases of eggs and haul them to the produce in Austinville. There was meat for the man who hoisted our 10-gallon cans of milk into his truck and hauled them off to co-ops in Plainfield, Benson or Hudson. Harley Parks, the tank wagon man who delivered gasoline, fuel oil and grease to our farm, was also given frozen home-butchered meat for Christmas.

And there were packages of meat, too, for neighbors. We could only convey farm products as gifts in appreciation for the abiding help and their friendship during the year.

We delighted in what the elevators, cooperatives, livestock buyers, egg produce and merchants in the area would give away as Christmas gifts. All of the items contained the businesses' names clearly printed on them. We kids complained that the giveaways too often were kitchen items.

We may have balked at doing some of the farm work that should have been accompanied over the long holidays, but when it came to Christmas morning itself, we worked with amazing speed at our chores. We always were up earlier than usual, stumbling into the December darkness to the barn, hog buildings and hen houses to get the work done as quickly as possible.

We weren't permitted to get to our presents until the chores were done, breakfast devoured and the Christmas Story from St. Luke read.

Our dog Buddy had been "trained" to carry things to family members on order, in this case Christmas presents. So he was skilled in delivering presents around the sitting room. Buddy, of course, had his own small packages of edible treats to pacify him amid the bedlam of flying wrapping paper and shrieks of unexpected surprises.

The volume and variety of gifts emerging from the boxes made it obvious that it was a *farm* family giving and receiving. For there were overalls and work gloves, tools and an electric shock livestock prod and other items picked up at a farm supply store.

It was all downhill from there. The rest of the vacation slipped away rapidly, and, before we wanted it, we were climbing back onto that school bus.

BEAVER NO. 2 AND BEYOND

EDUCATION AT THE EDGE OF A CORNFIELD

Atop the highest hill on our farm at a point where the two gravel roads intersect, a rural schoolhouse once stood as the seat of formal education for youngsters living in a 4-square-mile area.

It was officially known as Beaver No. 2, the "Beaver" coming from the name of the township.

Members of three generations of my family found our way to that simple, wood-frame building located on less than an acre of land on the southeast corner of that section of land in extreme north central Grundy County. Depending on our generation of school-going there, we arrived on foot or by wagon, bobsled, car, truck or tractor.

For a decade after World War II, Iowa's rural schools had their final flourish, as they co-existed with nearby town schools. Toward the end of the rural school era, many farm children were boarding buses bound to those town schools when, at the same time, just down the road, others were still walking to country school. But state-directed consolidation plans carried out in the early and mid-1950s brought an abrupt end to that time-worn, basic, yet respected, form of teaching and learning.

In the fall of 1955, the 15 of us who had been attending Beaver No. 2 were bussed to Parkersburg where we joined other somewhat bewildered and uprooted country school kids. Even my teacher, Viola Ulfers, was newly transplanted from country school instruction.

From a one-room school to a big brick building with three stories and many classrooms was daunting. Though I was to spend 18 years in schools and universities, ultimately earning a master's degree, I

considered my brief 1 ¼ years in country school to be an integral part of that learning process.

After they closed the rural school, the county school superintendent held a sale. My father was able to purchase the school building and grounds for just $300. The school would then spend its senility in the shade of great leafy elms, which were later killed by Dutch elm disease.

The schoolhouse must have been new when my Grandfather Bawn went to school there in the 1870s. During the First World War, Mother went to school there. On the eve of World War II, Dad bought the farm from which the schoolhouse had originally been cut.

Built with square nails by community farmer-settlers, the 35 by 20-foot building was planted at the center of the school ground. It faced south – down onto the Chicago & North Western Railroad track, which made a bend below the hill on a bead to Stout.

Freights used to thunder by twice daily, each time jarring the school and momentarily disrupting the teacher's discourse with one of her classes – or class of one, as often was the case.

At the last, there were 15 of us from nine families. When my twin brother and I enrolled in second grade in March 1954, we doubled the class size, making it the largest in the school.

Anyone entering the schoolhouse would first ascend two steps and then go into a cloakroom where lunch pails, coats, scarves and ball gloves hung on hooks or nails pounded in decades before. On the floor were graveled-covered overshoes, colored in dust or mud of the roads they tramped over to get to school.

The other side of the anteroom was a coal bin. Sparrows somehow got inside and made nests on the ceiling supports, and mice nested inside the walls and along the gnawed floor boards. Older boys used to capture mice in traps and dangle the partly paralyzed rodents in the faces of girls, who would scream and shrink and go tattling to the teacher.

Then Doris Allspach or Maida Davis, our teachers in separate years, would reprimand the boys. When their mischief was more roguish, they might be confined to their desks for recess.

The school grounds were not equipped as most school playgrounds were, but always did manage to find something to do during our two 20-minute recess periods each day.

A decrepit slide, its support legs bent, had to be braced against a pine tree to use. It served as the only piece of playground equipment for our use

The schoolhouse itself, however, became our biggest asset for recess entertainment. A hoop and basketball backboard was nailed up to its backside. We threw balls against its sides for fielding practice, and over the roof for "Annie, Annie Over."

One corner of the school's foundation always served as first base for softball. For any tag-type games, the school itself was the base where we were "safe" from becoming "it."

During recesses, Mrs. Davis was more rabid about softball than any of us students. She would kick off her high heels and play ball with youthful glee. In her nylon stockings, she would scamper around the bases with zeal. But we'd howl with the laughter whenever she'd step on a thistle or stone and hobble to base on one foot while grasping her pain-wracked other foot.

Another recreation was music.

Out vocal music department was found behind the stove. It was a hand-cranked phonograph kept on a table. Each morning, our teacher would put 78-rpm records on it and then stand cranking the phonograph while each student was required to take his or her turn singing a song from start to finish in front of other students. We had to be able to sing from memory before we could proceed to a new song. Our songbook was titled "Together We Sing," a book used by rural schools throughout Iowa and included many obscure songs I have never heard since.

The songs coming out of the phonograph had a Donald Duck sound, suggesting the records were probably going around at too many revolutions per minute, but they were never slowed down.

Every Monday afternoon at 2:30, the teacher turned on the radio that sat on the shelf on the wall behind her desk, and we listened to a radio program put together at the Department of Music at Iowa State Teachers College in Cedar Falls and broadcast over WOI Radio at Ames.

We dug out our "Songs in the Air" songbooks, cleverly illustrated by longtime Iowa cartoonist Herb Hake, who was also announcer for the program. Then ISTC assistant professor of music John W. Mitchell would tell us to turn to page 4, for example, and the professor would lead us in the singing "The Blue Tail Fly." And throughout rural Iowa,

tens of thousands of us country kids would simultaneously be singing, "Jimmy crack corn and I don't care...."

The radio was also turned on each noon when we would listen to the news while we ate the contents of our lunch buckets at our desks. They were the common school desks of the era – wooden tops and backs, supported by fancy iron castings. The desks were anchored to wooden slats to make it easy to keep the seats and desks in sections which could be slid around on the floor.

In the rear of the large main room of the rural school, near the door sat an earthenware jar with a spigot. It was our water cooler. Each morning two students were assigned the job of taking the badly chipped porcelain bucket out to the well. There together we would work the old, squeaky hand pump and fill the bucket with cold well water.

As a 60-pound second-grader, I had to reach up to the handle, wrap my own arms around the long pump arm, draw up my legs and hang onto the iron arm till my weight brought the heavy pump handle in a downward motion.

In the southwest corner of the schoolroom stood a five-shelf cupboard – the school library. In those days, I would not have doubted any statement that all the knowledge of the world was in the books on those shelves. I read avidly from that book collection. One year I read 40 books. That put me on the Grundy County Schools honor roll for reading achievement – and the first time ever that my name was published in a newspaper.

Our school had a central heating system. The black, pot-bellied stove near the center of the room always burned with a vicious roar in cold weather. Twisted circuits of stovepipe crawled along the ceiling until they plugged into the hole in the chimney. The teacher tried to arrive well before class time on winter mornings to get the fire blazing in the stove, but it took until mid-morning for the chill to be really gone.

When its educational role ended, my dad decided to use it to house hogs. For about 20 years, swine of all sizes found shelter in the old school.

In the temper of recent times, most property owners in the open spaces of rural Iowa have somehow fallen victim to the busy hands of deliberate destruction. Modern descendants of Attila the Hun and other Visigothic vandals still roam the countryside, blindly plundering what they can for some inexplicable reason.

Perhaps the combination of it being Halloween Eve and Saturday night gave the marauders enough cause to burn down Beaver No. 2 that night in 1976. The old white building was a good target when vandals poured a flammable substance on it about 10:30 p.m. that October 30. And it must have been a macabre thrill for them when it exploded into dizzy contagion.

If only that case of arson of the old school could have taught the "students of thrill" some kind of lesson. In time, it would have gone anyway – either by a storm or the decay of time. But that would have been a noble end for Beaver No. 2.

I sometimes wondered what I and others might have done vocationally had we been allowed to finish country school. Would five more years of rural education, then quitting school after the 8th grade, as was still common, have diminished my mental and creative development? I would have gone to town school starting in the 9th grade. Would I have been as well prepared? In the course of those five more years at Beaver No. 2 would I have learned less, dreamed less of bigger things or expected less of myself? How much further would I have gone with my education?

I can ponder such questions, but I can't answer them. However, the evidence that state officials had in the mid-1950s surely suggested it wasn't to my advantage to learn any longer in the school on the corner of our farm.

BEFORE THE BUS ARRIVED

When school started each fall, it always meant having to reschedule our morning and evening chores.

In late August, a few weeks before school started, the weekly newspaper carried the listings of school bus routes, and we always hoped the stop at our house would be near the end of the route. Not that we enjoyed getting off last at night, but, oh, the joy of getting a little more sleep in the morning before we had to get up and get outside to milk 20 cows, feed 1,500 hens and do hog chores.

But more often than not, the school bus was scheduled to make its stop at our driveway fairly early, usually about 7:50 a.m.

In the first week or two of school, Lincoln and I usually got up reasonably early – well before 6 a.m. – to make sure we had plenty of time to get the chores finished and have time to get ourselves ready for school. I milked, while Lincoln fed the chickens and did the morning pig chores. The goal was always to be done just as the barn radio came on with the 7:30 newscast.

In time, we were able to gauge just about how late we could stay in bed and still get done with chores by 7:30. We usually cut it all too close.

And when the unexpected occurred – the well pump malfunctioned or a stanchion broke and a cow got loose and hauled the milking machine and surcingle all over the barn – we would not get done in time.

At 7:30, there might well be several more cows waiting to be milked. Of course, there was only one way out: Scout around the farmstead or holler for Dad to come rescue us.

More than once, he could not be found—and I just pulled off all the milking machines, left the cows in the stalls, shut off the vacuum pump and headed to the house with semi-apologetic orders for Mother to find Dad and get him to the barn as soon as possible.

The 20 minutes or less we allowed ourselves to get cleaned up (that cow smell could hardly be washed off my hands) was a frantic rush. We jockeyed for a position around the sink to wash up, brush our teeth and comb our hair. On morning in his haste, Lincoln thought he had grabbed the tube of Brylcreem, put a little dab ("will do ya," as the TV commercial said) in his hand, and then rubbed it into his hair. But the peppermint smell exuding from his scalp told him he hadn't applied any of that super hair cream of the 1950s. Instead, he had grabbed the tube of Gleem toothpaste. Lincoln shrieked in disgust. The rest of us exploded in laughter. Mother got the shampoo and put his head under the faucet in the sink in the pantry. We now had one more obstacle jeopardizing catching the bus on time.

Once ready, I went upstairs, got dressed, then posted myself at either the west or east window depending on which way the bus came that year. Through openings in the trees, I could see about a half mile in either direction. The distance gave us early warning and usually gave the three of us time to scramble around, get our books gathered up, our shoes on, and all of us up the driveway before Jack Perry arrived there with the bus.

But all too often one of us couldn't find a shoe. In a furious frenzy, the shoeless kid crawled the floors and looked under the furniture. Meanwhile, he unleashed a litany of accusations that one of the rest of us somehow purposely hid the shoe.

Yet by then, the other two were out the door and climbing onto the bus. And if the shoe-seeking sibling continued to be missing, the other two of us, now seated on the bus, turned more and more shamefaced as we waited.

However, just before Jack's last threat that he would have to leave, the kid came hobbling out of the house, his foot partly stuffed into the shoe, the back of it being stomped down as he fumbled his way abashedly toward the bus. Sometimes, I was that straggler kid. And sometimes Jack Perry drove off, and our father had to make a trip to town with the kid who didn't get ready in time.

It's a wonder that I was absent from school only a half-day from 4th grade through my senior year of high school.

WITH A LITTLE HELP FROM A PIG

It was the age-old schoolboy's dilemma. The teacher said we had to give a speech in front of the class. But we didn't know of anything interesting enough to talk about. We were stumped. And our general indifference to becoming good speakers in the first place didn't help us come up with many ideas for a speech topic either.

When Lincoln and I were in the eighth grade, our teacher, Eloise Leavitt, set out to make us astute amateur orators. Mrs. Leavitt taught English. Sincere and determined, she was always trying out something new with us. Maybe it was that determination that prompted somebody to coin the phrase, "Leave it to Leavitt." She beamed with pride at the clever line.

That year, it seemed we had given numerous talks, each next expected to last longer. Then she wanted us to give show-and-tell talks.

Ugh! What could we do? We grumbled at home about the assignment. Suddenly Mother blurted, "Why don't you boys take one of the baby pigs from the barn to school and show the class how you give it vaccinations and iron shots and how you clip its teeth?"

At first, the idea seemed unexciting. To us, vaccinating pigs was just a common, everyday motion, and we doubted our fellow students would get much out of such a pedestrian demonstration.

But after more thought, we took hold of the idea.

First, we had to get Mrs. Leavitt's permission. After all, Mary, who had a little lamb, took it to school one day, which, we all know, was against the board of education policy, and she was put on something like mandatory probationary status. So we surely didn't want to cause an uproar that would make us the laughing stock that Mary was.

Mrs. Leavitt bought the idea.

Our English class started at 2 o'clock, or at the sixth hour. There was no way we could take the pig with us to school on the bus in the morning, then haul it around to five classes. It would be cold, hungry and tired by the time the little porker finally did arrive at Mrs. Leavitt's class in the southeast corner of the second floor of the old Parkersburg High School building.

So that morning, during chore time, Lincoln and I went down the line of farrowing pens, looking over newly born pig litters, eyeing each pig. We had to have the best pig possible to take to school. The piglet had to have the proper curl in its tail, ears keenly placed and proper body conformation. We wanted a pig that would have the right poise and personality in a classroom situation. Fortunately, we found one.

We put a chalk mark on him so that Dad would be able to find it and retrieve it about noon from its mother's farrowing stall and take it to the house to get the little oinker ready for school. Our timetable called for Mother to give it a bath immediately. All those piggy odors had to be gone, we insisted.

After the bath, the little white crossbred pig was to be put under a heat lamp in a cardboard box in the kitchen to dry off completely. Meanwhile, all necessary syringes, bottles of liquid iron and vitamins and paraphernalia had to be assembled. At about 1:30 p.m., our father loaded it all up in the car. The pig nestled in a paper box with towels under him and over him.

Dad drove to town and parked near the school and waited for one of us to come gather up the pig and the medicine.

The bell rang, and students shuffled off to new classes. Into the school came our oinking piglet. Everyone wanted a peek at him. He

grunted and jostled around in the box and wondered when all the nonsense would be over.

Without much delay, we started our demonstration talk. We explained the importance of disease prevention in baby pigs.

Next we proceeded with our work. One of us pulled the squirming pig from the box and locked him in a strong hold. Then we began snipping off his four tiny tusk-like teeth on the sides of his mouth. The squeals bounced off the classroom walls and could be heard down the school's corridors.

We next took a syringe and shot the terror-stricken pig under the right arm and pumped in a cubic centimeter of injectable iron. Under the other arm was shot a clear fluid vitamin, AD&E. Finally, down its throat, one of us plunged a plastic applicator of red, sticky Terramycin.

That shut him up. The whole thing was over in a brief time and only a bit longer than it would have taken in the barn at home. The 20 students in the classroom, many of them rural, laughed in fascination at the whole thing. We each received an "A" grade, and it sparked a variety of other lively demonstrations by other students in Mrs. Leavitt's eighth grade.

And speeches were always a little easier after that.

STUCK IN TOWN, WAITING FOR A RIDE HOME

Being stuck in town after school is a predicament most rural youths have been caught in. Whether it's just missing the bus and staying after school for an activity like sports practice or band practice, the situation often leaves parents and offspring both vexed.

When I stayed after school, I would walk two blocks to downtown Parkersburg and do my waiting at Dreyer Drug.

Dreyers always featured the best after-school party in town anyway.

Proprietor Louie Dreyer was always generous with his telephone by his desk in the back of the store where he prepared prescriptions and kept books. He would always let a stranded or beleaguered farm kid use the phone to call his parents and let the homefolks know he was at Dreyers, ready to be rescued – but "don't bother to be in too big of a hurry to come and get me."

From 3:30 until 5 o'clock, the stools and booths around the soda fountain were filled with teenagers sipping green rivers and cherry cokes, downing fries or getting ready for supper by swallowing malts. Every so often, Louie would shout through the clamor that someone was wanted on the telephone.

When the phone was for me, I usually found my mother on the other end saying she had finally gotten ahold of Dad. But he wouldn't be able to come until he could drive to New Hartford for a repair part before the implement there closed at 5 o'clock.

So, she said, just wait. Chores would have to wait. I'd have another coke, page through the "Mad" magazines and other more daring, adult pulp on the rack or just talk to the town kids who didn't have anything else to do until they wandered home for supper.

But Dreyers represented much more than an afterschool way station. It was more than a place where everyone in the family was expected to go whenever we came to town and split up to run our own errands.

Louie Dreyer operated a drug store for 30 years. My first memories of it was going into Dreyers with Dad in 1954 to buy the textbooks I needed for my country school classes. Louie would climb a ladder that wheeled along on a rail running along the south wall of the store. There near the top of the 14-foot tall ceilings, he would pull out the arithmetic and English books we wanted.

Dad always bought us five-cent cherry cokes, which we siphoned off sitting on the high stools and leaning on the black marble counter of the fountain. In 1958, the drug store doubled in size, when it expanded north in the area that the Princess Theater had occupied. It was at the Princess where I saw my first in-theater movie, "Gone with the Wind," in 1954 when I was 8.

Louie's Rexall drugstore was notoriously cluttered. Displays blocked out other displays, but his inventory was immense.

It was Dreyers where I went to buy my first camera and where I made numerous trips to take rolls of film to be developed. It was with great anticipation that I would return a few days later to pick up the pictures. There I bought thousands of baseball bubblegum cards as well as a lot of licorice, Kit candy and red-hots.

We went to Louie's to get syringes, needles, livestock penicillin, combiotic and a host of other animal medicines. He seemed to have more concoctions to treat a sick animal than a veterinarian. Louie even

mixed livestock treatments in 55-gallon barrels in the basement of the store.

Dreyers always rolled their popcorn machine out onto the sidewalk along Main Street on Wednesday and Saturday nights. Buying a bag of popcorn was as much a part of the evenings as getting groceries.

On weekdays, swarms of kids flocked to Dreyers for noon lunch as an alternative – or supplement—to the school's hot lunch program. For the entire noon hour on Wednesdays, it was standing room only, as Louie offered sodas for a penny for anyone ordering a sandwich.

For those who ate at school, a trip downtown always included at stop at Dreyers for a Pearson's Salted-Nut-Roll, Milk Duds or a Hershey bar, or just to be part of the hoopla and bustle inside.

A bespeckled, balding, short man of few words, Louie was respected and loved by the community's youth. He gave up the store for about five years and worked as a pharmacist in Cedar Falls. Then he returned to the store for a few months before he became gravely ill and wasted into death in April 1976.

About a year later, I stopped by at what had become the Parkersburg Pharmacy. That late afternoon, I ordered a green river, but they couldn't make one. So I ordered a malt. But the throng of teenagers I was familiar with was absent. Fifteen years before, a robust gang occupied the booths. But that day at 4:15 p.m., I was alone.

They later built the new high school on the east side of town – too far for a noon walk downtown and back.

So I sat on the old stools and leaned on the black marble of the fountain sipping my cold, thick malt. And I reflected on other late afternoons stuck in town waiting at Dreyers for a ride home.

NO MORE GETTING THE NURSE TO TOWN

Two times a week for 19 years, my mother left the demands of the farm to go 4 ½ miles to Parkersburg Community Schools. There she peered down the throats of school-age children, treated headaches and playground cuts and coordinated immunization programs in the schools. She weighed and measured students and posted it to their charts, and she gave occasional talks to girls in home economic classes about their physical maturation and changes with puberty.

Like rural students, she took the bus to school.

During her nearly two decades as school nurse, she followed a set routine of working each Tuesday and Thursday morning, then walking to the supermarket where she got her groceries and waited for my father to suspend his farm work to go to town to pick her up to take her home.

My mother couldn't drive. She wouldn't drive. She said she shouldn't drive. Mother said she would be a constant danger to every other driver on the road. Meanwhile, Dad never let her forget the inconveniences caused him and his farm work by her refusal to learn to drive a car. He told her that if she could drive, she could bring home a bigger sum of money working at a hospital in Waterloo.

But she still refused to learn to drive.

When she took up school nursing in the fall of 1956, she arranged to ride on the school bus with us three children. She always sat in the second seat on the right side of the bus. Even after we three had graduated from school in 1962 and 1964, Mother continued to go to work by school bus. It was part of the bus route to include a stop at our farm driveway twice a week.

Occasionally, she spent the entire day at school and would ride the bus home. The school district's courtesy, however, ended midway through her final year of school nursing. The rural neighborhood had changed. Different farms now had the school-age children. The district could no longer justify sending a bus well out of its way to pick her up. A neighbor woman who worked at a veterinary clinic in town provided her the ride to school twice a week.

At the end of the 1975 school year, Mother left the school system from which she had graduated as a student in 1929. She was 65 and had to retire. After high school, she had taken nurses training at Broadlawns General Hospital in Des Moines and served eight years as a registered nurse. She would often tell how Ronald Reagan was then a sports broadcaster at WHO-Radio in Des Moines and lived in an apartment near the nurses' housing where he was fond of flirting with the nurses as he washed his car bare-chested and Hollywood handsome.

Then at the age of 31, my mother quit full-time nursing and married a Des Moines dairy farmer, my father. Ironically, she and two other members of the same nursing school Class of 1932 married three Griffiths brothers, all farmers. The brothers operated Maple Leaf Dairy Co. in Des Moines.

When we were partly raised, Mother went back to light nursing as a school nurse. Until her last year, she never had a contract. She simply asked at the close of each school year whether she was wanted back the next year. Mother was always told yes.

But finally Doris Adelia Bawn Griffiths, R. N., reached mandatory retirement age. She finally became a full-time farmwife again and never had to worry about getting herself to town twice a week to look after the health of school-age youth.

GOING HOME TO CARMEN

In the late afternoon of weekdays when I would be driving in rural areas of Iowa as a newsman, I often came across a wistful scene.

A black-trimmed amber school bus was stopped beside a farm driveway, blinking like a pinball machine. A band of children, disheveled from a day of school and maybe a rowdy time on the trip home, clambered out of a side door. They stepped down to the gravel of home, caught the familiar scents of their farmstead and gave it all a quick is-anything-new glance before turning back just momentarily to wave to friends.

They began to walk up the driveway to the house. A little brother took off trotting. As the bus motor roared and the bus started up, some mouthy kid on the big vehicle stuck his head out the window and hollered an insult.

The farm dog came out to greet his pals whom he escorted that morning to the bus, sometimes climbing up onto the youngsters with muddy front paws to welcome them back.

I suppose getting home from school on a farm is really not much different from getting home from school anywhere, but more than anything else, it's different because the youths come home to a place where they are needed. In short, there is work waiting. They are just in time for chores.

My memories of getting off the school bus are congeries of individual experiences. I remember getting off many times in a state of nausea due to motion sickness gotten from reading too much of my homework during the bus ride home.

Or there were times that a big kid took my glove or hat and wouldn't give it back to me before I had to get off. I would plead in vain. "Look, I've gotta get off the bus now! Let me have it, please!" The bully scoffed at my pleas. I would get off in despair, only to see him fling my glove out onto the driveway as the bus drove off.

And there were days of dashing off the bus amid a downpour, scurrying without a raincoat or any protective cover for the many books that always went home with me at night.

Always exciting to me was getting home to see what major farm work had been done in my absence or whose strange car was parked in our driveway.

We were always hungry when we arrived home from school. We walked into the kitchen, plopped our books, jackets and anything else from school onto the table, then proceeded to scrape together a hearty snack.

My sister, Linda, turned on the television to Channel 9 to get Dick Clark's "American Bandstand," and somewhere between eating and changing our clothes, we heard the good and the forgettable music of the 1950s and early 1960s. Teens in Philadelphia danced to songs that Clark announced. He interviewed the kids to find out why this or that rock n' roll song hit or missed the mark.

I particularly remember a Bandstand regular named Carmen. Oh, lovely Carmen Jimenez.

It seemed that Dick Clark was repeatedly asking Carmen for her opinion on the latest single by Connie Francis or Jimmy Clampett. I thought Carmen was the cutest girl since Annette Funicello. She was so charming that to our most productive Holstein cow, the one that merited the first stall in the barn, I gave the name "Carmen."

Where now is that girl from Philadelphia, who in the early 1960s, charmed me after school just before I did my Iowa farm chores? Where is the namesake of our best cow back then?

She was a bridge to chore time. I had no trouble going from Carmen dancing the twist on television to Carmen the cow out in the barn.

They were both my afterschool friends, both with qualities that evoked something in me about grace and goodness.

FIRST HOMECOMING

Perhaps it's different now.

Maybe today when farm-raised college kids arrive home to the farm at homecoming time, there isn't that forlorn ache I experienced that October weekend in 1964.

I was strangely homesick at home.

I suspect a few rural-raised college freshmen each fall use their high school's homecoming football game as reason to make their first trips home from the halls of academia to visit the folks on the farm. It's likely they, too, feel passed up by events.

I caught a ride home with another Iowa State University student going to Cedar Falls that first homecoming after high school. It snapped just a five-week absence from the farm, my longest stretch away from home by far.

I went home to find I had been replaced.

A farm where I thought I had left my brand was functioning in new ways without me. My chore procedures had obviously been abandoned. Many changes were only subtle, yet still obvious to me.

While growing up, my domain had been the barn. During my high school years, particularly, I had asserted myself more and more on the ways things were done – and should be done – in that dairy barn.

I milked the cows in a certain order. Each cow was assigned her own stanchion, and I made sure they kept their places. The milking machines were hung up at night with a special tilt to drain and dry. Everything had its place in the milk house. The straps, or surcingles, that supported the milking machines, were kept at night on a wooden peg in a special way.

In short, a half dozen years as self-proclaimed "Chief of Dairy Operations" gave me time to establish a splendid order and protocol to barn activities. And I thought my superior methods would last for all time.

That weekend found me reconciled that I would never again be a part of the day-to-day operations on that farm. The cows were allowed to haphazardly take their places wherever in the various stanchions. Shelves, hooks, and corners of the barn contained tools and trappings of dairying and farming that belonged elsewhere.

The baby calves I had helped learn to nurse on their mothers' udders had grown into hay-chewing critters, their cuteness gone. Moreover, they ignored me.

I felt ambivalent and rueful that weekend. I felt a kind of melancholy gloom of seeing how ruthlessly time could change that place called home. I was in limbo about whether I should do any chores. The rules and procedures around the farm had changed. I was an outsider, a two-day guest at a place where I once lived. It was a weekend when I would normally be concentrating on the math and chemistry that Iowa State used to intimidate freshmen students and test their steel.

My parents convinced me not to waste a precious hour of my time home that weekend doing farm work. I should keep at my books.

The Sunday afternoon I packed up my clean clothes and loaded my pumpkin pies and other treats of home and went back to Ames. It was an ache and an estrangement that confounded me.

I don't remember a thing about the homecoming game or much about the dance that followed. Only the experience that the 18-year-old had of going home to the farm itself survives in my memories of my first homecoming.

Some six years later after I was discharged from the U.S. Army, I would spend the summer of 1971 on the farm awaiting the start of graduate school at Northwestern University. By then so much had changed on that farmstead, and I had grown up. I was 25, driving a '65 Ford Mustang convertible with all sights set on moving to the city and being a writer once I got my master's degree.

That summer would be the last time I got dirt under my fingernails from farming.

But by the end of the following year, I would be a daily newspaper editor writing about agriculture, traveling to many farms, interviewing U.S. secretaries of agriculture and judging pork queen candidates. I would be married, have two children, buy a small farm nearby with my siblings and sell that land years later.

For 25 more years my parents would live on their farms until death of my mother in 1997 and poor health of my father ended it.

Probably most of us who spent our formative years on working farms dream vividly at night about being back there, doing again what we were taught to do in the fields and barns. We return to the creek and the asparagus patches, the chicken houses and the feed salesmen,

the blizzards and the tornado warnings, tall silos and instruction to city kids on how to rake hay. I return to those places -- and more -- in those dreams.

Thoughts and dreams go back again and again to that patch of the planet – to that sacred land of nurture. Gone is the one-room school, the house and the barn, the fences and tractors, the guinea hens and the surcingles.

Despite the estrangement I felt so long ago coming back from college for high school homecoming, I came to realize the changes were taking place in me, and I had moved on.

Made in the USA
Middletown, DE
09 May 2016

19.99
5/12/16

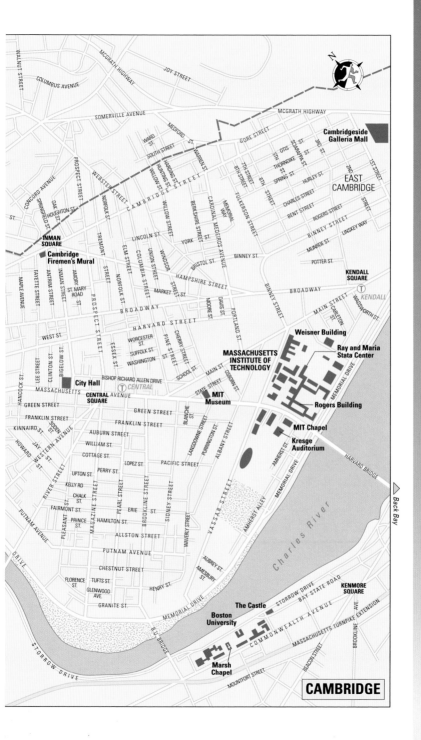

CAMBRIDGE

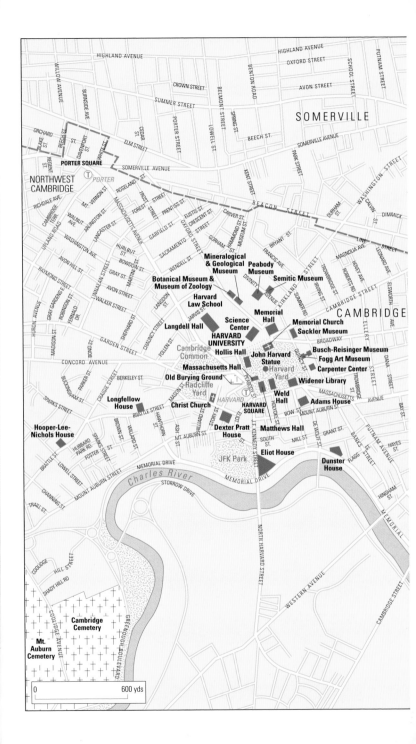

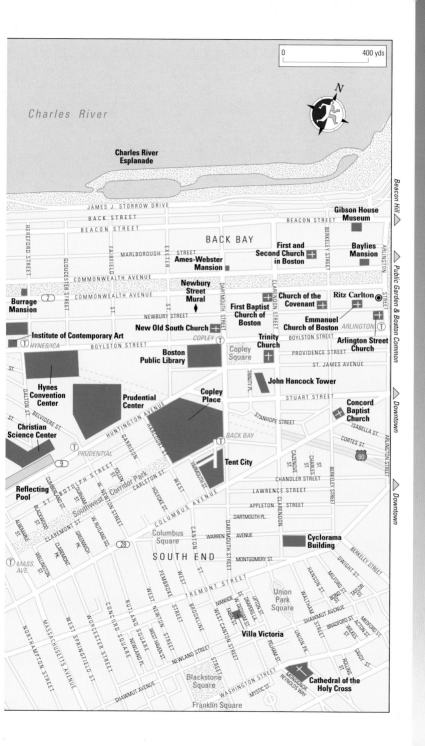

0   400 yds

N

Charles River

**Charles River
Esplanade**

JAMES J. STORROW DRIVE

BACK STREET

BEACON STREET

BEACON STREET

**Gibson House
Museum**

BACK BAY

HEREFORD STREET

FAIRFIELD STREET

EXETER STREET

MARLBOROUGH STREET

**Ames-Webster
Mansion**

**First and
Second Church
in Boston**

BERKELEY STREET

**Baylies
Mansion**

ARLINGTON STREET

COMMONWEALTH AVENUE

GLOUCESTER STREET

COMMONWEALTH AVENUE

**Newbury
Street
Mural**

DARTMOUTH STREET

CLARENDON STREET

**Church of the
Covenant**

Ritz Carlton

**Burrage
Mansion**

NEWBURY STREET

**First Baptist
Church of
Boston**

**Emmanuel
Church of Boston**

ARLINGTON

Institute of Contemporary Art

New Old South Church

**Trinity
Church**

BOYLSTON STREET

**Arlington Street
Church**

HYNES/ICA

BOYLSTON STREET

COPLEY

Copley
Square

PROVIDENCE STREET

**Boston
Public Library**

ST. JAMES AVENUE

TRINITY PL.

John Hancock Tower

**Hynes
Convention
Center**

**Prudential
Center**

**Copley
Place**

STUART STREET

STANHOPE STREET

**Concord
Baptist
Church**

DALTON ST.

BELVIDERE ST.

HUNTINGTON AVENUE

HARCOURT ST.

GARRISON ST.

BACK BAY

ISABELLA ST.

CORTES ST.

90

ARLINGTON STREET

**Christian
Science Center**

PRUDENTIAL

CAZENOVE ST.

CHARLES ST.

ST.

BERKELEY STREET

9

YARMOUTH ST.

Tent City

CHANDLER STREET

**Reflecting
Pool**

CLEARWAY ST.

BOTOLPH STREET

FOLLEN STREET

DURHAM ST.

CARLTON ST.

HOLYOKE ST.

W. NEWTON STREET

WEST

COLUMBUS

Southwest Corridor Park

AVENUE

LAWRENCE STREET

APPLETON STREET

DARTMOUTH PL.

CLARENDON STREET

ALBEMARLE ST.

CLAREMONT ST.

CLAREMONT PK.

GREENWICH ST.

W. RUTLAND SQ.

**Columbus
Square**

28

CANTON ST.

WARREN AVENUE

MONTGOMERY ST.

DARTMOUTH STREET

**Cyclorama
Building**

BERKELEY STREET

DWIGHT ST.

MASS.
AVE.

WELLINGTON ST.

SOUTH END

TREMONT STREET

PEMBROKE STREET

WEST NEWTON STREET

BROOKLINE STREET

WEST CANTON STREET

**Union
Park
Square**

IVANHOE ST.

UPTON ST.

W. DEDHAM ST.

DRAPERS LA.

FARM ST.

HANSON ST.

MILFORD ST.

BOND ST.

WALTHAM STREET

SHAWMUT AVENUE

BRADFORD ST.

UNION PK.

TAYLOR ST.

MEDFORD ST.

ACTON ST.

WYKES ST.

NORTHAMPTON STREET

MASSACHUSETTS AVENUE

WEST SPRINGFIELD ST.

WORCESTER SQUARE

CONCORD SQUARE

RUTLAND SQUARE

WEST NEWTON STREET

NEWLAND ST.

WEST HAVEN ST.

NEWLAND PL.

PELHAM ST.

Villa Victoria

SANDY ST.

ROLLINS ST.

SHAWMUT AVENUE

**Blackstone
Square**

WASHINGTON STREET

MYSTIC ST.

MONSIGNOR REYNOLDS WAY

**Cathedral of the
Holy Cross**

Franklin Square

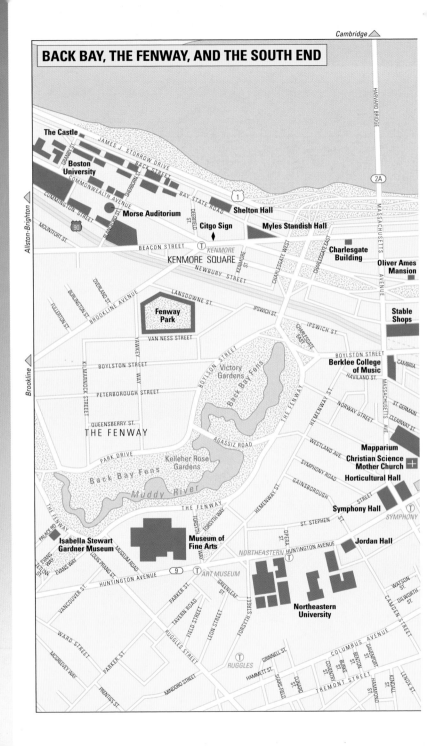

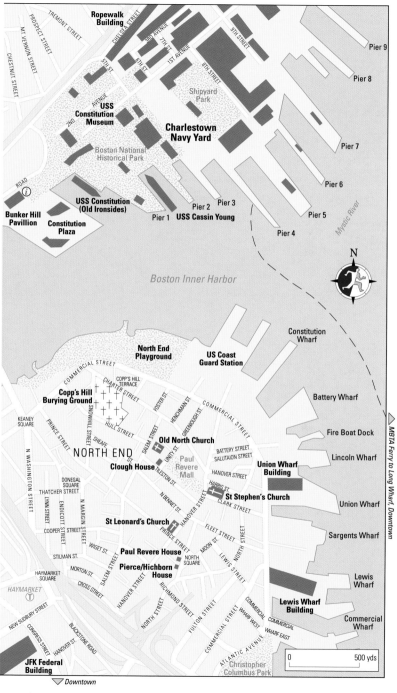

Ropewalk Building

Pier 9

Pier 8

CHELSEA STREET
TREMONT STREET
PROSPECT STREET
MT VERNON STREET
CHESTNUT STREET

3RD AVENUE
7TH ST
1ST AVENUE
6TH ST
5TH ST
2ND
AVENUE

8TH STREET

9TH STREET

Shipyard Park

Pier 7

USS Constitution Museum

Charlestown Navy Yard

Boston National Historical Park

Pier 6

ROAD ⓘ

USS Constitution (Old Ironsides)

Pier 3
Pier 2
Pier 1

Pier 5

Bunker Hill Pavillion

Constitution Plaza

USS Cassin Young

Pier 4

Mystic River

Boston Inner Harbor

N

Constitution Wharf

North End Playground

US Coast Guard Station

COMMERCIAL STREET

Battery Wharf

COPP'S HILL TERRACE
CHARTER STREET
FOSTER ST
HENCHMAN ST
GREENOUGH ST

Copp's Hill Burying Ground

SNOWHILL STREET
SHEAFE
HULL STREET

COMMERCIAL STREET

Fire Boat Dock

KEANEY SQUARE

SALEM STREET
UNITY ST
TILESTON ST

Old North Church

BATTERY STREET
SALUTAION STREET

Lincoln Wharf

PRINCE STREET

NORTH END

Clough House

Paul Revere Mall

HANOVER STREET

Union Wharf Building

N WASHINGTON STREET

DONEGAL SQUARE
THATCHER STREET

N BENNET ST

HARRIS ST
CLARK STREET

St Stephen's Church

Union Wharf

ENDICOTT STREET
LYNN STREET
COOPER STREET
N MARGIN STREET

St Leonard's Church

HANOVER STREET
FLEET STREET
NORTH STREET

Sargents Wharf

STILMAN ST.

PRINCE STREET

Paul Revere House

MOON ST.

LEWIS STREET

Lewis Wharf

HAYMARKET SQUARE
MORTON ST.
WIGET ST.
SALEM STREET

Pierce/Hichborn House

NORTH SQUARE

CROSS STREET

HANOVER STREET

RICHMOND STREET

NORTH STREET

FULTON STREET

COMMERCIAL STREET
WHARF WEST

Lewis Wharf Building

Commercial Wharf

HAYMARKET Ⓣ

NEW SUDBURY STREET
CONGRESS STREET
BLACKSTONE ROAD
HANOVER ST.

ATLANTIC AVENUE
COMMERCIAL
WHARF EAST

JFK Federal Building

Christopher Columbus Park

0   500 yds

▽ Downtown

△ MBTA Ferry to Long Wharf, Downtown

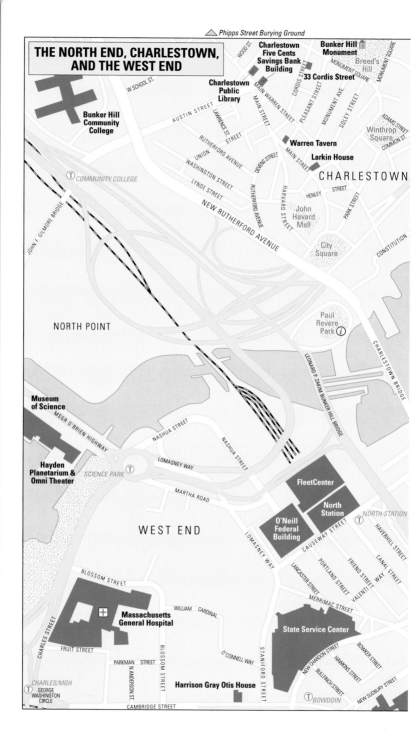

△ *Phipps Street Burying Ground*

THE NORTH END, CHARLESTOWN, AND THE WEST END

Charlestown Five Cents Savings Bank Building

Bunker Hill Monument 🏛

Breed's Hill

33 Cordis Street

Charlestown Public Library

Bunker Hill Community College

W SCHOOL ST.

AUSTIN STREET

LAWRENCE ST.

RUTHERFORD AVENUE

UNION

WASHINGTON STREET

LYNDE STREET

NEW RUTHERFORD AVENUE

Warren Tavern

Larkin House

CHARLESTOWN

WOOD ST.

MAIN STREET

MAIN WARREN STREET

PLEASANT STREET

CORDIS STREET

MONUMENT AVE.

MONUMENT SQUARE

MONUMENT SQUARE

ADAMS STREET

Winthrop Square

COMMON ST.

SOLEY STREET

DEVENS STREET

MAIN STREET

HARVARD STREET

HENLEY

STREET

PARK STREET

John Havard Mall

City Square

CONSTITUTION

JOHN F. GILMORE BRIDGE

Ⓣ COMMUNITY COLLEGE

NORTH POINT

Paul Revere Park ⓘ

LEONARD P. ZAKIM BUNKER HILL BRIDGE

CHARLESTOWN BRIDGE

Museum of Science

MSGR O'BRIEN HIGHWAY

NASHUA STREET

NASHUA STREET

Hayden Planetarium & Omni Theater

SCIENCE PARK Ⓣ

LOMASNEY WAY

MARTHA ROAD

FleetCenter

North Station

NORTH STATION

Ⓣ NORTH STATION

WEST END

O'Neill Federal Building

LOMASNEY WAY

CAUSEWAY STREET

HAVERHILL STREET

CANAL STREET

FRIEND STREET

VALENTI WAY

LANCASTER STREET

PORTLAND STREET

MERRIMAC STREET

BLOSSOM STREET

Massachusetts General Hospital ✚

WILLIAM CARDINAL

State Service Center

NEW CHARDON STREET

BOWKER STREET

HAWKINS STREET

BULFINCH STREET

CHARLES STREET

FRUIT STREET

PARKMAN STREET

N ANDERSON ST.

BLOSSOM STREET

O'CONNELL WAY

STANIFORD STREET

NEW SUDBURY STREET

CHARLES/MGH Ⓣ

GEORGE WASHINGTON CIRCLE

Harrison Gray Otis House

Ⓣ BOWDOIN

CAMBRIDGE STREET

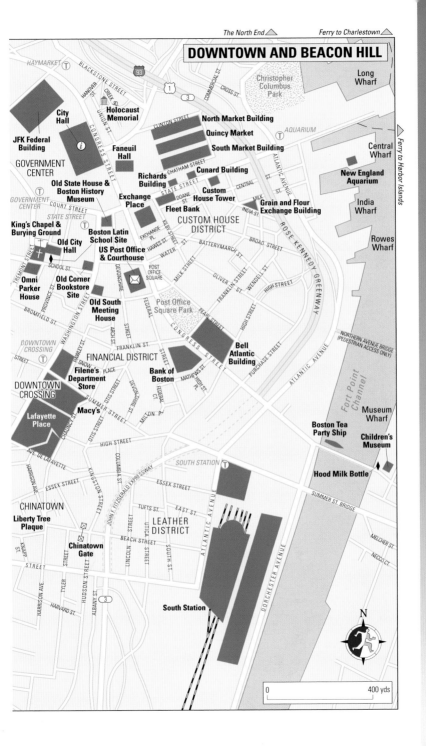

DOWNTOWN AND BEACON HILL

HAYMARKET Ⓣ

BLACKSTONE STREET

93

1

3

COMMERCIAL ST.

CROSS ST.

Christopher
Columbus
Park

Long
Wharf

City
Hall

Holocaust
Memorial

CLINTON STREET

North Market Building

AQUARIUM Ⓣ

AQUARIUM

Central
Wharf

JFK Federal
Building

ⓘ

Faneuil
Hall

Quincy Market

South Market Building

GOVERNMENT
CENTER

Ⓣ

GOVERNMENT
CENTER

COURT STREET

Richards
Building

CHATHAM STREET

Cunard Building

ATLANTIC AVENUE

New England
Aquarium

India
Wharf

Old State House &
Boston History
Museum

STATE STREET

DOANE ST.

Exchange
Place

Custom
House Tower

CENTRAL
ST.

MILK
ST.

Grain and Flour
Exchange Building

STATE STREET

Fleet Bank

INDIA ST.

King's Chapel &
Burying Ground

Old City
Hall

Boston Latin
School Site

EXCHANGE
PL.

KILBY STREET

CUSTOM HOUSE
DISTRICT

BROAD STREET

ROSE KENNEDY GREENWAY

Rowes
Wharf

SCHOOL ST.

US Post Office
& Courthouse

HAWES ST.

WATER ST.

BATTERYMARCH ST.

Omni
Parker
House

PROVINCE ST.

DEVONSHIRE ST.

POST
OFFICE
SQUARE

MILK STREET

OLIVER STREET

WENDELL ST.

HIGH STREET

BROMFIELD ST.

Old Corner
Bookstore
Site

Old South
Meeting
House

✉

Post Office
Square Park

FRANKLIN ST.

PEARL STREET

HIGH STREET

FEDERAL STREET

ARCH STREET

CONGRESS STREET

NORTHERN AVENUE BRIDGE
(PEDESTRIAN ACCESS ONLY)

DOWNTOWN
CROSSING Ⓣ

STREET

WASHINGTON STREET

FRANKLIN STREET

FINANCIAL DISTRICT

Bell
Atlantic
Building

ATLANTIC AVENUE

Fort Point Channel

HAWLEY ST.

SNOW PLACE

Filene's
Department
Store

Bank of
Boston

MATHEWS ST.

PURCHASE STREET

Museum
Wharf

DOWNTOWN
CROSSING Ⓣ

CHAUNCY ST.

OTIS STREET

Macy's

SUMMER STREET

DEVONSHIRE ST.

FEDERAL CT.

HIGH ST.

MILTON PL.

Lafayette
Place

HIGH STREET

Boston Tea
Party Ship

Children's
Museum

AVE. DE LAFAYETTE

COLUMBIA ST.

SOUTH STATION Ⓣ

Hood Milk Bottle

HARRISON AVE.

ESSEX STREET

KINGSTON STREET

JOHN F. FITZGERALD EXPRESSWAY

ESSEX STREET

SUMMER ST. BRIDGE

CHINATOWN

TUFTS ST.

EAST ST.

ATLANTIC AVENUE

Liberty Tree
Plaque

KNAPP ST.

STREET

Chinatown
Gate

BEACH STREET

LINCOLN STREET

UTICA STREET

SOUTH ST.

LEATHER
DISTRICT

DORCHESTER AVENUE

MELCHER ST.

NECCO CT.

STREET

HARRISON AVE.

TYLER STREET

HUDSON STREET

3

HARVARD ST.

ALBANY ST.

South Station

N

0   400 yds

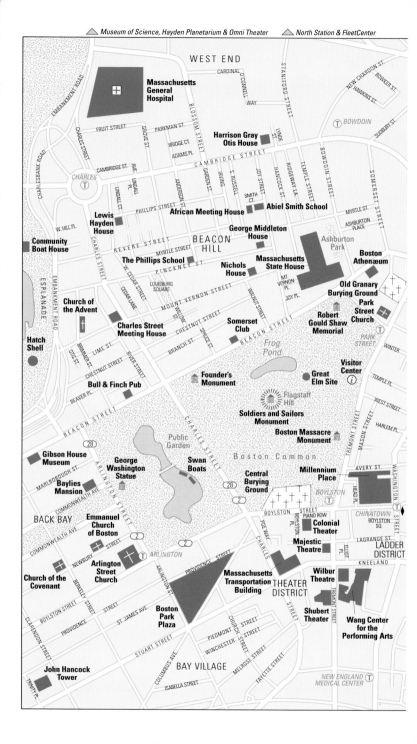

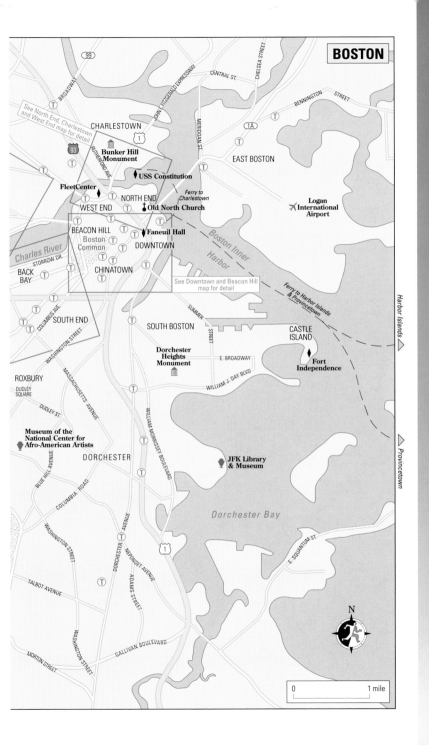

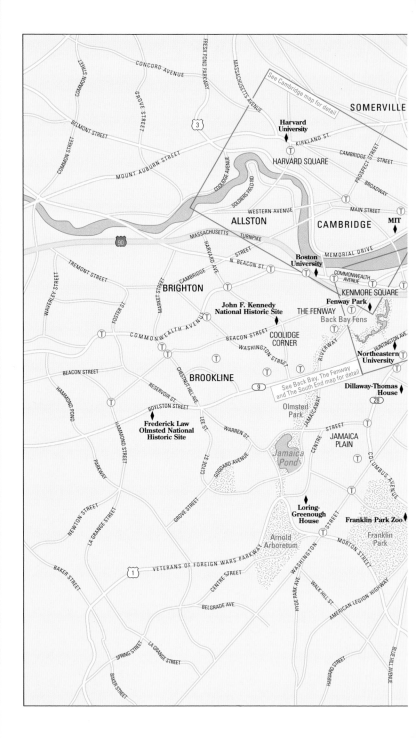

CONTENTS

Library of Congress Control Number: 2015908309
ISBN: Hardcover   978-1-5035-7284-3
                   Softcover   978-1-5035-7283-6
                   eBook   978-1-5035-7282-9

Print information available on the last page.

Rev. date: 09/15/2015

To order additional copies of this book, contact:
Xlibris
1-888-795-4274
www.Xlibris.com
Orders@Xlibris.com
713070

BATTING ROCKS
Over the Barn

An Iowa Farm Boy's Odyssey

LAWN GRIFFITHS

Five Stars (out of Five)

"Time is well spent within the pages of Griffiths's home run memoir, launching back to a place where imagination was ever-present.

.... In these high-tech, fast-paced times, Griffiths's recollections unfold like a warm blanket fresh out of the dryer.

.... His well-crafted narrative takes root in early childhood and stretches past his homecoming during his freshman year of college at Iowa State University.

What lies between are well-rendered recollections presented in a thematic structure that is narrated by a man who has had time to reflect on their value and their influence over his life."

—Foreword Reviews

"A debut collection of vignettes about the author's childhood on an Iowa farm.

... Griffiths lovingly details almost every aspect of the dairy farming, corn growing, and hog raising to which he was exposed, starting at age 4 when he rode a cultivator plowing through a cornfield. "My father believed all children had work potential, no matter how young they were," he recalls. "Play was okay for town kids, he'd say, but country youth had to learn responsibility." ... The author's collage of country life includes recollections of the schoolhouse he attended in second grade— "Older boys used to capture mice in traps and dangle the partly paralyzed rodents in the faces of girls"—and the local drugstore, where "the stools and booths around the soda fountain were filled with teenagers sipping green rivers and cherry cokes." ....

An affectionate but facile look at family farm life."

—Kirkus Reviews

" An inviting nostalgia permeates this collection of newspapers columns based upon the author's experiences growing up on an Iowa farm more than 50 years ago. The title alone will resonate with anyone who ever grabbed a flat stick and a handful of rocks and sent those rocks humming over a rooftop for imaginary game-winning home runs.

Writing with an assured touch and a journalist's keen eye for detail, he captures the natural rhythm of farming life with his essays based upon the four seasons. He describes, for example, how winter takes over "like a lazy polar bear about to relax on a floating mass of ice, burying us in smothering whiteness" and later only releases its grip reluctantly and deceptively.

"...This book will charm readers of a certain age—perhaps those upwards of 50—especially if they shared a similar rural childhood; many others will equally enjoy these well-crafted recollections from a bygone era."

—BlueInk Review

BATTING ROCKS
Over the Barn

19

How did these two dinosaurs end up like this? Perhaps a group of raptors attacked the Protoceratops. As it fought back, the Protoceratops clamped its jaws down on one raptor's arm and held on.

The other raptors
probably killed and ate
the Protoceratops and
went on their way.
The unlucky raptor
was left behind.

No one really knows what
color raptors, or any dinosaurs,
were. Many scientists think they
may have been as colorful as
snakes, lizards, and birds are today.

The dinosaurs' skin colors and patterns probably blended in with their surroundings. This allowed them to hide from enemies. These colors and patterns may also have helped the dinosaurs attract mates.

Some scientists think raptors might
even have had feathers. What do
you think raptors looked like?

Raptors lived in the late Cretaceous period (66 million years ago), which means that they were one of the very last kinds of dinosaurs to become extinct.

What happened to all the dinosaurs?
Did they all get sick and never
get well?

Did a huge chunk of space rock crash into Earth, killing the plants and animals that dinosaurs ate?

We may never know for sure. But what we do know is that the raptor was one of the fiercest, most terrifying dinosaurs of all.

Index